C000083669

1,000,000 Books
are available to read at

Forgotten Books

www.ForgottenBooks.com

Read online
Download PDF
Purchase in print

ISBN 978-0-365-25641-0
PIBN 11265284

This book is a reproduction of an important historical work. Forgotten Books uses state-of-the-art technology to digitally reconstruct the work, preserving the original format whilst repairing imperfections present in the aged copy. In rare cases, an imperfection in the original, such as a blemish or missing page, may be replicated in our edition. We do, however, repair the vast majority of imperfections successfully; any imperfections that remain are intentionally left to preserve the state of such historical works.

Forgotten Books is a registered trademark of FB &c Ltd.
Copyright © 2018 FB &c Ltd.
FB &c Ltd, Dalton House, 60 Windsor Avenue, London, SW19 2RR.
Company number 08720141. Registered in England and Wales.

For support please visit www.forgottenbooks.com

1 MONTH OF
FREE
READING

at

www.ForgottenBooks.com

By purchasing this book you are eligible for one month membership to ForgottenBooks.com, giving you unlimited access to our entire collection of over 1,000,000 titles via our web site and mobile apps.

To claim your free month visit:

www.forgottenbooks.com/free1265284

* Offer is valid for 45 days from date of purchase. Terms and conditions apply.

English
Français
Deutsche
Italiano
Español
Português

www.forgottenbooks.com

Mythology Photography **Fiction** Fishing Christianity **Art** Cooking Essays Buddhism Freemasonry Medicine **Biology** Music **Ancient Egypt** Evolution Carpentry Physics Dance Geology **Mathematics** Fitness Shakespeare **Folklore** Yoga Marketing **Confidence** Immortality Biographies Poetry **Psychology** Witchcraft Electronics Chemistry History **Law** Accounting **Philosophy** Anthropology Alchemy Drama Quantum Mechanics Atheism Sexual Health **Ancient History** **Entrepreneurship** Languages Sport Paleontology Needlework Islam **Metaphysics** Investment Archaeology Parenting Statistics Criminology **Motivational**

Ward 9—Precinct 1

CITY OF BOSTON

LIST OF RESIDENTS
20 YEARS OF AGE AND OVER

(NON-CITIZENS INDICATED BY ASTERISK)
(FEMALES INDICATED BY DAGGER)

AS OF

JANUARY 1, 1943

JOSEPH F. TIMILTY, *Chairman*
FREDERIC E. DOWLING, *Secretary*
WILLIAM A. MOTLEY, JR.
FRANCIS B. McKINNEY
EVERETT R. PROUT
Listing Board.

CITY OF BOSTON PRINTING DEPARTMENT

Page.	Letter.	Full Name.	Residence, Jan. 1, 1943.	Occupation.	Supposed Age.	Reported Residence, Jan. 1, 1942. Street and Number.

Canton Street Court

Page.	Letter.	Full Name.	Residence, Jan. 1, 1943.	Occupation.	Supposed Age.	Reported Residence, Jan. 1, 1942. Street and Number.
	B	Roberts Flora S—†	2	at home	71	here

Canton Street Place

Page.	Letter.	Full Name.	Residence, Jan. 1, 1943.	Occupation.	Supposed Age.	Reported Residence, Jan. 1, 1942. Street and Number.
	E	Marshall George	1	laborer	53	here
	F	White Thomas H	1	engineer	65	"
	G	*Tucker Bessie—†	1	at home	82	"
	H	Hawley Marie—†	1	waitress	26	
	K	Hawley Sarah—†	1	saleswoman	26	"

Draper's Lane

Page.	Letter.	Full Name.	Residence, Jan. 1, 1943.	Occupation.	Supposed Age.	Reported Residence, Jan. 1, 1942. Street and Number.
	L	Cummings Robert	31	laborer	60	here
	M	Murray Charlotte—†	31	housekeeper	63	"

Fabin Street

Page.	Letter.	Full Name.	Residence, Jan. 1, 1943.	Occupation.	Supposed Age.	Reported Residence, Jan. 1, 1942. Street and Number.
	R	*Brothers Joseph	3	retired	67	here
	S	Kitchenier Catherine—†	3	housekeeper	32	59 Corning
	T	Robinson Alberta—†	3	"	77	here
	U	Callison John	4	U S A	20	"
	V	Callison Joseph	4	"	23	"
	W	Callison Warren	4	"	25	
	X	Callison William	4	"	22	"
	Y	Coffee Honora—†	4	at home	36	58 W Dedham
	Z	*Coffee Mary—†	4	housekeeper	71	here
2	A	*Larsen Sigurd	4	retired	60	"
	B	Smith Augustus	4	laborer	30	Lynn
	C	Perry Carrie—†	16	housewife	67	here
	D	Perry John H	16	retired	64	"
	E	Roche Bartholomew	36	carpenter	47	"
	F	*Mouradian Catherine—†	36	housekeeper	69	"
	G	*Garabedian Mary—†	38	stitcher	47	"

Ivanhoe Street

Page.	Letter.	Full Name.	Residence, Jan. 1, 1943.	Occupation.	Supposed Age.	Reported Residence, Jan. 1, 1942. Street and Number.
	M	*Kazantzi Bessie—†	8	seamstress	34	here
	N	Kazantzi Luzeous	8	shoemaker	47	"
	R	*Smith Margaret—†	12	housewife	52	"

Page.	Letter.	Full Name.	Residence, Jan. 1, 1943.	Occupation.	Supposed Age.	Reported Residence, Jan. 1, 1942. Street and Number.

Ivanhoe Street—Continued

	S	Smith William	12	retired	68	here
	T	Santos Anthony	12	"	60	"
	U	Santos Mary E—†	12	housewife	61	"
	X	Alyward Arthur	24	laborer	30	
	Y	Alyward Julia—†	24	housewife	68	"
	Z	Howell John J	24	retired	67	
3						
	A	Howell Sarah—†	24	housewife	60	"
	B	Grady Arthur	26	retired	61	24 Ivanhoe
	C	Smith Charles W	26	"	65	24 Kirkland
	D	Collins Martin	28	"	69	here
	E	Riddle Bridget A—†	28	housekeeper	48	24 Milford
	1E	Williams Warner W	28	retired	67	here

Newland Street

	K	Maloof Richard	4	welder	23	696 Tremont
	L	Maloof Rose—†	4	housewife	22	696 "
	M	Merigan Violet—†	4	stamper	25	614 "
	N	Bezanson Annie—†	4	housekeeper	69	here
	O	Meulenaere Dorothy—†	4	housewife	23	4 Rutland
	P	Meulenaere Joseph	4	metalworker	23	4 "
	R	MacDonald Donald	4	carpenter	55	here
	S	MacDonald Margaret–†	4	housewife	54	"
	T	Meulenaere Camille—†	4	"	55	"
	U	Meulenaere Karel	4	manufacturer	60	"
	V	Meulenaere Leonard	4	laborer	29	
	W	*Curran Catharine—†	5	housewife	64	"
	X	Curran Dennie	5	retired	69	"
	Y	Zartman Birdie—†	5	housekeeper	72	"
	Z	Westcott Wanda—†	5	"	53	172 W Brookline
4						
	B	Lawless Christopher	6	retired	79	here
	A	Lawless Ellen—†	6	housewife	58	"
	C	Davis Fannie—†	6	laundress	45	"
	D	Rust Alfred P	6	retired	80	"
	E	Drew Joseph B	7	"	71	
	F	Bunker Edward	7	"	74	"
	G	Grant Horatio	7	"	70	3 Fabin
	H	Alker Lillian—†	8	housewife	20	here
	K	Alker Robert J	8	U S A	25	"

Page.	Letter.	FULL NAME.	Residence, Jan. 1, 1943.	Occupation.	Supposed Age.	Reported Residence, Jan. 1, 1942. Street and Number.

Newland Street—Continued

	L	McKenzie Irene—†	8	housewife	46	here
	M	Murtha Anna—†	8	"	43	"
	N	Murtha Arthur	8	salesman	46	"
	O	Gifford Mary—†	8	housekeeper	53	"
	R	Allen Harriett—†	15	"	68	677 Tremont
	S	Howard Andrew A	15	cook	76	here
	Y	Logan Albert	19	shoeworker	59	"
	Z	Logan Martha—†	19	housewife	48	"
5						
	A	Dimitropoulas Margaret—†	19	housekeeper	45	"
	E	Peterson Charles	22	blacksmith	63	"
	G	Ford Adeline A—†	23	housekeeper	47	"
	H	Boireau Margaret—†	24	"	56	"
	K	Davis Roger	24	clerk	24	
	L	*McCarty John	24	laborer	60	"
	M	*Shea James	24	"	63	
	N	Daley Catherine E—†	26	housewife	27	"
	O	Daley Frederick E	26	custodian	37	"
	P	Brown Annie—†	27	housekeeper	67	"
	R	Lee John	27	retired	78	"
	S	Martin Harold	29	janitor	38	
	T	Roisten Alice—†	29	laundress	35	"
	U	Roisten Harold	29	laborer	43	
	V	Roisten Joseph	29	"	40	
	W	Williams Fannie E—†	29	at home	77	"
	X	Durant Marie—†	33	housekeeper	33	"
	Y	McDonald Dorothy—†	33	waitress	37	98 W Newton
6						
	A	Tricone Frank	37	technician	48	1761 Wash'n
	B	Howard Elizabeth—†	37	housekeeper	71	here
	D	Clements Selena—†	41	"	69	"
	E	Brown Arthur	43	retired	68	"
	F	Brown Josephine—†	43	housewife	57	"
	G	Duffy Florence B—†	53	"	47	11 Norwell
	H	Duffy Florence L—†	53	electric'l work'r	24	11 "
	L	Alker James	53	insulator	27	77 Newland
	M	Alker Lillian—†	53	housewife	22	77 "
	N	O'Brien Mary—†	55	"	52	here
	O	O'Brien Thomas F	55	retired	75	"
	P	Abbott Caroline—†	55	housewife	55	77 Newland
	R	Murphy Arthur	55	chauffeur	24	Maine

Page.	Letter.	Full Name.	Residence, Jan. 1, 1943.	Occupation.	Supposed Age.	Reported Residence, Jan. 1, 1942. Street and Number.

Pelham Street

Page.	Letter.	Full Name.	Residence, Jan. 1, 1943.	Occupation.	Supposed Age.	Reported Residence, Jan. 1, 1942. Street and Number.
	S	Allen James	6	retired	84	12 Andrews pl
	T	*Currie Neil	6	laborer	64	436 Dudley
	U	Dennis John	6	draftsman	60	50 Union pk
	V	Dennis Mary—†	6	housewife	56	50 "
	W	Fisher Nathan	6	laborer	22	Walpole
	X	Fisher Pauline—†	6	housewife	20	"
	Y	Jenny Leo	6	metalworker	42	Newfoundland
	Z	*Latorio William	6	counterman	45	17 Rollins
7						
	A	LeNormand Robert J	6	retired	69	77 W Brookline
	B	Murphy Cora—†	6	factoryhand	51	20 Upton
	C	Brown Thomas C	8	retired	67	322 Shawmut av
	D	Chisholm Alfred T	8	painter	38	88 W Springfield
	E	Clink Richard	8	orderly	44	Taunton
	F	*Gairn Edward	8	cook	48	here
	G	Grant Elizabeth—†	8	at home	69	"
	H	Griffin Sumner	8	window washer	44	92 Compton
	K	Miskel Martin	8	laborer	49	here
	L	Murphy James	8	retired	48	Chelsea
	M	Regan Catherine—†	8	housewife	69	here
	N	Regan Michael	8	retired	70	"
	O	Russell James	8	waiter	45	"
	P	Anderson Anna K—†	10	housewife	70	"
	R	Anderson John	10	retired	72	Pittsfield
	S	Benson Alfred H	10	meatcutter	59	here
	T	Burns Mary—†	10	domestic	40	"
	U	Deal Howell E	10	packer	74	"
	V	Hagstrom Rudolph	10	painter	68	"
	[1]V	Jensen Peter	10	retired	78	398 Canterbury
	W	Larsen Eric	10	laborer	72	here
	X	*Lenahan Thomas	10	retired	77	"
	Y	MacLaren Robert	10	engineer	60	"
	Z	Murphy Jeremiah E	10	machinist	51	"
8						
	A	*Olson Marie—†	10	domestic	53	79 Bay State rd
	B	Wilhelmi Julia J—†	10	at home	64	here
	E	Freel Mary—†	16	"	73	"
	F	Huggins Ruth—†	16	housekeeper	43	"
	G	Kirby William	16	retired	55	31 W Dedham
	H	McCarthy James G	16	laborer	48	here
	K	Murray Samuel B	16	salesman	63	"

Page.	Letter.	FULL NAME.	Residence, Jan. 1, 1943.	Occupation.	Supposed Age.	Reported Residence, Jan. 1, 1942. Street and Number.
		Pelham Street—Continued				
	L	Carney John	18	retired	76	here
	M	Chabot Ephraim	18	draftsman	40	"
	N	Donnellan Michael	18	retired	79	"
	O	Fallon Henry F	18	"	72	"
	P	McFarnane Michael	18	porter	71	Canada
	R	O'Rourke William	18	retired	84	here
	S	*Smith William	18	cook	66	"
	T	Stickney Samuel	18	retired	82	"
	V	Devoy Isabel—†	22	at home	76	"
	W	Lee William	22	realtor	68	
	X	Slavin Mary—†	22	housekeeper	54	"
	Y	*Jacobs Fred J	22	orderly	66	1 Bush
	Z	Carr Patrick F	22	brushmaker	64	here
9						
	B	Bowers Thomas	24	salesman	42	"
	C	Corey Annie—†	24	housewife	38	"
	D	Corey Leslie	24	shoeworker	38	"
	E	Delome Alfred	24	retired	67	
	F	Dunne Robert	24	salesman	43	"
	G	Fitzgerald Michael	24	retired	65	21 Warren
	H	Holden Carl	24	U S A	28	here
	K	Theriault Beatrice—†	24	waitress	38	3 Hanson
		Pembroke Street				
	P	Barrett Marion—†	11	housewife	24	55 Newland
	R	Barrett Stephen	11	rigger	39	55 "
	S	Cloutier Leo	11	shipper	45	here
	T	Maher Helen—†	11	housewife	42	"
	U	Bowen Catherine—†	11	at home	64	"
	V	Dailey George	11	laborer	57	
	W	Dailey John	11	retired	62	
	X	Olander Irene—†	11	operator	44	
	Z	Peterson Marion—†	11A	housewife	40	"
10						
	A	Murphy Lomila—†	11A	"	56	
	B	Murphy Richard A	11A	machinist	66	"
	C	McCormack Sarah—†	15	at home	70	15 E Springfield
	D	Morton Della—†	15	"	71	here
	E	Coleman Lottie—†	15	"	66	"
	F	Hayden Harry V	15	laborer	60	"

Page.	Letter.	FULL NAME.	Residence, Jan. 1, 1943.	Occupation.	Supposed Age.	Reported Residence, Jan. 1, 1942. Street and Number.

Pembroke Street—Continued

Page.	Letter.	FULL NAME.	Residence, Jan. 1, 1943.	Occupation.	Supposed Age.	Reported Residence, Jan. 1, 1942.
	G	Trotman Eva—†	19	housewife	56	here
	H	Trotman Frederick	19	merchant	63	"
	K	Trotman George	19	U S A	24	"
	L	Trotman Robert C	19	"	21	"
	N	Holbrook Annie—†	21	housewife	31	37 Newland
	O	Holbrook Louis	21	machinist	34	37 "
	P	Lodge Blanche O—†	21	housewife	43	here
	R	Lodge Henry	21	clergyman	53	"
	T	Freeman Arthur	21	cook	49	"
	U	Driscoll Ann D—†	21	housewife	31	"
	Y	Eastman Gertrude—†	31	laundress	35	31 Rutland
	Z	Franklin Vivian B—†	31	housewife	38	767 Tremont
11						
	A	Malden William F	31	U S N	21	767 "
	B	McCue Margaret I—†	33	housewife	45	here
	C	Speath Joseph H	33	retired	70	"
	D	Clark Betty—†	47	housewife	34	"
	E	Clark Lewis W	47	chauffeur	40	"
	H	Efstathion Arthur	47	draftsman	27	"
	K	Efstathion Rena—†	47	housewife	27	"
	L	Shaw Diab	49	watchman	45	"
	M	Shaw Emma—†	49	housewife	40	"
	N	Acornley Francis	49	machinist	33	13 Upton
	O	Acornley Helen—†	49	housewife	30	13 "
	P	*Limberis Garoufalia—†	49	"	35	475 Shawmut av
	R	Limberis George E	49	electrician	42	475 "
	T	Moses Adele—†	51	housewife	22	70 Harvard
	U	Moses George	51	electrician	26	70 "
	V	Moneypenney Clara—†	51	housewife	60	107 Union Park
	W	Moneypenney Gladys—†	51	packer	25	107 "
	X	Moneypenney James O	51	U S A	22	107 "
	Y	Moneypenney Mandville	51	U S N	29	107 "
	Z	Moneypenney Owen J	51	machinist	22	107 "
12						
	A	*Thomas Etta—†	51	housewife	57	here
	B	Thomas Joseph	51	laborer	57	"
	C	Thomas Mary—†	51	waitress	33	"
	D	*DeVaio Nunziata—†	51	at home	65	7 Rollins
	E	Gray Anna—†	51	waitress	42	7 "
	F	Jordan Sarah—†	51	housewife	35	7 "
	G	Marra Bartholomew	53	packer	62	here

Page.	Letter.	FULL NAME.	Residence, Jan. 1, 1943.	Occupation.	Supposed Age.	Reported Residence, Jan. 1, 1942. Street and Number.

Pembroke Street—Continued

	H	Marra Jane—†	53	at home	64	here
	K	Marra Mary—†	53	"	66	"
	L	Harmoosh Lateefy M—†	53	housewife	62	"
	M	Harmoosh Mitry R	53	retired	61	
	N	Lewis Arthur	53	U S A	21	
	O	*Lewis George	53	shoemaker	60	"
	P	Lewis Samuel	53	welder	30	
	R	Lewis Thomas	53	laborer	32	
	S	Lewis William	53	U S A	22	
	T	*Kanan Jennie—†	53	housewife	43	"
	U	Kanan Joseph	53	U S A	21	
	V	Kanan Margaret—†	53	dressmaker	22	"
	W	Ballou Myra—†	57	at home	66	10 Julian
	X	Gray Helen—†	57	housewife	33	10 "
	Y	Gray William G	57	salesman	42	10 "
	Z	Siemlanski Edward	57	U S N	38	3 W Canton
13						
	A	Siemlanski Lillian—†	57	housewife	35	3 "
	B	Smart Mabel H—†	57	"	29	1486 Wash'n
	C	Smart Maurice	57	U S N	37	1486 "
	D	*Bendesky Max	57	laborer	52	here
	E	*LeFebvre Alice—†	57	housewife	21	122 W Canton
	F	LeFebvre Ludger	57	pipefitter	31	122 "
	G	*LeFebvre Mary—†	57	at home	62	Maine
	H	Gardner Victor	57	laborer	36	47 Bradford
	K	Leighton Irene M—†	57	housekeeper	36	47 "
	L	Leighton Irene V—†	57	laundress	21	47 "
	O	MacDonald Angus	65	retired	67	here
	P	MacDonald Hannah—†	65	at home	65	"
	R	Musgrave Alexander W	65	laborer	34	"
	S	Musgrave Jolena—†	65	housewife	32	"
	T	Kramer Elizabeth—†	65	"	29	60 E Springfield
	U	Kramer Norman	65	electrician	34	60 "
	V	Williams Blanche—†	65	housewife	36	here
	W	Williams Paul	65	U S N	20	"
	X	Conley Emily—†	65	housekeeper	70	"
	Y	Kelleher George	65	retired	60	"
	Z	*MacDonald Anna—†	65	housewife	63	35 Compton
14						
	A	MacDonald Harold	65	carpenter	36	35 "
	B	*MacDonald Malcolm	65	"	68	35 "

Page.	Letter.	Full Name.	Residence, Jan. 1, 1943.	Occupation.	Supposed Age.	Reported Residence, Jan. 1, 1942. Street and Number.
		Pembroke Street—Continued				
	C	Dargan Edward J	67	machinist	28	here
	D	Dargan Madeline—†	67	housewife	27	"
	E	Maxwell Elizabeth D—†	67	"	39	49 W Dedham
	F	Maxwell Harold J	67	engineer	39	49 "
	G	Maxwell Margaret I—†	67	housekeeper	59	80 Revere
	H	Hood Della—†	67	housewife	53	4 Milford
	K	Hood Walter J	67	machinist	54	4 "
	L	Torosian Armenooki—†	67	housewife	38	here
	M	Torosian Krikor	67	storekeeper	48	"
	N	Felger Marie—†	67	attendant	59	"
	O	Bonney Howard	69	painter	62	
	P	Chakils Michael	69	counterman	63	"
	R	Dewar George E	69	carpenter	57	"
	S	Drainis Arthur	69	manager	46	Florida
	T	Kellman Alton	69	machinist	51	745 Tremont
	U	MacKillop Orwell	69	bookkeeper	28	128 W Brookline
	V	Meuse Frances A—†	69	nurse	34	5 Louisburg sq
	W	Mistriotes Basil	69	waiter	52	here
	X	Norique Emanuel	69	salesman	58	"
	Y	Varotoutsos Athenasios	69	dishwasher	46	"
	Z	Walker Emma J—†	69	housekeeper	65	"
15						
	A	Yee Gingie—†	69	manager	26	New York
		Shawmut Avenue				
	B	O'Keefe Mary A—†	335	at home	68	here
	C	Reid Anna—†	335	housewife	34	"
	D	Reid James F	335	laborer	34	Lowell
	F	*Ahie Fadwa—†	335	at home	55	58 Dwight
	G	Donovan Stella—†	335	waitress	26	277 Silver
	H	Kalil Edna—†	335	housewife	59	14 Laconia
	K	Kalil Evelyn—†	335	stitcher	20	14 "
	L	Kalil Lawrence	335	machinist	26	14 "
	P	*Zidan Mary—†	335	at home	71	here
	R	*Lotif Melia—†	335	"	52	Virginia
	S	Aquino Casiano	335	U S N	38	New York
	T	Aquino Catherine—†	335	housewife	27	"
	U	*LaFauci Dorothy—†	335	"	41	here
	V	Huntley Mary—†	335	housekeeper	44	"
	W	Lotif Eva—†	335	stitcher	26	"

Page.	Letter.	Full Name.	Residence, Jan. 1, 1943.	Occupation.	Supposed Age.	Reported Residence, Jan. 1, 1942. Street and Number.

Shawmut Avenue—Continued

Page.	Letter.	Full Name.	Residence, Jan. 1, 1943.	Occupation.	Supposed Age.	Reported Residence, Jan. 1, 1942. Street and Number.
	X	Lotif Josephine—†	335	finisher	24	here
	Y	Lotif Victoria—†	335	stitcher	20	"
	Z	Gillis Neil	335	carpenter	61	"
16						
	A	Langford Earl	335	foundryman	21	143 Worcester
	B	Langford Mary—†	335	housewife	21	143 "
	C	*Kamer Nazer	335	merchant	53	here
	F	Black Lindsay	339	laborer	32	Ohio
	G	Brown Blanche—†	339	housewife	42	91 W Brookline
	H	Brown Clara—†	339	"	72	Cambridge
	K	Brown Joseph A	339	metalworker	39	91 W Brookline
	L	Cashin Charles H	339	retired	65	91 "
	M	Galvin Helen—†	339	housewife	26	106 E Brookline
	N	Goodwin Bernice D—†	339	housekeeper	34	91 W Brookline
	O	Hallisey Elmer E	339	porter	33	683 Tremont
	P	*Hallisey Eugene F	339	laborer	57	683 "
	R	Jackson John	339	shipper	29	New Jersey
	S	Jackson Margaret—†	339	housewife	28	here
	T	Wilcox Margaret E—†	339	domestic	53	111 Union Park
	U	Wilson Ansel	339	timekeeper	22	Ohio
	V	Wilson Gail—†	339	housewife	21	"
	W	Wilson Jerome L	339	laborer	29	"
	Z	Ganse Marion—†	341	at home	81	here
	X	Graham Christobel—†	341	housewife	38	"
	Y	Graham Moses	341	laborer	46	"
17						
	B	Salami Diab Y	345	expressman	51	"
	C	Salami Marie D—†	345	housewife	45	"
	D	Carbone Thomas	345	chauffeur	39	"
	E	Ferrullo Helen—†	345	housewife	33	"
	F	Ferrullo Henry	345	U S A	34	"
	G	Burns Hazel—†	345	stitcher	38	9 Union Park
	H	Burns Robert J	345	U S A	37	10 Milford
	K	*DeToma Nicolo	345	presser	64	360 Tremont
	L	Hassan Tabib	345	merchant	56	33 Newland
	M	Lewis Carrie F—†	345	waitress	57	here
	Y	Dunn William J	366	pedler	44	"
	Z	*Purland Cecil J	366	operator	60	"
18						
	A	Purland Marguerite—†	366	housewife	44	"

Page.	Letter.	Full Name.	Residence, Jan. 1, 1943.	Occupation.	Supposed Age.	Reported Residence, Jan. 1, 1942. Street and Number.

Shawmut Avenue—Continued

	B	Stephenson Catherine—†	366	housekeeper	36	here
	C	Fitzgerald Ada—†	366	housewife	39	"
	D	Fitzgerald Thomas	366	pipefitter	39	"
	E	Spring Lillian—†	366	housewife	28	21 W Dedham
	F	Spring Norman	366	chauffeur	26	111 W Brookline
	G	Diodati Angelo	366	laborer	26	109 E Canton
	H	Diodati Anna—†	366	housewife	27	109 "
	K	Thistle Clarence	366	chauffeur	23	here
	L	Thistle Marion—†	366	clerk	23	"
	M	McEachern Anna—†	366	stitcher	48	111 Union Park
	N*	Tatelbaum Sarah—†	367	housekeeper	66	here
	O*	Smith Bessie M—†	368	"	57	"
	P	Wilkins Elizabeth J—†	368	"	86	"
	R	Macharoni Louis	369	pedler	57	
	S	Ruland Laura—†	369	housekeeper	48	"
	U	McLeod Margaret—†	370	laundress	55	8 Union Park
	V	Peters James	370	laborer	50	here
	X*	Maher Joseph	370	"	53	"
	Y	Connelly Barbara—†	371	at home	79	"
	Z	Gagan Catherine—†	371	stitcher	63	
19						
	A	Croke Catherine—†	372	housewife	29	"
	B	Croke William	372	social worker	29	"
	C	Dee Thomas J	373	retired	68	
	D	Foster John	373	labcrer	68	
	E	McGaffigan John	373	retired	72	
	F	McGaffigan Rose—†	373	housewife	66	"
	G	Makros Anthony	374	chef	53	
	H	Makros Vina—†	374	housewife	57	"
	K	Blaher Theresa—†	375	"	60	"
	C	Ceely Frederick	375	inspector	39	N Hampshire
	M	Gorman Dennis	375	retired	61	here
	N	Nettles James	375	metalworker	42	"
	O	Bailey Mary—†	376	housekeeper	76	"
	P	Darlington Mary—†	376	"	52	"
	R	Prowse Mary—†	376	"	71	"
	S	Bergeron Albert	377	laborer	49	466 Shawmut av
	T	Christo Peter	377	"	61	295 "
	U	Conant Leander W	377	retired	71	here
	V	Earley Ellen—†	377	at home	69	10 Concord sq

Page.	Letter.	FULL NAME.	Residence, Jan. 1, 1943.	Occupation.	Supposed Age.	Reported Residence, Jan. 1, 1942. Street and Number.

Shawmut Avenue—Continued

	W	Hanrahan Michael J	377	laborer	54	1612 Columbia rd
	X	Moore Thomas	377	retired	72	18 Rutland
	Y	*Paolillo Salvatore	378	"	82	here
	Z	Santa Lucia Carmillo	378	U S N	29	"
20						
	A	*Santa Lucia Catherine–†	378	housewife	57	"
	B	*Santa Lucia Peter	378	barber	65	
	F	Dow Alice—†	385	housewife	57	"
	G	Soong Edward	385	U S A	24	Cambridge
	H	Soong Norah—†	385	manicurist	27	here
	K	Haw Harry	385	waiter	38	"
	L	Haw Nettie—†	385	housewife	31	"
	M	Harrington Edgar S	390	agent	56	
	N	Harrington Gertrude M–†	390	housewife	59	"
	O	Harrington Robert L	390	U S A	35	
	P	Harrington Thomas C	390	"	30	
	R	Harrington William	390	shoeworker	28	"
	S	Ustach Lois—†	390	operator	21	
	T	Aliki Joseph	391	storekeeper	52	"
	U	Aliki Mabel—†	391	housewife	30	"
	V	Aliki Stephen	391	manager	49	"
	W	Sterbach Josephine—†	391	housewife	40	"
	X	*DiCresci Bernardo	392	waiter	40	"
	Y	*DiCresci Josephine—†	392	housewife	39	"
	Z	Bodozian Harry	392	barber	40	
21						
	A	Bodozian Mary—†	392	housewife	38	"
	B	Sulfaro Constance—†	392	"	28	"
	C	Sulfaro Samuel	392	galvanizer	28	"
	D	Tikijian James S	392	cook	48	
	E	Tikijian Zaronkee—†	392	housewife	45	"
	H	Ferris Abraham	394	barber	46	
	K	Ferris Pauline—†	394	housewife	45	"
	L	Ferris Shaffe	394	laborer	20	"
	M	*Carlo George	394	shoeworker	49	"
	N	Carlo Joseph	394	welder	20	
	O	Hudba Mary—†	394	stitcher	24	"
	P	*Hoopes Bessie—†	394	housewife	53	"
	R	Hoopes Harry	394	laborer	21	
	S	Hoopes John	394	retired	65	

Page.	Letter.	Full Name.	Residence, Jan. 1, 1943.	Occupation.	Supposed Age.	Reported Residence, Jan. 1, 1942. Street and Number.

Shawmut Avenue—Continued

	T	Hoopes Thomas	394	laborer	22	here
	U	Dillon Mary—†	394	housewife	52	"
	V	Dillon Philip	394	laborer	28	"
	W	*Wong Louis R	394A	laundryman	70	369 Shawmut av
22						
	A	Barker Aram	401	janitor	48	New York
	B	Barker Celia—†	401	housewife	30	"
	K	Byrne Thomas	411	retired	69	20 Worcester sq
	L	Campbell Mary E—†	411	at home	66	here
	M	Daniels Helen—†	411	houseworker	35	54 Waltham
	N	Deraney Frederick G	411	machinist	31	here
	O	Deraney George	411	retired	63	"
	P	Deraney Josephine—†	411	stitcher	28	"
	R	Deraney Louis M	411	student	25	
	S	Deraney Nazira—†	411	housewife	51	"
	T	Elias George	411	laborer	46	
	U	Elias Mary—†	411	housewife	43	"
	V	Goulding Katherine—†	411	at home	60	19 Upton
	W	Green Frederick	411	retired	73	here
	X	Hoffman David	411	storekeeper	52	"
	Y	*Mannicrelli Gennaro	411	tailor	48	"
	Z	Poletski Jacob	411	factoryhand	52	Chelsea
23						
	A	Rogers Robert D	411	laborer	56	here
	B	*Samia Andrew	411	painter	55	"
	C	Curley Ethel—†	413	housewife	36	Malden
	D	Curley George	413	laborer	38	"
	E	Doherty Neil	413	printer	39	here
	F	Jones Alfred	413	laborer	49	"
	G	Lyons John J	413	"	29	112 Neponset av
	H	McLaughlin William	413	bartender	37	19 Myrtle
	K	Palmer Delia—†	413	housewife	30	here
	L	Palmer Francis	413	butcher	30	"
	M	Sidlauskas Leon	413	laborer	29	23 Pelham
	N	Tichler Clare—†	413	at home	79	here
	O	Tower Edward	413	U S A	33	"
	P	Tower Sadie—†	413	housewife	51	"
	R	Tower Sarah—†	413	cutter	24	
	S	Tower Thomas	413	U S A	22	
	T	Vzazanes John N	413	merchant	61	"
	U	Vzazanes Peter N	413	waiter	54	

Page.	Letter.	Full Name.	Residence, Jan. 1, 1943.	Occupation.	Supposed Age.	Reported Residence, Jan. 1, 1942. Street and Number.

Tremont Street

	W	Daly Catherine—†	592	housewife	62	328 Shawmut av
	X	Daly Daniel W	592	laborer	60	328 "
	Y	Oki Anna—†	592	housewife	51	351 Mass av
	Z	Oki Sozaburo	592	retired	62	351 "
24						
	A	Townsend Anna A—†	592	housewife	53	41 Upton
	B	Townsend Walter	592	painter	43	41 "
	C	Boreham Joseph M	594	"	54	here
	D	Chapman George	594	retired	51	616 Tremont
	E	Cochran Aubrey J	594	laborer	31	Kentucky
	F	Cochran Ruby G—†	594	housewife	26	"
	G	Coonley Alice—†	594	"	66	here
	H	Coonley John	594	cook	63	"
	K	Goodman Marie G—†	594	housewife	48	616 Tremont
	L	Hubbler Gladys M—†	594	"	41	Missouri
	M	Hubbler Rollie F	594	engineer	46	"
		Morefield Kenneth J	594	"	44	Kentucky
		Morefield Lela C—†	594	housewife	42	"
		Morefield Nelson W	594	carpenter	21	"
		Nadeau Eli M	594	cook	44	here
	N	Parker Marie—†	594	operator	55	"
	T	Peterson Lucille—†	594	housewife	38	"
	U	Peterson Theodore	594	porter	41	
	V	Angevine Millard	596	cook	48	
	W	Higgins Bernard M	596	laborer	24	
	X	Higgins Grace—†	596	housewife	28	"
	Y	O'Neil Jason	596	wool sorter	49	"
	Z	Pinney Mary—†	596	domestic	58	"
25						
	A	Wiles Annie—†	596	baker	53	
	B	*Becker Charles P	598	fireman	38	
	C	Carter Richard F	598	U S A	36	
	D	Dishon Leona—†	598	cook	46	
	E	Field Carroll	598	porter	39	
	F	Field Lillian—†	598	housewife	35	"
	G	Ford Perley K	598	packer	56	198 W Canton
	H	Henning Frederick	598	laborer	52	Plymouth
	K	Hunter Maude—†	598	at home	74	Maine
	L	King Russell	598	retired	77	9½ Leverett
	M	Layton Frank	598	actor	43	here
	N	Layton Victoria—†	598	actress	43	"

Page.	Letter.	Full Name.	Residence, Jan. 1, 1943.	Occupation.	Supposed Age.	Reported Residence, Jan. 1, 1942. Street and Number.

Tremont Street—Continued

	O	Markley Muriel—†	598	housewife	34	Maine
	P	Markley Thomas	598	U S N	34	"
	R	Perry Eugene C	598	carpenter	64	636 Tremont
	S	Perry Susanna M—†	598	housewife	58	636 "
	T	Reed Robert	598	U S A	43	here
	U	Regan Helen V—†	598	waitress	46	86 Albion
	V	Robinson Dorothy M—†	598	stenographer	24	86 "
	W	Robinson John C	598	assembler	25	86 "
	X	Robinson Ray H	598	U S N	22	86 "
	Y	Taylor Emma—†	598	domestic	38	here
	Z	Curran Charles G	600	laborer	56	143 W Newton
26						
	A	Curran Minnie—†	600	housewife	56	143 "
	B	Goyette Eva—†	600	at home	61	here
	C	*Green Elizabeth E—†	600	waitress	54	"
	D	*Green Margaret A—†	600	at home	79	"
	E	Johnson Mazie—†	600	clerk	39	163 Crescent
	F	LeBlanc Helen—†	600	domestic	42	here
	G	Mahoney Nicholas	600	porter	32	96 Lawn
	H	Martin Florence M—†	600	housewife	57	here
	K	Martin Thomas	600	engineer	63	"
	L	McNeill Kenneth	600	retired	73	"
	M	Melansky Michael J	600	machinist	31	"
	N	Nordling Ernest	600	retired	67	34 Navarre
	O	Shattucks Clyde	600	"	74	here
	P	Shattucks Dorothy—†	600	housewife	69	"
	R	Shaw George C	600	retired	72	Maine
	S	Shaw Georgia—†	600	at home	76	"
	T	Silverstein Harry	600	salesman	53	48 Lawrence av
	U	Bean Lena—†	602	waitress	49	684 Tremont
	V	*Corbin Albert	602	waiter	40	here
	W	Foster Angelina—†	602	housewife	25	98 Burrell
	X	Foster Herbert	602	clerk	29	98 "
	Y	*Gardiner Luke	602	retired	68	here
	Z	Glazier Harry A	602	"	78	"
27						
	A	Goodrich Albert	602	clerk	28	77 Worcester
	B	Goodrich Mary—†	602	housewife	26	77 "
	C	Korb Edward H	602	retired	73	here
	D	Korb Elizabeth—†	602	housewife	66	"
	E	*Murphy Annie—†	602	at home	62	32 Ash

Page.	Letter.	Full Name.	Residence, Jan. 1, 1943.	Occupation.	Supposed Age.	Reported Residence, Jan. 1, 1942. Street and Number.

Tremont Street—Continued

Page.	Letter.	Full Name.	Residence, Jan. 1, 1943.	Occupation.	Supposed Age.	Reported Residence, Jan. 1, 1942. Street and Number.
	F	Reardon Charles J	602	retired	61	here
	G	Washburn Everett G	602	waiter	30	“
	H	Washburn Mary I—†	602	housewife	33	“
	K	Wright Henry D	602	cook	49	36 Worcester
	L	Devine Gloucester P	604	janitor	60	here
	M	O'Keefe Daniel	604	engineer	50	“
	N	Shea Anna—†	604	stenographer	43	“
	O	Rodman Harold	604	mechanic	47	“
	P	Rodman James	604	retired	74	
	R	Rodman Minnie L—†	604	housewife	71	“
	S	Bellville Odessa—†	604	stitcher	33	
	T	Call Avis—†	604	“	36	
	U	Murphy Evelyn—†	604	housewife	42	“
	V	Payson George H	604	shoeworker	50	“
	W	Belzer Marie—†	606	nurse	72	“
	X	Donelly Frank	606	waiter	47	Waltham
	Y	Duggan William	606	clerk	53	674 Mass av
	Z	Fox Vera—†	606	waitress	28	36 Concord sq
28						
	A	Gray Arthur	606	painter	48	here
	B	Gray Lillian—†	606	housewife	37	“
	C	Heffernan Gerald	606	shipper	45	“
	D	*Huff Emily—†	606	cook	68	
	E	Koffard Henry	606	janitor	60	“
	F	*Lydon Beatrice—†	606	maid	36	18 W Newton
	G	Murphy John	606	janitor	65	616 Tremont
	H	Noonan John	606	waiter	40	here
	K	O'Keefe Albina—†	606	housewife	36	“
	L	O'Keefe James	606	attorney	53	“
	M	Parkinson Gertrude—†	606	nurse	65	“
	N	*Sharp Harry	606	bartender	45	Waltham
	O	Wales Fred	606	mechanic	72	here
	S	Anton Robert	610A	ironworker	42	308 Shawmut av
	T	Bannister Vincent	610A	rigger	52	85 Pembroke
	U	MacDonald Alice—†	610A	housewife	60	28 Upton
	V	MacDonald Sumner	610A	retired	60	28 “
	W	Manley Albert M	610A	clerk	48	here
	X	Manley Irene M—†	610A	housewife	52	“
	Y	*Oliver John T	610A	fisherman	38	“
	Z	*Santos Manuel	610A	janitor	59	

Page.	Letter.	Full Name.	Residence, Jan. 1, 1943.	Occupation.	Supposed Age.	Reported Residence, Jan. 1, 1942. Street and Number.

29

Tremont Street—Continued

Page.	Letter.	Full Name.	Residence, Jan. 1, 1943.	Occupation.	Supposed Age.	Reported Residence, Jan. 1, 1942. Street and Number.
29	A	Silva Charles A	610A	laborer	40	Winthrop
	B	Stratton George A	610A	retired	73	here
	C	Stratton Ida D—†	610A	housewife	59	"
	D	*Tzimopoulos Avangelos	610A	carpenter	59	"
	E	Valentine John B	610A	retired	65	24 Milford
	F	Valentine Mae J—†	610A	housewife	69	24 "
	G	Barr Margaret—†	612	at home	56	here
	H	Caswell William A	612	laborer	48	"
	K	Jansen Albert H	612	shipfitter	56	26 Union pk
	L	Jansen Etta A—†	612	housewife	35	26 "
	M	Kahaly Abraham	612	barber	43	here
	N	Kahaly Mary—†	612	housewife	34	"
	O	Moreau Cora—†	612	at home	51	"
	P	Bayside Thomas	614	retired	61	
	R	Bridgeford Rita—†	614	laundress	33	"
	D	Davies William	614	electrician	53	"
	T	Edelstein Hyman	614	retired	59	
	U	Ellis Frank	614	merchant	60	"
	V	Kent Ralph	614	cook	60	"
	W	Porhas Wilfred—†	614	painter	40	195 St Botolph
	X	Ruggier Joseph	614	laborer	58	here
	Y	Tessier John	614	painter	59	"
	Z	Young Frank	614	clerk	33	"
30						
	A	*Brady Margaret—†	616	at home	50	567 Tremont
	B	Castracane John	616	cook	66	622 "
	C	Grogan John	616	houseman	66	here
	D	Hoyt Walter	616	salesman	60	"
	E	Kaplan Charlotte—†	616	clerk	24	125 Boylston
	F	LaBrecque Yvonne—†	616	machinist	36	366 Centre
	G	LaPanne Euphemia—†	616	housekeeper	54	here
	H	Magee Gertrude—†	616	machinist	29	366 Centre
	K	*McDougall James	616	carpenter	62	here
	L	Raymond Joseph D	616	painter	51	462 Shawmut av
	M	Raymond Ruth—†	616	housewife	46	462 "
	N	St Peter Lottie—†	616	governess	34	Cambridge
	O	St Peter Priscilla—†	616	candymaker	20	"
	P	Soucy John B	616	retired	63	here
	R	Tiernan Kathryn—†	616	stitcher	35	249 W Newton

Page.	Letter.	Full Name.	Residence, Jan. 1, 1943.	Occupation.	Supposed Age.	Reported Residence, Jan. 1, 1942. Street and Number.

Tremont Street—Continued

	T	Abdelnour George	620	waiter	48	here
	U	Bryant Lydell D	620	retired	71	"
	V	Eldrich Georgia F—†	620	at home	79	"
	W	Fareta Catherine—†	620	stitcher	27	"
	X	Flynn Joseph	620	florist	28	550 Tremont
	Y	Marsh Florence—†	620	at home	63	here
	1Y	McShinsky Louis	620	farmer	55	N Hampshire
	Z	Ruby George N	620	retired	68	here
31						
	B	Sims Edith—†	620	housewife	38	Malden
	C	Sims Robert	620	cook	38	"
	D	Snow William	620	retired	76	here
	E	Bresnahan Thomas C	622	musician	47	196 St Botolph
	C	Cantinella Giuseppe	622	laborer	45	here
	G	Coyne Carol—†	622	nurse	32	Cambridge
	H	Fattibene Cosmos	622	chauffeur	32	626 Tremont
	K	Gordon Ruth M—†	622	secretary	52	196 St Botolph
	L	Gunderway Henry	622	chauffeur	52	here
	M	Hayes Rita M—†	622	waitress	27	95 Dakota
	N	*Johnstone Lydia—†	622	housewife	55	here
	O	Marshall Herbert	622	chauffeur	24	"
	P	Morse Flora—†	622	at home	72	Vermont
	R	*St Pierre Alma—†	622	housekeeper	45	here
	S	Williams Dorothy—†	622	laundress	37	"
	T	Brown William F	624	pipefitter	39	21 Dartmouth pl
	U	Clark Herbert S	624	clerk	47	here
	V	Coveney Harry	624	nurse	53	"
	W	Crevitz Henry J	624	clerk	57	573 Tremont
	X	Curry Charles	624	U S N	20	here
	Y	Curry Isabelle—†	624	housewife	40	"
	Z	Emono Omer J	624	shoemaker	47	Lawrence
32						
	A	Ford Clifford F	624	grinder	41	Cambridge
	B	Paiva Cedalia R—†	624	housewife	25	25 Dwight
	C	Paiva Edward S	624	foundryman	25	48 "
	D	Sullivan Harold G	624	U S N	34	New York
	E	Sullivan Kay—†	624	housewife	29	"
	F	Astensia Frank L	626	waiter	42	370 Col av
	G	*Baino Marcella—†	626	laborer	47	Cambridge
	H	Burgess Claire—†	626	housekeeper	28	1044 Wash'n

Page.	Letter.	Full Name.	Residence, Jan. 1, 1943.	Occupation.	Supposed Age.	Reported Residence, Jan. 1, 1942. Street and Number.

Tremont Street—Continued

	K	Damaceo Domingo	626	waiter	40	New York
	L	Dennis Nora—†	626	at home	64	89 Union Park
	M	Englis Elaine—†	626	housewife	28	here
	N	Lafond Charles	626	laborer	54	Harding
	O	Lew Young	626	laundryman	38	Wash'n D C
	P	Mallette Mary—†	626	waitress	22	31 Dartmouth
	R	McGilvary Isabel—†	626	domestic	52	78 W Dedham
	S	Rana Mikher M	626	waiter	42	New York
	T	Tedpago Jacqueline—†	626	waitress	30	340 Col av
	W	Cleary Edward F	634	bricklayer	65	here
	X	Cleary Henry	634	clerk	23	"
	Y	Taylor Eva—†	634	housewife	38	"
	Z	Taylor Howard	634	laborer	43	
33						
	B	Maksoodian Christy M	636	broker	58	"
	C	McDonald Agnes—†	636	housewife	43	Medford
	D	McDonald James	636	counterman	45	"
	E	O'Neil Catherine—†	636	housewife	28	here
	F	O'Neil James	636	molder	30	"
	G	Capillo Dominick	638	laborer	53	"
	H	*Capillo Margarite—†	638	housewife	49	"
	K	Champney Hilda—†	638	"	40	N Hampshire
	L	Champney Leonard	638	painter	50	12 Church
	M	Lamaco Donita	638	presser	45	here
	N	Logue Elizabeth—†	638	housewife	68	"
	O	Lohnes Madeline M—†	638	packer	34	53 Dudley
	P	Lohnes Robert E	638	mechanic	34	53 "
	R	Lynch Pauline—†	638	clerk	20	Newton
	S	Maginnes Anna—†	638	waitress	40	671 Mass av
	T	Moriarty John	638	laborer	50	214 W Newton
	U	Murphy Laura—†	638	at home	64	here
	V	Staples Fred	638	laborer	50	58 W Newton
	W	Connor Nora T—†	652	domestic	67	Marblehead
	X	Gill Elizabeth E—†	652	housewife	59	here
	Y	Hill Edward	652	retired	75	"
	Z	Jerome Edward	652	welder	33	"
34						
	A	Jerome Honora S—†	652	housewife	33	"
	B	McCarthy Josephine—†	652	at home	58	193 W Brookline
	C	Roche Carrie—†	652	housewife	72	here

Page.	Letter.	FULL NAME.	Residence, Jan. 1, 1943.	Occupation.	Supposed Age.	Reported Residence, Jan. 1, 1942. Street and Number.

Tremont Street—Continued

	D	Roche Frederick W	652	steamfitter	69	here
	F	*Akel Jamily—†	654	housewife	40	129 Hudson
	G	Akel Karan	654	cutter	50	129 "
	H	Kennison Fred M	654	physician	69	here
	K	Kennison Luella M—†	654	housewife	66	"
	L	Leidwell Mary—†	654	clerk	58	"
	M	Salemi Jeannette—†	654	housewife	28	Quincy
	N	Salemi Nahim J	654	attendant	30	35 Laconia
	O	Stevens Lillian—†	654	nurse	50	here
	P	Casey James O	656	retired	81	1521 Wash'n
	R	Hoban Luke	656	salesman	48	14 Rutland sq
	S	Hoban Sadie—†	656	housewife	50	14 "
	T	Lane Gercilder—†	656	at home	64	10 "
	U	Madden Patrick	656	operator	54	here
	V	Phillips Ella M—†	656	at home	59	"
	W	Rohan Francis D	656	physician	40	1521 Wash'n
	X	Rohan Mary C—†	656	housewife	32	1521 "
	Y	Toms Lola M—†	656	stitcher	62	here
	Z	Twiss David	656	clerk	24	"
35						
	A	Twiss Frederick	656	retired	64	
	B	Winn Helen—†	656	housewife	30	"
	C	Winn James	656	mechanic	32	"
	D	Andrews George	658	retired	60	627 Mass av
	E	Brown Lillian—†	658	waitress	34	here
	F	Campbell Gladys—†	658	housewife	39	"
	G	Campbell Peter	658	chef	40	"
	H	Clark Catherine—†	658	cook	40	
	K	Couch Ellen—†	658	at home	75	
	L	Day Ernest	658	retired	60	
	M	Murphy Delia—†	658	housekeeper	69	"
	N	O'Brien Lawrence	658	clerk	27	New York
	O	Ordiz Lionel	658	U S N	38	129 W Newton
	P	Ordiz Mary L—†	658	housewife	25	129 "
	R	Phelan Alice—†	658	seamstress	55	here
	S	Slesser Peter	658	mechanic	50	"
	T	Waters Georgianna M—†	658	housekeeper	52	167 Warren av
	U	Azzariti Ella—†	660	housewife	23	81 Amory
	V	Braley Everett	660	retired	66	here
	W	Chapman Alanson	660	engineer	48	"

Page.	Letter.	Full Name.	Residence, Jan. 1, 1943.	Occupation.	Supposed Age.	Reported Residence, Jan. 1, 1942. Street and Number.

Tremont Street—Continued

	X	Connor Maria—†	660	waitress	22	4 Union Park
	Y	Danford Daniel	660	laborer	39	here
	Z	Galiazzo Mary—†	660	operator	28	Somerville
36						
	A	Goodman Benjamin	660	seaman	64	here
	B	Haley Charles	660	laborer	66	"
	C	Harrington Theresa—†	660	stitcher	56	"
	D	Hunter Leroy	660	clerk	21	"
	E	Keefe Nellie—†	660	cook	60	Brookline
	F	Lock Charles	660	laborer	61	here
	G	Olsen Olaf	660	retired	65	"
	H	Richardson Herbert	660	toolmaker	66	"
	K	Smith Frank	660	painter	64	
	L	Akikie Chickory D	662	shoeworker	60	"
	M	Akikie Edward	662	U S A	22	"
	N	Akikie Freida—†	662	housewife	46	"
	O	Akikie Jennie A—†	662	stitcher	28	"
	P	Fitzgerald Patrick	662	mechanic	42	Cambridge
	R	Hall Sarah—†	662	at home	66	here
	S	Kearsley Alice—†	662	"	67	"
	T	Mahoney Edward	662	retired	71	"
	U	Malcolm Charles	662	"	69	"
	V	Rediker Harold	662	laborer	45	Cambridge
	W	Reilly Mary—†	662	at home	71	here
	X	Stevenson Martha—†	662	"	71	28 Upton
	Y	Yates Paul	662	chauffeur	27	Dedham
	Z	Leong Ham	662A	laundryman	47	here

Trumbull Street

37						
	A	Carr Laura—†	2	housewife	41	344 Shawmut av
	B	Carr William	2	retired	40	344 "
	C	Franklyn Hester—†	2	at home	67	344 "
	F	Housis Nicholas	8	waiter	42	here
	G	*Kaffetzaki Efdokia—†	8	housewife	61	"
	H	Kaffetzaki Manuel	8	porter	62	"
	K	Kaffetzaki Mary—†	8	seamstress	29	"
	L	Maronis George	14	laborer	58	
	M	*Polychronis Anna—†	14	housewife	62	"
	N	Polychronis Gregor	14	retired	59	

Page.	Letter.	Full Name.	Residence, Jan. 1, 1943.	Occupation.	Supposed Age.	Reported Residence, Jan. 1, 1942. Street and Number.
38		**Upton Street**				
	A	Binder Harry	10	retired	62	here
	B	Conard Claude	10	laborer	30	"
	C	Flynn David	10	retired	70	"
	D	Hickey Michael	10	laborer	40	
	E	Keenan Florence—†	10	housekeeper	55	"
	F	Manning Martin	10	chauffeur	50	"
	G	McDonnell Patrick	10	custodian	67	"
	H	Peverly Charles	10	retired	70	
	K	Sheehan Michael	10	laborer	64	
	L	Spear Frederick	10	"	40	"
	M	Azor Danius	12	"	50	548 Tremont
	N	*Eleopoulos Charles	12	laundryman	55	here
	O	Goldman Joseph	12	carpenter	60	19 Upton
	P	Patterson Helen—†	12	clerk	38	here
	R	Petrone Constantine	12	watchman	47	"
	S	Schoyios Mabel—†	12	housewife	50	"
	T	*Schoyios William	12	retired	54	
	U	Serfes Peter	12	watchman	48	"
	V	Spinney James	12	laborer	44	
	W	Murphy Annie—†	14	housekeeper	69	"
	X	Phillips Lillian—†	14	"	36	"
	Y	*Lehie Angeline—†	14	housewife	42	"
	Z	Lehie Henry	14	riveter	45	
39						
	A	*Affra Mary—†	14	stitcher	56	
	B	*Sahyoun George	14	operator	46	"
	C	Sahyoun Rita—†	14	housewife	35	"
	D	Trimmins Constantinos J	14	U S A	20	
	E	*Trimmins Fannie—†	14	housewife	48	"
	F	*Trimmins John	14	retired	70	
	G	Trimmins Peter	14	U S A	25	
	H	Trimmins Porta—†	14	stitcher	23	"
	K	Burlingame Emma—†	16	housewife	26	Cambridge
	L	Burlingame Robert	16	carpenter	36	"
	M	Cannara Genevieve—†	16	stitcher	23	here
	N	Hernon Thomas	16	bartender	40	"
	O	Jorgensen Frank	16	chef	37	New York
	P	Kelliher Dennis	16	clerk	47	616 Tremont
	R	MacKay Ann—†	16	housekeeper	34	New York
	S	McCarthy Florence J	16	chauffeur	35	616 Tremont

Page.	Letter.	Full Name.	Residence, Jan. 1, 1943.	Occupation.	Supposed Age.	Reported Residence, Jan. 1, 1942. Street and Number.

Upton Street—Continued

Page.	Letter.	Full Name.	Residence, Jan. 1, 1943.	Occupation.	Supposed Age.	Reported Residence, Jan. 1, 1942. Street and Number.
	T	Pavone Ann—†	16	stitcher	23	here
	U	Sullivan Edward	16	clerk	35	616 Tremont
	V	Wallace William	16	laborer	50	here
	W	Whitney Guy	16	chef	53	616 Tremont
	X	Armstrong Walter	18	laborer	45	here
	Y	Barros Joseph D	18	porter	40	72 Waltham
	Z	Cabral Charles	18	laborer	38	here
40						
	A	*Harfoush Joseph	18	"	53	
	B	Kudno Harry M	18	waiter	39	"
	C	LaFleur Lydia—†	18	attendant	42	28 Whitney
	D	Mendes Joseph	18	porter	40	Newton
	E	O'Connor Francis	18	laborer	45	Cambridge
	F	Thomas Alice—†	18	shoeworker	20	here
	G	Thomas Louise—†	18	clerk	22	"
	H	Thomas Michael	18	U S A	23	"
	K	*Thomas Nettie—†	18	stitcher	51	
	L	Thomas Roy	18	laborer	43	
	M	*Thomas Tofey	18	shoeworker	46	"
	N	Brunard Mary M—†	20	housekeeper	59	"
	O	*Chase Harry	20	retired	77	"
	P	Daws George H	20	"	68	"
	R	Dorr Bertha—†	20	housewife	59	Marblehead
	S	Dorr Henry P	20	machinist	51	"
	T	Elze Elizabeth—†	20	housekeeper	74	here
	U	Goodman Nellie—†	20	"	67	"
	V	Greathead Herbert B	20	machinist	51	144 W Concord
	W	Jellison John	20	laborer	60	602 Tremont
	X	*Lyddy Anna—†	20	housekeeper	61	here
	Y	Butterworth Harry	22	fireman	49	"
	Z	Colson Mary A—†	22	housekeeper	50	Chelsea
41						
	A	Domont Eliza—†	22	housewife	49	here
	B	Domont James	22	salesman	54	"
	C	Egan Nicholas	22	laborer	50	39 E Concord
	D	Firth Morris	22	fishcutter	32	here
	E	Galvin James F	22	painter	58	"
	F	*Kalalas Nicholas	22	laborer	61	Hingham
	G	Keough Anastasia—†	22	at home	84	here
	H	Sammis Eva J—†	22	housekeeper	66	"
	K	Thomas John J	22	printer	53	"

Page.	Letter.	Full Name.	Residence, Jan. 1, 1943.	Occupation.	Supposed Age.	Reported Residence, Jan. 1, 1942. Street and Number.

Upton Street—Continued

	L	Thomas Lena—†	22	waitress	32	616 Tremont
	M	Thomas Rose J—†	22	housewife	49	here
	N	Trabelsie Tofeek	22	barber	48	104 Union Park
	O	Booth Grace—†	24	housekeeper	64	here
	P	Delaney Gerald M	24	U S A	35	"
	R	Delaney Julia—†	24	housewife	59	"
	S	Delaney Viola M—†	24	technician	30	"
	T	Doherty John	24	U S A	33	
	U	Jenkins Alphus F	24	retired	70	
	V	Karestavren Harry	24	porter	56	
	W	MacDonald Daniel	24	watchman	57	"
	X	Sumner Sarah—†	24	housekeeper	82	"
	Y	Taylor Elmer E	24	laborer	55	"
	Z	Akuki Boulas A	26	retired	49	
42						
	A	Cosgrove Patrick	26	laborer	45	Maryland
	B	*Haddad Thomas	26	"	44	Waltham
	C	Lewis William A	26	bartender	49	25 Dartmouth
	D	Maher Gladys—†	26	nurse	36	Maryland
	E	Melanson Harry J	26	shoeworker	53	26 Union Park
	F	Montzores John E	26	cook	53	32 Hanson
	G	Olson Carl	26	retired	71	338 Shawmut av
	H	Olson Mina—†	26	housewife	73	338 "
	K	Simonton Sadie E—†	26	laundress	39	Maine
	L	Blake Edward	28	machinist	45	here
	M	Brunnell Leo	28	proprietor	32	"
	N	Canton Georgiana—†	28	maid	50	Rhode Island
	O	Connors Preston J	28	ironworker	44	16 Dartmouth pl
	P	Cook Jennie G—†	28	housewife	49	here
	R	Cook Mary J—†	28	housekeeper	80	"
	S	McGrath Joseph L	28	laborer	51	"
	T	*McManus James	28	"	38	"
	U	Monahan Mary—†	28	housewife	25	148 Warren av
	V	Monahan Paul	28	laborer	26	148 "
	W	Sedgly Gertrude—†	28	waitress	40	15 Decatur
	X	*Tucci Marco	28	cabinetmaker	63	here
	Y	Akle Mehanno	30	laborer	46	"
	Z	Allen Evelyn—†	30	waitress	32	Cambridge
43						
	A	Breen Mary—†	30	housekeeper	70	144 W Canton
	B	*Georgacopoulos Arthur	30	laborer	45	Newton

Page.	Letter.	Full Name.	Residence, Jan. 1, 1943.	Occupation.	Supposed Age.	Reported Residence, Jan. 1, 1942. Street and Number.

Upton Street—Continued

	C	Hurney Patrick	30	retired	69	here
	D	Leonard Patrick	30	shipper	62	"
	E	Martin John	30	retired	78	143 W Canton
	F	O'Brien Theresa—†	30	waitress	40	602 Tremont
	G	Tsangaris Peter	30	laborer	48	here
	H	Younis Evelyn—†	30	stitcher	21	"
	K	*Younis Helen—†	30	housewife	59	"
	L	Younis James	30	welder	20	
	M	Younis Joseph	30	"	26	
	N	Younis Nahoun J	30	laborer	58	
	O	Younis Sarah—†	30	housewife	48	"
	P	Younis Selma—†	30	teacher	23	"
	R	Davis Charles	32	laborer	32	Maine
	S	Fitzgerald William J	32	"	52	here
	T	Kelley Richard	32	retired	66	"
	U	*Lafferty Thomas	32	laborer	42	"
	V	Langan James T	32	mechanic	49	"
	W	Meaney Michael	32	retired	66	70 Montgomery
	X	Moffitt Edward	32	attendant	65	4 E Brookline
	Y	*O'Donnell Annabella—†	32	housewife	43	here
	Z	O'Donnell Joseph	32	laborer	51	"
44						
	A	Prior James	32		52	"
	B	Roach James M	32	"	50	68 Montgomery
	C	Young Michael	32	bartender	50	here
	D	Chluverus Anthony	34	chef	49	21 Upton
	E	Downey Julia M—†	34	housekeeper	34	here
	F	Fagan James E	34	cashier	43	43 Esmond
	G	Godfrey Anthony	34	manager	45	here
	H	Green Herman	34	retired	65	"
	K	Merrill Delwin	34	laborer	36	"
	L	Reardon Peter	34	engineer	55	222 Bennington
	M	Sim Alex	34	laborer	60	here
	N	Smith Francis N	34	B F D	32	"
	O	Smith Margaret F—†	34	housewife	32	"
	P	Vlachlas Harry	34	chef	50	
	R	Zaza Harry	34	cook	48	
	S	Brown Andrew	36	bottler	40	
	T	Casey John	36	laborer	51	
	U	Dluky Joseph	36	"	49	
	V	Donalek Adele—†	36	housekeeper	37	"

Page.	Letter.	FULL NAME.	Residence, Jan. 1, 1943.	Occupation.	Supposed Age.	Reported Residence, Jan. 1, 1942. Street and Number.

Upton Street—Continued

	W	Gorham Patrick	36	laborer	50	here
	X	Gust Anthony	36	"	48	"
	Y	*Matecko Albin	36	baker	51	"
	Z	*Minascian Leo	36	barber	50	"
45						
	A	Pasciuto Anely—†	36	housewife	21	"
	B	Pasciuto Darro	36	laborer	27	"
	C	Plates Charles	36	"	51	"
	D	Powers Mary—†	36	housekeeper	39	"
	E	Staskawicz Alexander	36	laborer	53	"
	F	*Staskawicz Anna—†	36	housewife	48	"
	G	Sullivan Daniel	36	laborer	31	"
	H	Sullivan Mary—†	36	collector	51	"
	K	Cole Mary—†	38	housekeeper	54	Hull
	L	Corchiara Alice J—†	38	attendant	57	here
	M	*Coull John	38	shipfitter	45	"
	N	Crowley James A	38	watchman	59	"
	O	Deuerer August	38	gasfitter	66	"
	P	*Fratus John	38	cook	52	"
	R	*Haldane Frank	38	steamfitter	62	"
	S	Harold William E	38	accountant	56	"
	T	Holland William	38	retired	66	695 Tremont
	U	Keaney Mary—†	38	housekeeper	62	here
	V	McHugh Annie—†	38	"	49	"
	W	Phelan John E	38	meatcutter	59	"
	X	Rosario Roy C	38	cook	41	"
	Y	Rubinovitz David	38	retired	78	"
	Z	Saghpossian Haig	38	stitcher	59	"
46						
	A	Albert John	40	plumber	35	Cambridge
	B	*Boujaily Mabelle—†	40	housekeeper	62	here
	C	Carberry James	40	attendant	55	"
	D	Chystynyz Michael	40	restaurateur	50	"
	E	Darrigo Angelo	40	laborer	41	"
	F	Fuchs William	40	"	60	"
	G	*Grambals John	40	restaurateur	71	"
	H	*Karapatakis John	40	laborer	68	"
	K	Nevets Joseph	40	"	68	Cambridge
	L	Sacks John	40	painter	65	here
	M	Saltes John	40	baker	36	"
	N	Aborjaily Frederick	42	electrician	43	"

Page.	Letter.	Full Name.	Residence, Jan. 1, 1943.	Occupation.	Supposed Age.	Reported Residence, Jan. 1, 1942. Street and Number.

Upton Street—Continued

Page.	Letter.	Full Name.	Residence, Jan. 1, 1943.	Occupation.	Supposed Age.	Reported Residence, Jan. 1, 1942. Street and Number.
		Aborjaily Katherine—†	42	clerk	24	here
		Akunis Peter	42	chef	43	"
		Frost Herbert	42	laborer	43	"
		Garey Stephen	42	roofer	54	
	R	Marcaudi Stephen	42	laborer	43	
	U	Pecci Orlando	42	painter	43	"
	W	Celley Evelyn—†	44	waitress	35	8 Dillaway
	V	*Cossaboom Annie B—†	44	housekeeper	70	8 "
	X	Cunningham Jerome	44	laborer	50	8 "
	Y	DeRosa Giuseppe	44	tailor	59	8 '
	Z	*Grant Joseph	44	retired	65	8 '
47						
	A	Green Thomas	44	freighthandler	55	8 "
	B	Miles Grace—†	44	musician	60	8 "
	C	Oliver Joseph	44	cook	37	91 Waltham
	D	Sanborn Christopher B	44	cashier	45	Melrose
	E	Sylvester Andrew	44	restaurateur	65	8 Dillaway
	F	Tichen Mary D—†	44	housekeeper	62	8 "

Washington Street

Page.	Letter.	Full Name.	Residence, Jan. 1, 1943.	Occupation.	Supposed Age.	Reported Residence, Jan. 1, 1942. Street and Number.
	M	Esparza Jennie—†	1435	housewife	28	1 Decatur
	N	*Esparza Joseph	1435	clerk	27	1 "
	P	McNally Rita—†	1435	housewife	48	107 Union Park
	R	McNally Thomas	1435	clerk	54	107 "
	S	McNally Thomas	1435	U S A	21	107 "
	T	Claessens Lilla—†	1435	housewife	37	107 "
	U	Claessens Oscar	1435	merchant	51	107 "
	V	Robishaw Clara—†	1435	housewife	47	36 Sharon
	W	Robishaw Francis	1435	laborer	38	36 "
48						
	A	Sylva Anthony	1445	waiter	67	20 Lovering
	B	Sylva Rose—†	1445	housewife	53	1 Decatur
	C	Barton Agnes—†	1445	maid	55	42 Hanson
	D	Kelly Bernice—†	1445	at home	29	42 "
	E	Sweet Albert	1445	laborer	51	328 Centre
	F	Sweet Mary—†	1445	housewife	49	328 "
	G	Dunton Margaret T—†	1445	at home	53	92 E Dedham
	H	*Hamdeed Abdul	1445	laborer	47	12 Genesee
	K	*Hamdeed Laura—†	1445	housewife	48	12 "
	M	Reardon Edward J	1445	chauffeur	32	4 Ringgold

Page.	Letter.	Full Name.	Residence, Jan. 1, 1943.	Occupation.	Supposed Age.	Reported Residence, Jan. 1, 1942. Street and Number.

Washington Street—Continued

	N	Reardon Mary R—†	1445	housewife	30	4 Ringgold
	P	Gu Wah Non	1449	laundryman	41	here
	R	*Carlson Marie—†	1453	at home	69	25 E Springfield
	S	*Smith George	1453	laborer	51	Grafton
	U	Raymond Edward	1453	manager	37	716 Harris'n av
	V	Raymond Helen—†	1453	housewife	35	716 "
	W	Stewart George	1453	machinist	32	Quincy
	X	Stewart Hilda—†	1453	housewife	29	"
	Y	Blacker Margaret—†	1453	at home	69	105 Union Park
	Z	Blacker Robert	1453	cablemaker	37	105 "
49						
	A	McKenna Catherine C—†	1453	at home	35	103 "
	E	Hoevelmann William	1463	stitcher	48	50 W Dedham
	F	Walsh Charles	1463	welder	23	50 "
	G	Walsh Jane—†	1463	housewife	23	50 "
	H	Halliday Frank	1463	janitor	41	here
	K	Rooney Mary—†	1463	at home	73	"
	L	Mullaney Margaret—†	1463	clerk	26	"
	M	Nichols Grace—†	1463	housewife	23	"
	N	Nichols Michael	1463	clerk	33	
	O	Konkokas Isabelle—†	1463	housewife	38	"
	P	Konkokas Leonidas	1463	merchant	51	"
	R	Pelzer Annette—†	1463	housewife	37	"
	S	Pelzer Ira	1463	shoeworker	40	"
	T	Byers Albert C	1463	buyer	58	N Hampshire
	U	Khirlla Helen—†	1463	dressmaker	35	here
	V	Hyder Manera—†	1463	at home	42	"
	W	Hyder Nicholas	1463	clerk	21	"
	X	Ayers Philomena—†	1463	at home	65	
	Y	Artes Violetta—†	1463	"	64	
50						
	A	Hughes George H	1469	painter	38	
	B	Hughes Lillian—†	1469	housewife	29	"
	D	Logue George	1469	clerk	20	
	E	Logue Molly—†	1469	at home	42	
	K	Campbell John	1475	shipper	55	
	L	Clarke Mary—†	1475	at home	67	
	M	Duggan Nora—†	1475	"	82	
	N	*Hamilton Charles	1475	cook	72	
	O	Nanostrom Angus	1475	messenger	60	"
	P	O'Brien Charles	1475	retired	66	

Page.	Letter.	FULL NAME.	Residence, Jan. 1, 1943.	Occupation.	Supposed Age.	Reported Residence, Jan. 1, 1942. Street and Number.

Washington Street—Continued

	R	Haddad Agnes—†	1479	housewife	26	here
	S	Haddad Ferris	1479	U S A	31	470 Centre
	T	Joseph Blanche—†	1479	at home	33	here
	U	Joseph George	1479	U S A	20	"
	V	Joseph James	1479	accountant	34	"
	W	Joseph Mageed	1479	merchant	58	"
	X	Joseph Sophie—†	1479	housewife	56	"
	Y	Maloof Louis	1479	shoeworker	58	"
	Z	Robertshaw James	1479	clerk	60	
51						
	B	Grossman Peggy—†	1483	at home	40	
	C	Massalam Linda—†	1483	housewife	35	"
	D	Massalam Metri	1483	shoemaker	49	"
	E	O'Connor Eugene	1483	retired	70	
	G	*Steed Annie—†	1485	housewife	43	"
	H	Steed Evelyn—†	1485	stitcher	27	
	K	*Spiliopoulos Anna—†	1485	housewife	48	"
	L	Spiliopoulos Limperios	1485	pedler	52	
	M	*Haddad Julia—†	1485	housewife	63	"
	N	Haddad Peter	1485	rigger	32	
	O	Haddad Mary—†	1485	housewife	30	"
	P	Haddad Paul	1485	laborer	31	
	W	Hewitt Harry	1503	pedler	58	
	X	Haddad George	1503	brazier	24	
	Y	Haddad Hallen	1503	student	22	
	Z	*Haddad Lena—†	1503	housewife	49	"
52						
	A	Haddad Nagila—†	1503	hairdresser	21	"
	B	Haddad Najib	1503	shoeworker	51	"
	C	*Najam Hajie—†	1503	hairdresser	35	"
	D	Khoury Adeeb N	1503	barber	50	
	E	Khoury Mary—†	1503	housewife	33	"
	G	Bethoney Ernest	1507	U S M C	20	"
	H	Bethoney George M	1507	U S A	22	
	K	*Bethoney Manson	1507	porter	61	"
	L	Bethoney Mary—†	1507	housewife	28	"
	M	Bethoney Michael	1507	shipper	32	
	N	*Bethoney Sarah—†	1507	housewife	54	"
	O	Bethoney Stephen	1507	electrician	29	"
	P	Bethoney Susan—†	1507	housewife	23	"
	R	Campbell John	1507	waiter	49	

Page.	Letter.	Full Name.	Residence, Jan. 1, 1943.	Occupation.	Supposed Age.	Reported Residence, Jan. 1, 1942. Street and Number.

Washington Street—Continued

	S	Canty John	1507	carpenter	54	265 Shawmut av
	U	Kraft Alfred	1513	laborer	50	here
	V	Kraft Lena—†	1513	clerk	24	"
	W	Kraft Marion—†	1513	housewife	52	"
	X	Dunkerton Sarah—†	1513	at home	68	
	Y	Hatch Fred	1513	tester	58	
	Z	Toomey Bessie—†	1513	at home	69	
53						
	A	Kelly John	1513	clerk	68	
	B	Kelly Maude—†	1513	housewife	57	"
	C	Glynn John	1513	ironworker	55	"
	D	Glynn Margaret—†	1513	housewife	46	"
	F	Magee Eleanor—†	1513	"	38	"
	G	Magee John E	1513	ironworker	38	"
	H	Harworth Gezar	1513	shipper	22	526 Mass av
	K	Harworth Mildred—†	1513	housewife	21	526 "
	L	Pratt Mary—†	1513	"	49	here
	M	Pratt Robert	1513	clerk	50	"
	N	Morancy Evelyn—†	1513	housewife	38	N Hampshire
	O	Morancy Homer	1513	shipfitter	36	3 Trenton
	P	O'Neil Margaret—†	1513	housewife	50	here
	R	O'Neil William F	1513	carpenter	62	"
	S	Ayoub Edward	1513	accountant	25	"
	T	Ayoub Marguerite—†	1513	housewife	30	"
	U	Hill Eva—†	1513	at home	54	Lowell
	V	Hill Lorraine—†	1513	nurse	24	"
	X	Murphy Dorothy M—†	1513	housewife	47	here
	Y	Murphy Harry T	1513	bartender	58	"
54						
	B	Marhar Lucy J—†	1513	at home	75	
	C	Quinn Henry M	1513	clerk	68	
	D	Stevens Catherine—†	1513	housewife	61	"
	E	Stevens John H	1513	manager	68	"
	F	Kubish John	1513	patternmaker	66	"
	G	*Kubish Victoria—†	1513	housewife	41	"
	H	Shamirian Samuel	1513	cook	58	
	N	Blair George P	1521	U S A	22	
	O	Gootner George	1521	salesman	45	"
	P	McGee Annie—†	1521	at home	65	
	R	Merrill Grace—†	1521	housekeeper	55	"
	S	Rigg John T	1521	salesman	54	"

Page.	Letter.	FULL NAME.	Residence, Jan. 1, 1943.	Occupation.	Supposed Age.	Reported Residence, Jan. 1, 1942. Street and Number.

Washington Street—Continued

Page.	Letter.	FULL NAME.	Residence, Jan. 1, 1943.	Occupation.	Supposed Age.	Reported Residence, Jan. 1, 1942. Street and Number.
	T	McArdle Dorothy—†	1521	housewife	24	here
	U	McArdle Henry P	1521	U S A	23	"
	V	McArdle Mary—†	1521	waitress	43	"
	W	McSweeney Hanorah—†	1521	at home	78	"
	Z	Finn Mary—†	1521	maid	76	Natick
55						
	A	Harper William	1521	laborer	55	here
	B	Kalick Leopold	1521	clerk	65	"
	C	Tomlinson Florence—†	1521	at home	65	"
	G	Edmunds Irene V—†	1521	housewife	41	"
	H	Edmunds Rodney J	1521	carpenter	41	"
	K	Oakes Henry E	1521	custodian	44	"
	L	Williams Rose—†	1521	waitress	53	

West Brookline Street

Page.	Letter.	FULL NAME.	Residence, Jan. 1, 1943.	Occupation.	Supposed Age.	Reported Residence, Jan. 1, 1942. Street and Number.
	O	Bartz Christine—†	61	clerk	58	here
	P	Bassett Agnes—†	61	at home	73	"
	R	Bassett Mary—†	61	"	76	"
	S	Buckley Hannah—†	61	"	73	
	T	Burke Mary C—†	61		72	"
	U	*Byrnes Margaret—†	61	"	71	5 Waterloo
	V	Cahill Hannah—†	61	"	73	here
	W	*Callahan Elizabeth—†	61	"	60	321 Longwood av
	X	Campbell Margaret—†	61	"	70	91 Walter
	Y	Clark Mary P—†	61	"	70	here
	Z	Clements Madeline—†	61	cook	29	"
56						
	A	*Coffey Nellie—†	61	at home	72	
	B	Coninix Mary—†	61	"	74	"
	C	Conneally Catherine—†	61	"	70	Brookline
	D	Counihan Margaret—†	61	"	83	here
	E	*Crossland Mary—†	61	"	75	"
	F	Daly Martha—†	61	maid	49	"
	G	Dermody Mary—†	61	at home	67	"
	H	Doherty Bridget E—†	61	"	74	
	K	Dolan Delia—†	61	"	74	
	L	Donovan Julia—†	61		76	
	M	Dooling Margaret—†	61	"	80	
	N	*Doyle Nora—†	61	"	73	
	O	*English Esther—†	61		65	

Page.	Letter.	Full Name.	Residence, Jan. 1, 1943.	Occupation.	Supposed Age.	Reported Residence, Jan. 1, 1942. Street and Number.
		West Brookline Street—Continued				
	P	Finn Esther—†	61	cook	39	here
	R	*Finnegan Catherine—†	61	at home	79	"
	S	Flynn Catherine—†	61	"	78	"
	T	Foley Annie F—†	61	"	73	
	U	*Garrity Margaret—†	61	"	58	
	V	*Hart Mary—†	61	"	52	
	W	*Hennessey Hannah—†	61	"	62	"
	X	*Herlihy Julia—†	61	"	78	25 Com av
	Y	*Higgins Catherine—†	61	"	63	here
	Z	*Hourihan Hannah—†	61	"	87	"
57						
	A	*Hourihan Julia—†	61	"	80	
	B	Hourihan Nora—†	61	"	69	
	C	Hughes Mary—†	61		79	
	D	Joyce Teresa—†	61		68	
	E	*Leonard Nora—†	61		62	
	F	Liddy Margaret—†	61		80	"
	G	*Lundy Catherine—†	61	"	70	Peabody
	H	Malley Anna—†	61	"	61	here
	K	McCarthy Joanna—†	61	"	84	"
	L	McDonald Annie—†	61	"	74	"
	M	McDonough Annie—†	61	"	78	
	N	*McGee Catherine—†	61	"	75	
	O	*McGee Mary—†	61	"	71	
	P	McGrail Mary—†	61		47	
	R	McGrath Elizabeth—†	61	"	86	
	S	McKenna Ellen—†	61		69	
	T	McLaughlin Mary—†	61	"	69	"
	U	*McPhelan Catherine—†	61	"	53	Cambridge
	V	McSweeney Margaret—†	61	cook	31	here
	W	Meehan Mary—†	61	at home	83	"
	X	Minezzi Alfred J	61	engineer	42	33 Lynde
	Y	Monagle Rose—†	61	maid	54	here
	Z	Murray Bridget—†	61	at home	83	"
58						
	A	Norton Mary—†	61	"	80	
	B	O'Brien Mary—†	61		69	
	C	*O'Connor Nellie—†	61		62	
	D	O'Hara Elizabeth—†	61	"	74	
	E	O'Reilly Georgianna—†	61	"	85	

Page.	Letter.	Full Name.	Residence, Jan. 1, 1943.	Occupation.	Supposed Age.	Reported Residence, Jan. 1, 1942. Street and Number.

West Brookline Street—Continued

Page.	Letter.	Full Name.	Residence, Jan. 1, 1943.	Occupation.	Supposed Age.	Reported Residence, Jan. 1, 1942. Street and Number.
	F	Paon Virginia—†	61	at home	87	here
	G	Partsch Barbara—†	61	"	80	"
	H	*Quinlan Margaret—†	61	"	82	"
	K	Raymond Alice E—†	61	clerk	26	Wellesley
	L	Rogers Nora—†	61	at home	70	here
	M	*Shanahan Ellen—†	61	"	74	Newton
	N	*Sullivan Ellen—†	61	"	74	here
	O	Sullivan Julia—†	61		70	"
	P	Sullivan Margaret M—†	61	"	83	"
	R	Sullivan Mary E—†	61	nurse	54	
	S	Triggs Rose—†	61	at home	73	"
	T	Wall Margaret—†	61	"	50	70 W Cedar
	U	Walsh Annie—†	61	"	75	here
	V	Walsh Catherine—†	61	"	77	"
	W	Wessler Ella—†	61	"	74	"
	X	Woods Ellen—†	61		74	
	Y	Wyman Mary—†	61	"	74	
	Z	Enright Victoria—†	73	housekeeper	51	"
59						
	A	Koop Ernest H	73	retired	74	"
	B	Robinson Norman L	73	chauffeur	54	"
	C	Hovsepian Eliazar	73	storekeeper	56	"
	D	Hovsepian Mary—†	73	housewife	43	"
	E	Tomkotonis Beatrice—†	73	"	33	Cambridge
	F	Tomkotonis John	73	laborer	29	"
	G	Torosian John	73	storekeeper	47	here
	H	*Torosian Nouvart—†	73	housewife	38	"
	K	*Ayvazian Stephen	73	retired	65	"
	L	*Ipasian Stephen	73	laborer	63	
	M	Torosian John	73	porter	58	
	N	Torosian Nereses	73	laborer	55	"
	P	Barbour Catherine—†	75	housewife	59	713 Tremont
	R	Barbour Mary—†	75	nurse	23	713 "
	S	Caddigan Charles E	75	linotyper	37	713 "
	T	*Cunningham Thomas P	77	realtor	38	here
	U	Dolan James	77	porter	59	"
	V	Firth Abraham	77	retired	82	82 W Newton
	W	Jess George R	77	porter	43	here
	X	Matifes Harry T	77	agent	70	"
	Y	McGloin Patrick M	77	janitor	52	44 E Newton

Page.	Letter.	Full Name.	Residence, Jan. 1, 1943.	Occupation.	Supposed Age.	Reported Residence, Jan. 1, 1942. Street and Number.

West Brookline Street—Continued

	z	Rubli Emil	77	retired	60	here
60						
	A	Allen Alice—†	79	seamstress	68	"
	B	*Harper Celia—†	79	at home	79	"
	C	Harrington Emma—†	79	housekeeper	72	"
	D	McNamara Frank	79	retired	64	"
	E	Nelson Forrest E	79	salesman	48	"
	F	*Nelson Maud E—†	79	housewife	51	"
	G	Olson Gustaf M	79	upholsterer	58	"
	L	McElmoyle Frances—†	82	housewife	33	16 Isabella
	M	McElmoyle Robert	82	checker	34	16 "
	N	Ahlquist Elvira—†	82	housewife	65	here
	O	Ahlquist Erik	82	retired	67	"
	P	*Alberth Sarah—†	82	waitress	52	"
	R	Larkin Josephine—†	82	laundress	57	"
	S	Doherty Andrew	82	engineer	45	
	T	Doherty Katherine—†	82	housewife	48	"
	U	Harvey Peter	82	laborer	49	
	V	Killion Clarence	83	"	48	
	W	*McKinnon Florence—†	83	domestic	45	"
	X	Seabury Harry	83	laborer	55	"
	Y	*Skwarck John	83	porter	55	"
	Z	Steele Angus	83	retired	69	Weymouth
61						
	A	Whelton Walter	83	laborer	56	here
	B	Williams Beatrice H—†	83	housewife	48	"
	C	Williams Harry J	83	salesman	58	"
	D	*Foley Delia—†	84	at home	61	"
	E	Williams Harry J	84	shipper	23	8 Pembroke
	F	*Williams Vera—†	84	housewife	21	8 "
	G	*Powers Annie—†	84	domestic	40	here
	H	Sawyer Carl	84	musician	52	"
	K	*Ferris Mary—†	85	housewife	52	"
	L	Ferris Samuel	85	watchman	63	"
	M	*Kurey Annagi—†	85	housewife	63	"
	N	Kurey Camilla—†	85	stitcher	29	
	O	Kurey John	85	laborer	28	
	P	Kurey Martha—†	85	stitcher	32	"
	R	Wadness Helen—†	85	housekeeper	36	58 Compton
	S	Gorlishian Helen—†	85	seamstress	40	here
	U	Frye Jack	87	chauffeur	45	"

Page.	Letter.	Full Name.	Residence, Jan. 1, 1943.	Occupation.	Supposed Age.	Reported Residence, Jan. 1, 1942. Street and Number.

West Brookline Street—Continued

	V	Lattimore John J	87	retired	65	here
	W	Shea Dennis	87	porter	60	"
	X	Reeves Mary E—†	88	housewife	38	82 W Brookline
	Y	Reeves Waldo M	88	woodworker	48	82 "
	Z	Carter Lydia—†	89	housekeeper	73	4 Decatur
62						
	A	Jones Cora—†	89	"	70	1475 Wash'n
	B	Voigt Ralph	89	salesman	52	here
	C	Voigt Rose—†	89	housewife	42	"
	E	Burton Mary A—†	91	housekeeper	45	15 Newland
	F	Shayeb Jessie—†	91	"	46	21 Waterford
	G	Wilton Effie—†	91	stitcher	60	38 Greenleaf
	K	*Knight Letitia—†	93	presser	63	here
	L	Norflett Almeta—†	93	housewife	45	"
	M	Norflett James D	93	porter	46	"
	O	Williams Annie—†	94	housewife	53	"
	P	Williams Edward	94	counterman	54	"
	R	Carter Marie—†	94	laundress	37	"
63						
	A	*Aulenback Berton	97	cook	42	
	B	Bixby Gertrude J—†	97	housewife	63	"
	C	Bixby Marvin	97	retired	65	"
	D	Hart Julia—†	97	housekeeper	78	"
	E	Ritter Louis	97	stagehand	58	"
	F	Cody Edna M—†	98	housekeeper	30	183 Shawmut av
	G	Hibbard Dolores—†	98	housewife	40	183 "
	H	Hibbard Lawrence M	98	chef	50	183 "
	K	Shamey Anna—†	98	cashier	28	here
	L	*Shamey Michael	98	pedler	62	"
	M	*Shamey Rose—†	98	housewife	56	"
	N	Shamey Samuel	98	pedler	24	"
	O	*Dalton Maude—†	98	housewife	39	109 E Newton
	V	Sander Carl	103	electrician	63	here
	W	Sander Marie—†	103	housewife	55	"
	X	Adams Theresa—†	103	housekeeper	55	"
	Y	Hook Franklin	105	retired	86	"
	Z	Best Martha—†	105	housekeeper	44	"
64						
	A	Ames Edgar J	105	retired	80	"
	C	Bofill Corinne C—†	111	housewife	36	758 Tremont
	D	Bofill Manuel L	111	riveter	41	758 "

Page.	Letter.	Full Name.	Residence, Jan. 1, 1943.	Occupation.	Supposed Age.	Reported Residence, Jan. 1, 1942. Street and Number.

West Brookline Street—Continued

	E	Harrington Charles E	111	shipper	33	98 Bowen
	F	Harrington George F	111	retired	52	98 "
	G	Harrington Rosanna—†	111	at home	74	98 "
	M	Kennedy John G	119	laborer	28	here
	N	Kennedy Sarah—†	119	housewife	70	"
	P	Bolio Arthur	119	rigger	56	1890 Wash'n
	R	Bolio Ella—†	119	housewife	57	1890 "
	O	Kane Annie—†	119	stitcher	43	here
	S	*Ross Rose—†	119	waitress	38	"
	T	Kyron Anna—†	119	housewife	56	"
	U	Kyron Bessie—†	119	stitcher	27	"
	V	Kryon George	119	photographer	23	"
	W	Kyron Helena—†	119	stenographer	24	"
	Y	Ellis Anna—†	121	stitcher	39	"
	Z	*Fick Freda—†	121	housewife	59	"
65						
	A	Fick Rudolph	121	painter	64	
	B	Cantello Otis S	124	janitor	45	
	F	Lapoint George	128	retired	74	
	G	*MacCuish Flora—†	128	at home	80	
	H	*MacLean Charles D	128	ironworker	61	"
	K	*MacLean Maude—†	128	housewife	56	"
	L	MacDonald Daniel A	128	steelcutter	57	"
	M	*MacDonald Mary—†	128	housewife	47	"
	N	Berntsen Sadie—†	128	stitcher	41	
	O	Deraney Sadie—†	128	housewife	74	"
	P	Deraney Samuel	128	chauffeur	49	"
	R	Malouf Nazla—†	128	housewife	35	Lynn
	S	Malouf Shibley	128	machinist	35	225 Shawmut av
	T	Donovan Sarah—†	128	housewife	58	here
	U	Donovan Timothy	128	laborer	61	"
	V	Ferguson Donald J	128	bookbinder	74	36 Coolidge rd
	W	MacKillop Daniel	128	porter	64	here
	X	MacKillop Effie—†	128	stitcher	57	"
	Y	Skillin Evelyn V—†	128	"	26	"
	Z	Blanchard Gladys—†	128	waitress	34	
66						
	A	Shine Jeremiah	128	retired	74	
	B	Sullivan Cecelia R—†	128	waitress	36	
	C	Morrison Evelyn—†	128	housewife	61	"
	D	Morrison William	128	baker	58	

Page.	Letter.	FULL NAME.	Residence, Jan. 1, 1943.	Occupation.	Supposed Age.	Reported Residence, Jan. 1, 1942. Street and Number.

West Brookline Street—Continued

	E	Cloyd Mildred—†	129	housekeeper	30	53 Symphony rd
	F	Pizzi Marion—†	129	housewife	29	50 "
	G	Pizzi Thomas	129	chauffeur	35	50 "
	H	Mackey Jefferson	129	laborer	40	522 Col av
	K	Mackey Lillie—†	129	housekeeper	38	522 "
	L	Davis Martha—†	129	housewife	47	here
	M	Davis Samuel	129	janitor	57	"
	N	Miller Beryl—†	130	housewife	32	"
	O	Miller Elmer	130	chauffeur	34	"
	P	Selig Hilda G—†	130	housewife	52	"
	R	Selig Theodore	130	retired	56	
	S	Willard Howard	130	radios	34	
	T	Willard Ruth—†	130	housewife	31	"
	U	Cunningham Charles	130	retired	73	"
	V	Gordon Joseph	130	"	75	
	W	Harris John	130	"	87	
	X	Jones Curwea	130	"	63	
	Y	Lajoie Nellie—†	130	at home	76	
	Z	Libby Lester	130	electrician	30	"
67						
	A	Daggert Roy	130	laborer	52	
	B	Hastings Everett	130	retired	81	
	C	*Laxon William	130	janitor	49	
	D	Milne Amy A—†	130	at home	71	
	E	*Sherman Herbert	130	cashier	68	"
	F	Brown Lena—†	130	domestic	52	14 Dartmouth pl
	G	Champlain William	130	retired	75	407 Col av
	H	Chapin Sarah—†	130	housekeeper	62	5 Dartmouth pl
	K	Arsenault Joseph O	130	carpenter	51	here
	L	*Charron Ferdinand	130	"	41	"
	M	Crowley Marie J—†	130	laundress	36	"
	N	Ellis Robert J	130	carpenter	36	1 Pevear pl
	O	*Harbour Eli	130	"	48	here
	P	Baronian Kachador H	130	storekeeper	59	"
	R	Baronian Mardiros	130	"	51	"
	S	*Baronian Virginia—†	130	housewife	40	"
	T	Manelian Sarkis	130	storekeeper	47	"
	V	Caggiano Michael	130	waiter	64	1 Union pk
	W	*Caggiano Palmia—†	130	housewife	52	1 "
	U	Johnson John	130	engineer	66	690 Harris'n av
	X	Gillis James	130	carpenter	52	here

Page.	Letter.	FULL NAME.	Residence, Jan. 1, 1943.	Occupation.	Supposed Age.	Reported Residence, Jan. 1, 1942. Street and Number.

West Brookline Street—Continued

	Y	Gillis Mary—†	130	housewife	48	here
	Z	MacLellan John J	130	lineman	54	"
68						
	A	Smith John H	130	mechanic	52	"
	C	*Blake Francis	133	janitor	76	
	D	Glendenning Gelenna A–†	133	housekeeper	53	"

West Canton Street

	N	Bennett Margaret—†	3	housewife	30	here
	O	Bennett William	3	machinist	32	"
	P	Cella Anthony R	3	seaman	30	"
	R	Frankle Fred	3	U S A	29	
	S	Frankle Sophie—†	3	housewife	25	"
	T	Frazier Augustus	3	painter	31	165 Com av
	U	Frazier Elsie M—†	3	housewife	20	165 "
	V	Lucas Dorothy—†	3	"	31	here
	W	Lucas Gabriel	3	counterman	50	"
	X	Mantos Diana—†	3	saleswoman	22	"
	Y	Molarelli Jennie—†	3	housewife	50	"
	Z	Molarelli Joseph	3	clerk	21	
69						
	A	*Weldon Eileen—†	3	housewife	32	"
	B	Weldon Thomas	3	engineer	40	
	C	Lamont Catherine—†	5	housewife	71	"
	D	Lamont Samuel	5	retired	70	
	E	Cleary Helen T—†	5	housewife	52	"
	F	Cleary James J	5	watchman	58	"
	G	Cleary James J	5	U S A	23	
	H	Spring Malcolm	5	U S N	30	
	K	Spring Ruth C—†	5	housewife	28	"
	L	Coggins Grace L—†	5	"	54	"
	P	Miller William	25	stableman	55	Waltham
	R	Boyle Abbie—†	29	at home	63	2064 Wash'n
	S	Mossey Lillian—†	29	"	70	here
	V	Kierce Daniel	31	laborer	31	"
	W	Kierce Freda—†	31	housewife	31	"
	X	Moran Pauline—†	31	housekeeper	31	"
	Y	Graham Phoebe—†	32	housewife	23	1 James
	Z	Olson Phoebe—†	32	housekeeper	49	1 "

Page.	Letter.	FULL NAME.	Residence, Jan. 1, 1943.	Occupation.	Supposed Age.	Reported Residence, Jan. 1, 1942. Street and Number.
70		**West Canton Street**—Continued				
	B	Drummond Edward	34	baker	37	here
	C	Drummond Ruth—†	34	housewife	33	"
	E	Green Nellie—†	46	housekeeper	66	"
	F	Holbrook Susan—†	48	"	70	
	G	*Kimball May—†	48	"	70	
	H	Lincoln Elizabeth—†	48	clerk	22	
	K	Nickerson William	48	retired	81	
	L	Doyle Gertrude—†	50	laundress	44	"
	M	Howard Marion—†	50	housekeeper	76	"
	R	Clarke John	58	U S A	30	"
	S	Clarke Mary—†	58	housewife	51	"
	T	Clarke Richard	58	U S A	26	
	U	Clarke William	58	"	23	"
	V	Parker Albert	58	clerk	30	Lynn
	W	Parker Eileen—†	58	housewife	27	here
	X	Walsh Anne—†	58	"	32	"
	Y	Walsh William	58	presser	33	"
	Z	Ahern Andrew	59	retired	81	
71						
	A	Erickson Matilda—†	60	housekeeper	85	"
	B	*Griffiths Eva—†	60	housewife	54	"
	C	Griffiths Mildred—†	60	saleswoman	27	"
	D	Griffiths Thomas	60	retired	67	
	E	Gould Anna—†	64	housewife	53	"
	F	Gould George	64	laborer	63	
	G	Gould Raymond	64	painter	68	"
	K	Blake Helen G—†	65	at home	65	89 Norfolk av
	L	Cummings Ann M—†	65	"	65	here
	M	Stanton Katherine M—†	65	domestic	52	21 Union Park
	N	Lambertson Winifred—†	65	at home	75	here
	P	*Natse Olymphia—†	67	housewife	55	"
	R	Blanchette Margaret—†	71	storekeeper	49	"
	S	Mauro Alfred	71	machinist	32	"
	T	Sheehan Annie—†	78	housewife	56	"
	U	Sheehan William	78	laborer	56	
	V	Kelly Marie—†	78	housekeeper	73	"
	W	Lans Edward	78	laborer	66	"
	X	Malone Mary—†	82	housekeeper	69	Brookline
	Y	Ross Harry	82	cook	50	here
	Z	Ross Mary—†	82	housewife	50	"

Page.	Letter.	Full Name.	Residence, Jan. 1, 1943.	Occupation.	Supposed Age.	Reported Residence, Jan. 1, 1942. Street and Number.
72		**West Canton Street**—Continued				
	A	Ross Mary C—†	82	clerk	21	here
	C	Clark Ferdi M—†	86	housekeeper	63	"
	D	Maloof James	86	clerk	44	"
	E	Maloof Lois—†	86	housewife	33	"
	F	Norton Mary—†	86	clerk	44	"
	G	Steinberg Louis	86	laborer	41	
	H	Orsley Iris—†	rear 88A	saleswoman	31	"
	K	Doucette Eva—†	" 88A	housewife	20	56 Compton
	L	Doucette James	" 88A	lineman	24	56 "
	M	Dimitri Arthur	" 88A	laborer	45	here
	N	DiPrisco Margaret—†	" 88A	housewife	21	109 E Canton
	O	DiPrisco Thomas	" 88A	ironworker	23	109 "
	P	Gittleman Samuel	" 88A	manager	39	here
	R	Moore Elizabeth—†	" 88A	housewife	46	14 James
	S	Moore William	" 88A	laborer	57	14 "
	T	Laham Jennie—†	90	housewife	22	here
	U	Laham Joseph	90	laborer	32	"
	W	McDonald Jeanette—†	90	housekeeper	91	"
	X	Hanscomb Hattie—†	90	"	64	"
	Y	Monahan Annie—†	90	"	71	"
	Z	Hull Alta—†	90		65	38 Rutland sq
73						
	A	Lewis John	90	laborer	51	here
	E	Thomas Alfred	94	printer	26	"
	F	Thomas Loranna—†	94	housewife	26	"
	G	Mitchell Stewart	94	laborer	65	Lowell
	H	Lehto Arvo	94½	painter	29	here
	K	Lehto Carl	94½	laborer	27	N Hampshire
	L	Lehto Lillian—†	94½	housewife	22	"
	M	Lehto Norma—†	94½	"	28	here
	N	Sheehan Catherine—†	98	laundress	36	"
	O	Sheehan Helen—†	98	housewife	79	"
	P	O'Leary Helen—†	98	"	41	"
	R	Maiolo Leo	98	tailor	47	15 Waltham
	T	Boucher Charles	100	iceman	48	here
	U	Boucher Geraldine—†	100	housewife	33	"
	V	Stevenson Lillian—†	100	housekeeper	60	11 North sq
	W	*Harkness Catherine—†	100	"	74	here
74						
	A	Barrows Albert	104	laborer	43	

Page.	Letter.	FULL NAME.	Residence, Jan. 1, 1943.	Occupation.	Supposed Age.	Reported Residence, Jan. 1, 1942. Street and Number.

West Canton Street—Continued

	B	Barrows Annie—†	104	housewife	40	here
	C	Dwyer Catherine—†	104	housekeeper	78	79 Emerald
	D	Thomas Margaret—†	104	stitcher	49	here
	F	Gaumont Thomas	108	laborer	66	"
	K	Roessel Clara—†	110	housewife	51	"
	L	Roessel John	110	chef	60	
	M	Healy Iran	110	carpenter	64	"
	N	Healy Loretta—†	110	housewife	59	"
	O	Pastuszek Adam	110	painter	47	
	P	Pastuszek Josephine—†	110	housewife	48	"
	X	Kirby David	116	inspector	57	"
75						
	B	Creed Arthur	120	laborer	48	
	C	Creed Bridie—†	120	housewife	37	"
	D	Moore Alice—†	120	"	38	
	E	Moore Leslie	120	laborer	37	
	G	*Douglas Daniel	122	"	65	
	H	LeFebvre Alice—†	122	housewife	21	"
	K	LeFebvre Ludger	122	cook	31	
	O	Aylward Irene—†	125	housewife	31	"
	P	Aylward James	125	shipper	34	"
	R	Duffy John	125	laborer	30	
	S	*Duffy Mary—†	125	at home	60	"
	T	Duffy Michael	125	laborer	27	64 Warren av
	U	Groober Howard	125	U S N	32	here
	V	Groober Mary—†	125	housewife	32	"
	Y	Kane George	128	chauffeur	33	"
	Z	Kane Nettie—†	128	housewife	34	"
76						
	A	Thayer Henry	128	operator	53	
	B	LeBeau Alden	128	clerk	43	
	C	LeBeau Rhea—†	128	housewife	32	"
	H	Strickland Daisy D—†	135	inspector	62	"
	K	Marsh Minerva—†	135	at home	69	
	L	Meserve Olive A—†	135	clerk	47	
	M	Handaka Paul	135	chef	48	
	O	Merritt Edward	135	janitor	48	
	P	*Contestabile Charles	135	chef	53	
	R	Sampson Alice—†	135	housewife	25	"
	S	*Sampson Raymond	135	musician	37	"
	T	Brousaides John	135	laborer	54	

Page.	Letter.	FULL NAME.	Residence, Jan. 1, 1943.	Occupation.	Supposed Age.	Reported Residence, Jan. 1, 1942. Street and Number.

West Canton Street—Continued

Page.	Letter.	FULL NAME.	Residence, Jan. 1, 1943.	Occupation.	Supposed Age.	Reported Residence, Jan. 1, 1942. Street and Number.
	U	Tardif Mabel—†	135	laundress	46	Maine
	V	Young Arthur	135	cutter	58	here
	W	Young Rose—†	135	housewife	56	"
	Y	Garland Laura—†	135	domestic	51	"

77 West Dedham Street

Page.	Letter.	FULL NAME.	Residence, Jan. 1, 1943.	Occupation.	Supposed Age.	Reported Residence, Jan. 1, 1942. Street and Number.
77	E	McEachern Lillian—†	14	at home	55	here
	F	Connors Anne—†	14	maid	52	"
	K	Hill William	15	retired	71	"
	L	*Lynch Hannah—†	15	at home	77	
	M	Smith Margaret—†	15	domestic	49	"
	P	Atkins Catherine—†	17	housewife	29	16 Rutland
	O	Atkins Lawrence	17	laborer	51	16 "
	R	Dietrich Joseph	17	blacksmith	55	here
	S	Jones Grace M—†	17	at home	65	56A Berkeley
	T	Potterson John	17	retired	67	15 Milford
	U	Smith Frank	17	laborer	50	here
	V	Yoe Annie—†	17	housewife	45	"
	W	Yoe George	17	clerk	50	"
	X	Molloy Elizabeth—†	18	at home	80	
	Y	Molloy Julia B—†	18	"	70	"
	Z	Burke Arthur	19	laborer	32	714 Tremont
78	A	Crotto Napolean	19	retired	67	20 Dartmouth
	B	Gaffney Frank	19	clerk	44	here
	C	LaFrance Gordon	19	"	42	146 W Canton
	D	Máloney Martin	19	cook	40	47 Dwight
	E	McLernon Edward T	19	shipper	58	Brockton
		McQuinlan John	19	retired	64	here
	G	Ramsden Fred	19	"	50	"
	H	Reiss Jacob	19	"	68	"
	K	Ryan Patrick	19	laborer	50	
	L	*Strang Mabel—†	19	housekeeper	49	"
	M	Turner Charles	19	retired	67	"
	O	Cronin Daniel	21	"	70	
	P	Domit Domit J	21	clerk	35	
	R	*Domit Sadie—†	21	housewife	65	"
	S	Domit Sophie—†	21	at home	30	"
	T	Gaddas Edwin H	21	painter	28	47 Warren av
	U	Gaddas Florence M—†	21	housewife	24	47 "

Page.	Letter.	FULL NAME.	Residence, Jan. 1, 1943.	Occupation.	Supposed Age.	Reported Residence, Jan. 1, 1942. Street and Number.

West Dedham Street—Continued

Page.	Letter.	FULL NAME.	Residence, Jan. 1, 1943.	Occupation.	Supposed Age.	Reported Residence, Jan. 1, 1942. Street and Number.
	V	Jackson Geoige	21	retired	60	Hanover
	W	Timlin James	21	laborer	44	here
	X	Cataldo George	22	chauffeur	48	26 W Dedham
	Y	Cataldo Mary—†	22	housewife	42	26 "
	Z	Egan Peter	22	waiter	46	26 "
79						
	A	Fotherbee Mary—†	22	at home	70	26 "
	B	Fotherbee William	22	retired	75	26 "
	C	Barrows William T	23	"	70	here
	D	*Berry Charles S	23	"	78	16 E Brookline
	E	Burke Walter J	23	cook	52	377 Shawmut av
	F	Chamberlain Raymond	23	painter	45	1463 Wash'n
	G	Farrell Charles	23	retired	72	here
	H	Hamaty Violet—†	23	housewife	24	"
	K	Hamaty Virgil	23	engineer	29	"
	L	John George	23	guard	27	
	M	*John Latiffy—†	23	housewife	49	"
	N	John Michael	23	U S A	29	
	O	*Shada Mary—†	23	clerk	37	"
	P	Stone William	23	cook	37	Rhode Island
	U	Keefe John	25	laborer	60	here
	V	Kincaid Rita A—†	25	housekeeper	62	"
	W	MacDonald John	25	machinist	59	"
	X	Meady Richard	25	printer	62	
	Y	Perkins Fred M	25	metalworker	70	"
	Z	Perry George V	25	retired	67	
80						
	A	Sanford Thomas	25	waiter	33	45 Milford
	B	Barry Della—†	26	at home	66	9 "
	C	King Patrick	26	laborer	43	9 "
	D	McAskill John	26	retired	68	here
	E	Palinkas Arthur	26	cook	37	16 Rutland
	F	Palinkas Leo	26	clerk	40	16 "
	G	Karacozian Charles	28	"	22	76 Intervale
	H	*Karacozian Martha—†	28	housewife	58	76 "
	K	Filchuk Lura—†	28	at home	22	9 Andrews
	L	Port George F	28	laborer	46	here
	M	Port Marion J—†	28	housewife	43	"
	N	Waterhouse Emma—†	28	at home	80	"
	O	White George	28	laborer	55	
	R	Graham David	29	"	24	

Page.	Letter.	Full Name.	Residence, Jan. 1, 1943.	Occupation.	Supposed Age.	Reported Residence, Jan. 1, 1942. Street and Number.

West Dedham Street—Continued

	S	Graham Mary—†	29	housewife	65	here
	T	Howe Frederick	30	laborer	34	"
	U	Howe Helen—†	30	housewife	33	"
	V	Tunnicliff Nancy—†	30	at home	32	Brockton
	W	Regan Lena—†	30	housewife	38	here
	X	Regan William A	30	laborer	40	"
	Y	Callahan Catherine R—†	30	housewife	43	1 Hubbard ter
	Z	Callahan Joseph P	30	laborer	22	1 "
81						
	A	Callahan Patrick J	30	"	46	1 "
	C	Casey Annie B—†	33	housewife	48	here
	D	Casey Mary C—†	33	laundress	22	"
	E	Casey Thomas T	33	laborer	48	"
	G	Rohan Isabella—†	43	at home	65	
	K	Moran Josephine—†	46	"	42	
	L	Fowler Verna—†	48	musician	40	"
	M	Selig Max	48	"	47	
	N	Selig Mildred—†	48	housewife	40	"
	O	Nealey Lucy L—†	49	at home	43	
	P	Nealey Sarah—†	49	"	86	
	R	Jopson Zanie M—†	49	"	59	
	S	Kelliher Florence—†	49	housewife	61	"
	T	Kelliher John	49	steamfitter	59	"
	U	Johnston Dorothy—†	49	housewife	52	"
	V	Johnston Frank	49	carpenter	54	"
	W	Patenaude Marie—†	49	housewife	43	"
	X	Patenaude Philip J	49	painter	52	
	Y	Hayes Alice—†	49	housewife	27	"
	Z	Hayes James	49	chauffeur	35	"
82						
	A	Antoine Hartwell	49	watchman	54	"
	B	Fickett Doris M—†	49	housewife	52	"
	C	Fickett George	49	entertainer	62	"
	D	Burnham Frank M	49	retired	70	
	F	Scantleberry William	52	laborer	64	
	G	Mercer Charles	53	retired	67	"
	H	Grant Harry	53	machinist	26	8A Dunlow
	K	Grant Louise—†	53	housewife	22	8A "
	M	Marren Mark	53	laborer	45	here
	O	Santy Catherine A—†	56	housewife	35	"
	P	Santy Joseph C	56	electrician	45	"

Page.	Letter.	Full Name.	Residence, Jan. 1, 1943.	Occupation.	Supposed Age.	Reported Residence, Jan. 1, 1942. Street and Number.

West Dedham Street—Continued

Page.	Letter.	Full Name.	Residence, Jan. 1, 1943.	Occupation.	Supposed Age.	Reported Residence, Jan. 1, 1942. Street and Number.
	R	Smith Edward	56	clerk	21	4 Newland
	S	Smith Eugenia—†	56	at home	22	4 "
	U	Dempsey Jeremiah	58	laborer	56	here
	V	McDonald Evelyn—†	58	housewife	33	"
	W	McDonald Henry	58	chauffeur	27	"
	X	McRae Anna—†	58	housewife	40	"
	Y	McRae James	58	chauffeur	42	"
83						
	A	DeSimone Brisco	62	bartender	28	"
	B	DeSimone Nancy—†	62	housewife	26	"
	C	Kaspert Rose—†	62	at home	63	
	D	McDonald George	62	retired	68	
	F	Gammell Mary A—†	66A	at home	56	"
	L	Post Charles	80	laborer	32	586 Mass av
	M	Post Vena—†	80	housewife	33	586 "
	N	Bedrosian Almas—†	80	"	54	here
	O	Bedrosian Derador	80	laborer	53	"
	P	Bedrosian Hovhanes	80	clerk	20	"
	U	Hayes Malina—†	84	housewife	42	"
	V	Hayes Ralph E	84	manager	42	"
	X	*Melad Adel—†	88	at home	43	
	Y	Joseph Mary—†	88	clerk	24	
84						
	B	Robitaille Edward	92	retired	69	
	C	Robitaille Stella—†	92	at home	70	
	D	Taylor Sarah—†	92	"	67	
	E	McDonald Elizabeth—†	92	clerk	20	
	F	McDonald Julia—†	92	"	27	
	G	McDonald Mary J—†	92	at home	62	
	H	McDonald Conrad	92	U S N	26	
	K	McDonald Margaret—†	92	clerk	24	
	L	MacComisky Florence—†	94	at home	65	
	M	McGovern Delia—†	94	"	54	
	N	Moohan Alice E—†	94	"	73	
	O	Moohan Margaret—†	94	"	59	
	P	Frawley Mary—†	96	"	67	"
	R	Harney Edward O	96	retired	70	19 W Dedham
	V	Jones Olive L—†	98	at home	60	here
	W	Hulse Ella—†	98	"	60	"
85						
	A	Ashline Lester	103	watchman	58	"

Page.	Letter.	Full Name.	Residence, Jan. 1, 1943.	Occupation.	Supposed Age.	Reported Residence, Jan. 1, 1942. Street and Number.

West Dedham Street—Continued

	B	Ashline May A—†	103	housewife	71	here
	C	Towers Sadie—†	103	at home	72	98 W Dedham
	D	Frederick Gretchen—†	103	domestic	58	here
	E	Carr Alice P—†	103	housewife	63	"
	F	Carr Edward	103	attorney	74	"
	G	Allen George	105	shipper	62	"
	H	Carney May—†	105	at home	52	
	K	Circeo Louis	105	chef	40	
	L	Circeo Matilda—†	105	housewife	38	"

2
3
4
6
7
8
9
10
11
12

Ward 9 Precinct 2

CITY OF BOSTON

LIST OF RESIDENTS
20 YEARS OF AGE AND OVER

(NON-CITIZENS INDICATED BY ASTERISK)
(FEMALES INDICATED BY DAGGER)

AS OF

JANUARY 1, 1943

JOSEPH F. TIMILTY, *Chairman*
FREDERIC E. DOWLING, *Secretary*
WILLIAM A. MOTLEY, JR.
FRANCIS B. McKINNEY
EVERETT R. PROUT
Listing Board.

CITY OF BOSTON PRINTING DEPARTMENT

Page.	Letter.	Full Name.	Residence, Jan. 1, 1943.	Occupation.	Supposed Age.	Reported Residence, Jan. 1, 1942. Street and Number.
200						
		Cumston Place				
	A	Crook Lena—†	1	housewife	46	here
	B	Joseph John	1	merchant	47	468 Shawmut av
	C	Joseph Mary—†	1	stitcher	24	468 "
	D	Joseph Shamas—†	1	housewife	49	468 "
	E	Nickerson Elmer	2	U S A	24	here
	F	Sissa Edith—†	2	housewife	26	Maine
	G	Sissa Rudolph	2	shipfitter	28	"
	H	Valenty Anthony	2	laborer	49	here
	K	Wheeler Minnie—†	2	housewife	48	"
	L	Diggs Frank	3	inspector	58	"
	M	Jackson Pearl E—†	3	housewife	51	"
	N	Collins Ellen E—†	4	domestic	65	"
	O	Flaherty Louis	4	porter	66	
	P	Flaherty Louis W	4	welder	30	
	R	Flaherty Mary—†	4	housewife	60	"
		Cumston Street				
	S	Thomson James W	8	laborer	58	731 Shawmut av
	T	Wormerly Alice—†	8	domestic	50	515 Tremont
		Haven Street				
	U	Abraham Frederick	1	welder	20	here
	V	Kaplan Nathan	1	bricklayer	42	"
	W	Kidder Margaret—†	1	cook	49	42 W Newton
	X	Atkins James H	2	machinist	52	here
	Y	Atkins Mary M—†	2	housewife	52	"
	Z	Martin Johanna—†	3	"	63	"
201						
	A	Kay Ida—†	4	laundress	47	"
	B	Wright Royal	4	janitor	40	
	C	Akikie George S	5	cutter	58	
	D	Akikie Helen S—†	5	dressmaker	21	"
	E	*Akikie Susan S—†	5	housewife	43	"
	F	Ayoub Solomon	5	cutter	46	
		Newland Street				
	G	Nutter Albert C	75	merchant	50	here
	H	Nutter Alice E—†	75	housewife	44	"

Page.	Letter.	FULL NAME.	Residence, Jan. 1, 1943.	Occupation.	Supposed Age.	Reported Residence, Jan. 1, 1942. Street and Number.

Newland Street—Continued

	K	Wilson Sarah A—†	75	domestic	46	here
	M	Burns Charles	77	laborer	59	57 Pembroke
	N	Burns Mabel—†	77	housewife	44	57 "
	P	Gavin Annie—†	88	matron	57	here
	R	O'Connell William	88	clerk	56	"
	S	Francis Helen—†	88½	housewife	37	"
	T	Francis Herbert	88½	chauffeur	42	"
	U	Corbett Katherine—†	90	matron	59	104 Mt Pleasant av
	V	Gavin James H	90½	operator	60	here
	W	Gavin Mildred—†	90½	housewife	44	"
	X	Lamy Ernest	92	machinist	45	"
	Y	Lamy Georgine—†	92	housewife	38	"

Pembroke Street

	Z	Alexander George W	8	engineer	56	here
202						
	A	Alexander Mary C—†	8	housewife	60	"
	B	Caswell Thomas	8	cook	60	"
	C	Jarrell Ann—†	8	clerk	34	187 Warren
	D	Jarrell Archibald K	8	electrician	35	187 "
	E	Voutiritsa Barbara—†	8	housewife	23	Maine
	F	Voutiritsa Whitney	8	seaman	28	"
	G	Andropoulos Andreas	10	laborer	58	here
	H	Bronnum Alma E—†	10	domestic	32	176 W Brookline
	K	Burrows George	10	waiter	51	here
	L	Dinn Charles	10	carpenter	48	"
	M	Edwards David	10	porter	55	91 Parker Hill av
	N	Ellis Bryant	10	carpenter	39	here
	O	Mahoney Francis J	10	manager	43	6 E Brookline
	P	McCarthy James	10	laborer	50	here
	R	McDonald Dudley	10	salesman	62	"
	S	McDonald James A	10	mover	39	"
	T	Monteith Annie—†	10	housewife	64	"
	U	O'Hare Joseph	10	retired	74	61 W Newton
	V	Pencille Theodore	10	baker	42	here
	W	Turio William H	10	retired	73	"
	X	*Abdou Jennie—†	12	housewife	32	"
	Y	Abdou Salama	12	boilermaker	43	"
	Z	Slamey Nabina—†	12	housewife	34	"
203						
	A	Aufiero Fredrick G	12	machinist	25	662 Tremont

Page.	Letter.	Full Name.	Residence, Jan. 1, 1943.	Occupation.	Supposed Age.	Reported Residence, Jan. 1, 1942. Street and Number.

Pembroke Street—Continued

	B	Aufiero Julia—†	12	housewife	25	662 Tremont
	C	Butera Laura—†	14	"	37	here
	D	*Lemanski Blanche—†	14	"	51	"
	E	Lemanski John	14	laborer	52	"
	F	Dooley Mary E—†	14	laundress	55	"
	G	Dooley William A	14	laborer	34	
	H	Bevis Anita—†	14	housewife	25	"
	K	Bevis Everett J	14	roofer	36	

Rutland Place

	L	Smith Bertha—†	1	clerk	37	here
	M	Peters Betty—†	3	housewife	24	28 Holyoke
	N	Peters Osmund	3	U S A	29	28 "

Rutland Street

	O	Hinton Ethel—†	1	housewife	28	here
	P	Hinton Garland	1	painter	34	"
	R	Sulvey Ethel—†	1	housewife	40	"
	S	Nembhard James	3	seaman	52	
	T	Nembhard Lillian—†	3	housewife	23	"
	U	Chase Dorothy—†	3	seamstress	30	"
	V	Williams Augusta R—†	3	"	43	
	W	Williams Frank J	3	retired	76	
	X	Tyter Margaret J—†	3	cook	44	
	Y	Tyter Stephen	3	"	44	
	Z	Bowen Betty—†	5	at home	72	
204						
	A	Battle Minnie—†	5	domestic	47	"
	B	Mars Jule	5	laborer	27	
	C	Mars Thelma—†	5	housewife	29	"
	E	Groves Langstron	7	porter	50	
	F	Groves Laurena †	7	housewife	31	"
	G	Taylor Carrie—†	7	"	60	
	H	Taylor Richard A	7	retired	67	"
	K	Sheppard Annie F—†	7	housewife	66	1 Hubert
	L	Sheppard Charles A	7	musician	68	1 "
	N	Brown John R	9	cook	41	15 Savoy
	O	Kelly Peter L	9	laborer	32	37 E Concord
	P	Kelly William	9	chauffeur	40	173 Boylston

Page.	Letter.	Full Name.	Residence, Jan. 1, 1943.	Occupation.	Supposed Age.	Reported Residence, Jan. 1, 1942. Street and Number.

Rutland Street—Continued

	R	Lynch Marie—†	9	housewife	39	96 Thornton
	S	Pelletier William	9	laborer	40	New York
	T	Cressman Margaret—†	11	at home	65	here
	U	O'Neil William	11	houseman	62	63 Rutland
	V	Sone Frank	11	retired	64	here
	W	Sweeney William J	11	lather	63	"
	X	Shing Dong Chuck	15–17	laundryman	43	16 Oxford
	Y	Etheridge Ida—†	16–18	seamstress	55	33 Rutland
	Z	Heeney Michael	16–18	laborer	52	here
205						
	A	Hopkins Herbert	16–18	retired	72	33 Rutland
	B	Mikelhalian Michael	16–18	laborer	56	here
	C	Penpraese Frank	16–18	foreman	68	21 E Concord
	D	Reisert Henry	16–18	steamfitter	60	here
	E	Rhodes Rebecca—†	16–18	housekeeper	67	"
	K	Gilman Joseph N	22	retired	66	6 Rutland
	L	McDermott Jennie E—†	22	housewife	58	here
	M	McDermott Thomas	22	laborer	62	"
	O	Nado Etta—†	24	at home	76	"
	P	Porter Frank	24	laborer	38	301 Shawmut av
	R	Rourke Charles	24	"	36	here
	S	Rourke Frances—†	24	housewife	23	"
	T	Clisham Michael J	27	laborer	55	"
	U	Connelly Michael	27	bricklayer	70	132 W Concord
	V	*Costello Catherine—†	27	housewife	31	here
	W	Costello Martin	27	painter	38	"
	X	Heath Richard F	27	brakeman	28	17 Dartmouth pl
	Z	Kissick William	27	roofer	56	here
	Y	McAvoy John J	27	mason	68	56 W Newton
206						
	A	Roberts Millard	27	bartender	47	here
	B	O'Toole William D	29	retired	58	"
	C	Titus Edward K	29	U S A	28	"
	D	Titus Edward M	29	retired	66	
	E	Berni Lazarus	31	cook	56	
	F	Berni Louise—†	31	clerk	27	
	G	Farrell Charles	31	retired	72	"
	H	Finocchiaro Joseph	31	barber	67	"
	K	*McGuire Mary—†	31	at home	68	
	L	Slattery Helen—†	31	housekeeper	42	"
	M	Lindgren Eric	32	janitor	46	

Page.	Letter.	FULL NAME.	Residence, Jan. 1, 1943.	Occupation.	Supposed Age.	Reported Residence, Jan. 1, 1942. Street and Number.

Rutland Street—Continued

	N	Lindgren Lilly—†	32	housewife	41	here
	O	Thornton Elizabeth—†	32	social worker	48	256 Newbury
	P	Crowley William	33	U S A	20	50 Gray
	R	Hallsworth Cecil	33	janitor	43	228 Shawmut av
	S	Hallsworth May—†	33	housekeeper	41	228 "
	T	Loveland Albert	33	laborer	65	24 Pelham
	U	Mahoney John J	33	"	45	228 Shawmut av
	V	Murphy William	33	retired	66	750 Tremont
	W	Savage Daniel	33	"	48	228 Shawmut av
	X	Savage Nora—†	33	housewife	40	228 "
	Y	Shallow Priscilla—†	33	at home	77	125 W Newton
	Z	Teagle Ernest	33	laborer	64	33 W Canton
207						
	A	Ward Meltha—†	33	housewife	21	56 Waltham
	B	DeHuff Arthur	45	retired	90	here
	C	Handy George	45	barber	29	"
	D	*Handy Mary—†	45	housekeeper	55	"
	E	Hines John	45	retired	70	"
	F	King Patrick	45	"	70	
	G	Mahoney Elizabeth—†	45	at home	53	
	H	Morris Edward	45	U S A	33	
	K	Morris Mabel—†	45	housewife	27	"
	L	Quimby Catherine—†	45	at home	68	"
	N	Bradley Ethel—†	48	social worker	62	Gloucester
	O	Griggs Catherine—†	48	"	60	here
	P	MacRae Catherine—†	48	housewife	61	"
	R	MacRae Donald	48	manager	61	"
	S	Sprague Priscilla—†	48	teacher	48	
	T	Sprague Sarah—†	48	clerk	44	
	U	Carlberg Arthur J	49	machinist	57	"
	V	Carlberg Ina W—†	49	housewife	65	"
	W	Connolly Joseph	49	laborer	60	"
	X	Granahan Mary—†	49	seamstress	55	Quincy
	Y	Lundquist Carl	49	laborer	66	here
	Z	Connolly Charles	51	retired	67	"
208						
	A	Donovan John	51	"	72	
	B	Lurvey Frederick	51	mechanic	65	"
	C	Reid Ellen—†	51	at home	74	
	D	Rooney Ann L—†	51	bookkeeper	48	"
	E	Solomon Evelyn—†	51	housewife	29	"

Page.	Letter.	Full Name.	Residence, Jan. 1, 1943.	Occupation.	Supposed Age.	Reported Residence, Jan. 1, 1942. Street and Number.

Rutland Street—Continued

Page.	Letter.	Full Name.	Residence, Jan. 1, 1943.	Occupation.	Supposed Age.	Reported Residence, Jan. 1, 1942. Street and Number.
	F	Solomon John	51	roofer	42	here
	G	Barkley Herbert	53	steward	45	"
	H	Barkley Rosena—†	53	housewife	34	"
	K	*Bergen Ralph	53	mechanic	50	"
	L	Brodeur George	53	"	65	Winchendon
	M	Buote Bertha—†	53	housewife	54	here
	N	Buote Henry	53	engineer	57	"
	O	Jackson Walter	53	inspector	61	"
	P	McDonald Albert	53	carpenter	66	"
	R	Rozando Emanuel	53	"	58	57 Rutland
	S	VanWart Leslie	53	machinist	44	here
	T	Carter Harry	55	cook	57	"
	U	Carter William	55	houseman	62	"
	V	Doyle Patrick	55	laborer	52	
	W	Lakeman Daniel W	55	retired	65	
	X	Lally John	55	mechanic	42	"
	Y	McCullough Frances—†	55	housekeeper	67	"
	Z	Montplaiser Louis D	55	mechanic	50	"
209						
	A	Montplaiser Margaret F—†	55	housewife	41	"
	B	Murphy James	55	plumber	60	
	C	O'Brien Catherine—†	55	at home	65	
	D	Roberts Nathaniel	55	machinist	50	"
	E	Bornback Anna—†	57	seamstress	63	"
	F	Cuminsky Edmund	57	cook	50	Maine
	G	Hughes Mary V—†	57	housekeeper	61	here
	H	Hurley Gertrude—†	57	clerk	56	"
	K	Kelly Catherine—†	57	at home	63	"
	L	Mara Nora—†	57	domestic	55	"
	M	McLaughlin Mary E—†	57	attendant	60	750 Harris'n av
	N	Mulino Anna—†	57	seamstress	64	here
	O	Regan Nellie—†	57	at home	63	89 Union Park
	P	Welsch Frank	57	cook	50	here
	R	Welsch Fred	57	"	45	Maine
	S	*Baisjaly Albert	58	painter	60	64 Rutland
	T	Carbanell Carl	58	musician	50	here
	U	Carbanell Doris—†	58	housewife	40	"
	V	*Carey Maxin	58	palmist	34	"
	W	Carey Vele—†	58	housewife	34	"
	X	Dwyer Charlotte—†	58	at home	61	
	Y	Elder John A	58	machinist	61	"

Page.	Letter.	Full Name.	Residence, Jan. 1, 1943.	Occupation.	Supposed Age.	Reported Residence, Jan. 1, 1942. Street and Number.

Rutland Street—Continued

	Z	Elder Mabel T—†	58	housewife	59	here
210						
	A	Evans Henry	58	chauffeur	45	"
	B	Mangine Frank	58	retired	63	7 James
	C	Sullivan George	58	painter	55	11 Gerald rd
	D	Ward Hubert	58	busboy	55	here
	E	Beaton Colin F	59	retired	70	27 Milford
	F	Cronin Julia—†	59	at home	66	New York
	G	DiRio Gaetano	59	carpenter	48	here
	H*	Domaney Abraham	59	retired	61	"
	K	Domaney George	59	U S A	25	"
	L*	Domaney Hasibe—†	59	housewife	51	"
	M	Domaney Mary—†	59	clerk	27	
	N	Domaney Nicholas	59	machinist	29	"
	O	Forslund Gustaff	59	tailor	66	300 Shawmut av
	P	Konko Kathleen—†	59	housewife	26	here
	R	Konko William	59	longshoreman	27	New York
	S	Bentley Mary—†	60	clerk	30	32 Marshfield
	T*	Cummisky Thomas	60	roofer	40	here
	U*	Cummisky Winifred—†	60	housewife	44	"
	V	Nickerson Joseph	60	laborer	32	102 Chandler
	W	Watson Sarah—†	60	at home	52	here
	Y	Coats Eloise—†	62	housewife	50	"
	Z	Coats Lewis	62	U S N	58	"
211						
	A	Jones Henry	62	chef	62	
	B	Jones Marie—†	62	housewife	63	"
	C	Thomas Carroll	62	embalmer	28	"
	D	Thomas Marie—†	62	housewife	25	"
	E	Concannon William	63	retired	73	"
	F	Dowd Ann—†	63	cook	50	85 Chandler
	G	Johnson Cora—†	63	at home	80	here
	H	Lyons Mary—†	63	housewife	60	"
	K	Lyons Michael	63	laborer	52	"
	L	Ransom Alice—†	63	at home	63	
	M	Reardon Edward	63	retired	75	"
	N	Sullivan Michael	63	"	72	Long Island
	O	Beddow John	64	laborer	43	65 St Stephen
	P*	Koylov Alfred	64	chef	51	here
	R	Legand Sadie—†	64	waitress	51	65 Appleton
	S*	McCollum Ingersoll	64	retired	83	here

Page.	Letter.	Full Name.	Residence, Jan. 1, 1943.	Occupation.	Supposed Age.	Reported Residence, Jan. 1, 1942. Street and Number.

Rutland Street—Continued

Page.	Letter.	Full Name.	Residence, Jan. 1, 1943.	Occupation.	Supposed Age.	Reported Residence, Jan. 1, 1942. Street and Number.
	T	Reed Frank	64	retired	81	71 Rutland
	U	Sullivan Jeremiah	64	"	68	71 "
	V	Williams Myrtle—†	64	housekeeper	61	377 Shawmut av
	W	Anderson Henry	65	retired	51	Quincy
	X	Baird Pauline—†	65	housewife	26	47 Fay
	Y	Boyter Leslie—†	65	"	23	Alabama
	Z	*Murphy Sally—†	65	housekeeper	27	74 Rutland
212						
	A	O'Connor Nora—†	65	waitress	32	133 Pembroke
	B	Accolitta Alfred	66	student	24	here
	C	Chamberland Dudley	66	waiter	39	198 St Botolph
	D	*Chamberland Frances—†	66	at home	73	here
	E	Chamberland Thelma—†	66	housewife	30	198 St Botolph
	F	Elward Gertrude—†	66	at home	67	here
	G	Matrell Mary A—†	66	"	79	"
	H	McDonell Frederick	66	physician	72	"
	K	Melinowski Theodore	66	student	24	Worcester
	L	*Mercer Gertrude—†	66	at home	75	here
	M	Reed Janet—†	66	clerk	27	27 Rutland
	N	*Reeve Anna—†	66	at home	74	here
	O	Wilson Ethel M—†	66	"	68	11 E Newton
	P	*Woodworth Minnie—†	66	"	67	Canada
	R	Ashey Elias	67	baker	55	Somerville
	S	*Ashey Zekia—†	67	housewife	50	97 Hudson
	T	Fitzgerald Edward	68	laborer	41	1522 Wash'n
	U	Gallant Marion—†	68	housewife	42	here
	V	Gallant Robert	68	machinist	40	"
	W	Hachey Agnes—†	68	waitress	35	"
	X	Hanson Phillip	68	lawyer	53	7 Concord
	Y	Hay James	68	chef	51	16 Dartmouth pl
	Z	Johnson Anna—†	68	housewife	51	here
213						
	A	Johnson Charles	68	janitor	56	
	B	Lacy Jennie—†	68	housewife	60	"
	C	Lacy Lewis	68	retired	74	
	D	McAnarney Evelyn—†	68	housewife	27	"
	E	McAnarney James	68	laborer	33	"
	F	McCloud Catherine—†	68	housekeeper	41	95 St Botolph
	G	Morris Isaac	68	gardener	61	here
	H	Porter Eva—†	68	clerk	27	"
	K	Porter Milford	68	"	42	"

Page.	Letter.	Full Name.	Residence, Jan. 1, 1943.	Occupation.	Supposed Age.	Reported Residence, Jan. 1, 1942. Street and Number.

Rutland Street—Continued

Page.	Letter.	Full Name.	Residence, Jan. 1, 1943.	Occupation.	Supposed Age.	Reported Residence, Jan. 1, 1942. Street and Number.
	L	Schaler William	68	machinist	51	Brookline
	M	Williams Hugh	68	stonecutter	50	682 Tremont
	N	Williams Lillian—†	68	housewife	51	682 "
	O	Worten Joseph	68	retired	74	here
	P	Loveland Bessie F—†	69	at home	61	656 Tremont
	R	Curtis Alice—†	69	seamstress	53	here
	S	Eistrup Albert	69	riveter	49	"
	T	Holstein Laura—†	69	clerk	64	"
	U	Pickering Rose T—†	69	at home	68	
	V	Connors Bessie T—†	69	housewife	45	"
	W	Connors William F	69	clerk	59	
	X	Savage David F	69	retired	70	
	Y	Callahan Charles	70	"	68	"
	Z	*Connellan John J	70	freighthandler	37	"
214						
	A	*Flynn Anne—†	70	domestic	73	63 Worcester
	B	Huston Marjorie—†	70	at home	75	here
	C	Ireland Jane R—†	70	housekeeper	60	"
	D	Kramer Ruth—†	70	seamstress	29	"
	E	*Rosendahl Walter	70	chauffeur	48	"
	F	Tierney Elizabeth—†	70	clerk	43	
	G	Bell Louis	71	retired	65	"
	H	Bristol Ernest	71	U S N	25	Maine
	K	Cotter James	71	laborer	60	here
	L	Downing James	71	"	50	"
	M	Fay Martin	71	"	50	"
	N	Galbo Celia—†	71	housewife	31	"
	O	*Galbo Nicholas	71	waiter	43	
	P	Hughes Margaret—†	71	maid	62	"
	R	LaCascia Theodore	71	chipper	34	703 E Fourth
	S	Porter Harry	71	laborer	63	425 Shawmut av
	U	Chabot Charles	73	electrician	26	9 Albemarle
	V	Chabot Eileen—†	73	housewife	30	9 "
	W	Curran Margaret—†	73	waitress	25	here
	X	McCarthy Arthur	73	painter	42	"
	Y	Nichols Rose—†	73	clerk	24	"
	Z	Rahal Anna—†	73	operator	21	300 Shawmut av
215						
	A	Rouvalis James	73	chauffeur	42	2 Union Park
	B	Thomas Marshall	73	"	43	here
	C	Thomas Sophie—†	73	housewife	38	"

Page.	Letter.	Full Name.	Residence, Jan. 1, 1943.	Occupation.	Supposed Age.	Reported Residence, Jan. 1, 1942. Street and Number.

Rutland Street—Continued

	D	Bielo Grace—†	74	waitress	25	here
	D	Elg Gustave	74	laborer	45	16 Rutland
	F	Elg Helen—†	74	housewife	45	16 "
	G	Fitzgerald Margaret—†	74	domestic	45	Newton
	H	Turbit Fredrick	74	porter	51	here
	K	Woodman Grace—†	74	housewife	27	Malden
	L	Woodman Richard	74	clerk	30	"
	M	Beard Thomas	75	chef	46	here
	N	Howard Agnes—†	75	at home	72	"
	O	Kennedy Martin	75	retired	75	"
	P	Powers Michael	75	laborer	38	137 W Concord
	S	Roach James	75	mechanic	50	here
	R	Shea Nellie T—†	75	housekeeper	68	"
	T	Young James	75	printer	29	126 Chandler
	U	Snow Paul	76	chipper	28	here
	V	Snow Sadie—†	76	housewife	24	"
	X	Henderson Ida—†	76	"	31	"
	Y	Henderson Roy	76	chef	33	"
216						
	B	Rynne Dole—†	76	housewife	30	Lowell
	C	Rynne John	76	chef	43	"
	D	Howard Rosie—†	76	waitress	22	1 Concord pl
	G	Bachman Catherine—†	77	housewife	46	Cambridge
	H	Bachman Grover	77	engineer	60	"
	K	Coughlin Catherine—†	77	waitress	35	here
	L	Dillon Clifford H	77	laborer	35	Rhode Island
	M	Kelliher Michael	77	retired	73	here
	N	Lareau Albert E	77	mechanic	34	Malden
	O	*Lareau Winifred—†	77	housewife	36	"
	P	Laycock Mary E—†	77	at home	72	40 Concord sq
	R	Lewis Margaret—†	77	housewife	42	here
	S	Neville Henry	77	chef	37	42 Rutland
	T	Osborne Warren E	77	painter	34	50 Dudley
	U	Shurey Nazeera—†	77	housekeeper	45	731 Tremont
	V	Shurey Tofik F	77	shoemaker	53	731 "
	W	Leonard Charles	78	fireman	25	here
	X	Leonard Muriel—†	78	housewife	22	"
	Y	Butler Mary—†	78	housekeeper	42	"
	Z	Crosby May—†	78	at home	60	"
217						
	A	Sculley Nellie—†	78	seamstress	58	"

Page.	Letter.	Full Name.	Residence, Jan. 1, 1943.	Occupation.	Supposed Age.	Reported Residence, Jan. 1, 1942. Street and Number.

Rutland Street—Continued

	B	Judge James	78	chef	41	here
	C	Chadbourne Rose—†	78	at home	63	"
	D	Goring Robert	78	welder	44	"
	E	Goring Rose—†	78	housewife	42	"
	F	*Marino Benjamin	78	laborer	61	"
	G	Marino Edith—†	78	housewife	37	"
	K	Baths Clara—†	79	"	26	W Virginia
	L	Baths Frank	79	U S N	26	"
	M	Cox Harold	79	"	35	Maine
	N	Cox Norma—†	79	housewife	22	"
	O	Damon Loretta—†	79	housekeeper	29	625 Tremont
	P	Haywood Forrest	79	U S A	22	Lawrence
	R	Haywood Lillian—†	79	housewife	22	"
	S	Porter Hazel—†	79	clerk	35	New York
	T	Searo John	79	"	45	Maine
	U	Waning Robert	79	laborer	29	Medford
	V	Gabriel Mary—†	80	housewife	42	here
	W	Gabriel Monsur	80	shoemaker	60	"
	X	Greeco Anthony	80	draftsman	42	"
	Y	Moore Jennie—†	80	housewife	32	"
	Z	Moore William	80	shipfitter	35	"

218 Shawmut Avenue

218	A	Odian Messak G	423	physician	49	here
	B	Odian Sonja—†	423	housewife	42	"
	C	Busch Henry	423	retired	80	27 Rollins
	D	Chatis Anastos	423	restaurateur	49	here
	E	McCloud Mary—†	423	housekeeper	70	"
	F	Roberts John	423	retired	73	16 W Dedham
	K	Boyson Rita—†	423	weaver	25	Somerville
	G	Little Frank	423	letter carrier	50	75 Rutland
	H	Little Mary E—†	423	housekeeper	88	75 "
	L	DePinko John	423	mechanic	42	here
	M	*DePinko Josephine—†	423	housewife	44	"
	N	Ricci Louis	423	chef	50	Belmont
	O	Dibious George	425	retired	83	224 Warren av
	P	Drew Joseph F	425	guard	47	here
	R	*Fitzpatrick Mary—†	425	housekeeper	60	441 Shawmut av
	S	Freskury Theodore G	425	laborer	48	757 Morton
	T	Gould Mary—†	425	housekeeper	78	here

Page.	Letter.	FULL NAME.	Residence, Jan. 1, 1943.	Occupation.	Supposed Age.	Reported Residence, Jan. 1, 1942. Street and Number.

Shawmut Avenue—Continued

Page.	Letter.	FULL NAME.	Residence, Jan. 1, 1943.	Occupation.	Supposed Age.	Reported Residence, Jan. 1, 1942. Street and Number.
	U	Kenen Edward	425	U S A	30	here
	V	Kenen George	425	retired	75	"
	W	*Kenen Zelfa G—†	425	housewife	65	"
	X	Lewenerk Jacob	425	machinist	31	18 Rutland sq
	Y	Norton Helen—†	425	clerk	38	here
	Z	Oakman George G	425	retired	74	683 Tremont
219						
	A	O'Connell John J	425	glazier	64	here
	B	Cliff Frederica—†	427	physician	60	"
	C	*Abraham Adballah	429	retired	72	"
	D	Abraham Aziz	429	manager	33	"
	E	Abraham Hassan	429	shipfitter	28	"
	F	Abraham James	429	laborer	26	
	G	Abraham Omar	429	"	48	
	H	Abraham Sara—†	429	housekeeper	27	"
	K	*Abraham Sarah—†	429	housewife	60	"
	L	*Mankin Ahmed	429	storekeeper	55	"
	M	Boultenhouse Charles	431	laborer	40	Cambridge
	N	Boultenhouse Leonard W	431	dishwasher	40	"
	O	*Doveston Hattie—†	431	domestic	56	here
	P	Johnson George W	431	machinist	40	"
	R	MacDonald William	431	laborer	49	"
	S	McGowan William	431	electrician	46	"
	T	Michelson Richard	431	paperhanger	50	"
	U	Patten Thomas	431	laborer	50	"
	V	Schaffer William	431	dishwasher	50	"
	W	Webb Robert W	431	laborer	43	11 Rutland
	X	Wesson Fulton P	431	deckhand	49	here
	Y	Wesson Laura E—†	431	housewife	42	"
	Z	Burns James H	433	retired	56	50 Waltham
220						
	A	Curry Margaret—†	433	laundress	50	here
	B	Eaton Charles	433	clerk	75	"
	C	Elliot William	433	retired	70	"
	D	Farrah George	433	chef	42	
	E	Farrah Nazeera—†	433	housekeeper	43	"
	F	Ferriear Augusta	433	cabinetmaker	48	1490 Wash'n
	G	Gugleatta Leonard	433	laborer	38	here
	H	Herberst Joseph	433	watchman	60	454 Broadway
	K	*Katrupes William	433	kitchenman	63	here
	L	Mannix Anna—†	433	housekeeper	69	"

Page.	Letter.	Full Name.	Residence, Jan. 1, 1943.	Occupation.	Supposed Age.	Reported Residence, Jan. 1, 1942. Street and Number.

Shawmut Avenue—Continued

	M	Miller John	433	clerk	60	here
	N	Stevens Lois—†	433	entertainer	35	"
	O	Thurston Eleanor—†	433	bookkeeper	36	"
	P	Brown James	435	retired	61	"
	R	Chapman Frank	435	chef	48	"
	S	*Chapolas Steven	435	laborer	47	9 Rutland
	T	*Cosras Charles	435	clerk	49	here
	U	Daley Ethel—†	435	housekeeper	58	122 W Concord
	V	Daley Joseph	435	draftsman	48	122 "
	W	Ettinden George W	435	carpenter	44	here
	X	*Geldings James	435	retired	60	"
	Y	Gilman Florence—†	435	housekeeper	62	"
	Z	Gorman John	435	retired	59	"
221						
	A	Holden Louise—†	435	cook	39	"
	B	Kelly John J	435	laborer	49	58 Bartlett
	C	LaChance Alice—†	435	housewife	42	N Hampshire
	D	LaChance Leo	435	painter	48	"
	E	McDowell Robert	435	laborer	38	here
	F	*Melechio Anthony	435	"	52	"
	G	Shamon Julia—†	435	housekeeper	60	"
	H	Vaitis Gustaf	435	retired	50	"
	K	Wright Mary—†	435	housekeeper	61	"
	L	*Areglado Mary—†	437	housewife	26	657 Tremont
	M	*Areglado Richard	437	bartender	36	657 "
	N	Demos Christos	437	chef	53	here
	O	Kinan Kalul	437	salesman	41	"
	P	*Kinan Rose—†	437	housewife	34	"
	R	O'Connor Lillian—†	437	maid	40	548 Tremont
	S	Sackell Alexander	437	housekeeper	68	here
	T	Sullivan Thomas	437	laborer	40	"
	U	Berger Rose—†	439	cleaner	54	24 E Brookline
	V	Downey Benjamin	439	laborer	50	here
	W	Hakim Edward	439	U S A	28	"
	X	*Hakim Rose—†	439	housekeeper	47	"
	Y	Hakim Shaffie	439	laborer	26	"
	Z	Hug Alice—†	439	stitcher	24	
222						
	A	Hug Eugene	439	U S A	29	"
	B	Johnson William	439	laborer	60	84 W Newton
	C	Scales Edwin	439	retired	69	88 "

Page.	Letter.	Full Name.	Residence, Jan. 1, 1943.	Occupation.	Supposed Age.	Reported Residence, Jan. 1, 1942. Street and Number.

Shawmut Avenue—Continued

	D	Sullivan Thomas M	439	photographer	70	579 Tremont
	E	Thomas Arthur	439	chef	53	568 Shawmut av
	F	Williams Charles M	439	machinist	49	33 Circuit
	G	Buckley James	441	retired	66	here
	H	Child Carrie—†	441	housekeeper	65	"
	K	Coleman George	441	retired	83	"
	L	Maloof Carl	441	U S A	22	
	M	*Maloof Mary—†	441	housewife	55	"
	N	*Maloof Samuel	441	retired	54	"
	O	Meegan Bridget—†	441	housekeeper	66	59 Rutland
	P	Morrissey Thomas	441	retired	70	here
	R	Murphy George	441	"	67	"
	S	Ambrose John	443	laborer	58	"
	T	Brophy Anna—†	443	housewife	51	Billerica
	U	Brophy John J	443	laborer	55	"
	V	Fitzpatrick Rebecca—†	443	housekeeper	58	63 Grant av
	W	Guertin Henry	443	painter	60	here
	X	Guertin Marie—†	443	housewife	62	"
	Y	Jordan Frank	443	pharmacist	83	"
	Z	Joseph Mary—†	443	housewife	28	"
223						
	A	Joseph Thomas G	443	manager	30	"
	B	Joy George E	443	retired	60	
	C	Kenny Benjamin	443	laborer	55	
	D	Kenny Mabel—†	443	housewife	52	"
	E	Kerrigan John	443	laborer	55	
	F	*Mansour Salen	443	roofer	65	"
	G	McCarthy Patrick	443	retired	70	658 Tremont
	H	Mugford Alexander	443	"	85	Quincy
	K	Scott Emma M—†	443	housekeeper	56	here
	L	Scott William M	443	retired	81	"
	M	Barnett Nathan	445	"	75	97 Appleton
	N	Brennan James	445	U S A	48	here
	O	Butler William P	445	"	24	"
	P	Cummings John	345	laborer	32	"
	R	Frazier Emma R—†	445	housekeeper	68	"
	S	*Germaine Mary—†	445	housewife	50	"
	T	*Germaine Richard	445	carpenter	52	"
	U	Germaine Samuel L	445	U S A	31	
	V	Gow David	445	carpenter	82	"
	W	Kenneary Patrick	445	U S A	26	50 Mercer

Page.	Letter.	Full Name.	Residence, Jan. 1, 1943.	Occupation.	Supposed Age.	Reported Residence, Jan. 1, 1942. Street and Number.

Shawmut Avenue—Continued

Page.	Letter.	Full Name.	Residence, Jan. 1, 1943.	Occupation.	Supposed Age.	Reported Residence, Jan. 1, 1942. Street and Number.
	x	Lermond Ernest A	445	chef	45	78 Rutland
	y	McGovern Alice—†	445	housekeeper	52	686 Tremont
	z	McGovern William	445	clerk	61	686 "
224						
	A	*McNulty Rose—†	445	housekeeper	87	here
	B	Nelson John	445	chef	85	"
	C	Porter Avis	445	clerk	31	526 Newbury
	D	Shapiro Max	445	retired	68	468 Shawmut av
	E	Talluback Nola—†	445	stitcher	36	here
	F	Walsh Abbie—†	445	housekeeper	71	"
	G	Dalton John J	446	salesman	47	19 Dover
	H	Freden Richard W	446	chef	52	52 W Newton
	K	Hicks Frank A	446	painter	55	here
	L	Jackman Francis A	446	chef	38	Littleton
	M	Marinelli Anthony	446	driller	37	here
	N	Marinelli Jennie—†	446	housekeeper	29	"
	O	*Milan John	446	shoemaker	62	"
	P	*Milan Sadie—†	446	housewife	56	"
	R	*Watson John	446	retired	76	
	S	Berrigan Nellie—†	447	housekeeper	63	"
	T	*Cyr Juliette—†	447	"	35	"
	U	*Cyr Patrick	447	laborer	38	
	V	Duffy Thomas J	447	retired	66	
	W	*Goulet Aurela—†	447	stitcher	55	
	X	*Haddad Anna—†	447	domestic	49	"
	Y	Haddad Richard	447	laborer	50	
	Z	Lizotte Demerice—†	447	housekeeper	44	"
225						
	A	Lizotte Joseph	447	carpenter	45	"
	B	*Maher Mary—†	447	housekeeper	56	"
	C	McLeod Carrie E—†	447	waitress	21	"
	D	McLeod Wallace J	447	retired	58	
	E	O'Neil Anastasia—†	447	housekeeper	58	"
	F	Sullivan Nora—†	447	"	67	"
	G	Walsh Hubert	447	watchman	60	"
	H	Xenos George	447	baker	54	
	K	Ham Stanley	448	laborer	55	
	L	Hanrahan Margaret—†	448	housekeeper	70	"
	M	Kelly George J	448	bartender	48	"
	N	Mitchell Alfred R	448	retired	68	"
	O	Pollard Joseph F	448	kitchenman	60	Tewksbury

Page.	Letter.	Full Name.	Residence, Jan. 1, 1943.	Occupation.	Supposed Age.	Reported Residence, Jan. 1, 1942. Street and Number.

Shawmut Avenue—Continued

Page.	Letter.	Full Name.	Residence, Jan. 1, 1943.	Occupation.	Supposed Age.	Reported Residence, Jan. 1, 1942. Street and Number.
	P	Sayre George	448	laborer	29	here
	R	*Sayre Joseph	448	retired	80	"
	S	*Sayre Mary—†	448	housekeeper	61	"
	T	Tetler Eva M—†	448	"	69	"
	U	Ayoub Catharine—†	449	"	59	
	V	Ayoub Elias	449	retired	72	"
	W	Bodden Steadman	449	laborer	50	Everett
	X	Brown Edward	449	chef	55	here
	Y	*Cavall John	449	laborer	55	10 Union pk
	Z	Clay Catherine—†	449	housekeeper	55	here
226						
	A	McCarty Francis	449	laborer	52	"
	B	McGillen John J	449	chauffeur	54	"
	C	*Morais James	449	restaurateur	53	"
	D	*Nasser Thomas	449	laborer	60	
	E	Siber Charles	449	retired	68	
	F	Simons Catherine—†	449	housekeeper	69	"
	G	Tellier Walter	449	retired	69	614 Mass av
	H	Clark Walter F	450	meatcutter	58	here
	K	Dinan Joseph J	450	retired	60	9 Rutland
	L	Foley Edward	450	laborer	42	15 Rollins
	M	Hayes Anna F—†	450	housekeeper	70	here
		Magee Elizabeth—†	450	waitress	42	"
		McIver Edwin J	450	grinder	60	"
		Nagle Anna—†	450	shoeworker	46	681 Tremont
	N O	Nagle Bartholomew J	450	painter	54	681 "
	S	O'Connell Emma L—†	450	housekeeper	65	19 E Concord
	T	*Pelton Grace—†	450	"	62	here
	U	Scully Dolores—†	450	secretary	44	27 Worcester sq
	V	Scully John F	450	inspector	45	27 "
	W	Vegneau Alexander J	450	retired	69	621 Mass av
	X	Cummings Carrie—†	451	housekeeper	61	here
	Y	DeEll Joseph H	451	salesman	67	"
	Z	*DeEll Mary—†	451	housekeeper	61	"
227						
	A	Jones Emily—†	451	clerk	23	
	B	*Lavery James	451	porter	48	"
	C	*Miller Harry	451	seaman	67	
	D	O'Brien Mary E—†	451	housekeeper	69	"
	E	Spear Frederick W	451	operator	59	"
	F	Spear Nellie—†	451	housekeeper	64	"

Page.	Letter.	Full Name.	Residence, Jan. 1, 1943.	Occupation.	Supposed Age.	Reported Residence, Jan. 1, 1942. Street and Number.

Shawmut Avenue—Continued

Page.	Letter.	Full Name.	Residence, Jan. 1, 1943.	Occupation.	Supposed Age.	Reported Residence, Jan. 1, 1942. Street and Number.
	G	Terrell Helen M—†	451	housekeeper	81	here
	H	Terrell Lillian F—†	451	"	52	"
	K	Woolf Edward	451	carpenter	57	"
	L	*Jadoun Alice M—†	452	housekeeper	54	"
	M	*Jadoun Joseph	452	retired	62	"
	N	King Patrick	452	"	62	468 Shawmut av
	O	Maloof Hatem G	452	operator	53	here
	P	Morgan John F	452	mason	69	"
	R	Thompson George	452	retired	73	"
	S	Ward Frank	452	laborer	50	
	U	Hanna Edythe A—†	453	social worker	59	"
	V	*Calen Elizabeth—†	456	housekeeper	52	"
	W	Harold Edward	456	custodian	45	"
	X	Harold Frances J—†	456	housekeeper	62	"
	Y	*ElDouaihy Mary—†	457	"	69	"
	Z	ElDouaihy Stephen	457	clergyman	60	"
228						
	A	Crashaw Alice—†	458	housekeeper	77	"
	B	Foley George	458	painter	56	"
	C	Foley Martha—†	458	housekeeper	54	"
	D	*Kelley Anna—†	458	housewife	51	"
	E	Kelley Corrine—†	458	stitcher	21	"
	F	*Kelley Maroon	458	retired	53	
	G	Kelley Mary—†	458	stitcher	27	
	H	Kelley Minnie—†	458	"	31	"
	K	Kelley Richard	458	laborer	24	"
	L	Mee Raymond C	458	"	48	56 E Springfield
	M	McHugh John	458	"	44	here
	N	Richman Mervin	458		57	"
	O	Sullivan Arthur	458	"	55	106 Chandler
	P	Sullivan Elizabeth—†	458	housekeeper	53	34 Fisher av
	R	*Wren Hannah—†	458	"	65	here
	S	*Cabrial Manuel J	460	laborer	61	"
	T	Hasson Margaret E—†	460	housekeeper	58	"
	U	McBride John	460	chef	39	Wayland
	V	Mullin George	460	laborer	57	16 Highland
	W	Naglemaher John	460	"	68	Long Island
	X	Perkins Michael	460	freighthandler	42	35 Wrentham
	Y	Reed William	460	painter	65	Long Island
	Z	*Rossi Alfred	460	baker	60	here

Page.	Letter.	FULL NAME.	Residence, Jan. 1, 1943.	Occupation.	Supposed Age.	Reported Residence, Jan. 1, 1942. Street and Number.
229						
		Shawmut Avenue—Continued				
	B	Harrington Benjamin	462	painter	61	here
	A	Harrington Elizabeth—†	462	housewife	60	"
	C	Cahill William J	463	laborer	52	"
	D	Choate Herbert	463	retired	73	
	E	Mulgrew Edward	463	"	76	
	F	*Walton Ella—†	463	housekeeper	46	"
	G	Zeigler Godfrey	463	retired	70	"
	H	Barlow Mary—†	464	housekeeper	75	370 Shawmut av
	K	Hanham Catherine—†	464	"	71	366 "
	L	Moscaritolo Fedele	464	tailor	48	19 Upton
	M	*Moscaritolo Mary—†	464	"	50	19 "
	N	Burke Michael	465	retired	67	104 W Concord
	O	Flynn John R	465	"	38	598 Tremont
	P	Guider William	465	laborer	60	1042 Harrison av
	R	Kelley George	465	rigger	34	here
	S	Kelley Margaret G—†	465	housekeeper	28	"
	T	Mattson George W	465	laborer	55	Dedham
	U	McLean John	465	"	35	968 Parker
	V	Regan James	465	retired	56	Maine
	W	Wall Edward	465	laborer	44	335 Shawmut av
	X	Drea Joseph T	466	barber	73	21 Maryland
	Y	Ghiz Amelia—†	466	housekeeper	62	here
	Z	Ghiz Lillian—†	466	laundress	27	"
230						
	A	Ghiz Michael	466	locksmith	32	"
	B	Ghiz Victor	466	"	21	"
	C	Jenkins Raleigh M	466	chef	50	Rhode Island
	D	O'Connor George	466	retired	70	here
	E	Richardson Arthur L	466	gasfitter	59	"
	F	Wheeler Edwin A	466	houseman	60	"
	K	Brochoven Agnes—†	469	housewife	45	"
	L	Brochoven Frank	469	laborer	46	
	M	Shaw Helen—†	469	housewife	21	"
	N	Shaw William	469	laborer	25	"
	O	Anderson Mary—†	469	domestic	61	49 Rutland
	P	Fenton Margaret—†	469	housewife	41	here
	R	Fenton Peter	469	laborer	40	"
	S	Grady Arlene E—†	469	housekeeper	58	"
	T	Grady Daniel H	469	waiter	55	"

Page.	Letter.	FULL NAME.	Residence, Jan. 1, 1943.	Occupation.	Supposed Age.	Reported Residence, Jan. 1, 1942. Street and Number.

Shawmut Avenue—Continued

	U	Hart Charles	469	painter	33	here
	V	Hart Theresa—†	469	housekeeper	31	"
	W	Dailey Annie M—†	469	"	58	"
	X	Dailey Lewis C	469	machinist	53	"
	Y	Bennett Rita—†	469	housekeeper	26	68 W Concord
	Z	Duane Madonna—†	469	"	28	here
231						
	A	Rushworth Mary—†	469	"	60	
	C	George Salem S	471	shoemaker	40	"
	E	McDonough Catherine—†	475	housewife	48	"
	F	McDonough Edward	475	chef	44	
	G	Welch Albe	475	shipfitter	35	"
	H	Welch Irene—†	475	housewife	31	"
	K	Brown Joseph	475	chauffeur	49	"
	L	Brown Rae—†	475	housewife	49	"
	M	Stearns Walter	475	U S A	32	
	N	*Zeber Alphonso	475	realtor	59	
	O	*Zeber Lottie—†	475	housewife	49	"
	P	Couchavles George	475	counterman	50	178 W Springfield
	R	*Couchavles Mary—†	475	housekeeper	36	178 "
	S	VanGemert Helen—†	475	housewife	49	here
	T	VanGemert Stephen	475	waterproofer	52	"
	U	Reardon Dorothy—†	475	housekeeper	33	"
	V	Reardon Joseph	475	bartender	35	"
	W	Khachadoorian Siony—†	475	housekeeper	38	"
	X	Khachadoorian Stephen	475	stitcher	48	"

Tremont Street

	Z	Galdi Clara—†	664	housewife	53	here
232						
	A	Galdi Frank	664	bookbinder	51	"
	B	*Makasian Annie—†	664	at home	77	
	D	Patten Richard	664	chauffeur	59	"
	E	Sherer August	664	printer	68	
	F	Sherer Isabelle—†	664	at home	68	
	G	Connolley Dudley	666	steamfitter	41	"
	H	Crowe Loretta—†	666	waitress	21	189 W Brookline
	K	DeYoung Albert	666	painter	50	here
	L	Fletcher Virginia—†	666	clerk	21	Iowa
	M	Greenwood Martha—†	666	"	20	here

Page.	Letter.	Full Name.	Residence, Jan. 1, 1943.	Occupation.	Supposed Age.	Reported Residence, Jan. 1, 1942. Street and Number.

Tremont Street—Continued

	N	Holms Joseph	666	U S N	30	Iowa
	O	Holms Mabel—†	666	housewife	42	"
	P	Maddox Ann—†	666	"	30	here
	R	Maddox Benjamin F	666	welder	40	"
	S	Smith Helen M—†	666	clerk	40	Winthrop
	T	Steele Benjamin	666	mason	38	41 Rutland sq
	U	Ladd Robert	666B	U S N	20	here
	V	Reynolds Arletta—†	666B	housewife	39	"
	W	Reynolds Frank	666B	laborer	54	"
	X	Stacker Gertrude—†	666B	housewife	22	"
	Y	Anderson Cora—†	668	waitress	27	Weston
	Z	Anderson Norman	668	counterman	38	here
233						
	A	Connors Alice—†	668	housewife	37	"
	B	*Gramash Thelma—†	668	domestic	34	Chelsea
	C	Holden Dorothy—†	668	housekeeper	29	Maine
	D	LaPete Robert	668	laborer	24	here
	E	Robertson Forrest	668	"	34	Malden
	F	Solomon Mary—†	668	housekeeper	48	here
	G	Sullivan Timothy	668	laborer	40	109 W Brookline
	H	Vien Emma—†	668	housekeeper	57	here
	K	Driscoll Mary—†	670	waitress	40	"
	L	Fadoul Stella—†	670	housewife	41	"
	M	*Levy Arthur J	670	ironworker	39	Maine
	N	Trainor Herbert	670	laborer	43	70 Burbank
	O	Blair William	672	counterman	39	8 Clarendon
	P	Bruno Eileen—†	672	housewife	48	536 Mass av
	R	Bruno Francis	672	laborer	28	536 "
	S	Edelson John	672	foreman	46	here
	T	Ferris Michael	672	machinist	26	"
	U	Ferris Sophie—†	672	housewife	35	"
	V	Hill Edward	672	salesman	50	Brookline
	W	Hill Nancy—†	672	housewife	34	"
	X	*Kerallah Bistros	672	retired	63	here
	Y	Preston Celia—†	672	at home	60	727 Tremont
	Z	Preston Thomas W	672	chauffeur	46	727 "
234						
	A	Robbins Beatrice—†	672	stenographer	29	here
	D	Angier Emma J—†	676	at home	77	"
	E	Bowles Emma—†	676	domestic	54	Newton
	F	Callan Jennie—†	676	at home	72	130 W Brookline

Page.	Letter.	Full Name.	Residence, Jan. 1, 1943.	Occupation.	Supposed Age.	Reported Residence, Jan. 1, 1942. Street and Number.

Tremont Street—Continued

	G	Clark Mary—†	676	at home	76	160 W Brookline
	H	Darling Ralph	676	janitor	62	here
	K	Gormley Michael J	676	retired	68	34 Calumet
	L	*Johnson Carl G	676	painter	51	here
	M	Johnson Greta—†	676	housewife	52	"
	N	Kelleher Caroline—†	676	at home	86	"
	O	Kelleher John T	676	retired	72	"
	P	Lynch Frank P	676	"	69	26 Concord sq
	R	O'Dell Minnie—†	676	at home	70	here
	S	Piper Rose—†	676	"	72	"
	T	Reardon Anna—†	676	"	63	433 Shawmut av
	U	Regan Mary—†	676	maid	54	here
	V	Roberts Calberath	676	retired	66	484 Col av
	W	Atwood Harry	678	laborer	64	here
	X	Cox Charles M	678	retired	67	Concord
	Y	Curley Michael J	678	laborer	38	Florida
	Z	Geoghegan Michael J	678	"	47	706 Mass av
235						
	A	*Hesketh Catherine—†	678	maid	56	here
	B	Ladd Louis	678	porter	52	"
	C	Quinlan Hammon W	678	mechanic	45	"
	D	Quinlan Katherine—†	678	housewife	65	"
	E	Quinlan William M	678	storekeeper	70	"
	F	Smith Blanche—†	678	at home	63	"
	G	*Bennett Joseph	680	laborer	47	"
	H	Blondin Gerald	680	waiter	37	"
	K	Brandt Catherine—†	680	housewife	39	"
	L	Brandt Charles	680	laborer	46	"
	M	Carroll Helen—†	680	domestic	58	"
	N	Dermerdi Sadie—†	680	housewife	58	"
	O	Dermerdi Thomas	680	retired	60	"
	P	Fay Michael	680	laborer	53	"
	R	*Lizzotte Leo	680	waiter	54	"
	S	McHugh Thomas J	680	machinist	60	602 Tremont
	T	Mulkern Catherine—†	680	housekeeper	56	569 Gallivan Blvd
	U	Roberto John	680	waiter	30	here
	V	Seams Archie A	680	janitor	71	"
	W	Trottier Vena—†	680	housewife	53	"
	X	Trottier William	680	barber	53	"
236						
	A	Butwell Louise—†	684	at home	72	"

Page.	Letter.	FULL NAME.	Residence, Jan. 1, 1943.	Occupation.	Supposed Age.	Reported Residence, Jan. 1, 1942. Street and Number.

Tremont Street—Continued

	B	Carr Charles	684	retired	73	here
	C	Carter Ida—†	684	at home	85	"
	D	Cohen Henry	684	salesman	57	"
	E	Cramer Eleanor—†	684	nurse	31	
	F	Cramer Louis	684	U S N	33	"
	G	*Deslites Eva—†	684	instructor	34	Salem
	H	Hewson Benjamin	684	painter	67	here
	K	Kilby Angus	684	conductor	45	Maine
	L	Lewis Evelyn—†	684	inspector	26	here
	M	Lewis Isaiah	684	manager	29	"
	N	Lewis Katherine—†	684	stitcher	49	"
	O	Lewis Virginia—†	684	housewife	26	"
	P	McLullan Neal	684	barber	40	
	R	Morgan Adeline—†	684	housekeeper	58	"
	S	Moses Frank	684	waiter	43	"
	T	Tarasaweitz Louis	684	cabinetmaker	47	"
	U	Brown Hattie—†	686	at home	74	
	V	Brown Henry V	686	retired	79	"
	W	Cahill William F	686	machinist	47	38 Carney ct
	X	Dubois Cephise—†	686	housewife	66	here
	Y	Dubois Omer E	686	salesman	65	"
	Z	Farrell James P	686	machinist	68	"
237						
	A	Foss Almon	686	chauffeur	36	"
	B	Foss Helen—†	686	housewife	39	"
	C	Garris Dorothy—†	686	"	29	Rhode Island
	D	Garris Edward	686	chef	42	"
	E	Haskell Herman	686	retired	68	here
	F	Jones Robert E	686	laborer	49	"
	G	Maslin Albert J	686	chauffeur	49	"
	H	Maslin Gertrude E—†	686	waitress	41	
	K	Moss Esther—†	686	cutter	53	"
	L	Robertson Catherine—†	686	laundress	28	156 W Canton
	M	Robertson John W	686	sailmaker	46	156 "
	N	Weld Mary—†	686	housewife	62	here
	O	Weld Joseph M	686	operator	61	"
	P	Welsh Catherine—†	686	cook	52	46 Pinehurst
	R	Wescott Eliza—†	686	at home	75	here
	S	Davenport Catherine—†	688	saleswoman	30	131 Pembroke
	T	Ferris Ella—†	688	housewife	44	268 Lamartine
	U	Ferris Harry B	688	welder	39	268 "

Page.	Letter.	Full Name.	Residence, Jan. 1, 1943.	Occupation.	Supposed Age.	Reported Residence, Jan. 1, 1942. Street and Number.

Tremont Street—Continued

	v	Quinn Irene—†	688	housewife	30	130 W Brookline
	w	Quinn Martin	688	chauffeur	34	130 "
	x	Scoppettuolo Thomas	688	laborer	55	8 Moon
	z	Foley Robert	690	"	48	here
238						
	A	Haley Charles E	690	"	40	168 Rutland
	B	Kelley Robert	690	"	62	here
	C	Lathan Daniel	690	retired	66	"
	D	Learmont Alexander	690	machinist	45	"
	E	Manning James	690	retired	72	"
	F	McGaw Emma B—†	690	housekeeper	84	"
	G	Shaw Jedediah	690	retired	77	"
	H	Smart James	690	laborer	50	"
	K	*Wah Lin	690	storekeeper	53	"
	L	Goodwin Bertha—†	692	at home	67	"
	M	Hanron Elisabeth—†	692	housewife	25	"
	N	Hanron John W	692	operator	26	"
	O	Kyle Mabel—†	692	waitress	49	"
	P	McCready William	692	draftsman	50	Florida
	R	Mellow Ernest M	692	welder	28	Lowell
	S	Ridge Ann—†	692	domestic	50	here
	T	Surrett Bertha—†	692	at home	67	"
	U	*Lee Charlie	692A	laundryman	48	Worcester
	V	Baker Jennie—†	694	clerk	28	here
	W	Bennett Addie—†	694	housekeeper	63	551 Mass av
	X	Bennett Everett	694	janitor	56	551 "
	Y	Brodeur Joseph E	694	counterman	63	237 Shawmut av
	Z	Carroll William	694	welder	47	here
239						
	A	Hayes Ruth—†	694	waitress	20	Connecticut
	B	Munroe Walter	694	painter	48	Gloucester
	C	Ponciroli Corinne A—†	694	housewife	37	7 Rand pl
	E	Carlson Edward	696	laborer	33	Ohio
	F	Jones Alice—†	696	saleswoman	38	560 Mass av
	G	Sundbergh John J	696	salesman	29	1849 Col av
	H	Sundbergh Josephine—†	696	housewife	27	1849 "
	K	Taylor Jane—†	696	domestic	35	here
	L	Towne George	696	laborer	47	Cambridge
	M	Allan Elizabeth J—†	698	housekeeper	79	here
	N	Clinton Thomas	698	laborer	43	"
	O	Jason Phillip	698	storekeeper	61	"
	P	Kelly Edward	698	plumber	50	"

Page.	Letter.	Full Name.	Residence, Jan. 1, 1943.	Occupation.	Supposed Age.	Reported Residence, Jan. 1, 1942. Street and Number.

Tremont Street—Continued

Page.	Letter.	Full Name.	Residence, Jan. 1, 1943.	Occupation.	Supposed Age.	Reported Residence, Jan. 1, 1942. Street and Number.
	R	LeRoy Robert	698	machinist	42	84 W Canton
	S	Locke Clarence	698	laborer	49	here
	T	McDonald Ruth—†	698	at home	50	139 Pembroke
	U	Perkins Mabel—†	698	"	69	52 Worcester
	V	Thompson Florence M–†	698	"	70	here
	W	Tibbitts Gladys—†	698	"	54	"
	X	Gordon Wendell	700	accountant	55	518 Mass av
	[1]Y	Bland George	704	laborer	54	Lowell
	Z	Cowen Irene—†	704	housekeeper	40	here
240						
	B	Anderson Helen D—†	704	waitress	30	84 St Botolph
	C	Colligan Lillian—†	704	at home	60	84 "
	D	McGrath Mary—†	704	"	81	here
	E	Sullivan Frederick	704	machinist	53	"
	F	Sullivan Lillian M—†	704	housewife	44	"
	G	Gorman Harold	704	laborer	41	
	H	Gorman Myrtle—†	704	housewife	40	"

Washington Street

Page.	Letter.	Full Name.	Residence, Jan. 1, 1943.	Occupation.	Supposed Age.	Reported Residence, Jan. 1, 1942. Street and Number.
	P	Murphy Elizabeth M–†	1561	housekeeper	73	48 E Springfield
	R	Dalton Mary M—†	1561	housewife	43	here
	S	Dalton William J	1561	mechanic	49	"
	T	Kane Jeanette—†	1561	clerk	51	"
	U	Karsen Kedah—†	1561	housewife	52	"
	V	Karsen Michael P	1561	chef	47	"
	W	Bushey Gertrude—†	1561	housewife	28	N Hampshire
	X	Bushey Walter, jr	1561	manager	28	"
	Y	Calam Esther—†	1561	housewife	40	here
	Z	Weber Segrid—†	1561	at home	70	"
241						
	A	Baldwin Emma E—†	1561	forewoman	60	"
	B	Baldwin Roland F	1561	U S N	24	
	G	Gianopoulos Arthur	1571	U S A	28	
	H	Gianopoulos Frances—†	1571	buyer	24	
	K	*Gianopoulos George	1571	chef	59	
	L	Gianopoulos James	1571	waiter	25	
	M	Gianopoulos Jennie—†	1571	housewife	54	"
	N	Gianopoulos Sophia—†	1571	dressmaker	22	"
	O	Trakas Christos J	1571	manager	53	"
	P	*Trakas Georgia D—†	1571	housewife	52	"
	R	Trakas John C	1571	student	24	

Page.	Letter.	Full Name.	Residence, Jan. 1, 1943.	Occupation.	Supposed Age.	Reported Residence, Jan. 1, 1942. Street and Number.

Washington Street—Continued

	S	Trakas Patricia C—†	1571	clerk	27	here
	T	Carpenter Charles	1573	laborer	21	"
	U	Carpenter Frank A	1573	chef	68	"
	V	Carpenter Frank E	1573	chauffeur	23	5 Gustin
	W	Carpenter Margaret—†	1573	housewife	59	here
	X	Carpenter Rita M—†	1573	"	21	5 Gustin
	Y	Geoghegan Michael	1573	laborer	52	330 Shawmut av
	Z	Kerwin Edward	1573	retired	74	374 "
242						
	A	King Michael	1573	chef	53	5 Gustin
	B	King William	1573	laborer	23	5 "
	C	Thompson Ernest	1573	chef	42	8 Pelham
	D	*Winecholm Sigrid—†	1573	housekeeper	59	Malden
	H	Dern Herman	1577	chauffeur	37	1690 Wash'n
	F	Hendrick Mary C—†	1577	housewife	26	here
	G	Hendrick Raymond J	1577	checker	38	"
	K	McGloin Anna—†	1577	housekeeper	39	1662 Wash'n
	L	McGloin Edward	1577	salesman	20	1662 "
	M	Munafo Juanita—†	1577	housewife	34	here
	N	Munafo Santo	1577	entertainer	30	"
	P	Adams Mildred—†	1581	housewife	22	45 Chadwick
	R	Adams Walter	1581	pipecoverer	33	45 "
	S	Nally Francis J	1581	chauffeur	34	57 E Springfield
	T	Nally Margaret F—†	1581	housewife	42	57 "
	U	Stamatopoulos Georgia–†	1581	"	32	here
	V	Stamatopoulos Takes	1581	salesman	36	"
	W	Vinios Asimo—†	1581	housekeeper	56	"
	Y	Bogige George	1585	retired	60	"
	Z	Bogige Lillian—†	1585	housewife	43	"
243						
	A	Taylor Frank	1585	tailor	33	
	B	Taylor Theresa—†	1585	stitcher	26	
	C	Harding Francis	1585	entertainer	35	"
	D	Lanzillo Louis M	1585	laborer	50	"
	E	Lanzillo Sarah J—†	1585	housewife	52	"
	F	Pliskin William G	1585	druggist	45	37 W Newton
	G	Manley Alice—†	1585	housewife	41	here
	H	Manley Clarence	1585	machinist	45	"
	K	Manley James	1585	U S A	23	"
	L	Sanders Dorothy—†	1585	housewife	33	"
	M	Sanders Edwin	1585	chauffeur	38	"

Page.	Letter.	Full Name.	Residence, Jan. 1, 1943.	Occupation.	Supposed Age.	Reported Residence, Jan. 1, 1942. Street and Number.

West Concord Street

	T	Jenkins Alice—†	101	housewife	41	here
	U	Jenkins Leland	101	mechanic	44	"
	V	Corbett Elizabeth—†	101	at home	65	"
	W	McKay John F	101	inspector	60	"
	X	McKay Mary A—†	101	housewife	55	"
	Y	LeDoux Clara—†	101	housekeeper	53	"
	Z	Petrous Anthony	101	chauffeur	23	"
244						
	A	Petrous Rose—†	101	housewife	23	"
	B	Newton Charles A	101	laborer	48	
	C	Newton Earl	101	"	52	"
	D	Cochran Charles N	106	"	34	Cambridge
	E	Cochran Mary—†	106	domestic	26	here
	F	Crowley James	106	retired	64	"
	G	Curran Beatrice—†	106	at home	47	"
	H	Daley Joseph	106	kitchenman	63	"
	K	Donovan Catherine—†	106	at home	70	"
	L	Joyce Martin	106	retired	67	121 W Concord
	M	Laurie Annie—†	106	maid	51	here
	N	Morse Grace—†	106	housewife	44	45 Worcester
	O	Murphy Patrick	106	retired	66	here
	P	Quinn Delia—†	106	housewife	56	"
	R	Roberts Walter J	106	cutter	60	"
	S	Connelly James	108	retired	73	"
	T	D'Amore Aroline B—†	108	clerk	46	Chelsea
	U	Haggerty Margaret—†	108	at home	73	here
	V	Nelson Alfred	108	retired	72	"
	W	O'Donnell John	108	laborer	68	258 Northampton
	X	Pereira Jordas P	108	paperhanger	48	Revere
	Y	Roberts Mary—†	108	housewife	58	here
	Z	Sullivan Michael	108	retired	73	"
245						
	A	Whooley Joseph J	108	clerk	44	
	B	Whooley Mabel—†	108	housewife	49	"
	C	Burns Agnes M—†	110	"	66	
	D	Donovan Ester—†	110	domestic	42	"
	E	Ehler Ernest	110	merchant	62	"
	F	Grove Catherine—†	110	housewife	74	1601 Wash'n
	G	Grove Harry	110	retired	70	1601 "
	H	Laemo Dominic	110	laborer	33	1082 Com av
	K	Laemo Earline—†	110	housewife	24	1082 "

West Concord Street—Continued

Page.	Letter.	Full Name.	Residence, Jan. 1, 1943.	Occupation.	Supposed Age.	Reported Residence, Jan. 1, 1942. Street and Number.
	L	Shea Mary—†	110	at home	87	here
	M	Tynen John J	110	laborer	63	"
	O	Ayer Lettie—†	114	housewife	60	"
	P	Ayer Palmer	114	salesman	56	"
	R	Bock Fredrick	114	mechanic	50	"
	S	Flynn Wallace	114	retired	68	
	T	Lowney John	114	mechanic	56	"
	U	Maloney Catherine—†	114	at home	66	46 Worcester
	V	Maloney Mary—†	114	"	68	110 W Concord
	W	McIsaac Annie—†	114	"	74	here
	X	McNara Mary—†	114		60	"
	Y	O'Hara Matilda—†	114	"	75	168 W Brookline
	Z	Rogers Jennie—†	114	housekeeper	64	here
246						
	A	Walsh Margaret—†	114	at home	73	
	B	Casey Marie L—†	116	housewife	76	"
	C	LaForme Charles W	116	retired	68	"
	D	LaForme Louis	116	"	65	"
	E	Maloney Arthur C	116	bookkeeper	40	New Jersey
	F	McPhee Lydia—†	116	housewife	54	here
	G	*McPhee Thomas	116	laborer	49	"
	H	Myers Edward F	116	"	35	Maine
	K	Rideout Douglas	116	U S A	27	8 Warren av
	L	Rideout Edmond	116	U S N	38	5 Col sq
	M	Rideout Edmond R	116	mechanic	68	8 Warren av
	N	Rideout Philip	116	U S A	34	here
	O	Tarris Charles	116	bartender	31	"
	P	Williams Augustus	116	photographer	63	"
	R	Joyce Edward P	118	laborer	42	161 Warren av
	S	Joyce Rose A—†	118	housewife	47	161 "
	T	LaForme Angelina—†	118	housekeeper	70	here
	U	*Long Daniel	118	retired	61	"
	V	McDonald James	118	"	68	"
	W	Morris Eugene J	118	cleaner	37	303½ Blue Hill av
	X	Walsh Patrick	118	laborer	52	11 Albemarle
	Y	Walsh William	118	storekeeper	46	here
	Z	Connolly James	119	retired	70	145 W Concord
247						
	A	Edwards Albert	119	porter	46	New York
	B	Ferguson Mary—†	119	at home	67	here
	C	Gordon Alexander	119	retired	76	"

Page.	Letter.	Full Name.	Residence, Jan. 1, 1943.	Occupation.	Supposed Age.	Reported Residence, Jan. 1, 1942. Street and Number.

West Concord Street—Continued

Page.	Letter.	Full Name.	Residence, Jan. 1, 1943.	Occupation.	Supposed Age.	Reported Residence, Jan. 1, 1942. Street and Number.
	D	Irwin Chester	119	nurse	46	here
	E	Lee Harry	119	laundryman	32	“
	F	Meyers Mary—†	119	at home	84	“
	G	Sawiuk Hazel—†	119	housewife	35	“
	H	*Sawiuk Michael	119	farmer	54	“
	K	Sawiuk Michael	119	U S A	27	331 Shawmut av
	L	Stuffle Laura—†	119	stitcher	26	17 Dartmouth pl
	M	Dean Ernest E	120	laborer	38	here
	N	Durney Edward	120	retired	75	653 Mass av
	O	Higgins Susan—†	120	at home	58	here
	P	Hunnefield Helen—†	120	clerk	64	“
	R	Kerins Mary A—†	120	at home	73	“
	S	Mathews James	120	chef	51	
	T	Osgood Harriet—†	120	housekeeper	62	“
	U	Peterson James	120	retired	72	127 W Concord
	V	Reardon James	120	laborer	46	27 Warren av
	W	Shea Edward	120	guard	51	758 Tremont
	X	Williams Louis J	120	retired	69	470 E Fourth
	Y	Blanche Robert	121	“	76	here
	Z	Logan John	121	operator	62	“
248						
	A	Losse Sadie—†	121	laundress	54	“
	B	Milosz Anthony	121	mechanic	46	“
	C	Milosz Konstanty	121	retired	51	
	D	O'Connell Margaret—†	121	at home	75	
	E	Richards Barbara—†	121	“	40	
	F	Richards Ernest	121	operator	51	..
	G	Williams Florence C—†	121	clerk	35	
	H	Williams Subina—†	121	housekeeper	66	“
	K	Ahern Oliver	122	painter	45	4 Worcester sq
	L	Burnham Edgar	122	retired	80	330 Shawmut av
	M	Couchaine Alfred	122	laborer	46	here
	N	Couchaine Marie—†	122	housewife	43	“
	O	McDonald Maurice	122	retired	67	102 W Concord
	P	Noonan David	122	“	67	134 “
	R	Sednoski Albert	122	shoeworker	50	here
	S	*Galvin Ellen—†	123	at home	65	45 Rutland
	T	*Galvin Mary—†	123	“	66	87 School
	U	Julian Charles	123	machinist	39	here
	V	Kelly Marie—†	123	housewife	30	103 Williams
	W	Kelly Maurice	123	mechanic	35	103 “

Page.	Letter.	Full Name.	Residence, Jan. 1, 1943.	Occupation.	Supposed Age.	Reported Residence, Jan. 1, 1942. Street and Number.

West Concord Street—Continued

	x	*MacDonald Pius	123	laborer	60	here
	Y	Mahoney John	123	watchman	72	24 Bigelow
	z	Mitchell Harry E	123	mechanic	52	22 Bradbury
249						
	A	Rymkiewicz Walter	123	machinist	46	here
	B	Duggan Mary—†	124	housekeeper	41	"
	C	Fanian Alfred	124	retired	66	"
	D	Kean Sallie—†	124	at home	76	"
	E	Knight Evelyn—†	124	domestic	42	46 Worcester
	F	McLean Archibald	124	laborer	61	here
	G	Weis Albert	124	painter	43	Quincy
	H	Allman Joseph H	125	chef	40	725 Tremont
	K	Frizzell Elizabeth—†	125	at home	66	128 W Concord
	L	Gallagher Joseph	125	chipper	27	144 Dudley
	M	Kreise Agnes—†	125	at home	78	61 W Brookline
	N	Mesparian Sarkis	125	shoemaker	40	89 W Concord
	O	Murray Margaret—†	125	cook	55	here
	P	Pitts George	125	retired	78	"
	R	Pitts Jennie E—†	125	housewife	57	"
	S	Pitts Lawrence J	125	chef	23	"
	T	Pitts Mary—†	125	housewife	23	5 Tupelo
	U	Sheehan William P	125	laborer	66	449 Shawmut av
	V	Dee Albert	126	"	63	here
	W	Dee Eva—†	126	housewife	61	"
	X	Duran John	126	laborer	64	"
	Y	Harrington Patrick	126	janitor	57	"
	Z	Johnson Christine—†	126	housewife	45	132 W Concord
250						
	A	Johnson David	126	retired	50	132 "
	B	Badock Chester	127	inspector	33	Wash'n D C
	C	*Galvin Eleanor—†	127	housewife	42	139 W Concord
	D	Galvin James	127	retired	68	139 "
	E	Byrne Helen—†	128	at home	65	485 Shawmut av
	F	Carney John C	128	U S A	37	here
	G	Carney John H	128	agent	68	"
	H	Daly Dennis H	128	clerk	79	"
	K	Daly Regina—†	128	housekeeper	40	"
	L	Monroe Harold J	128	clerk	62	485 Shawmut av
	M	Abey Edith—†	129	housewife	24	here
	N	Abey Potenciano	129	bartender	32	"
	O	Devine Bridget—†	129	housewife	48	"

Page.	Letter.	Full Name.	Residence, Jan. 1, 1943.	Occupation.	Supposed Age.	Reported Residence, Jan. 1, 1942. Street and Number.
		West Concord Street—Continued				
	P	Devine Michael	129	laborer	51	here
	R	Rosales Benjamin A	129	musician	42	"
	S	Rosales Rena—†	129	housewife	32	"
	T	Adams Charles	130	chef	44	
	U	*Cann Susan—†	130	stitcher	61	
	V	Cunningham Mary—†	130	housekeeper	62	"
	W	Donlon John	130	laborer	64	"
	X	Frenchville Charles	130	salesman	47	"
	Y	Harrington Catherine—†	130	domestic	49	"
	Z	Harrington Nellie—†	130	"	43	
251						
	A	Martin John	130	retired	75	
	B	Martin Mary—†	130	housewife	73	"
	C	*McKeever Josephine—†	130	housekeeper	51	"
	D	Westron Thomas	130	retired	77	"
	F	Dandelin Joseph	132	"	70	
	G	Dandelin Marie R—†	132	housewife	42	"
	H	Descranpie Joseph	132	laborer	31	
	K	Isa Georgianna—†	132	nurse	25	
	L	Kane Evelyn C—†	132	housewife	49	"
	M	Kane James W	132	chef	51	
	N	Kelley Agnes—†	132	housekeeper	60	"
	O	Konopocki Adam	132	laborer	48	"
	P	Slavin William T	132	"	51	"
	R	Viancour Arthur	132	clerk	45	"
	S	Viancour Mary—†	132	housewife	70	"
	T	Corcoran Julia—†	133	at home	67	37 Worcester
	U	Delaney John J	133	steamfitter	54	N Hampshire
	V	Flaherty Elizabeth—†	133	housewife	57	here
	W	Flaherty Patrick A	133	painter	55	"
	X	Leary Nora M—†	133	cook	64	16 Rutland sq
	Y	Phillips Wyart B	133	retired	75	here
	Z	Stanon Edward	133	laborer	49	4 E Brookline
252						
	A	Wyman Sarah E—†	133	at home	67	163 W Canton
	C	Henry Alfred M	135	retired	71	here
	D	Ironside James A	135	stonecutter	62	"
	E	*McIntosh Arthur	135	"	55	"
	F	*McIntosh Eleanor—†	135	housewife	52	"
	G	Nolan Johanna—†	135	at home	70	
	H	Ollendorf Edith—†	135	seamstress	56	"

Page.	Letter.	Full Name.	Residence, Jan. 1, 1943.	Occupation.	Supposed Age.	Reported Residence, Jan. 1, 1942. Street and Number.

West Concord Street—Continued

	K	Petty Susan E—†	135	at home	69	400 Col av
	L	Robertson Alexander	135	mechanic	51	Connecticut
	M	Trudo Clayton W	135	salesman	49	455 Dudley
	N	Trudo Suzanne E—†	135	nurse	38	455 "
	O	White Mary A—†	135	cook	64	here
	P	Wilson George	135	laborer	63	125 W Concord
	R	Baker Caroline—†	136	housekeeper	64	here
	S	Brett Althea R—†	136	instructor	39	"
	T	Carazo Oscar	136	mechanic	48	45 E Lenox
	U	Dias Anthony	136	chef	47	here
	V	Duffy Josephine—†	136	at home	65	127 W Concord
	W	Hamel Bertha—†	136	housewife	53	here
	X	Hamel Joseph	136	carpenter	61	"
	Y	McCarthy Arthur	136	chef	50	500 Morton
	Z	McDonald Catherine—†	136	housekeeper	64	here
253						
	A	Williams William R	136	fireman	62	114 W Concord
	B	Bryant George C	137	retired	67	16 Dartmouth
	C	Foley Herbert	137	"	45	here
	D	Grant Theresa—†	137	attendant	58	"
	E	Leaf Arthur	137	rigger	45	"
	F	MacNeil Marie—†	137	waitress	38	
	G	Maycock Thomas	137	laborer	58	
	H	*McInerney Margaret—†	137	at home	82	
	K	Sheehan Thomas	137	laborer	48	
	L	Brown Frank	138	musician	74	"
	M	Flaherty Delia M—†	138	at home	71	"
	N	Flannery Michael	138	gardener	52	60 Chandler
	O	Nephin Bridget—†	138	housewife	56	here
	P	Nephin Peter J	138	painter	53	"
	R	Rabbit John	138	chauffeur	48	31 Worcester sq
	S	Rogers Hugh	138	machinist	62	153 W Concord
	T	Allen Harold	139	chauffeur	31	14 Franklin
	U	Kalanicki Carl	139	blacksmith	49	53 Bradford
	V	Martell Wanda—†	139	housekeeper	23	53 "
	W	Chambers Ruth S—†	140	at home	77	here
	X	Clay Helen—†	140	nurse	40	"
	Y	Donohue Mary—†	140	domestic	64	"
	Z	Donovan John	140	clerk	68	
254						
	A	Drisko Harrison M	140	electrician	50	106 Norway

Page.	Letter.	Full Name.	Residence, Jan. 1, 1943.	Occupation.	Supposed Age.	Reported Residence, Jan. 1, 1942. Street and Number.

West Concord Street—Continued

Page.	Letter.	Full Name.	Residence, Jan. 1, 1943.	Occupation.	Supposed Age.	Reported Residence, Jan. 1, 1942. Street and Number.
	B	Fay Mary—†	140	at home	78	94 Worcester
	C	Johnson Augusta V—†	140	nurse	52	here
	D	Leary Helen—†	140	"	38	"
	E	McDonald Nellie—†	140	maid	67	"
	F	Murphy Louise M—†	140	nurse	68	
	G	Nephin Joseph R	140	retired	73	
	H	Nephin Julia A—†	140	housewife	72	"
	K	Nutting William C	140	chef	38	596 Tremont
	L	Sullivan Theresa B—†	140	domestic	61	here
	M	Allen Frank	141	window cleaner	45	10 Rollins
	N	Conley John	141	laborer	42	54 Westland av
	O	Hareguy Victor	141	pinboy	41	31 Worcester
	P	Howard Edward	141	retired	71	here
	R	LaPorte Minnie—†	141	at home	70	120 W Concord
	S	Oakley John J	141	operator	46	303 Summit av
	T	Thompson Glenn	141	window cleaner	45	10 Rollins
	U	Green Ruth D—†	142	housewife	47	here
	V	Green William	142	salesman	56	"
	W	Leslie Mary J—†	142	nurse	54	"
	X	McKenna Sarah J—†	142	housekeeper	68	"
	Y	McMartin Edward B	142	retired	84	"
	Z	Murray William E	142	salesman	45	"
255						
	A	Reynolds Percy W	142	"	59	
	B	Walsh Matthew A	142	retired	76	
	C	Donaldson George	143	"	69	
	D	*Peters Angelina—†	143	at home	59	
	E	Rice Edwin	143	salesman	67	"
	F	Williams Joseph W	143	welder	29	
	G	Williams Mary—†	143	housewife	30	"
	H	Bither Mabelle B—†	144	housekeeper	40	"
	K	Bragner Carl	144	laborer	42	Cambridge
	L	Cheever Patrick J	144	porter	47	Rhode Island
	M	Conway Anthony J	144	retired	77	here
	N	Elmore Cecelia—†	144	housekeeper	63	"
	O	MacDougall Duncan	144	mechanic	37	"
	P	Manthorn Theodore	144	chef	32	Hingham
	R	*Murphy Mary—†	144	domestic	50	here
	T	Alhard Hector E	146	plumber	59	"
	U	Bell Cora—†	146	at home	68	Quincy
	V	Bradbury Annie—†	146	domestic	52	here

Page.	Letter.	Full Name.	Residence, Jan. 1, 1943.	Occupation.	Supposed Age.	Reported Residence, Jan. 1, 1942. Street and Number.

West Concord Street—Continued

	W	Connor Martha—†	146	at home	68	468 Mass av
	X	Davis Rodeman	146	chauffeur	61	here
	Y	Gaynor Frank	146	retired	65	"
	Z	Hamilton Gertrude—†	146	waitress	44	Newton
256						
	A	Knight Margaret—†	146	at home	71	here
	B	Lawrence Frank M	146	laborer	64	"
	C	Long Mary—†	146	at home	53	Georgia
	D	McCarthy Elizabeth—†	146	housewife	59	here
	E	*McCarthy Henry T	146	barber	58	"
	F	McKewn Catherine—†	146	at home	72	85 Union Park
	G	McTiernan Bridget—†	146	"	72	75 Montgomery
	H	Sowerby Sarah E—†	146	housewife	68	here
	K	Walsh Freeman	146	mechanic	38	"
	L	Bessie Lillian B—†	147	housekeeper	65	Quincy
	M	Burr Louis	147	retired	59	here
	N	Cormier Dana	147	"	56	37 Upton
	O	Cronin Julia—†	147	stitcher	55	New York
	P	Donaghy Edward	147	rigger	56	here
	R	Hendry Thomas	147	retired	84	127 W Concord
	S	Lehmann Richard B	147	brakeman	66	Rhode Island
	T	Sanderson Loretta—†	147	waitress	30	174 W Brookline
	U	*Vaughan Michael	147	retired	75	here
	V	Beard Josephine—†	148	housekeeper	72	"
	W	Collins Etria E	148	retired	73	"
	X	Easton John	148	"	82	"
	Y	Gibbard Nellie—†	148	housewife	55	11 Rutland
	Z	McKeever James	148	painter	28	here
257						
	A	McKeever Margaret—†	148	housewife	29	"
	B	Summers Susan—†	148	housekeeper	54	"
	C	Banfill Harriette—†	149	housewife	39	N Hampshire
	D	Banfill Perley	149	machinist	50	"
	E	Boyd Helen—†	149	at home	39	49 Upton
	F	Burnham Dorothy—†	149	stitcher	30	here
	G	Dolan Caroline—†	149	housewife	58	151 W Concord
	H	Dolan William	149	retired	68	151 "
	K	Johnson Arthur	149	cher	60	471 Col av
	L	Kornheim Alexander	149	clerk	55	here
	M	Kornheim Esther J—†	149	housewife	50	"
	N	Mulholland Elizabeth—†	149	at home	60	49 Upton

Page.	Letter.	Full Name.	Residence, Jan. 1, 1943.	Occupation.	Supposed Age.	Reported Residence, Jan. 1, 1942. Street and Number.

West Concord Street—Continued

	o	Valley Ann—†	149	waitress	48	here
	p	Yassinski Irene—†	149	housewife	23	Illinois
	r	Yassinski Walter	149	U S C G	23	"
	s	Billings Anna K—†	150	housekeeper	66	here
	t	Bowen Patrick	150	laborer	56	"
	u	Chase Ida A—†	150	at home	80	"
	v	Diskin Ellen—†	150	"	66	Randolph
	w	Donovan Frances T—†	150	housewife	40	here
	x	Donovan Michael	150	laborer	57	"
	y	Fahey Edmund J	150	retired	70	"
	z	Kelley Ellen E—†	150	at home	71	
258						
	a	Ryan Sarah—†	150	domestic	40	Malden
	b	Dearth Blanche—†	151	at home	65	here
	c	Gould Daniel A	151	meatcutter	54	"
	d	Gould Harriet—†	151	housewife	50	"
	e	McConnell Sarah—†	151	seamstress	62	"
	f	McLaughlin George	151	engineer	49	"
	g	Mullen Georgianna—†	151	housewife	68	128 Pembroke
	h	Mullen William	151	steamfitter	55	128 "
	k	Roderick Florence—†	151	seamstress	58	80 Worcester
	m	Shurman Thomas	151	retired	53	here
	l	Small Rose—†	151	seamstress	70	"
	n	Tivnan Joseph B	151	retired	72	"
	o	Tivnan Margaret O—†	151	housewife	66	"
	p	Delong Bessie—†	152	stitcher	69	
	r	*Donovan Margaret—†	152	housekeeper	67	"
	s	Johnson Mary—†	152	domestic	53	"
	t	*Leonard Ida—†	152	housewife	56	"
	u	*Leonard Thomas	152	salesman	60	"
	v	Murphy Mary—†	152	housekeeper	71	"
	w	Pferdekamp Florence—†	152	stitcher	56	"
	x	Sheehan Agnes—†	152	nurse	51	
	y	Blarcom Van	153	attendant	49	"
	z	Cassidy Edith—†	153	housewife	52	N Hampshire
259						
	a	Cassidy Edward	153	machinist	58	"
	b	*Cross Arthur	153	janitor	35	11 Rutland sq
	c	Cross Lila—†	153	housewife	66	80 Rutland
	d	Cross William	153	retired	72	80 "
	e	Donlon Mary—†	153	domestic	68	here

Page.	Letter.	FULL NAME.	Residence, Jan. 1, 1943.	Occupation.	Supposed Age.	Reported Residence, Jan. 1, 1942. Street and Number.

West Concord Street—Continued

	F	Glennon Daniel	153	retired	69	80 Rutland
	G	Libby Ernest	153	"	69	172 W Brookline
	H	Melanson Raymond	153	U S N	28	Florida
	K	Snopley Zena—†	153	at home	49	159 Arlington
	L	Toomey Catherine—†	153	"	60	81 W Brookline
	M	Cash Lester K	154	U S N	26	Georgia
	N	Cash Marie M—†	154	housewife	23	"
	O	Dears Frank	154	chef	45	16 Dartmouth
	P	Gilbert Ceril E	154	U S N	30	Georgia
	R	Gilbert Louise E—†	154	housewife	22	"
	S	Goodwin Ellen—†	154	at home	76	167 W Brookline
	T	Graham Isabelle M—†	154	housewife	70	here
	U	Graham John F	154	retired	69	"
	V	Hinds Annie L—†	154	clerk	61	"
	W	Hoare Catherine—†	154	at home	75	"
	X	MacNeil George W	154	teacher	46	Braintree
	Y	Nichols Emma—†	154	stitcher	60	56 Rutland sq
	Z	Petit Annie B—†	154	at home	66	Newton
260						
	A	Conroy Margaret—†	155	"	75	27 Rutland sq
	B	Dolan Mary—†	155	"	68	11 E Newton
	C	Ellis Catherine—†	155	housewife	20	Wellfleet
	D	Ellis Warren	155	U S C G	38	"
	E	Hoffman Helen F—†	155	saleswoman	40	here
	F	Jones Elizabeth—†	155	stitcher	47	"
	G	Liever Elizabeth—†	155	at home	88	"
	H	Matol Rose—†	155	nurse	40	
	K	McNttt Cora—†	155	at home	73	
	L	McNutt William	155	retired	83	
	M	Roache Charles W	155	carpenter	57	"
	N	Shackley Angie—†	155	at home	89	
	O	Snyder Anna M—†	155	technician	26	"
	P	Snyder Charles H	155	salesman	69	"
	R	Snyder Mary A—†	155	housewife	61	"
	S	Tralinger Beatrice—†	155	"	23	Oklahoma
	T	Tralinger Homer	155	U S A	28	"
	U	Dillon Margaret—†	156	maid	35	here
	V	Eustis William	156	laborer	54	"
	W	Gens Frank	156	technician	25	"
	X	Jones John	156	electrician	35	725 Tremont
	Y	Jones Margaret E—†	156	waitress	31	here

Page.	Letter.	Full Name.	Residence, Jan. 1, 1943.	Occupation.	Supposed Age.	Reported Residence, Jan. 1, 1942. Street and Number.

West Concord Street—Continued

	Z	Manning Thomas	156	U S A	36	here
261						
	A	Martin Marcella—†	156	at home	72	10 Upland av
	B	Parsley Pearl—†	156	maid	30	here
	C	Shanley Nellie—†	156	housekeeper	51	"
	D	Shanley Rita M—†	156	clerk	25	"
	E	Watt Adam	156	"	40	"
	F	Anagnoston Haralampos	157	baker	65	10 Blackwood
	G	Flynn Patricia—†	157	waitress	28	1281 Mass av
	H	Friedman Louis	157	salesman	58	here
	K	Giles Arthur E	157	pharmacist	38	"
	L	Hawkins Mary E—†	157	at home	66	10 Blackwood
	M	Howie James	157	draftsman	53	here
	N	McCafferty Dominick	157	counterman	57	"
	O	Perry Gertrude—†	157	waitress	31	"
	P	Scanlon Francis J	157	inspector	49	1847 Col av
	R	Cronin John	158	retired	71	here
	S	Foster Louise J—†	158	operator	29	California
	T	Gubitosi Mario J	158	salesman	61	here
	U	Mazzonie Doris K—†	158	housewife	22	"
	V	McLean John F	158	U S N	23	"
	W	Stanley Margaret L—†	158	clerk	25	
	X	Sullivan Bridget L—†	158	housewife	57	"
	Y	Sullivan Eileen D—†	158	clerk	27	
	Z	Sullivan Evelyn—†	158	stitcher	20	
262						
	A	Sullivan Michael J	158	clerk	57	"
	B	Cable Helen—†	160	waitress	25	Wellesley
	C	Darcy Agnes—†	160	housewife	45	Vermont
	D	Darcy Hormisdas	160	carpenter	49	"
	E	Donovan Catherine—†	160	at home	60	2 Cedar
	F	Dunn William W	160	retired	72	here
	G	*Gold Rebecca—†	160	at home	58	449 Shawmut av
	H	Holmer Sadie—†	160	student	50	Maine
	K	Pooler Grace H—†	160	"	30	"
	L	Slamin Margaret—†	160	at home	68	Natick
	M	Buckley Julia—†	162	housewife	63	here
	N	Connolly Mary—†	162	domestic	45	90 Conant
	O	Grant Annie—†	162	clerk	48	here
	P	Harrison Nora—†	162	housekeeper	61	"
	R	Hughes Annie—†	162	at home	71	"
	S	MacGregor George A	162	retired	81	

Page.	Letter.	Full Name.	Residence, Jan. 1, 1943.	Occupation.	Supposed Age.	Reported Residence, Jan. 1, 1942. Street and Number.

West Concord Street—Continued

	T	McCarthy Beatrice—†	162	waitress	36	Cambridge
	U	McElroy Joseph	162	laborer	41	here
	V	Philips Ada N—†	162	at home	70	96 W Newton
	W	Philips Alice—†	162	stitcher	29	here
	X	Stacey Mary—†	162	clerk	49	"
	Y	Thompson Lucy—†	162	housewife	55	"
	Z	Thompson William	162	carpenter	56	"

263 West Newton Street

	C	Parker Nina L—†	36	nurse	33	Maine
	D	Girard Bertha M—†	36	"	30	here
	E	Ashby Amy—†	36	cashier	41	1302 Com av
	F	McGriel Frances—†	36	nurse	30	here
	H	Craig Richard J	37	letter carrier	55	"
	K	Dow Vivian A—†	37	cook	26	"
	L	Fitzgerald Mary E—†	37	housewife	65	"
	M	Fitzgerald Maurice E	37	physician	67	"
	N	Harrington Walter J	37	custodian	66	"
	O	Horowitz Morris H	37	stitcher	52	"
	P	Kolcoyne Bridget—†	37	cook	42	63 Berkeley
	R	McGillivray William	37	chauffeur	48	here
	S	Merrill Walter J	37	stagehand	52	"
	T	Russo Domenic	37	stitcher	42	"
	U	Dolan Henry J	38	retired	81	
	V	Gow George	38	cashier	62	
	W	Harvender Josephine—†	38	at home	50	
	X	Harvender William	38	retired	60	
	Y	Kane John	38	porter	60	
	Z	Kane Mary—†	38	at home	58	
264						
	A	Lipson Max	38	cutter	52	
	B	Newton Bessie—†	38	at home	60	"
	C	Rogers Albert	38	harnessmaker	78	"
	D	Rogers Mary—†	38	at home	72	"
	E	Stokes Albert	38	student	26	Connecticut
	F	Wyman Elsie—†	38	at home	52	here
	G	Wyman Ralph	38	waiter	57	"
	H	Galasso Lillian—†	39	operator	26	"
	K	Galasso William	39	pressman	28	"
	L	Tartar Deeb	39	clerk	49	

Page.	Letter.	Full Name.	Residence, Jan. 1, 1943.	Occupation.	Supposed Age.	Reported Residence, Jan. 1, 1942. Street and Number.

West Newton Street—Continued

	M	Tartar Nora—†	39	housewife	34	here
	N	Baccucci Ernest	40	laborer	30	"
	O	Bennett William	40	painter	40	"
	P	Bethoney Alice—†	40	at home	20	
	R	Bethoney Sabby	40	mechanic	26	"
	S	Blanchard Louise—†	40	nurse	21	
	T	Blow June—†	40	"	23	
	U	Donnelly Walter	40	retired	66	"
	V	Eitwuth Harry V	40	laborer	50	39 Dover
	W	Eitwuth Harry V, jr	40	"	30	39 "
	X	Griffin Helen J—†	40	nurse	23	here
	Y	Heffernan Eleanor—†	40	at home	65	"
	Z	Horming Joseph	40	salesman	50	"
265						
	A	*Larson Angelo	40	retired	44	"
	B	Melchitmas Alfred	40	laborer	45	518 Shawmut av
	C	Sinaris Constantine	40	chef	40	69 Appleton
	D	Zarthar Jennie S—†	40	at home	38	here
	E	Zarthar Saia	40	agent	41	"
	F	Benland Frank	41	laborer	53	"
	G	Brennan Margaret—†	41	maid	65	
	H	Cullinan Michael	41	retired	70	
	K	Doogan Paul	41	bartender	59	"
	L	Elias Albert	41	clerk	52	
	M	Hughes Katherine—†	41	at home	67	"
	N	Johnson Sven	41	laborer	66	134 W Concord
	O	Marchi James E	41	clerk	31	here
	P	Marchi Ruth E—†	41	"	29	"
	R	McGill John	41	salesman	55	"
	S	Newman Florence—†	41	at home	64	55 E Concord
	T	O'Connors Beatrice—†	41	maid	64	31 "
	U	Pearson Ella—†	41	housewife	63	here
	V	Pearson Gustave E	41	retired	67	"
	W	Taylor Elizabeth—†	41	laundress	62	"
	X	Farmer Ralph	42	laborer	59	
	Y	Garvey Catherine—†	42	at home	48	
	Z	Garvey Frederick	42	laborer	54	
266						
	A	Kashchian Michael	42	retired	62	
	B	Luskin Martin	42	laborer	49	"
	C	McLellan Archie	42	"	39	9 Rutland

Page.	Letter.	FULL NAME.	Residence, Jan. 1, 1943.	Occupation.	Supposed Age.	Reported Residence, Jan. 1, 1942. Street and Number.

West Newton Street—Continued

	D	McLellan Catherine—†	42	housewife	32	9 Rutland
	E	Mullen James	42	chef	31	1453 Wash'n
	F	Mullen John	42	"	37	1453 "
	G	Mullen Margaret—†	42	domestic	64	1453 "
	H	Munn Frank	42	laborer	25	14 Harvard
	K	Riley James P	42	"	32	Maine
	L	Sisco John	42	"	27	14 Harvard
	M	Sullivan Alice—†	42	housekeeper	53	here
	N	Walsh Michael	42	clerk	52	"
	O	Winston Susan—†	42	at home	53	39 Warren av
	P	McPhee Ethel—†	43	"	61	here
	R	Baz Naifie—†	44	stitcher	30	"
	S	Durocher Margaret E—†	44	housekeeper	60	674 Mass av
	T	Gardella Gladys—†	44	operator	45	here
	U	Gardella Joseph	44	painter	46	"
	V	Grennan Mollie—†	44	clerk	44	"
	W	Kingston Blanche—†	44	"	48	"
	X	Meade William	44	chauffeur	50	New York
	Y	Sheehan Daniel	44	retired	71	here
	Z	*Toohey Nellie—†	44	at home	64	"
267						
	A	Toohey Patrick	44	retired	76	
	B	Whalen Julia T—†	44	at home	68	"
	C	Baldesari Mary—†	45	clerk	26	10 McNulty ct
	D	Chambers David O	45	cutter	62	here
	E	Chambers James P	45	U S A	31	"
	F	Chambers Lillie—†	45	housekeeper	55	"
	G	Conroy Margaret—†	45	nurse	55	"
	H	Deshamps Blanche—†	45	stitcher	55	
	K	Hart Harriet—†	45	at home	67	
	L	Mahoney John	45	houseman	59	"
	M	McDonald Mary—†	45	checker	45	"
	N	McGonagle Annie—†	45	at home	65	25 W Concord
	O	McLain Daniel	45	orderly	55	here
	P	McNallis Bernard J	45	retired	50	"
	R	Morriscn Elizabeth—†	45	housewife	42	"
	S	Morrison Frank	45	clerk	45	
	T	Peacock Olive—†	45	waitress	37	
	U	Percy Harriet—†	45	clerk	32	"
	V	Boyd Ruth—†	46	waitress	35	39 W Newton
	W	Lee Annie—†	46	at home	67	here

Page.	Letter.	FULL NAME.	Residence, Jan. 1, 1943.	Occupation.	Supposed Age.	Reported Residence, Jan. 1, 1942. Street and Number.

West Newton Street—Continued

	X	McDonald Ida—†	46	maid	52	here
	Y	Duncan Archie	46	retired	79	599 Col av
	Z	Duncan Rachel—†	46	at home	65	599 "
268						
	A	Revens Emily—†	46	"	55	here
	B	Revens Mary—†	46	stitcher	57	"
	C	Howard Mary—†	46	at home	68	"
	D	Dolan Katherine—†	46	"	79	
	E	O'Leary Cornelius	46	bartender	64	"
	F	O'Leary Elizabeth—†	46	housewife	64	"
	G	Morgan Catherine C—†	46	at home	49	15 Worcester sq
	H	Morgan John J	46	welder	49	15 "
	K	Kelly Helen—†	46	maid	54	here
	L	Brewster Alice—†	46	clerk	49	"
	M	*Clifford Elizabeth—†	46	maid	44	"
	N	O'Neil Michael	46	blacksmith	53	"
	O	Hyman Harry	46	chauffeur	50	"
	P	Hyman Lena—†	46	housewife	42	"
	R	Arsenault Yvonne—†	46	clerk	23	71 Worcester
	S	Denisuk Alice—†	46	housewife	35	here
	T	Denisuk Luke	46	tailor	50	"
	U	Conway John	46	nurse	38	"
	V	Lowell Anna D—†	46	"	33	Onset
	W	Lowell Henry	46	U S A	34	"
	X	Nauss Robert	46	seaman	40	here
	Y	Paul Helen—†	46	nurse	45	"
	Z	McCarthy James	46	retired	67	"
269						
	A	Tweed Charles	46	clerk	54	"
	B	Downey Dorothy—†	46	"	22	11 E Springfield
	C	Downey Robert	46	U S N	25	11 "
	D	Ransom Aurelius C	46	janitor	57	here
	E	Ransom Lillian G—†	46	housewife	41	"
	F	Allen Frances—†	54	"	51	94 Waltham
	G	Allen John	54	longshoreman	55	94 "
	H	Conlon Michael	54	retired	68	258 Shawmut av
	K	Downes David	54	laborer	35	34 Wigglesworth
	L	Downes Dorothy—†	54	housewife	22	34 "
	M	Hazzard Albert	54	retired	68	here
	N	Healy Thomas	54	chef	35	625 Dudley
	O	Lener Joseph	54	retired	54	78 W Canton

Page.	Letter.	FULL NAME.	Residence, Jan. 1, 1943.	Occupation.	Supposed Age.	Reported Residence, Jan. 1, 1942. Street and Number.

West Newton Street—Continued

	P	Leslie Marion—†	54	housekeeper	45	here
	R	*Stewart Victoria—†	54	at home	60	"
	S	Toohey Patrick	54	retired	82	204 W Brookline
	T	Bernard John	56	"	72	here
	U	Christian Julia—†	56	domestic	49	10 Rutland
	V	Davis Edgar	56	clerk	50	20 Oak
	W	Foye Thomas	56	chef	66	76 Dover
	X	Hirsh Catherine—†	56	at home	68	74 W Newton
	Y	Kelley George	56	retired	67	here
	Z	MacFadden Mary—†	56	at home	68	"
270						
	A	Madden Thomas	56	laborer	53	63 Rutland
	B	Mangene Vincent	56	chef	60	51 "
	C	Martin Sadie—†	56	housekeeper	48	here
	D	Miller Frank	56	clerk	53	"
	E	Perry William	56	retired	68	"
	F	Turski Edward	56	clerk	35	6 Brown
	G	Turski Mary—†	56	housewife	27	6 "
	H	Ason George	58	clerk	38	242 W Newton
	K	Breen Gertrude—†	58	housekeeper	49	39 Upton
	L	David Nasim A	58	chemist	32	here
	M	Deurelle Madeline—†	58	laundress	38	"
	N	*Deurelle Theresa—†	58	at home	71	"
	O	Harris Helen—†	58	waitress	32	
	P	Jordan Frank J	58	chauffeur	64	"
	R	MacLeod George E	58	retired	70	
	W	*Meehan Vincent	58	merchant	50	"
	S	*Namey Edward	58	shoeworker	50	"
	T	Namey Fred	58	U S A	35	
	U	Namey Mary D—†	58	housewife	50	"
	V	Namey Nadra D	58	U S A	31	"
	X	Reid David H	58	retired	55	22 Upton
	Y	Reid Margaret—†	58	housewife	38	22 "
	Z	Riley Mary—†	58	at home	45	39 "
271						
	A	Shreenen Clara—†	58	housewife	30	here
	B	Shreenen Thomas	58	laborer	32	"
	C	Snowden Charles B	58	retired	70	"
	D	Coffey Leila—†	60	waitress	35	
	E	Dilboy John	60	chef	40	

Page.	Letter.	FULL NAME.	Residence, Jan. 1, 1943.	Occupation.	Supposed Age.	

West Newton Street—Continued

	F	Doherty Arthur	60	U S A	21	here
	G	Doherty William	60	janitor	55	"
	H	Doherty William J	60	U S A	23	"
	K	Freedman Priscilla—†	60	at home	43	
	L	Jean Arnold	60	laborer	56	
	M	LaPierre Alice—†	60	housekeeper	34	"
	N	LaPierre Ethel—†	60	beautician	32	"
	O	LaPierre Robert	60	U S N	30	
	P	Lutz Henry	60	engineer	50	
	R	Marshall Joseph	60	electrician	50	"
	S	Therault Eugene	60	janitor	45	
	T	Therault Mary—†	60	clerk	40	"
	V	Healey Frederick	62	messenger	30	40 E Newton
	W	Jensen Arthur	62	laborer	45	544 Tremont
	X	O'Keefe James	62	"	50	here
	Y	O'Neil Lawrence F	62	welder	43	"
	Z	O'Neil Mary—†	62	at home	66	61 St James
272						
	A	O'Neil William J	62	retired	75	61 "
	B	Evans John	63	clerk	46	here
	C	Fotos Esther—†	63	housekeeper	40	"
	D	Halsam Edward	63	laborer	42	"
	E	Kane Margaret—†	63	cook	61	
	F	McGarr Edward	63	realtor	62	"
	G	Mills Edward	63	welder	45	230 W Canton
	H	O'Melia Austin	63	engineer	56	here
	K	Pepin George	63	laborer	51	"
	L	Santoro William	63	barber	53	"
	M	Velvet Morris	63	laborer	45	
	N	Bernard Mary—†	64	housekeeper	63	"
	O	Burson Benjamin	64	chef	45	"
	P	Daley John C	64	retired	73	148 W Newton
	E	Egan Patrick	64	laborer	47	here
	S	Flynn Julia—†	64	at home	56	42 E Newton
	T	Hauser Henry	64	retired	72	here
	U	McGowan James	64	laborer	35	"
	V	Mullens John J	64	engineer	66	62 W Newton
	W	O'Shea Daniel	64	retired	70	98 Waltham
	X	*Rufus Rosa—†	64	at home	50	here
	Y	Sullivan Mary E—†	65	"	44	"

Page.	Letter.	Full Name.	Residence, Jan. 1, 1943.	Occupation.	Supposed Age.	Reported Residence, Jan. 1, 1942. Street and Number.

West Newton Street—Continued

	z	Sullivan Michael	65	blacksmith	45	here
273						
	A	Collins Cornelius	65	laborer	42	
	B	Collins James F	65	guard	52	
	C	Horgan Rose A—†	65	cashier	57	
	D	Poulos Kay—†	65	clerk	22	
	E	Poulos Sophie—†	65	at home	43	
	F	Hartman Juanita—†	65	entertainer	38	"
	G	*Anthony Philip	66	tailor	55	
	H	Collins Joseph F	66	carpenter	64	"
	K	Connolly Alfred	66	chef	58	
	L	Crowley Delia B—†	66	housewife	65	"
	M	Crowley Patrick H	66	retired	66	"
	N	Donahue Dennis	66	"	69	39 E Brookline
	O	Harrington William	66	"	70	76 W Newton
	P	*Kelly Michael	66	mechanic	54	here
	R	Lydon Mary A—†	66	housekeeper	58	"
	S	MacLeod William	66	retired	76	"
	T	McManus James	66	"	75	
	U	Meroth George	66	orderly	61	
	V	Burbridge Helen—†	67	at home	59	
	W	Worth Emmeline—†	67	"	72	
	X	Bowab Elias	67	merchant	45	"
	Y	Bowab Emily—†	67	at home	40	
	Z	Griffith Edith L—†	67	"	48	
274						
	A	Griffith Gernard F	67	electrician	52	"
	B	Archibald Greta C—†	67	clerk	46	
	C	Wiley Laura J—†	67	at home	67	
	D	Betts George F	68	laborer	62	
	E	Henehan Martin	68	brakeman	35	"
	F	Hewitt John J	68	pipefitter	40	Rhode Island
	G	Lyle Joseph	68	musician	35	"
	H	Mahoney Arthur	68	pipefitter	43	here
	K	Mandell Clara M—†	68	housekeeper	46	"
	L	McCluskey John M	68	machinist	53	"
	M	Binns Edgar	70	laborer	52	"
	N	Brewer Harry	70	"	49	48 Montgomery
	O	*Doucette Marie—†	70	housekeeper	44	here
	P	Durgin Frederick	70	clerk	38	"
	R	Farrell Mary—†	70	domestic	48	35 Worcester

Page.	Letter.	Full Name.	Residence, Jan. 1, 1943.	Occupation.	Supposed Age.	Reported Residence, Jan. 1, 1942. Street and Number.

West Newton Street—Continued

Page.	Letter.	Full Name.	Residence, Jan. 1, 1943.	Occupation.	Supposed Age.	Reported Residence, Jan. 1, 1942. Street and Number.
	S	Gray Helen—†	70	housewife	32	here
	T	Gray James	70	typist	23	"
	U	Gray John	70	steamfitter	55	Maine
	V	Moses Mary—†	70	entertainer	58	429 Shawmut av
	W	Wakins Florence—†	70	housewife	56	35 Worcester
	X	Watkins George	70	retired	64	35 "
	Y	Bransfield William	72	busboy	23	here
	Z	Callahan Jeremiah	72	watchman	45	"
275						
	A	Furlong Alice—†	72	housekeeper	62	"
	B	Furlong Edward	72	retired	71	"
	C	Gaudet Joseph	72	mechanic	33	98 W Concord
	D	Gaudet Lillian—†	72	housewife	30	98 "
	E	Jaquard Emil	72	U S A	36	here
	F	Jaquard Margaret C—†	72	housewife	33	"
	G	Jelloe Elizabeth—†	72	at home	70	123 W Newton
	H	Kerlin Agnes—†	72	"	59	here
	K	Landers Mary—†	72	"	50	"
	L	McGill Charles	72	retired	69	"
	M	Stiff Herbert	72	"	78	
	N	Turcotte Leo	72	realtor	59	
	O	Zacos John	72	retired	55	"
	P	Bezanson Florence—†	74	typist	46	372 Col av
	R	Bezanson Walter	74	waiter	46	372 "
	S	Bowers Clara—†	74	at home	67	here
	T	Cohan Dennis	74	waiter	60	372 Col av
	U	Collins Thomas	74	porter	55	183 Prentiss
	V	Devaney Ellen—†	74	at home	68	here
	W	Ford Mary—†	74	"	80	"
	X	Fraga Clara—†	74	housewife	50	"
	Y	Fraga William	74	druggist	52	
	Z	Harrington William	74	machinist	49	"
276						
	A	Hendricks Nellie—†	74	at home	68	80 W Newton
	B	Ogle Catherine—†	74	"	60	here
	C	Robertson Jean—†	74	housekeeper	47	"
	D	Anderson George	76	boilermaker	36	"
	E	Arnesen Harold	76	fisherman	40	Quincy
	F	Doyle Catherine—†	76	clerk	46	here
	G	Dubey Rose—†	76	housewife	38	Hingham
	H	Dubey Thomas	76	chef	40	"

Page.	Letter.	FULL NAME.	Residence, Jan. 1, 1943.	Occupation.	Supposed Age.	Reported Residence, Jan. 1, 1942. Street and Number.

West Newton Street—Continued

	K	Fiske Bessie—†	76	at home	75	here
	L	McManus Edward	76	shipper	36	132 Col av
	M	McManus Mary—†	76	housewife	35	132 "
	N	Melling Jennie—†	76	at home	68	here
	O	Melling Jessie—†	76	"	68	"
	P	Morrissey Winifred—†	76	waitress	28	"
	R	Osborn Elsie—†	76	at home	63	"
	S	Colbert Anna V—†	78	housekeeper	38	Brookline
	T	Finn Edward B	78	painter	47	70 W Newton
	U	Hurley Frederick	78	chauffeur	55	here
	V	O'Neil Edward	78	"	37	New York
	W	Ronayne Edith J—†	78	waitress	39	Somerville
	X	Antonio Gladys—†	80	clerk	26	Concord
	Y	Bergran Anna—†	80	housewife	51	Lynn
	Z	Bergran William	80	mason	47	"
277						
	A	Grady Thomas	80	retired	75	here
	B	Holbrook Ethel—†	80	maid	51	"
	C	Lord Josephine—†	80	housewife	56	"
	D	*Lydon Thomas	80	retired	63	
	E	Murphy Ellen—†	80	at home	66	
	F	Murphy William	80	retired	73	
	G	Rosengarton Philip	80	"	68	"
	H	Smith Leo J	80	salesman	48	Florida
	K	Thompson Mildred—†	80	at home	26	here
	L	Thompson Thomas	80	laborer	40	144 W Conco d
	M	Waters Julia—†	80	seamstress	52	here
	N	Wentworth Eugenia—†	80	housekeeper	61	"
	O	Wheeler Ruth—†	80	student	25	Maine
	P	White Alexander	80	clerk	44	here
	R	Cahill Harry T	82	"	58	4 E Brookline
	S	Campbell Margaret—†	82	at home	68	here
	T	Cloonan John F	82	chef	55	195 Warren av
	U	Farrell Margaret M—†	82	at home	65	735 Tremont
	V	Gillis George	82	mechanic	55	270½ Centre
	W	Gillis George E	82	machinist	28	270½ "
	X	Hunt Frank P	82	retired	70	here
	Y	Magulsky Joseph	82	"	72	61 W Newton
	Z	O'Brien James P	82	janitor	53	here
278						
	A	*Perry Daisy O—†	82	housekeeper	37	"

Page.	Letter.	Full Name.	Residence, Jan. 1, 1943.	Occupation.	Supposed Age.	Reported Residence, Jan. 1, 1942. Street and Number.

West Newton Street—Continued

	B	Perry George H	82	retired	76	here
	C	Smith Mary A—†	82	housekeeper	49	"
	D	Stoddard Anna—†	82	housewife	70	"
	E	Toohey Charles W	82	chauffeur	49	"
	F	Toohey Frances N—†	82	seamstress	44	"
	G	Veale Patrick J	82	porter	54	
	H	Campbell Archibald	84	ironworker	39	"
	K	*Chisholm Jessie—†	84	at home	70	
	L	*Gillis Bernice—†	84	clerk	45	"
	M	Keegan Louise—†	84	housewife	57	73 Bickford
	N	*MacDonald Jane—†	84	housekeeper	76	here
	O	McIsaac Louis	84	laborer	38	"
	P	McKenna Frank	84	plumber	32	4 E Brookline
	R	*McShane Nellie—†	84	waitress	40	here
	S	Seale Eleanor—†	84	at home	67	Ireland
	U	Bowen Ellen—†	86	housekeeper	45	here
	V	Cleary William	86	engineer	49	New York
	W	Conroy Edward	86	laborer	35	Cambridge
	X	Doherty Mary—†	86	waitress	40	here
	Y	Ellis Ralph	86	clerk	60	745 Tremont
	Z	*Haggerty Timothy	86	laborer	40	here
279						
	A	Kealey Patrick	86	"	62	
	B	Mahoney Mary—†	86	at home	80	
	C	McDermott Joseph M	86	laborer	55	"
	D	Davis Leota D—†	88	seamstress	58	10 Pembroke
	E	Foley John	88	operator	37	here
	F	Gould Helen—†	88	at home	80	"
	G	*Hamill Mary—†	88	"	65	103 Highland
	H	*Hamill Robert	88	machinist	65	103 "
	K	Hurley Jeremiah	88	laborer	56	here
	L	McCushing John M	88	orderly	58	45 W Newton
	M	McDonald Annie—†	88	housekeeper	75	here
	N	McDonald David	88	retired	80	"
	O	Newton Annie—†	88	at home	67	"
	P	Tahakjian Baulus	88	retired	81	"
	R	DeSchuytener John	90	chef	55	49 Upton
	S	English Frances—†	90	housewife	55	102 Allston
	T	English Marie—†	90	waitress	22	102 "
	U	*Fitzpatrick Daniel	90	porter	54	here
	V	Harrison Aaron H	90	retired	69	61 W Canton

Page.	Letter.	Full Name.	Residence, Jan. 1, 1943.	Occupation.	Supposed Age.	Reported Residence, Jan. 1, 1942. Street and Number.

West Newton Street—Continued

	W	Keenan Josephine R—†	90	housekeeper	44	here
	X	Keenan Michael J	90	manager	44	"
	Y	Sullivan Catherine—†	90	maid	56	86 Appleton
	Z	*Twohig Jeremiah	90	clerk	48	here
280						
	A	Carlson Evelyn B—†	92	secretary	42	New York
	B	Cohane John W	92	retired	55	here
	C	Delapole Carrie—†	92	housekeeper	61	"
	D	Doyle Grace—†	92	clerk	45	"
	E	Eberlein Ruth L—†	92	librarian	50	Springfield
	F	Gibbs Andrew A	92	salesman	62	here
	G	Gibbs Glendeane E—†	92	housewife	52	"
	H	Morse Helen P—†	92	secretary	43	Connecticut
	K	Patterson Paul	92	clerk	23	"
	L	Whitcomb Minerva—†	92	"	45	N Hampshire
	M	Bagley Mary—†	94	at home	65	here
	N	Beaman Norman H	94	retired	75	"
	O	Braym Samuel	94	plumber	55	432 Col av
	P	Donovan Elizabeth—†	94	housekeeper	64	here
	R	Flanetzer Rudolph	94	bartender	60	Lawrence
	S	Richards George	94	retired	70	here
	T	Sexton John	94	mechanic	40	15 Hanson
	U	Simpson Roy	94	chauffeur	40	Quincy
	V	Tobin Catherine—†	94	at home	65	here
	W	Young David	94	clerk	62	New York
	X	Baillergeon Albert	96	chef	30	here
	Y	Barrett Richard F	96	clerk	52	"
	Z	Berthol Henry	96	retired	64	"
281						
	A	Blacky Catherine—†	96	at home	68	"
	B	Borello Stella—†	96	"	35	Maine
	C	*Dupont Josephine—†	96	"	78	here
	D	Gwynn Martha—†	96	"	65	90 Mt Pleasant av
	E	Labrie Philip	96	chef	44	here
	F	McInnis George	96	ironworker	39	"
	G	McInnis Rose—†	96	housekeeper	36	"
	H	Smith Anna—†	96	at home	67	335 Shawmut av
	K	Vashon Aime	96	welder	24	422 Bowdoin
	L	Vashon Olga—†	96	housewife	28	19 Lucas
	M	Bagwell Frank	98	chauffeur	44	here
	N	Cefrey Mary—†	98	at home	66	"

Page.	Letter.	FULL NAME.	Residence, Jan. 1, 1943.	Occupation.	Supposed Age.	Reported Residence, Jan. 1, 1942. Street and Number.

West Newton Street—Continued

	O	Daly Gertrude E—†	98	housekeeper	54	here
	P	Daly Maurice A	98	toolmaker	54	"
	R	Falivan Ralph	98	shoemaker	42	"
	S	George Randall	98	pharmacist	43	72 E Brookline
	T	Gracier Mary—†	98	laundress	28	20 Rutland
	U	Haddigan Anna—†	98	at home	63	194 W Canton
	V	Haddigan Walter	98	painter	64	194 "
	W	McDonald Archie	98	bartender	34	118 Pembroke
	X	McDonald Clara—†	98	housewife	32	118 "
	Y	McGowan George	98	retired	72	Maine
	Z	Swethland Marvis—†	98	waitress	40	153 W Concord
282						
	A	Toutous James	98	chef	50	here
	B	Williams Walter	98	mechanic	44	20 Rutland
	C	Bryant Mildred—†	100	clerk	47	73 "
	D	Corkum Eva—†	100	at home	58	612 Tremont
	E	Daigle William	100	attorney	51	New York
	F	Delmonico Archibald	100	welder	50	Fitchburg
	G	Farnhan Vesta—†	100	housewife	46	700 Tremont
	H	Flynn Eleanor—†	100	housekeeper	42	20 Rutland
	K	Jackson Maxwell	100	detective	55	145 W Newton
	L	Massailes Joseph	100	cutter	47	20 Rutland sq
	M	Mullen Martin	100	laborer	57	53 Rutland
	N	Pittman John	100	mechanic	44	15 Nassau
	O	Reardon John	100	retired	78	80 Rutland
	P	Rolinson Joseph	100	bartender	41	695 Tremont
	R	Saul John	100	porter	57	Maine
	S	Brown Rose—†	102	at home	74	here
	T	Cram Henry	102	salesman	50	Holbrook
	U	Crane John G	102	bartender	56	70 W Newton
	V	*Granger Grace—†	102	housekeeper	44	here
	W	Kennedy Mary A—†	102	maid	33	"
	X	Leuchuck Peter	102	chef	47	"
	Y	Lyford Emily J—†	102	student	27	"
	Z	McHugh William	102	retired	69	667 Tremont
283						
	A	Morse Linley E	102	mechanic	57	here
	B	Naughton John	102	chef	60	66 W Newton

4
6
7
8
9
10
11
12

Ward 9—Precinct 3

CITY OF BOSTON

LIST OF RESIDENTS
20 YEARS OF AGE AND OVER

(NON-CITIZENS INDICATED BY ASTERISK)
(FEMALES INDICATED BY DAGGER)

AS OF

JANUARY 1, 1943

JOSEPH F. TIMILTY, *Chairman*
FREDERIC E. DOWLING, *Secretary*
WILLIAM A. MOTLEY, JR.
FRANCIS B. McKINNEY
EVERETT R. PROUT
Listing Board.

CITY OF BOSTON PRINTING DEPARTMENT

Page.	Letter.	FULL NAME.	Residence, Jan. 1, 1943.	Occupation.	Supposed Age.	Reported Residence, Jan. 1, 1942. Street and Number.
300						

Cumston Street

	D	Allen Dora E—†	5	housekeeper	84	here
	E	Allen John	5	carpenter	51	"
	F	Lyman Arthur L	5	laborer	50	"
	G	Norton Harriet—†	5	clerk	45	
	H	Norton Margaret—†	5	housekeeper	50	"
	K	Bezanson May L—†	6	"	53	"

Massachusetts Avenue

	N	Asplund Ernest	504	laborer	41	Connecticut
	O	Asplund Grace—†	504	assembler	34	"
	P	Crane James	504	brakeman	42	here
	R	Goyette Emile	504	cleaner	51	"
	S	Murphy Joseph E	504	painter	52	Maine
	T	Shurtleff Joseph L	504	U S A	45	here
	U	Bachoffner Edward	508	salesman	28	"
	V	Batiste Lawrence C	508	machinist	27	"
	W	Bernard Albert	508	chef	30	Vermont
	X	Grey Preston	508	chauffeur	50	"
	Y	Mackey Michael	508	rigger	74	here
	Z	Matroner Caesar	508	machinist	38	536 Mass av
301						
	A	Moors Archie	508	laborer	25	here
	B	Perry Rose—†	508	stitcher	38	"
	C	Ridley Freda—†	508	"	40	Somerville
	D	*Robbins William	508	retired	60	here
	E	Sanders Catherine—†	508	housewife	49	525 Mass av
	F	Sanders Charles	508	retired	55	525 "
	H	Colwell Emma L—†	512	at home	77	here
	K	Colwell Ward	512	retired	81	"
	L	Fitzsimmons Florence A–†	512	housewife	50	168 Hunt'n av
	M	Fitzsimmons Ralph L	512	clerk	47	168 "
	N	*Harris Ida M—†	512	housekeeper	59	here
	O	*Johnson Margaret—†	512	at home	50	"
	P	Lawlor Anne M—†	512	clerk	40	8 Johnson av
	G	*Lem Wing Chong	512	chef	35	21 Hudson
	R	McGarn Agnes—†	512	housekeeper	49	Braintree
	S	Brennan Annie—†	514	housewife	40	here
	T	Brennan Thomas	514	welder	40	"
	U	Carney Frank	514	chef	47	"

Page.	Letter.	Full Name.	Residence, Jan. 1, 1943.	Occupation.	Supposed Age.	Reported Residence, Jan. 1, 1942. Street and Number.

Massachusetts Avenue—Continued

	v	Cronin Bridget—†	514	at home	70	here
	w	Cronin Rose—†	514	"	73	"
	x	Folsom Helen—†	514	housewife	50	"
	y	Folsom Herbert	514	retired	64	"
	z	Griffin Patrick	514	"	74	
301A						
	A	Adams Howard	518	guard	48	309 Main
	B	Adams Lena R—†	518	housewife	62	here
	C	Adams Vernon G	518	janitor	57	"
	D	Anthony Alice—†	518	housewife	20	155 Mass av
	E	*Anthony Wilson T	518	U S A	30	155 "
	F	Hogquist Carl E	518	caretaker	52	512 "
	G	Hogquist Elva—†	518	housewife	32	512 "
	H	King Estelle—†	518	"	23	here
	K	King John	518	laborer	33	"
	L	Sample Jessie—†	518	cook	50	"
	M	Stafford Clara—†	518	stitcher	23	Rutland
	N	Stevens Elizabeth—†	518	housewife	50	here
	O	Stevens Frank	518	baker	53	"
	P	Stevens Frank, jr	518	U S A	23	"
	R	Stevens Winifred—†	518	stitcher	25	
	U	Collins Willa M—†	522	masseuse	27	"
	V	Dorsey William	522	musician	20	"
	W	Grant Earl	522	welder	20	
	X	Harris Cleveland	522	U S A	22	
	Y	Harris Gwendolyn—†	522	housekeeper	43	"
	Z	Holly Benjamin	522	waiter	47	"
302						
	A	Holly Kenneth	522	laborer	23	
	B	Jefferson Marcelle	522	welder	21	
	C	Knight Louis	522	barber	37	"
	D	O'Connor Joshua	522	welder	22	505 Col av
	E	Saunders Mary—†	522	at home	76	here
	F	Taylor Juanita—†	522	waitress	23	"
	G	Thompson Ralph	522	baker	38	"
	H	Antonopolos Mabel—†	524	housewife	48	"
	K	Antonopolos Paniotis	524	cook	47	
	L	Bloomberg Olaf	524	"	50	"
	M	Cammarato John	524	student	25	New York
	N	Cherone Joseph	524	barber	47	here
	O	Farnham Harold H	524	machinist	55	"

Page.	Letter.	Full Name.	Residence, Jan. 1, 1943.	Occupation.	Supposed Age.	Reported Residence, Jan. 1, 1942. Street and Number.

Massachusetts Avenue—Continued

	P	Felz Simon	524	salesman	44	here
	R	Foster Catherine—†	524	waitress	35	"
	S	Hurley Michael	524	solecutter	58	"
	T	Molloy John J	524	fisherman	59	"
	U	Moulton Elizabeth—†	524	housewife	58	"
	V	Moulton Percy C	524	machinist	58	"
	X	*Nicholas Anthony	524	cook	45	
	W	Nickerson Priscilla—†	524	waitress	31	"
	Y	Thompson Chester P	524	machinist	63	57 Horadan way
	Z	Wood Jessie—†	524	clerk	60	here
303						
	A	Brown Herman W	526	cleaner	55	678 Mass av
	B	Fish Alfred M	526	proprietor	43	43 Concord sq
	C	Harrison Olive—†	526	boxmaker	34	68 W Concord
	D	Harrison William	526	painter	35	68 "
	E	Herkert Ruth—†	526	clerk	30	Revere
	F	Keefe Elizabeth—†	526	housewife	48	34 Union pk
	G	Keefe Willis	526	engineer	56	34 "
	H	Kirby Helen—†	526	housekeeper	44	here
	K	Linart Edward	526	tailor	56	9 Col sq
	L	Lyman Lewellyn	526	chauffeur	46	9 "
	M	Rogers Elizabeth—†	526	dishwasher	45	947 Albany
	N	Henderson Fred C	528	retired	66	317 Northampton
	O	Jones Harriet A—†	528	at home	83	224 W Springfield
	P	Scott Maybelle—†	528	housekeeper	55	here
	R	Celester Edith—†	528	housewife	20	17 Benton
	S	Roach Lemuel	528	tailor	42	527 Col av
	T	Wynn Mary—†	528	operator	48	here
	U	Adler Gertrude—†	530	waitress	28	"
	V	Carlton Mary H—†	530	domestic	50	"
	W	Doucette Alice—†	530	"	32	
	X	Grobe Alice—†	530	housewife	44	"
	Y	Grobe William	530	machinist	45	"
	Z	Hilt Jennie—†	530	housekeeper	68	"
304						
	A	Leonard Elizabeth—†	530	housewife	50	"
	B	Leonard John	530	roofer	51	"
	C	Madden Mary—†	530	laundress	61	"
	D	McCoy William	530	painter	55	
	E	McKenzie Mary—†	530	clerk	40	
	F	Payson Daniel G	530	salesman	50	"

Page.	Letter.	Full Name.	Residence, Jan. 1, 1943.	Occupation.	Supposed Age.	Reported Residence, Jan. 1, 1942. Street and Number.

Massachusetts Avenue—Continued

	H	Puttie Laura—†	530	housewife	23	here
	G	Puttie William	530	chauffeur	38	"
	K	Ellis Anne—†	532	housewife	55	"
	L	Ellis Celia—†	532	stitcher	27	
	M	Ellis Doris—†	532	housewife	24	"
	O	Ellis Frederick	532	electrician	20	"
	N	Ellis Joseph	532	machinist	23	"
	P	Ellis Louis	532	clerk	35	
	R	Ellis Michael	532	laborer	58	
	T	Ellis Peter	532	U S A	28	
	S	Ellis Victoria—†	532	dressmaker	32	"
	U	Lyons Ethel—†	532	clerk	58	
	V	Meade Joseph	532	solecutter	58	"
	W	Sheposh Catherine—†	532	housewife	24	New York
	X	Sheposh John	532	U S N	25	Pennsylvania
	Y	Silver Carl	532	carpenter	65	here
	Z	Abbotson Anna—†	534	nurse	37	Lawrence
305						
	A	Barnes Agnes—†	534	"	61	here
	B	Berry Horace	534	retired	69	"
	C	Brown Herbert	534	"	75	Maine
	D	Brown William	534	"	80	Lexington
	F	Donahue John W	534		74	Everett
	E	Egan James J	534	"	71	8 Bulfinch pl
	G	Gustafson Carl F	534	superintendent	63	here
	H	Herbert William	534	retired	83	164 Hunt'n av
	K	Norman Sylvester	534	"	71	60 Carver
	L	O'Connor Mary—†	534	cook	41	39 Buswell
	M	O'Donnell Rose—†	534	at home	65	95 Chandler
	N	Olson Hilda—†	534	"	82	1066 Com av
	O	Sopp Erhard	534	retired	66	here
	P	Stackpole Arthur	534	"	64	"
	R	Swift Lena—†	534	at home	67	"
	S	Walden William	534	retired	59	194 W Canton
	T	Brigham Albert	536	guard	40	272 Hyde Park av
	U	Curran Mary—†	536	at home	73	here
	V	Delorey Vera—†	536	housewife	35	672 Tremont
	W	Fadale Helen—†	536	"	39	582 Mass av
	X	Fadale Ignatius C	536	molder	43	582 "
	Y	Gaul Charles	536	shipper	43	New York
	Z	Lockhart Lois E—†	536	housekeeper	58	here

Page.	Letter.	FULL NAME.	Residence, Jan. 1, 1943.	Occupation.	Supposed Age.	Reported Residence, Jan. 1, 1942. Street and Number.
306		**Massachusetts Avenue—Continued**				
	A	Lovejoy Arthur	536	shipper	45	Rhode Island
	B	Mackin William J	536	retired	71	here
	C	McIntyre Garnett	536	chef	61	"
	D	Taylor John	536	inspector	51	"
	E	Taylor Leonora—†	536	housewife	40	"
	F	Reinherz Charles	536	retired	69	"
	G	Walsh James	536	shipper	43	477 Shawmut av
	H	Beecher Lottie—†	538	housewife	48	N Hampshire
	K	Beecher Ralph	538	proprietor	50	"
	L	Conley William	538	machinist	38	46 Greenville
	M	Dacy Annie E—†	538	housekeeper	57	here
	N	Ellis John	538	clerk	60	"
	O	Farrell Mary—†	538	domestic	42	36 Worcester
	P	Flynn Agnes—†	538	clerk	60	79 "
	R	Flynn Philip	538	"	61	79 "
	S	Jensen Laura—†	538	domestic	55	here
	T	Martin Charles	538	salesman	43	New York
	U	Martin Isabelle—†	538	housewife	31	"
	V	McGonick Michael	538	retired	73	here
	W	McKenzie Jennie—†	538	clerk	60	"
	X	Nolan Catherine—†	538	at home	70	"
	Y	Nolan Clara—†	538	"	72	"
	Z	Pratt Phyllis—†	538	housewife	30	Duxbury
307						
	A	Ramsdell Stephen	538	retired	74	125 W Newton
	B	Tibbetts George	538	laborer	50	here
	C	Burkman Samuel	540	"	67	"
	D	Grimm Agnes—†	540	at home	60	Oak Bluffs
	E	Grimm Richard	540	bartender	51	"
	G	King Amelia—†	540	dressmaker	57	here
	F	Lannon Edward	540	cook	37	"
	H	McKay Phyllis—†	540	clerk	43	"
	K	Saver Armel R	540	U S N	25	Pennsylvania
	L	Saver Dolores—†	540	housewife	22	"
	M	St Lawrence Louis	540	laborer	36	496 Mass av
	N	Waldren Thomas	540	busboy	51	Vermont
	O	Bolster Carl W	542	U S C G	32	Virginia
	P	Bolster Laura E—†	542	housewife	33	Vermont
	R	Church Gertrude A—†	542	"	49	here
	S	Church Harold B	542	clerk	53	"

Page.	Letter.	FULL NAME.	Residence, Jan. 1, 1943.	Occupation.	Supposed Age.	Reported Residence, Jan. 1, 1942. Street and Number.

Massachusetts Avenue—Continued

	T	Griffe George A	542	U S C G	33	Iowa
	U	Griffe Joan P—†	542	typist	20	121 D
	V	Heath Annie I—†	542	housewife	53	here
	W	Heath Leo H	542	carpenter	53	"
	X	Heath Richard	542	manager	24	"
	Y	Louis Harry	542	machinist	62	"
	Z	Norman Alice—†	542	attendant	43	"
308						
	A	Barry William J	544	machinist	47	"
	B	Dunnie Philip	544	laborer	36	Lynn
	C	Hall Arthur	544	cook	46	36 Rutledge
	D	Koshkarian Sarkis	544	retired	46	here
	E	McInness Susan—†	544	at home	69	"
	F	Merritt Sadie—†	544	"	69	56 Worcester
	G	Moore James F	544	laborer	45	here
	H	Nickerson Ida—†	544	waitress	45	"
	K	Perkins Mary—†	544	domestic	40	"
	L	Sullivan John F	544	salesman	40	Rhode Island
	M	Taneelian Kerekor	544	laborer	45	here
	N	Tobin Bridget—†	544	housewife	46	"
	O	Tobin Michael F	544	carpenter	51	"
	R	*Arwashan Fannie—†	548	housewife	62	"
	S	Arwashan Helen—†	548	operator	23	"
	T	*Arwashan John N	548	manager	61	"
	U	Einhorn Evelyn—†	548	housewife	28	612 Tremont
	V	Einhorn Joseph	548	U S N	26	612 "
	W	Karam Michael	548	machinist	38	here
	X	Karam Sarah—†	548	housewife	33	"
	Y	Naymie Edward	548	student	20	"
309						
	A	Naymie George	548	U S A	28	
	[1]A	Naymie George J	548	manager	52	"
	B	Naymie Helen—†	548	at home	22	
	C	Naymie Nellie—†	548	"	30	"
	D	Naymie William R	548	U S A	26	
	E	Bernier Joseph	550	electrician	40	"
	F	Boutler Jerry	550	cook	40	673 Tremont
	G	Burke Anna—†	550	housewife	40	here
	H	Burke Bernard	550	porter	40	"
	K	Davidson Harry	550	waiter	48	"
	L	Dawe Noah	550	ironworker	46	"

Page.	Letter.	Full Name.	Residence, Jan. 1, 1943.	Occupation.	Supposed Age.	Reported Residence, Jan. 1, 1942. Street and Number.

Massachusetts Avenue—Continued

Page.	Letter.	Full Name.	Residence, Jan. 1, 1943.	Occupation.	Supposed Age.	Reported Residence, Jan. 1, 1942. Street and Number.
	M	Harvey Elizabeth—†	550	clerk	48	here
	N	Kelley James	550	retired	79	677 Mass av
	O	Kelliher Mary—†	550	maid	41	here
	P	MacLean Bernice—†	550	housekeeper	50	"
	R	Maynard Estelle—†	550	housewife	45	"
	S	McMannimin William	550	pressman	36	10 Wash'n
	T	Murphy Ellen—†	550	at home	71	here
	U	Ouelette William	550	welder	35	"
	V	Phillips James	550	pressman	33	10 Wash'n
	W	Schaeffer Albert	550	baker	50	Newton
	X	Williams Estelle—†	550	clerk	30	Malden
	Y	Crawford Bella E—†	552	pianist	65	here
	Z	Crooks Louise—†	552	clerk	36	16 Greenwich pk
310						
	A	Crooks Percival	552	painter	45	16 "
	B	Drummond George H	552	retired	74	here
	C	Hazzard Alvira—†	552	typist	38	504 Col av
	D	Jenkins Beaufort	552	shipper	40	here
	E	Jenkins Pauline—†	552	housewife	32	"
	F	Palmer Samuel B	552	U S N	47	"
	G	Palmer Sarah—†	552	housewife	42	"
	H	Rhodes William H	552	musician	36	"
	K	Woodard Elihu T	552	cook	36	
	L	Joslyn Grace—†	554	at home	68	
	M	Reid David	554	missionary	74	"
	N	Reid Lillian—†	554	at home	40	"
	O	Reid Marie—†	554	"	70	
	P	Reid Robert	554	draftsman	43	"
	S	Bailey Juanita—†	558	stitcher	27	
	T	Carberry Mary—†	558	"	30	
	W	Griffin Edith—†	558	clerk	28	
	U	Hammon Virginia—†	558	social worker	30	"
	V	Handy Mary C—†	558	at home	60	
	X	Jackson Eugenia—†	558	student	27	"
	Y	McCreary Doris—†	558	"	24	Michigan
	Z	Session Jeanette—†	558	stitcher	25	here
311						
	A	Thomas Maude M—†	558	matron	58	
	B	Veal Maude T—†	558	student	25	"
	C	Hamilton Gladys—†	560	at home	40	Malden
	D	*Langone Anthony	560	retired	75	here

Page.	Letter.	FULL NAME.	Residence, Jan. 1, 1943.	Occupation.	Supposed Age.	Reported Residence, Jan. 1, 1942. Street and Number.

Massachusetts Avenue—Continued

	E	Langone Julia—†	560	at home	31	here
	F	McElwain John J	560	clerk	58	"
	G	McElwain Josephine—†	560	housewife	54	"
	H	Roy Alfred	560	mechanic	40	"
	K	Roy Willa—†	560	at home	26	
	L	Sullivan May—†	560	clerk	31	
	M	Badger Helen—†	562	domestic	55	"
	N	Green Mary—†	562	at home	54	
	O	Murphy Michael	562	retired	65	"
	P	Toye John F	562	caretaker	57	572 Mass av
	S	Arsenault Frank J	566	salesman	50	17 Rutland sq
	T	*Bissonette John	566	retired	68	here
	U	*Bissonette Josephine—†	566	at home	75	"
	V	Cleveland Mary—†	566	operator	35	67 Sterling
	W	Cleveland Theodore	566	chauffeur	36	67 "
	X	Dapapalels Anthony	566	chef	45	here
	Y	Edmond Laurie—†	566	at home	24	36 Concord
	Z	Edmonds Ralph W	566	mechanic	65	36 "
312						
	A	Griffith Alice—†	566	at home	36	here
	B	Griffith Harold W	566	retired	46	Billerica
	C	Honaker Alice—†	566	operator	38	599 Col av
	D	Honaker Michael	566	U S A	40	here
	E	Hutchinson Charles	566	chauffeur	38	"
	F	MacCallum George D	566	operator	47	"
	G	Morrissey John	566	musician	33	37 Circuit
	H	Morrissey Mary—†	566	housewife	32	37 "
	K	Murphy Helen—†	566	at home	46	415 Mass av
	L	Pritchard Herbert	566	chauffeur	27	here
	M	Wilson Loretta—†	566	operator	40	202 Dudley
	N	Brady Grace—†	570	at home	51	Somerville
	O	Fatada Peter	570	agent	52	here
	P	Grutch Louis	570	chauffeur	35	"
	R	Hoyt Walter	570	barber	58	"
	S	Johnson John	570	mechanic	35	533 Shawmut av
	T	McDonald Margaret D—†	570	at home	58	here
	U	McKenna Elizabeth—†	570	operator	28	Stoughton
	V	McPherson Alex	570	mechanic	61	55 Dudley
	W	Oberg Carl	570	retired	67	here
	X	Ross Thomas H	570	operator	31	Cambridge
	Y	Scanlon Edith—†	570	housewife	68	here

Page.	Letter.	FULL NAME.	Residence, Jan. 1, 1943.	Occupation.	Supposed Age.	Reported Residence, Jan. 1, 1942. Street and Number.

Massachusetts Avenue—Continued

	Z	Scanlon John	570	agent	63	here
313						
	A	Stewart Myrtle—†	570	at home	66	"
	B	*Taylor Nora—†	570	"	65	"
	C	Turcotte Marie—†	570	operator	27	46 E Springfield
	D	Donlon Peter	572	bricklayer	60	here
	E	Donlon Theresa—†	572	operator	55	"
	F	Farrera Eileen—†	572	"	25	"
	G	Farrera Joseph	572	laborer	35	
	H	McShane Patrick	572	clerk	35	
	K	Murphy Anna—†	572	at home	52	
	L	Clifford Elizabeth—†	574	housewife	67	"
	M	Clifford Guy	574	retired	66	"
	N	Comstock Louis	574	"	64	"
	O	Johnston Raymond	574	cook	45	Everett
	P	McCourt Rose—†	574	at home	65	1466 Wash'n
	R	McKenzie Carrie—†	574	laundress	39	here
	S	Pettley Jean—†	574	housewife	27	"
	T	Pettley Lionel	574	chef	30	"
	U	Sparrow Wayne	574	"	52	
	V	Sweeney Mary—†	574	at home	39	
	W	Swensen Bertha—†	574	"	63	
	X	Vorterant Michael	574	clerk	57	"
	Y	Abbott Lester	578	mechanic	49	9 Blackwood
	Z	*Altoon Leo	578	painter	56	722 Shawmut av
314						
	A	Armour Margaret—†	578	at home	27	S Carolina
	B	Beeler Effie D—†	578	"	54	here
	C	Beeler Frank B	578	mechanic	57	"
	D	Grawdy Mary—†	578	at home	24	557 Mass av
	E	Gulowacz Frances—†	578	housewife	22	Rhode Island
	F	Gulowacz Walter	578	welder	25	696 Mass av
	G	Lacorara Dominic	578	student	24	here
	H	McDonald Anna—†	578	waitress	42	"
	K	Nalesnik Walter	578	student	23	Salem
	L	Olnick Gladys—†	578	operator	40	here
	M	Prysgodski Wanda A—†	578	nurse	39	52 E Springfield
	N	Stevens Harriet—†	578	at home	74	here
	O	Stevens Vassel	578	retired	92	"
	P	Weeks Edgar	578	salesman	50	"
	R	Woods Martin J	578	operator	52	

Massachusetts Avenue—Continued

S	Bergman Elna—†	582	at home	54	here
T	Bergman Lars	582	carpenter	50	"
U	Caplett George	582	mechanic	48	"
V	Goldstein Henry	582	laborer	59	
W	Gracia Florence—†	582	operator	38	"
X	Hubbard Lillian—†	582	"	23	44 Wilmington av
Y	Peterson Carl	582	mechanic	64	New York
Z	Tracy Edward	582	chauffeur	36	79 Heath
	315				
A	Tracy Grace—†	582	housewife	22	79 "
B	Courtney Margaret—†	586	operator	40	here
C	LaMarge Mary—†	586	domestic	65	"
E	Botaish Marianna—†	586	operator	28	"
F	Botaish Thomas	586	watchman	50	"
G	Pantazopoulos Peter	586	retired	66	"
H	Bosse Yvette—†	586	waitress	29	753 Tremont
K	Metz Stara—†	586	cashier	25	New York

Rutland Street

M	Blackstead Mary—†	2	housekeeper	38	here
N	McRobb Alice—†	2	housewife	32	"
O	McRobb James F	2	U S N	32	"
P	Namey Florence—†	2	housewife	24	"
R	Namey Phillip D	2	laborer	28	"
S	Sarris John	2	"	30	153 W Canton
T	Sarris Mary—†	2	housewife	28	152 "
U	Haley Ellen—†	4	housekeeper	68	here
V	Haley William	4	laborer	48	"
W	Johnson Arthur J	4	watchman	57	15 Milford
X	Johnson Bridget—†	4	housewife	58	15 "
Y	Nicoli Armando	4	laborer	33	485 Shawmut av
Z	Nicoli Marion—†	4	housewife	31	485 "
	316				
A	*Olsen John	4	painter	68	37 E Newton
B	Bott William	6	clerk	52	9 Rutland
C	Brown Albert	6	laborer	48	here
D	Cummings Martin	6	"	54	"
E	Hickey Agnes—†	6	domestic	42	"
F	McGrath John	6	chef	38	686 Tremont
G	McLaughlin Thomas	6	laborer	48	here

Page.	Letter.	FULL NAME.	Residence, Jan. 1, 1943.	Occupation.	Supposed Age.	Reported Residence, Jan. 1, 1942. Street and Number.

Rutland Street—Continued

	H	*McRae Olga—†	6	housekeeper	37	here
	K	McQuade Daniel	6	laborer	60	"
	L	Pimental Ola—†	6	housekeeper	38	"
	M	Goss Raymond A	8	laborer	36	"
	N	Goss Rose—†	8	housewife	32	"
	O	Fichter John	10	laborer	62	1123 Wash'n
	P	Geldert Arthur	10	retired	84	221 Shawmut av
	R	Hall Daniel	10	"	68	221 "
	S	Lombardi James V	10	chef	38	84 Prince
	T	Minns Mary—†	10	housekeeper	66	183 W Canton
	U	Morrison James	10	laborer	50	here
	V	Munroe Hugh	10	retired	66	"
	W	Regan Francis L	10	chef	30	1858 Wash'n
	X	Rollo Mary—†	10	housekeeper	35	Cambridge
	Y	Williams Adelbert G	10	retired	62	78 W Newton
	Z	Williams Lida—†	10	housewife	54	78 "
317						
	A	Dole Edward	12	agent	57	468 Shawmut av
	B	Harden Helen—†	12	housekeeper	55	468 "
	C	Lufty Frederick	12	laborer	21	here
	D	Lufty John	12	retired	81	"
	E	Lufty Sarah—†	12	housewife	49	"
	F	Mullen Michael T	12	retired	78	
	G	Nelson Emil J	12	"	60	
	H	Ready John	12	"	65	"
	K	Evans Harriett—†	14	housekeeper	38	Cambridge
	L	Mitchell Harriett—†	14	"	42	"
	M	Ewing John	14	U S A	23	here
	N	O'Bryant Elsie T—†	14	housekeeper	37	"

Shawmut Avenue

	O	Sreda Josephine—†	474	at home	38	here
	P	Forte Andrew	474	U S A	21	"
	R	*Forte Carmela—†	474	housewife	51	"
	S	Forte Frederick J	474	salesman	30	"
	T	Forte Joseph	474	U S A	23	"
	U	Forte Santo	474	"	25	
	V	*Petrou Helen—†	474	housewife	65	"
	W	Petrou Rena—†	474	at home	30	
	X	Petrou Stephen	474	salesman	29	"

Page.	Letter.	Full Name.	Residence, Jan. 1, 1943.	Occupation.	Supposed Age.	Reported Residence, Jan. 1, 1942. Street and Number.

Shawmut Avenue—Continued

Page.	Letter.	Full Name.	Residence, Jan. 1, 1943.	Occupation.	Supposed Age.	Reported Residence, Jan. 1, 1942. Street and Number.
	Y	*Petrou William	474	barber	67	here
	Z	Malocf Nicholas	474	laborer	30	"
318						
	A	Maloof Nora—†	474	housewife	22	"
	C	Constan Agathus	476	merchant	47	"
	E	*Druckerman Alice—†	476	at home	32	29 Compton
	F	Druckerman Herman	476	merchant	46	29 "
	G	Flynn Frank	476	laborer	32	224 Harris'n av
	H	Iles Margaret—†	476	at home	43	here
	M	Johnson Laura T—†	478	"	52	"
	N	Hebb James J	478	retired	73	"
	O	*Davis Julius	478	laborer	59	
	S	Murray Dorothy J—†	478	housewife	56	"
	R	Murray James H	478	laborer	60	"
	T	Doyle Catherine—†	478	at home	60	127 Roxbury
	U	Doyle Henry W	478	U S A	26	127 "
	V	Moore Francis	478	at home	29	60 Rutland
	W	Keegan James	478	rigger	29	3 Flagg
	Y	Fabery Beatrice—†	478	waitress	24	86 Springfield
	X	Foley William	478	machinist	59	482 Harris'n av
319						
	A	Brown Alton	480	U S A	25	here
	B	Brown Dana	480	"	21	"
	C	*Bullock Annie—†	480	at home	64	"
	D	Day Percy	480	laborer	54	
	E	Mardirosian Victoria—†	480	at home	50	
	G	Crowley Anna—†	480	"	38	
	K	Mills Alfred	480	laborer	21	
	L	Mills Anna—†	480	housewife	21	"
	N	McCausland George	480	shipfitter	42	"
	O	McCausland Helen S—†	480	housewife	31	"
	P	Porter Eva—†	480	domestic	32	"
	R	Baker Solomon	481	laborer	40	"
	S	Casey Thomas	481	clerk	35	15 Edgerly rd
	T	Cronin James	481	laborer	38	here
	U	Judge Mary—†	481	housewife	40	"
	V	*Lombardo Rocco	481	tailor	50	1094 River
	W	McDougall James	481	retired	65	here
	X	Menders John	481	tester	64	"
	Y	Moran Julia—†	481	at home	50	"
	Z	Salem Margaret—†	481	stitcher	24	

Page.	Letter.	FULL NAME.	Residence, Jan. 1, 1943.	Occupation.	Supposed Age.	Reported Residence, Jan. 1, 1942. Street and Number.
320		**Shawmut Avenue**—Continued				
	A	Shippy Carleton R	481	chauffeur	39	here
	B	Shippy Frances—†	481	housewife	30	"
	D	Davidson James A	483	merchant	29	Newton
	E	Driscoll James J	483	teamster	66	81 Rutland
	F	Hill Herbert L	483	at home	61	here
	G	Honlihan Mary J—†	483	"	68	140 W Canton
	H	*Kelly Catherine M—†	483	"	65	48 E Springfield
	K	McAuley Annie—†	483	"	64	here
	L	O'Connell Eleanor—†	483	"	73	"
	M	O'Connell Julia—†	483	housekeeper	70	"
	N	Reilly Rose A—†	483	domestic	59	139 W Newton
	O	Stanger Adolph	483	salesman	59	here
	P	Trainor Thomas	483	steamfitter	63	"
	R	Twoomey John	483	retired	68	876 Harris'n av
	T	Ambrose Edith—†	485	housekeeper	35	here
	U	Murphy Florence—†	485	at home	74	"
	V	Boitnott Julia—†	486	housewife	50	476 Shawmut av
	W	Boitnott William	486	barber	61	476 "
	X	Boitnott William W	486	U S A	20	here
	Y	Brownell Harold	486	painter	49	"
	Z	Brownell Kathleen—†	486	housewife	39	"
321						
	A	Sicalis George	486	chauffeur	53	"
	B	Sicalis Maria—†	486	housewife	50	"
	C	DeVinitas Grace—†	486	"	32	
	D	DeVinitas Joseph	486	clerk	34	
	E	Ford Frank	486	"	37	
	L	Purnell Christine—†	496	domestic	48	"
	M	Purnell Muriel—†	496	at home	21	"
	N	McGrath Margaret—†	496	"	29	478 Shawmut av
	O	Balinski Agnes—†	496	clerk	41	here
	R	Campbell Dositheous	499	chef	42	"
	S	Campbell Thelma—†	499	at home	30	"
	T	Mendes Evelyn—†	499	domestic	41	"
	U	*Burns Anne—†	499	at home	59	29 Wellington
	W	Green Elizabeth—†	499	cleaner	53	here
	Y	Polk Benjamin	501	laborer	53	"
	Z	Polk Dora—†	501	housewife	52	"
322						
	C	Stewart Jennie—†	501	at home	41	

Page.	Letter.	FULL NAME.	Residence, Jan. 1, 1943.	Occupation.	Supposed Age.	Reported Residence, Jan. 1, 1942. Street and Number.

Shawmut Avenue—Continued

Page.	Letter.	FULL NAME.	Residence, Jan. 1, 1943.	Occupation.	Supposed Age.	Reported Residence, Jan. 1, 1942.
	D	Thornton Joseph	501	janitor	60	here
	E	Whalen Angelina M—†	502	housewife	64	"
	F	Whalen Walter E	502	machinist	69	Worcester
	G	Brown May—†	502	at home	67	here
	H	Courtemanche Felix	502	retired	72	"
	K	Phiney John J	502	painter	60	"
	L	Ball Albert	502	janitor	66	
	M	Beaton Mildred—†	502	nurse	23	
	N	Coppellotti Peter	502	laborer	47	
	O	Moulton John J	502	janitor	67	
	P	Canada Herbert	503	chauffeur	30	"
	R	DeSoto Harry	503	"	46	
	S	Grant Edward	503	mechanic	29	"
	T	Holmes Alexander	503	porter	46	
	U	Holmes Marie—†	503	housewife	35	"
	V	Jones Melvin H	503	riveter	43	
	W	Lewis MacDonald	503	waiter	43	
	X	Little Arthur	503	printer	46	
	Y	Russell Breckenridge	503	laborer	58	
	Z	Smith Edward	503	welder	40	
323						
	A	Taylor Ira	503	dishwasher	53	"
	B	Trotman Albert	503	laborer	37	
	C	Bailey Walter	504	porter	42	
	D	Cook Emanda—†	504	saleswoman	32	"
	E	Cook James	504	clerk	33	
	F	Johnson Stark	504	laborer	43	
	G	Pack Lloyd	504	salesman	36	"
	H	Pack Nettie—†	504	at home	60	
	L	Silva Eva B—†	505	waitress	30	
	M	Silva William B	505	laborer	39	
	N	Leitao Antonio N	505	retired	66	
	O	Leitao Arthur	505	U S A	26	
	P	Leitao George	505	"	30	"
	R	Leitao Georgianna—†	505	housekeeper	30	"
	S	Leitao Virginia—†	505	waitress	22	"
	T	Low Jennie—†	505	at home	40	
	U	Robinson Celia—†	506	"	70	"
	V	Brooks Philip	506	chauffeur	54	"
	W	Mosbey Charles	506	clerk	45	
	X	Walker Lee	506	"	54	

Page.	Letter.	Full Name.	Residence, Jan. 1, 1943.	Occupation.	Supposed Age.	Reported Residence, Jan. 1, 1942. Street and Number.

Shawmut Avenue—Continued

Page.	Letter.	Full Name.	Residence, Jan. 1, 1943.	Occupation.	Supposed Age.	Reported Residence, Jan. 1, 1942. Street and Number.
	Y	Brown Corbett	506	janitor	26	here
	Z	Brown Mabelle—†	506	domestic	33	"
324						
	A	Batson Christine—†	507	clerk	35	"
	B	Jones William	507	laborer	51	33 Worcester
	C	Keith Hattie—†	507	housewife	32	New York
	D	Keith William	507	laborer	44	"
	E	Merrill Catherine E—†	507	housewife	66	here
	F	*Merrill James	507	retired	72	"
	G	Miller Catherine—†	507	housewife	27	New York
	H	Miller Reinhart	507	chauffeur	29	"
	K	Russell Lawrence	507	laborer	31	here
	L	Schuler Jennie—†	507	housewife	28	"
	M	Schuler Leroy	507	U S A	28	"
	N	Simpkins Earl	507	chauffeur	30	"
	O	Stewart Elizabeth—†	507	at home	54	
	P	Biele Maximilian	508	porter	46	
	R	Bourne John S	508	attorney	67	"
	S	Bourne Narka C—†	508	clerk	31	
	T	Cooke Anderson	508	laborer	47	
	U	Yee Aida—†	508	housewife	32	"
	V	*Yee Harry	508	laundryman	44	"
	Y	Sarkis Adele—†	515	typist	20	
	Z	*Sarkis Bashara	515	merchant	43	"
325						
	A	*Sarkis Mamie—†	515	housewife	40	"
	B	Doyle Agnes—†	515	laundress	41	"
	F	Cleveland Laura—†	521	housewife	34	"
	G	Cleveland Theodore	521	clerk	38	
	H	Diaz Manuel	521	laborer	50	"
	K	Hanna Alice—†	521	housewife	22	"
	L	Hanna Anthony	521	laborer	30	
	M	Mitchell Mary—†	521	clerk	28	
	N	Dean Marcus	521	laborer	39	
	O	Young Noel—†	521	waitress	40	"
	S	Corban Eustis	521	laborer	22	
	T	Corban Woodrow	521	"	28	
	P	Lewis Celise—†	521	housewife	25	"
	R	Lewis John	521	clerk	33	
	U	George Alice—†	521	cleaner	38	"
	V	Matthews Julia—†	521	at home	55	

Page.	Letter.	Full Name.	Residence, Jan. 1, 1943.	Occupation.	Supposed Age.	Reported Residence, Jan. 1, 1942. Street and Number.

Stevens Street

Page.	Letter.	Full Name.	Residence, Jan. 1, 1943.	Occupation.	Supposed Age.	Reported Residence, Jan. 1, 1942. Street and Number.
	Y	*Menzies Arthur	1	retired	73	here
	Z	*Menzies Mary—†	1	housewife	67	"
326						
	A	Bishop Joseph	1	retired	62	
	B	Bowen Anna—†	1	housekeeper	69	"
	C	Branagan Edward	2	U S N	35	"
	D	DeRossi Roy	2	laborer	54	
	E	*Quinlan Alice—†	2	housekeeper	59	"
	F	Splaine James	2	tailor	55	"
	N	Bailey Mattie—†	6	housekeeper	33	46 Northfield
	O	Booker Pearl—†	6	"	34	46 "

Tremont Street

Page.	Letter.	Full Name.	Residence, Jan. 1, 1943.	Occupation.	Supposed Age.	Reported Residence, Jan. 1, 1942. Street and Number.
	R	Allen Marie—†	748	housekeeper	45	105 Peterboro
	S	Arapahoe Bertha—†	748	housewife	71	here
	T	Cook Marie—†	748	housekeeper	71	"
	U	Foss Mary—†	748	cook	57	"
	V	Newcomb Frank	748	carpenter	69	"
	W	Jigarjian Nishan	748	clerk	55	
	X	Kazanjian Mardiros	748	janitor	46	"
	Y	Stavridis Ada—†	748	housekeeper	35	"
	Z	Stavridis George	748	chauffeur	45	"
327						
	A	David George	748	salesman	47	"
	B	Chaptell Lewis	750	mechanic	33	10 Marcella
	C	Hanna Edith—†	750	housewife	23	here
	D	Hanna Herbert	750	engineer	29	"
	E	Karmara Samuel	750	laborer	40	616A Shawmut av
	F	Langford Esther—†	750	housewife	30	214 W Canton
	G	Langford Philip	750	mechanic	35	214 "
	H	Lewis Catherine—†	750	housewife	41	here
	K	Lewis James	750	painter	41	"
	L	Teasley Larkin	750	clerk	56	"
	M	Williams Benjamin	750	porter	54	
	N	Williams Ella—†	750	cook	57	
	O	Belan Annette—†	752	clerk	44	
	P	Belan Theodore	752	chauffeur	47	"
	R	Brice Clara—†	752	housewife	42	Connecticut
	S	Brice Sherman	752	guard	42	"
	T	Junquist Carl	752	painter	45	Lawrence

Page.	Letter.	Full Name.	Residence, Jan. 1, 1943.	Occupation.	Supposed Age.	Reported Residence, Jan. 1, 1942. Street and Number.

Tremont Street—Continued

Page.	Letter.	Full Name.	Residence, Jan. 1, 1943.	Occupation.	Supposed Age.	Reported Residence, Jan. 1, 1942. Street and Number.
	U	Martelletti Henrietta—†	752	housewife	42	Maine
	V	Martelletti Joseph	752	chauffeur	43	here
	W	Rythen Fritiof H	752	mechanic	71	"
	X	Rythen Louise—†	752	student	22	"
	Y	Rythen Maria—†	752	housekeeper	73	"
	Z	Waterhouse Bertha—†	752	hairdresser	45	California
328						
	A	Derry Arthur	754	guard	56	here
	B	Duncan Edward	754	laborer	49	"
	C	Fuller Ruth—†	754	laundress	40	"
	D	Gage Thelma—†	754	housewife	30	"
	E	Gorman Audrey—†	754	laundress	38	"
	F	Gorman Joseph	754	mechanic	36	"
	G	Heaby Patrick	754	salesman	55	750 Tremont
	H	Hopwood Howard	754	mechanic	31	here
	K	Lawless William	754	clerk	58	"
	L	Lima Wilbur	754	mechanic	61	"
	M	Maloney James	754	laborer	47	"
	N	McKinnon John	754	porter	50	666 Tremont
	O	Philips Arthur	754	clerk	66	here
	P	Wigham Alexander	754	mechanic	47	"
	R	Winsor Susanna—†	754	housekeeper	60	"
	S	Brooker John	756	chauffeur	67	"
	T	Carmen George	756	laborer	45	
	U	Hatch Horace	756	steamfitter	53	"
	V	Jeffrey Margaret—†	756	housekeeper	61	"
	W	Jeffrey Walter	756	janitor	57	"
	X	Lyons Jennie—†	756	housekeeper	70	"
	Y	Maloney Annie—†	756	housewife	70	"
	Z	Maloney Frank	756	carpenter	43	"
329						
	A	Nevins Terrance	756	laborer	37	
	B	Peters Demitros	756	"	54	
	C	Trayers Mary—†	756	clerk	43	
	D	Whyte George	756	retired	62	
	E	Whyte Lillian—†	756	weaver	55	"
	H	Bloodworth William	758	U S N	24	Rhode Island
	F	Brookins John	758	porter	29	"
	G	Brookins Marie—†	758	housewife	29	"
	K	Byran Thelma—†	758	factoryhand	22	"

Page.	Letter.	Full Name.	Residence, Jan. 1, 1943.	Occupation.	Supposed Age.	Reported Residence, Jan. 1, 1942. Street and Number.

Tremont Street—Continued

	L	Clark Fanny—†	758	operator	23	Hingham
	M	Dolphus William	758	laborer	24	Florida
	N	Looke Bonne	758	presser	52	here
	O	Martindale Kenneth	758	entertainer	28	"
	P	McLaughlin Elizabeth—†	758	housewife	35	117 Brighton
	R	McLaughlin Frank	758	janitor	45	117 "
	S	McLaughlin James	758	U S A	20	117 "
	T	McLaughlin Paul	758	U S N	23	117 "
	U	Mondesire Maneria—†	758	housewife	45	175 Townsend
	V	*Pilgrim Mabel—†	758	laundryworker	37	New York
	W	Smith William	758	"	56	21 Arnold
	X	Wilson Eugene	760	chauffeur	41	here
	Y	Wilson Rebecca—†	760	housewife	36	"
	Z	Jackson Birdie—†	760	domestic	53	"
330						
	A	Jackson Selina—†	760	housekeeper	50	"
	C	Webb James	760	cook	42	"
	D	*Webber Rebecca—†	760	housekeeper	41	"
	E	Webber Roland	760	U S A	22	"
	F	Webber Wilfred	760	machinist	50	"
	G	Boyd Allan	760	porter	23	Connecticut
	B	Boyd Laura—†	760	housewife	21	203 W Springfield
	H	Robinson Mary—†	760	maid	25	662 Shawmut av
	L	Black Francis	762	porter	32	544 Col av
	M	Black Laura—†	762	housewife	23	544 "
	N	Gray Helen—†	762	domestic	43	here
	O	Peakes Peter	762	U S A	44	"
	P	Haggans Merie—†	762	student	25	610 Col av
	R	Readdy Helen—†	762	domestic	24	556 "
	S	Readdy Rosa—†	762	housewife	50	556 "
	T	Williams Alvin	762	U S A	51	610 "
	U	Smith Mabel—†	762	housewife	32	153 Worcester
	V	Smith Walter	762	molder	42	153 "
	W	Hopkins Alice—†	764	housekeeper	30	25 Claremont pk
	X	Hutchins Louis	764	U S A	22	25 "
	Y	Shank Ruth—†	764	housekeeper	44	25 "
	Z	Adams Bessie—†	764	domestic	51	here
331						
	A	Adams Frank	764	butler	62	
	B	Davis Ethelyn—†	764	housekeeper	43	"

Page.	Letter.	Full Name.	Residence, Jan. 1, 1943.	Occupation.	Supposed Age.	Reported Residence, Jan. 1, 1942. Street and Number.

Tremont Street—Continued

Page.	Letter.	Full Name.	Residence, Jan. 1, 1943.	Occupation.	Supposed Age.	Reported Residence, Jan. 1, 1942. Street and Number.
	C	Walker James	764	porter	43	here
	D	Cheatham Leroy	764	chef	39	19 Braddock pk
	E	Norwood Pearl—†	764	housekeeper	28	19 "

Washington Street

Page.	Letter.	Full Name.	Residence, Jan. 1, 1943.	Occupation.	Supposed Age.	Reported Residence, Jan. 1, 1942. Street and Number.
	O	Blackstead Gustava—†	1597	at home	59	here
	P	Hooley Gertrude—†	1597	clerk	27	27 Worcester sq
	R	Ramos Rachel—†	1597	at home	39	here
	S	Kosendos Mary—†	1597	"	26	467 Tremont
	T	Marquart Augusta—†	1597	"	85	467 "
	V	Pearson Elsie—†	1597	"	30	here
	W	*Peterson Tage	1597	laborer	35	"
	U	Ryan Augusta—†	1597	at home	61	467 Tremont
332						
	C	Hart Daniel F	1607	retired	73	here
	D	O'Donnell Marguerite-†	1607	at home	44	"
	E	O'Donnell Maurice J	1607	plumber	47	"
	L	Backman Mabel—†	1615A	at home	49	
	M	Backman William	1615A	manager	49	"
	H	Hart Daniel F, jr	1615A	musician	48	"
	O	Hart Rose—†	1615A	at home	66	"
	P	Newman William	1615A	laborer	39	
	S	Detry Harriet—†	1621	at home	77	"
	T	Detry Raymond	1621	laborer	41	
	U	Detry Ruth—†	1621	clerk	36	
333						
	M	Meaney James C	1675	laborer	46	
	N	Connaughton Dorothy-†	1675	clerk	22	
	O	Connaughton Eunice—†	1675	housewife	42	"
	P	Connaughton Joseph	1675	clerk	21	
	R	Connaughton Joseph E	1675	U S N	44	
	T	Stamatos Dennis	1677	student	23	
	U	Stamatos Nicholas	1677	manager	50	"
	V	Stamatos Paul	1677	U S A	27	
	W	Lalooses Constantine—†	1677	at home	38	
	X	Lalooses Demetrios	1677	manager	58	"

334 West Concord Street

Page.	Letter.	Full Name.	Residence, Jan. 1, 1943.	Occupation.	Supposed Age.	Reported Residence, Jan. 1, 1942. Street and Number.
	K	Medici Paul	68	janitor	55	here
	L	McGuinness Mary—†	68	housewife	45	5 Union pk

Page.	Letter.	FULL NAME.	Residence, Jan. 1, 1943.	Occupation.	Supposed Age.	Reported Residence, Jan. 1, 1942. Street and Number.

West Concord Street—Continued

Page.	Letter.	FULL NAME.	Residence, Jan. 1, 1943.	Occupation.	Supposed Age.	Reported Residence, Jan. 1, 1942. Street and Number.
	M	McGuinness Patrick	68	bartender	47	5 Union pk
	N	Kelly Agnes S—†	68	housewife	43	here
	O	Kelly James	68	machinist	56	"
	S	Seiberlich Lawrence A	68	painter	65	"
	T	Seiberlich Mary—†	68	housewife	60	"
	U	*Blasi James	68	retired	73	"
	V	MacDonald Edna R—†	68	housewife	44	8 Newland
	W	MacDonald Joseph A	68	ironworker	51	8 "
	X	Medici Anita—†	68	clerk	25	here
	Y	Medici Eleanora—†	68	seamstress	20	"
	Z	Medici Justina—†	68	housewife	52	"
335						
	A	Medici Virginia—†	68	cashier	22	
	B	*Cazzola Philomena—†	68	at home	83	"
	C	Tumbull John J	68	carpenter	52	32 Union pk
	D	Tumbull Louise S—†	68	clerk	21	32 "
	E	Tumbull Mary E—†	68	housewife	48	32 "
	G	Hening Laura—†	68	clerk	30	Indiana
	F	Morse Helen—†	68	"	24	"
	H	Benson Agnes—†	68	domestic	54	66 E Newton
	K	Benson Alexander	68	U S A	34	66 "
	L	Ryan Martha—†	68	domestic	56	66 "
	M	Ryan Mary—†	68	"	59	66 "
	N	*Sallios Christo	68	chef	39	Hyannis
	O	Packard Ada P—†	68	housewife	60	here
	P	Packard Edmund A	68	retired	70	"
	R	Shaw Dora M—†	68	seamstress	60	"
	S	O'Brien Francis W	68	U S A	25	
	T	O'Brien Ida S—†	68	housewife	61	"
	U	O'Brien Joseph E	68	bookkeeper	25	"
	V	Baker Lena—†	68	waitress	44	1 W Concord
	W	Sekulich Vasa	68	painter	54	1 "
	X	Barr Agnes—†	68	housewife	40	here
	Y	Howie Viola—†	68	operator	39	727 Tremont
	Z	Cronin Elsie—†	68	housewife	27	here
336						
	A	Cronin John J	68	manager	28	"
	B	Murphy Mary—†	68	housewife	25	"
	C	Murphy Thomas	68	U S A	44	"
	D	Pollard Marcia—†	68	housewife	37	N Hampshire
	E	Simoneau Edward	68	machinist	53	"
	G	Baxter Charles W	68	fireman	58	here

Page.	Letter.	Full Name.	Residence, Jan. 1, 1943.	Occupation.	Supposed Age.	Reported Residence, Jan. 1, 1942. Street and Number.

West Concord Street—Continued

	H	Baxter Lillian—†	68	housekeeper	65	here
	K	Tudor Mary J—†	68	at home	70	"
	L	Tudor Michael	68	salesman	63	"
	M	Hallstrom Robert	68	baker	40	Cambridge
	N	Calusdian Gladys E—†	68	housewife	44	here
	O	Calusdian Richard	68	meatcutter	44	"
	P	Reynolds Florence—†	68	teacher	47	"
	S	Kelman Marion—†	68	domestic	51	"
	T	*Quinn Ellen—†	68	laundress	36	"
	U	Sims Charles	68	retired	77	
	W	Astin Arlene—†	68	housewife	22	"
	X	Astin Roland	68	chauffeur	25	1 Hanson
	Y	Clough Leon	68	photographer	29	here
	Z	Clough Lillian—†	68	housewife	23	"
337						
	C	Vaara Charles	75	clergyman	57	"
	D	Vaara Elizabeth—†	75	at home	31	
	E	Vaara Freedom	75	clergyman	29	"
	F	Vaara Hattie—†	75	at home	65	
	H	Bellile Loretta M—†	78	clerk	36	"
	K	Buckley Michael W	78	retired	74	443 Shawmut av
	L	Butoym Lawrence M	78	mechanic	54	here
	M	Flaherty Mabel E—†	78	cook	57	"
	N	Lyons Jeremiah	78	laborer	47	"
	O	MacLean Angus H	78	"	45	"
	P	McGrath Hilda L—†	78	at home	68	5 Sharon
	R	Mullen John	78	painter	74	here
	S	Murray Abbie—†	78	at home	57	"
	T	Murray Robert	78	chauffeur	25	"
	U	Pooler Edmund J	78	mechanic	36	Maine
	V	Rogers Philip J	78	retired	60	here
	W	Simmonds Mary E—†	78	at home	68	"
	X	Shultz John	78	clerk	32	"
	Y	Shultz Josephine—†	78	housewife	62	"
	Z	*Shultz Peter	78	proprietor	64	"
338						
	A	Hanifer Harriet—†	78	clerk	38	"
	C	Campbell Florence—†	80	attendant	46	26 E Springfield
	D	Campbell Robert	80	operator	21	26 "
	E	Dirian Barbara—†	80	housewife	31	here
	F	Dirian Deeb	80	engineer	35	"

Page.	Letter.	Full Name.	Residence, Jan. 1, 1943.	Occupation.	Supposed Age.	Reported Residence, Jan. 1, 1942. Street and Number.

West Concord Street—Continued

Page.	Letter.	Full Name.	Residence, Jan. 1, 1943.	Occupation.	Supposed Age.	Reported Residence, Jan. 1, 1942. Street and Number.
	G	Lutfy Edward	80	brazier	25	12 Pembroke
	H	Lutfy Nettie—†	80	housewife	21	12 "
	K	Marcus Philip	80	chauffeur	29	here
	L	Marcus Winifred—†	80	housewife	28	"
	N	Boulanger Albert	84	chef	44	"
	O	*Boulanger Antoinette—†	84	at home	31	"
	P	Susky William	84	laborer	45	
	R	Granata Frances—†	84	stitcher	36	
	S	Granata Francesco	84	presser	53	..
	T	Lalooses Louis P	84	clerk	40	
	U	Lalooses Mary L—†	84	housewife	34	"
	X	*Anderson Francis	96	retired	67	102 W Concord
	Y	Duffy William H	96	"	75	31 Rutland
	Z	Farley Lawrence	96	"	71	here
339						
	A	Johnson Ernest A	96	mechanic	51	"
	B	*Maderio Anthony S	96	cook	44	462 Shawmut av
	C	Olsen George	96	porter	49	here
	D	Peterson Thomas	96	mechanic	60	"
	E	Shea Hazel M—†	96	hairdresser	33	"
	F	*Angelson Alberta—†	98	at home	43	
	G	Boas Romaine	98	baker	62	"
	H	Breen Joseph	98	roofer	34	10 Wendover
	N	Charisopolas Angelo	98	chef	54	here
	K	Conville John J	98	laborer	41	"
	L	Dunn Angus J	98	mover	33	469 Mass av
	M	Lonergan Albert J	98	clerk	53	here
	O	McCarthy Daniel E	98	laborer	58	55 Worcester
	P	Nelson John	98	painter	43	91 Hunneman
	R	Peters Walter	98	mover	56	here
	S	Sullivan Joseph	98	painter	69	"
	T	Williams Charles E	98	buffer	63	"
	U	*Connell Catherine—†	100	at home	77	
	V	Gillespie Charles	100	retired	68	"
	W	Hayes Josephine—†	100	at home	40	25 Worcester
	X	Kane Mary—†	100	"	73	here
	Y	*McDonald Catherine—†	100	domestic	40	"
	Z	*McDonald Raymond J	100	painter	42	"
340						
	A	O'Neil William	100	retired	76	41 W Newton
	B	*Walsh Thomas	100	roofer	58	here

Page.	Letter.	Full Name.	Residence, Jan. 1, 1943.	Occupation.	Supposed Age.	Reported Residence, Jan. 1, 1942. Street and Number.

West Concord Street—Continued

Page.	Letter.	Full Name.	Residence, Jan. 1, 1943.	Occupation.	Supposed Age.	Reported Residence, Jan. 1, 1942. Street and Number.
	C	Whitney Charles	100	mechanic	40	Cambridge
	D	*Christiansen Bernt	102	retired	72	here
	E	Driscoll Michael J	102	"	66	70 Rutland
	F	*Englbom Anna—†	102	at home	66	here
	G	*Jackson Lillian—†	102	"	81	"
	H	Murtaugh Edwin	102	retired	68	10 Rutland
	K	Peterson Harry	102	mechanic	63	here
	L	Robertson Elizabeth—†	102	at home	42	"
	M	Robertson George	102	retired	36	"
	N	Sholden Ruben	102	painter	55	
	O	Sorensen Conrad	102	retired	64	
	P	Austin Susan—†	104	at home	70	
	R	Benway Francis L	104	mechanic	48	"
	S	Benway Mary—†	104	at home	47	
	T	Boyle George	104	laborer	52	
	U	Burnett John	104	orderly	47	"
	V	Coughlin John	104	laborer	45	63 Rutland sq
	W	*Hart Daniel	104	porter	46	here
	X	Jacobs Samuel	104	manager	46	"
	Y	Kane Peter	104	porter	48	145 W Concord
	Z	McMorrow Charles	104	retired	70	here
341						
	A	*O'Connor David	104	porter	47	
	B	Pinkham William	104	retired	67	

West Springfield Street

Page.	Letter.	Full Name.	Residence, Jan. 1, 1943.	Occupation.	Supposed Age.	Reported Residence, Jan. 1, 1942. Street and Number.
	C	Jenkins Clarence	83	chef	49	here
	D	Jenkins Estelle—†	83	housewife	45	"
	E	Liggett Pauline—†	83	domestic	20	"
	F	Pina Joseph	83	laborer	28	New Bedford
	G	Stevenson John C	83	chauffeur	52	here
	H	Stevenson Pauline—†	83	housewife	40	"
	K	Amado Anna—†	85	"	52	"
	L	Amado Frank	85	laborer	62	
	M	Teixeira Ida—†	85	housewife	34	"
	N	Teixeira Roy F	85	attorney	49	"
	O	Clark Catherine—†	87	laundress	28	"
	P	Lee Harrison O	87	clerk	30	"
	R	Lee Ruth A—†	87	housewife	31	"
	S	Whitfield Theodore	87	clergyman	39	"

Page.	Letter.	Full Name.	Residence, Jan. 1, 1943.	Occupation.	Supposed Age.	Reported Residence, Jan. 1, 1942. Street and Number.

West Springfield Street—Continued

Page.	Letter.	Full Name.	Residence, Jan. 1, 1943.	Occupation.	Supposed Age.	Reported Residence, Jan. 1, 1942. Street and Number.
	T	Quatterbaum Georgia—†	89	hairdresser	38	here
	U	Smith Bertha—†	89	domestic	45	"
	X	Gibau Henry	91	chef	23	"
	Y	Gonsalves Robert	91	salesman	48	"
	Z	Mendelson Joseph	91	chef	38	
342						
	A	Pina Manuel	91	student	22	
	B	Senna George	91	chef	36	
	C	Tavares Aniceto	91	"	65	
	D	*Tavares Virginia—†	91	housekeeper	58	"
	E	Vierra Eugene D	91	chef	45	581 Mass av
	G	Bush Frank	99	laborer	26	here
	H	Bush Merriam—†	99	housewife	25	"
	K	McConnell Lottie—†	99	at home	62	"
	M	Sherman Andrew	101	laborer	52	
	N	Sherman Dorothy—†	101	housewife	24	"
	O	Noel Robert	101	U S N	26	976 Tremont
	P	Noel Ruth—†	101	housewife	26	976 "
	R	Strobhardt Gwendolyn—†	101	"	27	521 Shawmut av
	S	Monteiro Virginia—†	101	"	22	63 Hampden
	T	Atkins Charles	102	waiter	36	here
	U	Bryant Charles	102	laborer	30	Alabama
	V	Hall Charles J	102	"	58	here
	W	Hayes Julius	102	chef	30	504 Shawmut av
	X	Jones Clarence	102	laborer	36	here
	Y	Jones Mary—†	102	at home	43	"
	Z	Jordan Edward	102	waiter	38	47 Concord sq
343						
	A	Wright Herbert	102	clerk	41	10 Northfield
	B	Wright Lillian—†	102	housewife	34	10 "
	C	Bonapart Carol	103	engineer	60	here
	D	Bonapart Eugenia—†	103	housewife	52	"
	E	Braxton Gertrude—†	103	"	42	"
	F	Butler Dorothy I—†	103	waitress	21	"
	G	Rollins Catherine—†	103	housewife	45	Georgia
	K	Bailey Leon E	105	U S A	26	19 Dilworth
	L	Bailey Mabel V—†	105	housewife	45	19 "
	M	Bailey Mabel V—†	105	assembler	24	19 "
	N	Bailey Theodore L	105	blacksmith	50	19 "
	O	Bailey Theodore N	105	U S A	22	19 "
	P	Pinkney Pearl—†	105	domestic	45	549 Col av

Page.	Letter.	Full Name.	Residence, Jan. 1, 1943.	Occupation.	Supposed Age.	Reported Residence, Jan. 1, 1942. Street and Number.

West Springfield Street—Continued

	R	Anderson Richard	106	laborer	48	501 Shawmut av
	S	Braxton Clarence	106	"	32	32 Worcester
	T	Carter Neal	106	"	60	367 Northampton
	U	Cook John	106		60	535 Mass av
	V	Curtis Armond	106	"	36	741 Shawmut av
	W	Hinton Margaret—†	106	at home	69	here
	X	Johnson Louis	106	laborer	44	"
	Y	Perkins Margaret—†	106	at home	45	"
	Z	Seaborns Julius	106	laborer	38	
344						
	A	Randall Charles	108	retired	71	"
	B	West George	108	"	64	10 Northfield
	C	Blackwell Ida—†	110	at home	70	here
	D	Reddick Blanche—†	110	"	50	"
	E	Reddick Nellie—†	110	"	29	"
	F	Furman Charles	110	retired	69	
	G	Lewis Mabel—†	110	at home	41	
	H	Butler John	112	retired	71	
	K	Butler Sarah—†	112	at home	71	
	L	Collins Sarah—†	112	"	28	"
	M	Webster Vernice—†	112	"	28	34 Claremont pk
	O	Nickerson Helen—†	114	"	40	here
	P	Tavares Daniel	114	shipper	25	200 W Springfield
	R	Tavares Mary—†	114	housewife	21	200 "
	S	Turner James	114	laborer	50	here
	T	Bly Bernice M—†	118	at home	36	565 Col av
	U	Bly Samuel	118	clergyman	34	565 "
	V	Averett Catherine—†	133	domestic	65	Revere
	W	Bean Charles H	133	retired	74	here
	X	Beede Andrew W	133	"	76	"
	Y	Blaydon John	133	"	75	"
	Z	Bush Berthold C	133		75	
345						
	A	Butler Robert	133		76	"
	B	Cartwright Charles W	133	"	78	Milton
	C	Chadwick Edith F—†	133	clerk	39	here
	D	Clifford Clarence A	133	attendant	62	"
	E	Cressey Fred L	133	retired	67	"
	F	Cushman Frank H	133	"	85	
	G	Dudley Weston F	133	"	84	
	H	Dunn James	133	attendant	43	"

Page.	Letter.	Full Name.	Residence, Jan. 1, 1943.	Occupation.	Supposed Age.	Reported Residence, Jan. 1, 1942. Street and Number.

West Springfield Street—Continued

Page.	Letter.	Full Name.	Residence, Jan. 1, 1943.	Occupation.	Supposed Age.	Reported Residence, Jan. 1, 1942. Street and Number.
	K	Foote Walter H	133	retired	73	here
	L	Garland Curtis E	133	"	79	"
	M	Gore Theodore A	133	"	71	"
	N	Gould Samuel N	133		81	
	O	Guild Herbert L	133		76	
	R	Hartwell Frank W	133		81	
	P	Haven Charles E	133		84	
	S	Hayes Charles H	133		81	
	T	Heinzer Otto	133		79	
	U	Hill George H	133		80	
	V	Hill Harry H	133		88	
	W	Hood George H	133		76	
	X	Jacques George L	133	"	72	
	Y	Johnson Victoria—†	133	domestic	58	"
	Z	Joslin Horace W	133	retired	72	
346						
	A	Knowles Hilda P—†	133	domestic	49	"
	B	Knowles Robert	133	watchman	49	"
	C	Lord George W	133	retired	80	
	D	Lull George F	133	"	85	
	E	McDonald William R	133	"	74	
	F	Nickerson Margaret—†	133	cook	58	
	G*	Ostbery Nils	133	retired	85	
	H	Pike Frank E	133	"	76	
	K	Putnam David H	133	"	81	
	L	Richards Alfred R	133		80	
	M	Richards Louis M	133	"	91	
	N	Russell Ernest	133		71	
	O	Scott Charles T	133		85	
	P	Sprague William S	133		76	
	R	Swift Fred H	133	"	76	
	S	Tornsney John B	133	attendant	50	"
	T	Walker Warren T	133	retired	68	Brookline
	U	Walton Agnes A—†	133	superintendent	61	here
	V	Washburn Arthur	133	retired	76	"
	W	Willis Albert L	133	"	85	"
	Y	Butler Muriel—†	159	housewife	23	New York
	Z	Thompson Rena—†	159	"	43	45 Symphony rd
347						
	A	Thompson Richard N	159	technician	48	45 "
	B	Chandler Byron	159	bartender	25	here

Page.	Letter.	Full Name.	Residence, Jan. 1, 1943.	Occupation.	Supposed Age.	Reported Residence, Jan. 1, 1942. Street and Number.

West Springfield Street—Continued

	C	Chandler Frances A—†	159	housewife	22	here
	D	Young Margaret—†	159	at home	68	"
	E	Chadwick John	159	laborer	20	New York
	F	Rhodes Susie—†	159	at home	74	here
	G	Ross Ada—†	159	"	66	"
	K	Christian Pauline—†	159	domestic	21	"
	L	McIntyre Eliza—†	159	waitress	42	
	M	Graham Eleanor—†	159	stitcher	20	
	N	Graham Gertrude—†	159	housewife	46	"
	O	Graham Richard F	159	U S A	22	
	P	Graham Samuel	159	porter	47	
	R	Graham Samuel	159	laborer	25	
	S	Graham William	159	U S A	21	
	T	Johnson Dumas H	159	operator	47	"
	U	Johnson Iris M—†	159	housewife	35	"
	V	Collins Raphael D	159	riveter	45	396 Northampton
	W	Lewis Otelia—†	159	housewife	37	396 "
	X	Carrington Enid—†	159	domestic	40	here
	Y	Lleyne Eleanor—†	159	"	42	"
	Z	*Trotman Alice—†	159	housewife	54	"
348						
	A	*Trotman George	159	porter	50	
	B	Trotman Lena—†	159	student	20	
	C	Bates Ruth—†	160	housewife	22	"
	D	Bates Thomas	160	laborer	25	"
	E	Harris Nathan	160	"	40	"
	F	Johnson Henry	160	"	36	1051 Tremont
	G	Marlowe Bertha—†	160	at home	45	here
	H	White Armada—†	161	housewife	40	77 Highland
	K	White Frank G	161	janitor	57	77 "
	L	Holly Beatrice—†	161	housewife	31	here
	M	Holly Henry	161	porter	47	"
	N	Williams Adelia M—†	161	presser	44	"
	O	Evans Aubrey	161	porter	32	
	P	Evans Dorothy—†	161	clerk	32	"
	R	Kyles Harold N	161	U S A	28	192 W Springfield
	S	Kyles Margaret—†	161	housewife	21	192 "
	T	Lawrence Ann—†	161	"	33	21 Dilworth
	U	Fernandz Alice—†	162	at home	50	here
	V	Martin Frances—†	162	"	30	623 Col av

Page.	Letter.	FULL NAME.	Residence, Jan. 1, 1943.	Occupation.	Supposed Age.	Reported Residence, Jan. 1, 1942. Street and Number.

West Springfield Street—Continued

	W	Gamble Frederick	163	carpenter	52	here
	X	Haywood Irving	163	U S A	39	"
	Y	Haywood Julia M—†	163	housewfe	38	"
	Z	*Medley Anna—†	163	domestic	42	"
349						
	A	Greene Chesterfield	163	mortician	56	"
	B	Carew Nora—†	163	domestic	40	"
	C	Costello Elizabeth—†	164	at home	78	26 Warwick
	D	Jordon Lillian—†	164	"	67	here
	E	Jackson Lottie—†	164	"	40	"
	F	Henson Francis	164	janitor	53	"
	G	Henson Naomi—†	164	at home	53	
	H	Terry Lula—†	165	"	71	
	K	White Alfred	165	laborer	58	"
	L	Harper Elsie—†	166	at home	28	52 St Germain
	M	Howard Claretta—†	166	housewife	46	here
	N	Howard William A, jr	166	laborer	47	"
	O	Saunders Althea—†	166	at home	30	241 Northampton
	P	Moore Esther W—†	167	hairdresser	35	here
	R	Moore William	167	chauffeur	41	"
	S	Flynn Charles	167	mechanic	29	"
	T	Flynn Mamie—†	167	domestic	28	"
	U	Charles Cecile—†	167	housewife	44	"
	V	Charles Wright E	167	porter	48	"
	W	Dupree Alfred W	167	clerk	38	47 Symphony rd
	X	Bell Olivia M—†	168	at home	30	here
	Y	Stewart Mabelle—†	168	"	27	"
	Z	Sumpkin Marie—†	168	"	43	"
350						
	A	Thomas Alice C—†	170	housewife	36	"
	B	Thomas Arthur	170	laborer	42	
	C	Krigger Anselno	172	engineer	50	
	D	Taylor Mary G—†	172	seamstress	43	"
	E	Alleyne Charles	174	laborer	40	
	F	Alleyne Mary—†	174	housewife	36	"
	G	Green Helen—†	174	minister	71	
	H	Poindexter Alice J—†	174	at home	81	"
	L	Gibbs Lewis	178	laborer	39	New York
	M	Gibbs Lucretia—†	178	at home	63	Florida
	N	Gibbs William	178	laborer	70	"
	O	Williams Corine—†	178	at home	52	New York

Page.	Letter.	Full Name.	Residence, Jan. 1, 1943.	Occupation.	Supposed Age.	Reported Residence, Jan. 1, 1942. Street and Number.
		Worcester Street				
	P	Higgins Thomas E	7	porter	64	24 Worcester sq
	R	Hobbs Edward L	7	U S A	36	here
	S	Hobbs Margaret—†	7	housewife	45	"
	T	Kachulas Charles	7	laborer	41	"
	U	*Kachulas Tula—†	7	housewife	27	"
	V	Stamatos Aphrodite—†	7	"	34	
	W	Stamatos James	7	clerk	45	
	X	Arnold Adelaide—†	11	housekeeper	67	"
	Y	Madden Harvey J	11	musician	43	"
	Z	Madden William J	11	chauffeur	48	"
351						
	A	Fahey Christopher	11	laborer	51	
	B	Fahey Lillian—†	11	housewife	40	"
	C	O'Neil Annie L—†	11	"	54	
	D	O'Neil Daniel J	11	painter	57	
	E	O'Neil James F	11	U S A	22	
	F	Riordan Walter	13	laborer	52	
	G	Mumby Mary—†	13	housewife	58	"
	H	Mumby Robert	13	laborer	60	
	K	Jackson Lloyd E	13	U S A	36	
	L	Jackson Mary N—†	13	housewife	38	"
	M	Anderson Robert	14–18	laborer	40	33 Cliff
	N	Burns George	14–18	"	60	New Jersey
	O	Clark Frank	14–18	machinist	64	3 Glenwood
	P	Daly Stephen	14–18	"	62	12 Dwight
	R	Goode Patrick	14–18	retired	72	3 Glenwood
	S	Gordon Mary—†	14–18	waitress	24	3 "
	T	Graham Frank	14–18	machinist	60	14 Bond
	U	Hughes Joseph H	14–18	retired	72	143 Dudley
	V	MacKay James E	14–18	laborer	57	45 Rutland
	W	McDonald Daniel	14–18	retired	73	5 Dudley
	Z	McGlinchey Jeremiah	14–18	laborer	53	72 Waltham
	X	McNulty Mary—†	14–18	waitress	43	4 Boyd
	Y	McNulty William	14–18	laborer	43	4 "
352						
	A	Noyes Edward F	14–18	"	64	Danvers
	B	Oakley Thomas	14–18	foreman	54	68 W Concord
	C	Quinlan George	14–18	retired	66	3 Glenwood
	D	Riley John H	14–18	houseman	68	here
	E	Sandoris Charles	14–18	porter	34	3 Glenwood

Page.	Letter.	Full Name.	Residence, Jan. 1, 1943.	Occupation.	Supposed Age.	Reported Residence, Jan. 1, 1942. Street and Number.

Worcester Street—Continued

	F	Webster Frederick	14–18	laborer	53	56 W Newton
	H	Horgan Hanora—†	17	housewife	58	19 Haverford
	K	Horgan Maurice	17	janitor	61	19 "
	L	Regan Daniel	19	laborer	50	here
	M	*Ross Dora—†	19	housewife	37	485 Shawmut av
	N	*Ross John C	19	mechanic	42	485 "
	O	Underhill Henry	19	laborer	56	here
	P	Allison Emma—†	20	at home	64	"
	R	Bennett Iva—†	20	housekeeper	49	"
	S	Bennett Louis A	20	porter	46	"
	T	Clark Bessie—†	20	teacher	57	
	U	Clark Frank	20	plumber	62	
	V	King Thomas R	20	laborer	37	
	W	Payne Margaret—†	20	waitress	32	
	X	Van Orden Chester	20	waiter	25	
	Y	Van Orden Ellen—†	20	housewife	28	"
	Z	Weston Madelyne—†	20	waitress	26	31 Mass av
353						
	A	Galvin Mary—†	21	housekeper	72	here
	B	*Lee Nellie—†	21	"	70	"
	C	McAuley Grace—†	21	domestic	63	"
	D	*McPhee Pius	21	retired	78	
	E	Murphy John	21	laborer	53	
	F	Robertson Eleanor—†	21	housewife	63	"
	G	Robertson Thomas	21	laborer	56	
	H	Ross William	21	fisherman	60	"
	K	Sheridan Elizabeth—†	21	housekeeper	72	"
	L	Toohey James	21	laborer	51	"
	M	Wells Ina M—†	21	housekeeper	53	"
	N	Wells Jennie A—†	21	"	74	"
	O	Anderson John	22	salesman	46	"
	P	Crossman Herbert E	22	retired	80	
	R	Fitzpatrick Margaret—†	22	housewife	40	"
	S	Fitzpatrick Thomas	22	operator	43	"
	T	Grossman Cora E—†	22	housewife	74	"
	U	Haveland Ethel—†	22	stitcher	37	
	V	Hayes Margaret—†	22	at home	70	"
	W	Kemp Richard	22	laborer	59	28 Worcester
	X	Kemp Sarah—†	22	housewife	54	28 "
	Y	Linehan Theresa—†	22	at home	65	here

Page.	Letter.	Full Name.	Residence, Jan. 1, 1943.	Occupation.	Supposed Age.	Reported Residence, Jan. 1, 1942. Street and Number.

Worcester Street—Continued

Page.	Letter.	Full Name.	Residence, Jan. 1, 1943.	Occupation.	Supposed Age.	Reported Residence, Jan. 1, 1942. Street and Number.
	z	Moylan Alice—†	22	housewife	33	59 Burbank
354						
	A	Moylan Henry	22	clerk	44	59 "
	B	Richmond Edward	22	mechanic	45	here
	C	Richmond Helen—†	22	waitress	40	"
	D	Wetherbee Herbert	22	watchman	67	"
	E	Wetherbee Mary—†	22	housewife	65	"
	F	Carlson John	23	retired	72	
	G	Crouch Martha—†	23	at home	68	
	H	Hickey William J	23	salesman	42	"
	K	Kennedy James C	23	retired	67	
	L	*Kennedy Mary—†	23	housewife	64	"
	M	Schools George	23	retired	82	
	N	Schute Arthur	23	laborer	42	"
	O	Wark John	23	"	58	64 E Newton
	P	Kinch Coral—†	24	housekeeper	59	here
	R	Kinch William	24	laborer	68	"
	S	Wilerbury Alvin	24	salesman	35	"
	T	Wilerbury Harold D	24	"	37	
	U	Wilerbury Irene C—†	24	housewife	35	"
	V	Antaramian Marsoob	25	laborer	60	6 Rutland sq
	W	Barry Clara—†	25	housekeeper	73	here
	X	Burke Phillip	25	retired	74	"
	Y	Dutton Ernest	25	"	75	"
	Z	Kiley James	25	manager	50	"
355						
	A	Laird Charles	25	machinist	41	"
	B	O'Brien Daniel J	25	laborer	51	658 Mass av
	C	Payne George	25	foreman	48	here
	D	Payne Gladys—†	25	housewife	35	"
	E	Shabott Dolor	25	laborer	59	"
	F	Shaw John T	25	"	51	37 Upton
	G	Dolan Harry	26	chauffeur	44	here
	H	Jones Charles	26	carpenter	47	609 Mass av
	K	Murphy Michael	26	laborer	47	614 "
	L	Shellene John	26	mechanic	35	here
	M	*Shellene Mary—†	26	housewife	38	"
	N	Simones Christen	26	machinist	46	"
	O	Kern Carl	27	retired	68	"
	P	Auditore Frank	28	shipfitter	49	Dedham
	R	Brown Katherine—†	28	stitcher	36	45 Rutland

Page.	Letter.	FULL NAME.	Residence, Jan. 1, 1943.	Occupation.	Supposed Age.	Reported Residence, Jan. 1, 1942. Street and Number.

Worcester Street—Continued

	S	Chapman Charles	28	chauffeur	28	18 Northampton
	T	Corey Joseph	28	shipper	25	here
	U	*Corey Rose—†	28	housewife	46	"
	V	Corey Victoria—†	28	stitcher	23	"
	W	Curran Mary—†	28	at home	70	565 Mass av
	X	Deeb Joseph	28	shoeworker	45	here
	Y	Gannon Thomas	28	laborer	48	Swampscott
	Z	Nielsen Henry	28	meatcutter	58	148 W Canton
356						
	A	*Niks Domenic	28	chef	60	81 Worcester
	B	Parkinson Nora—†	28	at home	68	here
	C	*Langwith Frances—†	29	housewife	47	37 Worcester
	D	Langwith William	29	engineer	40	37 "
	E	Sales Mary—†	29	housekeeper	66	1675 Wash'n
	F	Sales William	29	laborer	32	1675 "
	G	Quinn Margaret—†	29	clerk	30	here
	H	Quinn Mary—†	29	housekeeper	66	"
	K	Quinn Thomas	29	laborer	46	"
	L	Downey Margaret—†	29	housekeeper	45	"
	M	White Evelyn A—†	30	housewife	61	"
	N	White John A	30	baker	44	
	O	Wadeoski Joseph	30	U S A	28	
	P	Wadeoski William	30	"	26	
	R	*Puccino Mary—†	30	housekeeper	29	"
	S	Wadeoski Mary—†	30	housewife	54	"
	T	Wadeoski Peter	30	steelworker	57	"
	U	Gabis Anthony	30	laborer	27	Newton
	V	Gabis Dorothy—†	30	housewife	26	"
	X	Costello Elizabeth—†	31	domestic	55	here
	Y	Daly Charles	31	laborer	60	"
	Z	Hall Albert W	31	"	60	"
357						
	A	Keane Margaret N—†	31	housekeeper	59	"
	B	Kirby Mary—†	31	"	67	"
	C	Mahoney Dennis	31	shipper	55	
	D	McCann James	31	retired	60	
	E	McGonagle Arthur	31	salesman	55	"
	F	McGonagle Michael	31	retired	90	
	G	*Page Martha—†	31	housekeeper	66	"
	H	Parechanian Manogg H	31	proprietor	58	435 Shawmut av
	K	Rauch Marion—†	31	housekeeper	66	here

Page.	Letter.	Full Name.	Residence, Jan. 1, 1943.	Occupation.	Supposed Age.	Reported Residence, Jan. 1, 1942. Street and Number.

Worcester Street—Continued

Page.	Letter.	Full Name.	Residence, Jan. 1, 1943.	Occupation.	Supposed Age.	Reported Residence, Jan. 1, 1942. Street and Number.
	L	Scheibe Mary—†	31	housekeeper	66	here
	M	Sinclair Thomas	31	laborer	40	555 Mass av
	N	Turner Harold	31	clerk	45	Mansfield
	O	Branch Edward	32	barber	27	419 Mass av
	P	Branch Leonora—†	32	housewife	24	419 "
	R	Burt Florence—†	32	domestic	40	419 "
	S	Cross Harry	32	retired	65	419 "
	T	Ford Richmond	32	musician	37	396 Northampton
	U	Johnson Minnie—†	32	seamstress	39	419 Mass av
	V	Lee Julia—†	32	at home	86	419 "
	W	Woods Minnie—†	32	"	60	419 "
	X	Abbott John	33	musician	25	37 Worcester
	Y	Curley Francis J	33	watchman	59	49 Rutland
	Z	Flynn Henry	33	painter	38	here
358						
	A	Manning Joseph	33	chauffeur	40	"
	B	*Ogonik Catherine—†	33	housewife	52	"
	C	Ogonik Frances—†	33	clerk	26	"
	D	*Ogonik John	33	proprietor	52	"
	E	Ogonik John	33	U S A	23	
	F	Ogonik Stella—†	33	teacher	28	
	G	Roche Albert	33	laborer	60	
	H	Whitney Fay E—†	33	housewife	51	"
	K	Whitney Harold E	33	laborer	39	
	L	Wilhere John	33	butcher	60	
	M	Wylie Edythe—†	33	domestic	55	"
	N	Dutton Emma—†	34	housekeeper	70	"
	O	Dutton William	34	laborer	49	"
	P	Birmingham Theresa—†	35	housekeeper	66	37 Rutland sq
	R	Brock Mary A—†	35	housewife	60	here
	S	*Brock Nicholas	35	painter	60	"
	T	Camberg Herbert	35	laborer	33	"
	U	Driscoll William	35	"	30	22 Wyoming
	V	Higgins Frederick R	35	salesman	55	435 Shawmut av
	W	*Kennedy Charles J	35	retired	67	here
	X	McCarthy John	35	laborer	35	5 Lovedeed ct
	Y	*McCarthy Nora—†	35	housekeeper	68	5 "
	Z	Silver Emanuel	35	chauffeur	40	here
359						
	A	Temple Alvin L	35	machinist	32	650 Mass av
	B	Wiley Frederick	35	laborer	45	100 W Springfield

Page.	Letter.	Full Name.	Residence, Jan. 1, 1943.	Occupation.	Supposed Age.	Reported Residence, Jan. 1, 1942. Street and Number.

Worcester Street—Continued

Page.	Letter.	Full Name.	Residence, Jan. 1, 1943.	Occupation.	Supposed Age.	Reported Residence, Jan. 1, 1942. Street and Number.
	C	Carroll Edith—†	36	seamstress	61	here
	D	Carroll Thomas	36	bartender	40	"
	E	Kohler Carl	36	"	63	"
	F	McIlwain Florence G—†	36	laundress	46	69 Worcester
	G	O'Hara James	36	retired	66	here
	H	Prince Katherine—†	36	housekeeper	59	"
	K	Toomey Frank	36	porter	53	"
	M	Carter Augustus	38	U S A	42	
	N	Carter Rowena—†	38	housewife	38	"
	O	Dickerson Clarence	38	machinist	43	"
	P	Henderson James	38	welder	37	New York
	R	Webzuish Louis	38	retired	72	here
	S	Ferguson Trudy—†	39	housekeeper	44	540 Mass av
	T	Johnson Ina—†	39	"	32	here
	U	McLeod Alice—†	39	housewife	38	91 Brookside av
	V	McLeod John	39	laborer	50	91 "
	W	Mollet Charles	39	"	60	8 Linden
	X	Sweeney Joseph	39	retired	64	here
	Y	Clark William	40	laborer	33	198 W Springfield
	Z	Johnson Harrison	40	"	36	Rhode Island
360						
	A	Reeves Moses	40	chef	45	3 Hubert
	B	Reid Lucy K—†	40	housekeeper	66	here
	C	Nicholas Matilda—†	41	"	45	"
	D	Hamway Mabel—†	41	shoeworker	41	Waltham
	E	DeBonis Daniel	41	machinist	50	627 Tremont
	F	Hill Harriet—†	41	housekeeper	42	627 "
	G	Kales Emily—†	41	housewife	40	539 Shawmut av
	H	Kales Harry	41	chef	47	539 "
	K	Lucireno Salvatore	42	"	44	here
	L	Monsour John	42	shoeworker	48	"
	M	Quinlan Frederick	42	seaman	60	3 Yeoman pl
	N	Thompson Howard	42	laborer	37	86 Waltham
	O	Wall Linda—†	42	clerk	24	here
	P	Wall Thomas	42	welder	27	"
	R	Yared George	42	machinist	21	"
	S	Yared Joseph	42	laborer	59	
	T	Yarad Linda—†	42	clerk	24	
	U	Yared Louis	42	U S A	23	
	V	Yared Nigmie—†	42	housewife	48	"
	W	Brasher George H	43	retired	72	1475 Wash'n

Page.	Letter.	Full Name.	Residence, Jan. 1, 1943.	Occupation.	Supposed Age.	Reported Residence, Jan. 1, 1942. Street and Number.

Worcester Street—Continued

	X	Cronan Josephine—†	43	housekeeper	53	here
	Y	Desmond Daniel B	43	laborer	40	17 Davis
	Z	Granger John J	43	retired	66	94 W Springfield
361						
	A	Granger Margaret—†	43	housekeeper	71	664 Mass av
	B	Greenhalgh Richard	43	laborer	50	here
	C	Lahage Habeeb	43	"	48	"
	D	Lahage Latife—†	43	housewife	39	"
	E	McCurdy John	43	laborer	52	778 Broadway
	F	McCurdy Margaret—†	43	housewife	46	778 "
	G	Sedgley Margaret—†	43	cook	45	Maine
	H	Aklund Holger	44	laborer	30	46 Dix
	K	Anderson Anna—†	44	housewife	69	here
	L	Applestam Charles	44	carpenter	57	"
	M	Buswell Barbara—†	44	housewife	30	37 Worcester
	N	Buswell William	44	U S A	32	37 "
	O	Commer Nellie—†	44	at home	64	here
	P	Concannon Joseph	44	laborer	51	"
	R	Engstrom Anna—†	44	at home	67	"
	S	Gamble James	44	laborer	57	
	T	Graham Joseph	44	"	56	
	U	Hally Eledia—†	44	at home	67	
	V	Perlson Anna L—†	44	"	64	"
	W	Swarplia Gertrude—†	44	"	73	17 Rutland sq
	X	*Urtia Stanley	44	laborer	48	40 Union pk
	Y	Albison Susan J—†	45	housewife	57	here
	Z	Albison Thomas	45	laborer	60	"
362						
	A	Berni Eleanor—†	45	clerk	26	31 Rutland
	B	Buckley Cornelius T	45	retired	61	here
	C	*Campbell Catherine—†	45	waitress	32	Cambridge
	D	Champ Ida—†	45	housekeeper	61	154 W Canton
	E	DeCoste Agnes—†	45	laundress	32	here
	F	DeCoste Margaret—†	45	"	20	Vermont
	G	Hartnett Charlotte—†	45	housekeeper	68	here
	H	Martin Peter	45	bartender	42	Lawrence
	K	Moore Catherine—†	45	clerk	29	14 Worcester sq
	L	Royal John T	45	retired	72	here
	M	Tuohy Alice—†	45	domestic	36	Salem
	N	Turco Martha—†	45	housekeeper	58	here
	O	Wall John S	45	laborer	54	"

Page.	Letter.	Full Name.	Residence, Jan. 1, 1943.	Occupation.	Supposed Age.	Reported Residence, Jan. 1, 1942. Street and Number.

Worcester Street—Continued

Page.	Letter.	Full Name.	Residence, Jan. 1, 1943.	Occupation.	Supposed Age.	Reported Residence, Jan. 1, 1942. Street and Number.
	P	Fagan Mary M—†	46	at home	71	here
	R	Gallagher Mary—†	46	"	66	"
	S	Gillespie Andrew	46	laborer	60	"
	T	*Kennedy Angus	46	roofer	38	37 Worcester
	U	Mannix Frances G—†	46	housewife	55	170 W Canton
	V	Mannix James E	46	salesman	59	170 "
	W	Wheeler Harry F	46	laborer	60	here
	X	Zion Selem	46	salesman	50	"
	Y	Zion Sophie—†	46	housewife	40	"
	Z	*Christi Peter	47	chef	54	"
363						
	A	Delory Michael	47	laborer	60	Saugus
	B	Hildreth Willard	47	U S N	36	here
	D	Deane Thomas	47	retired	67	"
	E	Killen Michael	47	laborer	42	"
	F	Knight Dixie—†	47	waitress	23	66 W Concord
	C	Lang Doris—†	47	"	23	Wellesley
	G	McDonald Harold	47	manager	50	here
	H	McManus Dennis	47	laborer	56	"
	K	Morse Julia—†	47	housekeeper	57	"
	L	Parks John W	47	retired	71	"
	M	Parks William H	47	clerk	33	"
	N	Ross Virginia G—†	47	"	47	"
	O	Steves Audrey—†	47	waitress	20	275 W Fourth
	P	Turner Lawrence	47	retired	69	here
	R	Anderson Carl	48	chauffeur	39	"
	S	Arensberg Harry	48	welder	41	"
	T	Baker Louise M—†	48	housewife	35	"
	U	Baker Ralph E	48	painter	49	
	V	Griffin Corbin C	48	"	57	
	W	Griffin Nellie M—†	48	housewife	54	"
	X	Hutchings Raymond C	48	U S A	34	"
	Y	Lewis William H	48	retired	72	
	Z	McCarty John J	48	inspector	64	"
364						
	A	McCarty Margaret—†	48	housewife	66	"
	B	McGuire Mary—†	48	saleswoman	62	"
	C	Parks John J	48	chauffeur	54	"
	D	*Wilson Edward J	48	retired	64	"
	F	Brow Joseph	50	mechanic	56	"
	G	Burke Thomas	50	machinist	32	"

Page.	Letter.	Full Name.	Residence, Jan. 1, 1943.	Occupation.	Supposed Age.	Reported Residence, Jan. 1, 1942. Street and Number.

Worcester Street—Continued

	H	Cameron Joseph	50	carpenter	54	here
	K	Cameron Mary—†	50	housewife	48	"
	L	Cichanowicz John	50	chef	48	"
	M	Daley Daniel	50	welder	51	"
	N	Driscoll Lawrence	50	operator	54	20 Dartmouth
	O	Fitzpatrick Herbert	50	laborer	40	here
	P	Kulick Joseph	50	cutter	46	"
	R	Lisay Florence—†	50	stitcher	52	"
	S	Pettipass Mary—†	50	domestic	48	"
	T	Strug Mary—†	50	housekeeper	45	"
	U	West Joseph	50	salesman	48	"
	V	Cruickshank Peter	51	foreman	55	
	W	Doherty Agnes—†	51	housekeeper	44	"
	X	Domit Anna—†	51	domestic	31	"
	Y	Feeney Martin	51	laborer	58	
	Z	Fitzgerald George	51	watchman	60	"
365						
	A	Lessier Edward	51	laborer	35	N Hampshire
	B	Little William	51	U S A	45	here
	C	MacDonald Alexander	51	"	40	"
	D	Morsky Stacia—†	51	nurse	29	"
	E	O'Neil James H	51	engineer	52	
	F	Peraria Jose J	51	fisherman	55	"
	G	Purcell Edmund	51	agent	60	"
	H	Boudreau Jeremiah	52	laborer	53	Somerville
	K	Cooney Michael	52	retired	75	here
	L	Malloy Stephen	52	meatcutter	38	"
	M	Maroon Elizabeth—†	52	stitcher	30	"
	N	*Maroon Helen—†	52	housekeeper	48	"
	O	Walsh Joseph	52	laborer	57	"
	P	Weeks Anna—†	52	at home	62	Rhode Island
	R	Johnson Elsie—†	53	domestic	49	here
	S	Johnson Louise—†	53	"	44	"
	T	Magnuson Albert G	53	retired	68	"
	U	Nuzzo Eva—†	53	domestic	36	"
	V	Poleo Theresa C—†	53	waitress	29	912 E B'way
	W	Pollard George	53	retired	78	here
	X	Pollard Inez M—†	53	housewife	74	"
	Y	Treanor Ethel B—†	53	"	57	54 Montgomery
	Z	Treanor James	53	clerk	59	54 "

Page.	Letter.	Full Name.	Residence, Jan. 1, 1943.	Occupation.	Supposed Age.	Reported Residence, Jan. 1, 1942. Street and Number.
366		**Worcester Street**—Continued				
	A	Feeley Delle—†	54	housekeeper	70	here
	B	Feeley Helen—†	54	at home	60	“
	C	Amory Barbara—†	55	waitress	28	“
	D	Barton Everett	55	laborer	40	561 Mass av
	E	Barton Susan—†	55	housewife	37	561 “
	F	Brown Helena W—†	55	clerk	23	here
	G	Brown Virgie—†	55	U S A	21	“
	H	Collin Edwin	55	laborer	46	928 Albany
	K	Doyle Margaret—†	55	housekeeper	70	here
	L	Forin Isabelle—†	55	housewife	63	“
	M	Forin John	55	laborer	64	“
	N	Jolly Albert	55	“	40	New York
	O	McBane Evelyn—†	55	waitress	25	154 W Newton
	P	*Pontillo Rocco	55	baker	48	here
	R	Rusicato Victor	55	clerk	29	Cambridge
	S	Shine John	55	painter	40	89 Worcester
	T	Shine Olga—†	55	housewife	25	89 “
	U	Wojtanski Henry	55	U S A	24	here
	V	Wojtanski Katherine—†	55	housewife	44	“
	W	Wojtanski Walter	55	laborer	47	“
	X	Wojtanski Wladyslawa—†	55	clerk	21	
	Y	Kelley John J	56	bartender	45	“
	Z	Kelley Mary—†	56	housewife	52	“
367						
	A	Hare Clarence F	56	retired	84	
	D	McDonald Marie—†	56	matron	56	
	E	Dinagan Barbara—†	56	“	52	..
	F	Richards James	56	baker	54	
	G	Chick Jennie—†	56	saleswoman	54	“
	H	Webster Ruth—†	56	at home	58	“
	K	Tillinghast Ruby—†	56	librarian	59	Connecticut
	L	*Bissett John	57	shipper	72	here
	M	Cassidy Clyde	57	“	61	Vermont
	N	Cohen Pearl—†	57	milliner	40	27 Worcester sq
	O	Healey Lena—†	57	housekeeper	72	here
	P	Heath Josephine—†	57	“	49	“
	R	Hunter Elizabeth—†	57	“	61	“
	S	Kimball Catherine—†	57	waitress	29	69 Braintree
	T	Kirby John	57	laborer	55	here

Page.	Letter.	Full Name.	Residence, Jan. 1, 1943.	Occupation.	Supposed Age.	Reported Residence, Jan. 1, 1942. Street and Number.

Worcester Street—Continued

Page.	Letter.	Full Name.	Residence, Jan. 1, 1943.	Occupation.	Supposed Age.	Reported Residence, Jan. 1, 1942. Street and Number.
	U	Miller Gertrude—†	57	housekeeper	66	here
	V	Nye Beatrice—†	57	nurse	32	400 Walk Hill
	W	O'Dwyer Jeremiah	57	laborer	60	here
	X	Walker Albert	57	"	57	560 Shawmut av
	Y	Ayles Joseph	59	clerk	43	here
	Z	Boyle Phillip	59	laborer	53	"
368						
	A	Brown Victor	59	chef	50	9 Eaton
	B	Davis Phillip	59	laborer	54	here
	C*	Davis Susie—†	59	housewife	57	"
	D	Duffy Edward	59	retired	75	"
	E	Eldridge Eva—†	59	housewife	45	27 Worcester sq
	F	Eldridge Harvey	59	retired	69	27 "
	G	Goodwin Frances—†	59	housekeeper	63	here
	H	Kenaman Carl	59	laborer	40	"
	K	Livingstone Jacob	59	retired	73	"
	L	Livingstone Mary—†	59	housewife	69	"
	M	Malard Thomas	59	carpenter	57	"
	N*	McKillopp Beatrice—†	59	waitress	27	"
	O	Boardman Mary—†	61	housekeeper	69	409 Marlboro
	P	Brown Charlotte E—†	61	hairdresser	28	Abington
	R	Donahue Agnes F—†	61	nurse	25	Taunton
	S	Doughi Mary—†	61	"	23	818 Harris'n av
	T	Goreynski Mary B—†	61	"	24	818 "
	U	Hatch Grace E—†	61	clerk	53	Medford
	V	Holt Florence S—†	61	housekeeper	62	Gardner
	W	Holt Louise H—†	61	clerk	32	11 E Newton
	X	Hunting Ada M—†	61	housekeeper	72	Gardner
	Y	Innocenti Mary E—†	61	nurse	21	818 Harris'n av
	Z	Lawrence Ruth B—†	61	"	22	Taunton
369						
	A	Wilcox Mabel P—†	61	housekeeper	60	36 W Newton
	B	Winston Murray R	61	physician	31	Brookline
	C	Costello Mary—†	63	housekeeper	58	here
	D	Gast Otto	63	retired	72	"
	E	Nelson Elizabeth—†	63	housekeeper	69	"
	F	Simons Samuel	63	retired	69	"
	G	Corcoran Lawrence	65	"	72	
	H*	Dawe Edgar	65	laborer	59	
	K	Dawe Grace M—†	65	housewife	62	"
	L	Gerry Frederick	65	retired	68	

Page.	Letter.	Full Name.	Residence, Jan. 1, 1943.	Occupation.	Supposed Age.	Reported Residence, Jan. 1, 1942. Street and Number.

Worcester Street—Continued

	M	*Peterson Sophie—†	65	housekeeper	72	here
	N	Rizzo Theodore	65	shoeworker	65	49 Worcester
	O	White Helen—†	65	domestic	40	16 Worcester sq
	R	Wright Clarence	65	retired	65	49 Worcester
	P	Wrin Charles H	65	laborer	42	here
	S	Austin Annie—†	67	housekeeper	68	"
	T	*Curhane Manuel	67	barber	62	"
	U	Heavey Theresa—†	67	housekeeper	68	4 Cortes
	V	McDougall Archibald	67	chauffeur	46	here
	W	McDougall Mary A—†	67	housekeeper	61	"
	X	Peterson Janen	67	musician	58	"
	Y	Torr Joseph M	67	retired	76	
	Z	Vellela Joseph	67	barber	60	
370						
	A	Williams Frederick	67	clerk	51	"
	B	Cook Gertrude—†	69	housekeeper	55	Maine
	C	Cook Irving	69	U S A	20	"
	D	Daney Clarice—†	69	housekeeper	29	"
	E	Demus Alice—†	69	housewife	35	61 Worcester
	F	Demus William	69	chef	50	61 "
	G	Edmond Mary—†	69	housekeeper	50	80 "
	H	Flemming Alexander	69	retired	65	65 "
	K	Garvey Thomas	69	laborer	50	462 Shawmut av
	L	Guider Sarah—†	69	housekeeper	70	735 Tremont
	M	Hammer Charles	69	janitor	42	65 Worcester
	N	Nera Kay	69	laborer	41	Cambridge
	O	Nye Dorothy—†	69	housewife	27	N Hampshire
	P	Nye Walter	69	U S N	26	"
	R	Stephens Everett	69	laborer	45	Maine
	S	Zyboski Christine—†	69	clerk	33	8 Rutland
	T	Brophy Elizabeth A—†	71	housekeeper	64	4 Emerald
	U	DeRose Irene—†	71	housewife	42	19 Rexford
	V	DeRose Joseph	71	chef	43	Plymouth
	W	Levy Louise—†	71	housekeeper	72	here
	X	McLean James	71	porter	67	21 Dwight
	Y	Reynolds William E	71	retired	74	470 Mass av
	Z	Rockteschel Oscar H	71	"	62	here
371						
	A	Thiers Ellen—†	71	housekeeper	69	"
	B	Abilio Anthony	73	U S A	39	"
	C	Buck Frederick	73	retired	63	

Page.	Letter.	Full Name.	Residence, Jan. 1, 1943.	Occupation.	Supposed Age.	Reported Residence, Jan. 1, 1942. Street and Number.

Worcester Street—Continued

	D	Buck George	73	U S N	32	here
	E	Buck Richard	73	student	22	"
	F	Busconi Anthony	73	clerk	28	"
	G	Busconi Mary—†	73	housewife	28	"
	H	*David Alfred	73	laborer	45	100 Blue Hill av
	K	Edwards John	73	"	56	here
	L	*Nagle William	73	retired	63	"
	M	*Rogers Anthony	73	chef	41	"
	N	Smith John J	73	manager	60	"
	O	*Thompson George	73	agent	49	
	P	Wilder Robert	73	cashier	43	"
	R	Williams Joseph	73	nurse	31	32 Old Harbor
	S	Anderson Margaret—†	75	housekeeper	68	here
	T	Donnelly Mary—†	75	waitress	30	154 Homes av
	U	Durval Alice—†	75	housekeeper	40	Hyannis
	V	*Frankowitz Anna—†	75	housewife	52	here
	W	*Frankowitz Daniel	75	chef	46	"
	X	McCormack James	75	laborer	60	Lexington
	Y	Worterman Stanley	75	"	26	here
	Z	Adler Charles	77	chauffeur	27	"
372						
	A	Adler Mary—†	77	housewife	27	"
	B	Costello Angelo	77	laborer	41	
	C	Costello Esther—†	77	housewife	39	"
	D	Gates Mary E—†	77	housekeeper	70	"
	E	Smith Daniel E	77	attorney	50	"
	F	Smith Irene—†	77	housewife	48	"
	G	Thorp Jane C—†	77	"	65	"
	H	Thorp William A	77	retired	67	
	K	Wallace Charles B	77	"	70	
	L	Aceves Arthur	79	chef	50	
	M	Allen Albert	79	painter	48	
	N	Anderson Bertha—†	79	housekeeper	48	"
	O	Harkins George	79	retired	72	"
	P	Keely Mary—†	79	housekeeper	65	"
	R	Keenan Nadine—†	79	housewife	20	Somerville
	S	Keenan William	79	laborer	25	"
	T	LaFauci Antonio	79	chef	50	here
	U	Lynch Frank	79	laborer	60	"
	V	Olsen Charlotte—†	79	housekeeper	72	41 Worcester
	W	Stone Charlotte—†	79	stitcher	40	N Hampshire

Page.	Letter.	Full Name.	Residence, Jan. 1, 1943.	Occupation.	Supposed Age.	Reported Residence, Jan. 1, 1942. Street and Number.

Worcester Street—Continued

	X	Vinal Willard	79	laborer	35	here
	Y	White Thomas	79	machinist	48	"
373						
	A	Chambers Elizabeth—†	80	housekeeper	53	"
	B	Donovan Nellie—†	80	at home	66	66 Rutland
	C	Foley Henry F	80	salesman	57	here
	D	Ford Elden A	80	laborer	42	Georgia
	E	Hamilton Mary E—†	80	domestic	58	Florida
	F	Hill Emily—†	80	seamstress	53	101 Warren
	G	Krieger Gustave	80	operator	62	here
	H	Mayo Daniel	80	"	64	"
	K	*Olive Ella S—†	80	at home	64	Canada
	L	Riley Gertrude—†	80	laundress	44	Cambridge
	M	Williams Elizabeth—†	80	at home	76	here
	N	Cheever Ralph	81	laborer	56	"
	O	Hickey Mary—†	81	stitcher	50	"
	P	Jones Earl	81	laborer	38	2 Sylvia
	R	Neville George	81	shoeworker	68	696 Tremont
	S	Nickerson Richard	81	chef	45	Chelsea
	T	Rhodenizer John	81	laborer	58	here
	U	Shulda Alma—†	81	housewife	52	Texas
	V	Shulda Frank M	81	laborer	55	98 Dartmouth
	W	Whittemore Arthur	81	retired	73	100 W Concord
	X	Ackles Helena—†	82	housewife	57	here
	Y	*Ackles John D	82	carpenter	56	"
	Z	Bertoldi Anthonio	82	laborer	59	"
374						
	A	Cobleigh Herbert	82	shipper	65	
	B	Nicholas Milton	82	chef	49	
	C	Mirakian Armon H	83	tailor	58	
	D	Mirakian Marjorie A—†	83	housewife	50	"
	E	Hopping Laura C—†	83	clerk	24	"
	F	*Lowery Cordelia L—†	83	housekeeper	78	23 Irving
	G	MacDonald Albina—†	83	"	77	here
	H	Goldthwait Austin H	83	retired	79	9 Col sq
	K	Goldthwait Mabel G—†	83	housewife	58	9 "
	L	Porter Annie—†	83	housekeeper	75	here
	M	Swift Ellen—†	83	housewife	49	"
	N	Swift Otis	83	laborer	65	"
	O	Connelly Mary—†	83	housekeeper	62	"
	P	Vinton John	83	laborer	48	"

Page.	Letter.	Full Name.	Residence, Jan. 1, 1943.	Occupation.	Supposed Age.	Reported Residence, Jan. 1, 1942. Street and Number.

Worcester Street—Continued

	R	Bagrowski Eldona—†	84	packer	22	61 Worcester
	S	Benoit Adrian D	84	mechanic	39	178 W Springfield
	T	Chausse Exilda I—†	84	housekeeper	48	1658 Wash'n
	U	Dolan Helen—†	84	housewife	28	Brookline
	V	Dolan Terry J	84	retired	70	613 Mass av
	W	Elsmer Ella—†	84	at home	82	7 Greenville
	X	Inenberg Bernard	84	salesman	52	519 Mass av
	Y	Morrissey Robert	84	retired	71	555 "
	Z	Murray Bernard	84	clerk	49	1658 Wash'n
375						
	A	Shore Evelyn—†	84	housewife	20	Iowa
	B	Shore John	84	laborer	32	"
	C	Walsh Arthur H	84	"	45	144 W Concord
	D	LaForge Leona—†	85	housewife	40	594 Tremont
	E	LaForge Wallace R	85	painter	59	594 "
	F	*Brennan Mary—†	85	housekeeper	67	56 Bromley
	G	McDermott Nora—†	85	"	39	here
	H	Clark Zetta C—†	85	"	67	"
	K	Chapman Harry	85	chauffeur	61	"
	L	Cole Anna—†	85	housekeeper	45	89 W Newton
	M	Brennan William	85	machinist	33	938 Parker
	N	Reynolds Lawrence	85	painter	54	Connecticut
	O	Williams Agnes—†	85	housekeeper	31	Brookline
	P	Hanley John	85	laborer	44	608 Mass av
	R	Hanley Mary—†	85	housewife	37	608 "
	S	Bokigian George	86	salesman	42	480 Shawmut av
	T	Coe Harry M	86	"	55	New York
	U	Coe Pearl—†	86	housewife	51	"
	V	Corbett Julia—†	86	at home	65	19 Concord sq
	W	Dwyer Anna B—†	86	"	63	here
	X	Hills Richard	86	mechanic	36	Newburyport
	Y	Holyoke Edward	86	waiter	41	here
	Z	Leary John P	86	porter	56	27 Parkman
376						
	A	Martin Alma—†	86	housekeeper	68	here
	B	McGuire Marie—†	86	waitress	25	Cambridge
	C	Packard Georginia—†	86	housewife	42	19 Concord sq
	D	Packard William	86	welder	47	19 "
	E	Peppard Jean—†	86	nurse	31	here
	F	Sullivan Lawrence E	86	laborer	35	Newton

Page.	Letter.	Full Name.	Residence, Jan. 1, 1943.	Occupation.	Supposed Age.	Reported Residence, Jan. 1, 1942. Street and Number.

Worcester Street—Continued

Page.	Letter.	Full Name.	Residence, Jan. 1, 1943.	Occupation.	Supposed Age.	Reported Residence, Jan. 1, 1942. Street and Number.
	G	White Eva M—†	87	housekeeper	58	here
	H	Taylor Gaynor	87	housewife	49	"
	K	Taylor Ralph	87	laborer	52	"
	L	Bullock Savina—†	87	housekeeper	42	70 Rutland sq
	M	Garcia Anna—†	87	domestic	20	70 "
	N	Stupple William	87	laborer	38	N Hampshire
	O	Graves Nellie—†	87	housekeeper	72	here
	P	Lord Catherine J—†	87	housewife	33	"
	R	Lord Harvey J	87	laborer	41	"
	S	*McLean Colen	87	retired	73	
	T	Webber Harriett W—†	87	housekeeper	46	"
	U	*Snyder George	87	laborer	58	"
	V	Gayton Arnold E	88	clerk	20	
	W	Gayton Chester E	88	U S A	34	
	X	Gayton David G	88	retired	67	
	Y	Gayton Ella A—†	88	housewife	61	"
	Z	Gayton Harold	88	U S A	28	
377	A	Sidorchuk Margaret—†	88	housewife	33	Rhode Island
	B	Sidorchuk Peter	88	chef	34	"
	C	Soule Maude—†	88	domestic	41	538 Mass av
	D	Caprarello Roeko	88	longshoreman	48	538 "
	E	Gerard Harold	88	painter	42	515 "
	F	Frances Catherine—†	88	housewife	45	New York
	G	Frances Joseph	88	painter	46	"
	H	Adams John W	88	U S A	21	Georgia
	K	Adams Mary E—†	88	housewife	45	"
	L	Adams William	88	welder	59	"
	M	Rosenberg Israel	88	rabbi	60	Medway
	N	Joyce Inez—†	88	seamstress	57	here
	O	Barkas Stephen	89	chauffeur	24	"
	P	Callahan Robert	89	retired	70	"
	R	Daly Russell	89	clerk	21	
	S	Fillmore Annette—†	89	housekeeper	48	"
	T	Hatfield William	89	retired	68	"
	U	Robinson Ethel—†	89	housekeeper	60	"
	V	Williams John	89	chef	50	"
	W	Anderson Elizabeth—†	90	at home	74	
	X	Bowes William F	90	engineer	55	"
	Y	Boyd Joseph A	90	retired	72	"

Page.	Letter.	Full Name.	Residence, Jan. 1, 1943.	Occupation.	Supposed Age.	Reported Residence, Jan. 1, 1942. Street and Number.

Worcester Street—Continued

Page.	Letter.	Full Name.	Residence, Jan. 1, 1943.	Occupation.	Supposed Age.	Reported Residence, Jan. 1, 1942. Street and Number.
	z	Collins Katherine—†	90	nurse	55	here
378						
	A	Crawshaw Benjamin	90	electrician	64	"
	B	Gough Byron	90	retired	75	
	C	Mullvery Helen—†	90	at home	61	
	D	Murphy Arthur	90	clerk	45	
	E	Powell Herbert	90	carpenter	68	"
	F	Sherar Elizabeth K—†	90	housekeeper	66	"
	G	Sutton Ethel—†	90	nurse	55	"
	H	Ward John	90	painter	65	
	K	Antill Florence C—†	91	housekeeper	55	"
	L	DeLong Garfield	91	retired	66	"
	M	Kyes Edwin C	91	butcher	53	
	N	Lloyd Elizabeth—†	91	housewife	34	"
	O	Lloyd Louis A	91	electrician	35	"
	P	McLaughlin Mary—†	91	housewife	40	"
	R	McLaughlin Stephen	91	laborer	45	"
	S	Tierney Thomas	91	"	42	2 Miles
	T	Acheson James	92	manager	59	here
	U	Foley John J	92	electrician	42	"
	V	Hendrickson Cyr	92	porter	57	"
	W	Hendrickson Ruth—†	92	housewife	56	"
	X	Kirby John	92	laborer	62	238 K
	Y	Shepard John	92	painter	52	562 Mass av
	Z	Upton Frederick	92	retired	62	here
379						
	A	Walker Mattie—†	92	housekeeper	64	"
	B	White James	92	bartender	35	Lowell
	C	Conway Amy—†	94	at home	68	here
	D	Dorr Annie J—†	94	"	70	"
	E	Edwards Louis	94	ironworker	72	"
	F	Edwards Mary—†	94	housewife	71	"
	G	Flanagan Margaret—†	94	at home	67	Malden
	H	Katz Sofie—†	94	"	65	24 Worcester sq
	K	Lyons Thomas	94	painter	61	here
	L	Markle Margaret—†	94	domestic	61	36 Alicia rd
	M	Mayers Jacob	94	salesman	83	here
	N	Poto Domenic	94	clerk	47	699 Mass av
	O	Ricker Mary E—†	94	at home	64	here
	P	Roncoe Gladys—†	94	seamstress	56	24 Rockville pk

4

5

6

7

8

9

10

11

12

1

1

1

Ward 9—Precinct 4

CITY OF BOSTON

LIST OF RESIDENTS
20 YEARS OF AGE AND OVER

(NON-CITIZENS INDICATED BY ASTERISK)
(FEMALES INDICATED BY DAGGER)

AS OF

JANUARY 1, 1943

JOSEPH F. TIMILTY, *Chairman*
FREDERIC E. DOWLING, *Secretary*
WILLIAM A. MOTLEY, JR.
FRANCIS B. McKINNEY
EVERETT R. PROUT
Listing Board.

CITY OF BOSTON PRINTING DEPARTMENT

Page.	Letter.	FULL NAME.	Residence, Jan. 1, 1943.	Occupation.	Supposed Age.	Reported Residence, Jan. 1, 1942. Street and Number.
400						

Camden Street

	A	Hunt Alexander	193	porter	24	here
	B	Hunt Lelia—†	193	housewife	54	"
	C	Hunt Richard B	193	porter	64	"
	D	Goudy Bertha—†	193	housewife	55	"
	E	Goudy Richard	193	laborer	50	
	F	Redmond Nathaniel A	193	"	26	
	G	Johnson Eugene	193	waiter	49	"
	H	Tomlinson Charles	193	laborer	30	Georgia
	K	Walker Bruce	193	rigger	24	here
	L	Walker Theopa—†	193	housewife	64	"
	M	Harris Mary—†	195	"	47	"
	N	Lewis Violet—†	195	"	20	223 W Springfield
	O	Lewis Walter R	195	shipper	25	here
	P	Lewis William S	195	musician	28	"
	R	Foss Ida—†	195	presser	60	"
	S	Lyle Susan B—†	195	housewife	35	"
	T	Lattimer Minnie—†	195	presser	35	
	U	Lattimer Nellie—†	195	domestic	58	"
	V	Michaels Desdemona—†	195	at home	85	"
	W	Allston Eldean—†	203	housewife	30	403 Mass av
	X	Allston Lucius	203	chef	35	403 "
	Y	Cooper Jennings	203	shipper	39	New York
	Z	Cooper Mary—†	203	domestic	37	"
401						
	A	Hartower Jennie—†	203	"	35	"
	B	Douglas Marguerite—†	203	housewife	21	1 Singleton
	C	Douglas Osmond	203	laborer	39	1 "
	D	Norwood Edward	205	molder	26	311 Hancock
	E	Norwood Flonda—†	205	housewife	24	311 "
	F	House Evelyn—†	205	laundress	35	23 Wellington
	G	Lewis Roscoe	205	laborer	33	N Hampshire
	H	Stewart Carolyn—†	205	domestic	40	58 Humboldt av
	K	Taylor Robert	205	retired	67	here
	L	Evans James	205	laborer	32	Newton

Columbus Avenue

	M	Colston Charles	561	welder	49	here
	N	Hester Robert	561	cook	45	"
	O	Johnson Lucy—†	561	waitress	26	"

Page.	Letter.	FULL NAME.	Residence, Jan. 1, 1943.	Occupation.	Supposed Age.	Reported Residence, Jan. 1, 1942. Street and Number.

Columbus Avenue—Continued

	P	McKenzie Anna R—†	561	housewife	54	here
	R	Moore James	561	mechanic	78	"
	S	Bert Dorothy—†	561	stitcher	32	"
	T	Davis Dorothy—†	561	domestic	32	Newton
	U	Garrett Mohala—†	561	stitcher	40	Florida
	V	Lewis Maude E—†	561	operator	21	"
	W	Lewis Walter A	561	"	25	"
	X	Lewis James E	561	janitor	65	here
	Y	Lewis Lillian—†	561	housewife	65	"
	Z	Floyd Rosa—†	561	cook	34	765 Tremont
402						
	A	Smith Alice B—†	561	housewife	36	415 Col av
	B	Smith Oscar	561	laborer	47	Mississippi
	C	Bowens Walter	561	"	27	Newton
	D	Munn Allen	561	"	32	here
	E	Munn Thelma—†	561	housewife	28	"
	F	Riley Gladys—†	561	clerk	22	"
	G	Wright Louise—†	561	stitcher	32	Florida
	H	King Anita—†	561	clerk	22	here
	K	King Barbara—†	561	domestic	23	"
	L	King Edwin	561	welder	20	"
	M	King Eldon	561	"	20	
	N	King Walter	561	U S A	25	
	O	*Batiste Bertina—†	561	housewife	44	"
	P	*Batiste Luther	561	laborer	46	"
	S	*Mouser Allie	563	painter	48	416 Mass av
	T	Ricker Ralph	563	janitor	55	here
	U	Taylor Bruce D	563	U S A	20	"
	V	Taylor Edgar R	563	chauffeur	47	"
	W	Taylor Laura—†	563	housewife	51	"
	X	Allen Charles H	563	welder	28	Virginia
	Y	Brown Elizabeth—†	563	maid	37	here
	Z	Dorroh Mary—†	563	"	56	"
403						
	A	Foster James O	563	salesman	49	"
	B	*Lewis Fitz	563	counterman	55	590 Col av
	C	*Mier Charles	563	waiter	42	New York
	D	Taylor Harvey	563	"	31	155 Worcester
	E	*Yee Henry	564	laundryman	41	here
	F	Wooding Frances—†	564	housewife	46	"
	G	Wooding James	564	realtor	61	"

Page.	Letter.	Full Name.	Residence, Jan. 1, 1943.	Occupation.	Supposed Age.	Reported Residence, Jan. 1, 1942. Street and Number.
		Columbus Avenue—Continued				
	H	Green Martha—†	564	domestic	50	here
	K	*Dominique Eliza—†	564	at home	84	"
	L	Webb Sylvia—†	564	"	75	"
	M	Reid Fannie—†	564	domestic	51	"
	N	Tate Matilda—†	564	stitcher	51	
	R	Davis Charlotte—†	565	domestic	50	"
	O	English Alma—†	565	housewife	21	Saugus
	P	English Edward	565	pipefitter	25	"
	S	Garcia Andrew	565	entertainer	21	Florida
	T	Garcia Antonio	565	"	42	New York
	U	Garcia Charles	565	actor	30	Florida
	V	Garcia Gloria—†	565	housewife	21	Brockton
	W	Hill Carolyn—†	565	"	22	113 Worcester
	X	Hill David	565	musician	30	113 "
	Y	Johnson Elizabeth—†	565	housewife	24	Cuba
	Z	Smith Frank L	565	porter	31	Georgia
404						
	A	Smith Martha—†	565	housewife	30	"
	B	Williams Robbie—†	565	maid	21	"
	C	Young Emily—†	565	presser	22	
	D	Young James	565	molder	24	"
	H	Nelson Florence—†	567A	housekeeper	34	here
	L	Benjamin Leo	568	mechanic	47	"
	M	Dupree Rosalie—†	568	domestic	41	Florida
	N	Perry Laura—†	568	operator	22	372 Mass av
	O	Vincensini Philippe	568	retired	73	here
	P	Wright Della—†	568	domestic	21	"
	S	Bentley Frank	570	U S A	27	"
	T	Bentley Lucille—†	570	housewife	22	"
	U	Famous Joseph	570	laborer	56	"
	V	Holland Mary—†	570	stitcher	21	Georgia
	W	Holland William	570	U S A	33	here
	X	Miller Enid—†	570	domestic	22	"
	Y	Miller Robert	570	janitor	34	"
	Z	Rattray Minnie—†	570	housekeeper	64	"
405						
	A	Schuman Max	570	pedler	64	
	B	Squires Lynch	570	laborer	49	
	C	VanName Evelyn—†	570	laundress	41	"
	D	Wong Frank	570	merchant	54	"
	E	Berry Robert H	571	clergyman	40	Missouri

Page.	Letter.	Full Name.	Residence, Jan. 1, 1943.	Occupation.	Supposed Age.	Reported Residence, Jan. 1, 1942. Street and Number.

Columbus Avenue—Continued

Page.	Letter.	Full Name.	Residence, Jan. 1, 1943.	Occupation.	Supposed Age.	Reported Residence, Jan. 1, 1942. Street and Number.
	F	Burns Robert	571	porter	58	here
	G	Castle Gertrude—†	571	stitcher	50	419 Mass av
	H	Harvey Cordelia—†	571	domestic	32	here
	K	Hatchor Catherine—†	571	dressmaker	28	"
	L	Haynes Florence—†	571	domestic	35	"
	M	Keil Jane—†	571	nurse	42	
	N	Prescott Ethel—†	571	housewife	35	"
	O	Riley Clifford	571	welder	30	
	P	Riley Grace—†	571	housewife	26	"
	R	Sadler Catherine—†	571	domestic	28	Alabama
	S	Timberlake Fred	571	clerk	38	here
	T	Timbers Charlotte—†	571	domestic	55	"
	U	Tracey Henrietta—†	571	"	48	"
	V	Williams Alice A—†	571	"	26	
	W	Williams Howard	571	waiter	30	"
	X	Williamson Ernest J	571	chef	38	Newton
	Y	Wyche Philip	571	"	34	New York
406						
	A	Allen Rita—†	573A	domestic	35	94 Camden
	B	Beauford Matilda—†	573A	laundress	35	75 W Rutland sq
	C	Crawford Edith—†	573A	domestic	30	405 Mass av
	D	Glover James	573A	machinist	55	4 Peter Parley rd
	E	Glover Mary—†	573A	housewife	46	4 "
	F	Hayes Arthur	573A	salesman	30	29 Wellington
	G	Hayes Mabel—†	573A	housewife	23	29 "
	H	Lillard Pearl—†	573A	domestic	35	here
	O	Mabbitt Alice—†	586	"	52	29 Wellington
	P	Mabbitt Julia—†	586	at home	70	29 "
	R	Gray Daniel	586	laborer	53	here
	S	Richardson Emma—†	586	housewife	51	"
	T	Richardson Herbert	586	laborer	53	"
	U	Taylor Harold	586	"	52	"
	V	Jones Daniel	586	janitor	50	2 Dilworth
	W	Jones Irene—†	586	domestic	47	2 "
	X	Davis Lillian—†	586	operator	34	618 Col av
	Z	Harris Learlean—†	588	beautician	27	here
407						
	A	Harris Louis	588	porter	31	610 Col av
	B	Wooten Gertrude—†	588	housewife	48	here
	C	Wooten Wilhelminia—†	588	dressmaker	20	"
	D	Wooten William H	588	laborer	64	"

Page.	Letter.	Full Name.	Residence, Jan. 1, 1943.	Occupation.	Supposed Age.	Reported Residence, Jan. 1, 1942. Street and Number.

Columbus Avenue—Continued

Page.	Letter.	Full Name.	Residence, Jan. 1, 1943.	Occupation.	Supposed Age.	Reported Residence, Jan. 1, 1942. Street and Number.
	E	Hector Mabel—†	588	housewife	43	11 Holyoke
	F	Hector Pauline—†	588	factoryhand	21	54 Elm Hill av
	G	Hector Winthrop	588	U S A	23	11 Holyoke
	H	Keen Earl	588	laborer	47	11 "
	K	Mendes Victor	588	chef	42	11 "
	L	Williams Rockwell	588	U S A	25	11 "
	M	Heggie George M	588	laborer	61	here
	N	Heggie Lucille M—†	588	housewife	46	"
	O	Gray Annie—†	590	at home	66	"
	P	*Reberio Louis	590	laborer	46	
	R	Reberio Virginia—†	590	cook	43	
	S	Physic Lena—†	590	student	22	
	T	Physic Leslie E	590	chauffeur	27	"
	U	Physic Vivian—†	590	housewife	22	"
	V	Williams David	590	clerk	52	
	W	Williams Jessie—†	590	housewife	52	"
	X	Reynolds Edith—†	592	"	29	
	Y	Reynolds James	592	janitor	29	
	Z	Lowden Alice—†	592	housewife	55	"
408						
	A	Nurse Arthur	592	porter	31	
	B	Nurse Evelyn—†	592	nurse	32	
	C	Polk Gladys—†	592	domestic	36	"
	D	Polk Helen—†	592	operator	32	"
	E	Polk Loretta—†	592	stitcher	38	
	F	Polk Mabel A—†	592	domestic	69	"
	G	Cedarblad Clara—†	599	housewife	52	"
	H	Cedarblad Oscar C	599	mechanic	53	"
	K	Erlendsen Einer	599	painter	55	
	L	Erlendsen Mary—†	599	housewife	70	"
	M	Cramer Alfred	599	welder	30	
	N	Cramer Mary—†	599	housewife	28	"
	O	Rumsey Alexander A	599	cook	40	"
	P	Gifford Barry W	599	mechanic	52	2 Champney
	R	Gifford Bertha F—†	599	housewife	59	2 "
	S	Mayer William H	599	operator	54	here
	T	Magee Herbert R	599	attendant	38	"
	U	Magee Hazel—†	599	housewife	42	"
	V	Shaw Eleanor—†	599	social worker	37	"
	W	Foley Edward	599	chauffeur	38	32 St Alphonsus
	X	Foley Ida—†	599	housewife	43	32 "

Page.	Letter.	FULL NAME.	Residence, Jan. 1, 1943.	Occupation.	Supposed Age.	Reported Residence, Jan. 1, 1942. Street and Number.

Columbus Avenue—Continued

Page.	Letter.	FULL NAME.	Residence, Jan. 1, 1943.	Occupation.	Supposed Age.	Reported Residence, Jan. 1, 1942. Street and Number.
	Y	Hanson Edward P	599	watchman	41	161 Brown av
	Z	Hillsdale Olive—†	599	checker	45	here
409						
	A	Lachinian Armen—†	599	housewife	50	"
	B	Lachinian Charles	599	storekeeper	50	"
	C	*Jordan Rena—†	599	saleswoman	35	"
	D	Steward Thomas	599	laborer	36	Maine
	E	Chute Ralph M	599	cook	44	here
	F	Leonard John	599	retired	71	"
	G	Leonard Mary B—†	599	housewife	62	"
	H	Halleran Mary—†	599	at home	70	
	K	Moody Oscar W	599	packer	55	
	L	Rodell Judith—†	599	stenographer	49	"
	M	Campbell Florence—†	599	housewife	32	"
	N	Campbell Peter	599	machinist	42	"
	O	Abbot Gloria—†	599	housewife	49	27 Sharon
	P	Kenney Anne M—†	599	"	45	here
	R	Kenney Carl E	599	machinist	48	"
	S	Bruce Chester	599	chauffeur	50	"
	T	Damon Mabel—†	599	maid	45	35 Hemenway
	U	Whitney Dora—†	599	housewife	55	here
	V	Whitney Frederick	599	plumber	65	"
	W	Walsh John P	599	welder	51	"
	X	Walsh Lillian—†	599	housewife	41	"
	Y	Hebsie William	599	watchman	48	"
	Z	Daniels William	599	salesman	47	"
410						
	A	Dood Frank E	599	electrician	44	420 Col av
	B	MacDonald Olive E—†	599	housewife	58	here
	C	MacDonald Ronald J	599	chauffeur	52	"
	D	Greer Ruth—†	599	housewife	22	"
	E	Greer William	599	student	24	
	F	Doherty Mary—†	599	waitress	30	"
	G	Remick Bernard S	599	janitor	68	22 Village
	H	Remick Ruth F—†	599	housewife	56	22 "
	K	Butters Bella—†	599	"	50	here
	L	Butters Herbert J	599	chauffeur	55	"
	M	Gould Clara—†	599	housewife	49	"
	N	Gould George	599	packer	45	
	O	Brooks Ida M—†	599	housewife	63	"
	P	Brooks William C	599	retired	73	

Page.	Letter.	Full Name.	Residence, Jan. 1, 1943.	Occupation.	Supposed Age.	Reported Residence, Jan. 1, 1942. Street and Number.

Columbus Avenue—Continued

Page.	Letter.	Full Name.	Residence, Jan. 1, 1943.	Occupation.	Supposed Age.	Reported Residence, Jan. 1, 1942. Street and Number.
	s	McKeever James L	599	clerk	48	48 School
	T	McKeever Mary—†	599	housewife	43	48 "
	U	*Soderbom Gustav	599	decorator	66	here
	V	Dionne Louise—†	599	housewife	42	"
	W	Swartz Linus	599	cook	34	"
	X	*Doherty Ruth—†	599	waitress	28	68 Springvale av
	Y	Wing Arthur	599	tailor	60	here
	Z	Wing Mabel—†	599	housewife	62	"
411						
	A	*Pinfold Mary—†	599		58	279 Princeton
	B	Hart Margaret—†	599	"	33	here
	C	Hart Thomas	599	laborer	55	"
	D	Watkins Bernice—†	599	housewife	44	"
	E	Watkins Clyde	599	chef	46	"
	F	Crowell Alfreda—†	599	waitress	43	11 Dalton
	G	Crowell William	599	chauffeur	41	11 "
	H	Flynn George L	599	salesman	52	122 St Stephen
	K	Glidden Perley F	599	"	36	109 "
	L	*Aganad Mariana J—†	599	housewife	42	here
	M	*Aganed Simplicio S	599	cook	34	"
	N	*Nakagawa Janet—†	599	at home	76	"
	O	*Nakagawa Yujiro	599	butler	54	Wayland
	P	Jances Charles	599	shoeworker	43	here
	R	Thomas Marion—†	599	at home	63	"
	S	Staikos Christos	599	chef	39	"
	T	Powers Adeline—†	599	housewife	30	"
	U	Powers George	599	manufacturer	42	"
	V	Goldstein Harry	599	storekeeper	46	"
	W	Goldstein Rose—†	599	housewife	45	"
	X	Goldstein Sidney	599	pharmacist	24	"
	Y	Cooper Mary—†	599	assembler	30	68 Springvale av
	Z	Brown Olivia L—†	599	at home	64	here
412						
	A	Grose Charles K	599	retired	65	
	B	Grose Elizabeth H—†	599	at home	65	
	C	*Weinstein Bella—†	599	housewife	38	"
	D	Weinstein Jacob	599	tailor	56	
	E	Jardine Romaine—†	599	waitress	28	
	F	Smyer Belle—†	606	domestic	33	"
	G	Starkey Isaac	606	pharmacist	41	"
	H	Starkey Rhoda—†	606	bookkeeper	39	"

Page.	Letter.	Full Name.	Residence, Jan. 1, 1943.	Occupation.	Supposed Age.	Reported Residence, Jan. 1, 1942. Street and Number.

Columbus Avenue—Continued

Page.	Letter.	Full Name.	Residence, Jan. 1, 1943.	Occupation.	Supposed Age.	Reported Residence, Jan. 1, 1942. Street and Number.
	K	Douglas Bertha—†	606	housewife	41	here
	L	Douglas George	606	retired	46	“
	N	Thomas Anita G—†	606	housewife	43	“
	M	Thomas William H	606	superintendent	54	“
	O	Wade James	606	steward	51	
	P	Wade Ursula—†	606	housewife	49	“
	R	Hawkins Iona—†	606	waitress	34	
	S	Hawkins Robert	606	barber	45	
	T	Clark David	606	laborer	45	“
	U	Clark Jeannette—†	606	waitress	43	708 Tremont
	V	Clark Mildred—†	606	domestic	43	here
	W	Waterhouse Daisy—†	606	“	41	“
	X	Waterhouse Joseph	606	cook	55	“
	Y	Gibson Cecil—†	606	housewife	43	“
	Z	Gibson John	606	porter	59	
413						
	A	Gibson Lloyd	606	clerk	22	
	B	Cummings Edna—†	606	domestic	47	“
	C	Edward Evelyn—†	606	waitress	41	
	D	Vickers George	606	porter	39	
	E	Vickers Pauline—†	606	housewife	37	“
	1E	Austin Luginia—†	606	domestic	45	“
	F	Mitchell Joseph	606	laborer	47	
	H	Keel Daniel	609	chauffeur	44	“
	K	Keel Daniel K	609	welder	20	
	L	West Elizabeth—†	609	hairdresser	53	“
	M	Cunningham Letitia—†	609	clerk	52	
	N	Dukes Edward M	609	“	55	
	O	Dukes Etta E—†	609	housewife	48	“
	P	Goodman George C	609	chef	42	
	R	Goodman Theodosia—†	609	housewife	36	“
	S	Grice Walton	609	laborer	52	“
	T	Jackson Nettie—†	609	entertainer	52	10 Kirkland
	U	May Nelson	609	laborer	32	here
	V	Tripp Charles F	609	retired	75	“
	W	White Joseph	609	welder	35	“
	X	Cleveland Alberta—†	609	housewife	21	Ohio
	Y	Jackson Louise—†	609	domestic	48	here
	Z	Jones Fannie—†	609	assembler	26	“
414						
	A	Lucas Samuel	609	butler	39	

Page.	Letter.	Full Name.	Residence, Jan. 1, 1943.	Occupation.	Supposed Age.	Reported Residence, Jan. 1, 1942. Street and Number.

Columbus Avenue—Continued

Page.	Letter.	Full Name.	Residence, Jan. 1, 1943.	Occupation.	Supposed Age.	Reported Residence, Jan. 1, 1942. Street and Number.
	B	Verter George	609	porter	36	here
	C	Verter Pearl—†	609	housewife	38	"
	D	Howard Edna—†	609	domestic	50	11 Claremont
	E	Sasser Allen	609	porter	59	here
	F	Sasser Ethel—†	609	housewife	42	"
	G	Chandler Gertrude—†	609	"	50	"
	H	Chandler Hubert	609	waiter	57	
	K	Morris Blanche—†	609	housewife	27	"
	L	Morris Kenneth	609	laborer	29	
	M	Atherton Charles	609	welder	46	
	N	Gardner Freda—†	609	"	45	
	O	Harris Charles	609	retired	74	
	P	Pitters Albert	610	cook	45	
	R	Gray Frederick I	610	dentist	40	"
	S	Gray Margaret—†	610	housewife	29	6 Hammond
	T	Ryner Edith—†	610	"	47	here
	U	Brown Albert	610	machinist	42	Rhode Island
	V	Brown Leon A	610	laborer	32	here
	W	Brown Pauline C—†	610	stitcher	47	"
	X	Styles Julius	610	laborer	54	"
	Y	Taylor Mildred—†	610	dressmaker	42	"
	Z	Wood John T	610	shipper	53	
415						
	A	Woody Henry	610	chef	47	
	B	Sanford Ida—†	610	domestic	25	"
	C	Sanford Taft	610	chauffeur	33	"
	D	Saunders Mary—†	610	domestic	62	"
	E	Gerald Arthur	610	laborer	36	
	F	Morris Fannie—†	610	housekeeper	26	"
	G	Morris Ruby—†	610	housewife	43	"
	H	Whitehead Josephine—†	610	housekeeper	48	"
	K	Stubblefield Abbie—†	612	housewife	27	"
	L	Stubblefield Harry	612	U S A	27	"
	M	Mitchell Agnes—†	612	housewife	39	"
	N	Mitchell Harry	612	laborer	43	
	O	Mitchell Leota—†	612	student	21	
	P	Jackson Abraham	612	laborer	67	
	R	Norman Maude—†	612	operator	38	
	S	Norman Turner	612	chauffeur	40	"
	T	Johnson Florence E—†	612	nurse	46	
	U	Adams Edith—†	612	housewife	42	"

Page.	Letter.	Full Name.	Residence, Jan. 1, 1943.	Occupation.	Supposed Age.	Reported Residence, Jan. 1, 1942. Street and Number.

Columbus Avenue—Continued

Page.	Letter.	Full Name.	Residence, Jan. 1, 1943.	Occupation.	Supposed Age.	Reported Residence, Jan. 1, 1942. Street and Number.
	V	Adams Jacob	612	laborer	42	here
	W	Forest Alberta—†	612	presser	30	“
	X	Forest Sarah—†	612	waitress	35	Georgia
	Y	Forest Woodson	612	cook	37	“
	Z	Grove Edward E	612	laborer	55	here
416						
	A	Thompson Erma—†	612	housewife	41	“
	B	Thompson John R	612	barber	39	
	C	Schuyler John T	612	inspector	41	“
	D	Sparrow Rose—†	612	housewife	38	“
	E	Sparrow William S	612	tailor	67	
	F	Butler Fred T	613	physician	38	“
	G	Hornsby Garret	613	porter	47	
	H	Hornsby Hattie—†	613	housewife	51	“
	K	Allen George W	613	policeman	47	“
	L	Schuyler Edith B—†	613	housewife	50	“
	M	Schuyler Raymond G	613	janitor	54	“
	N	Dorsey Alberta—†	613	nurse	42	431 Mass av
	O	Jenkins Ada—†	613	housekeeper	48	10 Braddock pk
	P	Roberts Mattie—†	613	housewife	44	here
	R	Roberts Samuel	613	clerk	45	“
	S	Reynolds Frederick	613	retired	64	“
	T	Reynolds Priscilla—†	613	housewife	63	“
	U	McKenzie Frank M	613	presser	38	
	V	McKenzie Ruth—†	613	housewife	35	“
	W	Wiley Ceola—†	613	“	29	
	X	Wiley Fred W	613	electrician	28	“
	Y	Wiley Sallie—†	613	at home	47	
	Z	Durant Daniel A	614	clergyman	50	“
417						
	A	Taylor Belle—†	614	housekeeper	46	“
	B	King Jennie—†	614	“	63	“
	C	Thomson Aubrey	614	laborer	24	
	D	Thomson Mattie A—†	614	teacher	27	
	E	Branker Charles K	614	tailor	42	
	F	Branker Helen E—†	614	housewife	37	“
	G	Perry Ebba S—†	614	waitress	62	
	H	Hayden James D	614	machinist	42	“
	K	Lewis May—†	614	factoryhand	45	“
	L	Lewis Robert	614	porter	69	
	M	Harper Ernest	614	retired	74	

Page.	Letter.	Full Name.	Residence, Jan. 1, 1943.	Occupation.	Supposed Age.	Reported Residence, Jan. 1, 1942. Street and Number.

Columbus Avenue—Continued

Page.	Letter.	Full Name.	Residence, Jan. 1, 1943.	Occupation.	Supposed Age.	Reported Residence, Jan. 1, 1942. Street and Number.
	N	Harper Juanita—†	614	beautician	28	here
	O	Harper Ralph	614	barber	45	“
	P	Haywood Emma—†	614	housekeeper	61	“
	R	Cannady James O	614	porter	37	“
	S	Cannady Ora L—†	614	dressmaker	48	“
	T	Garrett Julian L	614	cook	54	
	U	Addison Sally—†	615	at home	73	
	V	Robinson Everett	615	janitor	40	
	W	Robinson Jessie—†	615	housewife	48	“
	X	Oliver George	615	chef	52	
	Y	Gladden Virginia—†	615	housewife	38	“
	Z	Gladden Wallace	615	letter carrier	40	“
418						
	A	Lyles Olivia—†	615	housewife	34	“
	B	Lyles Oswald	615	laborer	35	
	C	*James David	615	cook	42	
	D	Lawrence Beatrice—†	615	housewife	40	“
	E	*Lawrence Ferdinand S	615	cook	42	“
	F	Handy Mattie—†	615	“	45	17 Westminster
	G	Dyett Patrick	615	salesman	37	here
	H	Dyett Susan—†	615	housewife	32	“
	K	Mujtaba Ali	615	boilermaker	51	81 Dartmouth
	L	Mujtaba Haleema—†	615	housewife	50	98 “
	M	Jackson Daniel	616	porter	47	here
	N	Jackson Mabel—†	616	housewife	47	“
	O	Blount Blinnie—†	616	finisher	20	“
	P	Blount Hattie—†	616	housewife	60	“
	R	Blount Jasper	616	U S A	28	“
	S	Blount Roscoe	616	“	23	
	T	Blount Rudolph	616	“	25	
	U	Blount William	616	retired	60	
	V	Farley Estelle—†	616	stitcher	24	
	W	Marsden Alphonse	616	laborer	44	
	X	Marsden Thelma—†	616	waitress	31	
	Y	Smith Anita—†	616	at home	59	
	Z	Ward Edward	616	laborer	50	
419						
	A	Ward Julia—†	616	housewife	48	“
	B	Edwards Harold B	616	chef	61	
	C	Edwards Mary—†	616	at home	77	

Columbus Avenue—Continued

Page.	Letter.	Full Name.	Residence, Jan. 1, 1943.	Occupation.	Supposed Age.	Reported Residence, Jan. 1, 1942. Street and Number.
	D	Hunt Pearl—†	616	housekeeper	48	here
	E	Brown Harry	616	cook	59	"
	F	Brown Lucy—†	616	housewife	60	"
	G	Burks William	616	waiter	29	
	H	Hinton Winnie—†	616	at home	77	"
	K	Davis Iola—†	616	housewife	26	29 Wellington
	L	Davis Theodore	616	U S A	31	29 "
	M	Johnson Maude—†	616	housewife	48	here
	O	Grant Viola—†	618	domestic	41	"
	P	Prioleau John	618	laborer	42	"
	R	Harris Howard F	618	"	33	355 Mass av
	S	Harris Ozepher B—†	618	waitress	26	355 "
	T	Jones Allie W—†	618	"	36	Florida
	U	Jefferson Adele—†	618	housewife	30	32 Greenwich pk
	V	Jefferson James	618	U S N	30	32 "
	W	Jones Clayton	618	"	26	32 "
	X	Jones Clifford	618	waitress	24	32 "
	Y	Brown James	619	machinist	45	here
	Z	Jordan Susan—†	619	cook	61	"
420						
	A	Muir Uriah	619	waiter	47	
	B	Richardson Herbert	619	"	57	
	C	Young Laura—†	619	at home	65	
	E	Foster Helen A—†	619	cook	47	
	F	Broadfield Barbara—†	620	housewife	51	"
	G	Broadfield Claudius J	620	teacher	57	
	H	Furly Elmo	620	waiter	58	
	K	Furly Eugenia—†	620	housewife	47	"
	L	Sinkler Phyllis—†	620	"	23	New Jersey
	N	Hayes Martha—†	622	domestic	46	here
	O	Logan Mamie B—†	622	seamstress	46	"
	P	Nelson Martha E—†	622	at home	71	"
	R	Green Cordelia—†	622	housewife	51	"
	S	Green Michael	622	waiter	47	
	T	Asbury Edwin V	623	physician	47	"
	U	Mann Dorothy—†	623	housewife	25	"
	V	McCoy Albert D	623	mechanic	58	"
	W	Nicholson Catherine—†	623	housewife	35	"
	X	Johns Sadie—†	623	domestic	36	"
	Y	Berry Roy	623	machinist	35	37 Greenwich pk

Page.	Letter.	Full Name.	Residence, Jan. 1, 1943.	Occupation.	Supposed Age.	Reported Residence, Jan. 1, 1942. Street and Number.

Columbus Avenue—Continued

Page.	Letter.	Full Name.	Residence, Jan. 1, 1943.	Occupation.	Supposed Age.	Reported Residence, Jan. 1, 1942. Street and Number.
	Z	Fisher Olive—†	623	housewife	39	here
421						
	A	Fisher Walter	623	waiter	40	
	B	Fowler Victor	623	clerk	45	
	C	Tucker Percy	623	janitor	48	"
	D	Jackson Gaston	623	laborer	35	625 Col av
	E	Johnson Esther—†	623	domestic	29	here
	F	Johnson William	623	retired	66	"
	G	Miles Edna—†	623	domestic	35	"
	H	Burrell Cynthia—†	623	at home	66	"
	K	Burrell Richard T	623	laborer	42	"
	L	Chase James R	623	waiter	54	27 Claremont pk
	M	Wilkins Amelia—†	623	housewife	25	Pennsylvania
	N	MacDonald Dolores—†	623	"	32	here
	O	MacDonald Ella—†	623	at home	65	"
	P	MacDonald Lloyd C	623	waiter	37	"
	R	Hayes Clarence A	625	physician	52	"
	S	*Ford Frances—†	625	housewife	56	"
	T	*Ford James	625	cook	60	
	U	*Henriques Lionel	625	chauffeur	60	"
	V	Tinney William R	625	watchman	52	"
	W	Washington Julius	625	laborer	42	
	X	Russell Robert	625	salesman	46	"
	Y	Smith Elizabeth—†	625	domestic	38	"
	Z	Underwood Robert	625	entertainer	39	New York
422						
	A	*Fuller Alphonso	625	mechanic	41	12 Claremont pk
	B	Fuller Richmond	625	"	39	94 Vernon
	C	Fuller Virginia—†	625	housewife	33	94 "
	D	Brown Anice—†	625	operator	27	here
	E	Brown Dora—†	625	housewife	55	"
	F	Brown Walter	625	porter	56	"
	G	Morris Jennie—†	625	housewife	40	"
	H	Morris Phillip	625	U S A	40	"
	K	Williams Walter	625	steward	50	New York
	L	Allen Griffin A	627	physician	66	here
	M	Colton Alice—†	627	domestic	55	"
	N	Long John	627	chauffeur	57	"
	O	Manuel Clifford B	627	porter	60	
	P	Manuel Lillian M—†	627	housewife	47	"
	S	Stevenson Arthur	627	waiter	53	

Page.	Letter.	Full Name.	Residence, Jan. 1, 1943.	Occupation.	Supposed Age.	Reported Residence, Jan. 1, 1942. Street and Number.

Columbus Avenue—Continued

	T	Hogg Lee	627	porter	39	here
	U	*Hogg Leona—†	627	housewife	38	"
	V	*Reid Jean—†	627	dressmaker	38	"
	W	*Ballantine Marion—†	627	cook	39	10 Moreland
	X	Soso George	627	molder	30	10 "
	Y	Soso Rose A—†	627	housewife	31	10 "

Dilworth Street

	Z	MacNeil James	1	U S A	23	here
423						
	A	Whitfield Fred	1	welder	25	Florida
	B	Whitfield Susan L—†	1	housewife	22	"
	C	Foreman Alfred	1	retired	71	here
	D	Foreman Frances—†	1	housewife	60	"
	E	Foreman Harriet—†	1	housekeeper	65	New Jersey
	F	Jackson Anita—†	1	domestic	35	here
	G	Jackson Evelyn—†	1	entertainer	24	Illinois
	H	Jackson Jesse	1	electrician	20	"
	K	Johnson Marguerite—†	2	domestic	29	610 Col av
	L	Rickes James	2	storekeeper	47	here
	M	Crite Allan	2	artist	32	"
	N	Crite Anna M—†	2	domestic	51	"
	O	Brady Georgia M—†	2	cook	45	11 Seneca
	P	Logan Margaret—†	3	housekeeper	34	here
	R	Parham Bertha—†	3	housewife	27	"
	S	Parham Otis	3	chef	30	"
	T	Handy Catherine—†	3	housewife	22	22 Concord sq
	U	Handy John H	3	rigger	22	22 "
	V	Hammond Leroy	3	baker	27	Georgia
	W	Hammond Mildred—†	3	housewife	23	"
	X	Hill Willa M—†	4	domestic	30	Wellesley
	Y	Hayes Margaret—†	4	housewife	42	here
	Z	Hayes Sebron	4	machinist	44	"
424						
	A	Smith Adina—†	4	housewife	45	"
	B	Smith William W	4	clergyman	54	"
	C	McLean Hilda—†	5	housewife	35	"
	D	Warrell Joseph	5	pedler	29	
	E	Warrell Mabel—†	5	housewife	52	"
	F	Wilson Anna—†	5	domestic	57	"

Page.	Letter.	Full Name.	Residence, Jan. 1, 1943.	Occupation.	Supposed Age.	Reported Residence, Jan. 1, 1942. Street and Number.

Dilworth Street—Continued

	G	Curtis Albert L	6	clerk	50	here
	H	Summers Henrietta—†	6	housewife	50	"
	K	Summers James H	6	fireman	60	"
	L	Moore Charles R	6	porter	67	"
	M	Moore May S—†	6	housewife	52	"
	N	Hill Amanda—†	7	"	41	
	O	Wake Martin L	7	chauffeur	48	"
	P	Wake Ora E—†	7	housewife	38	"
	R	Godfrey Alfred	7	laborer	44	
	S	Godfrey Gladys—†	7	housewife	41	"
	T	Goosby Ellsworth	7	messenger	24	"
	U	Goosby Franklin D	7	laborer	52	
	V	Goosby Lena—†	7	housewife	55	"
	W	Goosby Ruth—†	7	clerk	25	
	X	Crawford Ernest	8	porter	40	
	Y	Johnson Sarah—†	8	hairdresser	47	"
425						
	A	Smith Warren M	8	longshoreman	39	"
	1A	Williams Alice—†	8	housekeeper	30	"
	B	Gray Eugenia—†	8	shoeworker	21	"
	C	*Williams Fred	8	painter	52	"
	D	*Williams Marion—†	8	housewife	50	"
	H	Peters Lewis W	10	porter	35	16 Yarmouth
	K	Peters Ruth C—†	10	housewife	33	16 "
	L	Dowdy Catherine—†	10	domestic	56	here
	M	Dowdy James	10	janitor	24	"
	N	Jones John N	10	laborer	23	"
	O	Jones Maude—†	10	housewife	48	"
	P	Bosley Esther J—†	11	at home	91	
	R	Dickson Irene—†	11	operator	37	
	S	Tasco Lulu—†	11	housewife	52	"
	T	Tasco William	11	janitor	50	
	U	Ward Adele—†	11	housewife	42	"
	V	Ward George A	11	chauffeur	49	"
	W	Kerr Jennie—†	11A	housewife	56	"
	X	Kerr Victor E	11A	porter	62	"
	Y	Leonard Bertha—†	11A	housewife	35	80 W Rutland sq
	Z	Parks James	11A	waiter	32	here
426						
	A	Parks Olive—†	11A	housewife	32	"
	B	Parks William	11A	janitor	33	

Dilworth Street—Continued

Page.	Letter.	Full Name.	Residence, Jan. 1, 1943.	Occupation.	Supposed Age.	Reported Residence, Jan. 1, 1942. Street and Number.
	C	Parish Isabelle—†	12	cook	39	here
	E	Marsh Egbert	12	“	49	“
	F	Marsh Marion—†	12	student	22	“
	G	Marsh Zaida—†	12	housewife	43	“
	H	Johnson Gladys E—†	14	housekeeper	37	“
	K	Pinder Hugh	14	waiter	35	“
	L	Best Evelyn C—†	14	housewife	41	“
	M	Best Thomas W	14	laborer	53	“
	N	Price Grace—†	14	housewife	32	“
	O	Price John	14	porter	42	
	P	McAndrew Daniel	15	waiter	56	
	R	Purnell Martha—†	15	laundress	37	“
	S	King Jean—†	15	welder	20	
	T	King Samuel J	15	checker	64	
	U	King Samuel J, jr	15	ironworker	35	“
	V	Wolf Louis	16	porter	37	
	W	Wolf Mabel R—†	16	housewife	29	“
	X	Tasco Eula—†	16	“	52	
	Y	Tasco Stillman A	16	porter	52	
	Z	Boyd John	16	“	35	
427						
	A	Boyd Stella—†	16	housewife	32	“
	C	Brooks Henrietta—†	17	nurse	37	71 Camden
	D	Jones Fannie—†	17	at home	51	71 “
	E	Paige Hartley B—†	17	housewife	55	here
	F	Paige Jeremiah	17	laborer	63	“
	G	Paige Palmer	17	U S A	26	“
	H	Paige Russell	17	“	23	
	K	Paige Theresa—†	17	clerk	23	“
	L	Dukes Edward	18	welder	26	507 Shawmut av
	M	Dukes Lillian—†	18	housewife	21	507 “
	N	Tucker Claudia—†	18	“	27	507 “
	O	Tucker Royal	18	porter	30	507 “
	P	Ryalls Charles	18	“	41	here
	R	Ryalls Emanuel	18	chef	32	“
	S	Williams Edward	18	bellman	62	11 Marble
	T	Williams Mary—†	18	housewife	53	11 “
	U	Evans Eddy—†	19	domestic	42	here
	V	Frith Anna—†	19	housewife	35	“
	W	*Frith Edward	19	laborer	40	“
	X	Chambers Joseph R	19	waiter	69	

Page.	Letter.	FULL NAME.	Residence, Jan. 1, 1943.	Occupation.	Supposed Age.	Reported Residence, Jan. 1, 1942. Street and Number.

Dilworth Street—Continued

	Y	Chambers Mary M—†	19	housewife	62	here
	Z	Paris Eudora—†	19	at home	42	11 Elbert
428						
	A	Talbot Irene C—†	19	housewife	27	11 "
	B	Talbot John C	19	vulcanizer	33	11 "
	C	Dickson Alfred	20	mechanic	29	here
	D	Dickson Evelyn—†	20	housewife	30	"
	E	Craddock Elizabeth—†	20	"	44	"
	F	Craddock George	20	porter	55	
	G	Jones Austin	20	janitor	50	
	H	Jones Bessie—†	20	housewife	48	"
	K	Goode John L	21	welder	53	"
	L	Sharp Edna L—†	21	housekeeper	52	29 Wellington
	M	Kelly Albert	21	waiter	43	36 Symphony rd
	N	Winston Francis	21	machinist	33	Wellesley
	O	Winston Josephine—†	21	housewife	25	"
	P	Fuller Charles	21	waiter	40	here
	R	Fuller Gladys—†	21	housewife	34	"
	S	Dyett Alice—†	22	domestic	22	"
	T	Harper Alicia—†	22	"	37	"
	U	Wilson Esther—†	22	housewife	22	139 Worcester
	V	Wilson Ralph	22	welder	23	139 "
	W	Johnson Alitha—†	22	housewife	57	here
	X	Reddick Elaine—†	22	domestic	30	"
	Y	Foster Claudine—†	24	housewife	43	"
	Z	Foster Francis	24	laborer	50	
429						
	A	*Bassett Samuel	24	painter	58	New York
	B	*Lovell Charles	24	porter	54	"
	C	*Lovell Maude—†	24	housewife	44	"
	D	Harris Rosetta—†	24	"	42	here
	E	King George	24	barber	47	"
	F	Parton Clarence	24	porter	54	69 Hammond

Massachusetts Avenue

	L	Jacques Rudolph	393	superintendent	56	10 Pembroke
	M	Efter Harry	393	pipefitter	29	406 Mass av
	N	Roussell Jeanette—†	393	housewife	26	N Hampshire
	O	Roussell Louis	393	plater	33	34 Ditson
	P	Beals Charles L	393	bartender	46	here

Page.	Letter.	Full Name.	Residence, Jan. 1, 1943.	Occupation.	Supposed Age.	Reported Residence, Jan. 1, 1942. Street and Number.

Massachusetts Avenue—Continued

	R	Beals Savilla—†	393	housewife	35	here
	S	Edwards Rita—†	393	waitress	25	Missouri
	T	Johnson Ann—†	393	"	27	N Carolina
	U	Preble Ruth S—†	393	clerk	34	Medford
	V	Sullivan David D	393	operator	25	473 Mass av
	W	Sullivan James D	393	salesman	55	473 "
	X	Sullivan Marion T—†	393	housewife	55	473 "
	Y	Lundgren Martha—†	393	presser	29	75 Burbank
	Z	Ryan John H	393	diemaker	53	75 "
430						
	A	Herbert Irving	393	engineer	53	85 Worcester
	B	Davis Bertha L—†	393	cook	24	144 "
	C	Willson Donald R	393	painter	50	here
	D	Willson Lillian G—†	393	housewife	44	"
	F	Horton Louise W—†	393	"	44	84 Worcester
	G	Rooney Dorothy A—†	393	clerk	23	Florida
	H	Gambon George E	393	boilermaker	39	Somerville
	K	Gagnon Edward J	393	laborer	44	here
	L	Jobin Marie D—†	393	welder	49	"
	O	Evan Richard H	393	chauffeur	35	128 Bunker Hill
	P	Peterson Edmund	393	"	31	162 St Botolph
	R	Hyde Barbara—†	393	cook	50	here
	S	Nolan Dorothy P—†	393	housewife	32	48 Magnolia
	T	Nolan Lawrence J	393	clerk	29	48 "
	U	Cole Miley J	393	U S N	34	California
	V	Kostonis Bettina—†	393	housewife	41	here
	W	Kostonis Charles G	393	inspector	47	"
	X	Cooley John	393	electrician	45	"
	Y	*Cormier Patrick	394	janitor	73	499 Blue Hill av
	Z	Kohler Esther—†	394	housewife	35	3 Albemarle
431						
	A	Taylor Mary L—†	394	at home	63	here
	B	Kelley Francis E	394	painter	25	67 Westland av
	C	Kelley Mary—†	394	housewife	26	67 "
	D	Moriarty Irene M—†	394	supervisor	42	50 Province
	E	Reid Sarah B—†	394	housewife	62	34 Buswell
	F	Reid William J	394	salesman	32	34 "
	G	Sawyer Albert C	394	metalworker	82	34 "
	H	Rich Irma—†	394	teacher	59	70 Symphony rd
	K	Conroy Mary—†	394	stitcher	65	599 Col av
	L	Burns Violet—†	394	manager	39	39 Warren av

Page.	Letter.	FULL NAME.	Residence, Jan. 1, 1943.	Occupation.	Supposed Age.	Reported Residence, Jan. 1, 1942. Street and Number.

Massachusetts Avenue—Continued

	M	Manning Mary E—†	394	teacher	58	270 Hunt'n av
	N	Basche Elizabeth—†	394	at home	76	here
	O	Basche Mary—†	394	dressmaker	49	"
	P	DeBourbos Louis	394	laborer	22	"
	R	Rush Fred	394	mechanic	65	"
	S	Rush Grace—†	394	housewife	53	"
	T	Bather Margaret E—†	394	clerk	37	150 St Botolph
	U	Bather Mary A—†	394	"	39	150 "
	V	Tabor Beatrice—†	394	housewife	28	462 Mass av
	W	Tabor George	394	U S A	36	462 "
	X	MacCanna John F	394	machinist	63	here
	Y	MacCanna Prudent—†	394	housewife	60	"
	Z	Verrall Marie—†	394	nurse	39	"
432						
	A	Carney Agnes—†	394	assembler	21	"
	B	*Carney Ellen—†	394	at home	63	
	C	*Carney Matthew	394	laborer	59	"
	D	Kelliher Cornelius	394	cook	30	105 W Dedham
	E	Kelliher Sylvia E—†	394	housewife	37	105 "
	F	Amadei John	394	expediter	39	268 Norfolk av
	G	Sullivan Joseph M	394	engineer	52	here
	L	Deeg Edith M—†	394	nurse	49	"
	M	Harwood Gretchen—†	394	designer	30	Sharon
	N	Leonard Katherine J—†	394	attendant	50	here
	O	Therrien Mary J—†	394	at home	78	"
	P	Wolfgang Minna—†	394	"	60	743 Tremont
	R	Cotter Daniel	394	retired	72	here
	S	Shanklin Caroline—†	394	laundress	46	N Hampshire
	T	Dawley Jennie—†	394	at home	78	here
	U	Dawley William K	394	machinist	55	"
	W	Julian Frank	394	vulcanizer	27	Brookline
	X	Julian Irene—†	394	housewife	27	"
	Y	Aube Mary A—†	394	attendant	46	743 Tremont
	Z	Souza Henry P	394	seaman	52	743 "
433						
	A	Wheeler Calvin S	394	engineer	50	64 Hunt'n av
	B	Tinker Phyllis—†	394	waitress	24	here
	C	Gingras Eve—†	394	musician	38	"
	D	Pond Ethel M—†	394	presser	45	Milton
	E	Pond Jean L—†	394	librarian	21	Canton
	F	Hullum Laydon	395	mechanic	22	here

Page.	Letter.	Full Name.	Residence, Jan. 1, 1943.	Occupation.	Supposed Age.	Reported Residence, Jan. 1, 1942. Street and Number.

Massachusetts Avenue—Continued

	G	Pickens Catherine—†	395	domestic	36	here
	H	Pickens James	395	porter	39	"
	K	Singleton Bessie—†	395	laundress	45	Georgia
	L	Stickney Clara—†	395	hairdresser	28	here
	M	Stickney Edward	395	U S A	22	"
	N	Stickney Florence—†	395	housewife	63	"
	O	Stickney Mercer	395	janitor	38	
	P	Winston Electra—†	395	hairdresser	34	"
	S	Burton Henri B	397	realtor	60	65 Windsor
	T	Burton Roberta K—†	397	housewife	52	65 "
	U	Cook Charlotte—†	397	"	27	here
	V	Cook Rudolph	397	laborer	30	"
	W	Finn George	398	mechanic	47	"
	X	Finn Mildred—†	398	clerk	41	
	Y	Casipit Felix	398	mechanic	37	"
	Z	Casipit Mary—†	398	housewife	25	"
434						
	A	Valentin Isadore	398	U S A	38	New York
	B	Valentin Sarah—†	398	waitress	27	Framingham
	D	Brae Rose—†	399	maid	45	here
	E	Hamilton Kathleen—†	399	"	43	"
	F	Robinson Harry H	399	waiter	65	"
	G	Robinson Mabel A—†	399	hairdresser	53	"
	H	Willock Margaret—†	399	maid	56	
	N	Allen Nathaniel	403	porter	60	
	O	Burns Louis	403	"	68	
	P	Butler Edgar	403	retired	72	"
	R	Fernandez Dominga—†	403	waitress	21	18 Hubert
	S	Francis Charlotte—†	403	domestic	44	here
	T	Marshall Booker	403	chauffeur	34	"
	U	Merritt William H	403	presser	37	"
	V	Moore Elaine—†	403	typist	29	149 Worcester
	W	Tucker Mary—†	403	housekeeper	50	here
	X	Warren Clarise—†	403	clerk	32	804 Tremont
	Z	Lewis Florence—†	405	domestic	47	here
435						
	A	Russell Grant D	405	U S A	20	44 Cabot
	B	Russell Minnie—†	405	housewife	57	44 "
	D	McCormack Annie J—†	406	at home	55	here
	E	Monahan Alice—†	406	"	65	"
	F	Monahan Jennie Q—†	406	"	45	"

Massachusetts Avenue—Continued

Page.	Letter.	Full Name.	Residence, Jan. 1, 1943.	Occupation.	Supposed Age.	Reported Residence, Jan. 1, 1942. Street and Number.
	G	Chan Henry	406	manager	35	here
	H	Lutz Frederick	406	roofer	57	"
	K	Pringle Tina—†	406	at home	69	"
	L	Smith Alexander	406	cutter	74	
	M	Corey Trueman T	406	agent	53	
	N	DeCoste Sophie—†	406	operator	53	..
	O	Roberts Marcia E—†	406	at home	70	
	P	Soper Arthur W	406	retired	73	"
	R	Miles Veronica—†	406	housewife	30	Cambridge
	S	Miles William S	406	U S N	33	here
	T	Scott Elsie—†	406	clerk	37	41 Burbank
	U	Wilks Walter D	406	laborer	35	85 Roxbury
	V	Chin Cora—†	406	cashier	31	here
	W	Chin George	406	waiter	51	"
	X	Chin Leland	406	manager	43	"
	Y	Chin Paul	406	waiter	29	
	Z	Moy Charles	406	U S A	23	
436						
	A	Moy Conrad	406	waiter	33	
	B	Wong Lillina—†	406	operator	22	
	C	Conant Jennie S—†	406	at home	81	
	D	Conant Nettie M—†	406	"	58	
	E	Gould Nellie—†	406	"	45	"
	F	Chin Bing	406	manager	56	398 Mass av
	G	Chin May—†	406	at home	54	398 "
	H	Chin Rose—†	406	student	20	398 "
	K	DeCroteau Eugene F	406	U S A	24	here
	L	DeCroteau Florence M–†	406	milliner	43	"
	M	DeCroteau William E	406	merchant	57	"
	N	Finnegan James	406	chauffeur	56	"
	O	Galvin William	406	roofer	51	
	P	Monahan Martin J	406	manager	57	"
	R	Monahan Patrick J	406	chef	59	
	S	*Dame Lim—†	406	at home	40	
	T	Wong Goy	406	cook	45	"
	U	Bargasse Louis	407	laborer	40	378 Mass av
	V	Gomez Margo E—†	407	hairdresser	27	New York
	W	Hyatt Annie—†	407	housewife	21	"
	X	Hyatt Walter	407	machinist	21	"
	Y	Jackson Frank	407	laborer	50	378 Mass av
	Z	Johnson Estelle—†	407	maid	49	378 "

Page.	Letter.	Full Name.	Residence, Jan. 1, 1943.	Occupation.	Supposed Age.	Reported Residence, Jan. 1, 1942. Street and Number.
437		**Massachusetts Avenue**—Continued				
	A	Martin Emily—†	407	housekeeper	45	378 Mass av
	B	Nelson Lillian—†	407	machinist	33	378 "
	C	Nickerson Geneva—†	407	maid	32	Maine
	D	Thompson William A	407	laborer	45	"
	F	Daniels Lester L	409	machinist	32	here
	G	Daniels Pauline—†	409	maid	31	"
	L	Card Horatio S	411	physician	76	"
	M	Card Martha O—†	411	housewife	49	"
	N	Elliot Helen B—†	411	clerk	40	"
	R	Dubois Rudolph	413	cook	45	New York
	S	Hunter Robert	413	chauffeur	43	here
	T	Nura Manuel	413	cook	28	19 Dilworth
	U	Smith Matilda—†	413	housekeeper	55	here
	V	Talson Robert	413	clerk	40	Worcester
	W	Bean Helen—†	414	nurse	27	N Carolina
	X	Bean Walter	414	mechanic	35	"
	Y	Blanchard Lola—†	414	clerk	52	here
	Z	Braxton Rosanna B—†	414	domestic	63	"
438						
	A	Braxton Walter	414	retired	74	
	B	Dashwood Latricia—†	414	at home	72	
	C	*Johnson Stanley	414	mechanic	43	"
	D	*Morrison Herbert	414	janitor	55	
	E	Senio Frank	414	"	43	
	F	Stephens Edna—†	414	at home	36	
	G	Stephens William	414	cook	45	
	H	Williams Lillian—†	414	actress	35	"
	K	Franklin Herbert	415	clergyman	48	193 Humboldt av
	L	Johnson Elizabeth—†	415	housekeeper	63	115 "
	M	Moore Frank	415	janitor	52	Georgia
	N	Baker Mary—†	416	domestic	42	here
	O	Bonham Mary—†	416	clerk	30	465 Shawmut av
	P	Cantrell Mary—†	416	domestic	40	here
	R	Cousens Mary—†	416	"	41	"
	S	Gregory Edith—†	416	at home	21	Attleboro
	T	Gregory Walter L	416	welder	30	873 Harris'n av
	U	Harden Elizabeth—†	416	at home	65	here
	U	Harden William	416	retired	75	"
	V	Johnson Arthur	416	porter	55	"
	W	Johnson Edna—†	416	domestic	48	"

Page.	Letter.	Full Name.	Residence, Jan. 1, 1943.	Occupation.	Supposed Age.	Reported Residence, Jan. 1, 1942. Street and Number.

Massachusetts Avenue—Continued

Page.	Letter.	Full Name.	Residence, Jan. 1, 1943.	Occupation.	Supposed Age.	Reported Residence, Jan. 1, 1942. Street and Number.
	x	Jones Allen	416	baker	28	here
	y	Mitchell Mary—†	416	domestic	45	"
	z	Clark Ethel—†	417	waitress	20	431 Mass av
439						
	A	Jackson Charles W	417	driller	42	431 "
	B	Jackson Henry H	417	retired	75	here
	C	Jackson Mary C—†	417	housekeeper	43	431 Mass av
	D	Tate Charles E	417	cook	45	431 "
	E	Burton Bernice—†	418	at home	28	107 Quincy
	F	Burton Laselle	418	U S N	30	107 "
	G	Carr Rachel—†	418	domestic	55	here
	H	Chisholm Anna—†	418	"	43	"
	K	Houston Rita—†	418	"	30	"
	L	Houston Theodore	418	cook	35	
	M	Johnson Harriet—†	418	domestic	51	"
	N	Latham Herbert	418	operator	42	"
	O	Sampson Flora—†	418	cleaner	48	90 Camden
	P	Taylor Nina—†	418	at home	47	223 W Springfield
	R	Taylor William H	418	policeman	48	223 "
	S	Whelpley Fred	418	physician	65	here
	T	Averett Flora B—†	419	operator	25	Medford
	U	Cheesemond Walter	419	mechanic	58	397 Mass av
	V	Dean Ada E—†	419	domestic	21	Oklahoma
	W	Dickerson Vickie	419	musician	37	New York
	X	Ginn Marjorie—†	419	cook	27	429 Mass av
	Y	Kyser Marian—†	419	presser	48	here
	Z	Laney David	419	welder	25	84 W Rutland sq
440						
	A	Lee David	419	laborer	25	16 Hubert
	B	McFadden Harold	419	musician	26	383 Col av
	C	Russell William	419	machinist	25	897A Tremont
	D	Sullivan James	419	"	20	14 Harold
	E	Wolfork Julia—†	419	maid	23	10 Fairweather
	F	Yee N Yon	419A	laundryman	46	here
	G	Critchlow Erwin	420	porter	41	755 Tremont
	H	Daniels Annabelle—†	420	domestic	45	409 Mass av
	K	Harris Nicholas	420	porter	38	166 Walnut av
	L	Isaacs Robert	420	"	30	here
	M	Mundy Helen—†	420	waitress	39	"
	N	Richardson Barbara—†	420	operator	33	"
	O	Tappin James	420	porter	48	

Page.	Letter.	Full Name.	Residence, Jan. 1, 1943.	Occupation.	Supposed Age.	Reported Residence, Jan. 1, 1942. Street and Number.

Massachusetts Avenue—Continued

Page.	Letter.	Full Name.	Residence, Jan. 1, 1943.	Occupation.	Supposed Age.	Reported Residence, Jan. 1, 1942. Street and Number.
	P	Whitley Alfreda—†	420	domestic	43	here
	R	Bear Clyde	421	mechanic	39	New Jersey
	S	Luster Cleveland	421	clerk	30	355 Mass av
	T	Porter Harold	421	chipper	35	728 Tremont
	U	Ramsey Junious	421	laborer	32	Cambridge
	V	Stinson John	421	waiter	38	503 Col av
	W	Strobhart Lillian—†	421	housekeeper	39	355 Mass av
	X	Welles Carl	421	guard	42	305 Col av
	Y	Worthington Howard	421	laborer	29	499 "
	Z	Cheek Philip	422	packer	46	here
441						
	A	Gibbons Ida—†	422	domestic	39	"
	B	Harris Dorothy—†	422	"	40	Pennsylvania
	C	Holcomb Joseph	422	packer	42	522 Mass av
	D	Warner Ernest	422	mechanic	40	here
	E	Warner Rebecca—†	422	at home	38	"
	F	Williamson Norman G	422	laborer	40	"
	L	Barker Elizabeth—†	424	operator	29	91 W Rutland sq
	M	Barker Hattie—†	424	domestic	55	550 Col av
	N	Chavis Oleta—†	424	actress	28	here
	O	Cheesemond Ruth—†	424	domestic	44	623 Col av
	P	Ginn Theodore	424	retired	60	here
	S	Henderson Ollie—†	424	domestic	37	"
	R	Hendrickson Bena—†	424	actress	32	"
	T	Hendrickson Winfield	424	actor	35	
	U	Hicks Jesse	424	mechanic	53	"
	V	Monte Maude—†	424	at home	65	11 Albemarle
	W	Pitts Rosalie—†	424	actress	32	here
	Z	Conway Susan—†	426	laundress	40	586 Col av
442						
	A	Lavine Pearl—†	426	at home	48	here
	B	Marrow Hilda—†	426	"	38	"
	C	Marrow William	426	mechanic	39	"
	D	White Edith—†	426	operator	27	1A Hubert
	E	Douglas Jennie—†	427	cook	70	here
	F	Lewis Raymond	427	operator	48	"
	G	McKnight William A	427	upholsterer	29	2 Hubert
	H	Scott Randall	427	porter	37	401 Col av
	K	Warwick Henry	427	retired	70	here
	N	Berry Donald	429	mechanic	21	Onset
	O	Bowman Victoria—†	429	housekeeper	43	here

Page.	Letter.	Full Name.	Residence, Jan. 1, 1943.	Occupation.	Supposed Age.	Reported Residence, Jan. 1, 1942. Street and Number.

Massachusetts Avenue—Continued

	P	Chenault Oscar	429	houseman	20	Ohio
	R	Crump Helena—†	429	entertainer	37	here
	S	Dunham Oscar	429	musician	30	"
	T	Dunn Marie—†	429	cook	28	N Carolina
	U	Gordon Jesse	429	entertainer	31	here
	V	Hawkins Edgar	429	chauffeur	33	New York
	W	Headspeath Selma—†	429	entertainer	21	Pennsylvania
	X	Jarvis Theodore	429	chipper	25	90 Lenox
	Y	Lewis Oscar	429	waiter	29	414 Col av
	Z	Payne Constance—†	429	waitress	27	here
443						
	A	Rose James	429	welder	22	Connecticut
	B	Saunders Ella M—†	429	entertainer	33	here
	C	Saunders Richard	429	"	45	"
	D	Taylor Archibald	429	chef	38	"
	E	Terry Edith—†	429	domestic	62	"
	F	Vieira Herman	429	welder	25	Connecticut
	M	Stetson Ottie	433	retired	63	here
	O	Davis Josephine—†	433	at home	56	"
	R	Largy Frederick	433	chef	57	"
	S	Largy Nettie—†	433	housewife	52	"
	T	Hartman Hattie—†	433	clerk	59	
	U	Monroe Elizabeth—†	433	at home	73	"
	V	Keavy Michael F	433	longshoreman	46	88 Worcester
	W	Keavy Mildred—†	433	housewife	35	88 "
	X	Moore Annabelle—†	434	student	20	here
	Y	Moore Elmer E	434	clerk	46	"
	Z	Moore Margaret L—†	434	at home	43	"
444						
	A	Tsaggaris Adelaide—†	434	"	29	
	B	*Tsaggaris Charles	434	operator	41	
	C	Gordon Rose L—†	434	domestic	42	"
	D	Johnson Mary—†	434	cook	37	
	E	Norris Inez—†	434	operator	23	"
	F	Troupe Lucretia C—†	434	"	41	
	G	Tucker Ora L—†	434	cook	21	
	H	Young Nancy—†	434	domestic	23	"
	K	Bates Millie—†	434	at home	52	
	L	Bates Thomas R	434	cook	61	
	M	Bates Thomas R, jr	434	operator	21	"
	N	Wilkie Samuel	434	mechanic	45	"

Massachusetts Avenue—Continued

Page.	Letter.	Full Name.	Residence, Jan. 1, 1943.			
	T	Griffin Honora G—†	450	at home	80	here
	U	Griffin Katherine F—†	450	"	81	"
	V	Putnam Mary A—†	450	"	72	"
	W	Walther Bertha L—†	450	fitter	45	
	X	White Anna E—†	450	stitcher	52	
	Y	*Dykens Charles	451	laborer	57	
	Z	Dykens Ralph A	451	shipfitter	49	"
445						
	A	Dykens Victorian—†	451	housekeeper	40	"
	B	Eichel Albert	451	ironworker	36	"
	C	Eichel Catherine—†	451	housewife	29	"
	D	Hommel Robert	451	retired	74	
	E	Hughes Joseph	451	ironworker	34	"
	F	Pigeon Anna E—†	451	cashier	47	"
	G	Stanton Mary—†	451	waitress	39	92 Hemenway
	H	Doyle Peter	453	painter	38	N Hampshire
	K	Ellis Agnes—†	453	housewife	41	here
	L	Huber Frank	453	shipper	49	"
	M	Kelly Norris N	453	bartender	60	Belmont
	N	Leonard John	453	laborer	40	here
	O	Leonard Phoebe—†	453	at home	68	"
	P	Lydon Richard	453	brakeman	29	4 Parker pl
	R	Mangerian Gladys—†	453	clerk	36	here
	S	Pittman Mildred E—†	453	housekeeper	48	"
	T	Pittman Raymond L	453	U S C G	40	"
	U	Walton William	453	guard	47	
	V	Alperen Belle—†	454	at home	72	
	W	Beavis Kathleen—†	454	"	55	
	X	Beavis Michael	454	decorator	50	"
	Y	Bonzey LaForest	454	retired	65	406 Mass av
	Z	Dudley Annie—†	454	at home	70	here
446						
	A	Enwright Annie—†	454	"	77	
	B	Fitzgerald Bartholomew	454	retired	76	"
	C	Foley Joseph	454	"	68	50 Worcester
	D	Foster Edwin	454	"	74	here
	E	Fox Priscilla—†	454	at home	84	"
	F	Grant Alexander	454	retired	86	153 W Concord
	G	Green Henry	454	"	83	here
	H	Harrington Frank	454	"	66	252 Park
	K	*Johansen Edward	454	"	67	here

Page.	Letter.	FULL NAME.	Residence, Jan. 1, 1943.	Occupation.	Supposed Age.	Reported Residence, Jan. 1, 1942. Street and Number.

Massachusetts Avenue—Continued

	L	Johnson Miriam—†	454	at home	72	here
	M	Manning John J	454	retired	76	333 Mass av
	N	Prescott Orrin	454	"	83	here
	O	Tilton Matilda—†	454	at home	86	"
	P	Wishman Jennie—†	454	"	67	"
	R	Adshade Amy—†	455	nurse	40	N Hampshire
	S	*Adshade William	455	contractor	51	"
	T	Doherty Marion—†	455	operator	36	Somerville
	U	McDuffie George	455	cook	38	Georgia
	V	McDuffie Imogene—†	455	housewife	35	"
	W	Morrissey Albertina—†	455	laundress	55	211 W Newton
	X	Reardon Sarah—†	455	"	50	119 Appleton
	Y	Reiser Joseph	455	attendant	55	211 W Newton
	Z	Ross Anne—†	455	housewife	24	Arizona
447						
	A	Horan Agnes—†	457	at home	76	Quincy
	B	McNally Arthur	457	machinist	39	New York
	C	Plueff Sarah—†	457	stitcher	52	here
	D	Robertson William	457	shoeworker	67	459 Mass av
	E	Whalen John A	457	retired	74	here
	F	Whalen Mary L—†	457	housekeeper	66	"
	G	Bean Harry	458	retired	67	"
	H	Beens Thomas	458	"	69	
	K	Billington Alpheus	458	"	71	
	L	Coakley Charles	458	"	75	
	M	Coste Marie J—†	458	at home	60	
	O	Cregan James	458	retired	71	"
	N	Dowd Martin	458	"	74	
	P	MacEnerney Mary—†	458	at home	72	
	R	Marcus Louis	458	retired	82	
	S	*Sheehan William	458	"	73	"
	T	Thompson Anna—†	458	at home	74	"
	U	Wingate John	458	retired	80	"
	V	Cox Elizabeth F—†	459	at home	68	22 Westminster
	W	Jones Charles	459	laborer	34	N Hampshire
	X	Mitchell Virginia—†	459	clerk	23	7 Wellington
	Y	Ashton George	460	retired	67	here
	Z	Barrows Anna—†	460	domestic	25	"
448						
	A	Broderick Annie A—†	460	at home	50	
	B	Cashman John	460	printer	65	

Page.	Letter.	Full Name.	Residence, Jan. 1, 1943.	Occupation.	Supposed Age.	Reported Residence, Jan. 1, 1942. Street and Number.

Massachusetts Avenue—Continued

	c	Geran Jeremiah	460	retired	68	Tewksbury
	D	Mahoney Daniel	460	"	68	"
	E	Morey Patrick	460	"	71	here
	F	Mundy William	460	mechanic	63	"
	G	O'Connell Patrick	460	retired	65	"
	H	Ray Gertrude—†	460	domestic	50	"
	K	Rooney Thomas	460	retired	71	Tewksbury
	L	Walsh Patrick	460	"	70	"
	M	Wilbur James	460	"	71	here
	N	Barlow William H	461	salesman	62	459 Mass av
	O	Bousquet Joseph T	461	retired	68	here
	P	Bousquet Mellina—†	461	stitcher	62	"
	R	*Burke James	461	retired	69	"
	S	Burke James F	461	clerk	38	
	T	*Burke Margaret H—†	461	housewife	71	"
	U	*Christian Elizabeth—†	461	at home	74	
	V	Christian Rosalie—†	461	clerk	25	
	W	Green Michael T	461	porter	56	
	X	Hardiman James	461	"	34	
	Y	Hart Mary—†	461	housewife	60	"
	Z	*Matheson Sarah—†	461	retired	64	459 Mass av
449						
	A	Smith Edwin T	461	porter	42	N Hampshire
	B	Taylor Jessie—†	461	stitcher	50	here
	C	Andre Anthony	462	decorator	30	"
	D	Elifson Hilda—†	462	at home	77	"
	E	Ernest Florence—†	462	clerk	27	
	F	Ernest Ruth—†	462	at home	48	
	G	Fernandes Manuel	462	shipper	25	"
	H	Ferry George	462	welder	22	Onset
	K	Heraldo Alphonse	462	driller	42	570 Col av
	L	Lopes Augustus	462	barber	40	here
	M	Lopes Katherine—†	462	maid	28	"
	N	Miller Ruth—†	462	stitcher	38	26 Westminster
	O	Miller William	462	cook	39	26 "
	P	Parkinson Walter	462	"	44	here
	R	Valles Joseph	462	welder	21	New Bedford
	S	Valles Joseph J	462	"	28	Onset
	T	Valles Mary—†	462	at home	27	"
	U	Young Pauline—†	462	clerk	34	here
	V	Aylward John	463	mechanic	34	9 Tyler

Page.	Letter.	Full Name.	Residence, Jan. 1, 1943.	Occupation.	Supposed Age.	Reported Residence, Jan. 1, 1942. Street and Number.

Massachusetts Avenue—Continued

	W	Chick Mae—†	463	clerk	27	here
	X	Cullen Frank	463	chauffeur	41	"
	Y	*Delegeorges John	463	cook	55	"
	Z	Deviney David A	463	operator	66	"
450						
	A	Deviney Delia—†	463	housekeeper	62	"
	B	O'Neil Catherine—†	463	housewife	32	N Hampshire
	C	O'Neil Sherman	463	salesman	30	"
	D	Savage Mary D—†	463	at home	82	here
	E	Boyd Madeline—†	464	operator	23	"
	F	Lew Loretta—†	464	at home	50	94 Harrishof
	G	Pierce Frances—†	464	operator	29	here
	H	Weaks Hannah—†	464	cook	40	"
	K	Youngblood Margaret—†	464	director	48	"
	L	Bartlett Elizabeth—†	465	housewife	48	468 Mass av
	M	Bartlett Percy	465	mechanic	45	468 "
	N	Burke Joseph E	465	plumber	53	here
	O	Dern Walter	465	chauffeur	35	42 Waltham
	P	LeClerc Armand	465	mechanic	45	here
	R	LeClerc Helen—†	465	waitress	40	"
	S	Marlow Bernard	465	caretaker	60	"
	T	Marlow Bernard J	465	U S A	21	
	U	Marlow Edmund M	465	retired	75	
	V	Marlow Jennie A—†	465	housewife	64	"
	W	Marlow Leon F	465	student	29	
	X	Marlow Mary A—†	465	clerk	22	
	Y	Marlow Paul B	465	orderly	35	
	Z	Thornton Thomas J	465	chauffeur	31	"
451						
	A	Alexander John	466	messenger	68	"
	B	Bedell James	466	mechanic	42	Missouri
	C	Benjamin Laura—†	466	cook	46	here
	D	Bonner Ralph	466	porter	45	"
	E	Brown Walter	466	mechanic	62	"
	F	Christian Clara B—†	466	at home	50	
	G	Clark Alsona	466	clerk	40	"
	H	Gifford William	466	U S C G	23	Nantucket
	K	Johnson Walter	466	waiter	38	here
	L	Lombardi Joseph	466	roofer	40	"
	M	Lombardi Josephine—†	466	operator	35	"
	N	Miles Albert J	466	waiter	30	Missouri

Page.	Letter.	Full Name.	Residence, Jan. 1, 1943.	Occupation.	Supposed Age.	Reported Residence, Jan. 1, 1942. Street and Number.

Massachusetts Avenue—Continued

Page.	Letter.	Full Name.	Residence, Jan. 1, 1943.	Occupation.	Supposed Age.	Reported Residence, Jan. 1, 1942. Street and Number.
	O	Newton Ruth—†	466	operator	50	here
	P	Qualls Richard M	466	retired	70	"
	R	Randolph John	466	cook	50	40 Hollander
	S	Sims Arthur	466	"	40	here
	T	Woods Roosevelt	466	waiter	40	"
	U	Brosseau Henry	467	cook	50	"
	V	Bugby Celia—†	467	housekeeper	50	4 James
	W	*Gallagher Mary—†	467	at home	48	here
	X	Hamacher Elizabeth—†	467	housewife	57	"
	Y	Hamacher Robert	467	cook	31	"
	Z	Hamacher William	467	"	58	
452						
	A	Keenan Vincent	467	mechanic	27	54 John
	B	Leushier Charles	467	clerk	47	here
	C	Soloway Jean—†	467	housekeeper	27	"
	D	Soloway Joseph	467	cook	29	"
	E	Allen Ruth—†	468	actress	31	543 Col av
	F	Killian Albert	468	mechanic	25	here
	G	Killian Ruby—†	468	operator	22	"
	H	Martina Elizabeth—†	468	clerk	28	405 Mass av
	K	Taylor Violet—†	468	waitress	27	28 Hubert
	L	Watts Clara—†	468	operator	28	9 Holyoke
	M	Bailey Mary—†	469	housekeeper	67	here
	N	Borden Rosa—†	469	"	51	459 Mass av
	O	Byrnes Eden F	469	chauffeur	40	New York
	P	Carr Katherine—†	469	waitress	43	here
	R	Curtis Louis	469	mechanic	43	"
	S	Curtis Mae—†	469	housewife	32	"
	T	Kelly Gerald	469	painter	57	"
	U	Leonard Alice—†	469	domestic	55	459 Mass av
	V	Ritter Mary—†	469	clerk	64	459 "
	W	Weir Clarence	469	cook	63	453 "
	X	Winters Emil	469	baker	40	110 Pembroke
	Y	Dann Sofus F	470	retired	74	569 E Eighth
	Z	Henchey William J	470	"	70	here
453						
	A	Kazanjian Charles A	470	watchman	46	"
	B	McWilliams Robert A	470	retired	78	581 Mass av
	C	Nillson Carl	470	mechanic	56	here
	D	Parkhurst Edward	470	retired	72	38 Harvard
	E	Parkhurst Sadie—†	470	clerk	50	38 "

Massachusetts Avenue—Continued

Page.	Letter.	Full Name.	Residence, Jan. 1, 1943.	Occupation.	Supposed Age.	Reported Residence, Jan. 1, 1942. Street and Number.
	F	Saxer Emma F—†	470	at home	76	here
	G	Sherwin James J	470	laborer	60	"
	H	Brown James	471	retired	76	"
	K	*Byrnes Catherine—†	471	housekeeper	55	"
	L	Byrnes James A	471	manager	57	"
	M	Byrnes Sadie—†	471	operator	27	"
	N	Gillis Edgar	471	carpenter	38	7 Blackstone
	O	Moran Helen—†	471	housewife	35	here
	P	Moran John	471	mechanic	37	"
	R	Newhall Herbert C	471	chauffeur	34	459 Mass av
	S	Psyhages George	471	cook	50	here
	T	Sullivan Bessie—†	471	waitress	45	"
	U	Walsh John	471	boilermaker	58	"
	V	Wilson Mary—†	471	seamstress	55	"
	W	Cameron George	472	retired	76	99 Pembroke
	X	Chambers James	472	operator	50	here
	Y	Gillespie James	472	retired	56	460 Mass av
	Z	Healey William	472	"	45	here
454						
	A	Herney John	472	operator	55	"
	B	Madden Edward	472	clerk	50	"
	C	Marcille Mary—†	472	at home	55	"
	D	Scott George	472	retired	59	"
	E	Stone William	472	"	80	"
	F	Tonry John	472	"	68	"
	G	Topping Ann—†	472	at home	47	"
	H	Topping James P	472	printer	49	"
	K	Walker Henry	472	cook	55	"
	L	Cole Arthur W	473	janitor	76	New York
	M	Kawa Bonnelyn—†	473	housewife	27	Rhode Island
	N	Kawa Joseph	473	shipfitter	37	"
	O	Kelley Pauline—†	473	housewife	38	Maine
	P	Kelley Ray	473	printer	42	"
	R	Bryant James	474	retired	77	here
	S	Cody John	474	cook	56	472 Mass av
	T	Connolly Anna—†	474	at home	52	here
	U	Connolly John	474	student	22	"
	V	Connolly Michael	474	mechanic	53	"
	W	Connolly Michael G	474	"	20	"
	X	Creggs Edward	474	clerk	36	"
	Y	Creggs Mary—†	474	at home	60	"

Page.	Letter.	Full Name.	Residence, Jan. 1, 1943.	Occupation.	Supposed Age.	Reported Residence, Jan. 1, 1942. Street and Number.

Massachusetts Avenue—Continued

	Z	Croake Robert	474	retired	70	here
455						
	A	McCormack Charles	474	roofer	37	
	B	Murphy Charles	474	printer	55	
	C	Murphy Laura—†	474	at home	60	
	D	*O'Donnell Malcolm	474	retired	52	
	E	Steele Walter	474	surveyor	49	"
	F	Walsh William	474	retired	67	
	G	Brannagan Mary—†	475	at home	83	
	H	O'Brien Joseph P	475	retired	69	"
	K	Blaisdell Phillip	476	clerk	44	New Bedford
	L	Blaisdell Winola—†	476	"	25	"
	M	Bynum Ruth—†	476	maid	24	here
	N	Cheeks Alan D	476	dentist	68	"
	O	Cheeks Matilda—†	476	at home	67	"
	P	Chinn Pembroke B	476	mechanic	40	27 Cabot
	R	Downing Lillian—†	476	maid	41	here
	S	Farnham Della—†	476	at home	59	"
	T	Farnham Louis	476	retired	65	"
	U	Greenidge Edward	476	porter	55	
	V	Harrison Mary—†	476	maid	49	
	W	Hoxter Stanbury	476	waiter	69	
	X	*Doyle Amy—†	477	housewife	39	"
	Y	*Doyle John	477	carpenter	44	"
	Z	Kneicht Otto	477	"	30	
456						
	A	Martin Frank	477	clerk	41	
	B	Martin Lillian—†	477	housewife	32	"
	C	McDonald Jeanette—†	477	clerk	24	New York
	D	Olsen Hilda—†	477	housewife	50	here
	E	Olsen Simon	477	merchant	50	"
	F	Peters Celia—†	477	housewife	24	Maine
	G	Rowley Florence—†	477	clerk	24	Douglass
	H	Shores Jennie—†	477	housewife	56	N Carolina
	K	Shores Wallace	477	mechanic	56	"
	M	Blanchard Frederick	478	U S N	23	here
	N	Blanchard Ida—†	478	at home	51	"
	O	Moore Elwood	478	designer	43	6 Templeton way
	P	Moore Norma—†	478	at home	24	6 "
	R	Leroy Jane—†	478	"	47	here
	S	Leroy Mary—†	478	"	20	"

Page.	Letter.	Full Name.	Residence, Jan. 1, 1943.	Occupation.	Supposed Age.	Reported Residence, Jan. 1, 1942. Street and Number.

Massachusetts Avenue—Continued

Page.	Letter.	Full Name.	Residence, Jan. 1, 1943.	Occupation.	Supposed Age.	Reported Residence, Jan. 1, 1942. Street and Number.
	T	Baker Catherine—†	479	waitress	30	Maine
	U	Burke John	479	cook	37	New York
	V	Cowhig James A	479	clerk	47	here
	W	Foley Margaret—†	479	at home	76	26 Alpha rd
	X	Hubbard Ernest V	479	counterman	55	here
	Y	Mann George	479	chauffeur	33	"
	Z	Mann Gerard	479	clerk	40	"
457						
	A	Mann Katherine—†	479	retired	67	
	B	Merritt Clifford	479	salesman	35	"
	C	Moore Anna G—†	479	at home	66	717 Mass av
	D	Murdock John	479	mechanic	45	here
	E	Murdock Margaret—†	479	housekeeper	40	"
	F	Burke Jennie—†	480	at home	70	"
	G	Lane William	480	operator	65	563 Mass av
	H	Leonard Charles	480	retired	47	here
	K	Leonard John	480	plasterer	55	"
	L	Longa Joseph P	480	barber	56	"
	M	Marble Lawrence	480	fireman	60	"
	N	Mathewson Percy	480	porter	47	N Hampshire
	O	Mellish Leslie	480	carpenter	60	here
	P	Messick Christine—†	480	at home	52	"
	R	Parker William	480	retired	79	"
	S	Rivers Mary—†	480	at home	55	563 Mass av
	T	Rivers William	480	laborer	55	563 "
	U	Sutherland Christina—†	480	at home	60	here
	V	Sybil Jean—†	480	waitress	50	Rhode Island
	W	Tierney Anna—†	480	clerk	55	205 Com av
	X	Tierney James	480	watchman	56	205 "
	Y	Garrick Arthur	482	retired	62	here
	Z	Gilbert Flora—†	482	dressmaker	51	"
458						
	A	Gilbert Oswald	482	clerk	37	
	B	Johnson Adele—†	482	matron	75	
	C	Silva Richard	482	welder	23	
	D	Tasco Anna—†	482	at home	39	"
	E	Tasco Nathan	482	janitor	76	"
	F	Black Gertrude—†	483	waitress	28	Watertown
	G	Leach Louise—†	483	housekeeper	50	here
	H	MacCormick William	483	carpenter	54	Cambridge
	K	Madigan John	483	counterman	38	here

Page.	Letter.	Full Name.	Residence, Jan. 1, 1943.	Occupation.	Supposed Age.	Reported Residence, Jan. 1, 1942. Street and Number.

Massachusetts Avenue—Continued

	L	Manning George	483	shipper	64	here
	M	O'Connor Conelius	483	guard	51	"
	N	Richerson Gertrude—†	483	cook	55	"
	O	Salaries Charles	483	counterman	20	New York
	P	Schachter Maurice	483	retired	71	here
	R	Stevens Geraldine—†	483	maid	38	"
	S	Williams Bessie—†	483	housekeeper	53	453 Mass av
	T	Bayer Max	484	waiter	38	109 Walnut av
	U	Driscoll Helen—†	484	waitress	42	here
	V	Holbrook Florence—†	484	"	30	697 Mass av
	W	Holbrook Lawrence	484	mechanic	31	697 "
	X	Julinson Albian	484	painter	46	here
	Y	King Ernest	484	waiter	35	80 Hunt'n av
	Z	Marshall Marion—†	484	cashier	32	31 Melrose
459						
	A	Noyers Albert	484	fireman	40	33 Hillsdale
	B	Poirier Edward	484	operator	63	here
	C	Rancourt Evelyn—†	484	clerk	35	"
	D	Rancourt Irene—†	484	at home	25	"
	E	Rancourt Mary—†	484	"	56	
	F	Rancourt Norman	484	mechanic	26	"
	G	Rontier Albert	484	doorman	45	140 St Botolph
	H	Warren Joseph	484	mechanic	59	here
	K	Cole Henry	486	chauffeur	56	"
	L	Dilis Adrien	486	porter	65	"
	M	Dilis Elise—†	486	at home	64	
	N	Dilis Jeanette—†	486	waitress	24	"
	O	Enos Lena—†	486	laundress	48	460 Mass av
	P	Freeman William	486	painter	58	Littleton
	R	Golar Archibald	486	carpenter	66	here
	S	Good John	486	clerk	34	"
	T	Kelly Anne—†	486	waitress	52	"
	U	Lagoulis Anthony	486	cook	65	508 Mass av
	V	Lyons John	486	"	40	121 Warren av
	W	Marsella Carl	486	"	30	here
	X	Bakrison David	486	mechanic	58	Norwood
	Y	Smith Elmer	486	laborer	62	here
	Z	Sylva Charles	486	conductor	68	"
460						
	A	Bavineau Frank	487	retired	72	
	B	Byrne Alice—†	487	housewife	53	"

Page.	Letter.	Full Name.	Residence, Jan. 1, 1943.	Occupation.	Supposed Age.	Reported Residence, Jan. 1, 1942. Street and Number.

Massachusetts Avenue—Continued

	C	Byrne Walter	487	chef	43	here
	D	Collins Dennis	487	foreman	40	"
	E	*Ennis Frank	487	fireman	54	"
	F	Fennessy Helena—†	487	stitcher	39	Worcester
	G	*Flynn Catherine—†	487	maid	33	here
	H	*Greene Anna—†	487	laundress	45	37 Concord
	K	Greene James	487	houseman	44	37 "
	L	Hickey Maurice P	487	retired	72	here
	M	Kneeland Bernard	487	carpenter	68	14 Flagg
	N	*Kneeland Mary—†	487	at home	27	14 "
	O	McGrath Catherine—†	487	cook	59	144 Warren av
	P	Padden Mary E—†	487	stenographer	37	here
	R	Small Julia A—†	487	stitcher	66	"
	S	Chambers Bessie—†	491	housewife	55	"
	T	Chambers Gerald	491	machinist	23	"
	U	Powers Chester	491	entertainer	38	202 W Brookline
	V	Powers Dorothy M—†	491	housewife	36	202 "
	W	Wilson Anne—†	491	at home	50	here
	Y	Woodson Irene—†	493	housewife	20	Fall River
	Z	Woodson Newton	493	chauffeur	39	"
461						
	B	Smith Daniel J	493	plumber	69	here
	C	Smith Dolina—†	493	housewife	62	"
	D	Curtin John J	493	chef	49	"
	E	Flanders Emily—†	493	housewife	53	"
	F	Sullivan Frances—†	493	clerk	50	
	G	Stroyman Maurice	493	retired	72	"
	K	Locke Allison	493	clerk	47	508 Mass av
	N	Dobbins Chester	496	mechanic	35	N Hampshire
	O	Dobbins Eileen—†	496	at home	29	"
	R	Arda John	496	operator	47	Egypt
	S	McDermott Hugh	496	laborer	41	here
	T	Morin Grace—†	496	at home	60	"
	U	Cullen Dennis	496	mechanic	34	Maine
	V	Cullen Jean—†	496	waitress	30	"
	W	Matheson Elizabeth—†	496	at home	72	here
	X	Matheson Roderick D	496	retired	82	"
	Y	Mendengain Harry	496	mechanic	56	"
	Z	Walker George M	496	retired	77	"
462						
	A	Doherty Edward J	496	custodian	59	15 Gardner

Page.	Letter.	Full Name.	Residence, Jan. 1, 1943.	Occupation.	Supposed Age.	Reported Residence, Jan. 1, 1942. Street and Number.

Massachusetts Avenue—Continued

Page.	Letter.	Full Name.	Residence, Jan. 1, 1943.	Occupation.	Supposed Age.	Reported Residence, Jan. 1, 1942. Street and Number.
	B	Gray John D	496	nurse	38	15 Gardner
	C	Gray Marion—†	496	clerk	40	15 "
	D	Cullinan Edward N	496	chauffeur	36	here
	E	Cullinan Elizabeth J—†	496	at home	30	"
	F	Cullinan Mary J—†	496	"	69	"
	G	Green Mary J—†	496	clerk	39	
	H	Green Raymond F	496	watchman	42	"
	K	Burke John G	496	manager	43	"
	L	Heumiller George J	496	printer	47	
	M	Hull Eugene F	496	painter	61	
	N	Ross Charles A	496	contractor	38	"
	O	Sawtelle Della—†	496	at home	73	637 Dudley
	P	Gonzoulis George	496	salesman	50	here
	R	Lavis Charles J	496	manager	53	"
	S	Lavis Eleanor J—†	496	at home	48	"
	T	Corambis Alice M—†	496	"	57	
	U	Corambis Arthur S	496	manager	63	"
	V	Higgins Daniel	496	clerk	58	
	W	Kuntze Charles	496	watchman	50	"

463 Northampton Street

Page.	Letter.	Full Name.	Residence, Jan. 1, 1943.	Occupation.	Supposed Age.	Reported Residence, Jan. 1, 1942. Street and Number.
	G	Henry Robert C	363	tailor	45	here
	H	Henry Rose—†	363	maid	38	"
	K	Morgan Etta—†	363	domestic	35	"
	M	Smith Leonard	363	mechanic	30	"
	L	Waters Lillian—†	363	domestic	28	"
	N	Hayes Francis	365	laborer	38	
	O	Jarrett Homer	365	realtor	45	"
	P	Tunstell Lula—†	365	housekeeper	45	"
	R	Henderson Rosa—†	367	"	39	N Carolina
	S	Thomas Betty—†	367	domestic	21	New York
	V	Ramsay Martha—†	369	student	27	"
	W	Hathaway Martha—†	369	domestic	51	here
	X	Covington William	369	painter	62	"
	Y	Owens Anna—†	371	domestic	55	"
	Z	Pyhsic Agnes V—†	371	seamstress	33	249 River
464						
	A	Pyhsic Sarah—†	371	domestic	58	here
	B	Strickland Henry	371	laborer	33	"
	C	Strickland Nellie—†	371	housewife	23	"

Page.	Letter.	Full Name.	Residence, Jan. 1, 1943.	Occupation.	Supposed Age.	Reported Residence, Jan. 1, 1942. Street and Number.

Northampton Street—Continued

	D	Barber Nolan	373	laborer	46	12 Holyoke
	E	Caesar Jewell—†	373	housekeeper	38	25 Camden
	F	Poole Luther	373	laborer	50	Ohio
	G	Smith Bernard	373	cook	28	23 Wellington
	H	Wallace Anson A	373	laborer	23	25 Camden
	K	White Carleton C	373	porter	25	New York
	L	Wright Marion—†	373	laundress	36	42 Windsor
	M	Harris Carrie M—†	375	housewife	39	here
	N	Harris Walter T	375	merchant	49	"
	O	Satchebell Charles C	377	coppersmith	31	"
	P	Satchebell Eleanor J—†	377	housewife	31	"
	R	Satchebell Sarah—†	377	"	50	
	S	Wade Adolph	377	retired	70	"
	U	Brown Della—†	384	domestic	40	141 Lenox
	V	Gillette Martha—†	384	at home	76	3 Auburn
	W	Jackson Ida—†	384	"	67	18 Cunard
	X	Jackson Andrew	384	retired	71	here
	Y	Jackson Bessie—†	384	operator	23	"
	Z	Jackson Effie—†	384	housewife	61	"
465						
	A	Jackson Fannie—†	384	factoryhand	26	"
	B	Jackson Hattie—†	384	operator	36	
	C	Jackson Helen—†	384	housewife	38	"
	D	Jackson Robert	384	chauffeur	34	"
	E	Armstrong Joseph	384	porter	42	New York
	F	Darling Edward	384	laborer	45	here
	G	Edwards Alice—†	384	housekeeper	43	"
	H	Reason Lula—†	386	housewife	28	26 Holyoke
	K	Reason Pinkney	386	machinist	27	26 "
	L	Denby Martha—†	386	cook	56	here
	M	Holder Richard	386	seaman	63	"
	P	Harris Emily—†	392	operator	33	501 Col av
	R	Anderson Carrie—†	392	housewife	38	here
	S	Anderson McKerrow	392	baker	43	"
	T	Peters Clara—†	392	packer	34	"
	U	Peters Fred	392	machinist	22	"
	V	Peters George	392	engineer	45	"
	W	Dunkley Madeline—†	394	housewife	40	N Hampshire
	X	Decotea Connell	394	tailor	47	here
	Y	Decotea Jane—†	394	housewife	49	"
	Z	Foote Charles	394	laborer	24	Onset

Page.	Letter.	FULL NAME.	Residence, Jan. 1, 1943.	Occupation.	Supposed Age.	Reported Residence, Jan. 1, 1942. Street and Number.
466						

Northampton Street—Continued

Page.	Letter.	FULL NAME.	Residence, Jan. 1, 1943.	Occupation.	Supposed Age.	Reported Residence, Jan. 1, 1942. Street and Number.
	A	Lee Albercena—†	396	housewife	35	427 Mass av
	B	Lee Joseph	396	laborer	38	427 "
	C	Harris Georginia—†	396	housekeeper	51	here
	D	Powell Lloyd	396	porter	43	"
	E	Samuda Daniel	396	chef	54	"
	F	Samuda Roberta—†	396	housewife	43	"
	G	McCoy Jessie—†	396	"	36	
	H	McCoy Lee	396	porter	43	
	K	McCoy Lee, jr	396	U S A	22	
	L	Byrd May—†	396	domestic	40	"
	M	Downes Phoebe L—†	396	housekeeper	71	"
	N	Watson Annie B—†	396	"	70	
	O	Wanamaker Louella—†	396	"	31	
	P	Young Bessie—†	396	"	51	
	R	Mann Charles B	396	waiter	66	"
	S	Mann Wilhelmina—†	396	housewife	43	"
	T	Jackson Preston	396	chauffeur	41	"
	U	Jackson Rita—†	396	housewife	38	"
	V	Redwine Clara—†	396	maid	30	
	W	Jones Benedict	396	musician	42	"
	X	Jones Dorothy—†	396	housewife	39	"
	Y	White Henry	396	laborer	43	
	Z	White Marguerite—†	396	housewife	33	"
467						
	A	Matthews Alberta—†	396	housekeeper	42	"
	B	Spencer James	396	clerk	47	"
	C	Weedan William	396	retired	67	
	D	West Bessie—†	396	housewife	53	"
	E	West Milton	396	retired	55	
	F	Richardson Etta—†	396	domestic	45	"
	G	Mills Doris—†	396	housewife	37	"
	H	Mills Egbert	396	laborer	46	
	K	Custodio Cascilio	396	cook	29	
	L	Gordon Dell	396	U S A	26	
	M	McConney Donald	396	cook	33	
	N	Jeffers Lucille—†	396	housekeeper	53	"
	O	Smith Ann—†	396	housewife	30	"
	P	Smith Harry	396	laborer	29	
	R	Benson Lucille—†	396	housewife	28	"
	S	Benson William	396	porter	29	

Page.	Letter.	Full Name.	Residence, Jan. 1, 1943.	Occupation.	Supposed Age.	Reported Residence, Jan. 1, 1942. Street and Number.

Northampton Street—Continued

	T	Gomes Rudolph	396	waiter	38	here
	U	Gomes Virginia—†	396	housewife	28	"
	V	Lewis Edward	396	laborer	22	"
	W	Lewis Ellen—†	396	housewife	21	"
	X	Soars Lewis	396	chemist	45	
	Y	Soars Pearl—†	396	housewife	43	"
	Z	Kendricks Fannie—†	396	"	30	
468						
	A	Kendricks John	396	salesman	36	"
	B	Means Eastern	396	weigher	34	
	C	Whitted Marion—†	396	cook	37	"
	D	*Lopes Demasio	396	laborer	48	9 Dilworth
	E	*Lopes Eliza—†	396	housewife	48	9 "
	F	Rollins Hattie—†	396	cook	35	here
	G	Rollins Herman	396	entertainer	33	"
	H	Steele Elise—†	396	welder	26	"
	K	Steele John	396	laborer	24	
	L	Jones Della—†	396	housewife	30	"
	M	Murray Edward	396	laborer	39	
	N	Gordon Claude	396	clerk	46	
	O	Gordon Leonora—†	396	housewife	43	"
	P	Sealy David	396	presser	34	
	R	Sealy Ida—†	396	housewife	32	"
	S	McDowell Frederick	396	clerk	58	
	T	McDowell Vera—†	396	housewife	39	"
	U	Cosby Daisy—†	396	presser	38	757 Tremont
	V	Saunders Celeste—†	396	assembler	29	here
	W	Saunders Leon	396	U S A	38	"
	X	Wilson Catherine—†	396	waitress	33	"
	Y	Butcher Ernie—†	396	domestic	35	"
	Z	Bynoe Louise—†	396	housekeeper	32	"
469						
	A	Tudor John E	396	machinist	20	"
	B	Jackson Arthur C	396	laborer	42	
	C	Jackson Sarah—†	396	housewife	37	"
	D	McCoy Andrew	396	musician	22	"
	E	Ingram Edith—†	396	housewife	21	"
	F	Ingram Emma—†	396	"	63	"
	G	Ingram James	396	engineer	27	"
	H	Long George	396	porter	42	
	K	McKarney Carlton	396	mechanic	39	"

Page.	Letter.	Full Name.	Residence, Jan. 1, 1943.	Occupation.	Supposed Age.	Reported Residence, Jan. 1, 1942. Street and Number.

Northampton Street—Continued

	L	McKarney Hazel—†	396	machinist	27	Framingham
	M	Ricketts Byron J	396	seaman	43	here
	N	Ricketts Nellie—†	396	housewife	30	"
	O	Lewis Teresa—†	396	clerk	23	"
	P	Ricker Clara—†	396	housewife	26	"
	R	Ricker Edward	396	metalworker	29	32 Wellington
	S	Garner James A	396	letter carrier	46	here
	T	Garner Marie G—†	396	housewife	42	"
	U	Cook Bernice—†	396	"	41	"
	V	Cook Charles	396	porter	42	
	W	Cook Louise—†	396	seamstress	22	"
	X	Thomas Egbert	396	porter	32	
	Y	Thomas Olive—†	396	housewife	33	"
	Z	Contee James	396	waiter	33	
470						
	A	Contee Virginia—†	396	housewife	29	"
	B	Houston Fred C	396	laborer	34	"
	C	Houston Idella—†	396	housewife	33	44 Symphony rd
	D	Houston Nathaniel	396	messenger	35	Newton
	E	Somerset Carolyn—†	396	housewife	29	8 Royal
	F	Somerset Joseph	396	chipper	37	8 "
	G	Darrell Eric	396	welder	51	here
	H	Darrell Garnett—†	396	housewife	46	"
	K	Blair Edward	396	retired	70	"
	L	Blair Gertrude—†	396	housewife	29	"
	M	Blair Lewis	396	painter	35	

Tremont Street

	N	Daniel Diana—†	765	laundress	37	here
	O	Daniel Frank	765	retired	61	"
	P	Foster Samuel	765	operator	63	"
	R	Handy Isaac	765	laborer	35	"
	S	Pendleton Robert E	765	"	20	85 W Rutland sq
	T	Eccles Leona—†	765	domestic	45	here
	U	Hardy Beatrice—†	765	"	38	"
	V	Brownell Hattie—†	767	housekeeper	45	771 Tremont
	W	Edwards Edward	767	decorator	49	596 Col av
	X	Johnson Daisy L—†	767	housewife	27	66 Humboldt av
	Y	Taylor William H	767	meatcutter	56	771 Tremont
	Z	Festel August P	769	baker	56	here

Page.	Letter.	Full Name.	Residence, Jan. 1, 1943.	Occupation.	Supposed Age.	Reported Residence, Jan. 1, 1942. Street and Number.
471		**Tremont Street**—Continued				
	A	Festel Marie—†	769	housewife	54	here
	B	Hohberger Sophie—†	769	clerk	56	"
	C	Cotter Florette D—†	769	stitcher	61	"
	D	Cotter William M	769	barber	61	
	E	MacDougall Elizabeth—†	769	saleswoman	44	"
	F	Bowling Iola—†	771	housewife	46	"
	G	Bowling Ralph M	771	shipper	49	"
	H	Dotten Myrtle—†	771	operator	26	495 Col av
	K	Green Edith—†	771	waitress	27	here
	L	Milbourne Audrey—†	771	"	27	"
	M	Rogers Daisy—†	771	"	46	New York
	N	Taylor Lee V—†	771	housewife	24	"
	O	Taylor William E	771	U S A	27	Georgia
	P	Williams Cecelia—†	771	housewife	34	64 W Rutland sq
	R	Williams William K	771	melter	36	64 "
	S	Guiney Clarissa—†	773	housewife	43	here
	T	Guiney John A	773	engineer	57	"
	U	Sullivan Helen—†	773	housewife	36	"
	V	Sullivan James T	773	ironworker	45	"
	X	Jones Elmer H	775	electrician	42	201 W Springfield
	Y	Jones Gladys D—†	775	housewife	41	201 "
	Z	Cropp Neil L	777	realtor	50	427 Mass av
472		**Wellington Street**				
	E	Sephus Bertha—†	2	domestic	44	here
	F	Sephus Lawrence	2	operator	34	"
	G	Clifford Amelia—†	2	domestic	44	"
	H	Clifford William	2	laborer	54	
	K	Tyler George	2	janitor	42	
	L	Gladden Eliza—†	2	domestic	40	"
	M	Smithers Sadie—†	2	"	38	
	N	Trent Fannie—†	2	"	42	"
	O	Brown Ellis E	2	porter	52	
	P	Taylor Pauline—†	2	domestic	38	"
	R	Best Louise—†	2A	at home	65	
	S	Patrick William	2A	porter	49	
	T	Thompson Marion—†	2A	stitcher	32	"
	U	Samuda Alice—†	2A	dressmaker	53	"
	V	Samuda Sidney	2A	laborer	27	

Page.	Letter.	Full Name.	Residence, Jan. 1, 1943.	Occupation.	Supposed Age.	Reported Residence, Jan. 1, 1942. Street and Number.

Wellington Street—Continued

Page.	Letter.	Full Name.	Residence, Jan. 1, 1943.	Occupation.	Supposed Age.	Reported Residence, Jan. 1, 1942. Street and Number.
	W	Tomlinson Edith—†	2A	domestic	52	here
	X	Brown Ethel—†	2A	housewife	52	"
	Y	Brown Robert	2A	salesman	54	"
	Z	North Alice—†	2A	seamstress	47	"
473						
	A	Bell Dorothy L—†	2A	housewife	28	"
	B	Bell Ellis	2A	janitor	29	
	C	Thompson Harold	2A	"	37	
	D	Thompson Sarah—†	2A	housewife	72	"
	E	Bailey William G	4	porter	45	
	F	Evans Maude L—†	4	housewife	60	"
	G	Evans William H	4	retired	76	
	H	Martin John R	4	waiter	40	"
	K	Perkins Israel Z	4	pharmacist	50	Kansas
	L	Wade Manoah	4	porter	49	here
	M	Brooks Minerva—†	6	housewife	35	Kansas
	N	Cloud Clyde	6	mechanic	44	here
	O	Cloud India—†	6	housewife	42	"
	P	Cornwell Florance	6	manager	52	"
	R	King William	6	porter	69	"
	S	Mann Anna M—†	6	waitress	25	Lynn
	T	Overby Annette—†	6	domestic	23	here
	U	Overby Elizabeth—†	6	"	27	"
	V	Overby Fannie—†	6	"	25	"
	W	Sydnor Edmund F	6	porter	70	
	X	Sydnor Mamie—†	6	housewife	51	"
	Y	Isaacs Pansy M—†	8	"	53	
	Z	Isaacs Wilfred	8	chef	53	
474						
	A	Moore Gartrell R	8	usher	23	
	B	Overstreet Zanni T	8	U S A	27	
	C	Pear Ethel—†	8	domestic	51	"
	D	Harris Helen—†	10	clerk	34	
	E	Portlock Olive—†	12	housewife	36	"
	F	Kelley Emma—†	12	domestic	36	"
	H	Fennell Elaine—†	12	housewife	59	300 Tremont
	K	Fennell James T	12	retired	68	800 "
	L	Williams Lillian—†	14	housekeeper	41	here
	M	Jackson Eric	16	clerk	41	"
	N	Jackson Hilda—†	16	housewife	41	"
	P	Taylor Gloria—†	20	student	22	..

Page.	Letter.	Full Name.	Residence, Jan. 1, 1943.	Occupation.	Supposed Age.	Reported Residence, Jan. 1, 1942. Street and Number.

Wellington Street—Continued

Page.	Letter.	Full Name.	Residence, Jan. 1, 1943.	Occupation.	Supposed Age.	Reported Residence, Jan. 1, 1942. Street and Number.
	R	Taylor Lucius	20	musician	26	here
	S	Taylor Sarah—†	20	domestic	47	“
	V	Boddy Albert	22	cook	24	“
	W	Boddy Jane—†	22	housewife	60	“
	X	Boddy Martha E—†	22	domestic	28	“
	Y	Boddy Robert	22	porter	23	
	Z	Morris Annie—†	22	housewife	40	“
475						
	A	Morris Samuel	22	chef	43	
	B	Durant Beatrice—†	22	clerk	33	
	C	Durant John	22	waiter	62	
	D	Durant Joseph	22	retired	73	
	E	Durant Sarah—†	22	housewife	59	“
	F	Harris Henry P	24	retired	67	
	G	Harris Irene—†	24	housewife	23	“
	H	Harris Milton B	24	ironworker	38	“
	K	Cheek Hallie P—†	24	housekeeper	62	“
	L	Cheek Hazel L—†	24	stitcher	32	“
	M	Stubb Louis	24	mechanic	28	“
	N	Gillyourd Calvin	24	laborer	51	“
	O	Gillyourd Eulalie—†	24	housewife	39	“
	P	Dickinson Viola L—†	26	operator	47	“
	R	Hill Jasper F	26	porter	28	
	S	Lewis Sandifer	26	retired	72	
	T	Rice Ada C—†	26	housekeeper	52	“
	U	Schenck John W	26	attorney	77	“
	V	Lindsey Carrie—†	26	housewife	42	“
	W	Lindsey John	26	machinist	47	“
	X	Garrett Eliza—†	26	housekeeper	67	“
	Y	Garrett Margaret M—†	26	clerk	44	“
	Z	Garrett Theodore	26	laborer	43	
476						
	A	*Barry William	32	“	54	Lynn
	B	Dawson Delcia—†	32	housekeeper	66	here
	C	Duncan Muriel—†	32	stitcher	27	“
	D	Jenkins Catherine—†	32	at home	67	“
	E	Pryor Doris—†	32	waitress	30	
	F	Johnson Beresford	32	waiter	37	
	G	Johnson Ernest	32	carpenter	51	“
	H	Johnson Lawrence	32	porter	42	
	K	Johnson Marita—†	32	domestic	23	“

Page.	Letter.	FULL NAME.	Residence, Jan. 1, 1943.	Occupation.	Supposed Age.	Reported Residence, Jan. 1, 1942. Street and Number.

Wellington Street—Continued

	L	Miller Charles P	32	butler	44	here
	M	Miller Rosa—†	32	cook	58	"
	N	*Neufville Jean—†	32	"	47	"
	O	Osborne Burdett G	32	waiter	65	
	P	Gillyourd Edgar J	32	laborer	32	
	R	Gillyourd Mamie—†	32	waitress	33	
	S	Hardin Miriam—†	32	domestic	33	"
	T	Ricker Lillian—†	32	housewife	49	"
	U	Ricker Louis M	32	laborer	52	"
	V	Clarke John	32	janitor	42	
	W	Johnson Ella—†	32	housekeeper	54	"
	X	Reavis Mildred—†	32	clerk	27	
	Y	Samuda Albert	32	chef	42	
	Z	Samuda Joyce—†	32	stitcher	22	
477						
	A	Samuda Maude—†	32	housewife	40	"
	B	Thompson Sadie—†	32	domestic	59	"
	C	Tulley Roselyn—†	32	"	52	

West Springfield Street

	D	Banks Joseph	190	clerk	25	617 Shawmut av
	E	Brown Charles	190	laborer	55	45 Hammond
	F	Cummings George	190	"	56	here
	G	DeCordova Leopold	190	musician	57	"
	H	DeCordova Theresa—†	190	at home	43	"
	K	Dixon Edward	190	laborer	28	
	L	Griffin Arthur	190	"	42	
	M	Jones Irene—†	190	at home	46	"
	N	Bacon Doris—†	192	clerk	29	Florida
	O	Grant Emily—†	192	"	27	New Jersey
	P	Grant Ray	192	waiter	29	"
	R	Stafford Charles	192	"	31	New York
	S	Taylor Alice—†	192	at home	51	here
	T	Taylor Frank	192	laborer	55	"
	U	Taylor Frank M	192	clerk	27	"
	V	Taylor Harry	192	U S A	23	
	W	Taylor John	192	U S N	22	
	X	Taylor John V	192	clerk	21	
	Y	Tibbs Adelle—†	192	at home	26	
	Z	Tibbs Frederick	192	clerk	29	

Page.	Letter.	Full Name.	Residence, Jan. 1, 1943.	Occupation.	Supposed Age.	Reported Residence, Jan. 1, 1942. Street and Number.
478		**West Springfield Street**—Continued				
	A	Alexander Viola—†	194	at home	50	here
	B	Perry Frederick	194	clerk	43	"
	C	Perry Jessie—†	194	retired	53	"
	D	Perry Lucy—†	194	at home	72	
	E	Russell Alpheus	194	laborer	48	"
	F	Wilson Lucy—†	194	at home	42	Lexington
	G	Anderson Pauline—†	196	"	36	160 W Springfield
	H	Baldwin Etta—†	196	clerk	30	New York
	K	Brown Wolsie—†	196	"	38	Brookline
	L	Davis Thomas	196	laborer	50	here
	M	Gray Virginia—†	196	at home	48	"
	N	Hanson Earl	196	laborer	48	"
	O	Holmes James	196	retired	66	
	P	Holmes Mary H—†	196	at home	40	"
	R	Johnson Harold	196	laborer	43	170 Northampton
	S	March Edward J	196	waiter	43	here
	T	McLeod William	196	"	46	"
	U	Jackson Cephas W	198	clerk	25	Virginia
	V	Johnson William	198	"	38	here
	W	Lumpkin Irving	198	laborer	37	Virginia
	X	Page Melvin	198	waiter	24	"
	Y	Powell Cornelius	198	"	24	Maryland
	Z	Simmons LaBelle—†	198	at home	48	here
479						
	A	Solmon Robert	198	clerk	46	"
	B	Beckair Edmond	200	U S A	38	78 Middlesex
	C	Beckair Ruby—†	200	at home	33	78 "
	D	Cabral Anna—†	200	"	24	162 W Springfield
	E	Cabral Mahoney P	200	laborer	28	162 "
	F	Barker Norma—†	202	maid	38	here
	G	Hard Calvin W	204	waiter	37	New York
	H	Hyatt Helen M—†	204	at home	34	11 Westminster
	K	Jones George	204	waiter	48	413 Mass av
	L	Martin Maurice	204	"	23	24 Williams
	M	*Francis Ethel—†	206	at home	42	here
	N	*Hinds Ethlind—†	206	"	38	"
	O	*Wright Irene—†	206	"	79	"
	P	Babbitt Augustus	208	welder	25	Connecticut
	R	Edwin Amy—†	208	housewife	51	here
	S	Edwin Stephen	208	laborer	58	"

Page.	Letter.	FULL NAME.	Residence, Jan. 1, 1943.	Occupation.	Supposed Age.	Reported Residence, Jan. 1, 1942. Street and Number.

West Springfield Street—Continued

	T	Moore Coleman	208	laborer	40	here
	U	Morgan Leora—†	208	maid	51	"
	V	Roberts Daisy—†	208	"	35	"
	W	Viera John	208	laborer	24	Connecticut
	X	Williams Preston	208	musician	54	here
	Y	Grevious Hattie—†	210	housewife	38	"
	Z	Grevious Powhatan	210	watchman	58	"
480						
	A	Hale Inez—†	210	stitcher	20	Tennessee
	B	Harris Bertie—†	210	housewife	33	here
	C	Harris John D	210	machinist	43	"
	D	Williams Clifford C	210	laborer	32	"
	E	Williams Marie—†	210	housewife	30	"
	F	Allston Rose—†	212	housekeeper	52	"
	G	Brown Charles A	212	laborer	53	"
	H	Brown Charles L	212	retired	73	
	K	Brown Mary—†	212	housewife	30	"
	L	Desmond Mabel—†	212	maid	43	
	M	Holman Louise—†	212	housekeeper	65	"
	N	King Marcus	212	laborer	55	"
	O	Moody Doris—†	212	maid	28	
	P	Owens Cleveland	212	laborer	45	
	R	Owens Hattie—†	212	housewife	33	"
	S	Taylor Ruth—†	212	maid	40	
	T	Bennett Helen—†	214	stitcher	46	
	U	*Cassidy Ada—†	214	housekeeper	70	"
	V	Craig Charles—†	214	laborer	57	
	W	*Furlong Alice—†	214	housekeeper	41	"
	X	Hutchison Chester T	214	laborer	49	"
	Y	Kennelly John	214	"	62	
	Z	McGonigle John	214	"	45	
481						
	A	*Murphy Helen—†	214	stitcher	50	
	C	Quinn James	214	retired	84	"
	B	Rahenhijo Donald H	214	laborer	24	Malden
	D	Bennett Hermione—†	216	housewife	29	396 Northampton
	E	Bennett Ralph	216	porter	32	396 "
	F	Fryer Cecil	216	chauffeur	39	here
	G	Gibbons Edward	216	storekeeper	62	"
	H	Gibbons Edward, jr	216	laborer	22	"
	K	Gibbons Julius	216	U S A	28	

Page.	Letter.	Full Name.	Residence, Jan. 1, 1943.	Occupation.	Supposed Age.	Reported Residence, Jan. 1, 1942. Street and Number.

West Springfield Street—Continued

	L	Gibbons Victoria—†	216	housewife	54	here
	M	Jackson Walter	216	cook	41	"
	O	Johnson Joseph	216	retired	64	"
	N	Joseph Gertrude—†	216	housekeeper	39	"
	P	McCann Susie—†	216	maid	32	"
	R	McDougall Donald	216	laborer	30	
	S	McDougall Elizabeth—†	216	housewife	29	"
	T	Roundtree David	216	laborer	28	
	U	Roundtree Lillian—†	216	housewife	26	"
	V	Gibson John A	218	janitor	62	"
	W	Boyd Juanita M—†	220	housekeeper	50	"
	X	Harris Felix	220	laborer	46	"
	Y	Harris Joyce—†	220	housewife	44	"
	Z	Walker Mattie V—†	220	housekeeper	60	"
482						
	B	Carter Joseph	224	cook	48	530 Col av
	C	Clyatt Frances—†	224	housekeeper	35	60 Sterling
	D	Johnson Alice—†	224	maid	32	Cambridge
	E	Seager Phyllis—†	224	housekeeper	67	18 Greenwich pk

5

6

7

8

9

10

11

12

1

1

1

Ward 9—Precinct 5

CITY OF BOSTON

LIST OF RESIDENTS
20 YEARS OF AGE AND OVER

(NON-CITIZENS INDICATED BY ASTERISK)
(FEMALES INDICATED BY DAGGER)

AS OF

JANUARY 1, 1943

JOSEPH F. TIMILTY, *Chairman*
FREDERIC E. DOWLING, *Secretary*
WILLIAM A. MOTLEY, JR.
FRANCIS B. McKINNEY
EVERETT R. PROUT
Listing Board.

CITY OF BOSTON PRINTING DEPARTMENT

Page.	Letter.	Full Name.	Residence, Jan. 1, 1943.	Occupation.	Supposed Age.	Reported Residence, Jan. 1, 1942. Street and Number.
500						
		Camden Street				
	D	*Greco Samuel	12	laborer	56	here
	E	Lesha George	12	"	62	"
	F	Malouf Abraham	12	steamfitter	54	"
	G	Malouf Feris	12	U S A	21	
	H	Malouf Zaked—†	12	housewife	54	"
	K	Higgins Benjamin	14	laborer	40	
	L	Higgins Irene—†	14	housekeeper	41	"
	M	James Timothy L	14	laborer	41	"
	N	Penson Carrie—†	14	domestic	27	"
	O	Wills Edmund	14	chef	58	"
	P	Gailes Theophilus	16A	welder	28	5 Wellington
	R	Thompson Elliot	16A	mechanic	24	141 Lenox
	S	Thompson Helen—†	16A	housewife	23	141 "
	T	Thompson Lavinia—†	16A	"	31	141 "
	U	Hawkins Juanita—†	16A	"	43	here
	V	Singletera Georgia—†	16A	"	69	"
	W	Singletera Gerald	16A	laborer	28	"
	X	Proctor Herbert	18	plasterer	28	"
	Y	Proctor Thelma—†	18	housewife	33	"
	Z	Mason Florida—†	18	"	37	
501						
	A	Dickinson Dora—†	18	"	28	
	B	Dickinson Frank	18	retired	65	
	C	Dixon George	22	"	65	
	D	Myers Leah—†	22	housewife	70	"
	E	Myers Thomas	22	retired	73	
	F	Worthington Elmer C	22	laborer	40	
	G	L'Heureux Emeline—†	23	housewife	30	"
	H	L'Heureux Napoleon	23	baker	33	
	M	Allison Margaret—†	25	housewife	42	"
	N	*Silva Albert H	26	pedler	42	
	O	*Texeria Amata—†	26	housewife	59	"
	P	*Texeria Peter	26	laborer	66	
	R	McArthur Cyrus L	27	storekeeper	49	"
	S	Moore Mark	27	laborer	44	"
	T	Moore Ruth—†	27	housewife	25	"
	U	Rogers Alexander	28	machinist	60	"
	Z	Dixon Nathaniel	30	janitor	33	
502						
	A	Triplett Annabella—†	30	housewife	32	"

Page.	Letter.	Full Name.	Residence, Jan. 1, 1943.	Occupation.	Supposed Age.	Reported Residence, Jan. 1, 1942. Street and Number.

Camden Street—Continued

Page.	Letter.	Full Name.	Residence, Jan. 1, 1943.	Occupation.	Supposed Age.	Reported Residence, Jan. 1, 1942. Street and Number.
	B	Hall Agnes—†	32	dressmaker	22	here
	C	Hall Clara—†	32	"	20	"
	D	*Hall Harry	32	laborer	70	"
	E	*Hall Helen—†	32	housewife	52	"
	F	Albritten Amelia—†	34	"	20	1031 Tremont
	G	Albritten Zeb	34	laborer	28	1031 "
	H	Bouley Eleanor—†	34	cook	28	here
	K	Bouley Joseph	34	chauffeur	40	"
	L	Caution Mary—†	34	housewife	41	"
	M	Caution Owen	34	laborer	62	
	O	Belden Gertrude—†	53	domestic	30	"
	P	Noble Marie—†	53	waitress	45	
	R	Prince Edward	53	salesman	41	"
	S	Sealey Alice—†	53	housewife	33	"
	T	Sealey Cuthbert	53	U S A	40	
	U	Jordan John	57	painter	46	"
	V	Clayborne Frazier	57	laborer	46	38 Haskins
	W	Williams Thomas	57	"	59	here
	X	Alves Emma—†	59	domestic	40	"
	Y	Alves Louis	59	laborer	51	"
	Z	Francis Ethel—†	59	domestic	35	"
503						
	A	Herbert Peter	59	waiter	65	
	B	Lee Roland	59	retired	60	
	C	Robinson Arthur	59	porter	59	"
	D	Vaughan Lottie—†	59	housekeeper	60	"
	E	Venable James	59	laborer	48	"
	F	Warner John	59	retired	58	
	G	Slane Eugene	61	"	69	
	H	Williams Edward	61	"	64	
	K	Simmons Aurora—†	61	domestic	40	"
	L	Alexander Mary—†	61	"	45	
	M	Alexander Mattie—†	61	"	42	
	N	Dickerson Beverly	63	engineer	61	
	O	Dickerson Ruth—†	63	housekeeper	46	"
	P	Johnson Grace C—†	63	domestic	41	"
	R	Richardson Evelyn—†	63	at home	69	73 W Lenox
	T	Ess Mattie—†	65	housekeeper	46	here
	U	Campbell Gertrude—†	65	mechanic	47	"
	V	Campbell Robert	65	dishwasher	21	"
	W	Johnson Clarissa—†	65	assembler	43	"

Page.	Letter.	Full Name.	Residence, Jan. 1, 1943.	Occupation.	Supposed Age.	Reported Residence, Jan. 1, 1942. Street and Number.

Camden Street—Continued

	X	Johnson Rosmond	65	porter	34	here
	Y	Whitehead Arthur O	65	clerk	38	"
	Z	Whitehead Minnie—†	65	housewife	32	"
504						
	A	Lee Thelma—†	65	"	30	
	B	Lee William H	65	sandblaster	37	"
	C	King Bessie—†	67	housekeeper	57	"
	D	Hamilton Jessica—†	67	stitcher	44	"
	E	Jackson Albert	67	laborer	48	210 Wash'n
	F	Hewitt Charles	67	retired	89	here
	G	Turner Linnet—†	69	housewife	47	"
	H	Turner Pelmust	69	retired	57	"
	K	Smith Margaret—†	69	housewife	25	8 St Paul
	L	Smith Sidney	69	U S A	27	8 "
	M	Palmer Adina—†	69	housewife	42	here
	N	Palmer Arnold	69	barber	46	"
	O	Shields William	71	retired	80	572 Shawmut av
	P	White Annie—†	71	at home	73	98 Camden
	R	Mirandi Sarah—†	71	laundress	49	32 Lenox
	T	Brown Anna A—†	73	housewife	58	here
	U	Brown Thomas	73	porter	58	"
	V	Harris Frances—†	73	waitress	40	"
	W	Wentworth William	73	porter	62	9 Bower
	X	Riviere Louis	74	chef	51	here
	Y	Riviere Millicent—†	74	housewife	49	"
	Z	Roberts Alfred	74	retired	76	"
505						
	A	Virginia Henrietta—†	74	housewife	48	"
	B	Andrews William	75	engineer	80	"
	C	Donaldson Leola—†	75	housewife	60	203 Camden
	D	Donaldson Stanley	75	U S A	34	203 "
	E	Williams Leola J—†	75	housewife	29	203 "
	F	Kemp Henry A	76	porter	38	here
	G	Sparrow Elizabeth J—†	76	housewife	75	"
	H	Davies Louise J—†	76	"	55	"
	N	*Spinks Jacob	77	salesman	40	"
	O	*Spinks Sarah—†	77	housewife	47	"
	P	Bardonille Arline—†	78	"	60	
	R	Bardonille Luke	78	laborer	60	
	S	Bardonille Joseph	78	U S A	23	
	T	Bardonille Lawrence	78	"	25	

Page.	Letter.	FULL NAME.	Residence, Jan. 1, 1943.	Occupation.	Supposed Age.	Reported Residence, Jan. 1, 1942. Street and Number.

Camden Street—Continued

	U	Vaughn Gordon	78	machinist	40	here
	V	Vaughn Mabel—†	78	housewife	40	"
	W	Grant Dorothy—†	79	"	28	109 Sterling
	X	Grant Junius	79	welder	39	109 "
	Y	Newton Cora—†	79	at home	62	here
	Z	Randolph Agnes—†	79	housekeeper	66	"
506						
	A	Samuels Wilfred	79	laborer	54	
	B	Reid Cecil W	79	"	57	
	C	Skinner Minnie—†	80	housewife	80	"
	D	Taylor Ruth C—†	80	"	50	"
	E	Midgett William W	80	laborer	63	1126 Tremont
	F	Bennett Clifton J	81	oiler	59	here
	G	Bennett Mary F—†	81	housewife	56	"
	H	Reed Walter B	81	painter	35	"
	K	Taylor Anna F—†	81	housewife	65	"
	L	Wheatley Elizabeth—†	81	"	44	
	M	Wheatley George	81	laborer	42	"
	N	Manokey Josephine—†	82	housewife	68	24 Kendall
	O	Mack Lula—†	82	"	64	here
	P	Steele George G	82	plasterer	33	"
	R	Steele Martha—†	82	housewife	33	"
	S	King Frances—†	83	housekeeper	48	"
	T	Featherstone William B	83	janitor	64	"
	U	Green Maria—†	83	at home	65	
	V	Campbell Washington	83	laborer	48	
	X	Palmer Samuel	84	porter	46	
	Y	Palmer Zemerine—†	84	housewife	36	"
	Z	*Rickets Nina—†	84	domestic	40	29 Windsor
507						
	A	Furr Arthur	85	laborer	47	here
	B	Furr Harriet L—†	85	housewife	43	"
	C	Green Maria—†	85	domestic	64	"
	D	Manley Eleanor—†	85	housekeeper	53	"
	E	Miller Nonnie	86	attendant	37	"
	F	Parsons Laura M—†	86	housewife	55	"
	G	Kemp Dora M—†	86	factoryhand	37	"
	H	Chesbrough Israel	87	retired	84	
	K	Niles Adelaide—†	87	operator	45	
	L	Robinson Robert	88	retired	76	"
	M	Robinson Robert, jr	88	chauffeur	45	"

Page.	Letter.	Full Name.	Residence, Jan. 1, 1943.	Occupation.	Supposed Age.	Reported Residence, Jan. 1, 1942. Street and Number.
	N	Anderson Gladys—†	88	housewife	43	here
	O	Fuller Annie—†	88	"	28	"
	P	Fuller Ella—†	88	"	56	"
	E	Edmondson Janet—†	89	"	59	
	S	Edmondson Samuel	89	salesman	58	"
	T	Austin Lila—†	89	domestic	51	"
	U	Tomlin Hattie—†	89	housekeeper	47	"
	V	Murphy Charles	89	porter	48	"
	X	Stevens Lawrence A	90	laborer	53	"
	Y	Thomas Priscilla—†	90	housewife	30	16 Kendall
	Z	Thomas Roscoe	90	laborer	35	16 "
508						
	B	Ross Beulah—†	91	housewife	43	here
	C	Ross Carrie—†	91	stitcher	26	"
	D	Ross Emmett	91	laborer	46	"
	E	Johnson Flavella—†	91	housewife	41	"
	F	Johnson Seth W	91	U S A	58	
	G	Watson Charlotte—†	91	domestic	39	"
	H	Rogers Calie—†	92	housewife	54	"
	K	Collins Ruth—†	92	"	24	
	L	Smith Willie Mae—†	92	"	30	
	M	Brown Fannie—†	92	"	56	
	N	Adams Ruth—†	93	clerk	20	
	O	Jackson Harriett—†	93	singer	32	
	P	Jackson Irene—†	93	housekeeper	50	"
	R	Swann Hester—†	93	at home	74	
	S	Taylor William	93	laborer	41	
	T	Armour Rose—†	94	clerk	37	
	U	Davis Willie Mae—†	94	cook	40	
	V	Allen Alvin B	94	porter	54	
	W	Burton Eustace	95	operator	39	"
	X	Buron Minnie—†	95	housewife	37	"
	Y	Hobson Bessie—†	95	domestic	51	"
	Z	Taylor Snow P	95	laborer	60	
509						
	A	Walker Daniel	96	mechanic	55	"
	B	Marshall Caroline S—†	96	housekeeper	71	102 Camden
	C	Marshall Drusilla—†	96	housewife	42	here
	D	Marshall Earl L	96	mechanic	51	"
	E	Smith Chester	97	porter	53	"
	F	Smith Ruth L—†	97	housewife	36	"

Page.	Letter.	Full Name.	Residence, Jan. 1, 1943.	Occupation.	Supposed Age.	Reported Residence, Jan. 1, 1942. Street and Number.

Camden Street—Continued

Page.	Letter.	Full Name.	Residence, Jan. 1, 1943.	Occupation.	Supposed Age.	Reported Residence, Jan. 1, 1942. Street and Number.
	G	Counsel Eliza—†	97	domestic	67	here
	H	Williams Catherine—†	97	housewife	60	"
	K	Page Albert	98	retired	84	"
	L	Page India—†	98	housewife	80	"
	M	Covington Exodus P	98	laborer	43	Cambridge
	N	Meningal Clifton	98	U S A	25	here
	O	Meningal Sarah—†	98	laborer	42	"
	P	Scott Geraldine O—†	98	operator	26	589 Shawmut av
	R	Farrell Emma—†	99	housekeeper	75	here
	S	Brandon Alice—†	99	domestic	48	"
	T	Brown Ida—†	99	housekeeper	77	"
	U	Shelton Edna—†	100	clerk	37	"
	V	Shelton Ruth—†	100	"	35	
	W	Shelton William	100	janitor	76	
	X	Maddox Joseph	100	social worker	33	"
	Y	Maddox Maryland—†	100	clerk	26	
	Z	Carter Charles	101	porter	41	
510						
	A	Carter Marion—†	101	housewife	32	"
	B	Freeman Bertha—†	101	housekeeper	60	999 Tremont
	C	Marshall Ruth—†	101	domestic	50	here
	D	Johnson Margaret—†	101	operator	22	17 Claremont pk
	E	Greene Herbert E	102	laborer	27	here
	F	Greene May L—†	102	housewife	34	"
	G	Jackson Missouri—†	102	clerk	39	"
	H	Quarimley Theodore	102	janitor	41	
	K	White Clarence S	102	"	47	
	L	White Flossie S—†	102	clerk	39	"
	M	Parham Nannie—†	102	at home	68	24 Warwick
	N	Hipps Rebecca—†	103	housekeeper	65	119 Lenox
	O	Alleyne Cecelia—†	103	"	56	812 Tremont
	P	Noble Jannie—†	103	housewife	53	here
	R	Noble Wade	103	laborer	54	"
	S	Black William M	104	steward	61	"
	T	Hawkins Lee	104	checker	65	"
	U	Norris Junius	104	porter	61	
	V	Odom Charles	104	waiter	63	
	W	Pearson Alpha	104	porter	58	"
	X	Vilian Philip A	104	"	63	
	Y	Thomas Alice E—†	106	housekeeper	58	"
	Z	Reeves Rose—†	106	seamstress	66	"

Page.	Letter.	Full Name.	Residence, Jan. 1, 1943.	Occupation.	Supposed Age.	Reported Residence, Jan. 1, 1942. Street and Number.

511
Camden Street—Continued

	A	Howard Elizabeth—†	106	housewife	53	here
	B	Howard Frank	106	laborer	56	"
	C	Knox Herbert F	108	retired	41	"
	D	Knox Marguerite—†	108	housewife	60	"
	E	Waters Joseph	108	retired	79	
	F	Hall Alice A—†	108	seamstress	62	"
	G	Douglas Bertha—†	110	housewife	48	"
	H	Douglas William	110	laborer	37	"
	K	*Austin Gertrude—†	110	housekeeper	50	"
	L	Grudup Beulah—†	110	"	54	"
	M	Smith Anna M—†	112	housewife	64	"
	N	Smith James S	112	laborer	54	
	O	Upton Susie A—†	112	housekeeper	83	"
	R	Fairman Gladys—†	114	operator	42	"
	S	Burch Mabel L—†	114	"	59	
	T	King Mary E—†	114	housewife	63	"
	U	King William O	114	porter	73	
	W	Bracey Clara—†	116	housekeeper	38	"
	X	*Gomes Manuel	116	laborer	51	Plymouth
	Z	Mitchell Anna—†	118	housewife	42	here
512						
	A	Foster Mary—†	118	housekeeper	62	"
	C	Archey Blanche L—†	120	clerk	38	103 Sterling
	D	Johnson Catherine—†	120	housewife	77	here
	E	Johnson Cleophas J	120	retired	78	"
	F	Johnson Leroy	120	musician	52	"
	G	Johnson Viola—†	120	cashier	50	
	H	Thomas Joseph E	120	waiter	76	
	K	Thomas Lillian—†	120	student	43	"
	L	Maxwell Edward	122	tailor	52	31 Braddock pk
	M	Clark Samuel	124	clerk	46	here
	N	Freeman Susie—†	124	housekeeper	40	"
	O	Motley Martha H—†	124	housewife	47	"
	P	Motley Martin L	124	machinist	47	"
	R	Lumpkins Harriette—†	126	housewife	26	780 Shawmut av
	S	Lumpkins Robert L	126	cook	38	780 "
	T	Grant Clarence E	126	painter	28	here
	U	Grant Edna—†	126	housewife	28	"
	V	Gough Agnes L—†	126	"	28	"
	W	Gough Charles C	126	welder	35	

Page.	Letter.	FULL NAME.	Residence, Jan. 1, 1943.	Occupation.	Supposed Age.	Reported Residence, Jan. 1, 1942. Street and Number.

Camden Street—Continued

	X	Harris Celia A—†	128	clerk	63	here
	Y	Hargrow Rosetta—†	128	housekeeper	53	"
	Z	Hargrow Viola—†	128	presser	22	"
513						
	A	Garner Betty—†	128	at home	60	"
	B	Lopes Gaetano	130	realtor	52	5 Warwick
	C	Thomas Charles	130	clerk	32	here
	D	Thomas Marion—†	130	waitress	28	"
	E	Shepard Frances—†	130	housewife	21	6 Grinnell
	F	Shepard Lawrence	130	clerk	24	6 "
	G	*Skyers Leonora—†	132	housekeeper	68	23 Westminster
	H	Gladman Marion—†	132	housewife	32	here
	K	Gladman William	132	shipper	38	"
	L	Jones Pankie—†	132	housewife	34	"
	M	Jones Powell	132	laborer	38	

Comet Place

	O	Benny Charles	1	laborer	46	here
	P	Ward Mary—†	1	housewife	67	"
	R	Ward Robert	1	painter	57	"
	S	Wood Herman	1	laborer	56	Quincy
	T	*Lamason Alice—†	1	at home	68	36 Highland
	U	*Eklund Peter	2	retired	70	here
	V	*Johnson Einar	2	laborer	70	"
	W	Nixon Ralph	2	"	49	"
	X	*Locks Antonio	3	"	51	
	Y	*Merrill John	3		48	
	Z	*Nonus Robert	3		71	
514						
	A	Richardson Rebecca—†	3	housekeeper	49	"
	B	Tavares Lawrence	3	laborer	45	"
	C	VanTassel John	3	painter	66	"
	E	Montier Clarence	5	laborer	44	
	F	Winn Eugene	5	retired	63	"
	G	Williams Irene—†	5	housewife	57	14 E Lenox
	H	Williams William H	5	retired	67	14 "
	K	Williams Evelyn—†	5	housekeeper	32	106 Kendall
	L	Wray Frank T	5	baker	44	67 Ruggles
	M	Ryan John	10	laborer	47	here
	N	Ryan Winifred—†	10	housewife	37	"

Page.	Letter.	Full Name.	Residence, Jan. 1, 1943.	Occupation.	Supposed Age.	Reported Residence, Jan. 1, 1942. Street and Number.

Comet Place—Continued

	O	Kelly Sidney	10	retired	46	here
	P	Murphy Mary—†	10	at home	60	94 E Dedham
	R	*Murphy Nellie—†	10	housewife	80	94 "
	S	Handy Marion—†	10	teacher	47	here
	T	Whitmarsh George	10	laborer	57	"
	U	Cargo Ralph	10	U S A	21	"

Hampton Court

	W	Canada Viola—†	2	houseworker	45	here
	X	Jackson Clarence	2	entertainer	23	"

515 Lenox Street

515	E	*Fitz Frank	31	clergyman	65	here
	F	Senhouse Minnie B—†	31	housekeeper	54	"
	G	Brewster Margaret—†	33	housewife	56	"
	H	Brewster Richard	33	carpenter	57	"
	K	Schuyler Sarah C—†	33	housekeeper	68	"
	L	Sisco Eva—†	33	domestic	50	"
	M	Jones Lillian C—†	35	housekeeper	58	"
	N	Almeida Mayzie E—†	35	"	47	"
	O	Bolds Beatrice—†	35	"	71	
	P	Odum Mary—†	37	"	69	"
	R	Maddox Cecil	37	laborer	58	40 Worcester
	S	Maddox Helen—†	37	housekeeper	35	40 "
	T	Backus Mary—†	37	"	55	here
	V	Hayes Hattie—†	59	"	62	"
	W	Huggs Gilbert	59	clerk	67	"
	X	Huggs Minnie—†	59	housekeeper	72	"
	Y	Hind Alice—†	59	domestic	40	"
	Z	Cromwell Mildred—†	59	"	40	
516						
	A	Lovett Clara—†	59	"	51	
	B	West Harry	59	laborer	46	
	C	Nelson Harry	61	"	56	
	D	Cassette Carl	61	U S A	22	
	E	Cassette Lucy—†	61	housekeeper	68	"
	F	Harris Francis	61	laborer	45	"
	G	Washington Edward	61	"	53	
	H	Washington Ethel—†	61	housewife	51	"

Page.	Letter.	Full Name.	Residence, Jan. 1, 1943.	Occupation.	Supposed Age.	Reported Residence, Jan. 1, 1942. Street and Number.

Lenox Street—Continued

	L	Giles Estelle—†	63	housekeeper	36	130 Camden
	N	Brown Catherine—†	63	"	57	here
	O	Brown William	63	laborer	56	"
	P	Carey Eugenia—†	65	housewife	35	"
	R	Carey William F	65	U S N	46	
	S	Jones Lottie—†	65	housewife	67	"
	T	Jones William L	65	painter	62	"
	U	Nelson Florence—†	65	domestic	60	55 Clifford
	V	Wilson Elizabeth—†	65	"	60	here
	W	Chapman Joseph	65	porter	66	"
	X	Chapman Susan—†	65	housewife	66	"
	Y	Blackwell Eleanora—†	67	stitcher	48	
	Z	*Milano Agnes—†	67	housewife	69	"
517						
	A	*Milano Vincent	67	retired	76	
	B	Perry Martha G—†	67	housekeeper	62	"
	C	Waters Beatrice—†	67	domestic	50	24 E Lenox
	D	Waters Olifin	67	laborer	56	24 "
	E	Wilson George A	69	mason	68	here
	F	Wilson Rebecca S—†	69	housewife	70	"
	G	Mayers Dudley	69	seaman	53	"
	H	Zuill Lela—†	69	domestic	43	"
	K	Robinson Jacob	69	porter	69	"
	L	Joyner Consuelo—†	71	housekeeper	28	101 W Springfield
	M	Myles George	71	baker	46	here
	N	Myles Mamie—†	71	housewife	34	"
	O	Williams Clara—†	71	domestic	46	10 Worcester pl
	P	Haskins Vivian—†	71	housekeeper	21	New Bedford
	R	Valentine Laura—†	73	at home	65	38 Newcomb
	V	Lane Gwendolyn—†	75	beautician	32	813 Tremont
	W	Andrews Eva—†	75	housekeeper	62	here
	X	Brown Ella—†	75	housewife	65	"
	Y	Brown William	75	laborer	45	"
	Z	Evans Carrie—†	75	housekeeper	63	"
518						
	A	King Barney W	77	laborer	65	
	B	Kale Sarah—†	77	domestic	52	"
	C	Pena Anna—†	77	housekeeper	36	31 Middlesex
	D	Pena Joseph	77	laborer	39	31 "
	E	Cheatham Rose—†	77	domestic	38	here
	L	Lewis Arthur	109	electrician	37	"

Page.	Letter.	Full Name.	Residence, Jan. 1, 1943.	Occupation.	Supposed Age.	Reported Residence, Jan. 1, 1942. Street and Number.

Lenox Street—Continued

Page.	Letter.	Full Name.	Residence, Jan. 1, 1943.	Occupation.	Supposed Age.	Reported Residence, Jan. 1, 1942. Street and Number.
	M	Lewis Lucy—†	109	housewife	33	here
	N	Beasley James A	109	laborer	44	"
	O	Hill Theresa J—†	109	housekeeper	84	"
	P	*Thornell Elizabeth—†	111	domestic	50	109 Cabot
	R	Provo Helen—†	111	at home	74	here
	S	Randolph Frederick	111	laborer	60	"
	U	Harris Albert H	117	"	49	Woburn
	V	James Caroline—†	117	at home	81	here
	X	Randolph Fred S	117	laborer	56	"
	W	Randolph Lucy—†	117	housewife	58	"
	Y	Rosser Leroy	119	laborer	37	"
	Z	Rosser Marion—†	119	housewife	40	"
519						
	B	Blackwell Gerald	119	porter	58	1088 Tremont
	C	Robinson Leroy P	119	laborer	40	here
	D	Robinson Mary—†	119	at home	40	"
	E	Bolds George	123	laborer	56	"
	F	Moate Corinne—†	123	domestic	46	"
	G	Rickard Willis—†	123	"	39	
	H	Brown Mabel—†	123	clerk	21	
	K	Brown Mary—†	123	domestic	31	"
	L	Johnson Daniel	125	painter	68	
	M	Johnson Edith—†	125	domestic	52	"
	N	Lowe Barbara—†	125	"	42	Malden
	O	Murray Lillian—†	125	housekeeper	45	here
	P	Callender Rebecca—†	125	"	44	"
	R	Thomas Joseph	127	retired	73	"
	S	Hall Amanda—†	127	housewife	24	Georgia
	T	Hall Robert J	127	waiter	28	"
	U	Irving Alice R—†	127	housekeeper	50	here
	V	Irving Israel J	127	laborer	61	"
	W	Hill Virginia—†	127	housekeeper	47	"
	Y	Jones Celesta—†	129	housewife	30	"
	Z	Jones Joseph	129	laborer	34	
520						
	A	Fitch Hazel—†	129	domestic	35	"
	B	Thomas Carol—†	129	houseworker	30	"
	C	Thomas James	129	chauffeur	35	"
	D	Austin Marion—†	129	domestic	40	"
	E	Williams Walter	129	laborer	50	

Page.	Letter.	Full Name.	Residence, Jan. 1, 1943.	Occupation.	Supposed Age.	Reported Residence, Jan. 1, 1942. Street and Number.

Lenox Street—Continued

Page.	Letter.	Full Name.	Residence, Jan. 1, 1943.	Occupation.	Supposed Age.	Reported Residence, Jan. 1, 1942. Street and Number.
	F	Smith Margaret—†	129	housekeeper	69	1117 Harrison av
	G	Foster Irene—†	129	"	27	here
	H	Huizing Angeline—†	131	domestic	41	"
	K	Welles Marguerite—†	131	"	32	"
	L	*Mendez Anthony	131	laborer	53	
	M	Perry Joseph	131	"	25	
	N	Singleton Lucille—†	131	operator	47	"
	O	Mitchell Frank	131	laborer	46	
	P	Bonds Ada—†	131	domestic	25	"
	R	Bonds Oscar	131	chef	68	
	S	Bonds Sadie—†	131	housekeeper	59	"
	T	Spears Laura—†	131	domestic	41	"
	U	Johnson Jacob R	131	waiter	58	
	V	Hicks Ella—†	131	housekeeper	75	"
	W	Hunter Letitia—†	131	clerk	37	"
	X	Osborne Raymond	131	welder	39	
	Y	Reeves Fannie E—†	131	housekeeper	63	"
	Z	Canada Charles	131	laborer	47	"
521						
	A	Canada Johanna—†	131	housewife	45	"
	B	Green Delada—†	131	operator	21	
	C	Lewis May D—†	131	housekeeper	57	"
	D	Lewis Ophelia—†	131	domestic	38	"
	E	Lewis Walter J	131	laborer	58	"
	F	Scott Joseph H	131	waiter	56	119 Kendall
	G	Bookman Edith—†	131	clerk	27	here
	H	Hockaday Mary—†	131	cook	44	"
	K	Mitchell Genevieve—†	131	waitress	26	"
	L	Smith James	131	chauffeur	25	"
	M	Avelino Adele—†	131	at home	31	
	N	Smothers Lillian—†	131	"	64	
	O	Jackman Willy—†	131	housekeeper	65	"
	P	Flood Jeffrey	131	laborer	32	"
	R	West Elizabeth—†	131	housekeeper	35	"
	S	Taylor Lorenzo	131	waiter	65	"
	T	Bones Dorothy—†	141	domestic	30	"
	U	Landrum Anna M—†	141	housewife	32	34 Northfield
	V	Landrum Charles	141	laborer	37	34 "
	X	Singleton Nettie—†	141	housewife	45	here
	Y	Singleton Thomas	141	laborer	55	"

Page.	Letter.	Full Name.	Residence, Jan. 1, 1943.	Occupation.	Supposed Age.	Reported Residence, Jan. 1, 1942. Street and Number.
		Lenox Street—Continued				
	Z	Osborne Mary A—†	141	domestic	67	here
522						
	A	Diggs Clara—†	141		50	53 Humboldt av
	B	Wilkerson Edith—†	141	"	51	53 "
	C	Langford Wilhelmina—†	141	"	35	here
	D	Watkins Lemma—†	141	housekeeper	58	"
	E	Wagner Emma L—†	141	housewife	63	"
	F	Wagner Jasper	141	laborer	65	
	G	*Thibon Ernest M	141	chauffeur	45	"
	H	Woodson Mary L—†	141	houseworker	41	"
	K	Forsyth Edward	141	janitor	31	
	L	Forsyth Margaret—†	141	housewife	31	"
	M	Campbell David	141	laborer	61	
	N	Mendez Samuel	141	"	54	
	O	Kirk Viola—†	141	housekeeper	53	"
	P	Smith Ethel—†	141	waitress	35	"
	R	Clark Mabel—†	141	domestic	49	Newton
	S	Hector Lillian—†	141	baker	69	here
	T	McClendon Robert L	141	laborer	49	"
	U	Jackson Hilda—†	141	domestic	29	"
	V	Taylor Martha—†	141	"	50	90 Vernon
	W	Williams Nannie—†	141	"	45	here
523		**Massachusetts Avenue**				
	C	Barboza Caroline—†	505	clerk	23	Malden
	D	Davenport Margaret E—†	505	housewife	23	14 Westland av
	E	Davenport Thomas	505	U S M C	28	14 "
	F	Schofield Mary—†	505	at home	63	72 E Newton
	G	Schofield Reynolds	505	chauffeur	27	72 "
	H	Bartlett Chester B	505	cook	58	21 Leyland
	K	Bartlett Hazel G—†	505	housewife	52	here
	L	Smith Eli S	505	chauffeur	31	88 W Canton
	M	Smith Rita H—†	505	stitcher	33	1521 Wash'n
	N	Gill Josephine L—†	505	at home	58	here
	O	Hubbard Clive	505	U S A	40	"
	P	Quinn Ann V—†	505	at home	72	"
	R	Tucker Helena F—†	505	"	62	"
	S	Bath Michael	507	janitor	68	604 Mass av
	T	Connelly Marion—†	507	waitress	26	Quincy
	U	*Cummings Maurice	507	laborer	62	82 Bennet

Page.	Letter.	FULL NAME.	Residence, Jan. 1, 1943.	Occupation.	Supposed Age.	Reported Residence, Jan. 1, 1942. Street and Number.

Massachusetts Avenue—Continued

Page.	Letter.	FULL NAME.	Residence, Jan. 1, 1943.	Occupation.	Supposed Age.	Reported Residence, Jan. 1, 1942.
	v	*Cummings Rebecca—†	507	housewife	60	82 Bennet
	w	*Fallai Herbert	507	retired	63	here
	x	Huntley Lila—†	507	at home	48	"
	y	Libby Grover	507	laborer	40	55 Worcester
	z	*MacPherson Mary—†	507	at home	53	here
524						
	A	Mason William	507	retired	70	"
	B	O'Brien James	507	laundryworker	49	"
	C	Solomon Samuel	507	clerk	54	"
	D	Steward James	507	janitor	44	"
	E	Williams James	507	"	56	"
	F	Williams Mary—†	507	housewife	55	"
	G	Hergt Claire—†	511	proofreader	42	"
	H	King Peter	511	painter	24	"
	K	Lynch Catherine—†	511	clerk	28	"
	L	McGill Elsie—†	511	housewife	54	"
	M	McGill James	511	roofer	55	"
	N	Shapiro Barnard	511	manager	42	"
	O	Steele Mary—†	511	beautician	29	Maine
	P	Bellacqua Vincent	515	merchant	50	here
	R	Blackstead Peter A	515	painter	32	35 E Concord
	S	Dow David M	515	retired	70	493 Mass av
	T	Fanning David C	515	fireman	37	here
	U	Forte Beatrice—†	515	stitcher	30	529 Mass av
	V	Griswold Lorenzo, jr	515	bookkeeper	26	here
	W	Kieber Mary A—†	515	clerk	35	"
	X	Murphy James J	515	bartender	50	1042 Saratoga
	Y	Nepson Helen—†	515	housewife	30	here
	Z	Nepson Rudolph	515	U S N	40	"
525						
	A	Richmond Charles A	515	laborer	59	"
	B	Smith Robert H	515	salesman	55	"
	C	Twiss Charles K	515	chauffeur	33	"
	D	Wilkins Edwin	515	carpenter	42	124 Peterboro
	E	Wilkins Muriel—†	515	housewife	43	124 "
	F	Williams Morris	515	salesman	43	here
	G	Wright Katherine T—†	515	housekeeper	43	"
	H	Barney Donald	519	salesman	45	Malden
	K	Cameron Jacob	519	laborer	50	here
	L	Cameron Mary—†	519	housewife	50	"
	M	Curtis Grace—†	519	houseworker	23	New York

Page.	Letter.	Full Name.	Residence, Jan. 1, 1943.	Occupation.	Supposed Age.	Reported Residence, Jan. 1, 1942. Street and Number.

Massachusetts Avenue—Continued

Page.	Letter.	Full Name.	Residence, Jan. 1, 1943.	Occupation.	Supposed Age.	Reported Residence, Jan. 1, 1942. Street and Number.
	N	*Fenner Clara—†	519	housewife	71	here
	O	*Fenner Louis	519	retired	71	"
	P	Marinus John	519	janitor	50	210 W Newton
	R	Marquis Florence—†	519	forewoman	34	here
	S	Melille Angelo	519	bartender	36	Cambridge
	T	Pannica Anthony	519	merchant	40	here
	U	Pannica Arlene—†	519	housewife	23	"
	V	Steenblik Christine—†	519	at home	53	Burlington
	W	Steenblik Janna—†	519	clerk	20	"
	X	Walsh Richard	519	laborer	47	here
	Y	Aserdon Henry	521	retired	77	18 W Concord
	Z	Babban Robert	521	"	50	here
526						
	A	Connaughton Helen—†	521	nurse	46	
	B	Dawson Edward	521	machinist	56	"
	C	Gibson Edward	521	retired	68	Bellingham
	D	Johnson William	521	operator	56	Everett
	E	Mills Edward	521	waiter	32	Cambridge
	F	Park Samuel	521	salesman	48	Egypt
	G	Wieler Frank	521	retired	54	here
	H	*Aguate Nicholas	523	baker	52	520 Mass av
	K	Becker Gertrude—†	523	at home	65	here
	L	Carey Earl	523	butcher	34	"
	M	Coffey William	523	electrician	47	"
	N	Cotte Alfred	523	machinist	38	"
	O	*Cunningham Greta—†	523	clerk	44	Canada
	P	*Dieselkamp Henry	523	mechanic	34	here
	R	Fox Frank	523	salesman	58	471 Mass av
	S	Repucci Elizabeth—†	523	housewife	29	here
	T	Repucci William	523	mover	33	"
	U	Wessel Mary—†	523	at home	71	Medway
	V	Young Frank	523	policeman	31	here
	W	Braman Mildred—†	525	bookkeeper	40	"
	X	Brennan Thomas	525	watchman	50	3 Hansford pl
	Y	Carr Mary—†	525	at home	80	here
	Z	Carr Rosa—†	525	"	67	"
527						
	A	Douglass George	525	retired	80	
	B	McCowbry George	525	machinist	35	"
	C	Richardson Leroy	525	retired	90	"
	D	Sousa Leo	525	chemist	32	New Bedford

Page.	Letter.	Full Name.	Residence, Jan. 1, 1943.	Occupation.	Supposed Age.	Reported Residence, Jan. 1, 1942. Street and Number.
		Massachusetts Avenue—Continued				
	E	Wainwright Ivan	525	musician	26	Hingham
	F	Gillespie Carrie—†	527	at home	50	here
	G	Greeley Mary—†	527	domestic	38	"
	H	Jones Susan—†	527	clerk	24	"
	M	McAuley John	527	painter	30	
	K	*Menge Louis L	527	student	41	
	L	*Menge Mary—†	527	nurse	42	
	N	*Scarinci Domenico	527	finisher	53	
	O	Stephens Arnold B	527	woodworker	68	"
	P	*Fortunata Joseph	529	clerk	50	Malden
	R	*George John	529	cook	55	here
	S	Kay Jean—†	529	clerk	33	210 W Newton
	T	*Laflin Mabel—†	529	"	33	48 Wigglesworth
	U	Laflin Warren	529	chauffeur	40	47 Albany
	V	Looby Edward	529	clerk	45	559 Mass av
	W	Looby Mary—†	529	housewife	35	559 "
	X	Maloof David	529	shoeworker	55	here
	Y	McLaughlin Elsie—†	529	domestic	35	87 W Springfield
	Z	McLaughlin William	529	clerk	45	87 "
528						
	A	Scarpio Louis	529	stitcher	30	here
	B	Spranzo Michael	529	shoeworker	55	"
	C	*Yonnis Elizabeth—†	529	at home	56	"
	D	Yonnis Joseph	529	chauffeur	34	"
	E	Yonnis Phyllis—†	529	housewife	33	"
	F	Cyrus Patrick	531	cook	64	Wash'n D C
	G	Dean Anna—†	531	clerk	37	23 Ruggles
	H	Dean Elijah	531	"	52	23 "
	K	Dixon Wendell	531	laborer	65	here
	L	Edmunds Malcolm	531	"	48	100 W Springfield
	M	Hanna Louise—†	531	clerk	20	here
	N	Hanna Mary—†	531	housewife	48	"
	O	Hanna Michael	531	retired	64	"
	P	Harris Fred	531	mechanic	45	"
	R	Jackson Barbara—†	531	saleswoman	20	Wash'n D C
	S	Peters Elizabeth—†	531	waitress	28	Watertown
	T	Picney Dorothy—†	531	housewife	35	N Hampshire
	U	Picney Thomas	531	mechanic	40	"
	V	Reid Louise—†	531	domestic	58	Cambridge
	W	Austin Wade	533	laborer	40	Maine
	X	Capers George	533	U S A	40	Ayer

Page.	Letter.	Full Name.	Residence, Jan. 1, 1943.	Occupation.	Supposed Age.	Reported Residence, Jan. 1, 1942. Street and Number.

Massachusetts Avenue—Continued

	Y	Gay Elizabeth—†	533	housekeeper	59	here
	Z	Griffin James	533	newsdealer	65	"
529						
	A	Johnson David	533	chauffeur	31	205 Camden
	B	Johnson Thelma—†	533	housewife	21	205 "
	C	Kearney Robina L—†	533	waitress	21	New York
	D	Legette Casanna—†	533	domestic	21	547 Col av
	E	Mathias Elizabeth—†	533	at home	59	here
	F	McIntyre Patrick	533	clerk	60	"
	G	Moore Walter	533	presser	40	550 Col av
	H	Scott Ruben	533	clerk	39	here
	K	Thompson Nathan	533	laborer	30	"
	L	Alston Futue	535	mechanic	45	Nebraska
	M	Lee Beatrice—†	535	housewife	38	552 Shawmut av
	N	Lee Henry	535	shipfitter	47	552 "
	O	Noggins Beatrice—†	535	domestic	45	Newton
	R	Callahan Mary T—†	539	at home	51	here
	S	Callahan Stephen J	539	engineer	54	"
	T	Chiocchio Peter	539	"	54	"
	U	DeBell Sarah—†	539	at home	74	"
	V	Dillon Delia—†	539	laundress	57	"
	W	Ekberg John	539	retired	73	
	X	Ferguson Murray	539	waiter	50	
	Y	Harding William T	539	retired	76	"
	Z	O'Connell John J	539	nurse	63	4 Symphony rd
530						
	A	O'Neil Henry	539	retired	83	here
	B	Ostoff Phillip	539	mechanic	38	"
	C	Wetherbee Fred W	539	retired	78	"
	D	Anderson Benjamin J	541	clergyman	24	Newton
	G	Abram Sarah—†	547	at home	73	here
	H	Anderson Ruth—†	547	domestic	43	"
	K	Badge Martha—†	547	"	29	"
	O	Craig Blanche—†	547	"	55	
	L	Dart Jean—†	547	at home	64	
	M	Dustin Grace—†	547	housekeeper	71	"
	N	Gifford Madeline—†	547	domestic	43	"
	P	Hopkins Jennie—†	547	at home	83	"
	R	Landfire Harry	547	janitor	52	"
	S	Langerquist Augusta—†	547	at home	83	"
	T	*Morrill Charles	547	retired	80	"

Page.	Letter.	Full Name.	Residence, Jan. 1, 1943.	Occupation.	Supposed Age.	Reported Residence, Jan. 1, 1942. Street and Number.

Massachusetts Avenue—Continued

	U	Paine Susan—†	547	domestic	54	here
	V	*Scott Margaret—†	547	at home	67	"
	W	Stevens Jean—†	547	"	69	"
	X	Tonneson Carrie—†	547	"	84	
	Y	Tonneson Maria—†	547	"	76	
	Z	Chaplin Frederick	549	presser	50	
531						
	A	Chaplin Regina—†	549	housewife	38	"
	B	Connelly Mary C—†	549	waitress	39	11 E Springfield
	C	Cornell Mary T—†	549	at home	58	here
	D	Darling Chester	549	tanner	48	"
	E	Feinaur John R	549	nurse	38	N Hampshire
	F	Gaffrey Thomas	549	collector	51	557 Mass av
	G	Gilmore Francis	549	steamfitter	47	here
	H	Healey James F	549	bartender	50	9 Worcester sq
	K	O'Brien Mary P—†	549	housekeeper	58	here
	L	Riley Margaret—†	549	housewife	34	"
	M	Riley William	549	bricklayer	35	"
	N	Rimka John	549	stitcher	40	
	O	*Williams William	549	retired	72	
	P	Zahorakis Andrew	549	waiter	56	
	R	Brandley Margaret—†	551	housewife	36	"
	S	Brandley Paul	551	U S A	35	
	T	Flynn Martin	551	retired	85	"
	U	Kenny Leo	551	chauffeur	51	Chelsea
	V	Lyons Henry J	551	U S A	41	here
	W	Lyons Sarah A—†	551	at home	80	"
	X	Martin Anna—†	551	housewife	52	14 Union Park
	Y	Martin Charles	551	pressman	71	14 "
	Z	McGilfrey William	551	laborer	64	19 Rutland sq
532						
	A	Morgan Margaret—†	551	at home	75	here
	B	Richards Richard	551	orderly	45	"
	C	Daley Mary—†	553	nurse	55	"
	D	Flynn Patrick	553	guard	47	
	E	Helpard Ada—†	553	at home	42	"
	F	Hubley Benjamin	553	U S A	28	Maine
	G	Hubley Grace—†	553	clerk	27	"
	H	Lafferty John	553	mechanic	59	here
	K	Merrill Catherine—†	553	housewife	45	"
	L	Merrill John	553	cook	57	"

Page.	Letter.	Full Name.	Residence, Jan. 1, 1943.	Occupation.	Supposed Age.	Reported Residence, Jan. 1, 1942. Street and Number.

Massachusetts Avenue—Continued

	M	Perkins Bertha—†	553	housewife	63	572 Shawmut av
	N	Perkins George	553	laborer	66	572 "
	O	Whalen Sally—†	553	domestic	50	Newton
	P	Willis George	553	retired	74	here
	R	Daniels Efstratios	555	chef	55	"
	S	Daniels Jennie—†	555	housewife	69	"
	T	Hullburg Alec	555	toolmaker	59	"
	U	Kelly Arthur	555	laborer	56	
	V	Samuels Arthur	555	retired	69	"
	W	Banks Dorothy—†	557	waitress	40	Vermont
	X	Davies Theresa—†	557	nurse	25	818 Harris'n av
	Y	Demaris Alice—†	557	clerk	25	here
	Z	Demaris Norman	557	"	28	"
533						
	A	Jewett Alberta—†	557	"	45	Rhode Island
	B	Kiley Inez—†	557	housewife	40	here
	C	Kiley Vincent	557	laborer	40	"
	D	Marshner Betty—†	557	housewife	26	Newton
	E	Marshner Howard	557	electrician	26	"
	F	Moore John	557	janitor	49	here
	G	Moore Leah—†	557	waitress	28	"
	H	Newcomb Hazel—†	557	"	40	Vermont
	L	Smart Georgia—†	557	chauffeur	21	here
	K	Staples Sarah—†	557	at home	49	"
	M	Costos Nickolas	559	laborer	46	"
	N	Davenport Florence—†	559	housewife	59	"
	O	Davenport Horace	559	retired	60	
	P	Kiros John	559	laborer	49	
	R	*Livingston James	559	retired	59	
	S	Lynch Thomas	559	decorator	54	"
	T	McCarthy Delia—†	559	housewife	60	"
	U	McCarthy James	559	baker	61	"
	V	Mellon Mary—†	559	domestic	50	4 Moreland
	W	Powers Harriet M—†	559	housekeeper	62	here
	X	Smith Arlene—†	559	saleswoman	21	Maine
	Y	Wyatt John	559	musician	55	Billerica
	Z	Wyatt Sarah—†	559	housewife	50	"
534						
	A	Bissell Frank	561	bartender	55	619 Mass av
	B	Butts Augustus	561	carpenter	50	here
	C	Demour Marion—†	561	clerk	22	"

Page.	Letter.	FULL NAME.	Residence, Jan. 1, 1943.	Occupation.	Supposed Age.	Reported Residence, Jan. 1, 1942. Street and Number.

Massachusetts Avenue—Continued

	D	Glennon Joseph	561	U S A	32	here
	E	Glennon Ruth—†	561	housewife	29	"
	F	Hazelton Theodore	561	electrician	55	"
	G	Johnson Tobey	561	clerk	26	"
	H	Murphy Evelyn—†	561	"	30	40 Montgomery
	K	Tanner Wilbur	561	fisherman	45	here
	L	Chidzinski Chester J	563	busboy	28	"
	M	Conley Robert	563	laborer	52	"
	N	Krikorian Helen—†	563	housewife	67	"
	O	Krikorian Morris	563	laborer	72	"
	P	Lorenzo Herbert	563	chauffeur	50	"
	R	Lyagen Edna—†	563	stenographer	33	"
	S	Rivers Albert	563	porter	60	"
	T	Robart Mary—†	563	laundress	31	Worcester
	U	Sheridan Ellen—†	563	at home	65	here
	V	Anderson Theodore	565	laborer	46	New Jersey
	W	Czerniawsk Eugenia—†	565	clerk	24	4 James
	X	*Czerniawsk Felicia—†	565	housewife	56	4 "
	Y	Czerniawsk Natalie—†	565	clerk	26	4 "
	Z	Glynn Robert	565	U S N	21	Wakefield
535						
	A	Hayes Walter	565	busboy	55	1413 Wash'n
	B	Janski Henry	565	laborer	29	Danvers
	C	Jeansonne Adam	565	U S N	36	New York
	D	Lavell Chester	565	waiter	49	60 Temple
	E	Morgan Lester	565	salesman	27	46 W Newton
	F	Pardy Robert C	565	guard	24	Mississippi
	G	Wasserman Helen—†	565	housewife	24	Somerville
	H	Wasserman Neil	565	laborer	26	"
	K	Wilberg Olga—†	565	seamstress	60	480 Mass av
	L	Arrenault Evelyn—†	567	stitcher	54	44 Worcester
	M	Collins Elizabeth—†	567	seamstress	63	here
	N	Cotter George E	567	machinist	42	Maine
	O	Cotter Martha—†	567	housewife	35	"
	P	Flynn Mary—†	567	nurse	46	here
	R	Joyce Frederick M	567	editor	49	132 W Concord
	S	Kerber Leon A	567	clerk	44	Pennsylvania
	T	Lewis Albert	567	bartender	48	here
	U	Lewis Josephine—†	567	housewife	34	"
	V	Robinshaw Margaret A–†	567	domestic	46	14 Highland
	W	Scott Marion E—†	569	housekeeper	51	here

Page.	Letter.	FULL NAME.	Residence, Jan. 1, 1943.	Occupation.	Supposed Age.	Reported Residence, Jan. 1, 1942. Street and Number.

Massachusetts Avenue—Continued

	X	Asakura Evelyn—†	571	housewife	37	here
	Y	*Asakura Thomas	571	cook	51	"
	Z	Bestecki Max	571	lawyer	38	"
536						
	A	Dolan John	571	clerk	61	581 Mass av
	B	Doucette Paul	571	seaman	45	Maine
	C	Hilton Fred	571	salesman	78	here
	D	McGinnis Daniel	571	retired	68	"
	E	Parson Thomas C	571	student	23	New Jersey
	F	Provin Annie—†	571	domestic	53	here
	G	Rogers Andrew	571	baker	46	"
	H	Rogers Florence—†	571	housekeeper	63	"
	K	Shea John	571	clerk	32	Brookline
	L	Shea Mary—†	571	housewife	27	"
	M	Bannun Margaret—†	573	waitress	23	Lawrence
	N	Bappastergion Mary—†	573	"	23	Rhode Island
	O	Caswell Irene—†	573	cashier	53	577 Mass av
	P	*Donnelly John P	573	salesman	66	567 "
	R	Doucette Rose—†	573	clerk	30	Revere
	S	Freeman John	573	"	59	577 Mass av
	T	Hollingsworth Frederick	573	manager	54	Revere
	U	Keith Rubin	573	janitor	71	here
	V	Mahoney Arthur	573	porter	55	"
	W	McCarthy Frank	573	waiter	49	New York
	X	Monks Helen—†	573	domestic	51	here
	Y	O'Connor Charles T	573	clerk	52	567 Mass av
	Z	Armour Ida—†	577	housewife	40	here
537						
	A	Armour Melvin	577	machinist	50	"
	B	Esterbrook Phyllis—†	577	clerk	26	Lawrence
	C	Gardner Harold	577	waiter	29	Connecticut
	D	Johnson Frederick	577	student	22	17 Union Park
	E	Jordan Charles	577	salesman	61	here
	F	Jordan Isabelle—†	577	housewife	53	"
	G	Munroe Anna—†	577	"	61	Somerville
	H	Munroe George	577	retired	66	"
	K	Phinney Freeman	577	machinist	44	Rhode Island
	L	Pipen George	577	laborer	36	"
	M	Rothrock David	577	student	25	New York
	N	Tortici James	577	tailor	27	"
	O	Yost George	577	student	27	New Jersey

Page.	Letter.	Full Name.	Residence, Jan. 1, 1943.	Occupation.	Supposed Age.	Reported Residence, Jan. 1, 1942. Street and Number.

Massachusetts Avenue—Continued

	P	Adams George	581	laborer	48	Malden
	R	Brennan Hilda—†	581	nurse	40	543 Mass av
	S	Brown Anna—†	581	housewife	40	Norwell
	T	Brown Harold	581	plumber	39	"
	U	Johnson Frank	581	laborer	48	New York
	V	Olson Victor	581	"	46	63 Worcester
	W	Orr Edna—†	581	housekeeper	45	New York
	X	Ottie Edwin	581	laborer	52	here
	Y	Cunningham Arthur	585	operator	50	"
	Z	Cunningham Margaret J–†	585	housewife	46	"
538						
	A	Cunningham Ruth—†	585	clerk	24	
	B	Davis George W	585	electrician	49	"
	C	Hickey Charles E	585	retired	60	
	D	Hickey Josephine—†	585	housewife	59	"
	E	McCort John	585	retired	73	
	F	Sargent Elizabeth—†	585	housewife	47	"
	G	Sargent Richard	585	U S A	21	"
	H	*Barukas Bessie—†	585	housewife	47	"
	K	*Barukas Cocotas	585	baker	48	"
	L	Spear Leslie	585	laborer	32	
	M	Spear Margaret—†	585	housewife	26	"
	P	Fortune Frances—†	602	clerk	30	
	R	Fortune Harold	602	laborer	41	
	S	James Bruce A	602	machinist	40	"
	T	James Irene—†	602	housewife	39	"
	U	Williams Cora L—†	602	musician	32	21 Rutland sq
	V	Williams Theodore S	602	U S A	30	369 Northampton
	W	Clark Alonzo M	603	embalmer	59	here
	X	Cochran Laura—†	603	housekeeper	42	34 Northfield
	Y	Cochran Lawrence	603	chauffeur	20	34 "
	Z	Cochran Todd	603	shipper	22	34 "
539						
	A	Cochran Zenoba—†	603	beautician	21	34 "
	B	Parris Datha L—†	603	domestic	36	here
	C	*Ardine Samuel	604	laborer	56	39 Worcester
	D	Bell Michael	604	"	60	here
	E	Desdane John	604	"	62	"
	F	Farrell James	604	retired	87	"
	G	Hanson John	604	laborer	57	
	H	Hawley Mary—†	604	at home	76	

Page.	Letter.	FULL NAME.	Residence, Jan. 1, 1943.	Occupation.	Supposed Age.	Reported Residence, Jan. 1, 1942. Street and Number.

Massachusetts Avenue—Continued

	K	McCarthy Charles	604	laborer	61	here
	L	O'Connell Sadie—†	604	housewife	61	"
	M	O'Connell William	604	laborer	61	"
	N	Pressey Harry C	604	retired	62	
	O	Pressey Mary—†	604	housekeeper	57	"
	P	Stevens Fred	604	retired	62	
	R	Whitaker Agnes—†	604	housewife	56	"
	S	Whitaker Ernest	604	painter	62	
	T	*Glavo Catherine—†	605	housewife	45	"
	U	Glavo Joseph	605	manager	49	"
	V	Gouzoules Arthur	605	salesman	37	"
	W	Gouzoules Margaret—†	605	housewife	27	"
	X	Gordon Alma—†	605	"	40	
	Y	Gordon Edgar F	605	manager	44	"
	Z	Constatine James G	605	engineer	34	"
540						
	A	Constaine Louise—†	605	housewife	24	"
	B	Vartervian Mihran	605	salesman	57	"
	D	Baker Helen—†	608	housewife	50	"
	E	Baker Vernon L	608	operator	49	"
	F	*Barnett Louise—†	608	at home	35	
	G	Beres Burt	608	laborer	57	
	H	*Buchanan Betty—†	608	at home	38	
	K	Condon Nellie—†	608	domestic	55	"
	L	*Doane William H	608	painter	59	
	M	*Dorey Walter	608	porter	70	"
	N	Gardner John	608	laborer	35	"
	O	O'Brien Earl	608	"	30	"
	P	O'Brien Timothy	608	"	55	
	R	Sagatosky Anthony J	608	retired	69	
	S	Waddell Myette—†	608	at home	60	
	T	Andres Esther—†	609	seamstress	48	"
	U	*Guinnasso Frank	609	retired	84	"
	V	Hogan Thomas	609	"	71	Salem
	W	Marler Robert	609	clerk	53	1534 Wash'n
	X	McPherson John	609	boilermaker	52	here
	Y	Morris Winston	609	coremaker	56	110 Gibson
	Z	Murdock William	609	laborer	54	here
541						
	A	Parker Herbert	609	counterman	48	"
	B	*Trainor Frederick	609	boilermaker	39	"

Page.	Letter.	Full Name.	Residence, Jan. 1, 1943.	Occupation.	Supposed Age.	Reported Residence, Jan. 1, 1942. Street and Number.

Massachusetts Avenue—Continued

	C	Berry Thomas	612	retired	90	here
	D	Burrows Elizabeth—†	612	housekeeper	66	"
	E	*Croger Francis	612	laborer	65	"
	F	Cronin Jeremiah	612	"	48	"
	G	Danielson George	612	retired	64	664 Mass av
	H	Finn James	612	"	68	here
	K	Kennedy Patrick	612	"	70	8 Concord sq
	L	Murphy Mary—†	612	housekeeper	50	562 Mass av
	M	Ryan Mary—†	612	clerk	55	785 Old Colony P'kway
	N	Smith Charlotte—†	612	shoeworker	37	here
	O	Walsh Herman	612	laborer	49	"
	P	Walsh Jessie—†	612	housewife	49	"
	R	*Alexavich Davie	613	shoeworker	52	"
	S	*Burns Michael J	613	laborer	55	"
	T	Hanchuk Dement	613	machinist	50	617 Mass av
	U	Lukaszewicz Frances—†	613	teacher	31	here
	V	Morgan Paul T	613	steelworker	26	"
	W	Murphy Frederick	613	laborer	58	"
	X	*Okoniewski Marie—†	613	laundress	38	"
	Y	Sartoris Herman J	613	clerk	61	"
542						
	A	Scho Joseph S	613	laborer	28	
	B	Smith Sadie W—†	613	stitcher	51	
	C	Symanski Walter	613	laborer	44	
	D	Vigneau Frank E	613	"	58	"
	E	Burke Thomas J	614	"	56	677 Mass av
	F	Burns David	614	"	50	here
	D	Burns Helen L—†	614	clerk	23	"
	H	Burns John T	614	operator	35	Canada
	K	Durant Louise—†	614	waitress	35	42 St Stephen
	L	Greeley Henry	614	chauffeur	53	27 Tower
	M	*Johnson John F	614	cabinetmaker	59	here
	N	MacDonald Andrew	614	carpenter	50	406 Col av
	O	McAllister Marie W—†	614	factoryhand	39	32 Worcester sq
	P	*McInnis Elizabeth—†	614	waitress	42	42 "
	R	*McInnis Robert	614	laborer	42	42 "
	S	*O'Neil Julia M—†	614	housekeeper	44	here
	T	Paulson Carl	614	laborer	57	"
	U	*Toma Samuel	614	shoemaker	58	"
	V	Zandotes Harry	614	chef	48	"
	W	Brindmour Homer	615	cook	40	"

Page.	Letter.	FULL NAME.	Residence, Jan. 1, 1943.	Occupation.	Supposed Age.	Reported Residence, Jan. 1, 1942. Street and Number.

Massachusetts Avenue—Continued

	X	Fidrocki Alfred V	615	U S A	21	here
	Y	Fidrocki Marie—†	615	housewife	43	"
	Z	Fidrocki William	615	manager	56	"
543						
	A	Goddard Marie E—†	615	beautician	39	"
	B	Killin Grace—†	615	housewife	47	"
	C	Killin Thomas	615	chauffeur	42	"
	D	Taura Anna—†	615	laundress	60	"
	F	Cullen Mary—†	617	at home	69	
	G	Daley William	617	laborer	65	
	H	Fat Lee T	617	chef	32	
	K	*Maas George A	617	manager	64	"
	L	McIntosh Mildred—†	617	operator	34	"
	M	Middleton Ralph J	617	letter carrier	37	"
	N	Norton Clara—†	617	at home	66	
	O	Patrick Arthur	617	retired	74	
	P	Sarette Edward	617	laborer	34	
	R	Sarette Eugenia—†	617	housekeeper	62	"
	S	Sarette Wanda—†	617	housewife	38	"
	T	Sarette William	617	laborer	36	
	U	*Senna Joseph	617	waiter	51	
	V	Williams Ina M—†	617	seamstress	62	"
	X	Condlin John	619	laborer	55	617 Dor av
	Y	Crowley Helen—†	619	domestic	42	here
	Z	Flynn Daniel A	619	salesman	59	"
544						
	A	Flynn Mary J—†	619	housewife	50	"
	B	Hanson Melvin	619	shoeworker	62	152 Warren av
	C	Langham George	619	printer	45	Springfield
	D	Langham Lena—†	619	housewife	37	"
	E	Leach John	619	retired	75	here
	F	Mason Harry	619	shoeworker	55	848 Mass av
	G	Ryan Frederick W	619	retired	75	here
	H	Shakley Anna—†	619	at home	67	"
	K	Smith Mabel—†	619	housekeeper	59	15 W Dedham
	L	Stanley Rubin	619	carpenter	60	here
	M	Turner William J	619	cook	51	680 Mass av
	O	Booth Carl	621	designer	68	here
	P	Booth Sylvia—†	621	housewife	67	"
	R	Carroll Joseph	621	retired	73	604 Mass av
	S	Cawley Alice—†	621	seamstress	57	here

Page.	Letter.	FULL NAME.	Residence, Jan. 1, 1943.	Occupation.	Supposed Age.	Reported Residence, Jan. 1, 1942. Street and Number.

Massachusettts Avenue—Continued

Page.	Letter.	FULL NAME.	Residence, Jan. 1, 1943.	Occupation.	Supposed Age.	Reported Residence, Jan. 1, 1942. Street and Number.
	T	Donohue Thomas	621	laborer	40	450 Centre
	U	Dyer Lena M—†	621	housekeeper	61	here
	V	Gagnas John	621	baker	54	70 Hunneman
	W	O'Donnell Marie—†	621	matron	40	Nantucket
	X	Tarbox Anna P—†	621	seamstress	55	here
	Y	Thompson James	621	retired	67	"
	Z	Thompson Joseph	621	upholsterer	61	"
545						
	A	Workman Mary—†	621	matron	65	619 Mass av
	C	Carlson Mary E—†	623	at home	70	here
	D	Crowley Louise—†	623	packer	28	4 Worcester sq
	E	Fowler Ethel M—†	623	housewife	55	485 Shawmut av
	F	Fowler William L	623	mechanic	55	485 "
	G	Grant Michael J	623	engineer	57	here
	H	Griffin May—†	623	domestic	41	233 Warren av
	K	Hall Etta—†	623	laundress	55	here
	L	McPherson Albert	623	rigger	44	Brookline
	M	Mulkern Joseph H	623	machinist	40	here
	N	Mulkern Mary J—†	623	housewife	40	"
	O	Whitney Mary—†	623	housekeeper	41	"
	S	Allen Edith M—†	627	waitress	36	"
	T	Angel Walter	627	laborer	51	"
	U	Evans Maude—†	627	housekeeper	36	"
	V	Fedellia Edward	627	bartender	41	"
	W	Hennessey Andrew	627	engineer	52	
	X	O'Neil Agnes—†	627	housekeeper	55	"
	Y	Lantz Helena I—†	628	typist	30	"
	Z	Lantz Jennie C—†	628	stitcher	54	
546						
	A	Lantz Walter H	628	retired	62	"
	B	Goldstein Max	628	U S M C	46	Medford
	C	Goldstein Virginia—†	628	housewife	29	"
	D	Bray Mary—†	628	operator	45	here
	E	Peterson Florence—†	628	waitress	58	"
	F	Peterson William F	628	laborer	31	"
	G	Canner Max	628	merchant	51	"
	H	Guiffrida Margaret —†	628	housewife	20	"
	K	Guiffrida Sebastian	628	laborer	24	"
	L	Bates Gwendolyn—†	628	clerk	30	1761 Wash'n
	M	Bates Thomas H	628	clergyman	33	1761 "
	N	Hoo Soo	628	waiter	35	here

Northampton Place

Page.	Letter.	Full Name.	Residence, Jan. 1, 1943.	Occupation.	Supposed Age.	Reported Residence, Jan. 1, 1942. Street and Number.
	R	Sisco Fred	1	laborer	42	here
	S	Taten Ophelia—†	1	laundress	39	“
	T	Thurston Mary—†	1	housekeeper	76	“

547 Northampton Street

Page.	Letter.	Full Name.	Residence, Jan. 1, 1943.	Occupation.	Supposed Age.	Reported Residence, Jan. 1, 1942. Street and Number.
547	C	Mosby Pearl—†	142	domestic	42	here
	D	Small Susan—†	142	“	68	“
	E	Singletary Goldie—†	142	housewife	27	561A Shawmut av
	F	Singletary Theodore	142	laborer	29	561A “
	G	Wilder Augustus	142	“	26	561A “
	H	Wilder Julia—†	142	domestic	20	178 Northampton
	K	Wilder Raymond	142	laborer	25	178 “
	L	Wyatt Sarah—†	142	domestic	57	561A Shawmut av
	O	Douglas Elizabeth—†	143	at home	78	here
	P	Gaines Bertha—†	143	housekeeper	50	“
	R	Miranda John	143	laborer	39	“
	S	Miranda Louise—†	143	housewife	38	“
	T	Mazzone Domenic	143	cook	51	
	W	Walker Emily—†	145	domestic	32	“
	Y	Lee Baldwin	145	sorter	32	
	Z	Lee Edward	145	retired	64	“
548						
	D	Williams Roberta E—†	147	at home	70	35 Woodbury
	E	Bane Sadie—†	147	“	69	here
	F	Stokes Anthony	147	retired	68	“
	G	Stokes Estelle L—†	147	housewife	66	“
	H	Robbins James L	147	packer	22	
	M	Reardon Emma—†	149	housekeeper	53	“
	N	Ealey Eugene	149	retired	50	“
	O	Jackson Estelle—†	149	storekeeper	53	“
	P	Jones Richard	149	laborer	44	“
	S	Lucas Daniel	150	retired	70	“
	T	Duncan William	150	“	70	
	U	Childs Annie—†	150	at home	91	
	Y	MacDonald Mary—†	152	housekeeper	72	“
	Z	MacMillan William	152	packer	70	“
549						
	A	Peyton Hattie—†	152	at home	60	“
	B	Washington Carol	153	shipper	48	Virginia
	C	Washington Mabel—†	153	housewife	32	Pennsylvania

Page.	Letter.	Full Name.	Residence, Jan. 1, 1943.	Occupation.	Supposed Age.	Reported Residence, Jan. 1, 1942. Street and Number.

Northampton Street—Continued

Page.	Letter.	Full Name.	Residence, Jan. 1, 1943.	Occupation.	Supposed Age.	Reported Residence, Jan. 1, 1942. Street and Number.
	E	*Montague Zachariah	153	laborer	47	here
	H	Blackshear Elizabeth—†	155	at home	37	"
	L	Brown Kenneth	155	porter	59	"
	P	King Harriet R—†	157	at home	64	
	R	Haynes Rebecca—†	157	housewife	37	"
	S	Milton Barney	157	salesman	53	30 Newcomb
	V	Dickson Alice—†	160	housewife	44	552 Shawmut av
	W	Dickson James	160	laborer	56	552 "
	X	Dickson James	160	U S A	21	552 "
550						
	B	Tolliver Daisy—†	175	housewife	23	here
	C	Tolliver James	175	barber	24	"
	D	Smith Evelyn—†	175	housewife	49	"
	E	Smith Thomas	175	laborer	52	
	G	Jones Eunice—†	175	housewife	42	"
	H	Jones Henry	175	porter	48	
	K	Drayton Renee—†	176	storekeeper	52	"
	L	Robinson James	176	laborer	27	N Carolina
	M	Robinson Viola—†	176	housewife	29	"
	N	Jones Emma—†	176	domestic	25	here
	O	Smith Harry	176	clerk	45	"
	P	Todd Mattie—†	176	housewife	25	"
	R	Todd Norris	176	laborer	27	
	S	Wigfall Joseph	176	plumber	49	
	T	Thomas Ethel—†	177	housewife	53	"
	U	Thomas John O	177	laborer	50	
	V	Jones James	177	"	44	
	W	Jones Laura—†	177	housewife	44	"
	X	Stephens Matthew	177	seaman	42	
	Y	Stephens Myra—†	177	domestic	39	"
	Z	Catherwood Claudius	177	laborer	53	
551						
	A	Catherwood Estelle—†	177	housewife	53	"
	B	*Clark Anna N—†	178	"	58	
	C	Clark George N	178	chauffeur	44	"
	D	Arnold Florence—†	178	housewife	30	"
	E	Arnold William	178	laborer	33	
	F	Wilson Hattie—†	178	domestic	39	"
	G	Camp John	179	mechanic	36	203 W Springfield
	H	Camp Zelma—†	179	housewife	36	203 "
	K	Jones Emma—†	179	at home	55	Texas

Page.	Letter.	Full Name.	Residence, Jan. 1, 1943.	Occupation.	Supposed Age.	Reported Residence, Jan. 1, 1942. Street and Number.

Northampton Street—Continued

Page.	Letter.	Full Name.	Residence, Jan. 1, 1943.	Occupation.	Supposed Age.	Reported Residence, Jan. 1, 1942. Street and Number.
	L	James Louise—†	179	housewife	27	here
	M	*James Ormond	179	janitor	52	"
	N	*Small Augustus	179	laborer	31	"
	O	*Small Thelma—†	179	housewife	28	"
	P	Bushfan Hilary	179	laborer	42	
	R	Bushfan Mildred L—†	179	housewife	24	"
	T	Jeffress Robert	181	porter	42	
	U	Williams Annie—†	181	domestic	40	"
	V	*Folkes Almanda—†	181	housewife	44	"
	W	Folkes Calvin	181	laborer	21	
	X	Folkes McDonald	181	machinist	43	"
	Y	Quinn Curley	181	mechanic	38	12 Greenwich pk
	Z	Quinn Elizabeth—†	181	housewife	20	12 "
552						
	A	Hamm Edgar A	181	U S A	28	229 W Canton
	B	Hamm Gladys—†	181	housewife	48	229 "
	C	Hamm Ralph C	181	laborer	25	229 "
	D	Hamm Ruth H—†	181	clerk	20	229 "
	E	Bland James	182	molder	42	668 Shawmut av
	F	Chappell Edith M—†	182	cook	36	Connecticut
	G	Lewis Margaret—†	182	domestic	30	here
	H	Spell Bernice—†	182	housewife	32	"
	K	Spell Louis	182	laborer	32	"
	L	Strother Mary—†	182	at home	48	5 Woodbury
	M	Frazier Ida—†	184	housewife	35	here
	N	Frazier Isaiah	184	ironworker	38	"
	O	Miller Katherine—†	184	housewife	21	"
	P	Montier Della—†	184	"	49	
	R	Montier Sidney W	184	laborer	49	
	S	Ridley Fred	184	"	50	
	T	Ridley Margaret—†	184	housewife	48	"
	U	Collymore Alice—†	186	at home	50	
	V	Collymore Gwendolyn—†	186	stitcher	22	
	W	Collymore Ismay—†	186	beautician	20	"
	X	Collymore Ruby—†	186	stitcher	24	
	Y	*Brotherson Samuel	188	painter	54	
	Z	Lewis Henry	188	paperhanger	43	"
553						
	A	DeGroat Douglas	190	plumber	48	46 Northfield
	B	DeGroat Raymond	190	gardener	49	46 "
	C	Rahn Chester	190	retired	61	163 W Springfield

Page.	Letter.	Full Name.	Residence, Jan. 1, 1943.	Occupation.	Supposed Age.	Reported Residence, Jan. 1, 1942. Street and Number.

Northampton Street—Continued

	D	Taylor Stanley P	190	clerk	42	here
	E	Washington Joseph P	190	clergyman	58	"
	F	Coleman Annie M—†	192	at home	65	"
	G	Canada Daisy—†	192	laundress	28	"
	H	Canada Dobbie	192	welder	30	
	K	Peak Ruby—†	192	laundress	34	"
	L	Bryan Adelaide—†	192	at home	83	
	M	Hall Adelaide—†	192	stitcher	21	
	N	Hall Helen—†	192	"	20	
	O	Briggs Carrie—†	194	domestic	60	"
	P	Williams Florence—†	194	at home	55	
	R	Hayes Marguerite—†	194	housekeeper	40	"
	S	*Mendes Antonio	194	laborer	35	Wareham
	T	*Perry Manuel	194	"	64	here
	U	Gomes John	196	"	51	"
	V	Gomes Lillian—†	196	housewife	41	"
	W	Knight Charlotte—†	196	domestic	30	"
	X	*Taylor Ellen—†	196	at home	71	25 Arnold
	Y	Garro Charles A	198	chauffeur	32	here
	Z	Garro Lydia—†	198	housewife	36	"
554						
	A	Smith Mary—†	198	at home	50	"
	B	Seymour Mary—†	198	housewife	20	339 Shawmut av
	C	Seymour William	198	chauffeur	35	339 "
	D	Lockwood Letitia—†	198	domestic	70	here
	E	Barber Vivian—†	200	"	39	"
	F	Haynes Vida—†	200	cook	53	"
	G	Fontaine Barbara—†	202	housewife	34	"
	H	Fontaine Oliver	202	longshoreman	33	"
	K	Palmer Mabel—†	202	domestic	48	59 Windsor
	L	Pina Michael	202	laborer	38	Newton
	M	Silva Sabina—†	202	housewife	37	Ohio
	N	Singletary Collier	204	cook	40	4 Claremont
	O	Singletary Irene—†	204	housewife	37	4 "
	P	Cooper Lillian—†	204	dressmaker	48	here
	R	Gray Mary E—†	204	housewife	56	"
	S	Gray Robert E	204	porter	46	"
	T	Holliday Helen—†	204	musician	47	"
	U	Lee Glen L	206	U S C G	25	Florida
	V	Lee Mamie—†	206	housewife	23	"
	W	Warner Ida—†	206	domestic	55	"

Page.	Letter.	Full Name.	Residence, Jan. 1, 1943.	Occupation.	Supposed Age.	Reported Residence, Jan. 1, 1942. Street and Number.

Northampton Street—Continued

Page.	Letter.	Full Name.	Residence, Jan. 1, 1943.	Occupation.	Supposed Age.	Reported Residence, Jan. 1, 1942. Street and Number.
	x	McLean Beulah—†	206	domestic	28	681 Shawmut av
	z	Davis Eva E—†	208	housewife	67	here
555						
	A	Davis George H	208	engineer	75	
	B	Laws Emma—†	208	at home	74	
	C	Hillard Parthenia—†	208	"	67	
	D	Irving Elizabeth—†	208	"	75	"
	E	Brown Chester	210	cook	22	15 Wellington
	F	Campbell William	210	tailor	46	here
	G	Dean George	210	machinist	47	"
	H	Howard Helen—†	210	stitcher	23	215 W Springfield
	K	Nelson Arthur	210	porter	25	758 Tremont
	L	Robinson Herbert	210	welder	47	here
	M	Warwick Gladys—†	210	housekeeper	44	"
	N	Webster Daniel	210	retired	66	"
	O	Williams Clara—†	210	stitcher	37	
	P	Ballieu Norman	212	vulcanizer	27	"
	R	Hayes Harry	212	realtor	50	
	S	Anderson Melvin S	212	conductor	43	"
	T	Anderson Pauline—†	212	housewife	45	"
	U	*Woodson Glenora—†	212	at home	35	"
	V	Emrich William	212	laborer	42	Cambridge
556						
	A	Robinson James	216	U S A	39	39 Newcomb
	B	Robinson Laura—†	216	housewife	37	39 "
	C	Sims Bertha—†	216	domestic	40	39 "
	D	Brookins Frank G	216	clergyman	67	here
	E	Braxton Charles P	216	retired	66	"
	G	Harding Edmund	218	porter	50	"
	H	Coleman Junius	218	laborer	41	
	K	Coleman Margaret E—†	218	housewife	32	"
	L	*Eastmond Caswald	218	operator	31	"
	M	Eastmond Ophelia—†	218	housewife	27	"
	N	Harding Edward	218	welder	24	
	O	Harding Rose—†	218	housewife	23	"
	P	Chambliss Sally—†	220	stitcher	51	
	R	Grant Minnie M—†	220	domestic	58	"
	S	Manley Celia F—†	220	housewife	66	"
	T	Manley John T	220	mechanic	61	"
	U	Mason Charles	222	laborer	56	
	V	Mason Wilhelmina—†	222	housewife	55	"

Page.	Letter.	FULL NAME.	Residence, Jan. 1, 1943.	Occupation.	Supposed Age.	Reported Residence, Jan. 1, 1942. Street and Number.

Northampton Street—Continued

	W	Simmons Agnes—†	222	housewife	37	here
	X	Simmons Robert A	222	dentist	61	"
	Y	Wright Franklin	222	laborer	36	"
	Z	Wright Mildred—†	222	housewife	33	"
557						
	A	Ford Mary—†	224	at home	38	
	B	Harris Nellie—†	224	domestic	54	"
	C	Lockett Eleanor—†	224	at home	66	"
	D	Griffin Isaac	224	U S A	23	19 Albemarle
	E	Griffin Marie—†	224	housewife	22	here
	F	Holmes Helen—†	224	"	46	"
	G	Holmes Richard	224	chef	48	"
	H	Hinton James	225	laborer	28	
	K	Hinton Jane—†	225	housewife	21	"
	L	Moore Annie G—†	225	"	25	Georgia
	M	Moore James	225	porter	23	"
	N	Pettie Benjamin	225	U S A	28	here
	O	Pettie Robert	225	laborer	60	"
	P	Pettie Wesley	225	U S A	23	"
	R	Hamilton Annie—†	225	at home	75	
	S	Hayes Ruth A—†	225	stitcher	45	
	T	Kennedy Daisy—†	225	"	48	
	U	Kennedy Edward	225	tailor	47	
	W	Crawford Henry	229	laborer	34	
	X	Crawford Mamie S—†	229	domestic	40	"
	Y	Davis Harold	229	barber	39	
	Z	Davis Thelma—†	229	domestic	23	"
558						
	A	Johnson Harold A	229	laborer	33	
	B	Johnson Ruth E—†	229	domestic	31	"
	C	Matthews Jackie—†	229	entertainer	40	"
	D	Walters Emmeline—†	229	domestic	23	"
	E	Hatch William	231	salesman	40	"
	F	Hill Louis	231	retired	73	
	G	McRae Anna—†	231	at home	65	
	H	Simms Roberta—†	231	"	64	
	K	Elijah Peaceful	233	laborer	52	
	L	Fairfax Robert	233	"	61	
	M	Ford John	233	barber	42	
	N	Gray Arthur	233	laborer	66	"
	O	Lewis George	233	"	44	42 Kendall

Page.	Letter.	Full Name.	Residence, Jan. 1, 1943.	Occupation.	Supposed Age.	Reported Residence, Jan. 1, 1942. Street and Number.

Northampton Street—Continued

	P	Mallory Lola—†	233	at home	50	here
	R	McLennie Harold	233	laborer	36	"
	S	Morris Josephine—†	233	housekeeper	69	"
	T	Smith Stewart	233	decorator	46	"
	U	Braxton Clarence	235	laborer	46	
	V	Reid George	235	"	47	
	W	Reid William	235	retired	71	
	X	Sewell Violet—†	235	housewife	48	"
	Y	Sewell Wilson	235	laborer	49	"
	Z	Valentine Marjorie—†	235	housewife	27	17 Pompeii
559						
	A	Valentine Warren	235	chauffeur	30	17 "
	B	Moore Edwin	237	U S A	24	687 Shawmut av
	C	Moore Mary—†	237	housewife	58	687 "
	D	Moore May—†	237	laundress	21	687 "
	E	Moore Walter	237	laborer	58	687 "
	F	Fairfax Martha—†	239	operator	50	here
	G	Miles Arthur J	239	clerk	31	"
	H	Miles Ruth E—†	239	housewife	26	"
	K	Westmoreland Isaac	239	clerk	58	616 Col av
	L	Westmoreland Jean—†	239	"	28	616 "
	M	Westmoreland Marion—†	239	teacher	57	616 "
	N	Worthy Helen V—†	239	student	23	here
	O	Worthy Mabel R—†	239	housewife	59	"
	P	Worthy Myrtle A—†	239	at home	28	"
	R	Worthy William	239	physician	62	"
	S	Worthy William, jr	239	student	21	"
	T	Zellner Curtis	239	seaman	22	Illinois
	U	Carter Rosa—†	241	domestic	46	here
	V	Henson George	241	sorter	39	140 Camden
	W	Nairne Alfred S	241	dentist	62	here
	X	Rose Manuel	241	laborer	35	Falmouth
	Y	Osborne Louise—†	241	housewife	24	here
	Z	Osborne Milton	241	seaman	27	"
560						
	A	Stokes James	241	welder	26	Virginia
	B	Wilson Catherine—†	241	housekeeper	45	here
	C	Dyer Elizabeth—†	243	"	59	"
	D	Hampton Ruby—†	243	dressmaker	39	"
	E	Johnson Bertha—†	243	cook	47	

Page.	Letter.	Full Name.	Residence, Jan. 1, 1943.	Occupation.	Supposed Age.	Reported Residence, Jan. 1, 1942. Street and Number.

Northfield Street

	R	Barros Beatrice—†	11	waitress	29	here
	S	Barros Anna—†	11	housekeeper	27	"
	T	Barros Anthony	11	painter	38	"
	U	Watson Andrew	11	rigger	32	
	V	Watson Dorothy—†	11	housekeeper	27	"
	W	Pells Florence—†	13	domestic	44	"
	X	Jenkins Esther—†	13	"	50	571 Col av
	Y	Squire Catherine—†	13	housekeeper	67	182 Northampton
	G	Cannon Jesse	14	kitchenman	51	here
	H	Ashton Ruth—†	14	housewife	36	"
	K	Stinson Arthur	14	laborer	35	"
	L	Stinson Leila—†	14	housewife	29	"
	M*	Berry John	14	laborer	63	
	Z	Brown Selina—†	15	domestic	55	"
561						
	B	Reggins Esther—†	15	at home	75	
	C	Bowen Emery	16	laborer	58	
	D	Hawkins Margaret—†	16	housewife	74	"
	E	Hawkins William F	16	laborer	57	
	F	Taylor Susie M—†	16	housewife	76	"
	O	Rogers Elizabeth—†	19	domestic	58	"
	P	Mitchell Elma—†	19	housekeeper	60	"
	R	Alston Eary	19	laborer	59	"
	S	Alston Lucille—†	19	housekeeper	42	"
	T	Wright Rachel—†	20	factoryhand	52	"
	U	Holloway Sarah—†	20	housewife	42	"
	V	Owens Ethel—†	20	"	39	
	W	Owens Prince	20	janitor	50	"
	X	Bozeman Carolyn—†	20	presser	31	Georgia
	Y	Bozeman Melvin	20	chipper	34	"
	Z*	Lopez Edna—†	21	housewife	47	here
562						
	A*	Lopez John	21	retired	48	
	B	Fields Anna B—†	21	housekeeper	60	"
	C*	Mendez Joseph	21	laborer	47	"
	D	Harrison Quillar	22	mechanic	52	"
	E	Holland Leila—†	22	housewife	58	"
	F	Monterio Ida—†	22	housekeeper	28	"
	G	Robinson James	22	plumber	55	"
	H	Allen Florence—†	23	domestic	46	"

Page.	Letter.	Full Name.	Residence, Jan. 1, 1943.	Occupation.	Supposed Age.	Reported Residence, Jan. 1, 1942. Street and Number.

Northfield Street—Continued

Page.	Letter.	Full Name.	Residence, Jan. 1, 1943.	Occupation.	Supposed Age.	Reported Residence, Jan. 1, 1942.
	K	Nixon Harry	23	laborer	29	Wellesley
	L	Nixon May—†	23	housekeeper	21	"
	N	Wallace Clara—†	24	at home	71	here
	O	Brown Ethel—†	24	domestic	52	"
	P	Dennis John H	24	clergyman	58	"
	R	Dennis Sadie—†	24	housewife	56	"
	T	Robinson James L	25	laborer	37	
	U	Osborne Lillian V—†	25	domestic	40	"
	V	Matthews Elizabeth—†	25	waitress	42	"
	W	Dabbs Maria S—†	27	housekeeper	59	27 Arnold
	X	Kirby Carrie—†	27	domestic	50	here
	Y	Marshall George A	27	laborer	47	"
563						
	G	O'Brien Louise—†	31	housekeeper	27	"
	H	O'Brien Reginald	31	laborer	43	"
	K	Barton Betty B—†	31	housekeeper	74	"
	L	Saunders Robert J	31	laborer	46	506 Shawmut av
	M	Wallace Mary L—†	31	domestic	44	14 Rutland
	S	Bryant Elizabeth—†	33	housekeeper	47	here
	T	McCrae James	33	laborer	60	"
	U	Quattlebaum Furman	33	"	43	"
	V	Curry Charles E	33	"	40	
564						
	A	Morrison Henry	39	porter	58	"
	B	Morrison William	39	"	52	"
	C	Cole Vashti C—†	39	domestic	55	"
	D	Griffith Gwendolyn—†	39	"	25	129 Lenox
	E	Peters Anna—†	39	"	56	here
	G	Johnson Lila—†	40	housewife	42	565 Col av
	H	Wolcott Josephine—†	40	waitress	47	Pennsylvania
	K	Reed Harriet—†	40	housewife	50	here
	M	Williams Leroy	41	laborer	42	"
	N	Robinson May E—†	41	domestic	45	"
	O	Gray Beatrice—†	41	housekeeper	44	"
	P	Gray Robert	41	laborer	30	"
	R	Jones Henry	41	"	46	"
	S	King John W	42	cook	46	43 Northfield
	T	Smith James	42	retired	97	43 "
	U	Linton Hilda—†	42	housewife	63	here
	V	Jones Samuel	42	packer	42	"

Page.	Letter.	Full Name.	Residence, Jan. 1, 1943.	Occupation.	Supposed Age.	Reported Residence, Jan. 1, 1942. Street and Number.

Northfield Street—Continued

Page.	Letter.	Full Name.	Residence, Jan. 1, 1943.	Occupation.	Supposed Age.	Reported Residence, Jan. 1, 1942.
	W	Foster Alonzo	42	retired	66	here
	X	Warner Herbert	43	laborer	65	"
	Y	Brown Martha—†	43	housekeeper	49	"
	Z	Edwards John	43	mechanic	45	"
565						
	A	Wiley Susan—†	43	at home	76	109 W Canton
	B	Holmes William	43	laborer	62	23 E Canton
	E	Hunt Edgar S	44	"	53	570 Col av
	F	Perry Catherine—†	44	maid	49	567 "
	H	Moody George	45	laborer	28	68 Northfield
	K	Moody Mildred—†	45	domestic	29	11 Marble
	L	Freeman Charles	45	laborer	30	here
	M	Freeman Marie—†	45	domestic	30	"
	N	Calliste J Alexander	45	mason	41	"
	O	Lee Mildred—†	45	domestic	46	"
	P	Jett Mary—†	46	housewife	56	32 Northfield
	R	Jones Julia—†	46	"	39	here
	S	Hampton Gwendolyn—†	46	"	27	34 Trotter ct
	T	White Ruth—†	46	"	22	Brookline
	U	Johnson Paul	46	mover	47	44 Northfield
	V	Gary Adolphus	47	laborer	46	here
	W	Gary Emma—†	47	housekeeper	45	"
	X	White Cora L—†	47	storekeeper	31	"
	Y	White John W	47	chemist	28	"
566						
	A	Hicks Eula—†	47	domestic	51	"
	[1]A	Hicks Lillian—†	47	"	26	
	B	Lane Benjamin F	48	realtor	57	
	C	Lane Benjamin F, jr	48	U S A	22	
	D	Lane Estella A—†	48	housewife	45	"
	E	Richards Arthur	48	chauffeur	49	"
	F	Richards Eva—†	48	housewife	47	"
	G	Brown Harold	48	laborer	44	
	H	Brown Maude—†	48	seamstress	45	"
	K	Thurston Florence—†	48	housewife	66	"
	R	Brown Josephine—†	51	domestic	57	"
	S	Gross Herbert	51	salesman	47	"
	T	Smith Arthur	51	porter	24	
	U	Smith Charles	51	cook	62	
	V	Smith Charles, jr	51	porter	23	

Page.	Letter.	Full Name.	Residence, Jan. 1, 1943.	Occupation.	Supposed Age.	Reported Residence, Jan. 1, 1942. Street and Number.

Northfield Street—Continued

	W	Smith Marion—†	51	domestic	20	here
	X	Smith Mary—†	51	housekeeper	44	"
	Y	Smith Thomas	51	machinist	25	"
	Z	Saunders Edward	52	cook	34	39 Northfield
567						
	A	Saunders Louise—†	52	housewife	35	39 "
	B	Alivierre Maude—†	52	"	50	here
	C	Armstrong Lucille—†	52	"	28	"
	D	Beckles Laura—†	52	factoryhand	28	"
	E	Innis Colletta—†	52	"	45	
	F	Keys Eula M—†	52	operator	25	"
	G	Williams Elinor—†	53	laundress	40	"
	H	Williams George	53	laborer	54	
	K	Teixeira Julio	53	"	49	
	L	Teixeira Margaret—†	53	housekeeper	47	"
	M	Teixeira Martha—†	53	W A A C	22	"
	N	Teixeira Raymond	53	chauffeur	28	"
	P	Churchill Alice—†	54	housewife	52	"
	R	Church Grace—†	54	"	66	
	T	*Smith Jemina—†	54	"	72	
	U	Coles Lola A	55	domestic	45	"
	V	Jackson Anna—†	55	at home	57	
	W	Perkins Harry	55	laborer	40	
	X	Green James E	56	gardener	53	"
	Y	Hudlin Shepard	56	foreman	50	
	Z	Cross Emma—†	56	housewife	60	"
568						
	A	Jasey James E	56	kitchenman	44	"
	B	Cardozo Albert	57	laborer	39	
	C	Wheary Jennie—†	57	domestic	43	"
	D	Wheary Myrtle—†	57	housekeeper	41	"
	E	Edwards Emma—†	57	domestic	39	"
	L	Hamilton Eva—†	59	"	40	
	M	Miller Albert	59	laborer	39	"
	N	Rock Hannah G—†	59	housekeeper	64	"
	T	Williams James V	61	laborer	40	103 Camden
	U	Gary Gladys—†	61	operator	23	68 Northfield
	V	Gary James	61	laborer	26	68 "
	W	Joynor Jonathan	61	cook	45	here

Page.	Letter.	Full Name.	Residence, Jan. 1, 1943.	Occupation.	Supposed Age.	Reported Residence, Jan. 1, 1942. Street and Number.
		Northfield Street—Continued				
	X	Rose Christine—†	62	housewife	21	14 E Lenox
	Y	Milligan Bertha—†	62	"	54	14 "
	Z	Milligan Bertha—†	62	"	36	14 "
569						
	A	*Hamilton Georgina—†	62	"	38	here
	C	Paschall Luella—†	63	housekeeper	55	"
	D	Diamond Harvey	63	laborer	44	Everett
	E	Robinson Robert	63	cook	57	here
	F	Robinson Sarah—†	63	housekeeper	64	"
	G	Minton Harriet L—†	63	laundress	60	"
	H	Minton Herbert G	63	laborer	59	"
	O	Johnson James	65	"	47	16 Munroe
	P	Prevos Elizabeth—†	65	domestic	62	here
	R	Braxton Ernest	65	chauffeur	49	"
	S	Battle Harry	66	laborer	40	"
	T	Gray George R	66	retired	73	
	U	Fletcher Tessie—†	66	housewife	62	"
	V	Sharp Hazel—†	66	"	36	
	W	*Lidner Louise—†	66	"	65	"
	X	Fryerson Edward	66	laborer	56	
	Y	Fryerson Mary A—†	66	domestic	42	"
	Z	Roseme John	68	factoryhand	54	"
570						
	B	Thomas Clifton	68	laborer	33	76 Westminster
	A	Thomas Florence M—†	68	housewife	38	76 "
	C	Lee Erma—†	68	"	44	36 Kendall
	D	Silva Joseph	68	laborer	50	here
	H	Peterson Charles C	70	retired	72	"
	K	Peterson Grace A—†	70	housewife	65	"
	L	Peterson Ruby I—†	70	"	43	
	M	Davis Mordecai A	70	porter	49	
	N	Peterson Grace D—†	70	operator	35	"
	O	Peterson Leroy G	70	cook	36	
	P	Reid Clara—†	70	operator	26	
	S	Wheeler Helen—†	71	housekeeper	52	"
	T	Benjamin Charles	71	retired	68	
	V	Blakey Benjamin F	72	painter	71	
	W	Collins Lela M—†	72	operator	46	"
	X	Henderson David	72	laborer	50	

Page.	Letter.	Full Name.	Residence, Jan. 1, 1943.	Occupation.	Supposed Age.	Reported Residence, Jan. 1, 1942. Street and Number.

Shawmut Avenue

Page.	Letter.	Full Name.	Residence, Jan. 1, 1943.	Occupation.	Supposed Age.	Reported Residence, Jan. 1, 1942. Street and Number.
	Z	Williams Edith B—†	516	housewife	35	here
571						
	C	Burgo John	518	seaman	50	27 E Lenox
	D	Cummings George E	518	retired	68	here
	E	Faria Evelyn—†	518	at home	39	"
	F	Haines Helen—†	518	housewife	22	542 Mass av
	G	Haines Lionel	518	laborer	30	542 "
	H	Siber Edward	518	pipefitter	43	here
	K	Siber Julia—†	518	housewife	43	"
	L	Wentworth Linwood	518	chauffeur	26	59 Rutland
	M	Fletcher John	520	"	22	here
	N	Fletcher Katherine—†	520	at home	20	"
	O	Fletcher May—†	520	housewife	43	"
	P	Hall James	520	inspector	43	"
	R	Hall Virginia—†	520	stitcher	38	
	S	Robinson Agnes—†	520	housewife	70	"
	T	Robinson Herbert P	520	seaman	20	
572						
	D	Hunter Stewart	539	engineer	58	660 Tremont
	E	Joslin Lawrence	539	chef	39	11 Pembroke
	F	*Joslin Marie—†	539	housewife	28	11 "
	K	Myers James A	542	cook	52	Revere
	L	Williams Joshua	542	entertainer	54	Brockton
	M	Jones Adolph	542	U S C G	22	New Jersey
	N	Jones Mary—†	542	housewife	22	"
	O	Thompson Beatrice—†	542	"	31	58 Compton
	R	Banks Ada—†	544	beautician	40	here
	S	Parris Florence—†	544	housewife	63	"
	T	Parris James	544	painter	57	"
	U	Andrews John	544	laborer	24	Florida
	V	Henney Margaret—†	544	domestic	29	here
	W	Taylor Edward	546	retired	87	"
	X	Adams Myrtle—†	548	housewife	30	"
	Y	Anderson Pauline—†	548	cook	41	N Carolina
	Z	Carew Edna—†	548	"	39	here
573						
	A	Carew Harry	548	"	43	"
	B	Clark Doris—†	548	housewife	22	5 Wellington
	C	Clark George	548	laborer	23	5 "
	D	Wynn Carrie—†	548	housewife	22	625 Shawmut av
	E	Wynn Harold	548	welder	23	625 "

Page.	Letter.	Full Name.	Residence, Jan. 1, 1943.	Occupation.	Supposed Age.	Reported Residence, Jan. 1, 1942. Street and Number.
		Shawmut Avenue—Continued				
	K	Butler Caroline—†	552	domestic	21	159 Cabot
	L	Butler Mary—†	552	"	24	159 "
	M	Butler Minnie—†	552	"	50	159 "
	N	Smith Sally—†	552	housewife	35	here
	O	Smith Stephen	552	laborer	36	"
	R	DeBoise Harry	554	U S A	27	"
	S	DeBoise Margaret—†	554	housewife	31	"
	T	Robinson Beatrice—†	554	"	27	
	U	Robinson Godfrey	554	chauffeur	31	"
	V	Dixon Louis	554	U S A	32	
	W	Dixon Thomasina—†	554	housewife	27	"
	X	Ford Jane—†	554	"	26	
	Y	Barnard John	555	retired	65	
	Z	Cassell Samuel K	555	laborer	43	
574						
	A	Collins Beatrice—†	555	housewife	62	"
	B	Collins Hubert C	555	laborer	61	
	C	Jones Theodore	555	"	56	"
	D	Young Joseph	555	porter	30	Florida
	F	Goring Lillian—†	557	housewife	64	here
	G	Oxley Benjamin	557	retired	75	"
	H	Simpson Edward	557	cook	59	202 Northampton
	K	Simpson Minnie—†	557	housewife	52	202 "
	M	McAlister David	559	laborer	27	here
	N	McAlister Plassie—†	559	housewife	28	"
	O	Brown Ellen—†	559	domestic	39	"
	P	McCree Michael	559	chauffeur	56	"
	S	*Yee Hong	561	laundryman	42	"
	T	Corr John M, jr	561A	mechanic	42	"
	U	Francis Clifford	561A	barber	38	New Jersey
	V	Francis Mabel—†	561A	housewife	30	"
	W	Smith Pearl—†	561A	teacher	30	here
	X	Williams Evelyn—†	561A	domestic	55	"
	Z	Whittier Dorothy E—†	572	housewife	23	189 Quincy
575						
	A	Whittier Leroy	572	laborer	30	189 "
	B	Walker John	572	clerk	23	here
	C	Walker Maurice	572	laborer	24	"
	D	Walker Ralph	572	"	21	"
	E	Walker Sallie—†	572	housekeeper	47	"
	F	Andrews Manuel	572	laborer	54	Plymouth

Page.	Letter.	Full Name.	Residence, Jan. 1, 1943.	Occupation.	Supposed Age.	Reported Residence, Jan. 1, 1942. Street and Number.

Shawmut Avenue—Continued

	P	Johnson Florence—†	589	housewife	60	here
	R	Johnson James	589	laborer	65	"
	S	Wilks Laura G—†	589	housekeeper	74	"
	T	*Blaun Clara—†	589	at home	69	"
	U	Crichlow Ellsworth	589	laborer	20	"
	V	Crichlow Harold F	589	U S A	24	
	W	*Crichlow Mary M—†	589	housewife	47	"
	X	Gordon Frances—†	589	housekeeper	66	"
	Y	Jeltz John E	589	clergyman	68	"
	Z	Johnson Helen R—†	589	cook	46	
576						
	A	Russell Johnie B—†	589	housekeeper	30	"

Tremont Street

	L	Pankey Annie—†	786	housekeeper	65	here
	M	Ringold Esther—†	786	domestic	62	"
	N	Thomas Elizabeth—†	786	"	67	"
	S	Fogg Thomas	792	laborer	63	
	T	Miller Jesse	792	"	44	
	U	Pinder Algha—†	792	housekeeper	54	"
	V	Rollins Thomas	792	laborer	37	"
	W	Smith Louis	792	"	55	"
	X	Woodrow Benjamin	792	mechanic	50	"
	Z	Kitchener Vita—†	794	domestic	42	"
577						
	A	Haughton Alfred	794	printer	53	
	B	Haughton Mildred—†	794	housewife	36	"
	C	Johnson Martin	796	printer	45	
	D	Lane Daisy—†	796	domestic	43	"
	E	Kelui John	796	retired	69	"
	F	Bobb James	796	laborer	50	Cambridge
	G	Brackett Irene L—†	798	at home	68	here
	H	Christian Jack	798	butler	36	"
	K	Christian Maggie—†	798	housewife	33	"
	L	Williams Emma—†	798	"	32	
	M	Williams Harry	798	laborer	33	
	O	Gainville Walter	800	"	38	
	R	Spear Elsie—†	800	at home	60	"
	S	Anderson Emma—†	800	housekeeper	55	108 W Springfield

Tremont Street—Continued

Page.	Letter.	Full Name.	Residence, Jan. 1, 1943.	Occupation.	Supposed Age.	Reported Residence, Jan. 1, 1942. Street and Number.
	T	Byrd Charles	800	porter	64	112 W Springfield
	U	Rocheford Sarah—†	802	housekeeper	65	here
	V	Lewis Jennie—†	802	operator	42	"
	W	Ramsey Ethel—†	802	domestic	37	"
	X	Rosser Richard	802	laborer	43	"
	Y	Harris Margaret—†	804	housekeeper	40	42 Cabot
	Z	Howard Sarah—†	804	housewife	61	here
578						
	A	Howard William	804	retired	71	
	B	Smith Margaret—†	804	domestic	61	"
	C	Mascarinhas Evelyn—†	806	beautician	45	"
	D	Mascarinhas Januario	806	barber	49	
	E	Freeman Beulah—†	806	domestic	45	"
	F	Clough Charles	808	laborer	50	
	G	Arrington Geneva—†	808	beautician	47	"
	H	Gibson Althea—†	808	domestic	29	"
	K	Bryan Drusilla—†	808	"	50	
	L	Francis Daisy—†	808	"	55	
	M	Pope Gertrude—†	808	"	39	
	N	Brown Bessie—†	810	housewife	56	"
	O	Brown Bessie G—†	810	dressmaker	24	"
	P	Brown Clarissa—†	810	waitress	30	
	R	Brown Glenn	810	pedler	61	"
	S	Coleman Ethel B—†	812	nurse	57	896 Tremont
	T	Thompson Callie D—†	812	housewife	73	896 "
	U	Glenn Magnolia—†	812	domestic	49	here
	V	Patten Mamie—†	812	at home	57	"
	W	Tucker Martha—†	812	domestic	28	"
	X	Austin Harriet—†	812	at home	72	"
	Y	Woodson Pauline—†	812	domestic	22	"
579						
	N	Myers Arthur	896	mechanic	29	21 Rutland sq
	O	Myers Flossie—†	896	housewife	26	21 "
	P	Dickerson Daniel	896	laborer	54	here
	R	Dickerson Ethel—†	896	domestic	38	"
	S	Carrillo Mary—†	896	housewife	80	"
	T	Clayborne Rose—†	896	domestic	50	"
	U	Dutton Benjamin	896	laborer	50	
	V	Dutton Emma—†	896	housewife	60	"
	X	Crawford Ernest R	896	laborer	46	
	Y	Crawford Mary—†	896	housewife	66	"

Page.	Letter.	Full Name.	Residence, Jan. 1, 1943.	Occupation.	Supposed Age.	Reported Residence, Jan. 1, 1942. Street and Number.
580		**Washington Street**				
	P	Boatman Samuel	1761	janitor	66	30 Summit av
	S	Prior Sumner G	1761	agent	48	here
	T	Rice Caroline L—†	1761	housewife	63	"
	U	Rice Nathan F	1761	clerk	22	Chelsea
	V	Andrew Nellie G—†	1761	housewife	71	here
	W	Kenney Lizzie F—†	1761	housekeeper	83	"
	X	Broadbent Anne E—†	1761	housewife	64	"
	Y	Broadbent Herbert S	1761	retired	70	"
	Z	Farrell Ethel A—†	1761	housewife	34	Cambridge
581						
	A	Pearson John	1761	cementworker	61	here
	B	Maguire Louise—†	1761	housekeeper	64	"
	C	Mullen Bernard F	1761	retired	59	"
	D	Tibbetts John F, jr	1761	salesman	49	Everett
	E	Beckman Albert B	1761	shipfitter	25	here
	F	Beckman Jennie—†	1761	housewife	50	"
	G	Beckman Paul S	1761	U S A	21	"
	H	Linder Bergitta V—†	1761	housewife	30	"
	K	*Linder Harry S	1761	waiter	34	New York
	L	Carlson Arvid	1761	fireman	42	here
	M	Diamond James	1761	barber	47	Cambridge
	N	Eastland Hattie—†	1761	housekeeper	41	here
	O	Maroney Evelyn—†	1761	operator	22	"
	S	Huntoon Catherine—†	1767	housewife	27	"
	T	Huntoon Ricardo	1767	physician	34	"
	U	Anderson Joseph	1767	retired	63	
	V	Anderson Maude E—†	1767	housewife	64	"
	W	Bouboulias Georgia—†	1767	domestic	46	"
	Y	Carey Claire—†	1767	housewife	32	"
	Z	Carey Edward F	1767	masseur	33	"
582						
	A	Carey Mary—†	1767	factoryhand	20	Cambridge
	F	Donovan Anna—†	1779	housewife	37	here
	G	Donovan Patrick	1779	pressman	43	"
	H	*Simonetti Emilio	1779	retired	69	"
	K	*Simonetti Fidelma—†	1779	housewife	64	"
	L	Simonetti Italia—†	1779	housekeeper	28	"
	N	Simonetti Eva—†	1779	dressmaker	38	"
	O	*Simonetti Peter	1779	clerk	73	

Page.	Letter.	Full Name.	Residence, Jan. 1, 1943.	Occupation.	Supposed Age.	Reported Residence, Jan. 1, 1942. Street and Number.
583		**Washington Street**—Continued				
	B	Dillon Elmer M	1821	laborer	59	here
	C	Dillon Mary N—†	1821	housekeeper	64	"
	D	Barnes Kenneth	1821	painter	24	"
	E	Choquett Anna—†	1821	housewife	53	"
	F	Choquett Clifford	1821	storekeeper	63	"
	G	Clukey Marion—†	1821	housekeeper	44	"
	S	Celcil Theresa—†	1829	"	55	"
	T	Pinsent Charles W	1829	retired	75	
	U	Pinsent Mary B—†	1829	housekeeper	71	"
	V	Waite Mary P—†	1829	nurse	57	"
	W	Tait Pearl—†	1829	at home	68	
584						
	F	Henry Colon	1845	laborer	59	"
	G	Johnson Cazelma—†	1845	cook	30	Georgia
	H	Johnson Narcissus—†	1845	housekeeper	52	"
		Wentworth Place				
	V	Jackson Hattie—†	2	housewife	62	here
	W	Jackson William	2	laborer	36	"
	Y	Morrison Ethel—†	2	housekeeper	61	"
585						
	A	Stewart Vera—†	3	housewife	36	"
	B	Stewart William R	3	laborer	44	
	C	Richardson Alfred J	3	"	21	
	D	Richardson Arthur	3	U S A	22	
	E	Richardson Charles C	3	carpenter	53	"
	F	Richardson Charles L	3	U S A	25	
	G	Richardson Winifred—†	3	housewife	42	"
		West Springfield Street				
	K	Schmelling Sophina—†	84	at home	78	here
	L	Schmelling William	84	laborer	55	"
	M	*King Annie—†	84	cook	51	"
	P	Griffiths Charles F	84	painter	57	
	R	Griffiths Mary—†	84	at home	62	
	U	McGinty Mary—†	84	operator	53	"
	X	Austin Frederick	86	porter	60	22 Worcester sq

Page.	Letter.	Full Name.	Residence, Jan. 1, 1943.	Occupation.	Supposed Age.	Reported Residence, Jan. 1, 1942. Street and Number.

West Springfield Street—Continued

	Y	Bilodeau Henry	86	porter	63	673 Mass av
	Z	Cavey Ralph	86	mechanic	42	143 O
586						
	A	Daniels Phillip	86	mechanic	60	Woburn
	B	Galvin Johanna—†	86	at home	73	here
	C	Haynard Joseph	86	painter	63	"
	D	Hull William	86	retired	66	"
	E	Purdy Davis	86	fisherman	57	"
	F	Purdy Ellen—†	86	at home	60	"
	G	Sheehan John J	86	laborer	48	88 W Springfield
	H	Brooks Clara—†	88	at home	50	here
	L	Clark Kathleen—†	88	waitress	42	377 Dorchester
	K	Clark William	88	laborer	46	377 "
	M	Duffy William	88	mechanic	66	705 Mass av
	N	Griffin David R	88	laborer	47	868 Col av
	O	Havey Elizabeth—†	88	operator	29	31 Armstrong
	P	McNamara Joseph	88	porter	53	24 Eliot
	R	Sawyer Elizabeth—†	88	at home	38	46 Symphony rd
	S	Sawyer Elmer	88	chauffeur	47	46 "
	T	Thatcher James	88	porter	52	482 Shawmut av
	U	*Burrows Benson	90	mechanic	36	612 Mass av
	V	Burrows Nina—†	90	operator	34	612 "
	W	*Burroughs Nora—†	90	"	38	here
	X	Crane William	90	retired	75	"
	Y	Haddix Florence—†	90	clerk	42	"
	Z	Haddix Samuel	90	mechanic	41	"
587						
	A	Lovins Elmer F	90	operator	50	"
	B	Bubaro Louis	92	cook	43	678 Mass av
	C	Gibbons Elizabeth—†	92	operator	40	here
	D	Hamilton Anna—†	92	at home	60	"
	E	*Hamilton Harry	92	molder	56	"
	F	*Handrahan Byron	92	retired	67	
	G	*Jinolowski Peter	92	mechanic	60	"
	H	Litchfield Milton	92	student	26	28 Worcester
	K	*Lundeen John	92	painter	58	here
	L	Smith Viola—†	92	waitress	51	"
	M	Walsh Alice—†	92	"	41	"
	N	Weightman Walter	92	porter	56	"
	O	Compton Peter	94	mechanic	63	Milton
	P	MacDougall Daniel	94	roofer	47	here

Page.	Letter.	Full Name.	Residence, Jan. 1, 1943.	Occupation.	Supposed Age.	Reported Residence, Jan. 1, 1942. Street and Number.

West Springfield Street—Continued

Page.	Letter.	Full Name.	Residence, Jan. 1, 1943.	Occupation.	Supposed Age.	Reported Residence, Jan. 1, 1942. Street and Number.
	R	McCaul John E	94	dispatcher	42	here
	S	McDonough Emma—†	94	operator	55	"
	T	Moritz Charles G	94	mechanic	59	"
	U	Paul Laura—†	94	at home	49	
	V	*Phessaroulis Peter	94	baker	52	
	X	White Alice—†	94	domestic	45	"
	W	Williams Fred E	94	mechanic	63	Somerville
	Y	Abrams Jacob	96	laborer	45	330 Shawmut av
	Z	Barrett Thomas	96	clerk	55	here
588						
	A	Doherty Eugene	96	mechanic	43	"
	B	Doherty Genevieve—†	96	at home	39	"
	C	Grogan Austin F	96	painter	54	15 Cedar
	D	Grogan Mary L—†	96	at home	42	15 "
	F	*Salazar Louis	96	cook	70	here
	G	Clifford Jeremiah	98	porter	37	"
	H	Clifford Mary—†	98	at home	38	"
	K	Coveney Clarence	98	cook	25	
	L	Coveney Marie—†	98	housewife	22	"
	M	Daniels Samuel	98	printer	58	"
	N	Ferguson Archibald	98	teacher	35	"
	O	Ford James	98	retired	68	4 Bishop
	P	Glennon John	98	nurse	50	28 Allen
	R	McGinnis Allen	98	laborer	60	here
	S	Rock Joseph	98	cook	45	"
	T	Sweeney Harriet—†	98	laundress	65	"
	U	LaTourneau Lafayette	100	manager	52	
	V	Burton Edgar	100	retired	76	"
	W	Mento James	100	carpenter	64	2 Fellows ct
	X	Mento William	100	mechanic	59	2 "
	Y	Nelson Maud—†	100	at home	78	here
	Z	*Peale Russell	100	cook	63	"

589 Willard Place

Page.	Letter.	Full Name.	Residence, Jan. 1, 1943.	Occupation.	Supposed Age.	Reported Residence, Jan. 1, 1942. Street and Number.
589	B	Robinson Bertha—†	2	housekeeper	34	here
	C	Hall Catherine—†	4	"	61	"
	D	Hall Grandison	4	retired	73	"
	E	Mitchell Walter	4	U S A	22	
	F	Howell Henry	8	laborer	61	
	G	Howell Henry, jr	8	"	28	"

Page.	Letter.	Full Name.	Residence, Jan. 1, 1943.	Occupation.	Supposed Age.	Reported Residence, Jan. 1, 1942. Street and Number.
		Willard Place—Continued				
	H	Howell Martha—†	8	housekeeper	52	here
	K	Morgan Dorothy—†	8	"	21	"
	L	O'Bryant Richard L	10	U S A	24	23 Northfield
	M	O'Bryant Samuel T	10	"	22	23 "
	N	O'Bryant Ula—†	10	housekeeper	43	23 "
	O	O'Bryant William	10	laborer	21	23 "
	P	Frederick Florence—†	10	housekeeper	32	here
	R	Penn Caroline—†	10	"	62	53 Camden
	S	Penn William H	10	retired	82	53 "
	T	Hoffman David	10	pipefitter	40	here
	U	Hoffman Lawrence	10	U S A	23	"
	V	Hoffman Margaret—†	10	housekeeper	42	"
	W	Nichols Luzone—†	10	"	50	"
	X	Grant David	10	cook	53	
	Y	Grant Gladys—†	10	housekeeper	42	"
	Z	Robinson Catherine—†	10	"	43	612 Shawmut av
590						
	A	Robinson David	10	clerk	23	612 "
	B	Montario Frances—†	10	housekeeper	37	Duxbury
	C	McIntyre Clara—†	10	"	47	here
	D	Lee Charles	10	painter	48	"
	E	Lee Myrtle—†	10	waitress	47	"
	G	Foster Annie B—†	25	housekeeper	51	"
	H	Foster Matthew	25	laborer	51	"
	K	Hodge Rachel—†	25	housekeeper	57	Georgia
	L	Hodge William H	25	laborer	57	"
	M	Turner Ola M—†	25	waitress	26	"
	N	Porter Edward	25	laborer	41	190 Northam o
	O	Porter Ida—†	25	housewife	37	190 "
	P	McPhail James	27	laborer	38	here
	R	Ward Kenneth	27	U S A	35	"
	S	Ward Margaret—†	27	housewife	37	"
	T	Freeman Melvin	27	laborer	55	981 Tremont
	U	McQueen Cyrus	27	"	60	here
	V	Moore Leonard	27	porter	56	"
		Wirth Place				
	Z	Garnett Alice—†	1	housewife	48	here
591						
	A	Garnett Samuel	1	laborer	50	New Jersey
	C	Augustus William	1	retired	75	22 Camden

Ward 9—Precinct 6

CITY OF BOSTON

LIST OF RESIDENTS
20 YEARS OF AGE AND OVER

(NON-CITIZENS INDICATED BY ASTERISK)
(FEMALES INDICATED BY DAGGER)

AS OF

JANUARY 1, 1943

JOSEPH F. TIMILTY, *Chairman*
FREDERIC E. DOWLING, *Secretary*
WILLIAM A. MOTLEY, JR.
FRANCIS B. McKINNEY
EVERETT R. PROUT
Listing Board.

CITY OF BOSTON PRINTING DEPARTMENT

Page.	Letter.	Full Name.	Residence, Jan. 1, 1943.	Occupation.	Supposed Age.	Reported Residence, Jan. 1, 1942. Street and Number.
600						
		Ditmus Court				
	A	Brooks Willie—†	1	housewife	32	here
	B	Long Hazel—†	1	secretary	32	"
	C	Long Lilly—†	1	housewife	57	"
	D	White Doris A—†	1	"	31	
	E	White Nathaniel E	1	laborer	31	
	F	Wooten Mary A—†	1	housewife	55	"
	G	Camrell Gertrude B—†	1	"	71	
	H	Camrell Rose L—†	1	laundress	56	"
	K	Camrell Walter J	1	retired	74	"
	L	Carney Blanche—†	1	housewife	33	418 Mass av
	M	Carney Calvin W	1	laborer	32	418 "
	N	Alford Francis M	1	porter	32	here
	O	Alford Luella—†	1	nurse	36	"
	P	Holmes Hugh	1	waiter	27	"
	R	Holmes Ruth—†	1	housewife	23	"
	S	Bates Rose—†	1	waitress	49	87 Hammond ter
	T	Lomax Celeste—†	1	housewife	21	18 Trotter ct
	U	Lomax Walter W	1	carpenter	28	18 "
	V	Williams Annetta—†	1	operator	21	here
	W	Williams Westmeath—†	1	housewife	51	"
	X	Montero Dorothy—†	1	"	33	"
	Y	Ponds Alice—†	1	"	25	
	Z	Williams Josephine—†	2	"	76	
601						
	A	Williams Thomas	2	retired	79	
	B	Monroe Beatrice—†	2	housewife	30	"
	C	Monroe Edward	2	porter	34	
	D	Quarles Harry	2	retired	82	
	E	Quarles Josephine—†	2	housewife	69	"
	F	Wood Irving	2	letter carrier	25	"
	G	Wood Ruth—†	2	housewife	24	"
	H	Thomas Edward	2	laborer	23	
	K	Thomas Ethel—†	2	housewife	21	"
	L	Nichols Harold	2	laborer	31	
	M	Nichols Lillian—†	2	housewife	24	"
	N	Walker William	2	janitor	68	"
	O	McLaughlin Georgie—†	2	housewife	24	"
	P	McLaughlin Richard	2	laborer	23	
	R	Kemp Dorothy—†	2	housewife	28	"
	S	Kemp Robert E	2	messenger	30	"

Page.	Letter.	Full Name.	Residence, Jan. 1, 1943.	Occupation.	Supposed Age.	Reported Residence, Jan. 1, 1942. Street and Number.

Ditmus Court—Continued

	T	Bracy Charles	2	operator	20	here
	U	Bracy Hilda—†	2	housewife	21	"
	V	Buford Helen—†	2	domestic	32	"
	W	Buford Schuyler	2	laborer	36	
	X	Davis Beatrice—†	2	housewife	39	"
	Y	Jeffress Hannah—†	2	"	73	
	Z	Jeffress Robert	2	operator	41	"
602						
	A	Jeffress Willa—†	2	housewife	37	"
	C	Ford Cornelia—†	9	"	32	
	D	Ford Howard	9	porter	39	
	E	Hill Daisy—†	9	domestic	42	"
	F	Hill Elizabeth—†	9	housewife	93	"
	G	Phoenix Alice—†	9	"	41	2 Lattimore ct
	H	Phoenix Robert	9	laborer	43	2 "
	K	Green Dorothy—†	9	domestic	43	here
	L	Williams Robert	9	pipefitter	27	"
	M	Williams Theola—†	9	housewife	27	"
	N	Collymore Beatrice—†	9	"	63	
	O	Collymore Edwin	9	retired	68	
	P	Simms Helen—†	9	housewife	25	"
	R	Simms William	9	laborer	31	
	S	Talbot Hilda M—†	9	housewife	48	"
	T	Moore Velver—†	9	domestic	34	"
	U	Gomes Grace—†	9	housewife	54	"
	V	Gomes Lillian—†	9	clerk	20	
	W	Wood Helen—†	9	housewife	20	"
	X	Wood John	9	welder	21	
	Y	White Bertha—†	10	housewife	44	"
	Z	Bolling Nellie—†	10	"	53	
603						
	A	Wilson Beatrice—†	10	"	26	
	B	Wilson George	10	chauffeur	27	"
	C	Jones Ruth—†	10	housewife	33	"
	D	Jones Virgil	10	laborer	28	
	E	Tillman Mary—†	10	housewife	69	"
	F	Jackson Emmanuel	10	retired	71	
	G	Jackson Lena—†	10	housewife	55	"
	H	Tulloch Mazie—†	10	"	29	
	K	Tulloch Sidney	10	machinist	36	"
	L	Bracy Paul N	10	welder	24	

Page.	Letter.	Full Name.	Residence, Jan. 1, 1943.	Occupation.	Supposed Age.	Reported Residence, Jan. 1, 1942. Street and Number.

Ditmus Court—Continued

	M	Bracy Ruth—†	10	housewife	22	here
	N	Sutton Hallie—†	10	"	32	"
	O	Sutton Richard	10	welder	46	"
	P	Bell Daniel	10	laborer	25	
	R	Bell Emma—†	10	housewife	22	"
	S	Foster Grace—†	10	"	37	
	T	Gohring Phillip	10	laborer	27	
	U	Dixon Lawrence	10	janitor	31	
	V	Dixon Veronica—†	10	housewife	28	"
	W	Miles Gladys—†	10	"	32	
	X	Ridley Daniel I	10	clerk	39	
	Y	Ridley Mary—†	10	housewife	21	"
	Z	Williams Annie—†	18	"	21	
604						
	A	Williams Isaac	18	welder	26	
	B	Graham Rossie	18	molder	37	
	C	Graham Theresa—†	18	housewife	31	"
	D	Lumpkins Celeste—†	18	"	20	
	E	Lumpkins George	18	welder	23	
	F	Barros Mildred—†	18	housewife	24	"
	G	Bolt Clara—†	18	"	31	
	H	Bolt Walter	18	clerk	35	
	K	Diggs Edwin U	18	musician	44	"
	L	Diggs Grace M—†	18	housewife	42	"

Hammond Street

	P	Hoar Annie—†	15	at home	56	857 Col av
	R	Hoar Queenie—†	15	domestic	50	857 "
	T	Norton Matilda—†	15	housewife	36	here
	U	Norton William N	15	porter	44	"
	V	Wiggins Albert C	15	"	24	"
	W	Wiggins Beatrice S—†	15	at home	24	
	X	Wiggins Lula C—†	15	housewife	48	"
	Y	Benjamin Ruth—†	17	at home	66	19 Hammond
	Z	Bracy Dock C	17	retired	83	here
605						
	A	Poole Jesse S	17	packer	58	
	B	Poole Susie E—†	17	housewife	56	"
	C	Welch Emma—†	17	"	46	
	D	Welch Gladys R—†	17	"	20	

Page.	Letter.	Full Name.	Residence, Jan. 1, 1943.	Occupation.	Supposed Age.	Reported Residence, Jan. 1, 1942. Street and Number.

Hammond Street—Continued

	E	Welch William W	17	laborer	62	here
	F	Collins Blanche—†	17	domestic	44	Everett
	G	Austin Mary—†	19	housewife	59	here
	K	Austin Vance	19	fireman	54	"
	H	Wiggins Inez—†	19	domestic	35	"
	L	Harris Clara—†	19	at home	70	"
	M	Harris Enoch	19	retired	72	
	N	Benders Eleanor—†	19	housewife	25	"
	O	Benders Malcolm	19	technician	34	"
	P	*Phillips Beatrice—†	19	housewife	41	"
	R	Phillips Reuben	19	porter	43	"
	T	Rollins Dora—†	21	housewife	38	216 W Canton
	U	Rollins Harold	21	oiler	38	216 "
	V	Lambert Lucy R—†	21	at home	74	Virginia
	W	Lambert William W	21	laborer	40	Randolph
	X	Hill Frank	23	mason	38	here
	Y	Hill Mattie—†	23	housewife	36	"
	Z	Smith Benjamin	23	laborer	56	"
606						
	A	Smith Ida—†	23	housewife	60	"
	B	Anderson Ishmael E	25	chef	51	
	C	Anderson Sarah E—†	25	housewife	44	"
	D	Cox William G	25	retired	80	
	E	Jones Caroline D—†	25	at home	68	"
	F	Walker Margaret A—†	25	housewife	68	100 Harrishof
	G	Walker William L	25	retired	73	100 "
	H	Neale Pauline—†	27	domestic	35	here
	K	Foy Mamie—†	27	at home	65	"
	L	Taylor Evelyn H—†	27	domestic	39	"
	M	Brooks Lillian—†	27	"	51	
	N	Fordham Percy	27	policeman	54	"
	O	Jackson Edward	29	porter	42	
	P	Jackson Margaret—†	29	housewife	33	"
	R	White Martha—†	29	cook	46	
	U	Fraser Ethel—†	29	housewife	51	"
	T	Fraser Joslin	29	painter	54	"
	V	Smith Eleanor—†	31	housewife	20	67 Lenox
	W	Burris Frank	31	retired	68	here
	X	Barbara Clara—†	31	domestic	50	"
	Y	Batson John	31	laborer	46	"
	Z	Batson Julia—†	31	housewife	46	"

Page.	Letter.	Full Name.	Residence, Jan. 1, 1943.	Occupation.	Supposed Age.	Reported Residence, Jan. 1, 1942. Street and Number.
607						

Hammond Street—Continued

	C	Pitts Catherine—†	33	housewife	37	here
	D	Pitts Raymond	33	laborer	37	"
	E	Fisher Margaret—†	33	housewife	46	"
	G	Johnson Irene—†	35	"	61	
	H	Johnson Stephen	35	retired	69	
	K	Collins Bertha—†	35	maid	43	
	L	Clark Sarah—†	35	housewife	53	"
	M	Hackett Ernest	35	retired	77	
	N	Taylor Evelyn—†	35	domestic	38	"
	P	Harrod William	37	U S A	31	
	R	Nelson Alfred	37	shipper	35	"
	S	Nelson Bradford L	37	U S A	33	
	T	Ward Lewis	37	waiter	55	
	U	Watts Rosa—†	37	housewife	52	"
	V	Frank Annie—†	37	"	55	
	W	Frank Henry	37	retired	52	
	X	Morris Nelson	37	porter	45	
	Y	Nichols George	37	machinist	61	"
	Z	Williams Isabelle—†	37	housewife	39	"
608						
	A	Williams Lucy L—†	37	mechanic	37	"
	B	Ruddman Abraham	39	storekeeper	57	"
	D	Munroe Bessie—†	39	at home	61	"
	E	Roberts Thelma—†	39	operator	35	"
	F	Lee Ernest	39	laborer	27	
	G	Lee Mabel—†	39	housewife	26	"
	K	*Pina Gertrude—†	41	"	46	
	L	*Pina Joseph	41	laborer	59	
	M	Williams Alfred N	41	fireman	41	
	N	Williams Leon N	41	machinist	23	"
	O	Williams Lewis	41	retired	78	"
	P	Williams Mary C—†	41	at home	75	
	R	Brown Jacob	41	laborer	36	
	S	Brown Susie—†	41	housewife	36	"
	U	Hill Mary L—†	43	"	43	
	V	Hill William H	43	laborer	49	
	W	Tuft Louise—†	43	at home	50	
	X	Pearson Annie—†	43	housewife	37	"
	Y	Pearson William	43	porter	41	
	Z	Dixon Joseph	43	laborer	62	

Page.	Letter.	FULL NAME.	Residence, Jan. 1, 1943.	Occupation.	Supposed Age.	Reported Residence, Jan. 1, 1942. Street and Number.
609		**Hammond Street**—Continued				
	A	Fredericks Charles	43	laborer	46	here
	B	Fredericks Nellie—†	43	housewife	43	"
	C	Miller Joseph	45	realtor	56	616 Col av
	D	*Sievewright Edith A—†	45	housewife	44	here
	E	*Sievewright Henry	45	seaman	47	"
	F	*Wright Clarissa—†	45	at home	66	"
	G	*Wright Keziah—†	45	domestic	49	"
	H	Green Israel	45	mechanic	30	"
	K	Green Rosalie—†	45	domestic	24	"
	L	Hunter Evelyn—†	45	operator	22	S Carolina
	M	McGill Sidney	45	laborer	20	here
	N	Brightman Rosa—†	45	domestic	42	"
	O	Richardson Rosalie—†	45	at home	69	"
	P	Amis Helen—†	47	clerk	21	
	R	Amis Lewis	47	U S A	24	"
	S	Amis Rosetta—†	47	operator	26	Brookline
	T	Dukes Annie—†	47	housewife	27	here
	U	Dukes Jack	47	porter	27	"
	V	Jarvis Dorothy—†	47	at home	24	17 Trotter ct
	W	Watson Zella—†	47	housewife	39	here
	X	Bullock Luke	47	laborer	60	"
	Y	Bullock Lula—†	47	housewife	55	"
	Z	Grimes F Millett	47	machinist	24	"
610						
	A	Palmer Sarah—†	47	housewife	43	"
	B	Smith Cleo—†	47	domestic	43	"
	C	Adams Henry	47	waiter	48	
	D	Taylor Joseph	47	mechanic	48	"
	E	Taylor Lorena—†	47	housewife	46	"
	F	Ince Delcine—†	47	"	56	
	G	Ince James R	47	cook	65	"
	H	Johnson Charles	47	shipper	49	
	M	Jefferson Marjorie L—†	47	stitcher	56	
	K	*Harris Hattie—†	49	at home	65	"
	L	Ranforth William	49	operator	40	Georgia
	N	*Shanks Hattie—†	49	"	35	"
	O	*Stevens Ella—†	49	domestic	33	here
	P	Hyatt George W	49	operator	68	"
	R	Hyatt Helen W—†	49	housewife	65	"
	S	Hyatt John A	49	U S A	23	

Page.	Letter.	Full Name.	Residence, Jan. 1, 1943.	Occupation.	Supposed Age.	Reported Residence, Jan. 1, 1942. Street and Number.

Hammond Street—Continued

	T	Hyatt William E	49	laborer	33	here
	U	Alleyne Althea—†	49	housewife	27	15 Sarsfield
	V	Alleyne Wesley	49	chipper	28	15 "
	W	Elliott Ella—†	49	housewife	55	here
	X	Elliott Marietta—†	49	clerk	28	"
	Y	Johnson Ruth—†	49	folder	29	"
611						
	A	Taylor Beulah—†	49	housewife	34	"
	B	Taylor James W	49	laborer	49	
	C	Adams Charles C	49	janitor	50	
	D	*Adams Louise—†	49	housewife	50	"
	E	Eastmond Elzear	49	laborer	46	
	F	Eastmond Jessie—†	49	housewife	52	"
	G	Alleyne Glaston	51	laborer	43	
	H	Alleyne Lolita—†	51	housewife	35	"
	K	Dodson James	51	retired	69	
	M	Reid Irene W—†	51	housewife	37	"
	L	Reid Julian H	51	houseman	40	"
	N	*Cargill Edith—†	51	domestic	52	"
	O	*Marstons Rowena—†	51	"	41	"
	P	*McCooty Margaret—†	51	housewife	43	77 Hammond ter
	R	Pickett James C	53	laborer	22	here
	S	Wilson Olive—†	53	domestic	56	"
	T	O'Neil Ernest	53	laborer	45	"
	U	O'Neil Victoria—†	53	housewife	32	"
	V	Williams Eva—†	53	"	46	
	W	Williams George	53	laborer	47	
	X	Tyler Minnie K—†	57	housewife	51	"
	Y	Tyler William K	57	laborer	51	
	Z	*Thompson Alfred	57	cook	50	
612						
	A	*Thompson Keturah—†	57	housewife	48	"
	B	Johnson Ada—†	57	"	28	"
	C	Fisher Elvetta—†	57	clerk	32	34 Highland
	D	Harriston Alyce—†	57	student	21	34 "
	E	Harriston Sally—†	57	housewife	54	34 "
	F	Brown Birtie—†	59	"	50	here
	G	Brown Frances—†	59	stitcher	26	"
	H	Robinson Jennie—†	59	operator	35	"
	K	Brown Donald	59	U S A	23	33 Westminster
	L	Kennedy William	59	"	21	33 "

Page.	Letter.	FULL NAME.	Residence, Jan. 1, 1943.	Occupation.	Supposed Age.	Reported Residence, Jan. 1, 1942. Street and Number.
		Hammond Street—Continued				
	M	Robinson Geraldine—†	59	housewife	35	33 Westminister
	N	Robinson Ralph	59	molder	45	33 "
	O	Brown Everett J	59	U S A	36	here
	P	Brushingham James E	59	meatcutter	53	"
	R	Brushingham Mary E—†	59	housewife	61	"
	S	Fanell Mildred—†	59	factoryhand	25	"
	T	Tillman Albertha—†	59	housewife	30	"
	U	Greene Dorothy—†	61	"	23	
	V	Irving Freeman H	61	shipworker	28	"
	W	Irving Serena M—†	61	housewife	61	"
	X	Davis Cora—†	61	cook	51	810 Tremont
	Y	Davis James C	51	seaman	22	810 "
	Z	Daniel Benjamin I	61	laborer	27	32 Munroe
613						
	A	Daniel Edna R—†	61	housewife	25	32 "
	B*	Mair Florence L—†	61	"	49	here
	C*	Mair Thomas H	61	waiter	53	"
	D	Parker Addie V—†	61	housewife	63	"
	E*	Parker Samuel K	61	laborer	60	
	F	Thorpe Simeon	63	porter	31	
	G*	Alves Fidell	63	laborer	47	
	H	Alves Mamie—†	63	housewife	51	"
	K	Alves Vincent	63	student	20	
	L	Drumgold Erma—†	63	housewife	32	"
	M	Harrison Joseph	63	retired	83	"
	N	Brown Jesse J	63	machinist	29	2 Williams St ter
	O	Brown Zoe—†	63	cleaner	26	2 "
	S	Dymond Margaret—†	95	housewife	38	here
	T	Cooper George W	95	retired	70	"
	U	Cooper Jennie—†	95	housewife	64	"
	V	Enslow Alice—†	97	"	72	
	W	Enslow Joseph	97	retired	72	
	X	Jenkins Lulu—†	97	housewife	64	"
	Y	Sealey Richard	97	cook	50	
	Z	Fernandez Inga—†	97	"	41	
614						
	A	Barnwell Lawrence M	99	retired	52	
	B	Byron Carrie—†	99	domestic	60	"
	C	Clark Williemae—†	99	"	38	
	D	Turner John	99	laborer	31	
	E	Turner Mabel—†	99	housewife	35	"

Page.	Letter.	Full Name.	Residence, Jan. 1, 1943.	Occupation.	Supposed Age.	Reported Residence, Jan. 1, 1942. Street and Number.

Hammond Street—Continued

	F	Turner Mamie—†	99	domestic	63	here
	G	Turner Marge—†	99	factoryhand	29	"
	H	Buckley James M	99	laborer	46	39 Greenwich
	K	Hogeland Lila—†	99	housewife	50	here
	L	Barnett Timothy	101	laborer	52	"
	M	Warren Rhoda C—†	101	domestic	52	"
	N	Burnett Carrie—†	101	housewife	62	"
	O	Burnett James	101	laborer	46	
	P	Burnett Mark	101	restaurateur	44	"
	R	Burnett Minnie—†	101	housewife	35	"
	S	Branch Nannie W—†	101	"	69	
	T	Ericson Alice—†	101	agent	37	
	U	Reese Rosalie—†	103	housewife	38	"
	V	Anthony Mildred—†	103	domestic	30	"
	W	Anthony Ruth—†	103	millhand	24	Milford
	X	Lang Monzella—†	103	housewife	35	here
	Y	Thomas Dessie—†	103	"	32	"
	Z	Thomas Norman	103	photographer	34	"
615						
	A	Johnson Louise—†	105	cook	29	
	B	Martin Luther N	105	car cleaner	50	"
	C	Martin Wilhelmina—†	105	housewife	48	"
	D	Payne James	105	cook	39	
	E	Sneed Estelle—†	105	housewife	37	"
	F	Campbell Donald	107	laborer	55	
	G	Nelson Erva—†	107	housekeeper	47	"
	H	Stewart Altermont	107	cook	50	"
	K	Stewart Edythe—†	107	housewife	55	"
	M	Mackeris Mary—†	111	"	32	
	N	Roberts Lee—†	111	"	43	
	O	Roberts Simeon	111	mechanic	45	"
	P	Smith Harry D	111	shipper	25	"
	R	Smith Sylvia—†	111	housewife	27	"
	S	Taws Lillian—†	111	domestic	60	"
	U	Slade Renner	113	restaurateur	61	"
	V	Brannon Fannie—†	113	housewife	42	"
	W	Brannon Garrison	113	fireman	56	
	X	James H James	113	baker	40	
	Y	James Nellie—†	113	housewife	33	"
	Z	Pridgen Nichols	113	U S A	26	

Page.	Letter.	FULL NAME.	Residence, Jan. 1, 1943.	Occupation.	Supposed Age.	Reported Residence, Jan. 1, 1942. Street and Number.
616		**Hammond Street**—Continued				
	A	Pridgen Pearl—†	113	clerk	26	here
	B	Watson Marie A—†	113	housewife	25	"
		Hammond Terrace				
	D	Willis Alice—†	77	housewife	45	here
	E	Castelle Warren C	77	U S A	21	"
	F	Proctor Ada—†	77	housewife	48	"
	G	Johnson Evelyn—†	77	"	28	50 Cabot
	H	Johnson William P	77	porter	50	50 "
	K	Brown Lester	79	garageman	47	9 Burke
	L	Thomas John	79	janitor	59	here
	M	Brewer Irene—†	79	housewife	36	"
	N	Curry Domingo	81	retired	56	"
	O	Moore Anna F—†	81	housewife	56	"
	P	Davis Julian	81	cook	48	30 Greenwich
	R	Williams Ruth—†	81	housewife	29	here
	S	Davis Jeanette L—†	81	"	21	79 Sterling
	T	Davis Walter	81	shipfitter	23	79 "
	U	Johnson Benjamin E	83	U S A	28	23 Hammond
	V	Moore Theodore	83	porter	51	here
	W	Tappen Catherine—†	83	housewife	47	"
	X	Tappen Clarence L	83	U S A	25	"
	Y	Harding Bessie—†	83	domestic	30	Malden
	Z	Johnson Florence—†	85	waitress	23	23 Hammond
617						
	A	Cureton Adelaide—†	85	housewife	24	11 Claremont pk
	B	Cureton Woodrow	85	laborer	28	11 "
	C	Cogswell Helen—†	85	domestic	28	91 Sterling
	D	Ralston David W	87	retired	76	here
	E	Ralston Vera—†	87	housewife	42	"
	F	Andrews Adeline—†	87	"	28	186 Chambers
	G	Andrews Louis	87	welder	28	586 Col av
	H	Arthur Clarabelle—†	87	housewife	36	30 Newcomb
	L	*Irving Gladys—†	89	"	50	here
	M	Knight Doris—†	89	"	21	184 Cabot
	N	Knight Robert, jr	89	butcher	26	184 "
	O	*Als St Clair E	91	laborer	43	here
	P	*Sealey St Clair	91	porter	58	"

Page.	Letter.	Full Name.	Residence, Jan. 1, 1943.	Occupation.	Supposed Age.	Reported Residence, Jan. 1, 1942. Street and Number.

Hammond Terrace—Continued

	R	Foreman Daisy—†	91	domestic	46	here
	S	Foreman Frank	91	barber	51	"
	T	Foreman Henrietta—†	91	housewife	40	"
	U	Rebiera Doris—†	91	domestic	31	Cambridge

Kendall Street

	V	Gibbons James H	3	clerk	41	here
	W	Gibbons Margaret T—†	3	housewife	36	"
	X	Campbell David A	3	U S A	29	"
	Y	Campbell Dorothea—†	3	housewife	27	"
	Z	Francis Cleora V—†	3	"	22	
618						
	A	Francis Richard	3	janitor	22	
	C	Rowe Naomi G—†	3	domestic	37	"
	B	Woodhouse Eleanora C—†	3	housewife	62	"
	D	Erickson Carl F	3	clerk	36	
	E	Erickson Helen E—†	3	housewife	33	"
	F	O'Connor Edmund F	3	laborer	61	
	G*	O'Connor Mary J—†	3	housewife	58	"
	H	Brown Anna D—†	4	laundress	63	"
	K	Terrell Henderson	4	laborer	25	
	L	Terrell Mabel—†	4	housewife	60	"
	M	Brown Rosie—†	4	"	65	
	N	Harris Walter	4	retired	65	
	R	Celia Myrtle B—†	8A	at home	65	
	S	Cobbs Suzetta—†	8A	housewife	77	"
	T	Jones Maud—†	8A	operator	59	"
	U	Saunders David	8A	retired	68	
	V	Fernandes Joseph	8A	pedler	50	
	W	Greer Hamilton	8A	"	32	"
	X	Lima Antonasio	10	laborer	60	12 Kendall
	Y	Edison Laura—†	10	housewife	70	here
	Z	McClain Joshua	10	chauffeur	48	"
619						
	A	McClain Viola—†	10	housewife	40	"
	B	Mantero Frank	10	laborer	50	
	F	Clark Squire	14	"	50	
	G	Henry Rose—†	14	housewife	35	"
	H	Nobles Mary—†	14	"	20	S Carolina
	K	Edwards Sarah H—†	16	"	64	here

Page.	Letter.	Full Name.	Residence, Jan. 1, 1943.	Occupation.	Supposed Age.	Reported Residence, Jan. 1, 1942. Street and Number.

Kendall Street—Continued

Page.	Letter.	Full Name.	Residence, Jan. 1, 1943.	Occupation.	Supposed Age.	Reported Residence, Jan. 1, 1942. Street and Number.
	L	Hunter Elijah	16	mechanic	64	here
	M	Brothers Bessie—†	18	housewife	54	"
	N	Brothers George	18	laborer	25	"
	O	Nunes Hortense—†	18	housewife	41	"
	P	Nunes John	18	laborer	39	
	R	*Costa Albert	20	"	37	
	S	Costa Lena—†	20	housewife	49	"
	T	Hardrick Edward T	20	laborer	45	
	U	Hardrick Ester L—†	20	nurse	47	
	V	Hardrick Milton	20	laborer	20	
	W	McKenzie Adolphus	20	"	60	
	X	Loman Martha—†	22	housewife	53	"
	Y	Loman Milton—†	22	laborer	62	
	Z	Haywood James	22	"	46	
620						
	A	Haywood Mary—†	22	housewife	45	"
	B	Brown Lillian—†	22	"	26	"
	C	Rowland Henry	24	mover	39	Pennsylvania
	D	Rowland Maud—†	24	housewife	39	"
	E	Thompson Amy—†	24	"	42	here
	F	Thompson James	24	laborer	49	"
	G	*Loftman Gladys—†	24	housewife	27	"
	H	*Loftman Oswald	24	porter	24	
	K	Robinson Minnie—†	26	housewife	52	"
	L	Robinson Sturgis	26	chemist	55	
	O	Evans Gilbert	26½	laborer	42	
	P	Evans Isabella—†	26½	housewife	72	"
	R	Howland Ernest	26½	laborer	72	
	S	Craig Mable—†	28	housewife	48	"
	U	Hill George W	28	porter	56	
	V	Manor Julia—†	28	housewife	72	"
	Y	Devine Elizabeth—†	36	"	75	"
	Z	Addison Sarah—†	36	"	54	84 Sterling
621						
	A	Turner Robert E	36	retired	74	19 Madison
	B	Jones Edith—†	36	housewife	32	here
	C	Clark Sterling	38	laborer	72	"
	D	Johnston Alma—†	38	tailor	28	26 Westminster
	K	Williams George	42	laborer	52	here
	L	Blue Lena—†	42	housewife	42	673 Shawmut av
	M	Blue Lucy J—†	42	domestic	21	673 "

Page.	Letter.	Full Name.	Residence, Jan. 1, 1943.	Occupation.	Supposed Age.	Reported Residence, Jan. 1, 1942. Street and Number.

Kendall Street—Continued

Page.	Letter.	Full Name.	Residence, Jan. 1, 1943.	Occupation.	Supposed Age.	Reported Residence, Jan. 1, 1942. Street and Number.
	N	Weeden Ora—†	42	housewife	42	here
	O	Birdsong Susan L—†	60	"	70	"
	P	Adams Reginald	60	laborer	55	"
	R	Fuller Frederick	60	"	66	"
	S	Hugley May W—†	66	domestic	42	47 Northfield
	T	Payne Samuel B	66	laborer	62	here
	V	Burt Annie S—†	68	at home	38	"
	X	Burt Louis	68	laborer	41	"
	Y	Spenorourd Jenell L	68	watchman	44	"
	W	Daniels Eva—†	72	"	60	
	Z	Gorene Lorenzo	72	pianist	40	
622						
	B*	Price David T	72	porter	59	
	D	Norwood Avarel—†	74	domestic	41	"
	E	Skinner Harriet—†	74	"	34	
	F	Moore Lila—†	74	at home	30	
	G*	Hamlett Lurline—†	76	"	43	"
	H*	Israel Minnie—†	76	domestic	56	41 Sterling
	K	Branch George	76	baker	68	here
	L	Badreaux Louis	78	retired	81	"
	M	Budd Gabrielle—†	78	at home	76	"
	N	Clark Nellie—†	78	"	73	
	O	Purnell Annie—†	78	"	74	
	R*	Dyer Catherine—†	80	"	71	
	S	Glover Lawrence E	80	mechanic	60	"
	T	Pigott Austin	80	laborer	66	
	U	Payne Ethelbert T	82	watchman	51	"
	V*	Payne Violet—†	82	at home	48	
	W	Payne Ruth C—†	82	teacher	22	
	X	Payne Rubinetta E—†	82	beautician	25	"
	Z	Simpkins Lillie—†	88	domestic	40	Cambridge
623						
	A	Averette Helen—†	88	at home	49	here
	B	Averette James B	88	porter	54	"
	C	Belle Mary—†	88	at home	69	"
	D*	Williams Muriel—†	90	"	30	
	E	Marsman Evelyn W—†	90	shoeworker	23	"
	F	Ray Sarah R—†	90	at home	68	
	G	Barry John	92	retired	78	"
	H	Mosson Albert	92	mover	60	
	K	Mosson Julia—†	92	messenger	20	"

Page.	Letter.	Full Name.	Residence, Jan. 1, 1943.	Occupation.	Supposed Age.	Reported Residence, Jan. 1, 1942. Street and Number.

Kendall Street—Continued

Page.	Letter.	Full Name.	Residence, Jan. 1, 1943.	Occupation.	Supposed Age.	Reported Residence, Jan. 1, 1942. Street and Number.
	L	Mosson Sybil—†	92	at home	48	here
	M	Bracy George H	94	U S N	52	"
	N	Bracy Hazel V—†	94	at home	44	"
	O	Lucas Margaret—†	94	domestic	60	"
	P	Lucas Palmer	94	cooper	60	
	R	Suggs Hilliard E	94	retired	72	"
	S	Suggs Percy E	94	porter	43	21 Claremont pk
	T	Bascom James C	96	retired	70	here
	U	Towner Mary—†	98	at home	70	"
	V	Towner Abraham L	98	retired	75	"
	W	Green Lavina—†	100	domestic	50	"
	X	Fisher Melinda—†	100	at home	65	43 Braddock pk
	Y	*Halliburton Caroline—†	100	waitress	25	here
	Z	*Halliburton William	100	laborer	45	Texas
624						
	A	Austin Mahala—†	102	at home	70	here
	B	*Holmes Dora—†	102	domestic	40	"
	C	*Palmer Louisa—†	102	at home	53	"
	D	*Palmer Sarah—†	102	beautician	32	"
	E	*Scott Leonard	102	fisherman	58	"
	F	Jordan Fred	104	laborer	64	
	G	Frazier Julia—†	104	at home	53	
	H	Brown Samuel	104	watchman	64	"
	K	Dixon Goldie L—†	106	waitress	23	Winchester
	L	Johnson Grace—†	106	at home	73	68 Kendall
	M	Alexandria Cora—†	108	cook	50	here
	N	Loatman Hazel—†	108	waitress	29	"
	O	Saunders Edward	108	painter	35	15 Sarsfield
	P	Polland Hattie—†	108	laundress	35	here
	R	Polland Lilla—†	108	at home	55	"
	S	Coss Amy—†	108	waitress	39	"
	T	Lee Robert A	108	U S A	44	
	U	Bennett Ersaline—†	108	operator	27	"
	V	*Bennett Nathaniel	108	cook	46	
	W	Barbosa Nicholas	110	U S A	30	
	X	Barbosa Philomena—†	110	stitcher	28	"
	Y	Fernandes Frances—†	110	"	33	Egypt
	Z	Armstrong Arthur E	110	longshoreman	65	here
625						
	A	Armstrong Frederica—†	110	seamstress	60	"
	B	Baptist Joshua T	110	porter	45	

Page.	Letter.	Full Name.	Residence, Jan. 1, 1943.	Occupation.	Supposed Age.	Reported Residence, Jan. 1, 1942. Street and Number.
		Kendall Street—Continued				
1	B	Baptist Mary D—†	110	housewife	42	here
	C	Durant Ollie—†	110	at home	30	"
	K	Shands Elizabeth—†	114	"	31	924 Tremont
	L	Shands William	114	welder	47	here
	M	Washington Rena—†	114	at home	53	"
	N	DeVoe Earilee—†	114	domestic	28	Brookline
	O	Lewis Dorothy—†	114	"	26	33 Walnut av
	P	White Frank	119	retired	70	here
	R	White Lula—†	119	housewife	60	"
	S	Woodbury Eva—†	119	"	22	Florida
	T	Woodbury Jesse	119	laborer	23	"
	U	Woodbury Lorraine—†	119	housewife	30	"
	V	Royal Ola—†	119	laundress	48	here
	W	Thompson Doctor R	119	operator	67	"
	X	Hoyt Arthur	119	laborer	52	"
	Y	Sampson Flora—†	119	housewife	64	"
	Z	Sampson William	119	laborer	66	
626	A	Kinder James	119	"	34	
	B	Kinder Roberta—†	119	housewife	36	"
	C	Roberts Helen—†	119	"	34	
	D	Thompson Leverett	119	laborer	34	
	E	Thompson Sally B—†	119	housewife	32	"
	F	Dyer Mary—†	119	"	38	
	G	Dyer Philip	119	laborer	40	
		Lattimore Court				
	K	Westmoreland Alice—†	1	housewife	29	here
	L	Ruffen Julia—†	1	domestic	45	"
	M	Jackson Arthur G	1	laborer	35	"
	N	Jackson Bertha C—†	1	housewife	32	"
	O	Hurley Arnold	1	laborer	29	
	P	Hurley June—†	1	housewife	26	"
	R	Bird Dora—†	1	"	40	
	S	Bird William M	1	laborer	38	
	T	Chandler Grace—†	1	clerk	21	
	U	Chandler Joseph	1	laborer	22	"
	V	Lambert Irene—†	1	housewife	46	"
	W	Paige Anna L—†	1	"	29	
	X	Paige Milton	1	laborer	32	

Page.	Letter.	Full Name.	Residence, Jan. 1, 1943.	Occupation.	Supposed Age.	Reported Residence, Jan. 1, 1942. Street and Number.

Lattimore Court—Continued

	Y	Williams Elizabeth—†	1	housewife	57	here
	Z	Jones George, jr	1	welder	25	"
627						
	A	Jones Thelma—†	1	housewife	29	"
	B	Patterson Eva—†	1	"	34	
	C	Patterson Herbert W	1	laborer	34	
	D	James Ethelda—†	1	housewife	35	"
	E	Allen Charles	1	machinist	25	"
	F	Allen Mary—†	1	housewife	23	"
	G	Gordon Frederick	1	laborer	36	
	H	Gordon Gladys—†	1	stitcher	35	
	K	West Lucy—†	2	factoryhand	28	"
	L	West Rena—†	2	housewife	51	"
	M	Janey Benetta—†	2	"	26	
	N	Janey Charles	2	machinist	27	"
	O	Farrell Eva—†	2	housewife	50	"
	P	Lawrence Thelma—†	2	"	33	
	R	Robinson Benjamin	2	tester	36	
	S	Robinson Thelma—†	2	housewife	26	"
	T	Ryner Edwina—†	2	"	38	
	U	Ryner John	2	janitor	44	
	V	Campbell Edward	2	musician	25	"
	W	Campbell Ruth—†	2	housewife	21	"
	X	Gomes Bessie—†	2	"	50	
	Y	Gomes Manuel	2	janitor	50	
	Z	Lisle Andrew	2	shipper	36	
628						
	A	Lisle Annie N—†	2	housewife	26	"
	B	Moss Earl	2	welder	32	9 Lattimore ct
	C	Moss Elva—†	2	housewife	29	9 "
	D	Hilton Louise—†	2	"	21	here
	E	Hilton Roy E	2	laborer	27	"
	F	Davis Beatrice—†	2	housewife	35	"
	G	Davis Lorenzo	2	laborer	29	
	H	Brown Ellen—†	9	housewife	35	"
	K	Washington Amos	9	laborer	25	
	L	Washington Edith—†	9	housewife	24	"
	M	Freeman George	9	porter	24	"
	N	Freeman Mary—†	9	housewife	22	"
	O	Rust Edward	9	counterman	37	"
	P	Rust Geraldine—†	9	housewife	27	"

Page.	Letter.	Full Name.	Residence, Jan. 1, 1943.	Occupation.	Supposed Age.	Reported Residence, Jan. 1, 1942. Street and Number.

Lattimore Court—Continued

Page.	Letter.	Full Name.	Residence, Jan. 1, 1943.	Occupation.	Supposed Age.	Reported Residence, Jan. 1, 1942. Street and Number.
	R	Trouit Clarence	9	cook	35	here
	S	Trouit Thelma—†	9	housewife	30	“
	T	Wayne Ethel J—†	9	“	38	“
	U	Wayne Walter C	9	porter	42	
	V	Roberts Harold W	9	laborer	25	“
	W	Roberts Lucille—†	9	housewife	22	“
	Y	Fletcher Alice—†	9	“	62	15 Hammond
	Z	Fletcher Edward H	9	porter	66	15 “
629						
	A	Bonner Gladys—†	9	housewife	35	here
	B	Bonner Isaac	9	coppersmith	39	“
	C	Rhoden Calvin	9	operator	43	“
	D	Rhoden Martha—†	9	housewife	26	“
	E	Hester Dorothy E—†	9	“	37	
	F	Hester Luther M	9	porter	49	
	G	Randolph John	10	retired	63	
	H	Randolph Lillie—†	10	housewife	50	“
	K	Tyson Artice	10	laborer	32	
	L	Tyson Mary—†	10	housewife	29	“
	M	Barbosa Louise—†	10	“	36	
	N	Barbosa Michael	10	welder	35	“
	O	Pierce Frank	10	retired	52	
	P	Pierce Mattie—†	10	seamstress	40	“
	R	Nutter Georgia L—†	10	housewife	34	“
	S	Nutter May—†	10	domestic	31	“
	T	Henderson Gertrude—†	10	cleaner	47	
	U	Henderson Irene—†	10	laundress	27	“
	V	Bowden Ernest	10	laborer	48	
	W	Bowden Rita—†	10	housewife	35	“
	X	Reed Clarence S	10	U S A	25	
	Y	Reed George	10	laundryworker	48	“
	Z	Reed Josephine—†	10	housewife	39	“
630						
	A	Cook Jasper G	10	retired	72	
	B	Middleton Josephine—†	10	housewife	25	“
	C	Middleton Melvin	10	laborer	27	
	D	Jackman Christiana—†	10	housewife	50	“
	E	Jackman Edward	10	porter	57	
	F	Randolph Harold	10	garageman	31	“
	G	Randolph Rose—†	10	housewife	27	“
	H	Teixeira Phyllis—†	10	“	27	

Page.	Letter.	Full Name.	Residence, Jan. 1, 1943.	Occupation.	Supposed Age.	Reported Residence, Jan. 1, 1942. Street and Number.

Lattimore Court—Continued

	K	Blacklock Daniel	17	laborer	32	here
	L	Blacklock Sarah—†	17	housewife	28	"
	M	Franklin Charles E	17	laborer	24	"
	N	Franklin Sarah—†	17	housewife	20	"
	O	Burch Grace—†	17	waitress	25	
	P	Williams Harriet G—†	17	housewife	56	"
	R	Stokes Bessie—†	17	"	55	
	U	Porter Bennie W	17	laborer	25	
	V	Porter Ruth—†	17	operator	31	
	S	Wolff Herbert L	17	machinist	33	"
	T	Wolff Mary A—†	17	housewife	33	"
	W	Hogue Carrie—†	17	"	40	
	X	Hogue Lawrence	17	fireman	59	
	Y	Grant Carrie—†	17	housewife	22	"
	Z	Grant John	17	laborer	24	
631						
	A	Sealy Keturah—†	17	housewife	58	"
	B	Sealy Rita—†	17	stitcher	27	
	C	Warren Ariel—†	17	inspector	23	"
	D	Warren Isaac F	17	laborer	26	
	E	Manton June—†	17	housewife	20	"
	F	Manton Raymond	17	laborer	24	
	G	McKenney John D	17	"	26	
	H	McKenney Marguerite—†	17	housewife	22	"
	K	Johnson Henson T	17	porter	62	
	L	Johnson Sadie—†	17	housewife	64	"
	M	Beard Leora—†	18	"	35	
	N	Beard Maurice	18	waiter	43	
	O	Brown Mary—†	18	housewife	28	"
	P	Brown Richard	18	painter	32	
	R	Harding Edna—†	18	secretary	23	"
	S	Harding George	18	operator	27	"
	T	Harding Juanita—†	18	housewife	27	"
	U	Jeffreys Otho	18	porter	35	
	V	Jeffreys Viola—†	18	housewife	32	"
	W	Jones Bernetta—†	18	"	25	
	X	Jones Francis	18	watchman	23	"
	Y	Kennard Madeline—†	18	housewife	28	"
	Z	Kennard Ralph	18	cook	30	
632						
	A	Overstreet Martha—†	18	cashier	37	

Page.	Letter.	Full Name.	Residence, Jan. 1, 1943.	Occupation.	Supposed Age.	Reported Residence, Jan. 1, 1942. Street and Number.

Lattimore Court—Continued

	B	Overstreet Zannie	18	U S A	28	8 Wellington
	C	Tyler Grace—†	18	waitress	38	here
	D	Wray Addie—†	18	housewife	65	"
	E	Wray Josiah Z	18	waiter	65	"
	F	Randolph Edith—†	18	housewife	24	"
	G	Phillips George	18	chipper	29	"
	H	Phillips Marion—†	18	housewife	26	"
	K	Gibson Elizabeth—†	18	at home	21	
	L	Gibson Marguerite—†	18	housewife	52	"
	M	Jones Margaret—†	26	"	46	
	N	Horne Manuel	26	electrician	35	"
	O	Horne Mary—†	26	housewife	33	"
	P	Rose Kathleen—†	26	domestic	26	"
	R	Rose Quentin	26	laborer	28	
	S	Hester Angela—†	26	housewife	24	"
	T	Hester Benjamin	26	welder	25	
	U	Clark Eva—†	26	housewife	29	"
	V	Clark Ralph	26	welder	31	
	W	Milburn Octavia—†	26	housewife	33	"

633 Lenox Street

633	A	Taylor Eliza—†	144	housewife	82	here
	B	Taylor Robert	144	laborer	39	"
	C	Abbott Louise—†	144	housekeeper	49	"
	D	Jasper Benjamin G	144	retired	76	"
	E	Johnson Margaret—†	144	housewife	71	"
	F	Johnson Lauretta—†	144	"	36	"
	G	Johnson Mortimer	144	porter	46	
	H	Bovill James	144	painter	46	
	K	Herbert Dorothy—†	144	housekeeper	32	"
	L	Stewart Hyman	144	cook	50	"
	M	Stewart Isabel—†	144	housewife	50	"
	S	Pettyjohn Isaiah	156	chef	67	
	T	Pettyjohn Nellie—†	156	housewife	58	"
	U	Ward John T	156	cleaner	52	
	V	Ward Leila E—†	156	housewife	53	"
	W	Coleman John B	156	cook	77	
	X	Coleman Lena—†	156	housewife	49	"
	Y	Batson John	156	tester	23	630 Shawmut av
	Z	Batson Ruth—†	156	housewife	21	630 "

Page.	Letter.	Full Name.	Residence, Jan. 1, 1943.	Occupation.	Supposed Age.	Reported Residence, Jan. 1, 1942. Street and Number.
634		**Lenox Street**—Continued				
	A	Smith Marion—†	156	housekeeper	69	here
	B	Jenkins Ora C	156	porter	57	"
	C	Jenkins Viola—†	156	housewife	52	"
	D	White Ida—†	156	"	48	
	E	White Joshua	156	machinist	48	"
	F	Greenidge Julia—†	156	housewife	43	"
	G	Greenidge Walter B	156	janitor	54	"
	H	*Trotman Fitzroy A	156	painter	38	17 Hammond
	K	*Williams Frances—†	156	housewife	58	687 Shawmut av
	L	Williams Zachariah	156	seaman	58	681 "
	M	Henderson Carrie—†	156	housewife	44	here
	N	Henderson Robert	156	sandblaster	42	"
	P	Sisco Alma—†	156	housewife	43	"
	O	Sisco Benjamin	156	laborer	52	
	R	Finch Rosetta—†	156	domestic	50	
		Shawmut Avenue				
	T	Mayo Clementine H—†	601	housewife	24	here
	U	Mayo Earl F	601	clerk	26	"
	V	Bowers Lorraine—†	601	domestic	39	"
	W	Diggs Gladys E—†	601	housewife	33	"
	X	Diggs James O	601	porter	39	"
	Y	Duncan Alice E—†	601	housewife	63	"
	Z	Duncan Charles H	601	retired	73	
635						
	A	Hurley Lloyd W	601	mechanic	27	"
	B	Hurley Rose M—†	601	housewife	24	"
	C	Shephard George A	601	laborer	26	
	D	Shephard Julia M—†	601	housewife	29	"
	E	Hood Benjamin F	601	machinist	26	1 Ditmus ct
	F	Hood Evelyn V—†	601	housewife	27	1 "
	G	Carden Sabina M—†	601	laundress	37	here
	H	Still Elaine H—†	601	housewife	25	"
	K	Still William	601	laborer	30	"
	L	Robinson Alice E—†	601	housewife	47	"
	M	Robinson Fitzgerald	601	operator	49	"
	N	Joy Geraldine A—†	601	housewife	32	"
	O	Joy Raymond E	601	porter	36	
	P	Baldwin George A	601	painter	58	

Page.	Letter.	FULL NAME.	Residence, Jan. 1, 1943.	Occupation.	Supposed Age.	Reported Residence, Jan. 1, 1942. Street and Number.

Shawmut Avenue—Continued

	R	Baldwin Julia A—†	601	housewife	66	here
	S	Smith Julia—†	609	domestic	50	"
	T	*Springer Beatrice A—†	609	housewife	54	"
	U	Springer James A	609	chipper	60	
	V	Bisbee Annie I—†	609	housekeeper	51	"
	W	Coleman Lucy C—†	609	housewife	32	"
	X	Coleman Raymond P	609	U S N	35	
	Y	Goode Edward J	609	coppersmith	23	"
	Z	Goode Juanita—†	609	housewife	22	"
636						
	A	Kershaw Henrietta—†	609	"	28	
	B	Kershaw William	609	janitor	35	"
	C	Gilkes Ernest A	609	waiter	64	2 Trotter ct
	D	Gilkes Hilda C—†	609	housewife	60	2 "
	E	Reid Clarence W	609	janitor	40	here
	F	Reid Ovetta—†	609	housewife	29	"
	G	Clark Agnes M—†	609	"	24	"
	H	Clark Paul M	609	cook	26	
	K	Woodhouse Enoch O	609	clergyman	36	"
	L	Woodhouse Gertrude T-†	609	housewife	34	"
	M	Diggs Richard A	609	clerk	50	
	N	Diggs Rosanna D—†	609	housewife	42	"
	O	Wharton Archibald A	609	cook	25	
	P	Wharton Laurene D—†	609	housewife	31	"
	R	Harrison Eloise—†	617	"	29	
	S	Harrison James A	617	laborer	54	
	T	Augustine Emma B—†	617	"	60	
	U	Augustine Matthew	617	waiter	67	
	V	Banks Blanche—†	617	housewife	22	"
	W	Banks Joseph M	617	chipper	24	
	X	Ferguson Conrad Y	617	retired	60	
	Y	Ferguson Mary E—†	617	housewife	62	"
	Z	Richardson Martin D	617	operator	36	"
637						
	A	Richardson Mary R—†	617	housewife	32	"
	B	Plummer Ernestyne V—†	617	"	32	
	C	Plummer Jesse B	617	inspector	34	"
	D	Burns Edward J	617	chauffeur	30	"
	E	Burns Sarah E—†	617	housewife	27	"
	F	Langford Gladys A—†	617	"	32	

Page.	Letter.	Full Name.	Residence, Jan. 1, 1943.	Occupation.	Supposed Age.	Reported Residence, Jan. 1, 1942. Street and Number.

Shawmut Avenue—Continued

	G	Langford Oscar J	617	entertainer	31	here
	H	Contee Ethel S—†	617	housewife	28	“
	K	Contee Maurice	617	cutter	30	“
	L	Blunt Leonard N	617	shipper	31	
	M	Blunt Mary A—†	617	housewife	26	“
	N	Hill Clarence A	617	operator	22	
	O	Hill Maizie E—†	617	housewife	23	“
	P	Weeks Arthur E	617	presser	30	
	R	Weeks Ruby L—†	617	housewife	20	“
	S	Johnson Helen K—†	625	“	46	
	T	Johnson Richard J	625	laborer	48	
	U	Dudy Cora L—†	625	housekeeper	70	“
	V	Dudy Kenneth A	625	laborer	32	“
	W	Harris Ada E—†	625	housekeeper	49	“
	X	Coulthurst George B	625	molder	43	“
	Y	Coulthurst Mary A—†	625	housewife	41	“
	Z	Warrenton Susan—†	625	“	35	
638						
	A	Warrenton Vincent	625	laborer	37	
	B	Brown Aaron	625	painter	30	
	C	Brown Thelma—†	625	housewife	28	“
	D	Tucker Charles E	625	laborer	31	
	E	Tucker Gertrude J—†	625	housewife	28	“
	F	Walker Bertha—†	625	“	26	
	G	Walker Jesse	625	laborer	28	
	H	Pope Barbara C—†	625	housewife	23	“
	K	Pope James N	625	clerk	23	
	L	King Eva A—†	625	housewife	29	“
	M	King Joseph J	625	welder	29	
	N	Jones Albert	625	laborer	24	
	O	Jones Elizabeth—†	625	housewife	23	“
	P	Garner Ethany—†	625	operator	29	755 Tremont
	R	Allen Anita G—†	633	housewife	30	here
	S	Allen Ervin	633	laborer	30	“
	T	O'Neil Helen—†	633	housekeeper	20	“
	U	Mayo Doris—†	633	housewife	30	“
	V	Mayo James R	633	plumber	38	“
	W	Reavis Lloyd J	633	janitor	24	8 Elbert
	X	Reavis Shirley M—†	633	housewife	22	8 “
	Y	Johnson Constance B—†	633	“	27	here

Page.	Letter.	FULL NAME.	Residence, Jan. 1, 1943.	Occupation.	Supposed Age.	Reported Residence, Jan. 1, 1942. Street and Number.

Shawmut Avenue—Continued

	Z	Johnson Louis L	633	laborer	35	here
639						
	A	Key Ella J—†	633	housewife	25	"
	B	Key John H	633	mechanic	26	"
	C	Gibbs Doris F—†	633	housewife	27	"
	D	Gibbs William H	633	shipper	33	
	E	Reynolds Bernice M—†	633	housewife	20	"
	F	Reynolds Delos A	633	boilermaker	23	"
	G	Fairfax Charles E	633	proofreader	35	"
	H	Fairfax Marion C—†	633	housewife	27	"
	K	McIntyre Theodora—†	633	"	25	"
	L	McIntyre William J	633	laborer	26	
	M	Marshall Hazel A—†	633	housewife	26	"
	N	Marshall Ralph W	633	laborer	30	"
	O	Murray Frances W—†	633	housewife	22	"
	P	Murray James T	633	laborer	24	
	S	Hickman Elsie—†	643	domestic	52	"
	T	Thomas Jesse	643	longshoreman	42	"
	U	Thomas Mattie—†	643	housewife	43	"
	V	Washington Daisy E—†	643	housekeeper	50	"
	W	Landy Patience—†	643	"	51	64 Sterling
	X	Landy Wilma—†	643	"	21	64 "
	Y	Thomas Ida—†	643	"	25	55 "
	Z	Joesoonon Winnie—†	645	housewife	22	here
640						
	A	Joesoonon Wong	645	laundryman	28	"
	B	Greggs Lillian N—†	645	domestic	42	"
	C	Greggs Martha A—†	645	housekeeper	73	"
	D	Middleton James	645	laborer	50	S Carolina
	E	Somers Lottie F—†	645	housewife	62	here
	F	Somers Wallace	645	retired	78	"
	G	Tobey Eugene W	645	laborer	41	7 Cunard
	H	Scott Louise—†	647	housekeeper	71	here
	K	Graham Lucy—†	647	domestic	46	"
	L	Vass Beulah—†	647	housewife	28	"
	M	Vass Domingo	647	laborer	45	
	O	Lathrop Ella—†	649	housekeeper	76	"
	P	McDavid Lucinda—†	649	at home	81	"
	R	Boyd Alice—†	649	housewife	27	"
	S	Boyd Matthew	649	laborer	27	
	T	Greer Robert	651	carpenter	48	"

Page.	Letter.	Full Name.	Residence, Jan. 1, 1943.	Occupation.	Supposed Age.	Reported Residence, Jan. 1, 1942. Street and Number.

Shawmut Avenue—Continued

	U	Haines Daisy—†	651	at home	73	here
	V	Colbourne Hezekiah	651	machinist	46	"
	W	Colbourne Mahala—†	651	operator	23	Pennsylvania
	Y	Foster Walter	653	chauffeur	50	here
	Z	Parks Mildred—†	653	housekeeper	65	"
641						
	A	Sparks Edward L	653	blacksmith	44	"
	B	Smith James	655	clergyman	80	"
	C	Smith Katherine—†	655	housewife	42	"

Tremont Street

	N	Walker Bertha—†	924	housewife	48	here
	O	Walker Frederica—†	924	clerk	27	"
	P	Walker Kenneth	924	laborer	25	"
	R	George Katherine—†	924	houseworker	47	"
	S	Richardson Etta—†	924	"	42	
	T	Brown Mary—†	924	housewife	42	"
642						
	A	Stewart Charles G	932	dentist	65	"
	B	Stewart Maude—†	932	editor	63	
	E	Greene John	932	retired	67	
	C	Young Frederick M	932	laborer	45	
	D	Young Gladys—†	932	housewife	41	"
	F	Bellden Dorothy—†	932	"	30	
	G	Bellden George	932	machinist	35	"
	H	Murray Lottie—†	932	houseworker	44	"
	K	Walcott Allen B	932	laborer	64	"
	M	Harris Laurie—†	936	housewife	43	83 Hammond ter
	N	Harris Richard	936	laborer	42	83 "
	O	James Ella—†	936	laundress	50	here
	P	Saphie Charles	936	clerk	28	"
	R	Pina Joseph	936	machinist	48	"
	S	Pina Julia—†	936	housewife	46	"
	T	Eppe Ida—†	936	operator	43	"
	V	Hotaling Anna—†	940	housewife	42	"
	W	Williams Rachael—†	940	"	48	
	X	Farrier Julia—†	940	houseworker	23	"
	Y	Williams Harold	940	laborer	24	"
	Z	Jones Edward	940	"	37	111 Ruggles
643						
	A	Jones Wilhelmina—†	940	housewife	30	111 "

Page.	Letter.	FULL NAME.	Residence, Jan. 1, 1943.	Occupation.	Supposed Age.	Reported Residence, Jan. 1, 1942. Street and Number.

Tremont Street—Continued

	C	Leonard Alberta—†	944	housekeeper	22	here
	D	Leonard Earl	944	laborer	28	"
	E	Leonard Joseph R	944	"	30	"
	F	Leonard Robert	944	retired	63	
	G	Braxton Edith—†	944	at home	40	"
	H	Moore Margaret—†	944	housewife	58	57 Hammond
	K	Campbell Thomas	944	laborer	42	here
	L	Campbell Victoria—†	944	housewife	40	"
	N	Hopkins Annie E—†	948	"	50	"
	O	Hopkins John G	948	laborer	61	
	P	Heathman Joseph E	948	chauffeur	43	"
	R	Paul Avis M—†	948	housewife	39	"
	S	Webster Walter	948	attendant	51	135 Cabot
	T	Martin Cora—†	948	housewife	52	Plymouth
	U	Martin Francis	948	laborer	24	"
	V	Martin Manuel	948	retired	52	"

644 Trotter Court

	A	Bonds Essie L—†	1	housewife	24	here
	B	Bonds Harold J	1	laborer	28	"
	C	Warner Estelle—†	1	domestic	54	122 Camden
	D	Rose George W	1	cook	44	here
	E	Rose Ida—†	1	housewife	33	"
	F	Johnson Beatrice E—†	1	"	43	"
	G	Johnson George O	1	chauffeur	41	"
	H	Parris Gertrude M—†	1	housewife	22	"
	K	Parris Robert H	1	welder	24	
	L	Thomas Joyce A—†	1	housewife	20	"
	M	Thomas William E	1	laborer	25	
	N	Callender Mabel—†	1	domestic	45	"
	O	Dugger Joseph	1	laborer	41	
	P	Dugger Ruth—†	1	housewife	40	"
	R	Wolff Earl C	1	janitor	28	
	S	Wolff Marguerite—†	1	housewife	27	"
	T	Saunders Mary E—†	1	"	21	12 Cunard
	U	Saunders Thomas C	1	laborer	28	here
	V	Morris Ruth E—†	1	housewife	33	"
	W	Walters Ernest J	1	chauffeur	27	"
	X	Walters Hilda G—†	1	housewife	27	"
	Y	Meuillon Amy M—†	2	"	60	

Page.	Letter.	Full Name.	Residence, Jan. 1, 1943.	Occupation.	Supposed Age.	Reported Residence, Jan. 1, 1942. Street and Number.

Trotter Court—Continued

	Z	Meuillon James J	2	porter	64	here
645						
	A	Clark Hattie P—†	2	housewife	35	"
	B	Clark Paul C	2	butler	35	
	C	Pina Viola—†	2	domestic	40	"
	D	Underwood Richard B	2	porter	27	18 Trotter ct
	E	Underwood Viola—†	2	housewife	26	18 "
	F	Underwood Joseph J	2	porter	33	Everett
	G	Underwood Mary E—†	2	housewife	29	"
	H	Henderson William	2	chauffeur	36	here
	K	Daise Booker	2	cook	34	"
	L	Daise Florence—†	2	housewife	32	"
	M	Johnson Antonia A—†	2	"	25	633 Shawmut av
	N	Johnson Theodore M	2	welder	26	633 "
	O	Burton Embrue	2	laborer	31	here
	P	Burton Ruth—†	2	housewife	30	"
	R	Bracy Charlotte—†	2	"	56	"
	S	Bracy Paul S, jr	2	porter	58	
	T	Johnson Edwina—†	2	housekeeper	36	"
	U	Mainer Bettie P—†	2	housewife	20	9 Lattimore ct
	V	Mainer Robert	2	welder	25	9 "
	W	Thomas Louis	9	mechanic	21	here
	X	Thomas Olga L—†	9	housewife	21	"
	Y	Dixon Elizabeth—†	9	"	39	"
	Z	Dixon Robert	9	laborer	34	
646						
	A	Powell Henry C	9	"	34	
	B	Powell Violette D—†	9	housewife	30	"
	C	Moore Frances—†	9	"	29	
	D	Moore Kenneth G	9	laborer	30	
	E	Wilson Dorothy—†	9	housewife	40	"
	F	Wilson Leonard	9	laborer	30	
	G	Johnson Evelyn—†	9	housewife	29	"
	H	Johnson Joseph	9	laborer	30	
	K	Wise Josephine R—†	9	housewife	22	"
	L	Wise Stokes N	9	chipper	29	
	M	Royall Bessie O—†	9	domestic	54	"
	N	Royall Constance—†	9	housewife	25	"
	O	Royall John N	9	laborer	29	
	P	Taylor Rose M—†	9	housewife	21	"
	R	Taylor Wesley R	9	laborer	23	

Page.	Letter.	Full Name.	Residence, Jan. 1, 1943.	Occupation.	Supposed Age.	Reported Residence, Jan. 1, 1942. Street and Number.

Trotter Court—Continued

Page.	Letter.	Full Name.	Residence, Jan. 1, 1943.	Occupation.	Supposed Age.	Reported Residence, Jan. 1, 1942. Street and Number.
	s	Seaforth Robert R	9	laborer	29	here
	T	Seaforth Sophia E—†	9	housewife	27	“
	U	Smith Virginia E—†	9	housekeeper	34	“
	V	Jackson John H	9	laborer	28	“
	W	Jackson Millicent A—†	9	housewife	26	“
	X	Pontes Domingo	10	laborer	31	
	Y	Pontes Vera M—†	10	housewife	31	“
	Z	Williams Chester M	10	welder	26	
647						
	A	Williams Edna E—†	10	housewife	26	“
	B	Goodman Guernsey	10	laborer	40	
	C	Goodman Viola—†	10	housewife	39	“
	D	Isaacs Louise C—†	10	“	54	135 Chiswick rd
	E	Isaacs Robert H	10	retired	73	135 “
	F	Richardson Charles	10	laborer	50	here
	G	Richardson Lucille—†	10	housewife	37	“
	H	Drewery Helen—†	10	“	30	“
	K	Drewery Thomas	10	laborer	39	
	L	Mitchell Alice M—†	10	housewife	34	“
	M	Mitchell Thoedore H	10	laborer	36	
	N	Rose Antonia—†	10	housewife	28	“
	O	Rose Lindo J	10	chipper	28	
	P	Emerson Ruth—†	10	housewife	27	“
	R	Emerson Vincent	10	laborer	40	“
	S	Wilkerson Shedric	10	busboy	23	21 Greenwich pk
	T	Wilkerson Zerita A—†	10	housewife	21	77 Humboldt av
	U	Cox Ethel A—†	10	“	44	here
	V	Cox Stanley H	10	waiter	54	“
	W	Thomson James W	10	electrician	22	789 Shawmut av
	X	Thomson Thelma J—†	10	housewife	21	789 “
	Y	Watkins Dominga—†	17	“	27	here
	Z	Watkins John V	17	laborer	26	“
648						
	A	Sisco Dempsey	17	welder	29	
	B	Sisco Florence G—†	17	housewife	20	“
	C	Jett Evelyn M—†	17	“	32	
	D	Jett Willis T	17	laborer	43	“
	E	Edwards Archie	17	bootblack	47	18 Trotter ct
	F	Edwards Hattie M—†	17	housewife	47	18 “
	G	Wood Hilda C—†	17	“	20	1 “
	H	Wood Samuel C	17	laborer	23	1 “

Page.	Letter.	Full Name.	Residence, Jan. 1, 1943.	Occupation.	Supposed Age.	Reported Residence, Jan. 1, 1942. Street and Number.

Trotter Court—Continued

Page.	Letter.	Full Name.	Residence, Jan. 1, 1943.	Occupation.	Supposed Age.	Reported Residence, Jan. 1, 1942. Street and Number.
	K	Curry Fannie A—†	17	housekeeper	55	here
	L	Pope Nellie O—†	17	laundress	39	"
	M	Bryant Hilda F—†	17	housewife	29	"
	N	Bryant John A	17	electrician	32	"
	O	Dupee Alexander	17	laborer	29	
	P	Dupee Evelyn—†	17	housewife	25	"
	R	Chase Charlotte F—†	17	"	29	
	S	Chase Randolph S	17	machinist	31	"
	T	Holmes Richard M	17	fireman	23	
	U	Holmes Thelma J—†	17	housewife	24	"
	V	Bailey Hester—†	17	"	53	Malden
	W	Bailey William	17	laborer	58	"
	X	Stanley John	17	"	50	here
	Y	Stanley John C	17	"	41	67 Mountfort
	Z	Smith Anita—†	18	housewife	20	here
649						
	A	Smith James	18	U S A	33	
	B	Madden Gwendolyn—†	18	housewife	24	"
	C	Madden Joseph P	18	chipper	24	
	D	Underwood Charles C	18	boilermaker	28	"
	E	Underwood Lavinia—†	18	housewife	22	"
	G	Robinson Dorothy A—†	18	"	25	
	H	Robinson Jacob W	18	laborer	24	
	K	Moody Bessie G—†	18	housewife	23	"
	L	Moody Wilbert G	18	welder	25	"
	M	Foskey George A, jr	18	laborer	28	32 Sarsfield
	N	Foskey Gladys L—†	18	housewife	22	32 "
	O	Creed Donald G	18	laborer	25	here
	P	Creed Johanna—†	18	housewife	23	"
	R	Benjamin Jacqueline—†	18	"	29	"
	S	Benjamin James	18	laborer	29	
	T	Benders Clarence	18	"	34	
	U	Benders Dorothy—†	18	housewife	32	"
	V	Thomas John B	18	retired	69	62 Harold
	W	Thomas Mary M—†	18	housewife	69	62 "
	X	Watkins Kate M—†	18	"	29	here
	Y	Watkins Robert P, jr	18	dentist	29	"
	Z	Averett Albert A	25	chipper	52	62 Sherman
650						
	A	Averett Barbara E—†	25	housewife	55	62 "
	B	Byrd Barbara O—†	25	laundress	38	here

Page.	Letter.	FULL NAME.	Residence, Jan. 1, 1943.	Occupation.	Supposed Age.	Reported Residence, Jan. 1, 1942. Street and Number.

Trotter Court—Continued

	C	Gibbs Esther—†	25	at home	72	here
	D	Ware Daniel	25	retired	72	"
	E	Ware Ella L—†	25	housewife	67	"
	F	Cabral Louise—†	25	"	30	
	G	Cabral Theodore	25	chipper	36	
	H	Smith Arthur W	25	laborer	59	
	K	Smith Mary K—†	25	housewife	41	"
	L	Massey Isabel F—†	25	"	29	
	M	Massey James I	25	waiter	34	
	N	Lomax William S	25	electrician	21	"
	O	Mason Fannie L—†	25	housekeeper	55	528 Mass av
	P	Slaymon George W	25	chauffeur	32	here
	R	Slaymon Hortense O—†	25	housewife	29	"
	S	Scott Odessa—†	25	domestic	31	"
	T	Jones Rebecca—†	25	"	33	
	U	Whitfield Clara—†	25	housekeeper	30	"
	V	Jones John	25	laborer	25	"
	W	Jones Virginia—†	25	housewife	22	"
	X	Graham Andrew	25	laborer	28	
	Y	Graham Willie M—†	25	housewife	28	"
	Z	Browning Richard E	26	chauffeur	62	"
651						
	A	Browning Rose L—†	26	housewife	52	"
	B	Henderson Charles J	26	welder	28	
	C	Henderson Helen C—†	26	housewife	24	"
	D	Morrison Garfield E	26	chipper	25	
	E	Morrison Iona A—†	26	housewife	29	"
	F	Watts Alonzo F	26	chauffeur	26	"
	G	Watts Josephine P—†	26	housewife	23	"
	H	Jones James	26	laborer	27	
	K	Jones Sally—†	26	housewife	25	"
	L	Butler Agnes L—†	26	"	27	
	M	Butler Robert S	26	welder	28	
	N	Redd Estelle—†	26	housewife	22	"
	O	Redd Leslie S	26	laborer	27	"
	P	Jackman Clara—†	26	housewife	29	"
	R	Jackman Ivan	26	laborer	32	
	S	Bostick Claudia—†	26	housewife	32	"
	T	Bostick Delano	26	painter	39	
	U	Isaacs Louis S	26	clerk	26	
	V	Paige Florence M—†	26	housewife	29	"

Page.	Letter.	FULL NAME.	Residence, Jan. 1, 1943.	Occupation.	Supposed Age.	Reported Residence, Jan. 1, 1942. Street and Number.

Trotter Court—Continued

	W	Paige Henry E	26	chauffeur	30	here
	X	Merchant Marion T—†	26	housekeeper	26	"
	Y	Francis Christina—†	34	housewife	57	"
	Z	Francis Richard	34	laborer	62	
652						
	A	Jones Doris—†	34	housewife	38	"
	B	Jones Ira	34	laborer	26	
	C	Parker Elijah	34	retired	84	
	D	Parker Emily C—†	34	housewife	71	"
	E	Nickerson Carmen—†	34	"	21	"
	F	Nickerson Joseph	34	mechanic	22	"
	G	Wright Edgar	34	laborer	36	
	H	Wright Martha—†	34	housewife	36	"
	K	McMullen Christopher	34	waiter	26	
	L	McMullen Louise—†	34	housewife	22	"
	M	Gittens Audrey—†	34	"	26	
	N	Gittens Charles	34	U S A	30	
	O	Thompson Katherine L—†	34	housewife	34	"
	P	Thompson Norman S	34	barber	38	
	R	Peters Edith—†	34	housekeeper	46	"
	S	Peters Louis	34	laborer	55	"
	T	Rickson George	34	"	23	
	U	Rickson Roslyn—†	34	housewife	21	"
	V	Parris Georgia—†	34	"	37	
	W	Parris Stanley	34	laborer	37	
	X	Williams Charles	34	clerk	39	
	Y	Williams Esther—†	34	housewife	29	"

Ward 9—Precinct 7

CITY OF BOSTON

LIST OF RESIDENTS
20 YEARS OF AGE AND OVER

(NON-CITIZENS INDICATED BY ASTERISK)
(FEMALES INDICATED BY DAGGER)

AS OF

JANUARY 1, 1943

JOSEPH F. TIMILTY, *Chairman*
FREDERIC E. DOWLING, *Secretary*
WILLIAM A. MOTLEY, JR.
FRANCIS B. McKINNEY
EVERETT R. PROUT
Listing Board.

CITY OF BOSTON PRINTING DEPARTMENT

Page.	Letter.	Full Name.	Residence, Jan. 1, 1943.	Occupation.	Supposed Age.	Reported Residence, Jan. 1, 1942. Street and Number.
700						
		Cabot Street				
	A	Cummings Ella—†	34	housewife	22	here
	B	Cummings Richard	34	factoryhand	21	Maine
	C	Williams McCleary	34	laborer	21	1086 Tremont
	D	Dorsey Catherine L—†	34	domestic	38	here
	E	Dorsey Edward	34	U S A	23	"
	F	Dorsey Louis J	34	"	21	"
	G	Kennedy Walter	36	laborer	62	
	H	Thomas Elsie—†	36	at home	64	
	K	Harriston Robert	36	laborer	56	
	L	Whiteside Anna M—†	38	housewife	52	"
	M	Whiteside Thomas W	38	retired	58	
	N	Ferguson Ruby—†	40	factoryhand	30	"
	O	Jameson Rachel—†	40	at home	70	
	P	Quow Edna—†	40	housewife	67	"
	R	Hinton William	42	retired	72	
	T	Linzey Ruby—†	42	domestic	38	"
	U	Snowden Eleanor—†	44	"	29	
	V	McAdam Molly—†	44	"	59	
	W	Sanford Lena—†	44	housewife	59	"
	X	Sheffield Julia—†	44	at home	26	78 Sterling
	Y	Small Josephine—†	44	cook	23	12 Marble
	Z	Small Lila—†	44	"	28	12 "
701						
	A	Trouit Bernice—†	44	housewife	28	Everett
	B	Trouit Harold	44	laborer	32	991 Tremont
	C	Jones Dorothy—†	46	laundryworker	33	80 Windsor
	D	Jones William	46	porter	33	80 "
	E	Lewis Edna—†	46	housewife	48	here
	F	Lewis Robert	46	laborer	61	"
	G	Thomas Richard	46	"	27	59 Camden
	H	Thomas Rosalie—†	46	housewife	21	59 "
	K	Taylor Charles	46	laborer	55	Lynn
	L	Taylor Edna—†	46	housewife	32	"
	M	Gellighen Maggie—†	48	at home	68	here
	N	Hawkins Annie—†	48	laundryworker	38	"
	O	Lewis Vernon	48	painter	47	"
	P	Walton Jennie—†	48	domestic	53	"
	R	Fuller Della—†	48	at home	63	
	S	Ragland Abraham	48	laborer	35	
	T	Ragland Louise—†	48	housewife	30	"

Page.	Letter.	Full Name.	Residence, Jan. 1, 1943.	Occupation.	Supposed Age.	Reported Residence, Jan. 1, 1942. Street and Number.

Cabot Street—Continued

	U	Proctor Louisa—†	48	domestic	57	here
	V	Smith Edith E—†	50	"	34	"
	W	Smith Henry S	50	laborer	33	"
	X	Brown Charles	50	"	29	79 Williams
	Y	Brown Mary E—†	50	housewife	44	79 "
	Z	Burns Agnes—†	50	"	25	here
702						
	A	Rosser John	50	laborer	56	"
	B	Rosser Roy	50	"	38	119 Lenox
	C	Cardoza Bras C	52	"	46	here
	D	Pratt Howard	52	"	43	22 Lansing
	E	Pratt Rosamond—†	52	housewife	33	22 "
	F	Turner John	52	laborer	42	Georgia
	G	Turner Mamie—†	52	housewife	40	"
	L	Baker Lavenia—†	54	"	78	here
	M	Smith Albert	54	retired	83	"
	N	Smith Sarah P—†	54	housewife	64	"
	O	Johnson Belle—†	54	"	60	
	P	Johnson Edward M	54	laborer	62	
	R	Woods Gladys—†	54	seamstress	34	"
	U	Swain Rosena—†	56	housekeeper	41	"
	W	Brown Susie—†	58	domestic	58	"
	X	Brennan Pauline—†	58	"	45	
	Y	Dupee Alexander	58	janitor	57	
	Z	McQueen Beulah—†	58	domestic	29	"
703						
	A	Lane Charles F	58	steward	52	
	B	Lane Henrietta—†	58	housewife	45	"
	D	*Paris Frances—†	60	"	39	
	E	Paris James	60	porter	44	
	F	Jackson Mary—†	60	housewife	39	"
	G	Richardson Henry	60	porter	65	
	H	*De Palma Natalie—†	62	housewife	65	"
	K	Mahan Agnes—†	62	housekeeper	63	"
	L	Mahan Margaret—†	62	"	71	"
	M	Stockwell Fannie M—†	62	housewife	69	"
	N	Sidberg Elizabeth—†	64	"	74	
	O	Woods Cecelia—†	64	"	51	
	P	Baker Ada—†	64	"	62	
	S	Jennings Walter	66	packer	37	
	T	Johnson Alma—†	66	finisher	28	

Page.	Letter.	Full Name.	Residence, Jan. 1, 1943.	Occupation.	Supposed Age.	Reported Residence, Jan. 1, 1942. Street and Number.

Cabot Street—Continued

Page.	Letter.	Full Name.	Residence, Jan. 1, 1943.	Occupation.	Supposed Age.	Reported Residence, Jan. 1, 1942. Street and Number.
	U	Johnson Helena—†	66	stitcher	57	here
	V	Manuel Rose—†	66	trimmer	29	"
	W	Quow Angela M—†	66	maid	37	"
	X	Zinfolino Grace—†	68	housewife	52	"
	Y	Zinfolino Joseph	68	laborer	57	"
	Z	Taylor Alice—†	68	domestic	55	1088 Tremont
704						
	B	Ingersoll Marie—†	70	checker	69	here
	C	Ingersoll Roberta—†	70	operator	31	"
	D	Hart Jane—†	70	housewife	87	"
	F	Bibby William	72	painter	58	"
	H	Johnson James R	74	cook	37	
	K	Williams John	74	"	41	
	M	Lambert Blanche A—†	84	housewife	45	"
	N	Lambert Josephine—†	84	student	20	
	O	Pollard Eva W—†	84	presser	50	
	P	Byars Albertina—†	94	housewife	48	"
	R	Byars George	94	chauffeur	49	"
	S	Byars George	94	U S A	21	
	T	McKissick Stanford	94	entertainer	69	"
	U	Gillis Robert J	94½	janitor	65	
	V	Lydston Sarah—†	94½	housewife	71	"

Greenwich Street

Page.	Letter.	Full Name.	Residence, Jan. 1, 1943.	Occupation.	Supposed Age.	Reported Residence, Jan. 1, 1942. Street and Number.
	X	Johnson Addie E—†	2	cook	53	here
	Y	Johnson Herman A	2	messenger	35	"
	Z	Sims Edna—†	2	domestic	32	"
705						
	A	Sims Russell	2	presser	33	
	B	Harris Alma—†	4	seamstress	60	"
	C	Thompson Ephraim	4	machinist	33	81 Sterling
	D	Thompson Thelma—†	4	housewife	30	74 Hammond
	F	Moore Phoebe—†	6	clerk	26	here
	H	Sysco William	6	musician	34	772 Shawmut av
	K	Miller James	6	porter	37	here
	G	Jackman Phillip	6	"	49	"
	L	*Barbour Cecelia—†	7	domestic	62	"
	N	*Thorpe Phyllis—†	7	housewife	28	"
	O	*Wade Clement F	8	foundryman	55	"
	P	*Warner Walter	8	chef	56	

Page.	Letter.	Full Name.	Residence, Jan. 1, 1943.	Occupation.	Supposed Age.	Reported Residence, Jan. 1, 1942. Street and Number.

Greenwich Street—Continued

	R	Harris Dolores F—†	8	housewife	23	here
	S	Harris James M	8	machinist	24	"
	T	Casneau Alice A—†	9	at home	76	"
	U	Hyman Annie L—†	10	housewife	30	"
	V	Hyman Sybalye	10	chef	31	
	W	Howe Lela M—†	11	domestic	56	"
	X	Smith Laura A—†	11	at home	67	"
	Y	Terry Virginia—†	11	manager	26	22 Windsor
	Z	Burgess Nannie H—†	12	housekeeper	66	here
706						
	A	Elliott Margaret E—†	12	"	73	
	B	Bryant Lela—†	13	at home	72	"
	C	Green Julia—†	13	"	72	26 Claremont pk
	D	Wilson Cornelius J	14	janitor	61	here
	E	Wilson Dora—†	14	housewife	66	"
	F	Davis Bessie—†	15	domestic	53	"
	G	Jones Elizabeth—†	15	"	49	
	H	Wells Susan A—†	16	housekeeper	74	"
	K	Reddick Eliza—†	17	housewife	61	"
	L	Reddick Gladys M—†	17	secretary	30	"
	M	Reddick Robert	17	garageman	62	"
	N	Bryant Muriel L—†	18	housewife	29	"
	O	Jones Annie—†	18	housekeeper	60	"
	P	Brim Amelia—†	19	domestic	58	"
	R	Jeter Lillian—†	19	at home	61	"
	S	Lewis Emma—†	19	"	55	127 Centre
	T	Buchanan Laura—†	20	housewife	47	here
	U	Cephas George	20	painter	58	"
	V	Davis Bertie—†	21	housewife	51	20 Warwick
	W	Davis Thomas	21	retired	65	20 "
	X	Craddock Elizabeth—†	21	housewife	30	here
	Y	Craddock Hyman	21	welder	35	"
707						
	A	Hill James E	22	janitor	65	
	B	Jefferson John	22	"	63	
	C	Byndloss Florence M—†	23	stitcher	21	
	D	Byndloss Lillian A—†	23	housewife	46	"
	E	Byndloss Peter	23	carpenter	51	"
	F	Lee Lucinda A—†	24	housewife	70	"
	G	Lee Riley A	24	retired	72	"
	H	Christy Dorcas—†	25	presser	22	25 Westminster

Page.	Letter.	Full Name.	Residence, Jan. 1, 1943.	Occupation.	Supposed Age.	Reported Residence, Jan. 1, 1942. Street and Number.

Greenwich Street—Continued

	K	Christy Dorothy—†	25	presser	34	25 Westminster
	M	Anderson Roy	27	clerk	20	New Jersey
	N	Brown Thomas H	27	retired	72	here
	O	Dawson Robert	27	welder	20	Wash'n D C
	P	Talley William A	27	"	20	Georgia
	R	Edwards Mollie E—†	28	housewife	61	here
	S	Edwards Wilbur	28	waiter	65	"
	T	Dowd Charles	29	U S A	21	"
	U	Dowd Laura—†	29	housewife	41	"
	V	Tillman Rose—†	29	at home	72	
	X	Grant William	31	laborer	52	
	Y	Markum Myrtle N—†	32	student	21	
	Z	Markum Willa E—†	32	housewife	52	"
708						
	A	Markum William B	32	mechanic	60	"
	B	Markum William B	32	U S A	27	
	C	Benders George	33	laborer	24	
	D	Benders John	33	"	25	"
	E	Benders Mattie—†	33	at home	67	
	F	Benders Stewart	33	welder	38	
	G	Gooding William A	34	musician	32	"
	H	Watson Louise A—†	34	housewife	28	"
	K	Cromwell Malzetta—†	35	factoryhand	24	Lynn
	L	MacCleave Josephine—†	35	"	30	here
	M	Reid Fannie—†	35	domestic	66	"
	N	Taylor Julia J—†	35	"	52	"
	O	McGirt Frank R	36	porter	67	
	P	McKnight Alexander	36	"	64	"
	R	Satterfield Mary—†	36	domestic	44	Connecticut
	S	Williams Frank	37	laborer	65	here
	T	Taliaferro Della—†	38	housewife	67	"
	U	Taliaferro Matthew F	38	U S A	31	"
	V	Lewis Mabel—†	39	housewife	24	"
	W	Lewis Parker	39	laborer	24	
	X	Bacchus Lucy—†	39	at home	72	"
	Y	Hudson Hettie K—†	39	"	72	28 Adams pl
	Z	Beverly William A	39	retired	77	23 Windsor
709						
	A	Barnes Lucille C—†	40	housewife	56	35 Warwick
	B	Barnes Walter D	40	waiter	56	35 "
	C	Jones Lucius F	40	retired	56	here

Greenwich Street—Continued

Page.	Letter.	Full Name.	Residence, Jan. 1, 1943.	Occupation.	Supposed Age.	Reported Residence, Jan. 1, 1942. Street and Number.
	D	Haughton Rachel O—†	41	at home	69	here
	E	*Richards Agnes—†	41	"	82	"
	F	*Samuels Richard	41	porter	54	"
	G	Stewart Hattie—†	41	domestic	57	"
	H	Hayes Jesse	43	laborer	72	
	K	Hayes Josephine—†	43	at home	72	"
	L	Smith Minnie—†	43	student	42	14 Gertrose
	M	Dowell Malzene—†	45	housewife	56	here
	N	Guyton Lucretia—†	45	"	53	"
	O	Walker Emma S—†	45	"	38	47 Ottawa
	P	Gray Esther—†	47	domestic	51	here
	R	Richey Ella W—†	49	at home	76	"
	S	Johnston Grace—†	51	housewife	70	"
	T	Cunningham Isabelle—†	53	housekeeper	67	New York
	U	Jones Sarah P—†	53	"	67	here
	V	Pritchett John E	53	mechanic	41	"
	W	Austin Ernest	55	janitor	46	"
	X	Williams Bessie L—†	55	clerk	32	

Hammond Street

Page.	Letter.	Full Name.	Residence, Jan. 1, 1943.	Occupation.	Supposed Age.	Reported Residence, Jan. 1, 1942. Street and Number.
710	B	Howell Blanche F—†	12	housewife	26	here
	C	Barry Margaret E—†	12	housekeeper	78	"
	D	Chandler Lula E—†	12	"	58	"
	E	Evans William T	12	machinist	36	"
	F	Kearse Henry	12	seaman	46	
	G	May Clement W	12	engineer	59	
	H	May Inez F—†	12	housewife	47	"
	K	Crawford Charles	12	waiter	69	
	L	Crawford Charles, jr	12	laborer	45	
	M	Crawford Julia C—†	12	housewife	68	"
	N	Mitchell Elizabeth—†	12	housekeeper	37	"
	O	Mitchell Isabel—†	12	housewife	29	689 Shawmut av
	P	Curtis Cecil	14	laborer	48	here
	R	Curtis Esther—†	14	housewife	48	"
	S	Jackson Adelaide—†	14	"	30	"
	T	Surrey Gladys M—†	14	"	67	
	U	Gough Margaret S—†	14	operator	23	"
	V	Gough Rebecca H—†	14	housekeeper	28	"
	W	Gough Stanley B	14	U S A	21	"
	Y	Moran Clarence G	16	shipfitter	20	"

Page.	Letter.	Full Name.	Residence, Jan. 1, 1943.	Occupation.	Supposed Age.	Reported Residence, Jan. 1, 1942. Street and Number.

Hammond Street—Continued

	z	Moran Julia Z—†	16	housewife	49	here
		711				
	A	Goode Blanche E—†	16	"	55	
	B	Porter Leslie E—†	16	mechanic	59	"
	C	Floyd Bertha—†	16	operator	51	"
	E	Chestnut Herbert A	24	janitor	35	
	F	Russell Olivene—†	24	housewife	44	"
	G	Russell Theodore G	24	janitor	40	"
	H	Brown Mabel E—†	24	housewife	62	"
	K	Taylor Ethel M—†	24	laundress	38	"
	L	Taylor Horace T	24	porter	38	
	M	Walker Alfred J	24	U S A	22	
	N	Walker William F	24	"	29	
	O	Green Ada M—†	24	housewife	22	"
	P	Green Leroy H	24	meatcutter	29	"
	R	Brown Harvey W	24	U S N	29	Ohio
	S	Brown Willie V—†	24	actress	23	"
	T	Smith Maggie—†	24	housewife	84	"
	U	Falden Elizabeth M—†	24	"	37	here
	V	*Johnston Elizabeth—†	24	"	45	"
	W	Blizzard Alice—†	24	waitress	52	"
	X	Johnson Christina—†	24	laundress	51	"
	Y	Johnson Pauline—†	24	stenographer	32	"
	Z	Payne Nelson N	24	rigger	35	
		712				
	A	Payne Olive A—†	24	housewife	35	"
	B	Tyrell Henry B	24	cutter	31	
	C	Tyrell Margaret E—†	24	housewife	26	"
	D	Davis John	24	painter	68	"
	E	Hudson Robert	24	chauffeur	46	"
	F	Smith Eunice O—†	24	housewife	50	"
	G	Luke Gerald E	24	longshoreman	46	"
	H	Luke Mary E—†	24	housewife	32	"
	K	Smith Ernest	24	U S A	43	5 Col av
	L	Sykes Georgianna—†	24	presser	46	here
	M	Drew Minnie—†	24	finisher	40	51 Westminster
	N	Porter Mary—†	24	operator	22	51 "
	O	Toney Pierce	24	miner	38	1051 Tremont
	P	Toney Thelma—†	24	stitcher	26	1051 "
	R	Carter Budd C	24	porter	31	here
	S	Clark Grace—†	24	hairdresser	31	"

Page.	Letter.	Full Name.	Residence, Jan. 1, 1943.	Occupation.	Supposed Age.	Reported Residence, Jan. 1, 1942. Street and Number.

Hammond Street—Continued

	T	Kendricks Caroline M—†	24	housewife	25	34 Rochester
	U	Kendricks Leethan	24	welder	34	34 "
	V	Butler Lydia A—†	24	housekeeper	59	here
	W	Varrs Aubrey G	24	chipper	29	"
	X	Varrs Dorothy—†	24	housewife	28	"
	Y	Butcher Charlotte—†	24	"	45	
	Z	Butcher Edwin	24	attendant	48	"
713						
	A	Jones Edith L—†	24	seamstress	57	"
	B	Bell Charles M	24	baker	39	
	C	Bell Flora N—†	24	housewife	33	"
	D	Barrows Ina—†	24	presser	39	
	E	*Perry Joseph	24	factoryhand	46	"
	F	Perry Stella—†	24	housewife	36	"
	G	Johnson Edward	24	leatherworker	40	"
	H	Johnson Evelyn B—†	24	housewife	36	"
	K	Allen Jesse	24	waiter	51	
	L	Brown Gladys—†	24	domestic	42	"
	M	Seales Marguerite—†	24	housewife	22	22 Dilworth
	N	Sweeney Sarah—†	24	"	44	here
	O	Williams Richard	24	operator	45	"
	P	Caradine Nancy—†	24	housewife	25	32 Ball
	R	Caradine Robert	24	laborer	36	774 Col av
	S	Washington Alta V—†	24	clerk	28	Cambridge
	T	Washington Clarence W	24	welder	31	"
	U	Coffey Maude—†	24	domestic	57	Milton
	V	Dawson Eva M—†	32	housewife	41	here
	W	Dawson James W	32	laborer	45	"
	X	Moffitt Mary J—†	32	housewife	51	"
	Y	Moffitt William H	32	retired	68	
	Z	Seldon Rosetta M—†	32	waitress	30	
714						
	A	*Tarpin Anna E—†	32	housekeeper	28	"
	B	Williams Alexander	32	seaman	25	"
	C	Williams Annie B—†	32	housewife	49	"
	D	Williams David R	32	seaman	26	"
	E	Williams Ida E—†	32	domestic	27	59 Hammond
	F	Barnett Edna L—†	32	housewife	35	here
	G	Barnett Norvell	32	laborer	47	"
	H	McClain John A	32	porter	40	"
	K	McClain Ruth E—†	32	housewife	40	"

Page.	Letter.	FULL NAME.	Residence, Jan. 1, 1943.	Occupation.	Supposed Age.	Reported Residence, Jan. 1, 1942. Street and Number.

Hammond Street—Continued

	L	Ross Ellen L—†	32	housewife	55	here
	M	Ross John R	32	houseman	59	"
	N	Chinn Gilbert J	32	U S A	20	29 Wellington
	O	Chinn Margaret M—†	32	housewife	42	29 "
	P	Chinn Pembroke B	32	U S A	22	29 "
	R	Sanford Georgiana—†	32	housewife	40	here
	S	Sanford Irene—†	32	clerk	23	"
	T	Sanford Oswald	32	garageman	43	"
	U	Smith Beatrice A—†	34	housewife	37	"
	V	Smith Paul A	34	U S A	39	New Jersey
	W	Saunders Malcolm	34	laborer	21	15 Sarsfield
	X	Wimberly Adolph	34	butler	44	here
	Y	Wimberly Roselle—†	34	housewife	43	"
	Z	Stewart Edmonia—†	34	"	57	23 Arnold
715						
	A	Stewart Eva D—†	34	"	26	23 "
	B	Stewart William C	34	porter	61	23 "
	C	Stewart William E	34	laborer	32	23 "
	D	Lopes Christian C	34	U S A	20	here
	E	Lopes Emma E—†	34	housewife	49	"
	F	Martin Aristine T—†	34	clerk	27	"
	G	Johnson Ernest E	34	bricklayer	44	"
	H	Johnson Henrietta—†	34	housewife	24	"
	K	Green Richard	34	embalmer	22	"
	L	King Herbert	34	U S A	30	
	M	Smith Blanche—†	34	housewife	60	"
	N	Smith Joseph	34	retired	74	
	O	Barrows Antonio	34	laborer	27	"
	P	Barrows Gertrude M—†	34	housewife	50	"
	R	Barrows Peter	34	laborer	59	
	S	Dunbar Ethel—†	34	housewife	46	"
	T	Dunbar Hezekiah	34	waiter	47	
	U	King Ellen—†	36	operator	60	"
	V	Hoyte Rhoda M—†	36	housewife	64	"
	W	Hoyte Robert J	36	operator	70	
	X	Austin Druscilla—†	36	housewife	61	"
	Y	Austin Mark A	36	porter	63	
	Z	Gilbert Moses	36	millwright	48	"
716						
	A	Wilson Bertha M—†	36	housewife	43	"
	B	Booker Sarah A—†	38	housekeeper	45	"

Page.	Letter.	Full Name.	Residence, Jan. 1, 1943.	Occupation.	Supposed Age.	Reported Residence, Jan. 1, 1942. Street and Number.

Hammond Street—Continued

Page.	Letter.	Full Name.	Residence, Jan. 1, 1943.	Occupation.	Supposed Age.	Reported Residence, Jan. 1, 1942. Street and Number.
	C	Bryant John	38	porter	50	here
	D	Randolph Amelia—†	38	domestic	53	"
	E	Wallace Susie C—†	38	housewife	47	"
	F	Murray Victoria—†	38	domestic	42	6 Elbert
	G	Halfpenny Myrtle—†	40	maid	48	here
	H	Brown Elizabeth S—†	40	domestic	50	"
	K	Brown Mary—†	40	"	62	"
	L	Oliver Gloria L—†	40	waitress	20	
	M	Oliver Lottie M—†	40	domestic	42	"
	N	Thomas Alice M—†	40	housewife	22	"
	O	Thomas Jerome E	40	laborer	22	
	P	Thomas Matilda S—†	40	housewife	53	"
	R	Bartley Ethelind—†	40	"	40	
	S	Lewis Thomas A	42	retired	63	
	T	Newton Tempie—†	42	domestic	49	"
	U	Heal Mary P—†	42	dressmaker	49	"
	V	*Janvier Clara—†	42	housekeeper	60	"
	W	Brewster Nellie L—†	42	"	65	
	X	Carson Alexander	42	shipper	60	
	Y	Black Lillian—†	42	domestic	52	"
	Z	Ware Anna E—†	42	at home	75	"
717						
	A	Gale Charles N	42	porter	52	
	B	Gale Mary E—†	42	housewife	49	"
	C	White Charlotte—†	60	"	22	
	D	White Leroy	60	porter	28	
	E	Gatewood Herman F	60	laborer	35	
	F	Gatewood Marion—†	60	housewife	28	"
	G	*Harper Evelyn—†	60	"	27	"
	H	Harper Thornton	60	laborer	33	
	K	Forsyth Sadie—†	60	cashier	54	
	L	Wilson Charles	60	U S A	28	
	M	Wilson Ernest	60	laborer	26	
	N	Wilson Victory—†	60	housewife	56	"
	O	Caines Eugene	60	electrician	26	"
	P	Caines Lottie—†	60	housewife	26	"
	R	*Murray Clarissa—†	60	"	38	
	S	Murray Edward M	60	laborer	34	
	T	Wade Estelle—†	60	housewife	30	"
	U	Wade George	60	laborer	32	
	V	Cidolip Virginia—†	60	housewife	48	"

Page.	Letter.	FULL NAME.	Residence, Jan. 1, 1943.	Occupation.	Supposed Age.	Reported Residence, Jan. 1, 1942. Street and Number.

Hammond Street—Continued

	W	Hall John F	60	cook	23	here
	X	Hart Vivian—†	62	domestic	29	"
	Y	Williams Lewis	62	chauffeur	54	"
	Z	Williams Winifred—†	62	housewife	49	"
718						
	A	*Murray Beresford	62	dyer	53	
	B	*Murray Viola—†	62	operator	46	"
	C	*Harper Esther—†	62	domestic	53	"
	D	James Peter	62	chipper	50	
	E	*Bryant Hilda—†	62	domestic	51	"
	F	Johnston Annie W—†	62	housewife	50	"
	G	Johnston David A	62	tailor	60	
	H	Johnston Ralph E	62	U S A	29	
	K	Johnston Mary C—†	66	housewife	53	"
	L	Royster Frank	66	tailor	48	7 Braddock pk
	M	Jackson Howard T	66	miner	42	here
	N	Jackson Margaret—†	66	housewife	32	"
	O	Joseph James	66	waiter	59	"
	P	Joseph Narcessa—†	66	housewife	49	"
	R	McDonald Gladys—†	66	stitcher	41	
	S	Moore Dorothy E—†	66	dressmaker	51	"
	T	Moore William H	66	laborer	61	"
	U	Green Anita—†	66	housewife	32	Cambridge
	V	Green Jacob	66	laborer	42	"
	W	Bennett William	66	machinist	21	here
	X	*Isles Constance—†	66	housewife	44	"
	Y	Isles John	66	cook	46	"
	Z	Griffith Archibald	66	molder	49	
719						
	A	Richardson Randolph	66	U S N	41	California
	B	Richardson Vera—†	66	domestic	42	here
	C	Midget Annie—†	66	"	59	"
	D	Munroe Cicero	66	porter	27	"
	E	Rageland Moses	66	"	69	34 Windsor
	F	Hinds Georgie—†	68	domestic	64	here
	G	Wright Fred D	70	porter	62	"
	H	Kelly Gwendolyn A—†	72	housewife	23	"
	K	McIlvaine Howard F	72	U S A	25	
	L	McIlvaine John F	72	manager	66	"
	M	Harvey Cordelia M—†	74	housewife	65	"
	N	Moxley Fentress J—†	74	"	35	

Page.	Letter.	Full Name.	Residence, Jan. 1, 1943.	Occupation.	Supposed Age.	Reported Residence, Jan. 1, 1942. Street and Number.

Hammond Street—Continued

	o	Prioleau Chester	74	U S A	25	here
	p	Roundtree Eugene S	74	laborer	38	"
	r	Roundtree Grace M—†	74	housewife	42	"
	s	Elliott Augusta—†	76	"	66	
	t	Elliott Moses	76	shipper	60	"
	u	Elliott Robert B	76	musician	35	"
	v	McIlvaine Bessie—†	78	housewife	60	"
	w	McIlvaine Helen F—†	78	clerk	30	
	x	McIlvaine John C	78	agent	33	
	y	McIlvaine Leah—†	78	housewife	25	"
720						
	a	Sewell Betsy—†	86	domestic	58	768 Col av
	b	Willis Joseph H	86	chauffeur	58	here
	c	Willis Katherine—†	86	housewife	52	"
	d	Caldwell Lillian M—†	86	"	50	"
	e	Caldwell Walter G	86	porter	58	
	f	Carney Olivia L—†	86	housewife	53	"
	g	Carney William L	86	garageman	54	"
	h	Monroe Sara—†	88	housewife	55	"
	k	Jones Lula V—†	88	domestic	59	"
	l	Kirkland Arizona—†	88	stock woman	27	"
	m	Holt Mary—†	88	operator	30	
	n	Holt Rogers	88	machinist	35	"
	o	Jackson John	88	laborer	63	
	p	Jackson Lena—†	88	housewife	55	"
	r	DeWitt Alfredo B	90	porter	41	
	s	DeWitt Phyllis L—†	90	housewife	52	"
	t	Warner Alfred H	90	retired	59	
	u	Howard Francis H	90	superintendent	53	"
	v	Howard Laura M—†	90	housewife	53	"
	w	Jackson Charlotte R—†	90	dishwasher	59	"
	x	Brooks Mary E—†	90	housewife	68	"
	y	Jackson Annie—†	90	houseworker	30	"
	z	Jackson Moxley Z	90	salesman	32	"
721						
	a	Hall Anna—†	92	housewife	73	"
	b	Hall Esther E—†	92	at home	30	
	c	Brown Ada B—†	92	houseworker	70	"
	d	*Nichol Evelyn—†	92	"	64	"
	e	Smith Daniel W	92	barber	42	
	f	Smith Sybil L—†	92	housewife	34	"

Page.	Letter.	FULL NAME.	Residence, Jan. 1, 1943.	Occupation.	Supposed Age.	Reported Residence, Jan. 1, 1942. Street and Number.

Hammond Street—Continued

	G	Santos Francisco	92	laborer	41	here
	H	*Santos Isolene A—†	92	domestic	41	"
	K	Barker Donie—†	94	laundress	55	"
	L	Famous Alfred	94	porter	46	
	M	Nelson Alfred C	94	checker	20	
	N	*Nelson Beryl E—†	94	housewife	37	"
	O	Bradley Ollie M—†	94	at home	24	646 Shawmut av
	P	Goode Alice B—†	94	"	52	646 "
	R	Oakley Joseph S	94	U S A	28	646 "
	S	Oakley Mary M—†	94	housewife	27	646 "
	T	Walker William	96	porter	65	here
	U	Freckleton Evelyn A—†	96	housewife	40	"
	V	Glover Gilbert G	96	porter	61	"
	W	Watkins Belle W—†	96	houseworker	46	"
	X	Batchelder Henry M	96	musician	48	"
	Y	Kelley Willie A—†	96	at home	39	
	Z	Beal Frank	96	kitchenman	60	"
722						
	A	Green John	96	porter	48	
	B	Sneed Violet—†	96	cook	43	
	C	Taylor Robert M	96	porter	52	
	E	Branche Mary F—†	102	at home	65	
	F	Carter Elinor M—†	102	grinder	29	
	G	Grason Harrison W	102	cook	54	
	H	Grason Maude W—†	102	housewife	52	"
	K	Jones Margaret—†	102	maid	57	
	L	Grice Anna B—†	102	at home	58	
	M	McLaurin Erma E—†	102	housewife	37	"
	N	McLaurin James E	102	cutter	41	"
	O	Anderson Emma—†	102	laundress	41	10 Fairweather
	P	Carter Annie—†	102	houseworker	58	here
	R	Consalves Blanche—†	104	stitcher	31	18 Cunard
	S	Johnson Charles S	104	retired	39	here
	T	Johnson Francis R	104	U S A	26	"
	U	Johnson Lucille B—†	104	at home	56	"
	V	Trice Mortimer W	104	riveter	39	
	W	Lewis Elsie—†	106	houseworker	31	"
	X	Lewis Ethel—†	106	"	34	
	Y	Johnson Ella—†	106	at home	61	
	Z	Johnson Thomas L	106	retired	71	

Hammond Street—Continued

A	Holloman Harriet—†	106	stitcher	46	here
B	Nelson Avery L	106	longshoreman	37	"
C	Brown Dora—†	108	domestic	48	"
D	Wells Certhus	108	porter	50	
E	Belton Mary—†	108	seamstress	38	"
F	Overton Cloritia—†	108	domestic	50	41 Dale

Shawmut Avenue

N	Johnson Eleanor B—†	665	housewife	51	here
O	Lance Christopher	665	retired	78	"
P	Hanson Charles	665	laborer	64	"
R	Hanson Georgia—†	665	housewife	45	"
S	Logan George	665	janitor	59	
T	Fury Edna—†	665	clerk	47	
U	Fury Ernest	665	mechanic	25	"
V	Golden Albert	667	porter	40	1 Clarmont pk
W	Collins Alice C—†	667	housewife	47	Revere
X	Collins Harry P	667	cook	47	"
Y	Reed Margaret—†	667	at home	65	Cambridge
Z	Rollie Viola—†	667	houseworker	40	"
	724				
A	Elliott Almena—†	667	stitcher	33	605 Shawmut av
B	Hines John	667	laborer	21	S Carolina
C	Feeney Violet—†	667	houseworker	47	82 E Lenox
D	Holloway Gladys M—†	667	matron	40	Randolph
E	McKarney William	667	checker	51	"
G	Robbins Charles	669	laborer	53	here
H	Reed George	669	machinist	72	"
K	Reed Rachel—†	669	waitress	24	"
L	Joseph Alma B—†	669	stitcher	31	25 Arnold
M	Layne Daisy—†	669	dressmaker	49	796 Tremont
N	Marshall Everton	669	waiter	34	796 "
O	Miller May D—†	669	attendant	60	667 Shawmut av
P	Smith Frances—†	669	housewife	30	New York
R	Smith Kenneth	669	cook	35	"
S	Armstrong Lillian F—†	669	stitcher	25	29 Wellington
T	Granville Walter L	669	waiter	45	New Bedford
U	Westley Abigail A—†	669	operator	20	29 Wellington

Page.	Letter.	FULL NAME.	Residence, Jan. 1, 1943.	Occupation.	Supposed Age.	Reported Residence, Jan. 1, 1942. Street and Number.

Shawmut Avenue—Continued

	W	Davenport Lillian—†	671	at home	69	here
	Y	Allen Marietta—†	671	laundress	50	"
	Z	Phillips Lawrence	671	porter	50	"
725						
	A	Cooper Elizabeth—†	671	seamstress	22	"
	B	Liggins Bessie—†	671	houseworker	45	"
	C	Washington Archie	671	laborer	46	"
	E	White Fannie—†	673	presser	39	7 Rutland
	K	Bacote Daisy—†	679	clerk	54	here
	L	Bacote Harriett—†	679	at home	95	"
	M	Hall Viola—†	679	houseworker	31	"
	N	Williams Franklin B	679	porter	34	
	O	Williams Juanita—†	679	pharmacist	33	"
	P	Williams Mable B—†	679	at home	51	
	R	Makel Florence V—†	679	housewife	68	"
	S	Makel Harold D	679	laborer	29	
	T	Makel Luther M	679	retired	80	
	U	Guscott Ruby—†	679	seamstress	42	"
	V	Bunch Julia—†	681	housekeeper	56	"
	W	Foster Lennie—†	681	cook	36	"
	X	Davis Mary E—†	681	housewife	63	"
	Y	Davis Walter A	681	janitor	65	
	Z	Waddell Bessie J—†	681	at home	70	
726						
	A	Fletcher Florence R—†	683	housewife	77	"
	B	Fletcher James H	683	retired	79	
	C	Jordan Minnie L—†	683	at home	64	
	D	Kenney David D	683	retired	73	
	G	Collinder Sarah A—†	683	at home	71	"
	E	DeBoise Charles J	683	U S A	28	379A Warren
	F	DeBoise Gertrude E—†	683	maid	31	here
	H	Myers Aubrey H	683	operator	33	"
	K	Myers Hortense M—†	683	housewife	29	"
	L	Austin Everett	685	laborer	23	"
	M	Austin Samuel	685	porter	42	New York
	N	Nicholson Frances—†	685	laundress	36	here
	O	Nicholson Guy	685	barber	46	"
	P	Cleland Beatrice—†	685	stenographer	24	"
	R	Cleland John M	685	porter	58	"
	S	Cleland Marie—†	685	housewife	50	"
	T	Cleland Thomas A	685	student	20	
	U	Brown Isabelle—†	685	at home	42	

Page.	Letter.	Full Name.	Residence, Jan. 1, 1943.	Occupation.	Supposed Age.	Reported Residence, Jan. 1, 1942. Street and Number.
		Shawmut Avenue—Continued				
	V	Leoney Augustus	685	laborer	57	here
	W	Leoney Charles	685	attendant	20	"
	X	Leoney Susie—†	685	houseworker	33	"
	Y	Davenport Suleta—†	687	operator	28	726½ Shawmut av
	Z	Mathis Alma—†	687	houseworker	58	726½ "
727						
	A	Smith Louise—†	687	operator	20	726½ "
	B	Sousa Celia M—†	687	housewife	28	Canton
	C	Sousa Vernon	687	welder	31	"
	D	Clarke Mary S—†	687	dressmaker	42	here
	E	Thomas Albert	687	laborer	50	"
	F	Thomas Virginia—†	687	housewife	36	"
	G	Dewey Helen A—†	689	student	48	
	H	Dewey Miles Z	689	retired	57	
	K	Dewey William H	689	porter	62	"
	L	Martin Audrey—†	689	dressmaker	22	New York
	M	Pitter John B	689	laborer	48	here
	N	Pitter Marie E—†	689	housewife	43	"
	O	Johnson Lucinda—†	689	"	52	"
	P	Johnson William G	689	foundryman	62	"
	R	Mickey Johnsie—†	689	stenographer	27	"
	S	*Walcott Eloise—†	689	housewife	37	"
	T	*Walcott Robert	689	chauffeur	38	"
	U	Bernard Albemarle	691	U S A	26	
	V	Pinckney Inez B—†	691	at home	26	"
	W	Fennell Gladys—†	691	housewife	25	716 Shawmut av
	X	Fennell John	691	steelworker	37	716 "
	Y	Fennell William	691	laborer	28	716 "
	Z	Benders Esther B—†	691	housewife	42	here
728						
	A	Benders Melvin S	691	laborer	20	
	B	Benders William H	691	"	42	
	D	Hasgrow Rose—†	693	housekeeper	36	"
	E	Robinson Benjamin	693	laborer	55	"
	F	Robinson Viola—†	693	houseworker	44	"
	G	Hixon Lillian C—†	693	housewife	43	"
	H	Hixon William H	693	porter	46	
		Sterling Street				
	M	Howard Charles F	53A	welder	54	667 Shawmut av
	N	Howard Georgianna E—†	53A	housewife	50	667 "

Page.	Letter.	Full Name.	Residence, Jan. 1, 1943.	Occupation.	Supposed Age.	Reported Residence, Jan. 1, 1942. Street and Number.

Sterling Street—Continued

Page.	Letter.	Full Name.	Residence, Jan. 1, 1943.	Occupation.	Supposed Age.	Reported Residence, Jan. 1, 1942. Street and Number.
	O	Pruett Martha S—†	53A	housewife	34	here
	P	*McIntyre Arthur	55	laborer	65	38 Sterling
	R	Busquine Caroline—†	55	stitcher	56	here
	S	Snipes Lillian F—†	55	domestic	32	"
	T	Casminski Ella—†	55	"	49	"
	U	Dupree Esther F—†	61	housewife	62	"
	V	Dupree Frank R	61	realtor	64	
	W	Jones Frederica—†	61	clerk	41	
	X	Isham Lena—†	61	stitcher	50	
	Y	Randolph James R	63	laborer	40	
	Z	Randolph Winifred—†	63	typist	36	
729						
	A	*Garro Bertha—†	63	housewife	51	62 Ruggles
	B	*Garro John A	63	laborer	53	62 "
	C	Britto Cornelius	63	"	32	11 Paul
	D	Britto Sylvia—†	63	housewife	24	11 "
	H	Morris Charles H	67	retired	72	here
	K	Morris Rose L—†	67	housewife	68	"
	L	Cleveland Esther M—†	67	laundress	25	"
	M	Smith Izetta—†	67	housewife	67	"
	O	Eppinger Ellen H—†	69	domestic	70	"
	P	Wedge Frank	69	laborer	70	
	R	Murphy Marie—†	69	laundress	26	"
	T	Manning Richard	71	laborer	49	
	S	Woolson Emma—†	71	laundress	25	"
	U	Woolson Harry	71	laborer	28	"
	V	Kelson Manda—†	71	housekeeper	31	Pennsylvania
	W	Solomon Eileen—†	71	cook	48	here
	X	Sparks Clarence W	71	laborer	36	"
	Y	Sparks Jeanette M—†	71	housewife	35	"
	Z	Jackson Lucius M	73	laborer	58	
730						
	A	Jackson William B	73	machinist	45	"
	B	Sayles William	73	porter	49	
	C	Smith Thomas S	73	cook	48	
	D	Jones Helen—†	75	housewife	42	"
	E	Jones William	75	janitor	57	
	F	Allen Jasper R	75	laborer	66	
	G	Allen Mary P—†	75	housewife	58	"
	H	Terry Mary—†	75	operator	41	105 Sterling
	K	Terry Matthew	75	laborer	62	105 "

Page.	Letter.	Full Name.	Residence, Jan. 1, 1943.	Occupation.	Supposed Age.	Reported Residence, Jan. 1, 1942. Street and Number.

Sterling Street—Continued

	M	Thornton Elizabeth—†	77	housewife	30	40 Sterling
	N	Thornton Thomas	77	laborer	32	40 "
	O	Betts Edna L—†	77	housewife	37	40 "
	P	Betts William W	77	machinist	38	40 "
	R	Washington Adeline B—†	79	nurse	38	here
	S	Little Mozella—†	79	domestic	39	"
	T	Drysdale Gertrude P—†	79	housekeeper	62	"
	U	Sanders Joseph P	79	laborer	53	"
	V	Williams Florence—†	81	cook	59	27 Hopeburn av
	W	Washington Pauline—†	81	housewife	25	here
	Y	Washington Warren	81	presser	33	"
	X	*Groce Ethel—†	81	"	42	"
	Z	Luacaw Edward J	81	machinist	44	"
731						
	A	Luacaw Nancy—†	81	housewife	43	"
	C	Middleton James	83	janitor	35	73 Williams
	D	Middleton Marie—†	83	waitress	32	73 "
	F	Johnson Annie M—†	85	housekeeper	74	here
	G	Slappy Lillian V—†	85	stitcher	51	"
	H	Dunston Henrietta—†	85	housekeeper	60	"
	K	Bayne Leonard N	87	laborer	53	"
	L	Bayne Martha—†	87	housewife	31	"
	M	Bright Louise—†	87	housekeeper	58	"
	N	*Hayes Gertrude—†	87	"	61	"
	O	Mitchell Mattie—†	89	"	60	"
	P	Coles Gertrude—†	89	laundress	27	703 Shawmut av
	R	Thomas Florence—†	89	"	44	here
	S	Trimble Katherine—†	89	housewife	24	"
	T	*Perry Robert	89A	laborer	47	"
	V	Lewis Beatrice—†	101	housewife	26	68 Ruggles
	W	Lewis George	101	machinist	46	68 "
	X	Quarles Anna—†	101	housekeeper	77	here
	Y	Wilson Beatrice—†	101	"	37	"
	Z	Foster Alice—†	101	stitcher	59	"
732						
	A	Foster Charles	101	porter	64	
	B	Foster George	101	cook	21	
	C	Mayfield Lawrence	101	U S A	28	
	D	Mayfield William	101	cook	31	
	E	Ramos Lillian—†	101	stitcher	33	"
	F	Littles Lola M—†	103	clerk	22	Brookline

Page.	Letter.	FULL NAME.	Residence, Jan. 1, 1943.	Occupation.	Supposed Age.	Reported Residence, Jan. 1, 1942. Street and Number.

Sterling Street—Continued

	G	Still Gertrude—†	103	housewife	50	here
	H	Still Rita L—†	103	machinist	26	"
	K	Beckette John	103	porter	42	"
	L	Beckette Laura—†	103	clerk	42	
	M	King Israel	103	laborer	53	
	N	King Mercedes—†	103	clerk	33	
	O	Merrill Bessie—†	105	housewife	39	"
	P	Huggins Alice J—†	105	"	27	
	R	Huggins Arthur L	105	laborer	29	
	S	Hinds R Sylvester	105	cook	33	
	T	Hinds Thelma J—†	105	housewife	31	"
	U	Burrill Alice—†	107	"	26	
	V	Burrill Rollins	107	shoeworker	55	"
	W	Burrill Roy	107	fireman	30	
	X	Green Benjamin	107	seaman	47	
	Y	Green Callie—†	107	housewife	42	"
	Z	Jennings William P	107	shoeworker	32	45 Symphony rd
733						
	A	Bassett Martha—†	107	housewife	32	here
	B	Bassett Theodore	107	welder	38	"
	C	Collins Alfred	109	"	34	"
	D	Collins Isabelita—†	109	housewife	35	"
	E	Corbin Lillian—†	109	housekeeper	24	"
	F	Davis Everett	109	porter	62	"
	1F	Davis Gertrude—†	109	housewife	55	"
	G	Harper Sarah—†	109	laundress	37	"
	H	Chambers Chauncey W	109	meat packer	28	38 Warwick
	K	Singleterry Nora—†	109	domestic	34	here
	L	Benjamin Albert L	109	laborer	27	"
	M	Benjamin Frederick R	109	U S A	25	"
	N	Benjamin Lucy—†	109	housewife	52	"
	O	Miles Barbara—†	109	housekeeper	20	"
	P	Miles James	109	welder	46	"
	R	Roberts Alice—†	109	housewife	31	"
	S	Roberts Frank	109	laborer	41	
	T	White Millicent—†	109	housewife	47	"
	U	White Reginald	109	machinist	59	"
	V	Grant Carol	109	housewife	27	"
	W	Grant William, jr	109	janitor	27	

Page.	Letter.	Full Name.	Residence, Jan. 1, 1943.	Occupation.	Supposed Age.	Reported Residence, Jan. 1, 1942. Street and Number.

Sterling Street—Continued

	x	Walker Bernice—†	109	maid	35	here
	y	Clark Henry M	109	watchman	53	"
	z	Clark Susan—†	109	housewife	53	"
734						
	A	Wells Joseph J	109	clergyman	41	"
	B	Wells Lena E—†	109	housewife	54	"
	C	McIver Eva E—†	109	"	38	
	D	McIver James G	109	clerk	45	
	E	Kirton Stanley D	109	student	21	
	F	Kirton St Clair	109	tailor	47	
	G	Kirton Willie B—†	109	dressmaker	37	"
	H	Allen Grace—†	109	housewife	22	23 Walpole
	K	Allen John	109	welder	24	23 "
	L	Jones Arlette—†	109	entertainer	25	407 Col av
	M	Jones Richard	109	laborer	29	407 "
	N	Snypes Marguerite—†	109	housekeeper	30	here
	O	Davis Charles	109	barber	50	"
	P	Davis Emma—†	109	housewife	49	"
	R	Lee Marie—†	109	"	22	
	S	Ingliss Annie—†	109	"	60	
	T	Ingliss Lynch	109	laborer	61	
	U	Laing Emma—†	109	housekeeper	63	"
	V	Bisphan Milton	109	cook	40	"
	W	Damouras Grace—†	109	housewife	45	11 Greenwich
	X	Damouras Peter	109	stripper	51	11 "
	Y	Steele Charles	109	chauffeur	32	34 Highland
	Z	Steele Louise—†	109	clerk	31	34 "
735						
	A	Frye Alma—†	109	housewife	31	12 Elbert
	B	Frye Arthur	109	laborer	32	12 "
	C	Scott Ralph H	133	chauffeur	52	here
	E	Wills Alice—†	133	housewife	29	"
	F	Slayman Henrietta—†	133	"	60	"
	G	*Kennealy Charles	133	janitor	54	
	H	McPherson Clement	133	porter	51	
	K	Snow Elaine—†	133	operator	25	
	L	Parker Blanche—†	133	cook	55	
	M	Parker Robert	133	"	25	
	N	Johnson Emerson	133	machinist	32	"

Page.	Letter.	Full Name.	Residence, Jan. 1, 1943.	Occupation.	Supposed Age.	Reported Residence, Jan. 1, 1942. Street and Number.

Sterling Street—Continued

Page.	Letter.	Full Name.	Residence, Jan. 1, 1943.	Occupation.	Supposed Age.	Reported Residence, Jan. 1, 1942. Street and Number.
	O	Johnson Vivian A—†	133	housewife	31	here
	P	Blair Lillie B—†	135	"	65	"
	R	Blair Ralph C	135	salesman	37	"

Sussex Street

Page.	Letter.	Full Name.	Residence, Jan. 1, 1943.	Occupation.	Supposed Age.	Reported Residence, Jan. 1, 1942. Street and Number.
	S	Fields Copeland W	1	janitor	33	here
	T	Fields Elizabeth—†	1	domestic	33	"
	U	Fields John	1	cook	64	"
	V	Chapman Parnell—†	3	operator	48	"
	W	Chapman William A	3	janitor	72	
	X	Goins Rosetta—†	3	domestic	64	"
	Y	Goldstein Esther—†	4	housewife	35	"
	Z	Goldstein Samuel	4	proprietor	38	"
736						
	A	Davis Edward D	4	"	47	
	B	Davis Margaret R—†	4	tailor	44	
	C	Gilbert Ada E—†	5	domestic	45	"
	D	Gilbert Lavinia—†	5	housekeeper	43	"
	E	Heggie Phillip	5	mechanic	58	"
	F	Jackson Maurice	6	laborer	47	
	G	Woods, James	6	baker	44	
	H	Stubbs Julian R	7	clerk	59	
	K	Stubbs Marion B—†	7	housewife	56	"
	L	Brandom Junius	8	houseman	45	"
	M	Smith Nellie—†	8	housewife	62	"
	N	Dias Annie L—†	9	cook	54	"
	O	Williams Alcora—†	9	dressmaker	50	"
	P	Estes Nannie—†	10	housewife	70	"
	R	*Saunders Joseph	10	laborer	51	
	S	Varco James W	11	"	49	
	U	Whaley Beatrice—†	14	housewife	57	"
	V	Whaley James T	14	retired	82	"
	W	Ransom Ralph	16	musician	36	"
	X	Ransom Louis	18	clerk	32	
	Y	Ransom Marvis—†	18	housewife	31	"
737						
	A	Crawford Lawrence	24	laborer	47	
	B	Elliott Florence—†	24	housewife	61	"
	C	Ringels Raymond	24	electrician	43	"
	D	Walters Leroy	24	dishwasher	48	Vermont

Page.	Letter.	FULL NAME.	Residence, Jan. 1, 1943.	Occupation.	Supposed Age.	Reported Residence, Jan. 1, 1942. Street and Number.

Sussex Street—Continued

	E	McClean Geneva—†	26	matron	45	here
	F	Cox Reginald	28	U S A	34	"
	G	Jones Arthur	28	laborer	52	"
	H	Jones Arthur H, jr	28	U S A	22	
	K	Jones Emma L—†	28	housewife	57	"
	L	Jones Gertrude—†	28	clerk	26	
	M	Addition Mary—†	30	domestic	43	"
	N	McMullen Julia—†	30	housewife	45	"
	O	McMullen Julius	30	U S A	30	
	P	Cunningham Annie—†	32	housewife	55	"
	R	Cunningham Eleanor—†	32	cook	40	
	S	French George	32	U S A	20	
	T	French Mary—†	32	housewife	39	"
	U	Williams Gertha—†	32	waitress	23	
	V	Hoyte Hiram	34	cabinetmaker	60	"
	W	Worrell Lester	34	engineer	56	
	X	Powell Eunice—†	36	stenographer	21	"
	Y	Powell Imogene—†	36	beautician	41	"
	Z	Alison Edna H—†	38	domestic	58	58 Windsor
738						
	A	Parish George J	38	janitor	50	here

Warwick Street

	C	Slade Anne—†	1	housewife	37	here
	E	Allston Bristol	3	welder	27	"
	F	Allston Catherine—†	3	housewife	47	"
	G	Hodsdon James R	3	operator	41	"
	H	Hodsdon Mary J—†	3	clerk	38	
	K	*Burke Cleveland	3	cook	51	
	L	*Burke Iona—†	3	housewife	43	"
	M	Patterson Carl	5	chauffeur	49	24 Hammond
	N	Patterson Doris I—†	5	housewife	34	24 "
	O	Arnold Sarah—†	5	hairdresser	56	here
	P	Hunter Cecelia—†	5	housewife	31	"
	R	Hunter George	5	bartender	31	"
	S	Williams Samuel	5	welder	21	29 Rose
	T	Williams Wilhelmina—†	5	housewife	21	794 Shawmut av
	U	Carter Irene—†	7	domestic	30	here
	V	Carter Oscar	7	operator	35	"
	W	Shelton Philip	7	chauffeur	43	"

Page.	Letter.	Full Name.	Residence, Jan. 1, 1943.	Occupation.	Supposed Age.	Reported Residence, Jan. 1, 1942. Street and Number.

Warwick Street—Continued

	X	Shelton Phyllis—†	7	housewife	43	here
	Y	McReynolds Atlee—†	7	waitress	36	"
	Z	Rosser Carrie—†	7	housewife	48	"
739						
	A	Rosser James T	7	dentist	48	"
	B	Banks Alice—†	9	housewife	65	"
	C	Banks Elsie A—†	9	stenographer	38	"
	D	Castile Ethel—†	9	domestic	38	"
	E	Garnett Alice—†	9	"	37	
	F	Gerald Una—†	9	seamstress	56	"
	G	*Howard Sarah—†	9	housewife	30	"
	H	Howard William	9	welder	28	
	K	Frye Bessie—†	14	operator	40	"
	L	Hathaway Julia—†	14	housewife	57	"
	M	Nelson Lulu—†	14	housekeeper	42	"
	N	Byrd Lillian A—†	15	domestic	56	"
	O	Mosley Mary—†	15	waitress	40	
	P	Mosley Westerly	15	welder	40	
	R	Winter Willard	15	porter	22	"
	S	Gardner James L	16	"	51	4 Wellington
	T	Walters William	16	"	47	here
	U	Bannon Edith P—†	17	housewife	39	"
	V	Bannon William D	17	baggageman	39	"
	W	Jones Albion S	17	operator	48	
	X	Lane Allen S	17	porter	46	
	Z	Hankinson Myrtis L—†	19	housewife	61	"
740						
	A	Hankinson Thomas B	19	retired	73	
	B	Pleasant Florence—†	20	housewife	71	"
	C	Kettler Pansy—†	20	factoryhand	21	"
	D	Satchell Marion H—†	20	seamstress	50	"
	E	Stephens Margaret P—†	20	waitress	42	46 Dale
	F	Valentine Doris—†	20	typist	20	46 "
	G	Campbell Arthur W	21	welder	23	here
	H	Campbell Hazel N—†	21	clerk	29	"
	K	Page Jennie—†	21	housewife	51	"
	L	Page William R	21	laborer	62	
	M	Anderson Mildred—†	23	domestic	26	"
	N	Graves John	23	repairman	62	"
	O	Graves May—†	23	housewife	60	"
	P	Malloroy Eugene	23	fireman	50	

Page.	Letter.	Full Name.	Residence, Jan. 1, 1943.	Occupation.	Supposed Age.	Reported Residence, Jan. 1, 1942. Street and Number.

Warwick Street—Continued

	R	Malloroy Lula—†	23	housewife	45	here
	S	Malloroy Junius	23	fireman	53	"
	T	Malloroy Mabel—†	23	housewife	40	"
	U	Bryan Gertrude—†	24	housekeeper	24	2741 Wash'n
	V	Bryan Hazel—†	24	clerk	21	2741 "
	W	Bryan Mildred—†	24	housewife	40	2741 "
	X	Bryan William	24	U S A	26	2741 "
	Y	Mills Henry	24	chauffeur	38	2741 "
	Z	Murray Beatrice—†	24	housewife	40	here
741						
	A	Hendrickson Hazel—†	24	"	35	
	B	Hendrickson Joel	24	porter	35	
	C	Stewart Malinda C—†	25	housewife	59	"
	D	Elliott Georgia A—†	25	domestic	54	"
	F	Hollowell Isabella—†	26	housekeeper	66	"
	G	Noble Laura—†	26	domestic	60	"
	H	Gay Lillian—†	26	housekeeper	54	11 Marble
	K	Pope Lincoln G	26	steward	54	26 Greenwich
	L	Jones Daisy—†	27	housewife	33	11 Marble
	M	Jones Robert H	27	porter	43	11 "
	N	Mead Hattie—†	27	housekeeper	66	119 Kendall
	O	Brown Henry F	27	laundryworker	45	22 Dilworth
	P	Lattimore Alfonzo S	28	attendant	63	here
	R	Spriggs Georgie L—†	28	housekeeper	79	"
	S	Taylor Silas F	28	pharmacist	57	"
	T	Branch Charles	29	plumber	50	
	U	Branch Zuleka—†	29	domestic	49	"
	V	Hughes Janet—†	29	"	45	
	W	Lane Herbert	29	clerk	43	
	X	Walters King A	30	butler	63	
	Y	Walters Mary E—†	30	housewife	57	"
	Z	Fraction Dorothy—†	30	clerk	31	
742						
	A	Herrold Arthur B	30	"	56	
	C	Roberts Lillian—†	31	at home	72	"
	B	Harris Mabel—†	31	domestic	40	10 Windsor
	E	Miller Emma J—†	32	housekeeper	63	here
	F	Tattoon Fannie M—†	32	"	59	"
	G	Senna Anthony J	32	U S A	24	"
	H	*Senna Joaquim J	32	cook	49	
	K	Russell Emma—†	33	housewife	75	"

Page.	Letter.	Full Name.	Residence, Jan. 1, 1943.	Occupation.	Supposed Age.	Reported Residence, Jan. 1, 1942. Street and Number.

Warwick Street—Continued

	L	Walker Charlotte—†	33	at home	47	here
	M	Williams Edna C—†	33	operator	43	"
	N	Williams Thelma F—†	33	nurse	27	"
	O	Stewart Minnie—†	34	housewife	64	"
	P	Stewart William A	34	porter	50	
	R	Mentor Anne—†	35	operator	31	"
	S	Mentor John	35	laborer	35	
	T	Henry Anne—†	35	housewife	30	"
	U	Henry James	35	porter	36	
	V	Melton Mary—†	35	operator	35	"
	W	Melton Stephen	35	domestic	37	"
	X	Moore Mary E—†	36	housewife	47	"
	Y	Edwards Florence—†	37	domestic	27	10 Windsor
	Z	Fowler Martha—†	37	at home	59	here
743						
	A	Reilly Priscilla—†	37	seamstress	56	"
	B	Franks Louis	37	chauffeur	59	"
	C	Collins James	38	clerk	26	"
	D	Jones Woodward	38	laborer	21	36 Hammond
	E	Lake Edmund C	38	porter	46	here
	F	Lake Rhoda M—†	38	housewife	40	"
	G	Skipper Rufus	38	laborer	21	36 Hammond
	H	Childs Barbara L—†	39	student	21	here
	K	Childs Nettie E—†	39	housewife	55	"
	L	Childs Oscar	39	waiter	64	"
	M	Sanders Ida E—†	39	housewife	43	Pennsylvania
	N	Sanders William K	39	clerk	45	"
	O	Stafford Sophie—†	39	domestic	35	here
	P	Smith Nannie—†	40	housekeeper	65	"
	R	Boyd Mabel—†	40	stitcher	21	"
	S	Hicks Harry	40	laborer	55	
	T	Brown Effie—†	41	housewife	37	"
	U	Brown Frederick	41	houseman	38	"
	V	Brown Helen—†	41	housewife	58	"
	W	Brown John H	41	pedler	60	
	X	Hudson Charles	41	laborer	35	
	Y	Landrum Elijah	41	porter	48	
	Z	Jones Harriet—†	42	at home	50	
744						
	A	VanDerzee Agnes—†	42	teacher	49	"
	B	Hill Bennett	43	machinist	47	"

Page.	Letter.	Full Name.	Residence, Jan. 1, 1943.	Occupation.	Supposed Age.	Reported Residence, Jan. 1, 1942. Street and Number.

Warwick Street—Continued

Page.	Letter.	Full Name.	Residence, Jan. 1, 1943.	Occupation.	Supposed Age.	Reported Residence, Jan. 1, 1942. Street and Number.
	C	Hill Ednora—†	43	housewife	44	here
	E	Budd James H	43	chauffeur	63	"
	F	Budd Viola—†	43	domestic	55	"
	G	Reed Mary—†	43	"	34	940 Tremont
	H	Greenidge Joseph N	44	carpenter	61	here
	K	Greenidge Vivian E—†	44	domestic	43	"
	L	*Moore Lawrence	45	cook	53	"
	M	Gill Isabella—†	45	housewife	45	"
	N	Wallace Jennie B—†	45	nurse	24	
	O	Peters Gladys—†	45	entertainer	44	"
	P	Williams Isabella—†	46	housewife	72	"
	R	Foster George	47	laborer	30	
	S	Foster Phyllis—†	47	housewife	59	"
	T	Carr Margaret—†	47	domestic	27	Virginia
	U	Carr Theodore	47	U S C G	29	Maine
	V	Hunter Helen—†	47	housewife	23	here
	W	Hunter William	47	operator	27	"
	X	Williams Jennie—†	48	housewife	67	"
	Y	Williams Vivian C	48	laborer	46	
	Z	Shaw Louise—†	48	housewife	55	"
745						
	A	Shaw William	48	laborer	64	
	B	Collins Evelyn M—†	49	domestic	47	"
	C	Read Alice—†	49	at home	78	
	D	Roberts Alice—†	49	typist	25	
	E	Smith Rose—†	49	domestic	70	"
	F	Farley Edgar	51	laborer	51	
	G	Farley Mary—†	51	housewife	37	"
	H	Mitchell Cordelia—†	51	operator	31	34 Williams
	K	Edmondson George W	51	waiter	66	here
	L	Lewis Florence L—†	53	at home	55	"
	M	Ware Barbara—†	53	housewife	28	Wash'n D C
	N	Ware Preston	53	laborer	32	"
	O	Pompeli Laura—†	53	nurse	25	here
	P	Pompeli Lawrence	53	U S A	25	"
	R	Minor James A	53	laborer	65	"
	S	Minor Nettie R—†	53	housewife	59	"
	T	Irish Rebecca J—†	55	at home	71	"
	U	Schuyler Mary E—†	55	housewife	65	43 Warwick
	V	Johnson Susan—†	55	matron	40	here
	W	Christiani Vincenzo	59	retired	58	"

Page.	Letter.	Full Name.	Residence, Jan. 1, 1943.	Occupation.	Supposed Age.	Reported Residence, Jan. 1, 1942. Street and Number.

Warwick Street—Continued

Page.	Letter.	Full Name.	Residence, Jan. 1, 1943.	Occupation.	Supposed Age.	Reported Residence, Jan. 1, 1942. Street and Number.
	X	Pruitt Jacob	59	laborer	40	here
	Y	Pruitt Susie—†	59	housewife	28	"
	Z	Christiani Anna—†	59	"	54	"
746						
	A	Christiani Salvatore	59	welder	20	
	B	Voss Ella—†	64	housekeeper	45	"
	C	Allen Quizella C—†	64	housewife	32	"
	D	Williams Viola—†	64	"	27	"
	E	Alexander Helen—†	66	"	29	New York
	F	Alexander Henry	66	mechanic	35	"
	G	Allen Charles	66	laborer	53	122 Sterling
	H	Allen Irene—†	66	housewife	45	122 "
	K	Lawrence Evelyn—†	66	"	35	here
	L	Lindsay Florence—†	68	dressmaker	55	"
	M	Woodson Carrie—†	68	housewife	58	"
	N	Woodson Edward	68	laborer	32	
	O	Woodson Eunice—†	68	housewife	28	"
	P	Reid John	69	millhand	34	53 Camden
	R	Reid Loretta—†	69	housewife	22	53 "
	S	Belden Lillian—†	69	"	31	here
	T	Roe Elizabeth—†	69	housekeeper	63	"
	U	Rollins Pauline—†	69	housewife	42	"
	V	Berryman Jennie—†	69	"	50	
	W	Bell Una—†	69	"	38	"
	X	Morgan Willa C—†	69	laundress	34	1051 Tremont
	Y	Grimes Lottie—†	69	housekeeper	62	here
	Z	Brown Gladys—†	69	housewife	43	"
747						
	A	Grace Rose—†	69		25	
	B	Hawksworth Eugenia—†	69	"	28	
	C	Waithe Ellen L—†	69	"	52	
	D	*Waithe George H	69	shoeworker	56	"
	E	Lehtonen John	69	painter	47	
	F	*Alves Caesar	69	laborer	42	
	G	Johnson Lillian—†	69	housewife	43	"
	H	Johnson Walter K	69	U S A	22	
	K	Langford Alma—†	69	housewife	27	"
	L	Langford Joseph	69	U S A	39	"
	M	Lockett Helen A—†	69	housewife	40	73 Warwick
	N	Lockett John M	69	laborer	42	73 "
	O	Grant Mary—†	69	housekeeper	27	here

Page.	Letter.	Full Name.	Residence, Jan. 1, 1943.	Occupation.	Supposed Age.	Reported Residence, Jan. 1, 1942. Street and Number.

Warwick Street—Continued

	P	Loatman Cora J—†	70	housewife	58	here
	R	Loatman John	70	clergyman	57	"
	S	Gabourel Sarah—†	70	housewife	67	"
	T	Woods Sylvester	70	cook	48	
	U	Jones David	71	painter	42	
	V	Jones Helen—†	71	housewife	35	"
	W	Tyler Bertha E—†	71	"	45	Medford
	X	Tyler Walter J	71	porter	47	"
	Y	Wright Catherine—†	71	housewife	27	"
	Z	Wentworth Arthur A	71	porter	53	here
748						
	A	Wentworth Margaret—†	71	housewife	53	"
	B	Wentworth Thelma—†	71	houseworker	22	"
	C	Anderson Essie—†	71	housekeeper	56	"
	D	Noble Jacob	71	cook	57	"
	E	Young Frederick	73	laborer	31	
	F	Young Louise—†	73	housewife	24	"
	G	Anderson Amanda—†	73	"	42	
	H	Anderson Joseph	73	laborer	43	
	K	Hayes James	73	porter	37	
	L	Jackson Eleanor—†	73	housewife	33	"
	N	Gainey Elizabeth—†	73	clerk	20	
	O	Gainey Mabel—†	73	cook	42	
	P	Kennedy Etta M—†	73	housewife	23	"
	R	Kennedy Eugene	73	U S A	31	
	S	Valentine Rose—†	73	housewife	73	"
	T	Valentine William P	73	laborer	49	"
	U	Morrison Arthur	73	"	56	61 Lenox
	V	Morrison Jennie—†	73	housewife	44	61 "

Westminster Street

	X	Fisher Lorreta M—†	11	housewife	74	here
	Y	Fisher William A	11	laborer	80	"
	Z	Seabrooks Dolores F—†	11	clerk	21	"
749						
	A	Seabrooks Mabel L—†	11	domestic	41	"
	B	*Neil Grace E—†	11	housewife	43	"
	C	*Neil Joseph W	11	laborer	48	
	D	*Small Maude V—†	11	housewife	50	"
	E	*Small Sydney I	11	cook	59	

Page.	Letter.	Full Name.	Residence, Jan. 1, 1943.	Occupation.	Supposed Age.	Reported Residence, Jan. 1, 1942. Street and Number.

Westminster Street—Continued

Page.	Letter.	Full Name.	Residence, Jan. 1, 1943.	Occupation.	Supposed Age.	Reported Residence, Jan. 1, 1942. Street and Number.
	F	Hawkins Henrietta M—†	11	housewife	47	58 Windsor
	G	Hawkins Mingo H	11	janitor	49	58 "
	H	Hayes Frances—†	11	clerk	35	here
	K	Ponton Edward	11	waiter	78	"
	L	Syms Edward P	11	"	27	"
	M	Syms George B	11	mechanic	30	N Carolina
	N	Syms Thelma W—†	11	housewife	27	here
	O	Walker Horace	11	cook	20	"
	P	Joseph Raymond P	11	U S A	32	"
	R	Onley Irene E—†	11	domestic	33	"
	S	Chowell Mildred B—†	12	housewife	68	16 Westminster
	T	Lewis Mabel—†	12	domestic	47	16 "
	U	Green Lucy—†	12	housewife	56	here
	V	Flint Comphy C—†	12	"	62	"
	W	Jeffress Margaret—†	12	waitress	41	"
	X	Brown Edna—†	12	domestic	47	"
	Y	Morris Florence—†	12	housewife	68	"
	Z	Young Catherine—†	12	"	28	
750						
	A	Young Walter	12	chauffeur	30	"
	B	Brown Persis L—†	12	housewife	30	1016 Tremont
	C	Brown Robert G	12	porter	47	1016 "
	D	Dickinson Phyllis L—†	12	clerk	24	1016 "
	F	Harris James E	12	mechanic	35	here
	G	Harris Lula M—†	12	housewife	35	"
	H	Willis James M	14	mechanic	44	"
	K	Willis Louise M—†	14	housewife	70	"
	L	Hall Evelyn—†	14	"	29	"
	M	Smart Marian E—†	14	seamstress	56	65 Ruggles
	N	Barrett Samuel S	16	pedler	59	here
	O	Guardini Louise—†	16	operator	48	Mansfield
	P*	Webb Henry	16	porter	53	here
	R*	Webb Marie A—†	16	housewife	53	"
	T	Thoms Florence H—†	17	"	70	15 Hammond
	U	Armstrong Henry	17	laborer	65	here
	V	Brown Mary J—†	17	housewife	58	"
	W	McLaughlin Marie—†	17	domestic	54	"
	X	Williams Mamie F—†	17	"	53	
	Y	Parks Lillian—†	18	housewife	65	"
	Z	Clark Hilda—†	18	"	53	

Page.	Letter.	Full Name.	Residence, Jan. 1, 1943.	Occupation.	Supposed Age.	Reported Residence, Jan. 1, 1942. Street and Number.
751		**Westminster Street**—Continued				
	A	*Edmonds Italene I—†	18	housewife	31	192 Northampton
	B	Edmonds James R	18	porter	39	192 "
	C	Broadnax Pauline L—†	19	stenographer	33	60 Ruggles
	D	Pierce Mildred N—†	19	maid	28	56 Lenox
	E	Woodley Harold	19	mechanic	37	here
	F	*Mills Victor A	20	seaman	55	"
	G	Wood Mallie C—†	20	housewife	68	"
	H	Johnson Carrie B—†	20	"	28	
	K	Johnson Columbus	20	cook	29	
	L	Bowman John	21	laborer	61	
	M	Mills Rhoda R—†	21	housewife	56	"
	N	Lewis Sidney A	21	laborer	49	"
	O	Badgett Laura E—†	21	housewife	44	24 Westminster
	P	Badgett William H	21	chef	46	24 "
	S	Prince Ruth—†	22	domestic	52	here
	T	Garner Lola—†	22	"	34	243 Northampton
	U	Parks Lumonia—†	22	"	38	243 "
	V	*Crichlow Hyacinth—†	23	"	30	31 Westminster
	W	Valentine Clark	23	housewife	42	Malden
	X	Anderson Julia C—†	24	"	66	23 Northfield
	Y	Field Julia D—†	24	"	42	Amherst
	Z	Fox Carey	24	welder	22	24 Ball
752						
	A	Carter Cecil W	25	porter	40	here
	B	Carter Mae—†	25	housewife	35	N Carolina
	C	Smith Marion N—†	25	clerk	35	here
	D	Summers Nathaniel	25	U S A	25	"
	E	Summers Priscilla J—†	25	housewife	24	New York
	F	Williams Frances—†	25	factoryhand	38	1 Marble
	G	Murphy Robert	26	laborer	69	here
	H	Dames Gertrude R—†	26	housewife	36	"
	K	Dames Joseph A	26	presser	34	"
	L	Jones Louise—†	26	laundress	37	977A Tremont
	M	Murray Julia C—†	27	domestic	60	here
	N	Green Annie—†	27	housekeeper	65	"
	O	Young Bertha—†	27	"	49	"
	P	Paul Silas	28	teacher	46	117 Ruggles
	R	Gordon Douglas	28	pipefitter	43	62 Sterling
	S	Stokes Jennie L—†	28	housewife	36	New York

Page.	Letter.	Full Name.	Residence, Jan. 1, 1943.	Occupation.	Supposed Age.	Reported Residence, Jan. 1, 1942. Street and Number.

Westminster Street—Continued

	T	Stokes Townsend	28	mechanic	42	New York
	U	Hall Alan J	29	chef	64	here
	V	World Charles T	29	retired	77	"
	W	Carmichael Myrtle—†	29	housekeeper	37	"
	X	Williams John	29	chef	35	33 Weston
	Y	Williams Rose—†	29	domestic	40	33 "
	Z	Vass Peter	30	laborer	37	here
753						
	A	Green Martha—†	30	housewife	58	"
	B	Williams Robert J	30	operator	44	
	C	*Payne Fitz H	31	clergyman	49	"
	D	*Payne Naomi M—†	31	housewife	47	"
	E	*Mattis Ernest	31	chef	40	
	F	*Mattis Mildred—†	31	housewife	30	"
	G	Williams Lloyd O	31	machinist	29	Newton
	H	Williams Mabelle A—†	31	housewife	27	806 Tremont
	L	Heald Herbert	33	laborer	37	here
	M	Boston Beverley—†	33	housewife	26	224 W Canton
	N	Boston George M	33	laborer	24	224 "
	O	Taylor Edith A—†	33	housewife	63	here
	P	Taylor William T	33	clerk	32	"
	R	Addison Benjamin	35	painter	44	"
	S	Tabb Ella C—†	35	housewife	46	"
	T	Tabb Robert L	35	chauffeur	66	"
	U	Tabb Virginia—†	35	stenographer	20	"
	W	Rutledge William	35	U S A	23	"
	V	Shay Martha A—†	35	domestic	48	"
	X	Weeks Edith—†	35	housewife	52	"
	Y	Weeks William G	35	dentist	58	
	Z	Neville David J	35	chef	40	
754						
	A	Neville Evelyn—†	35	housewife	38	"
	B	Jones Jennie—†	51	domestic	48	551 Col av
	C	Rice Ina M—†	51	waitress	43	Hull
	F	Arnold Eleanor F—†	52A	housewife	21	45 Waumbeck
	G	Arnold George P	52A	porter	21	45 "
	H	Cardozo Marcelino	52A	proprietor	47	here
	K	Privoa Frances—†	52A	waitress	42	"
	L	*Santo Samuel	52A	laborer	56	"
	M	Edney Marion L—†	53	housewife	37	"
	N	Benders Harold J	53	presser	34	1947 Wash'n

Page.	Letter.	Full Name.	Residence, Jan. 1, 1943.	Occupation.	Supposed Age.	Reported Residence, Jan. 1, 1942. Street and Number.

Westminster Street—Continued

	O	Benders Louise F—†	53	housewife	32	1947 Wash'n
	P	Morgan Lunette—†	53	"	42	here
	R	Morgan Robert J	53	janitor	42	"
	S	Howell Ruthena F—†	55	housewife	25	"
	T	Riley Rose—†	55	"	38	
	U	Williams James	55	U S A	28	
	V	Williams Lucille—†	55	domestic	31	"
	W	Williams Maria—†	55	housewife	69	"
	X	McAllister Ida M—†	55	"	39	64 Ruggles
	Y	McAllister Pinkston	55	mechanic	39	64 "

Windsor Street

755						
	B	Williams Bertha—†	14	laundress	65	here
	C	Hunter Frances—†	14	dressmaker	58	"
	D	Hunter Rhoda—†	14	examiner	21	"
	E	Wood Fannie E—†	14	domestic	59	"
	F	Taylor Inez—†	14	housewife	63	"
	G	Taylor William H	14	porter	52	
	H	Bembery Carrie—†	14	cook	70	
	K	Blake Benjamin	14	waiter	52	
	L	Gale Ernest	14	retired	53	
	M	Jackson Marilla—†	14	journalist	41	"
	N	Scott Annie S—†	14	teacher	52	"
	O	Wood Elizabeth—†	14	housewife	24	8 Williams St ter
	P	Wood John B	14	laborer	24	8 "
	R	Peachy Elizabeth—†	14	housekeeper	60	here
	S	Robinson Munroe	14	janitor	49	"
	T	Davis Emily—†	14	at home	68	"
	U	Kelton Frances A—†	14	saleswoman	20	"
	V	Kelton Gillie M—†	14	housewife	42	"
	W	Stanfield Booker T	14	custodian	38	"
	X	Stanfield Harriet E—†	14	housewife	34	"
	Y	Wright Libby—†	14	domestic	55	"
	Z	Williams Ruby E—†	14	housewife	43	63 Windsor
756						
	A	Hoffman James E	14	porter	36	here
	B	Hoffman Winifred—†	14	housewife	37	"
	C	Tolbert Jessie—†	14	operator	38	"
	D	Smith Clifton L	14	tailor	40	
	E	Smith Grace—†	14	housewife	35	"

Page.	Letter.	Full Name.	Residence, Jan. 1, 1943.	Occupation.	Supposed Age.	Reported Residence, Jan. 1, 1942. Street and Number.

Windsor Street—Continued

	F	Sealy Anna L—†	14	laundress	23	29 Westminster
	G	Sealy Benjamin, jr	14	U S A	26	here
	H	Ford Martha L—†	14	housewife	30	"
	K	Huggins Laura—†	15	at home	78	"
	L	Grant Egbert F	15	machinist	58	"
	M	Grant Mary—†	15	housewife	48	"
	N	Ellis Adriana—†	15	domestic	61	"
	O	Walker Edward A	16	waiter	59	14 Windsor
	P	Leftwich Ica—†	16	domestic	31	here
	R	Leftwich Ola—†	16	"	30	"
	S	Etchison Leola—†	16	housewife	39	"
	T	Wilkhelms Wilhelmina—†	17	presser	57	
	U	Jones Lillian G—†	17	stitcher	46	
	V	Harris Lulu—†	17	domestic	55	"
	W	Harris Katherine E—†	18	housewife	62	"
	X	Harris Samuel A	18	laborer	60	
	Y	Ross Althea E—†	18	domestic	28	"
	Z	Mapp Zylpha O—†	18	clerk	52	508 Shawmut av
757						
	A	Wilder Crudella—†	18	housewife	30	here
	B	Wilder Horace W	18	welder	26	"
	C	Ward Esther—†	19	housewife	39	"
	D	Ward James	19	operator	41	"
	E	Wright George M	19	retired	84	
	F	Horne Alfreda—†	19	stitcher	53	
	G	Belgrave Alice—†	20	cook	29	"
	H	Belgrave Fritz	20	laborer	23	
	K	Bligen Abraham	20	"	50	
	L	Prescod James	20	retired	63	
	M	Prescod Joffre	20	clerk	29	
	N	Prescod Nella—†	20	operator	20	"
	O	Prescod Winston	20	U S A	21	
	P	VanHise Alonzo	21	retired	78	
	R	VanHise Julia A—†	21	housewife	68	"
	S	Jones Irving	21	laborer	50	
	T	Jones Tharo—†	21	housewife	47	"
	U	Caution Katherine A—†	22	at home	68	"
	V	Smallwood Anna E—†	22	"	70	3 Carleton
	W	Smallwood John S	22	U S A	22	3 "
	X	Smallwood Malcolm G	22	laborer	25	3 "
	Y	Wallace Frank	22	U S A	33	here

Page.	Letter.	Full Name.	Residence, Jan. 1, 1943.	Occupation.	Supposed Age.	Reported Residence, Jan. 1, 1942. Street and Number.

Windsor Street—Continued

	Z	Wallace Marie—†	22	operator	53	here
758						
	A	Nelson Arthur M	23	janitor	32	"
	B	Anderson George W	23	porter	63	14 Windsor
	C	Anderson Marie—†	23	housewife	52	14 "
	D	Crawford Priscilla E—†	23	at home	54	here
	E	Harris Winthrop C	23	machinist	57	"
	F	Francis Laura A—†	24	housekeeper	62	"
	G	Gordon Florence—†	24	at home	69	"
	H*	Greenway Jane—†	24	"	71	"
	K	Dixon James W	25	U S A	25	49 Hammond
	L	Dixon John H	25	laborer	22	49 "
	M	Dixon Joseph N	25	"	21	49 "
	N	Dixon Leslie	25	"	58	49 "
	O	Dixon Mary—†	25	domestic	45	49 "
	S	Jones Ella S—†	26	clerk	50	here
	T	King Dorothy—†	26	housewife	42	"
	U	Huggins Anita—†	26	"	32	"
	V	Archer Ada—†	27	domestic	33	69 Warwick
	W	Archer Robert A	27	seaman	27	69 "
	Y	Braxton Margaret E—†	27	housewife	40	here
	Z	Brown Charles A	28	student	26	"
759						
	A	Brown Charles S	28	laborer	50	
	B	James Mabel—†	28	seamstress	43	"
	C*	Hurley William	28	porter	37	
	D	York Joseph	28	decorator	36	"
	E	Barnett Violet—†	29	laundress	37	"
	F	Parker Myretta—†	29	domestic	35	"
	G	Trotman Beatrice—†	29	housewife	49	"
	H	Trotman Samuel	29	foundryman	55	"
	K	Henry Ethel M—†	30	operator	21	"
	L	Jones Mary—†	30	at home	50	
	M	Raynor Bessie—†	30	domestic	54	"
	N	Raynor George H	30	janitor	66	"
	O	Whitehead Belle—†	30	operator	35	"
	P	Banks Catherine M—†	30	housewife	35	"
	R	Banks Charles S	30	chipper	32	
	S	Stewart Margaret—†	30	at home	83	
	T	Brown Mary C—†	31	housewife	70	"
	W	Durbin Hannah A—†	32	at home	68	

Page.	Letter.	FULL NAME.	Residence, Jan. 1, 1943.	Occupation.	Supposed Age.	Reported Residence, Jan. 1, 1942. Street and Number.

Windsor Street—Continued

Page.	Letter.	Full Name.	Residence, Jan. 1, 1943.	Occupation.	Supposed Age.	Reported Residence, Jan. 1, 1942.
	X	Perez Antonio	32	barber	38	here
	Y	Brittain Daisy—†	32	laundress	33	"
	Z	*Goode Bertha—†	32	clerk	38	"
760						
	A	*Taylor Mary—†	32	at home	59	
	B	Johnson Martha K—†	33	domestic	47	"
	C	Thompson John	33	retired	78	
	D	Perry Lila—†	33	stitcher	54	"
	E	Bailey Lucy—†	34	domestic	40	26 Davenport
	F	Gatewood Robert	34	porter	21	547 Tremont
	G	Harrison Howard	34	carpenter	67	here
	H	Herbert Arthur T	34	painter	70	"
	K	Hopes Mary A—†	34	at home	73	"
	L	Hopes Winthrop	34	laborer	43	
	M	Prialeu Daisy—†	34	at home	59	
	N	Hoskins Eugene	35	chef	64	
	O	Hoskins Josephine—†	35	housewife	60	"
	P	Rice Dorothy—†	35	domestic	28	"
	R	Eller Dorothy M—†	36	musician	26	"
	S	Eller Sarah E—†	36	domestic	50	"
	T	Lombard David	36	plumber	39	
	U	Lombard Hazel—†	36	housewife	30	"
	V	Marrow Bernita—†	36	"	30	Wash'n D C
	W	Marrow Carl K	36	presser	31	"
	X	Reed Rosa—†	37	domestic	66	39 Waumbeck
	Y	Wise Carrie—†	37	"	62	39 "
	Z	Avant Clarence	37	laborer	28	here
761						
	A	Avant Marie—†	37	housewife	28	"
	B	Chew Bella—†	37	at home	78	
	C	Connelly Laura—†	38	housewife	67	"
	D	Forney Hattie L—†	38	domestic	40	"
	E	Monte Alice—†	38	at home	80	Maryland
	F	Perkins Grandell	38	porter	60	here
	G	Quattlebaum Lucille—†	39	domestic	39	"
	H	Beatty Henry	39	porter	33	"
	K	Simmons Elizabeth—†	39	at home	90	
	L	Morris Frederick	39	clerk	36	
	M	Morris Louise—†	39	matron	32	
	N	Washington Paul	40	chef	41	
	O	Izett Catherine P—†	40	at home	62	

Page.	Letter.	FULL NAME.	Residence, Jan. 1, 1943.	Occupation.	Supposed Age.	Reported Residence, Jan. 1, 1942. Street and Number.

Windsor Street—Continued

Page.	Letter.	FULL NAME.	Residence, Jan. 1, 1943.	Occupation.	Supposed Age.	Reported Residence, Jan. 1, 1942. Street and Number.
	P	Hardrick Claudia—†	40	clerk	45	here
	R	Hardrick Virginia—†	40	housewife	71	"
	T	Tucker Marietta—†	41	stitcher	61	57 Windsor
	U	Davis Lula—†	41	domestic	58	here
	V	Hill Hattie—†	42	housewife	65	"
	W	Hill Robert	42	welder	26	"
	X	Hill Samuel	42	porter	34	
	Y	Chisholm John	42	retired	67	
	Z	Robinson Clara—†	42	domestic	58	"
762						
	A	Jones Talmadge	42	laborer	47	
	B	Lloyd Henry M	42	porter	46	
	C	Lloyd Rosa L—†	42	housewife	47	"
	D	*Perry John	42	laborer	53	"
	E	Morris Elsie—†	43	housewife	30	1182 Tremont
	F	Morris Oscar	43	porter	41	118 "
	G	McCullough Julia—†	43	stitcher	51	here
	H	*Lamos Alfred	44	seaman	47	"
	K	*Lamos Grace—†	44	housewife	46	"
	L	*Johnson Elizabeth W—†	44	"	65	
	M	Johnson Robert	44	janitor	68	
	N	Hing Qung Leong	44A	laundryman	26	"
	P	Dance Robert	50	clerk	37	Cambridge
	R	Gatlin Robert	50	bartender	47	89 Sterling
	S	Jones Jessie T—†	50	housewife	42	here
	T	Jones Richmond F	50	porter	49	"
	U	Harraway Arthur	52	attendant	40	403 Mass av
	V	Trotman Ernest	52	U S A	22	here
	W	Trotman Lambert	52	teacher	48	"
	X	*Trotman Lillian—†	52	housewife	45	"
	Y	Trotman Stanley	52	chauffeur	21	"
	Z	Hamilton Mollie—†	53	stitcher	59	
763						
	B	Reddick Cornelius T, jr	53	laborer	22	
	C	Dennis Minnie—†	54	housewife	68	"
	D	Satham Margaret—†	54	"	24	41 Ruggles
	E	Satham Thomas	54	draftsman	27	41 "
	F	Kamran Beatrice—†	54	domestic	35	102 W Springfield
	G	Martin Clifford	55	fireman	40	here
	H	Martin Ella—†	55	housewife	42	"
	K	Boddie Erie—†	56	clerk	24	"

Page.	Letter.	Full Name.	Residence, Jan. 1, 1943.	Occupation.	Supposed Age.	Reported Residence, Jan. 1, 1942. Street and Number.

Windsor Street—Continued

	L	Bryant Edwina—†	56	teacher	24	here
	M	Bryant Geraldine—†	56	"	21	"
	N	Bryant Roscoe W	56	tailor	56	"
	O	Bryant Roscoe W, jr	56	U S A	21	
	P	Parkhurst Ella—†	56	at home	70	
	R	Parkhurst James	56	chef	38	
	S	Covington Irma L—†	57	domestic	53	"
	T	Covington Seymour	57	retired	65	"
	U	Jackson Julia P—†	57	housewife	66	"
	V	Jackson Robert	57	adjuster	70	
	W	Bailey Kathleen—†	58	domestic	52	"
	X	Campbell Rosamond—†	58	teacher	28	
	Y	Williams Richard	58	boilermaker	45	"
	Z	Williams Viola—†	58	housewife	47	"
764						
	A	Smith Chester	58	chipper	27	
	B	Smith Muriel—†	58	housewife	27	"
	C	Flack Mary—†	59	domestic	38	34 Greenwich pk
	D	Hawkins Maggie—†	59	housewife	70	N Carolina
	E	Jones Julia—†	59	domestic	30	Connecticut
	F	Burnett Helen—†	59	stitcher	39	here
	H	Davis Elizabeth B—†	60	clerk	37	"
	K	Hall Harriet C—†	60	housewife	58	"
	L	Hall John B	60	physician	66	"
	M	Rayford Narka L—†	60	clerk	47	
	N	Wood Anne R—†	60	typist	21	
	O	Wood L Fern—†	60	teacher	25	
	P	Manuel Isaac	61	porter	60	
	R	Payne Clarence	61	waiter	52	
	S	Payne Rebecca—†	61	housewife	40	"
	T	Alves John	61	laborer	29	
	U	Alves Virginia—†	61	stitcher	25	"
	V	Norris James	63	machinist	34	"
	W	Norris Rosetta—†	63	housewife	27	"
	X	Scott Ruth E—†	63	domestic	21	Virginia
	Y	Gomez Andrew L	63	realtor	45	195 W Newton
	Z	Gomez Edna—†	63	housewife	22	195 "
765						
	A	Hicks Joseph	63	laborer	25	18 Hubert
	B	Ball Evelyn—†	65	housewife	37	69 Warwick

Page.	Letter.	Full Name.	Residence, Jan. 1, 1943.	Occupation.	Supposed Age.	Reported Residence, Jan. 1, 1942. Street and Number.

Windsor Street—Continued

Page.	Letter.	Full Name.	Residence, Jan. 1, 1943.	Occupation.	Supposed Age.	Reported Residence, Jan. 1, 1942. Street and Number.
	C	Ball Newton L	65	musician	42	here
	D	Williams Elita—†	65	domestic	35	“
	E	Gaines Ada—†	65	at home	66	11 Greenwich
	F	Johnson Mary—†	67	“	77	here
	G	Blount Robert	69	caterer	67	“
	H	Wilkinson Harriet—†	69	domestic	64	“
	K	Williams James E	69	retired	72	
	L	Williams Josephine—†	69	typist	26	“
	M	Williams Louisa—†	69	housewife	65	“
	N	Smith Mary E—†	71	“	49	
	O	Smith Robert	71	manager	49	“
	R	Harris Jessie—†	71	housewife	44	“
	S	Harris Maceo	71	U S A	22	
	T	White Frederick	73	musician	79	“
	U	White Myrtle—†	73	housewife	49	“
	V	Whiteman Alice—†	73	domestic	51	“
	W	Cotton Margaret—†	73	stitcher	41	
	X	Jackson James E	75	retired	74	
	Y	Jackson Mattie F—†	75	housewife	74	“
	Z	Nobles Paul	75	laborer	69	
766						
	A	Saunders Rachael—†	75	domestic	42	“
	B	Jones Henrietta—†	77	housewife	68	“
	C	Washington Benjamin	77	chauffeur	46	“
	D	Washington Mary O	77	housewife	42	“
	E	Cain Emma—†	79	“	58	
	F	Cain Shellie F	79	porter	60	
	G	*Davis Lydia—†	80	at home	65	
	H	*Gloster Lena—†	80	“	70	“
	K	Avant Octavia—†	80	housewife	25	Mashpee
	L	States Cecil	80	molder	44	here
	M	States Jean—†	80	housewife	44	“
	N	States Winifred—†	80	student	21	“
	O	Hollingsworth Cyril	80	carpenter	61	“
	P	Hibbler Charles	80	agent	66	
	R	Hibbler Mary—†	80	housewife	47	“
	S	Gunn Anna—†	80	“	36	
	T	Gunn Neville	80	laborer	52	
	U	Gupton William T	81	porter	68	“
	V	Browne Henry	83	molder	43	

Page.	Letter.	Full Name.	Residence, Jan. 1, 1943.	Occupation.	Supposed Age.	Reported Residence, Jan. 1, 1942. Street and Number.

Windsor Street—Continued

	W	Johnson Fred D	83	laborer	56	here
	X	Jones Charles F	83	"	60	"
	Y	*Jones Clara M—†	83	housewife	44	"
767						
	A	Taylor Charlotte—†	96	housekeeper	67	"
	B	Belt Charles C	96	barber	75	"
	C	Belt Hattie M—†	96	housewife	66	"
	D	Morris Alice—†	96	housekeeper	67	"
	E	Steadman Bertha—†	96	housewife	40	"
	F	Steadman James	96	chef	49	

Ward 9—Precinct 8

CITY OF BOSTON

LIST OF RESIDENTS
20 YEARS OF AGE AND OVER

(NON-CITIZENS INDICATED BY ASTERISK)
(FEMALES INDICATED BY DAGGER)

AS OF

JANUARY 1, 1943

JOSEPH F. TIMILTY, *Chairman*
FREDERIC E. DOWLING, *Secretary*
WILLIAM A. MOTLEY, JR.
FRANCIS B. McKINNEY
EVERETT R. PROUT
Listing Board.

CITY OF BOSTON PRINTING DEPARTMENT

Page.	Letter.	Full Name.	Residence, Jan. 1, 1943.	Occupation.	Supposed Age.	Reported Residence, Jan. 1, 1942. Street and Number.
800						

Benton Street

Page.	Letter.	Full Name.	Residence, Jan. 1, 1943.	Occupation.	Supposed Age.	Reported Residence, Jan. 1, 1942. Street and Number.
	A	Coreia Hilario	4	laborer	48	15 Windsor
	B	Williams Alfred	4	"	33	here
	C	Williams Cordelia—†	4	domestic	60	"
	D	Frye Hortense—†	4	operator	41	"
	E	Frye Layton B	4	laborer	51	
	F	Rutherford Charles	6	chauffeur	45	"
	G	Rutherford Grace B—†	6	housewife	43	"
	H	Harris Anderson	6	laborer	58	
	K	Harris Georgia—†	6	domestic	55	"
	L	Watkins Lewis T	6	U S N	21	"
	M	Morse Anne—†	6	at home	73	
	N	*Ford Charles A	8	pedler	60	
	O	Ford Stella—†	8	housewife	58	"
	P	Yancey Sofia—†	8	operator	60	
	S	Boggs Emma—†	9	domestic	38	"
	T	Talton Lulu—†	9	at home	56	
	U	Mayers Bessie—†	9	housewife	50	"
	V	Mayers David	9	porter	50	
	W	Scott Charles	9	meatcutter	27	"
	X	Scott Thelma—†	9	at home	25	"
	Y	Tyler Carrie—†	9	housewife	49	"
	Z	Tyler Warren	9	laborer	51	
801						
	A	Wright Rose—†	11	domestic	49	"
	B	Wright William	11	boilermaker	49	"
	C	Hill Ida M—†	11	housewife	54	"
	D	Hill Richard A	11	retired	67	
	E	Myles Mildred—†	11	at home	60	"
	F	Ridley Rose—†	11	housewife	49	"
	G	Ridley Vernice R—†	11	operator	24	
	M	Eastly Effie—†	19	laundress	55	"
	P	Taylor Frank	21	retired	63	
	R	Taylor Margaret M—†	21	at home	62	
	S	Caswell George	21	U S N	22	
	T	Fuller Edward	27	retired	75	
	U	O'Brien Louisa—†	27	at home	69	
	V	Kimball Annie—†	27	"	66	
	W	Straim Gertrude—†	27	"	57	"
	X	Buck Eulalia M—†	29		78	5 Pratt ct
	Y	Fisher Fannie E—†	29		70	here

Page.	Letter.	Full Name.	Residence, Jan. 1, 1943.	Occupation.	Supposed Age.	Reported Residence, Jan. 1, 1942. Street and Number.

802

Benton Street—Continued

Page.	Letter.	Full Name.	Residence, Jan. 1, 1943.	Occupation.	Supposed Age.	Reported Residence, Jan. 1, 1942. Street and Number.
	A	Hassett James J	29	retired	71	here
	B	Hassett Mary—†	29	at home	73	“

Burke Street

Page.	Letter.	Full Name.	Residence, Jan. 1, 1943.	Occupation.	Supposed Age.	Reported Residence, Jan. 1, 1942. Street and Number.
	C	Eckles Barbara—†	4	housewife	27	here
	D	Eckles George	4	cook	30	“
	E	White Leroy	4	baker	35	“
	F	White Nora—†	4	housewife	33	“
	G	Randall Elsie—†	5	“	40	Cambridge
	H	Randall James	5	laborer	47	“
	K	Wolfson Julius H	5	attorney	46	Newton
	L	Burtin Alfred	5	laborer	50	Cambridge
	M	Ward Elsie—†	5	housewife	42	“
	N	Ward James	5	laborer	50	“
	O	Jones Dora B—†	7	domestic	56	here
	P	Fairier Lucy—†	7	housekeeper	72	“
	R	Johnson Dora B—†	7	“	58	“
	S	Jones Mattie—†	7	housewife	62	“
	T	Jones Walter E	7	waiter	62	
	V*	Moore Gwendolyn—†	9	housekeeper	39	“
	W	McKnight Florence—†	9	“	51	“
	X	Centeio Julio G	16	weaver	41	
	Y	Centeio Lettie—†	16	housewife	36	“
	Z	Purcell John J	16	cook	44	62 Harold
803						
	A	Purcell Ora—†	16	housewife	42	62 “
	B	Campbell Sylvanus	16	janitor	58	here
	C	Campbell Vera—†	16	housewife	49	“
	D	Pearson Bismark	16	porter	52	159 W Springfield
	E	Pearson Irene—†	16	housewife	36	159 “
	F	Priest Lillian—†	16	housekeeper	35	N Carolina
	G	Augustus Jack W	18	porter	26	here
	H	Augustus Mayetta—†	18	housewife	27	“
	K	Jackson Hilda—†	18	“	68	“
	L	Jackson William	18	chauffeur	56	“
	M	Beckett Alfred	18	porter	29	
	N	Beckett Clara—†	18	housewife	27	“
	O	Word Frances—†	18	“	54	
	P	Word James H	18	porter	56	

Page.	Letter.	Full Name.	Residence, Jan. 1, 1943.	Occupation.	Supposed Age.	Reported Residence, Jan. 1, 1942. Street and Number.

Cabot Street

	v	Parker Eliza—†	41	housewife	66	159 Cabot
	y	Johnson Arthur E	67	U S A	21	here
	z	Johnson Helen L—†	67	clerk	24	"
804						
	A	Johnson Mary—†	67	housewife	52	"
	B	Johnson Walter H	67	laborer	56	
	C	Bitetti Clara—†	67	clerk	32	
	D	Bitetti Donato	67	retired	59	
	E	Bitetti Fabruzio	67	laborer	20	
	F	*Bitetti Therese—†	67	housewife	58	"
	G	Roderick Julia—†	67	"	43	129 Lenox
	H	Holmes Arlene—†	69	"	26	95 Camden
	K	Holmes Joseph	69	laborer	26	95 "
	L	Thomas Charles E	69	machinist	24	1045 Tremont
	M	Thomas Pauline D—†	69	housewife	24	1045 "
	N	Stanyan William H	69	retired	76	here
	P	Eaton May—†	75	housewife	38	93 Belvidere
	T	Collins Etta—†	77	"	71	here
	U	Mahoney Edward	77	retired	66	"
	V	Mahoney Mary E—†	77	housewife	67	"
	W	Thomas Cora E—†	79	"	76	
	X	Sanford Jennie T—†	79	"	77	
	Y	Stark Etta E—†	79	"	53	
	Z	Stark William F	79	finisher	60	
805						
	A	Salisbury Arthur L	81	retired	65	"
	B	Salisbury Catherine—†	81	housewife	69	"
	C	Palmisano Gerardo P	81	porter	27	
	D	Palmisano Josephine—†	81	housewife	36	"
	E	Fraser Joseph	81	U S A	24	75 Cabot
	F	O'Rourke Mary—†	81	operator	21	75 "
	G	Rowe Catherine I—†	81	housewife	47	75 "
	H	Rowe Edward R	81	porter	50	75 "
	M	Miller Emma—†	99	housewife	38	here
	O	Johnson Mary C—†	99	"	25	Marshfield
	P	Johnson Thomas C	99	laborer	27	"
	R	Andersen Agnes S—†	101	housewife	67	here
	S	Andersen Blanche E—†	101	operator	25	"
	T	Andersen Karl	101	lineman	63	"
	U	Marr Charles W	101	U S A	23	
	V	Marr Lillian V—†	101	housewife	44	"

Page.	Letter.	Full Name.	Residence, Jan. 1, 1943.	Occupation.	Supposed Age.	Reported Residence, Jan. 1, 1942. Street and Number.

Cabot Street—Continued

	W	Marr Raymond A	101	entertainer	45	here
	X	Green William F	101	chauffeur	48	"
	Y	Hassett Katheryn M—†	101	stenographer	46	"
	Z	Latti Margaret M—†	101	housewife	88	"
806						
	A	*Pendergast Bernard	101	retired	79	
	B	Green Charles W	101	trainer	50	
	C	Green Genevieve M—†	101	housewife	43	"
	F	Myrick John S	109	clergyman	67	992 Tremont
	M	Everett Laura—†	113	housewife	62	here
	N	Hobart Elizabeth—†	113	"	66	"
	O	Howard Marcus	113	retired	80	"
	P	Hill William	115	laborer	56	
	S	Westgate Charles	117	"	66	
	V	Ferris George	119	cook	60	
	W	Monagle Charles	119	plumber	64	"
	X	Lewis Josephine—†	121	operator	48	5 McLellan
	Y	Grimes Marie—†	135	housewife	73	here
	Z	Weston Pauline A—†	135	"	33	"
807						
	A	Weston Sebron W	135	machinist	44	"
	B	*Lesley Mosley	135	riveter	49	66 Williams
	C	Lesley Olivina—†	135	cook	21	66 "
	D	Casciottolo Mary—†	135	housewife	73	here
	E	*Donelan Gertrude—†	135	"	38	"
	F	Simons Mary I—†	135	domestic	55	35 Weston
	G	Brandford Ada—†	135	maid	55	here
	H	*Brooks Angelina T—†	135	missionary	56	"
	K	Perkins Marjorie—†	135	operator	21	"
	L	Thorpe Helena—†	135	housewife	65	8 Hubert
	M	Emery Sarah E—†	137	"	69	here
	O	Skidmore Francis C	141	laborer	28	"
	P	*Skidmore Jane—†	141	housewife	85	"
	R	Welsh Edna I—†	141	"	27	
	S	Welsh John	141	shipper	36	
	T	Reed Sarah A—†	141	housewife	62	"
	U	*Reed William H	141	retired	77	
	W	O'Donnell Alice—†	143	housewife	73	"
	X	O'Donnell Gerard	143	laborer	30	"
	Y	O'Donnell Henry E	143	chauffeur	43	"
	Z	O'Donnell Robert	143	retired	76	

Cabot Street—Continued

Page.	Letter.	Full Name.	Residence, Jan. 1, 1943.	Occupation.	Supposed Age.	Reported Residence, Jan. 1, 1942. Street and Number.
808	A	O'Donnell Robert T	143	laborer	46	here
	B	O'Donnell William J	143	"	50	"
	C	McCauley Lillian E—†	143	housewife	44	"

Columbus Avenue

Page.	Letter.	Full Name.	Residence, Jan. 1, 1943.	Occupation.	Supposed Age.	Reported Residence, Jan. 1, 1942. Street and Number.
	P	Bell James F	706	retired	76	here
	R	Ridley Clara—†	706	waitress	36	"
	S	Gordon Joseph H	706	chef	58	"
	T	Gordon Nellie—†	706	housewife	44	"
	U	Parks Adelaide—†	706	"	56	
	V	Parks James A	706	porter	55	
	W	Milmore Amanda—†	708	housewife	58	"
	X	Milmore Martin	708	realtor	72	
	Y	Milmore Vivian—†	708	teacher	36	
	Z	Lindo Daphne—†	708	housewife	28	"
809	A	Lindo Urbain A	708	chauffeur	38	"
	E	Nunes Florence—†	748	housewife	38	"
	F	Nunes Theophilus	748	clerk	47	
	H	Reid Mattie L—†	748	undertaker	34	"
	G	St Hilari Edward	748	doorman	50	"
	K	Austin Agnes—†	748	housewife	48	"
	L	Austin Lorenzo H	748	investigator	56	"
	M	Gibson Joseph	750	welder	36	
	N	Gibson Rose—†	750	housewife	30	"
	O	Flowers Amanda—†	750	"	63	"
	P	Flowers Frank	750	porter	63	
	R	Gorey John	750	shipper	41	"
	S	Gorey Mildred—†	750	housewife	42	"
	T	Harris Aubrey	752	mechanic	24	"
	U	Harris Clothilde—†	752	housewife	26	"
	V	Frazer Bernice—†	752	"	49	
	W	Frazer Charles	752	cook	55	
	X	Cuzzens Marguerite—†	752	housewife	45	"
	Y	Cuzzens Richard	752	decorator	56	"
	Z	Vanderbilt Sarah—†	752	housewife	73	"
810	A	Lyken Ethelbert	768	custodian	54	"

Page.	Letter.	Full Name.	Residence, Jan. 1, 1943.	Occupation.	Supposed Age.	Reported Residence, Jan. 1, 1942. Street and Number.

Columbus Avenue—Continued

Page.	Letter.	Full Name.	Residence, Jan. 1, 1943.	Occupation.	Supposed Age.	Reported Residence, Jan. 1, 1942. Street and Number.
	B	Robinson Mathilda—†	768	housewife	73	here
	C	Woodfork Agnes—†	768	domestic	54	"
	D	Woodfork George	768	porter	56	"
	E	Douglas Stephan	768	printer	45	76 Worcester
	F	Valentine Mary—†	768	domestic	67	here
	G	Stephens Joseph	768	porter	28	426 Col av
	H	Stephens Thelma—†	768	housewife	24	426 "
	K	Wade Marion—†	768	domestic	32	here
	L	Wade Vera—†	768	"	28	"
	M	Watkins John	768	porter	52	"
	N	Watkins Rose—†	768	housewife	42	"
	O	Dilworth Doris—†	768	beautician	28	"
	P	Dilworth Wesley	768	cook	45	"
	R	Samuels Felix	768	"	36	421 Col av
	S	West Maude—†	768	housewife	59	here
	T	West Willis	768	porter	35	"
	W	Burgo Margaret—†	772	housewife	28	34 Northampton
	X	Faria Louise—†	772	trimmer	23	8 Greenwich
	Y	Barnett Mamie—†	772	housekeeper	50	here
	Z	Lynch Herbert	772	porter	32	"
811						
	A	Lynch Verdell—†	772	housewife	29	"
	B	Singleton Harry	772	welder	32	
	C	*LeVatt Elma—†	772	housewife	50	"
	D	LeVatt Thomas	772	janitor	49	"
	E	Smythwick John	774	calker	34	26 Davenport
	F	Smythwick Nancy—†	774	housewife	38	26 "
	G	*Wilson Claude	774	porter	41	here
	H	*Wilson Mildred—†	774	housewife	39	"
	K	Clark Anne L—†	774	"	47	"
	L	Clark George L	774	laborer	70	
	N	Bailey Lawrence H	776	"	58	
	O	Reynolds Beulah—†	776	stenographer	26	"
	P	Reynolds Margaret—†	776	housewife	64	"
	R	Reynolds Wyatt	776	retired	66	
	U	Smith Elmer W	813	U S N	33	"
	V	Smith Wilhelmina F—†	813	housewife	32	"
	W	Pridgen James	813	laborer	29	
	X	Pridgen Louise—†	813	domestic	24	"
	Y	Pridgen William	813	waiter	34	

Page.	Letter.	FULL NAME.	Residence, Jan. 1, 1943.	Occupation.	Supposed Age.	Reported Residence, Jan. 1, 1942. Street and Number.

Columbus Avenue—Continued

	Z	Evora Norwell	813	painter	23	here
812						
	A	Evora Phyllis—†	813	housewife	25	"
	B	Armstrong Irene—†	815	"	35	
	C	Bonnello Albert	815	laborer	40	
	D	Bonnello Margaret—†	815	housewife	40	"
	E	*Seales Alberta—†	815	"	43	"
	F	Smith Frederick	815	U S A	29	166 Walnut av
	G	Smith Wilhelmina—†	815	assembler	25	here
	H	Harmon Grace—†	819	domestic	44	"
	K	Armstead Joseph	819	retired	73	"
	L	Armstead Mary—†	819	housewife	68	"
	M	Ferguson Mary—†	819	domestic	40	"
	N	Ferguson Mary—†	819	assembler	21	"
	O	Bailey Claude	819	typist	26	
	P	Stuart Alexander B	819	porter	46	
	R	*Stuart Hilda—†	819	housewife	45	"
	T	Stephenson David J	834	laborer	60	
	U	*Stephenson Gertrude—†	834	housewife	54	"
	V	Williams Edythe—†	834	operator	27	936 Tremont
	W	Williams John	834	chef	56	936 "
	X	Williams Lenora—†	834	housewife	44	936 "
	Y	Henry George	834	mechanic	50	here
	Z	Ward Amelia—†	836	housewife	32	"
813						
	A	Ward Orie	836	laborer	34	"
	B	Ezell Lucille—†	836	housewife	22	11½ Sarsfield
	C	Ezell William	836	welder	26	11½ "
	D	Cotter Gilbert	836	machinist	42	37 Windsor
	E	Cotter Ruby—†	836	housewife	28	37 "
	G	*Henry Reginald	853	cook	49	here
	H	Henry Ruth—†	853	housewife	40	"
	K	Jefferson Lewis H	853	U S A	22	"
	L	Jefferson Olive E—†	853	housewife	52	"
	M	Jefferson Walter H	853	operator	53	
	N	Mindoza Edeline—†	853	housewife	20	"
	O	Butler Adele—†	853	"	61	
	P	Butler John A	853	mechanic	63	"
	R	Bell Catherine—†	855	housewife	39	"
	S	Bell Theodore	855	baker	39	
	T	Henderson James	855	mechanic	48	"

Page.	Letter.	Full Name.	Residence, Jan. 1, 1943.	Occupation.	Supposed Age.	Reported Residence, Jan. 1, 1942. Street and Number.

Columbus Avenue—Continued

	U	Henderson Ruby—†	855	housewife	48	here
	V	Adams Phyllis—†	855	"	43	"
	W	Adams Seth	855	janitor	23	"
	X	Brown Bruce	856	U S A	33	
	Y	Brown Frederick	856	printer	56	
	Z	Brown Gertrude—†	856	housewife	54	"
814						
	A	Thomas Eric	856	U S A	29	"
	B	Thomas Miriam—†	856	domestic	52	"
	C	Dewey Frances—†	857	housewife	28	"
	D	Dewey Wallace	857	guard	28	
	E	Joseph Alfred	857	U S A	26	
	F	Joseph Burt	857	cook	44	
	G	Joseph Jennie—†	857	housewife	38	"
	H	Joseph John	857	decorator	20	"
	K	Gill Frank M	857	electrician	55	24 Warwick
	L	Gill Vivian—†	857	housewife	40	24 "
	M	Maloney James	860	painter	51	222 W Newton
	N	Momian Laura—†	860	housekeeper	36	222 "
	O	Morrow John F	860	laborer	27	here
	P	Morrow Josephine M—†	860	housewife	27	"
	R	Conway Agnes—†	860	"	80	"
	S	Strynk Fanny F—†	860	folder	33	Cambridge
	T	Graham Ethel M—†	860	housewife	45	here
	U	Graham James L	860	mechanic	34	"
	V	Hogan Francis J	860	"	20	18 E Springfield
	W	Hogan Margaret—†	860	housewife	52	18 "
	X	Regan Frances E—†	860	"	38	here
	Y	McCarthy Josephine A-†	860	forewoman	50	"
	Z	Blethan Virginia W—†	860	domestic	37	"
815						
	A	Farrell Frank J	860	guard	40	
	B	*Farrell Louise A—†	860	housewife	40	"
	C	Barrett Mary A—†	864	housekeeper	61	"
	D	Fusoni Harold F	864	operator	34	"
	E	Jacquith Beatrice—†	864	housewife	51	"
	F	Jacquith John T	864	U S N	60	
	G	Weiland Joseph F	864	chauffeur	54	"
	H	Weiland Mary—†	864	housewife	49	"
	K	Murphy Catherine—†	864	"	21	30 Tavern rd
	L	Murphy Martin	864	fireman	30	30 "

Page.	Letter.	Full Name.	Residence, Jan. 1, 1943.	Occupation.	Supposed Age.	Reported Residence, Jan. 1, 1942. Street and Number.

Columbus Avenue—Continued

Page.	Letter.	Full Name.	Residence, Jan. 1, 1943.	Occupation.	Supposed Age.	Reported Residence, Jan. 1, 1942. Street and Number.
	M	Murphy Winifred—†	864	technician	60	30 Tavern rd
	N	Turner Clara—†	864	stenographer	43	here
	O	Turner Herbert	864	mechanic	48	"
	P	Morrow Elizabeth—†	864	housewife	47	872 Col av
	R	Andrews Agnes—†	864	"	20	here
	S	Andrews George	864	U S A	26	"
	T	Devine Joseph	864	U S N	22	"
	U	Devine Mary—†	864	assembler	52	"
	V	Joy Marjorie L—†	864	operator	29	177 Shawmut av
	W	Joy Raymond S	864	counterman	36	177 "
	X	*Crekos Demetris—†	864	housewife	43	here
	Y	Crekos Stephen	864	cook	49	"
	Z	Glynn Alice V—†	864	operator	36	"
816						
	A	Glynn William	864	storekeeper	39	"
	B	Conaletta Carmen M—†	868	housewife	32	"
	C	Conaletta William R	868	laborer	32	
	D	Walsh Patrick J	868	"	52	
	E	Walsh Sarah A—†	868	housewife	52	"
	F	Barry Dorothy M—†	868	secretary	23	"
	G	Barry Leonard T	868	mechanic	55	"
	H	Barry Leonard T, jr	868	U S A	22	
	K	Snyder Charles	868	"	23	
	L	Snyder Eleanor—†	868	housewife	22	"
	M	McDonough James E	868	chauffeur	48	"
	N	McDonough Mary—†	868	housewife	45	"
	O	Coulson William F	868	janitor	45	60 Brighton av
	P	Bradbury Helen G—†	868	attendant	40	here
	R	Dempsey Johanna A—†	868	at home	70	"
	S	Dempsey Mary L—†	868	clerk	35	"
	T	Bollgol Georgia—†	868	housewife	22	45 Field
	U	Bollgol Peter J	868	waiter	25	45 "
	V	Johnson Amy E—†	868	housewife	25	here
	W	Johnson Harold J	868	rigger	31	"
	X	Manchester Loyola B—†	868	stitcher	55	"
	Y	Phillips Cora—†	868	housekeeper	75	"
	Z	Maminos John G	872	manager	69	"
817						
	A	*Markos Angelos	872	cook	46	
	B	Panizzi Carido A	872	butcher	38	

Page.	Letter.	Full Name.	Residence, Jan. 1, 1943.	Occupation.	Supposed Age.	Reported Residence, Jan. 1, 1942. Street and Number.

Columbus Avenue—Continued

	c	*Panizzi Irene—†	872	stitcher	36	here
	D	Mamoli Mario	872	grocer	43	878 Col av
	E	Ricard Bertha—†	872	"	45	878 "
	F	Bridges Harold F	872	bartender	34	60 Linwood sq
	G	Bridges Lena L—†	872	housewife	29	60 "
	H	McEttrick James F	872	operator	36	here
	K	McEttrick Loretta M—†	872	boxmaker	35	"
	L	Ramsdell Alice—†	872	housewife	36	178 Hillside
	M	Ramsdell Horace	872	operator	48	178 "
	N	Randall Albert M	872	soapmaker	40	22 Alaska
	O	Randall Annie—†	872	housewife	38	22 "
	P	Hedges Georgia—†	872	waitress	25	here
	R	Hedges James	872	mechanic	26	"
	S	Neill Oscar O	872	chauffeur	46	"
	T	Nelson Mildred A—†	872	waitress	44	
	V	Connor Charles T	880	U S A	26	
	W	Connor Joseph A	880	"	28	
	X	Glynn Elizabeth—†	880	housewife	48	"
	Y	Glynn John T	880	lineman	48	
	Z	Davenport Edith—†	902	laundryworker	38	"
818						
	A	Fisher Charles H	902	painter	60	
	B	Fisher Josephine—†	902	housewife	60	"
	D	Newton William	904	longshoreman	51	"
	E	Scostopoulos George	904	baker	40	
	F	O'Donnell William	904	retired	74	
	G	Ingersol Jeremiah	906	operator	55	
	H	Ingersol Rose—†	906	housewife	38	"
	K	Wheelock Charles	906	mechanic	34	"
	L	Wheelock Florence—†	906	domestic	52	"
	M	Condos Charles	906	florist	50	"
	N	Sheehan Lawrence	908	guard	30	9 Bainbridge
	O	Sheehan Myrtle—†	908	housewife	25	9 "
	P	Daylor Ellen—†	908	housekeeper	65	here
	R	Banks Catherine—†	908	housewife	65	"
	S	Banks James	908	retired	65	"
	T	Stengle Minnie—†	910	housewife	66	"
	U	Murphy Catherine—†	910	housekeeper	88	"
	W	*Johnson Josephine—†	912	"	70	"
	Y	Buckley Mary—†	912	housewife	65	"

Page.	Letter.	Full Name.	Residence, Jan. 1, 1943.	Occupation.	Supposed Age.	Reported Residence, Jan. 1, 1942. Street and Number.

Columbus Avenue—Continued

	z	Lohnes Alice—†	914	housewife	33	303 Dudley
819						
	A	Lohnes Charles	914	chauffeur	35	303 "
	B	Prentiss William	914	retired	66	here
	C	Rogers Lillian—†	914	laundress	45	"
	D	Croker Laverne L—†	916	housewife	61	76 Westland av
	E	Clark Charlotte—†	916	housekeeper	62	here

Coventry Street

	H	Barber Alice R—†	7	at home	60	here
	K	Barber Robert A	7	retired	72	"
	L	Johnson Courtney	7	janitor	42	"
	M	Johnson Madge—†	7	housewife	42	"
	N	Debnam Anna—†	7	domestic	40	"
	O	Allen Charlotte—†	7	cook	55	
	P	Allen Jean—†	7	domestic	30	"

Cunard Street

	S	Buchanan James O	3	waiter	67	1015 Tremont
	T	Hill Willis H	3	carpenter	61	1015 "
	U	Jones Dolores B—†	3	housewife	30	Illinois
	V	Jones Maxwell U	3	entertainer	37	"
	W	Jones Harold C	3	"	29	Malden
	X	Jones Hattie L—†	3	domestic	54	200 W Springfield
	Y	Jones Kathleen R—†	3	housewife	30	Malden
	Z	Lane Edward C	5	clerk	43	here
820						
	A	Miller Delia—†	5	housewife	49	"
	B	Miller William	5	laborer	21	
	C	Holman Mary L—†	5	social worker	36	"
	D	Yarde Edgar S	5	janitor	39	
	E	Yarde Enid F—†	5	housewife	38	"
	F	Mayes Bessie—†	7	"	41	Illinois
	G	Mayes David	7	laborer	46	"
	H	Hays Lillian—†	7	housewife	29	91 Warwick
	K	Hays Wilfred R	7	U S N	24	91 "
	L	Billings Ruth M—†	7	housewife	33	3 Cunard
	M	Johnson Clara—†	8	housekeeper	29	75 Ruggles
	N	Blair Sarah—†	8	waitress	45	10 Greenwich

Page.	Letter.	Full Name.	Residence, Jan. 1, 1943.	Occupation.	Supposed Age.	Reported Residence, Jan. 1, 1942. Street and Number.

Cunard Street—Continued

	O	Desmond Anna H—†	8	housewife	73	10 Greenwich
	P	Whitted Florence O—†	8	maid	65	10 "
	R	Smith Mabel—†	8	domestic	50	14 Windsor
	S	Sisco Dorothy—†	9	housewife	39	here
	T	Sisco Leon	9	laborer	42	"
	U	Smith Herbert	9	shipper	43	"
	V	Smith Josephine—†	9	housewife	38	"
	W	Stone Bessie B—†	9	"	35	
	X	Stone Robert L	9	clergyman	50	"
	Z	Alston Mattie—†	10	housewife	57	"
821						
	A	Alston Stephen	10	laborer	47	
	B	Jones John	10	clerk	60	
	C	Jones Kate—†	10	housewife	58	"
	D	Fontes John	10	laborer	42	"
	E	Fontes Sallie—†	10	housewife	29	"
	F	Robinson Anna—†	10	"	60	
	G	Robinson James R	10	U S A	22	
	H	*Perry Emanuel J	10A	cook	60	
	K	Johnson Pearl—†	12	housewife	32	"
	L	Saunders Catherine—†	12	housekeeper	60	"
	M	Davis Ethel V—†	12	housewife	28	"
	N	Davis Stanley	12	welder	27	
	O	Harrington Charlotte—†	12	housewife	68	"
	P	Colvin Loretta—†	12	laundress	50	"
	R	Jackson Alzatta—†	12	maid	31	
	S	Johnson Beatrice—†	12	waitress	33	
	T	Royal Gussie—†	12	maid	23	"
	V	Sullivan John	16	retired	70	118 W Concord
	W	*Payne Joseph	18	janitor	47	here
	X	Sampson Albert	18	laborer	39	16 Newcomb
	Y	Sampson George	18	dishwasher	47	16 "
	Z	Sampson Rosa—†	18	housewife	76	16 "
822						
	A	Walker Edythe—†	18	"	57	here
	B	Walker Joseph	18	laborer	47	"
	C	Crishlow Nellie—†	18	domestic	47	Brookline
	D	Eastman Alma—†	18	housekeeper	24	8 E Lenox
	E	Eastman Charles	18	laborer	53	here
	F	Eastman Loretta—†	18	stitcher	20	8 E Lenox
	G	Haynes Annie V—†	18	domestic	53	69 Northfield

Page.	Letter.	FULL NAME.	Residence, Jan. 1, 1943.	Occupation.	Supposed Age.	Reported Residence, Jan. 1, 1942. Street and Number.

Cunard Street—Continued

	H	Stubbs Hazel—†	18	cook	37	68 Cabot
	K	Edwards Corrine—†	18	domestic	50	here
	P	Ward Alma—†	30	housekeeper	29	141 Lenox
	R	Holloran Margaret—†	30	at home	64	Cambridge
	S	Martin Cornelius	30	chauffeur	36	here
	T	Martin Eva—†	30	housewife	34	"
	U	Gallman Ida—†	30	presser	24	"
	V	Gallman Odessa—†	30	housewife	43	"
	W	Dillingham Edith—†	30	housekeeper	32	"
	X	Simpson Myrtle—†	30	domestic	50	"
	Y	Mitton James	31	laborer	55	
	Z	Watson Christopher C	31	porter	44	
823						
	A	Watson Marion F—†	31	housewife	40	"
	B	Youngblood Grace I—†	31	"	38	
	C	Youngblood Joseph S	31	woodworker	20	"
	D	Youngblood Offie D	31	janitor	40	
	E	Wilson Clarence	31	laborer	39	
	F	Wilson Norma—†	31	housewife	38	"
	G	Landrum Ophelia—†	31	"	23	"
	H	Landrum Pres	31	U S A	20	
	K	Smith Robert	31	laborer	38	
	L	Duarte Antonio M	31	"	40	
	M	Bowden Kenneth	31	janitor	50	"
	N	Fisher Mary—†	31	housewife	39	"
	O	Horner Bradford	31	presser	21	8 Hubert
	P	Horner Priscilla—†	31	housewife	21	8 "
	R	Brown William	32	U S A	36	here
	S	Bell Irene—†	32	housewife	42	"
	T	Bell Peter	32	porter	50	"
	U	Butler Adelaide—†	32	domestic	29	"
	V	Butler Ruth—†	32	"	46	
	W	Johnson Lucinda—†	32	housekeeper	56	"
	X	Thomas Henry	32	laborer	26	"
	Y	Stanley Nebraska—†	33	domestic	50	"
	Z	Howard Frances F—†	33	presser	38	
824						
	A	Tavaris Januario M	33	pedler	58	
	B	Whittier Agatha—†	33	housewife	49	"
	C	Whittier James	33	laborer	55	
	D	Horner Irene—†	33	housewife	51	"

Page.	Letter.	FULL NAME.	Residence, Jan. 1, 1943.	Occupation.	Supposed Age.	Reported Residence, Jan. 1, 1942. Street and Number.

Cunard Street—Continued

	E	Howell Freeman	33	retired	75	New York
	F	Ford Mary—†	33	presser	32	here
	G	Ford Walter	33	clerk	38	"
	H	Green Annie—†	34	domestic	38	"
	K	Merandus Grace—†	34	presser	59	
	L	Redmond Lydia—†	34	housewife	35	"
	M	Redmond Robert	34	bartender	23	527A Col av
	N	Bleckley Leila—†	34	waitress	35	here
	O	Brown Mae—†	34	"	53	"
	P	Goosby Julia—†	34	housewife	33	"
	R	Goosby Louie	34	engraver	37	"
	S	Hughes Arthur L	35	welder	31	
	T	Hughes Gladys—†	35	housewife	25	"
	U	Snipes Abraham	35	laborer	46	
	V	Snipes Gertrude L—†	35	housewife	40	"
	W	Tynes Edith—†	35	"	49	
	X	Tynes Robert	35	electrician	46	"
	Y	Belcher Parker	35	cook	37	
	Z	Tyler Julia—†	35	housewife	46	"
825						
	A	Tyler Nathan	35	U S A	21	746 Shawmut av
	B	Tyler Rita—†	35	housekeeper	21	746 "
	C	Tyler William	35	rigger	47	here
	D	Chapman Elizabeth F—†	35	housewife	46	"
	E	Chapman Paul F	35	waiter	49	"
	F	Johnson Daisy—†	36	domestic	31	New York
	G	Williams Eula	36	laborer	49	here
	H	Wilson Louise—†	36	housewife	50	"
	K	Wilson Samuel	36	laborer	46	"
	L	Clark Elliot	36	cook	30	
	M	Clark Frederick H	36	U S A	32	
	N	Clark Nellie—†	36	domestic	60	"
	O	Matthews Mildred—†	36	housewife	35	"
	P	Bishop Iris—†	36	seamstress	43	38 Cunard
	R	Reid Nathaniel	36	janitor	53	31 Warwick
	S	Jenkins Walter	37	laborer	47	here
	T	Jones Francis	37	"	46	"
	U	Lucas Minnie—†	37	housewife	46	"
	V	Lucas Thelma K—†	37	maid	30	"
	W	Bruton Mack	38	waiter	49	31 Eustis
	X	Shorts Benjamin	38	boilermaker	46	here

Page.	Letter.	Full Name.	Residence, Jan. 1, 1943.	Occupation.	Supposed Age.	Reported Residence, Jan. 1, 1942. Street and Number.

Cunard Street—Continued

	Y	Shorts Phoebe—†	38	housewife	44	here
	Z	Kelly David W	38	cook	49	"
826						
	A	Kelly Margaret—†	38	housewife	32	"
	B	Eagle Robert	38	U S A	29	"
	C	Irving Fannie—†	38	domestic	46	"
	D	Irving Inez—†	38	clerk	22	"
	E	O'Bryant Alethia—†	39	housewife	27	31 Cunard
	F	O'Bryant Charles	39	welder	28	31 "
	G	Somerville Alice—†	39	domestic	58	Newton
	H	Williams Hannah—†	39	housewife	51	here
	K	Williams James	39	porter	65	"
	L	Rhoderick Emma V—†	39	housewife	47	"
	M	Rhoderick Francis A	39	cook	49	
	N	*Butcher James	39A	retired	60	
	O	Clark Cleophas N	41	U S A	22	
	P	Clark Edwin	41	"	20	
	R	Clark Othniel	41	"	24	
	S	Clark Samuel	41	retired	71	
	T	Clark Xenophon	41	U S A	30	
	U	Clark Zelmar—†	41	housewife	62	"
	V	Johnson Charles	41	laborer	45	
	W	Johnson Elma—†	41	housewife	42	"
	X	Gray Beatrice—†	41	"	45	41 Northfield
	Y	Gray Robert A	41	U S A	24	41 "
	Z	Powell Frank	42	sorter	37	here
827						
	A	Powell Margaret—†	42	housewife	34	"
	B	Lynch Gertrude—†	42	"	54	801 Tremont
	C	Lynch Hazel—†	42	typist	21	801 "
	D	Nichols Lottie L—†	42	housewife	49	here
	E	Nichols Robert L	42	attendant	51	"
	F	Brown Louie	42	bellboy	34	"
	G	Neblett Emma—†	42	housewife	33	"
	H	Neblett McDonald	42	porter	42	"
	K	Cromwell Fred S	42	mechanic	49	65 Ruggles
	L	Ellis George W	42	retired	75	65 "
	M	Ellis Gertrude—†	42	shoeworker	40	65 "
	N	Matthews Lilly M—†	42	at home	57	here
	O	Hopes Helen—†	42	housewife	45	"
	P	Hopes Maude—†	42	presser	49	"

Page.	Letter.	Full Name.	Residence, Jan. 1, 1943.	Occupation.	Supposed Age.	Reported Residence, Jan. 1, 1942. Street and Number.

Cunard Street—Continued

	R	Hopes Queena—†	42	shoeworker	42	here
	S	Jordan Dudley	42	laborer	28	"
	T	Bell Julius A	42	retired	69	"
	U	Bell Mollie L—†	42	housewife	55	"
	V	Carney Harry F	42	sorter	59	
	W	Carney Jennie H—†	42	housewife	53	"
	X	Cox Etta—†	42	"	58	
	Y	*Cox Thomas	42	laborer	60	
	Z	West Lillian—†	42	domestic	26	"
828						
	A	Moody Elizabeth—†	42	cook	35	66 W Rutland
	B	Pierce Lillian—†	42	"	27	79 "
	C	Williams Laura—†	42	at home	72	29 Hollander

Davenport Street

	D	Bush Charles	14	laborer	56	here
	E	Hunter Eliza—†	14	housewife	62	"
	F	Hunter Henry L	14	garageman	56	"
	G	Pasteur Allida P	14	porter	49	"
	H	Pasteur Emma L—†	14	housewife	47	"
	K	Robinson Bessie E—†	14	"	42	
	L	Robinson Robert	14	waiter	53	"
	M	Johnson Charles K	16	presser	24	71 Warwick
	N	Johnson Esther L—†	16	housewife	20	71 "
	O	Parker Joseph	16	longshoreman	47	here
	P	Parker Memi—†	16	housewife	47	"
	R	Binyard Clara—†	16	domestic	48	73 Bower
	S	Binyard Clarence	16	laborer	49	73 "
	T	Parsons Edmond A	16	"	49	87 W Rutland
	U	Church Harry	18	"	49	here
	V	Mayo Lottie—†	18	housekeeper	44	"
	W	Russell Mary—†	18	at home	73	"
	X	Grainger Hazel—†	18	housekeeper	46	"
	Y	Simper John	18	machinist	22	"
	Z	Simper Lillian—†	18	domestic	28	"
829						
	A	Simper Mildred—†	18	clerk	20	
	B	Simper William	18	laborer	26	"
	C	Walker Alice—†	20	housewife	42	505 Col av
	D	Walker William	20	porter	39	505 "

Page.	Letter.	Full Name.	Residence, Jan. 1, 1943.	Occupation.	Supposed Age.	Reported Residence, Jan. 1, 1942. Street and Number.

Davenport Street—Continued

	E	Fortune Donald F	20	presser	23	here
	F	Fortune Edna M—†	20	housewife	47	"
	G	Fortune William E	20	laborer	27	"
	H	Reed Silvia—†	20	at home	83	
	K	Stevens Aleathia—†	20	housewife	47	"
	L	Stevens Radcliffe	20	laborer	46	
	N	Varrs Joseph	22	chauffeur	48	"
	O	Varrs Leonora—†	22	at home	70	
	P	Janey Carrie—†	22	"	70	
	R	Janey Mary—†	22	clerk	40	
	S	Janey Paul R	22	barber	45	
	T	Skinner Thomas	22	laborer	54	
	U	Francis Ann L—†	22	dressmaker	23	"
	V	Francis Frank J	22	cook	54	
	W	Francis Joseph E	22	laborer	25	
	X	Francis Susan M—†	22	housewife	54	"
	Y	Bennett Hattie—†	24	laundress	44	"
	Z	Bennett Junian	24	laborer	47	
830						
	A	Buckley Georgetta—†	24	at home	65	
	B	Drewery Luella—†	24	dressmaker	20	"
	C	Drewery Mollie—†	24	housewife	50	"
	D	Felton William	24	carpenter	68	"
	E	Briggs Gladys O—†	26	housewife	26	29 Wellington
	F	Briggs James L	26	laborer	28	29 "
	G	Davis Hattie—†	26	housekeeper	50	here
	H	Haywood Henry	26	laborer	44	"
	K	Wilson Mary—†	26	housekeeper	39	"
	L	Furtado Josephine—†	26	housewife	44	"
	M	Furtado Peter	26	laborer	56	
	N	Shefton Anna—†	28	housewife	49	"
	O	Shefton Ethel—†	28	typist	32	
	P	Shefton Laura—†	28	"	30	
	R	Husband Joseph	28	waiter	67	
	S	Lovel Malvina—†	28	housekeeper	58	"
	T	Bishop Helen D—†	28	housewife	39	87 Munroe
	U	Bishop Peter	28	laborer	42	87 "

Drew Place

	V	Belyea Evelyn—†	1	maid	44	here
	W	Doyle Augustine	1	retired	74	"

Page.	Letter.	FULL NAME.	Residence, Jan. 1, 1943.	Occupation.	Supposed Age.	Reported Residence, Jan. 1, 1942. Street and Number.

Drew Place—Continued

	X	Waterhouse Melvin E	1	engineer	26	8 Gore
	Y	Waterhouse Melvin F	1	retired	79	8 "
	Z	Chamberlain Albert	2	"	65	19 Newland
831						
	A	Chamberlain Alice—†	2	housewife	47	19 "
	B	*Kopper Sigrid—†	2	housekeeper	79	here
	C	Sullivan Michael	2	attorney	69	"
	D	Kenyon Margaret—†	3	nurse	64	"
	E	*Daly Lena—†	3	housewife	61	"
	F	Horton Mary A—†	3	"	58	"
	G	Boyle James	4	retired	80	"
	H	Adley Blanche—†	4	housewife	62	311 Hunt'n av
	K	Adley Edgar	4	chauffeur	54	311 "
	L	Kay Winifred—†	4	clerk	42	Worcester

Grinnell Street

	M	Whitly Alonzo	6	laborer	45	11 Weston
	O	Dorsey Marion—†	6	domestic	48	here
	P	Ingraham Laura M—†	8	housekeeper	30	"
	R	Howard Anne—†	8	domestic	24	13 Hubert
	S	Howard Robert	8	painter	32	560 Shawmut av
	T	Schlappi Christian	8	retired	76	here

Hammett Street

	U	Skinner Erwin	1	retired	68	here
	V	McGee Catherine—†	1	housewife	66	"
	W	McGee Charles W	1	U S A	30	"
	X	McGee Dorothy F—†	1	clerk	31	
	Y	McGee Ellen—†	1	nurse	27	
	Z	Fitzgerald Mary K—†	1	housewife	50	"
832						
	A	Winn Anna—†	1	clerk	65	
	B	Sonneman Bessie—†	1	housewife	70	"
	C	Sonneman Fred	1	retired	74	"
	D	Butler Marjorie E—†	3	housewife	21	30 Valentine
	E	Butler William	3	painter	27	30 "
	F	Gordon Paul	3	chauffeur	33	here
	G	Gordon Pearl R—†	3	housewife	32	"
	H	Connolly Edward V	3	U S A	34	"
	K	Connolly Mary A—†	3	housewife	64	"

Page.	Letter.	Full Name.	Residence, Jan. 1, 1943.	Occupation.	Supposed Age.	Reported Residence, Jan. 1, 1942. Street and Number.

Hammett Street—Continued

Page.	Letter.	Full Name.	Residence, Jan. 1, 1943.	Occupation.	Supposed Age.	Reported Residence, Jan. 1, 1942. Street and Number.
	L	Connolly Patrick J	3	laborer	64	here
	M	Donegan Bridget M—†	3	housewife	58	"
	N	Balise Arline C—†	3	"	23	"
	O	Balise Stamslaus	3	U S A	30	
	P	Preeper Charlotte—†	3	housewife	43	"
	S	Brinkert Edward	4	U S A	28	
	T	Brinkert Emma—†	4	housewife	66	"
	Y	Brinkert Richard R	4	laborer	71	
	V	Brinkert Theodore	4	U S A	32	
833						
	C	Fitzgerald John	7	laborer	52	
	D	Poirier Joseph J	7	"	50	
	E	Poirier Mary—†	7	housewife	50	"
	F	Poirier Thomas	7	U S A	21	

Howe Court

Page.	Letter.	Full Name.	Residence, Jan. 1, 1943.	Occupation.	Supposed Age.	Reported Residence, Jan. 1, 1942. Street and Number.
	K	Garabedian Sophie—†	1	at home	80	here
	L	Byrne James T	2	U S A	37	"
	M	Keating John	2	laborer	57	"

Newbern Street

Page.	Letter.	Full Name.	Residence, Jan. 1, 1943.	Occupation.	Supposed Age.	Reported Residence, Jan. 1, 1942. Street and Number.
	O	Hagen Charles E	15	painter	51	96 Westminster
	P	Hagen Nona—†	15	housewife	76	96 "
	R	Green Julia—†	15	"	35	here
	S	Green William E	15	laborer	33	"
	T	Holford Leo C	15	retired	42	"
	U	Holford Minnie—†	15	housewife	36	"
	V	Harrington Emily E—†	16	"	39	Needham
	W	Harrington James W	16	laundryworker	54	503 Shawmut av
	X	Sisco Marion—†	16	clerk	43	here
	Y	Ellis Albert	16	"	52	"
	Z	Ellis Lillian—†	16	housewife	55	"
834						
	B	Webb Henry	18	chauffeur	60	"
	C	Offley Charles	18	laborer	58	
	D	Thompson Frances—†	18	domestic	53	"
	E	Howell Rosa—†	18	at home	68	"
	F	Wesley Ethel—†	19	housewife	50	23 Newbern
	G	Small Goldie—†	19	at home	32	29 Oakburn av

Page.	Letter.	FULL NAME.	Residence, Jan. 1, 1943.	Occupation.	Supposed Age.	Reported Residence, Jan. 1, 1942. Street and Number.

Newbern Street—Continued

	K	Jones Gussie—†	19	housewife	38	here
	L	Jones John W	19	welder	51	"
	M	Wines Constance—†	19	domestic	22	"
	N	Wines Mary E—†	19	at home	24	
	O	Saunders Mildred—†	19	housewife	35	"
	P	Saunders Roy E	19	retired	47	"
	R	Jackson Martha—†	19	domestic	40	83 Sterling
	T	Allston Sadie—†	23	"	33	here
	U	Dudley Edward	23	retired	70	"
	V	Dudley Mattie—†	23	housewife	51	"
	W	Hawkins Emma—†	23	at home	66	
	Z	Hayes Helen M—†	30	domestic	42	"
835						
	A	Taylor Elsie—†	30	at home	20	"
	B	Barnes Frank A	31	buffer	53	Concord
	C	Barnes Hope—†	31	housewife	43	"
	D	Ellis George	32	laborer	43	here
	E	Ellis Lucille—†	32	housewife	38	"
	F	Ellis Mary L—†	32	domestic	20	"
	H	Watkins Bertie L—†	34	housewife	67	15 Ball
	G	Pearson Mary—†	34	"	30	here
	K	Jackson Howard	36	carpenter	56	"
	L	Jones Charlotte J—†	36	at home	94	"
	M	Lindsay Geraldine—†	36	"	23	
	N	Dubin Jacob	38	storekeeper	55	"
	O	Dubin Sarah—†	38	housewife	45	"

Pratt Court

	R	Moores Alice—†	1	housewife	39	120 W Canton
	S	Moores Leslie C	1	fireman	38	120 "
	T	Merolla Conrad	2	pedler	48	224 Eustis
	U	Merolla Jeremiah	2	florist	50	224 "
	V	Kelly William	3	porter	43	136 Cabot
	W	*MacNeil Francis J	4	clerk	60	58 Northampton
	X	MacNeil Margaret E—†	4	seamstress	57	58 "
	Y	Edwards Rose—†	5	at home	70	683 Tremont
	Z	Smith Agnes—†	6	housewife	38	here
836						
	A	Smith Harvey W	6	oiler	36	

Page.	Letter.	Full Name.	Residence, Jan. 1, 1943.	Occupation.	Supposed Age.	Reported Residence, Jan. 1, 1942. Street and Number.

Ruggles Street

Page.	Letter.	Full Name.	Residence, Jan. 1, 1943.	Occupation.	Supposed Age.	Reported Residence, Jan. 1, 1942. Street and Number.
	E	Rose Alvin R	175	laborer	30	here
	F	Rose Michael H	175	retired	64	"
	G	Rose Sarah F—†	175	housewife	56	"
	H	True George D	177	clerk	36	
	K	True Jennie—†	177	housewife	62	"
	L	True Ruth—†	177	secretary	26	"
	O	Neas Helen—†	205	at home	88	63 Birchwood
	P	Irwin Anna F—†	205	housewife	55	here
	R	Irwin Edward A	205	salesman	60	"
	S	Derler Anna—†	205	packer	55	4 Drew pl
	T	Carey Claire B—†	207	artist	58	Cambridge
	U	Egan Margaret—†	207	seamstress	46	88 Lambert av
	V	Harrington John	207	laborer	63	here
	W	Harrington Ruth—†	207	housewife	60	"

Sarsfield Street

Page.	Letter.	Full Name.	Residence, Jan. 1, 1943.	Occupation.	Supposed Age.	Reported Residence, Jan. 1, 1942. Street and Number.
	Z	Daley Ethel—†	8	clerk	21	here
837						
	A	Daley Mildred—†	8	"	20	
	B	Cross Marie—†	8	at home	80	
	C	Holmes Charles E	8	laborer	44	
	D	Lofkin Henrietta—†	8	at home	71	
	F	Jones Junius	10	shipper	39	
	G	Jones Myrtle—†	10	housewife	34	"
	H	Spencer Bernard	10	laborer	29	
	K	Spencer Ruth—†	10	housewife	32	"
	L	Greenage Harriet E—†	10	at home	67	
	M	Paull Anna—†	11	housewife	53	"
	N	Paull Charles M	11	retired	54	
	R	Pitters Mabel—†	11½	at home	45	"
	S	Pina Angeline—†	11½	housewife	32	16 Burke
	T	Pina Edward	11½	cook	42	16 "
	U	Pina Mildred—†	11½	at home	21	16 "
	V	Rose Charles H	11½	operator	51	here
	W	Silver Annette M—†	11½	domestic	36	"
	X	Rankin Ada—†	12	housewife	27	"
	Y	Rankin William	12	laborer	36	
	Z	Bean Anna—†	12	at home	73	
838						
	A	Bean Lawrence	12	laborer	36	

Page.	Letter.	Full Name.	Residence, Jan. 1, 1943.	Occupation.	Supposed Age.	Reported Residence, Jan. 1, 1942. Street and Number.

Sarsfield Street—Continued

	B	Bean Thomas	12	retired	76	here
	C	Bowen Anna—†	12	waitress	30	“
	D	Doyle May—†	14	dressmaker	60	“
	E	Pullen Frances—†	14	domestic	35	“
	F	Fowler Elizabeth—†	14	operator	25	“
	G	Arnold Annie E—†	15	at home	57	“
	H	Nicholson George	15	welder	45	
	K	Nicholson Kathryn—†	15	housewife	30	“
	L	Remsen Barbara—†	15	laundryworker	27	36 Newbern
	M	Reynolds Imogene—†	20	at home	67	here
	N	Tillman William	20	watchman	65	“
	O	Williams Bessie—†	20	clerk	27	“
	P	Worlock Joseph	20	mover	45	
	R	McPherson Bessie M—†	22	seamstress	45	“
	S	*McPherson Margaret—†	22	at home	76	
	T	Nicholson Alexander	22	retired	80	
	U	Merrill Frederick H	24	“	70	
	V	Westwood Esther M—†	24	stenographer	41	“
	W	Westwood Nettie A—†	24	housewife	71	“
	X	Bradshaw Mary—†	27	“	25	
	Y	Bradshaw Oscar	27	laborer	28	
	Z	Davis John	27	“	36	
839						
	A	Williams Rosa—†	27	domestic	46	“
	B	Hall Consuella—†	27	housewife	50	“
	C	Hall Elder H	27	clergyman	50	“
	D	Steffe Theresa—†	29	housewife	36	“
	E	Steffe William	29	painter	48	
	F	*Maxwell Alberta—†	29	domestic	40	“
	G	Maxwell Chester	29	typist	22	
	H	Maxwell Gwendolyn—†	29	ropemaker	25	“
	K	*Maxwell Leo	29	laundryman	26	“
	M	Saunders Lawrence	30	janitor	48	Cambridge
	N	Trent Abigail—†	30	at home	73	here
	O	Henderson Mack G	30	fireman	49	“
	P	Henderson Viola H—†	30	housewife	40	“
	R	Hewett Harold	32	operator	40	1045 Tremont
	S	Goodman Louella—†	32	waitress	50	here
	T	Prevo Cora—†	32	housewife	44	“
	U	Prevo Eugene	32	clerk	26	“
	V	Prevo Myrtle—†	32	“	23	

Page.	Letter.	Full Name.	Residence, Jan. 1, 1943.	Occupation.	Supposed Age.	Reported Residence, Jan. 1, 1942. Street and Number.

Sarsfield Street—Continued

	Z	Foster Wilfred—†	42	at home	47	here
840						
	A	Mintus Aurelius	42	laborer	56	
	B	Ingram Emma—†	42	housewife	46	"
	C	Joseph Clayter—†	42	at home	23	
	D	Winborn Watson	42	checker	58	"
	E	Arcord James	44	rigger	31	20 Greenwich pk
	F	Faggett Nettie—†	44	at home	72	here
	G	Barnett Christine—†	44	housewife	30	"
	H	Barnett Ellsworth	44	metalworker	48	"

Sterling Street

	L	Fonseca Fred	142	laborer	45	here
	M	Fonseca Gladys—†	142	housewife	31	"

Tremont Street

	S	Alcorn Marie—†	795	housewife	44	here
	T	Alcorn William	795	laborer	42	"
	U	Gibson Amos	795	electrician	44	"
	V	Gibson Doris—†	795	housewife	40	"
	W	Davis Milton	795	barber	42	"
	X	Mouzon George W	795	laborer	29	416 Mass av
	Y	Thompson Milton	795	porter	29	14 Camden
	Z	Brown Athalia J—†	795	housewife	40	here
841						
	A	Brown Patrick M	795	laborer	42	"
	B	Cheery Consevella—†	795	waitress	24	
	C	Morrison Benjamin	795	laborer	46	
	D	Morrison Viola—†	795	housewife	45	"
	E	Rutledge Eula L—†	795	"	38	757 Tremont
	F	Rutledge Lindsey	795	laborer	45	757 "
	G	Jenkins Australia H—†	795	housewife	30	here
	H	Jenkins R Benjamin	795	laborer	30	"
	K	Bullock Audrey L—†	795	housewife	28	"
	L	Bullock Benjamin L	795	porter	31	
	N	Brown Farona—†	799	hairdresser	32	"
	O	Hicks Eula M—†	799	housewife	32	"
	P	Hicks Walter	799	barber	39	
	R	Coulston Samuel E	799	presser	47	

Page.	Letter.	Full Name.	Residence, Jan. 1, 1943.	Occupation.	Supposed Age.	Reported Residence, Jan. 1, 1942. Street and Number.

Tremont Street—Continued

	S	Ward Charles D	799	machinist	51	here
	T	Williams Dorothy—†	799	housekeeper	43	"
	U	Moore Claude	799	laborer	32	"
	V	Moore Dorothy M—†	799	waitress	23	
	W	Willis Albert A	799	mechanic	63	"
	X	Willis Anna—†	799	housewife	55	"
	Y	Franks Horace H	799	retired	66	
	Z	Tutt Elsie M—†	799	housewife	27	"
842						
	A	Tutt Wesley E	799	U S A	33	
	B	Ross Deed	801	laborer	44	
	C	Ross Lucy M—†	801	housewife	40	"
	E	Jacobs Christina—†	801	"	44	
	F	Jacobs Nathan E	801	laborer	50	"
	G	White Georgia—†	801	housewife	27	New York
	H	White Louis E	801	welder	44	"
	L	Ramsey Claude	803	laborer	42	here
	M	Ramsey Sophronia—†	803	housewife	30	"
	N	Coffey Lillie M—†	803	operator	30	"
	O	Reed Josephine—†	803	housewife	51	"
	P	Wiley Etoye—†	803	domestic	27	"
	R	Jordan Edward	803	retired	73	
	S	Jordan Josephine M—†	803	housewife	68	"
	T	Warren Florence I—†	803	domestic	52	"
	U	Crick Keziah K	803	housekeeper	53	"
	V	Harris Arthur W	803	janitor	51	"
	W	Harris Mildred C—†	803	domestic	21	"
843						
	A*	Richards Georgianna—†	813	housekeeper	52	"
	B	Johnson Anthony	813	engineer	56	"
	C	Johnson Edna—†	813	housewife	53	"
	D	Jones Dorothy—†	813	maid	21	
	E	Jones Julia I—†	813	housewife	47	"
	G	Anderson Carlotta—†	819	"	38	28 Kendall
	H	Anderson Edward	819	presser	37	28 "
	K	Johnson Richard	819	"	33	New York
	L	Payne Daisy M—†	819	housewife	56	here
	M	Payne Humphrey	819	waiter	61	"
	N	Sweeney Ann—†	819	domestic	50	"
	O	Kelley Margaret—†	957	housewife	31	29 Wellington
	P	Rhode Ethel—†	957	domestic	33	9 Ashland

Page.	Letter.	Full Name.	Residence, Jan. 1, 1943.	Occupation.	Supposed Age.	Reported Residence, Jan. 1, 1942. Street and Number.

Tremont Street—Continued

	R	Thomas Lavania H—†	957	domestic	34	Maryland
	S	Selden Laura—†	957	"	67	here
	T	Davis Nellie—†	957	housekeeper	65	"
	V	Spencer Daniel	959	retired	75	"
	W	Spencer Mary J—†	959	housewife	67	"
	X	Dotson Ellen—†	959	housekeeper	69	"
	Y	Lynch Adelle—†	959	domestic	60	"
844						
	C	Johnson Rose A—†	961A	laundress	55	"
	D	Davis Martha—†	961A	domestic	50	"
	E	Akins Annie—†	963	"	50	
	F	Lawton Emma—†	963	housekeeper	59	"
	G	Powell Edward	963	laborer	57	"
	H	Meranda Dorothy—†	963	housewife	48	"
	K	Meranda Frank D	963	laborer	57	
	L	Meranda Louise E—†	963	stitcher	20	
	M	Meranda Raymond F	963	U S A	22	"
	N	Bazemore Beatrice M—†	963	clerk	27	
	O	Bazemore Rosa B—†	963	housewife	70	"
	S	Edwards Audrey B—†	965	"	22	
	T	Edwards Clarence T	965	electrician	26	"
	U	Smith Frances—†	965	at home	69	
	V	Lawrence Andrew J	965	laborer	65	
	W	Lawrence William H	965	U S A	36	
	Z	Washington Dora—†	967	housekeeper	62	"
845						
	A	Ripley Hattie—†	967	at home	69	
	B	Smith Mabel C—†	967	housekeeper	60	"
	D	Day Eugene W	968	shoeworker	60	"
	E	Jackson Robert D	968	retired	68	
	F	Themea Ruby E—†	968	operator	52	"
	G	Carden Alice—†	968	housewife	67	671 Shawmut av
	H	Carden Clifton	968	laborer	32	671 "
	K	Carden James S	968	chauffeur	36	here
	L	Clark Frances—†	968	housewife	52	Newton
	M	Clark Stuart	968	U S A	26	Revere
	P	Hansley Cecelia—†	971A	domestic	42	here
	R	Taylor Josephine—†	971A	housewife	59	"
	S	Taylor Samuel	971A	laborer	58	"
	T	William Ellen—†	971A	at home	76	"
	U	Brown Walter E	971A	packer	33	1025 Tremont

Page.	Letter.	Full Name.	Residence, Jan. 1, 1943.	Occupation.	Supposed Age.	Reported Residence, Jan. 1, 1942. Street and Number.

Tremont Street—Continued

	v	Noka Gideon A	971A	laborer	61	here
	w	Noka Hattie M—†	971A	housewife	59	"
	x	Davis Lulu—†	971A	housekeeper	58	"
	y	*Martin Jeremiah	972	chef	58	"
	z	*Martin Minnie—†	972	housewife	53	"
846						
	A	Banks Joseph	972	retired	65	
	B	Thompson William	972	laborer	45	
	D	Lynch Richard	973A	"	47	
	E	Williams Catherine—†	973A	domestic	50	"
	F	Russell Harold W	973A	electrician	22	"
	G	Russell Lorena L—†	973A	housewife	45	"
	H	Russell William J	973A	laborer	23	
	K	Sampson George	973A	laundryman	47	"
	L	Henry George	973A	laborer	49	
	M	Jones Mary E—†	973A	domestic	46	"
	P	*Murray David W	975A	laborer	47	
	R	Nelson Irene—†	975A	domestic	37	"
	S	Peart Ada—†	975A	"	50	
	T	Barnes Ottelia—†	975A	"	42	
	U	Parks Eleanor—†	975A	"	20	
	V	Parks John	975A	U S A	21	
	W	Parks Marion F—†	975A	housewife	49	"
	X	Parks Zora—†	975A	domestic	22	"
	Y	Gomes Edith B—†	976	maid	62	
	Z	Carter Ella—†	976	at home	80	
847						
	A	Pina Emma—†	976	housewife	52	"
	B	Pina Zachariah	976	laborer	57	"
	C	Houser William	976	"	67	8 Benton
	D	Snow Florence—†	976	maid	34	Hyannis
	F	Lucas William	977A	chauffeur	50	here
	G	Alston Benjamin	977A	"	39	"
	H	Anderson Evelyn—†	977A	domestic	32	"
	K	Anderson George	977A	clerk	40	
	L	Nunley Regina J—†	977A	housekeeper	24	"
	M	Sivewright Earl R	977A	laborer	23	"
	N	Sivewright Florence V—†	977A	housewife	47	"
	O	Sivewright Reginald W	977A	clerk	26	"
	S	Burse Albert S	979A	musician	46	"
	T	Burse Beatrice—†	979A	housewife	64	"

Page.	Letter.	Full Name.	Residence, Jan. 1, 1943.	Occupation.	Supposed Age.	Reported Residence, Jan. 1, 1942. Street and Number.

Tremont Street—Continued

Page.	Letter.	Full Name.	Residence, Jan. 1, 1943.	Occupation.	Supposed Age.	Reported Residence, Jan. 1, 1942. Street and Number.
	U	Burse Margaret A—†	979A	housewife	27	here
	V	Burse Veal W	979A	laborer	63	"
	W	Burse Veal W	979A	shipfitter	26	"
	X	Pearce Ethel—†	979A	domestic	34	"
	Y	Rainey Dorothy—†	979A	presser	36	
	Z	Rainey Sarah—†	979A	housewife	64	"
848						
	A	Washington William	979A	laborer	20	
	B	Monroe Ada J—†	979A	housekeeper	57	"
	C	Williams Bernard	979A	porter	47	"
	D	Bell Florence J—†	980	housewife	64	"
	E	Bell Irving H	980	porter	54	
	F	Williams Ida B—†	980	at home	70	"
	G	Reid Edith—†	980	housewife	20	111 Ruggles
	K	Williams Elizabeth—†	981A	domestic	50	here
	L	Lomax Lillian A—†	981A	housewife	47	"
	M	Lomax Lillian F—†	981A	domestic	21	"
	N	Robinson Bertha—†	981A	laundress	47	"
	P	Foster Ellen—†	984	at home	89	
	R	Henderson Edna—†	984	clerk	50	
	S	Plenty Austin	984	laborer	49	
	U	*Hunt Adora—†	984	housewife	61	"
	V	Hunt Constance—†	984	presser	32	
	W	Hunt Curtis	984	clerk	31	
	Z	Woodward Helen—†	987	housewife	33	"
849						
	A	Woodward Thomas	987	porter	68	
	B	Scoltock Adeline—†	987	housewife	51	"
	C	Mackay James	987	retired	69	"
	E	Anderson Hattie—†	988	maid	59	56 Cabot
	F	Sorrels James D	988	porter	44	217 W Canton
	G	Crawford Helena B—†	988	saleswoman	36	here
	H	Engerman Daniel	988	laborer	49	"
	K	Murray Ruby—†	988	waitress	24	"
	L	Randolph Edith—†	988	clerk	38	967 Tremont
	M	Braxton Ruth E—†	989	domestic	37	here
	N	Lindsay Anna D—†	989	florist	60	"
	O	Luacaw Clinton A	989	U S A	20	"
	P	Hudlin Vera—†	989	housekeeper	43	"
	R	Ford Lillian—†	989	maid	30	"
	S	Glover Geneva—†	989	laundress	27	"

Page.	Letter.	Full Name.	Residence, Jan. 1, 1943.	Occupation.	Supposed Age.	Reported Residence, Jan. 1, 1942. Street and Number.

Tremont Street—Continued

Page.	Letter.	Full Name.	Residence, Jan. 1, 1943.	Occupation.	Supposed Age.	Reported Residence, Jan. 1, 1942. Street and Number.
	V	Bryant Jennie G—†	991	domestic	64	531 Mass av
	W	Bryant Richard C	991	laborer	23	750 Tremont
	X	Powell Florence—†	991	at home	35	here
	Y	Henderson Preston	991	cutter	35	"
	Z	Robinson Alexander	992	retired	62	"
850						
	A	Robinson Estella—†	992	housewife	57	36 Cunard
	C	Canada Charles S	992	welder	21	34 Cabot
	D	Canada Maud—†	992	housewife	20	34 "
	E	Dorsey Frances—†	992	"	21	9 Ditmus ct
	F	Dorsey Jacob L	992	U S A	21	9 "
	H	Davis Cleo—†	994	housewife	31	here
	K	Davis Gertrude—†	994	maid	34	"
	L	Davis Joel	994	laborer	32	"
	M	Gillespie Louisa—†	994	housewife	68	"
	N	Jones George	994	laborer	50	
	O	Jones Phillip	994	"	46	
	P	Andrews Peter	994	chipper	35	
	R	Andrews Rose—†	994	housewife	28	"
	S	Rollins Alberta—†	994	"	25	
	T	Rollins Lonnie	994	waiter	30	
	W	*Smith Myrtle—†	998	maid	26	
	X	*Smith Samuel O	998	chef	37	
	Y	*Smith Sarah—†	998	housewife	62	"
	Z	*Kirton Florence—†	998	"	61	"
851						
	A	*Kirton Nathaniel	998	janitor	70	
	B	Snape Susie—†	998	housewife	38	"
	C	Snape Thomas	998	laborer	47	
	D	*Downes Edna—†	998	operator	25	"
	E	*Downes Rose—†	998	housewife	56	"
	F	Hannon Willie—†	999	at home	65	
	G	Allston Sterling	999	chef	32	
	H	Smith Almira—†	999	housekeeper	69	"
	M	Seay Edward	1003	laborer	43	"
	N	Seay Freddie—†	1003	housewife	43	"
	O	Sykes Anna—†	1003	"	31	
	P	Sykes Raymond	1003	laborer	47	
	R	Anderson John E	1004	attendant	48	"
	S	Anderson Mildred—†	1004	housewife	39	"
	T	Smith Mary—†	1004	operator	54	

Page.	Letter.	FULL NAME.	Residence, Jan. 1, 1943.	Occupation.	Supposed Age.	Reported Residence, Jan. 1, 1942. Street and Number.

Tremont Street—Continued

	Z	Hill Alice L—†	1010	housewife	49	here
852						
	A	Guy Cora—†	1010	maid	58	"
	B	Wimbish Rose—†	1010	housewife	78	Woburn
	H	Marshall Rebecca J—†	1015	"	58	here
	K	Brooks Florence E—†	1016	"	50	"
	L	Brooks Robert E	1016	clergyman	52	"
	M	Brooks Robert E	1016	welder	29	"
	N	Foster Irene—†	1016	clerk	30	70 Westminster
	O	Mosley Ellen—†	1016	housewife	78	70 "
	S	Crawford Edward	1019	clerk	42	here
	T	Crawford Jane—†	1019	packer	41	"
	U	Boyle John	1019	U S A	21	"
	V	Hill Della—†	1019	housewife	41	"
	W	Hill William	1019	U S C G	20	"
	X	Strong Clarence	1019½	waiter	38	
	Y	Strong Gladys—†	1019½	housewife	36	"
	Z	Blair Harriet—†	1019½	"	68	
853						
	A	Thompson Albina—†	1019½	"	38	
	B	*Thompson William A	1019½	porter	41	
	C	Corbin John D	1019½	mechanic	63	"
	D	Porter Anthony	1019½	U S A	21	
	E	Roachford Claudia—†	1019½	clerk	53	
	F	Robinson Elizabeth—†	1019½	maid	38	
	K	Caines Sarah—†	1022	housewife	45	"
	L	Precia Beulah—†	1022	"	31	
	M	Precia Spencer	1022	laborer	40	
	N	Precia Walter	1022	dentist	49	
	T	Parker Jacqueline—†	1025	stenographer	23	"
	U	Parker John	1025	janitor	62	"
	V	Parker Nellie V—†	1025	housewife	62	"
	W	Springer Dana	1025	U S A	24	
	X	Springer Elsie—†	1025	stenographer	24	"
	Y	Springer Gertrude—†	1025	housewife	48	"
	Z	Springer Joseph	1025	steamfitter	47	"
854						
	A	Springer Robert	1025	student	20	
	B	Springer Vincent	1025	welder	21	
	C	Brown Naomi—†	1025	housewife	32	"
	D	Brown Walter	1025	musician	33	"

Page.	Letter.	Full Name.	Residence, Jan. 1, 1943.	Occupation.	Supposed Age.	Reported Residence, Jan. 1, 1942. Street and Number.

Tremont Street—Continued

	E	Rue Belle—†	1026	at home	79	here
	F	Rue Eva—†	1026	housewife	52	"
	G	Rue John	1026	retired	52	"
	H	Harris Louise—†	1026	hostess	39	Illinois
	K	Williams James	1026	laborer	55	here
	L	Williams Mary L—†	1026	housewife	60	"
	M	Rannie Anita—†	1026	"	40	"
	N	Rannie Leon A	1026	chauffeur	42	"
	O	Williams Mary R—†	1026	housewife	65	"
	P	Conway Anna—†	1026	"	42	
	R	*Conway Edward	1026	janitor	50	
	S	Smith William	1026	laborer	47	
	T	Stile Katie—†	1026	presser	24	
	U	Jones Lucille—†	1026	housewife	45	"
	V	Mitchell Belle—†	1026	"	64	
	W	Williams Louise—†	1026	"	48	
	X	Leach Wendell L	1027	porter	46	
	Y	Grant Howard	1027	chef	33	
	Z	Grant Thomasina—†	1027	housewife	23	"
855						
	D	*Douglin Aberna—†	1029½	housekeeper	48	"
	E	Herron Cyril	1029½	painter	48	"
	F	Herron Lucy—†	1029½	housewife	42	"
	H	Henry Earl	1031	laborer	28	
	K	Henry Mildred—†	1031	clerk	26	
	L	Fox Carey	1031	chauffeur	52	"
	M	Fox Helen J—†	1031	housewife	49	"
	N	Cauley Bobbie—†	1031	"	32	14 Watson
	O	Cauley Romilles	1031	assembler	40	14 "
	U	McDonald Theresa—†	1037	factoryhand	47	here
	V	Aronson Esther—†	1037	bookkeeper	28	"
	W	*Ruvich Julius	1037	storekeeper	53	"
	X	Ruvich Louis	1037	shipfitter	22	"
	Y	*Ruvich Mary—†	1037	housewife	52	"
	Z	Ruvich Mary—†	1037	housekeeper	24	"
856						
	A	Curtis Kathleen—†	1037	clerk	23	
	B	Curtis Philip	1037	"	50	
	C	Curtis Sofie—†	1037	housewife	50	"
	D	Lewis Margaret—†	1037	housekeeper	61	"
	N	Oliver Laura—†	1043	operator	24	"

Page.	Letter.	Full Name.	Residence, Jan. 1, 1943.	Occupation.	Supposed Age.	Reported Residence, Jan. 1, 1942. Street and Number.

Tremont Street—Continued

	o	Smith Estelle—†	1043	housewife	38	10 Cunard
	p	Smith Henry	1043	clerk	39	10 "
	r	Rollins Hattie J—†	1043	housewife	65	here
	s	Rollins Lillian E—†	1043	dressmaker	30	"
	t	Rollins Thomas H	1043	retired	70	"
	u	Springer Louis	1043	porter	30	Michigan
	v	Springer Myrtle—†	1043	housewife	28	"
	w	Goode Carrie—†	1043	"	30	here
	x	Goode Edward J	1043	welder	32	"
	y	Butler Alice—†	1045	housekeeper	45	46 Hammond
	z*	Williams Jacob	1045	laborer	50	here
857						
	a	Hood Elaine—†	1045	housewife	39	"
	b	Hood Thomas	1045	operator	36	"
	c	Bland Rose—†	1045	housekeeper	43	1029½ Tremont
	d	Butler Arthur	1045	plumber	53	Rockland
	e	Dockett Bennie—†	1045	operator	53	here
	g	Hunt Agnes R—†	1045	housewife	35	"
	h	Hunt St Aubyn	1045	painter	47	"
	k	Langford Henrietta—†	1045	housekeeper	38	"
	l	Marsh Irene—†	1045	"	20	"
	r	Piper Bertha L—†	1050	housewife	54	"
	s	Piper Elsie W—†	1050	clerk	38	
	u	Clark Eula—†	1051	housewife	35	"
	v	Clark Joseph	1051	chauffeur	49	"
	w	Jackson Mamie—†	1051	operator	33	"
	x	Walker Addie—†	1051	housewife	43	"
	y	Lomax Phillip	1051	chauffeur	26	"
	z	Graham Mamie F—†	1051	housewife	58	"
858						
	a	Graham William H	1051	carpenter	60	"
	b	Smith Frederick	1051	laborer	37	12 Oakburn av
	c	Colston Flora—†	1051	laundress	47	here
	d	Lewis Adelle—†	1051	housekeeper	30	"
	e	Braxton Geraldine—†	1051	domestic	27	1059 Tremont
	f	Braxton John	1051	laborer	30	1059 "
	g	James Charles	1051	"	48	1022 "
	h	Louis Derather D	1052	dentist	46	here
	k	Brown William H	1052	clerk	45	"
	l	Louis Ernest A	1052	"	51	"
	n	Ingram Henry	1053	laborer	28	

Page.	Letter.	Full Name.	Residence, Jan. 1, 1943.	Occupation.	Supposed Age.	Reported Residence, Jan. 1, 1942. Street and Number.
		Tremont Street—Continued				
	O	Ingram Mary—†	1053	housewife	27	here
	P	Bowen John	1053	mechanic	49	New York
	R	Flowers Clara—†	1053	housewife	54	571 Col av
	S	Flowers James P	1053	porter	55	571 "
	T	Butner Hazel—†	1053	housekeeper	30	here
	U	Thomas Alderwin	1053	laborer	25	"
	V	Thomas Virginia—†	1053	housewife	27	"
859						
	B	LeSueur James	1059	physician	46	"
	C	LeSueur Olive—†	1059	housewife	35	"
	D	Tucker Artemus I	1059	dentist	40	
	E	Tucker Julia V—†	1059	housewife	38	"
	F	Lopes Antonette—†	1059	"	27	
	G	Lopes William	1059	laborer	25	
	K	Nurse Frank	1059	porter	41	
	L	Nurse Ruth—†	1059	housewife	43	"
	M	Brown Gertrude—†	1059	housekeeper	40	"
	N	Goodrich Curtis	1059	U S N	29	"
	O	Goodrich Florence—†	1059	housewife	28	Virginia
	P	Johnson Pauline—†	1059	maid	27	Ohio
	R	Wagg Marcus	1059	retired	42	here
	S	Ashley Angella—†	1059	housewife	38	"
	T	Ashley Ernest	1059	seaman	49	"
	U	Thomas Joseph	1060	porter	41	
	V	Parker Moses	1060	laborer	49	"
	W	Cole Gilbert	1060	U S A	26	37 Kent
	X	Lowry Betty—†	1060	domestic	53	here
	Y	Davis James P	1060	janitor	65	"
	Z	Wyns Olga L—†	1060	hairdresser	29	"
860						
	A	Foy Wyoma—†	1060	maid	40	
	B	Vass Paul	1060	laborer	54	
	C	Vass Viola—†	1060	housewife	40	"
	D	Jones Elizabeth—†	1060	"	24	52 Cabot
	E	Jones Samuel	1060	printer	42	52 "
	F	Jefferson Dora L—†	1060	housewife	23	Florida
	G	Jefferson James	1060	laborer	25	"
	M	Brown Albert S	1064	"	53	here
		Clarke Nellie H—†	1064	cook	45	"
		Peters Prince	1064	retired	44	"
	N O	Burke Augustus	1064	laborer	33	

Page.	Letter.	Full Name.	Residence, Jan. 1, 1943.	Occupation.	Supposed Age.	Reported Residence, Jan. 1, 1942. Street and Number.

Tremont Street—Continued

Page.	Letter.	Full Name.	Residence, Jan. 1, 1943.	Occupation.	Supposed Age.	Reported Residence, Jan. 1, 1942. Street and Number.
	R	Burke Augustus	1064	retired	68	here
	S	Burke Cato M	1064	laborer	43	"
	T	Burke Rachel—†	1064	housewife	65	"
	X	Langford Joseph	1066	laborer	60	
	W	Tanner Walter	1066	tailor	48	
	Y	Smith Florence—†	1066A	housewife	59	"
	Z	Pendleton Catherine—†	1066A	"	86	
861						
	B	Allen Charles	1068	printer	22	
	C	Allen Gloria—†	1068	housekeeper	23	"
	D	Allen Sarah—†	1068	housewife	55	"
	E	Isaacs James	1068	chef	56	"
	F	Isaacs Winifred—†	1068	housewife	64	"
	P	Washington Annie—†	1080	"	38	
	R	McIntyre Larnie	1080	retired	76	
	S	McIntyre Larnie	1080	porter	44	
	T	McIntyre Martha—†	1080	housewife	76	"
	U	Ferribaugh Jennie—†	1080	domestic	68	"
	V	Henry Robert T	1080	porter	55	119 Lenox
	X	Thompson Harvey M	1081	manager	55	here
	Y	Thompson Ora—†	1081	housewife	39	"
	Z	Cartwright Matilda—†	1081	housekeeper	68	"
862						
	A	Overton William	1081	laborer	59	
	B	Wise Hattie—†	1081	dressmaker	68	"
	C	Berry George A	1081	retired	70	"
	D	Berry Laura M—†	1081	housewife	45	"
	E	Clark Etheline—†	1081	"	41	
	F	Clark Melville	1081	porter	48	"
	G	Morrison Julius	1081	"	31	
	H	Morrison Ruth—†	1081	housewife	29	"
	K	Dozier Clarence	1081	janitor	48	
	L	Dozier Virginia—†	1081	housewife	48	"
	M	Remy Clarence	1081	laborer	23	
	N	Remy Rhoda—†	1081	housewife	44	"
	O	*Silcott Joseph	1081	chef	42	
	P	*Silcott Louise—†	1081	housewife	41	"
	R	Cantave Alice—†	1083	"	34	
	S	Cantave Nelson	1083	chef	38	
	T	Adams Etta—†	1083	housekeeper	55	"

Page.	Letter.	Full Name.	Residence, Jan. 1, 1943.	Occupation.	Supposed Age.	Reported Residence, Jan. 1, 1942. Street and Number.

Tremont Street—Continued

	U	Fields William	1083	retired	70	here
	V	Moody Inez—†	1083	dressmaker	23	"
	W	Moody Violet—†	1083	waitress	25	"
	X	Fitzgerald Edith—†	1083	presser	22	
	Z	Crocker Anna M—†	1086	maid	38	
863						
	A	Crocker Charles	1086	laborer	62	"
	B	Crocker Hattie—†	1086	housewife	61	"
	C	Duarte Carolina—†	1086	"	55	New Bedford
	D	Duarte Frank	1086	laborer	52	"
	E	Allen Albert	1086	window cleaner	47	19 Newbern
	F	Allen Mary—†	1086	housewife	33	19 "
	K	McDonald Bertha—†	1090	"	58	here
	L	McDonald Frederick	1090	laborer	60	"
	M	Williams Annie L—†	1090	maid	51	"
	N	Williams Frederick L	1090	U S A	22	
	P	Smith Clifford	1090	janitor	59	
	R	Smith Matilda—†	1090	housewife	57	"
	Y	Reid Mary—†	1096	waitress	25	1090 Tremont
	Z	Spencer Josephine—†	1096	housewife	56	here
864						
	A	Greene Elizabeth—†	1096	"	35	1060 Tremont
	B	Couto Eunice—†	1096	"	20	66 Humboldt av
	E	Flynn Anna—†	1117	housekeeper	51	here
	F	Eastwood George L	1117	laborer	54	1309 Tremont
	G	Eastwood Nellie—†	1117	housewife	56	1309 "
	H	McAvoy Patrick J	1117	mechanic	73	here
	K	Hand Elizabeth—†	1117	housewife	74	"
	L	Hand Robert	1117	draftsman	34	"
	M	Manning Edwin F	1117	musician	53	"
	N	Manning Ellen A—†	1117	housewife	53	"
	O	Currier Anna—†	1117	waitress	45	"
	P	Currier Helen—†	1117	factoryhand	32	"
	R	Hare Josephine—†	1117	housekeeper	40	"
	T	*Christian Paul	1117	laborer	62	
	U	Cornell James P	1117	"	32	
	V	Cornell Maud—†	1117	housewife	38	"
	W	*Chotourian Margaret-†	1118	"	35	
	X	Chotourian Nishan	1118	laborer	47	
	Y	Lynch Anna—†	1118	housewife	56	"

Page.	Letter.	Full Name.	Residence, Jan. 1, 1943.	Occupation.	Supposed Age.	Reported Residence, Jan. 1, 1942. Street and Number.

Tremont Street—Continued

Page.	Letter.	Full Name.	Residence, Jan. 1, 1943.	Occupation.	Supposed Age.	Reported Residence, Jan. 1, 1942. Street and Number.
	z	Lynch William	1118	laborer	62	here
865						
	D	Carter Cleora—†	1122	housewife	52	"
	E	Carter James	1122	laborer	56	
	F	Manning Bertha L—†	1122	housewife	49	"
	G	Manning John F	1122	retired	46	
	H	Croxan Charles	1122	laborer	24	
	N	Green Celia—†	1125A	housewife	62	"
	O	Green Isaac	1125A	storekeeper	64	"
	P	Thayer Effie D—†	1125A	stitcher	64	"
	T	Dulong Virginia—†	1125A	housekeeper	49	"
	R	Gillion Gladys—†	1125A	housewife	29	"
	S	Gillion James	1125A	U S N	34	
	U	Sullivan Catherine—†	1125A	housewife	54	"
	V	Sullivan James J	1125A	U S A	28	
	W	Sullivan Patrick J	1125A	laborer	61	
	X	Sullivan Thomas P	1125A	U S A	21	
	Y	Hetherington Ethel—†	1125A	housewife	34	"
	Z	Riley Mary E—†	1125A	"	65	
866						
	A	Riley William L	1125A	custodian	64	"
	B	Riley William L, jr	1125A	U S A	26	"
	C*	Andrews Julia—†	1125A	housekeeper	73	Canada
	D	Queen Katherine—†	1125A	"	67	here
	E	Devlin Henry	1125A	clerk	50	21 Wensley
	F	Devlin Mary—†	1125A	housewife	47	21 "
	O	Melaski Veronica—†	1132	storekeeper	49	here
	R	Elliot Mary—†	1133A	housewife	23	1137 Tremont
	S	Elliot Robert	1133A	inspector	25	1137 "
	T	Lord Mary—†	1133A	housewife	53	here
	U	Lord William	1133A	laborer	47	"
	V	Smith Dora M—†	1133A	housekeeper	68	"
	W	Hurder Benjamin J	1133A	chauffeur	31	"
	X*	Hurder Elvira—†	1133A	housewife	28	"
	Y	Murray Alice—†	1133A	housekeeper	65	"
	Z	Costello Mary M—†	1133A	housewife	42	"
867						
	A	Costello Thomas F	1133A	machinist	51	"
	B	Costello William F	1133A	U S A	25	
	C	Coates Eleanor G—†	1133A	housewife	54	"
	D	Coates Harry	1133A	foreman	50	

Page.	Letter.	Full Name.	Residence, Jan. 1, 1943.	Occupation.	Supposed Age.	Reported Residence, Jan. 1, 1942. Street and Number.

Tremont Street—Continued

	E	Tornberg Ann E—†	1133A	housewife	58	here
	F	Tornberg Per F	1133A	boilermaker	60	"
	G	*Grant Hildred—†	1133A	housewife	34	"
	M	Sullivan Mildred—†	1137A	"	22	14 Beethoven
	N	Sullivan Patrick F	1137A	electrician	26	14 "
	O	Reardon Herbert	1137A	liquors	45	478 Shawmut av
	P	Reardon Nellie—†	1137A	housewife	54	478 "
	R	King George	1137A	chef	58	here
	S	Knoblock Burton J	1137A	manager	52	Michigan
	T	O'Brien Jessie M—†	1137A	clerk	33	here
	U	Harding Mary—†	1137A	housewife	24	"
	V	Harding William	1137A	laborer	30	"
	W	Walters Annie—†	1137A	housewife	51	"
	X	Walters Frank	1137A	clerk	26	
	Y	Walters Mary—†	1137A	saleswoman	22	"
	Z	Walters Oliver E	1137A	chef	61	
868						
	A	Walters Rita—†	1137A	saleswoman	24	"
	B	Dorr Norman L	1138	retired	86	
	D	*Goon Lee	1140	laundryman	74	"

Walpole Street

	O	Rose Elizabeth—†	17	at home	41	here
	P	Cox Cecil C	17	laborer	35	"
	R	Cox Sarah D—†	17	housewife	29	"
	S	Hart Curtis	17	laborer	38	
	T	Hart Lois—†	17	housewife	37	"
	U	Goodman John R	17	janitor	40	
	V	Goodman Mary B—†	17	at home	60	
	W	Johnson Perley	17	laborer	38	
	X	Raynor Hazel G—†	17	dressmaker	36	"
	Y	Carter Lillian—†	17	laundress	46	27 Warwick
	Z	Sivewright Adelaide—†	17	waitress	28	27 "
869						
	A	Barrett Charles P	17	operator	62	here
	B	Barrett Lelia B—†	17	housewife	65	"
	C	Manley Ella—†	17	laundress	50	"
	D	Brown Benjamin	17	laborer	42	
	E	Brown Ruth—†	17	at home	24	
	F	Cummings Isaac	17	gatetender	22	"

Page.	Letter.	FULL NAME.	Residence, Jan. 1, 1943.	Occupation.	Supposed Age.	Reported Residence, Jan. 1, 1942. Street and Number.

Walpole Street—Continued

	G	Ward Carrie—†	22	housewife	48	here
	H	Ward Gladys—†	22	domestic	26	"
	K	Ward Joseph A	22	laborer	56	"
	L	Edwards Charles	22	barber	76	
	M	Francis Annie L—†	22	domestic	56	"
	N	Gumes Minnie—†	22	"	42	
	O	Peachey Charles R	22	porter	53	
	P	Peachey Nettie A—†	22	housewife	52	"
	R	Benders Joseph	23	laborer	38	262 Blue Hill av
	S	Benders Zaida—†	23	housewife	36	262 "
	T	Scott James	23	pickler	26	262 "
	U	Green Georgie M—†	23	domestic	44	here
	V	Green William H	23	sexton	52	"
	W	Heyward William	23	U S A	25	"
	X	Monroe Kate—†	23	housewife	37	"
	Y	Monroe Paul	23	painter	39	
	Z	Faust Eugene	23	welder	54	
870						
	A	Faust Lillian—†	23	domestic	44	"
	B	Faust Pavilla—†	23	at home	22	
	C	Faust Raymond	23	welder	23	"
	D	Garner Sally—†	23	at home	48	10 Willard pl
	E	Cromwell Anthony	23	welder	27	here
	F	Cromwell Archebell—†	23	housewife	24	"
	G	Suggs Laura—†	23	cook	52	"
	H	Lesueur Arthur D	23	laborer	46	
	K	Lesueur Esther M—†	23	clerk	24	
	L	Lesueur Florence R—†	23	housewife	44	"
	M	Lesueur Virginia E—†	23	clerk	23	
	N	Thrower Susan—†	23	cook	53	
	O	Wray Ann—†	23	housewife	40	"
	P	Wray William E	23	chauffeur	47	"
	R	Nichols Frances E—†	23	laundress	36	68 Harold
	S	Rankin Agnes E—†	23	"	27	here
	T	Thomas Florence C—†	23	at home	47	"
	U	Thomas Russell H	23	shipfitter	38	"
	V	Mitchell Inez—†	23	housewife	35	"
	W	Mitchell Raymond	23	mechanic	45	"
	X	*Allen Abraham	23	laborer	50	
	Y	Allen Emily—†	23	housewife	58	"
	Z	Allen William	23	U S C G	20	"

Page.	Letter.	Full Name.	Residence, Jan. 1, 1943.	Occupation.	Supposed Age.	Reported Residence, Jan. 1, 1942. Street and Number.
871		**Walpole Street**—Continued				
	A	DesSuze Marion—†	23	clerk	23	9 Catawba
	B	Myers Joseph D	24	retired	73	here
	C	Myers Selina E—†	24	at home	69	"
	D	Harvey Edith M—†	24	operator	41	"
	E	St Laurent Mercedes—†	24	clerk	40	
	F	Brewster Ethel—†	24	at home	36	"
	G	Hudlin Jesse A	24	porter	39	
	H	Middleton Mary—†	24	at home	50	
		Weston Place				
	M	Perry Charles C	2	mechanic	45	here
	N	Perry Dagmar W—†	2	wrapper	39	"
	P	Conniff Agnes R—†	4	housewife	36	"
	R	Dorr Vera V—†	5	"	29	67 Field
	S	*Pike William T	6	tailor	41	here
	T	Barrett John F	7	cleaner	60	"
	U	Barrett Nellie—†	7	housewife	61	"
	V	Barrett Thomas S	7	laborer	26	New York
	W	Dooley Annie E—†	8	at home	58	here
	X	Lynch Grace E—†	8	housewife	32	"
	Y	Lynch Jesse R	8	mechanic	37	"
	Z	O'Connor Roger J	9	chauffeur	44	57 Pembroke
872						
	A	Schmidt Francis	9	laborer	47	57 "
	B	Schmidt Mary L—†	9	housewife	43	57 "
	C	Ducharme Leonard E	10	baker	48	here
	D	Ducharme Mae A—†	10	housewife	45	"
	F	Vergakes Madelon H—†	12	"	37	"
	G	Vergakes Paul E	12	chef	42	"
	H	Connell Joseph E	13	brakeman	40	"
	K	Connell Mildred V—†	13	housewife	40	"
	L	Buckley Theresa—†	14	waitress	38	Quincy
	M	Lowe Ilene M—†	14	housewife	38	908 Col av
	N	Baumann Christina A—†	15	"	24	here
	O	Baumann William F	15	rigger	29	"
	T	Walnut Dorothy E—†	17	clerk	22	"
	U	Walnut Etta E—†	17	housewife	60	"
	V	Walnut Frederick C	17	U S A	25	"

Page.	Letter.	FULL NAME.	Residence, Jan. 1, 1943.	Occupation.	Supposed Age.	Reported Residence, Jan. 1, 1942. Street and Number.
		Weston Place—Continued				
	W	Walnut George E	17	painter	23	here
	X	Mischler Frank	18	retired	74	11 Armstrong
	Y	Cunniff James J	18	watchman	64	here
		Weston Street				
	Z	Hinds Leslie A	22	storekeeper	21	1053 Tremont
873						
	A	Hinds Ruth J—†	22	housewife	24	1053 "
	B	Scott Sarah J—†	22	at home	83	1053 "
	C	Latham Louis	22	clerk	50	here
	D	White Eleanor L—†	22	at home	24	"
	E	White Roxelina—†	22	presser	40	"
	F	White William	22	laborer	45	
	G	Walker Clara V—†	22	housewife	43	"
	H	Walker James B	22	laborer	20	
	K	Jefferson Katherine—†	23	stitcher	40	
	L	Jones Mary A—†	23	housewife	73	"
	M	Smith Elizabeth—†	23	domestic	51	"
	N	Pearson Bertha M—†	23	housewife	32	"
	O	Pearson George H	23	operator	32	"
	P	Covell Alfred L	27	rigger	35	
	R	Covell Grace A—†	27	inspector	22	"
	S	Covell Walter R	27	shipper	25	
	T	Covell Anna L—†	27	housewife	57	"
	U	Covell Lee R	27	rigger	62	
	V	Austin Edward	28	retired	65	
	W	*Fitzpatrick Hattie—†	28	domestic	41	"
	X	*Mason Mary—†	28	at home	80	"
	Y	Scrivner Anna A—†	29	"	64	50 Phillips
	Z	Mackay Emily E—†	29	"	65	here
874						
	B	Remy Lucy V—†	33	housewife	26	"
	C	Remy Stanton W	33	machinist	28	"
	D	Wilson Ida M—†	33	at home	24	
	F	Reed Perlenia B—†	35	"	68	"
	G	Bell Bessie L—†	35	housewife	22	Fitchburg
	H	Bell Charles W	35	operator	26	"
	K	Coles Lillian E—†	35	housewife	20	here
	L	Coles William M	35	laborer	25	"
	M	Francis Lillian C—†	35	at home	23	Virginia

Page.	Letter.	FULL NAME.	Residence, Jan. 1, 1943.	Occupation.	Supposed Age.	Reported Residence, Jan. 1, 1942. Street and Number.

Weston Street—Continued

	N	Williams Carrie M—†	37	trimmer	23	981 Tremont
	O	Williams John	37	laborer	25	981 "
	P	Payton Annie—†	37	housewife	54	here
	R	Payton Frank	37	porter	74	"
	S	Weeks Beatrice—†	37	packer	33	"
	T	Weeks Gladstone	37	student	35	"
	U	*Busby Cecil M	41	machinist	45	28 Davenport
	V	*Busby Mabel E—†	41	housewife	43	28 "
	W	Schuyler Georgiana—†	41	at home	74	here
	Z	Allen Ernest B	62	engineer	54	"
875						
	A	Burt Eliza—†	63	at home	74	24 King
	B	Myers Georgiana—†	63	"	27	27 Beech Glen
	C	Raiklen Harold	65	U S A	22	here
	D	Raiklen Hyman	65	"	27	"
	E	Raiklen Matthew	65	"	21	"
	F	Raiklen Michael	65	painter	52	
	M	Dorbe Ernest	69	machinist	60	"
	N	Hart Thomas	69	laborer	60	"
	O	Jordan Catherine—†	69	counter girl	60	Chelsea
	P	Kelley William	69	retired	66	here
	R	Mills Daniel W	69	steamfitter	73	1182 Tremont
	S	Murray Emma—†	69	housekeeper	44	here
	T	Sheehan Joseph	69	chauffeur	46	"
	U	Snell Samuel J	69	"	48	"
	V	Stiefel Robert	69	carpenter	53	"
	X	Granger Ethel—†	74	at home	32	
	Y	Janeves Baidzar—†	76	"	37	
	Z	Janeves Mary—†	76	housewife	63	"
876						
	A	Janeves Peter J	76	U S N	32	

Ward 9—Precinct 9

CITY OF BOSTON

LIST OF RESIDENTS
20 YEARS OF AGE AND OVER

(NON-CITIZENS INDICATED BY ASTERISK)
(FEMALES INDICATED BY DAGGER)

AS OF

JANUARY 1, 1943

JOSEPH F. TIMILTY, *Chairman*
FREDERIC E. DOWLING, *Secretary*
WILLIAM A. MOTLEY, JR.
FRANCIS B. McKINNEY
EVERETT R. PROUT
Listing Board.

CITY OF BOSTON PRINTING DEPARTMENT

Page.	Letter.	Full Name.	Residence, Jan. 1, 1943.	Occupation.	Supposed Age.	Reported Residence, Jan. 1, 1942. Street and Number.

900 Adams Place

	A	Glennon Patrick	20	laborer	65	here
	B	Hennessey Mary—†	20	housekeeper	69	"
	C	Merrigan Delia—†	20	houseworker	72	"
	D	Matthewson Gertrude—†	20	housewife	48	2622 Wash'n
	E	Matthewson John	20	laborer	46	2622 "
	F	Wambolt Daniel	22	"	24	here
	G	Wambolt James	22	U S A	25	"
	H	Wambolt Martha—†	22	housewife	47	"
	K	Wambolt Mary—†	22	clerk	21	
	L	Wambolt William	22	laborer	53	
	M	Dickinson Frederick	24	painter	68	
	O	DiDico Peter	26	retired	82	
	P	Lynch Mary L—†	28	housekeeper	70	"
	R	Davis Eva—†	28	housewife	73	Illinois
	S	Hines Lily—†	28	laundryworker	39	"
	T	Hughes George W	28	retired	82	here
	U	Hughes Virginia V—†	28	housekeeper	74	"
	V	Hughes William E	28	laborer	55	"
	W	Lewis Byrd C	28	retired	65	"
	X	Lewis Jennie F—†	28	housewife	62	"
	Y	Davis Millard	28	blacksmith	39	"
	Z	Smith Emma—†	28	domestic	38	"

901 Arnold Street

	B*	Norman Harry	1	laborer	63	here
	C	Norman Margaret—†	1	housewife	62	"
	F	Petitpas Emma—†	1½	"	31	"
	H	Giannini Anthony	3	retired	79	
	K	Robbins Madeline—†	3	operator	26	"
	M	Lopes Viola—†	5	clerk	44	Duxbury
	N	Stephens Beatrice—†	5	sorter	40	here
	O	Stephens Thaddeus H	5	laborer	38	"
	P	Morris Elinor—†	5	housewife	21	2 Forest
	R	Green Alice—†	6	"	45	here
	S	Green Paul	6	sandblaster	36	"
	V	Wormley Bessie—†	8	housewife	56	"
	W	Wormley Dorothy—†	8	stitcher	20	
	X	Wormley Lillian—†	8	"	24	
	Y	Smith Joseph	8	U S A	22	

Page.	Letter.	Full Name.	Residence, Jan. 1, 1943.	Occupation.	Supposed Age.	Reported Residence, Jan. 1, 1942. Street and Number.

Arnold Street—Continued

Page.	Letter.	Full Name.	Residence, Jan. 1, 1943.	Occupation.	Supposed Age.	Reported Residence, Jan. 1, 1942. Street and Number.
	Z	Smith Marion—†	8	laundress	50	here
902						
	A	Meade Henry	9	printer	69	
	B	Meade Pauline—†	9	housewife	52	"
	D	Lewis Bernard P	10	student	25	
	E	Lewis Charles D	10	U S A	22	
	F	Lewis Eva—†	10	laundress	48	"
	G	Crawford Margaret E—†	11	at home	66	
	H	Orr Sarah—†	11	"	54	
	K	Sarno Delia—†	12	housewife	62	"
	L	Sarno Guerino	12	clerk	69	
	M	Foster Arlene—†	13	housewife	30	"
	N	Foster Ethel—†	13	maid	33	
	O	Foster Norman A	13	chauffeur	36	"
	P	Porziale Gerald	14	clerk	28	
	R	Porziale Ida—†	14	housewife	29	"
	S	Moakley Edward	16	retired	88	
	T	Shinick Ellen—†	16	housekeeper	69	"
	U	Barnes Hattie—†	17	housewife	40	"
	V	Barnes Walter	17	laborer	38	
	W	Taylor Clarence	17	"	42	
	X	Braxton Julia—†	18	housewife	55	"
	Y	Braxton William J	18	clergyman	62	"
	Z	Jones Annie—†	19	housewife	52	"
903						
	A	Jones Ezekiel	19	carpenter	57	"
	B	Sumpter Daniel	19	retired	68	
	E	Plummer Levi	20	student	21	"
	F	Stephenson Joseph	20	"	23	
	G	White Emma—†	20	housekeeper	46	"
	H	Olmsted Daniel, jr	21	laborer	37	"
	K	Olmsted Daniel	21	clerk	63	
	L	Olmsted Henrietta—†	21	housewife	68	"
	N	Dooley Edward	22	porter	56	
	O	Dooley Ruth—†	22	operator	42	
	S	Faulk Anna—†	23	laundress	56	"
	U	O'Neil James W	24	student	20	
	V	O'Neil Judah	24	laborer	25	
	W*	O'Neil Martha—†	24	housewife	52	"
	X*	O'Neil Samuel	24	laborer	72	
	Y*	Harrison Joseph	25	"	47	

Page.	Letter.	FULL NAME.	Residence, Jan. 1, 1943.	Occupation.	Supposed Age.	Reported Residence Jan. 1, 1942. Street and Number.

Arnold Street—Continued

Page.	Letter.	Full Name.	Residence, Jan. 1, 1943.	Occupation.	Supposed Age.	Reported Residence Jan. 1, 1942. Street and Number.
	Z	Williams Ella—†	25	houseworker	41	Cambridge
904						
	A	James Alberta—†	25	housewife	29	84 Westminster
	B	Huff Martha—†	25	"	24	31 Eustis
	C	Craighead Rebecca—†	27	houseworker	66	131 Bower ct
	D	Ward Ada V—†	27	housekeeper	68	here
	E	Dobbs Maria L—†	27	"	52	"
	F	Wilson Sarah A—†	27	"	74	"
	G	Brown Martha—†	29		61	
	H	Williams Henritta—†	29	"	68	
	K	Smith Bettina—†	29	"	54	
	L	Walker Andrew	29	laborer	63	

Ball Street

Page.	Letter.	Full Name.	Residence, Jan. 1, 1943.	Occupation.	Supposed Age.	Reported Residence Jan. 1, 1942. Street and Number.
	M	Clark George	5	guard	55	here
	N	Day Gertrude—†	5	housewife	66	"
	O	Whitaker Margaret—†	5	"	69	"
	P	*Belyea Gertrude—†	7	"	72	2550 Wash'n
	R	*Anderson Cecilia—†	7		70	here
	S	Collins Mary R—†	7		71	"
	T	Morris Isabella—†	9	"	83	"
	U	Davidson Albert	9	shipper	46	
	V	Davidson Louise—†	9	housekeeper	48	"
	W	*Lindo Walkino—†	10	at home	55	"
	X	Arnett Beatrice—†	10	housekeeper	32	"
	Y	Milner Hazel—†	10	cook	20	"
	Z	Willis Corrine—†	10	domestic	40	"
905						
	A	Horrigan John	10	salesman	52	"
	B	Horrigan Lucy—†	10	housewife	40	"
	C	*Horton Matilda—†	10	domestic	82	"
	D	Clifton Harriet—†	10	housekeeper	71	"
	E	Johnson Edward	10	packer	51	"
	F	Martin Harriet—†	10	housekeeper	32	"
	G	*Cabral Frank M	10	laborer	56	"
	H	Cabral Louisa—†	10	housewife	52	"
	K	Decourcey William	10	retired	58	
	L	Hoffman Savannah—†	10	domestic	57	"
	M	Bryant Eleanor—†	11	machinist	33	"
	N	Bryant Mark	11	chauffeur	42	"

Page.	Letter.	FULL NAME.	Residence, Jan. 1, 1943.	Occupation.	Supposed Age.	Reported Residence, Jan. 1, 1942. Street and Number.

Ball Street—Continued

Page.	Letter.	FULL NAME.	Residence, Jan. 1, 1943.	Occupation.	Supposed Age.	Reported Residence, Jan. 1, 1942. Street and Number.
	P	Loud Helen—†	14	domestic	83	here
	R	Maloney Edward J	14	milkman	43	"
	S	Maloney Frances E—†	14	housewife	48	"
	T	Jones Iris—†	15	housekeeper	33	Cambridge
	U	Jones John	15	machinist	49	here
	V	Rice Margaret—†	15	housekeeper	64	"
	X	Frye Jerry	16	retired	76	"
	Y	Garfield Edward	16	waiter	38	
	Z	Garfield Vera—†	16	housewife	37	"
906						
	A	Leake Corrella—†	16	at home	70	
	B	Leake William	16	retired	72	"
	C	Widdiss Gladys—†	17	artist	28	Provincetown
	D	Widdiss Henry	17	laborer	27	here
	E	Widdiss Leonard	17	letter carrier	34	"
	F	Widdiss Lucille—†	17	housekeeper	64	"
	G	Carrier Grace L—†	18	housewife	37	"
	H	Carrier Howard	18	porter	41	
	K	Fitzgerald Edith M—†	18	housewife	42	"
	L	Fitzgerald M McFarland	18	porter	50	
	M	Gibson George	19	retired	56	
	N	Gibson Mary—†	19	housekeeper	64	"
	O	Regan Martha—†	19	"	68	"
	P	Elliott Cecilia—†	20	housewife	28	Vermont
	R	Elliott Lawrence	20	operator	38	"
	S	Henderson Ella—†	20	domestic	33	here
	T	Henderson Robert	20	cook	45	"
	U	Henderson Wanda—†	20	housekeeper	65	"
	V	Higgins Mattie—†	20	"	35	"
	W	Spencer George	20	chauffeur	38	"
	X	Spencer Maude—†	20	domestic	35	"
	Y	Francis Esther—†	21	housekeeper	67	"
	Z	Lattimer Henry	21	U S A	39	
907						
	A	Borden John	21	laborer	44	22 Windsor
	B	Mayfield Alice—†	21	housewife	32	22 "
	C	Rivers Esther—†	21	domestic	47	22 "
	D	Rivers George	21	porter	46	22 "
	E	Jennings Harold	22	packer	25	32 Ball
	K	Ruff Robert	22	orderly	53	here
	F	Scott William	22	rigger	30	Oregon

Page.	Letter.	FULL NAME.	Residence, Jan. 1, 1943.	Occupation.	Supposed Age.	Reported Residence, Jan. 1, 1942. Street and Number.

Ball Street—Continued

	G	Wilson George	22	retired	64	here
	H	Wilson Rebecca—†	22	housewife	50	"
	L	Young Sylvester	22	cook	40	666 Shawmut av
	M	Goode Mabel—†	23	packer	32	here
	N	Goode Robert	23	welder	36	"
	O	Jackson Edna—†	23	packer	34	"
	P	*Jacobsen Jennie—†	23	housekeeper	62	Maine
	R	Williams Archie G	23	welder	24	17 Hammond
	S	Williams Mary L—†	23	housewife	25	17 "
	T	Etts Bertha—†	23	attendant	29	Brookline
	U	Claderbuck Lubernet—†	24	housekeeper	58	here
	V	Fox Florence—†	24	clerk	20	"
	W	Fox Herbert	24	teamster	24	"
	X	Fox Ottoway	24	retired	63	"
	Y	Murchison Elijah	24	porter	52	131 Everett
	Z	Simmons Christine—†	24	dishwasher	25	Brookline
908						
	A	Richards Arlene—†	25	domestic	35	here
	B	Miller Earle	25	laborer	27	"
	C	Miller Robert	25	salesman	55	"
	D	Hepbourne Blanche—†	25	operator	30	
	E	Hepbourne Lillian—†	25	housekeeper	72	"
	F	Dooley Edward	26	porter	55	"
	G	Drayton Clarence	26	fireman	49	"
	H	Drayton Naomi—†	26	clerk	27	
	K	Drayton Sarah—†	26	housekeeper	48	"
	L	Fickens Robert	26	laborer	56	"
	M	Johnson Cornelius	26	packer	55	"
	N	Thomas Blanche—†	26	waitress	50	"
	O	Clarke Hubert	27	welder	48	35 Hammond
	P	Ezell James	27	retired	72	here
	R	Montero Samuel	27	mechanic	23	Provincetown
	S	Sheridan Jackson	27	retired	71	here
	T	Taylor Charles	27	"	66	"
	U	Taylor Elizabeth—†	27	housewife	69	"
	V	Adams Anne—†	28	"	29	"
	W	Adams William	28	electrician	24	Virginia
	X	Alcorn Harold	28	laborer	45	here
	Y	Cooper John E	28	janitor	70	"
	Z	Diggs Charles	28	retired	82	"
909						
	A	Small Celia—†	28	housewife	43	"

Page.	Letter.	FULL NAME.	Residence, Jan. 1, 1943.	Occupation.	Supposed Age.	Reported Residence, Jan. 1, 1942. Street and Number.

Ball Street—Continued

	B	Small Jacob	28	packer	51	here
	C	Works Horace	28	laborer	40	32A Humboldt av
	D	Jones Margaret—†	29	waitress	35	44 Kendall
	E	Jones Paul	29	U S A	35	here
	F	Hudson Edna—†	29	housekeeper	49	64 Dover
	G	Merritt Fannie—†	29	"	65	64 "
	H	Franklin Charles	29	mover	48	691 Shawmut av
	K	Taylor Ezera—†	29	clerk	38	691 "
	L	Doiley Gladys—†	30	waitress	22	N Carolina
	M	Goldman Virginia—†	30	clerk	23	here
	N	Hicks Alfred	30	porter	31	"
	O	Hicks Marion—†	30	housewife	26	"
	P	Sessons Thelma—†	30	"	46	
	R	Clark Mary—†	31	"	26	
	S	Clark Ralph	31	printer	38	
	T	Andrews James	32	laborer	38	
	U	Harris Wilfred	32	porter	61	
	V	Haskins Roger	32	waiter	60	"
	W	Hester Philip	32	cook	70	64 Kendall
	X	Johnson Henry	32	laborer	40	Brookline
	Y	Snyder Lester	32	mechanic	40	here
	Z	Young James	32	machinist	50	"
910						
	A	Russell Alice—†	33	domestic	49	"
	B	Russell James	33	laborer	49	
	C	Montero Angela—†	33	housewife	33	"
	D	Montero Earl	33	caretaker	33	"
	E	Montgomery Charles	33	machinist	34	"
	F	Montgomery Marion—†	33	domestic	34	"
	G	Goodman Charles	34	laborer	37	Winthrop
	H	Goodman Irene—†	34	housewife	26	"
	K	Beckwith Joshua H	34	porter	52	43 Windsor
	L	Beckwith Lucy M—†	34	housewife	54	43 "
	M	Dickerson John	34	cook	44	here
	N	Dickerson Julia—†	34	"	46	"

Cabot Street

	O	Clay Lillian—†	rear 108	housekeeper	54	here
	S	Matthews Ada—†	" 108	housewife	62	"
	V	Taylor Lucille—†	110	housekeeper	65	17 Benton

Page.	Letter.	Full Name.	Residence, Jan. 1, 1943.	Occupation.	Supposed Age.	Reported Residence, Jan. 1, 1942. Street and Number.
		Cabot Street—Continued				
	X	Loatman Susan—†	110	housewife	74	here
	Y	Loatman William C	110	laborer	59	"
911						
	B	Bennett Benjamin	124	machinist	21	"
	C	Brown Pauline—†	124	housewife	21	"
	D	Brown Thomas	124	musician	23	"
	E	Tate Robert	124	laborer	28	
	F	Norris Gertrude—†	124	housekeeper	64	"
	G	Hart Ella—†	124	housewife	47	"
	H	Hart Fred	124	waiter	48	"
	K	Hill Roscoe L	126	cook	75	29 Weston
	L	Davis James	126	stockman	37	here
	M	Fitzgerald Edith—†	126	operator	22	"
	N	Williams Inez—†	126	housewife	35	"
	O	Coffey Mary—†	126	domestic	46	"
		Champney Place				
	R	Leighton George	1	clerk	33	here
	S	Leighton Rita—†	1	housewife	28	"
	T	Hagerty Arthur	2	laborer	59	"
	U	Hagerty Beatrice—†	2	housewife	42	"
	V	Hagerty Frederick G	2	foreman	56	
	W	Norian George	3	chauffeur	36	"
	X	Norian Lillian—†	3	housewife	35	"
	Y	Heggie John J	4	laborer	58	
	Z	Jackson Fred T	4	garageman	50	"
912						
	A	Jackson Marion M—†	4	operator	40	
	B	Jackson Maud E—†	4	housewife	82	"
	C	Doran Joseph P	5	laborer	61	
	D	Doran Sadie E—†	5	housewife	57	"
	E	Post Lotta—†	6	housekeeper	75	"
	F	St Germaine Henrietta—†	7	"	36	"
	G	Jansky Elizabeth—†	8	"	53	
	H	Brown Gladys G—†	9	housewife	30	"
	K	Brown William P	9	carpenter	33	"
	L	Hurley Anna J—†	10	housekeeper	40	"
	M	O'Toole Helen—†	10	tel operator	22	"
	N	O'Toole Mary—†	10	housewife	45	"
	O	O'Toole Thomas	10	foreman	47	

Page.	Letter.	Full Name.	Residence, Jan. 1, 1943.	Occupation.	Supposed Age.	Reported Residence, Jan. 1, 1942. Street and Number.

Clifton Place

Page.	Letter.	Full Name.	Residence, Jan. 1, 1943.	Occupation.	Supposed Age.	Reported Residence, Jan. 1, 1942. Street and Number.
	P	Morris John	1	salesman	35	20 Madison
	R	Morris Josephine—†	1	housewife	29	20 "
	S	Bruce Ella—†	2	"	67	here
	T	Tucker Marion—†	2	"	34	"
	U	Baldwin Mimi—†	3	housekeeper	77	"
	V	Earle Edith—†	3	clerk	54	"
	W	McDermott Warren R	3	U S A	27	"
	X	Connors Agnes—†	4	housewife	66	3 Flagg
	Y	Wishart James J	4	machinist	68	3 "
913						
	A	Webber Mary—†	5	housekeeper	75	here
	E	Dyer Viola—†	7	"	70	"
	F	Quint James E	7	laborer	65	826 Mass av
	G	Quint Theresa—†	7	housewife	50	826 "
	M	McVay Mable—†	9	housekeeper	76	here
	N	*Connell Ellen—†	10	"	75	"
	O	Tobin Calvin P	10	laborer	40	"
	P	Conte Pasquale	11	splicer	34	
	R	Conte Rachel—†	11	housewife	29	"
	S	Ardolino Margaret J—†	12	waitress	48	"
	T	Colley Ernest	12	laborer	37	42 W Newton
	U	Colley Frances—†	12	housewife	20	42 "
	W	Morse Francis M	13	"	47	16 Madison
	X	Morse Phillip C	13	retired	68	16 "
	Y	Dunnell Albert S	14	"	69	here
914						
	A	*Minard Jean—†	14	housewife	35	"
	B	Conklin Mae—†	15	"	57	
	C	Conklin Norval	15	operator	60	
	D	Gould Georgia—†	15	housewife	73	"
	E	Gould Helen—†	15	bookbinder	35	"
	F	Franklin Mary H—†	16	housekeeper	80	"
	G	Knowles Queenie—†	17	housewife	43	"
	H	Scarborough Joseph	17	inspector	37	8 Clifton pl
	K	Scarborough Mary—†	17	housewife	36	8 "
	L	Bishop Catherine—†	18	"	48	19 "
	M	Bishop Joseph S	18	guard	40	19 "
	N	Scott Mary—†	18	housekeeper	68	21 Bartlett
	O	Drury William	19	laborer	63	17 Clifton pl
	P	Jones Lucy—†	19	housewife	58	11 Thorndike
	R	*Jackson Annie—†	20	"	63	6 Clifton pl

Page.	Letter.	Full Name.	Residence, Jan. 1, 1943.	Occupation.	Supposed Age.	Reported Residence, Jan. 1, 1942. Street and Number.

Clifton Place—Continued

	S	Drinkwater Fred	20	painter	66	here
	T	Kellett Ella—†	20	housewife	65	"
	U	Kellett Frederick	20	U S A	26	"
	V	Kellett Lawrence	20	painter	36	
	W	Kellett William	20	"	34	
	X	Sallinger Sadie—†	21	housekeeper	50	"
	Y	Smarkowitz Anna—†	21	"	46	
	Z	Homsey Annie—†	21	housewife	46	"
915						
	A	Homsey Joseph	21	retired	57	
	B	Marks Harry	22	carpenter	54	"
	C	*Marks Ruth—†	22	housewife	42	"
	D	McSwain John	22	carpenter	53	"
	E	Killen Francis	22	messenger	25	"
	F	Killen Katherine—†	22	housewife	50	"
	G	Starkey Howard E	22	tinsmith	62	
	H	*Yair Mary—†	23	housewife	42	"
	K	Ginsberg Louis	23	salesman	32	"
	L	Ginsberg Mary—†	23	housewife	59	"
	M	Barsell Margaret—†	23	"	48	
	N	Barsell William	23	inspector	50	"

Derby Place

	O	Flynn Mary—†	A	housekeeper	71	here
	P	Eaton Mary E—†	B	domestic	56	"
	R	Huber Frederick H	B	cook	46	"
	S	Painter Florence—†	B	cleaner	61	
	T	Scarborough Florence—†	B	housewife	36	"
	U	Scarborough Joseph	B	U S C G	20	"
	V	Lyons Edith—†	C	housewife	60	"
	W	Lyons Walter M	C	carpenter	65	"
	X	Wood Hazel—†	C	housewife	39	1829 Wash'n
	Y	Pimental Anna—†	D	clerk	43	here
	Z	Strauser John J	1	laborer	28	"
916						
	A	Strauser Mary A—†	1	attendant	26	"
	B	Strauser Thomas	1	laborer	27	
	C	Dann Carl	2	machinist	26	"
	D	Dann Carmella—†	2	housewife	32	"
	E	Brown Ernest	3	retired	66	

Page.	Letter.	FULL NAME.	Residence, Jan. 1, 1943.	Occupation.	Supposed Age.	Reported Residence, Jan. 1, 1942. Street and Number.

Derby Place—Continued

	F	Bylsma Bertha—†	3	housewife	31	here
	G	Bylsma Peter D	3	painter	35	"
	K	Leighton Dorothy—†	5	housewife	23	"
	L	Leighton Jesse	5	floorman	28	"
	M	Izzo Angelo	6	chef	50	
	N	Izzo Anna—†	6	housewife	40	"
	O	Izzo Anthony	6	chauffeur	22	"
	P	Hooper Annie—†	7	housewife	42	"
	R	Hooper Nelson	7	laborer	42	"
	T	Purcell Joseph D	8	"	56	4 Brookline
	U	Rourke Robert M	8	"	61	here
	W	Tobin Jane—†	9	housewife	72	"
	X	Tobin John J	9	retired	70	"
	Y	White James C	9	laborer	42	
	Z	White Mary—†	9	housewife	39	"
917						
	C	Young James	10	laborer	61	"
	D	Danforth Alexandrina—†	11	housewife	67	187 Dudley
	E	Danforth Frank	11	welder	64	187 "
	F	Danforth Margaret—†	11	housekeeper	26	187 "
	G	Sonia Frances—†	11	housewife	22	59 W Brookline
	H	Sonia Herbert	11	U S A	26	59 "

Hubert Street

	K	Peters Henry	1A	druggist	36	here
	L	Peters Mary—†	1A	housekeeper	65	"
	M	Green Portia—†	1A	housewife	44	"
	N	Ivey Joseph	1A	painter	45	
	O	Jett Catherine—†	1A	housewife	21	"
	P	Jett Willis	1A	laborer	23	"
	R	Noiles Edith—†	3	housekeeper	33	102 Hammond
	S	Edmunds Ada—†	3	domestic	40	here
	T	Edmunds Jacob	3	laborer	53	"
	U	Turner Charles H	3	gardener	59	"
	V	Turner Mary—†	3	housewife	49	"
	W	Blunt Augustus	5	laborer	54	17 Haskins
	X	Coppen Helen—†	5	domestic	55	here
	Y	Brown George	5	laborer	37	"
	Z	Douglas Gladys—†	7	stitcher	44	"

Page.	Letter.	Full Name.	Residence, Jan. 1, 1943.	Occupation.	Supposed Age.	Reported Residence, Jan. 1, 1942. Street and Number.
918						

Hubert Street—Continued

Page.	Letter.	Full Name.	Residence, Jan. 1, 1943.	Occupation.	Supposed Age.	Reported Residence, Jan. 1, 1942. Street and Number.
	A	Horton Mary E—†	7	housekeeper	77	here
	B	Beckett Mary—†	7	"	50	"
	C	Horner Cora—†	7	housewife	30	"
	D	Horner Howard	7	laborer	36	
	E	Marshall Charles	9	"	31	
	F	Marshall Nettie—†	9	housewife	31	"
	G	Gardner George	9	laborer	46	
	H	Drayton Edward	9	"	29	
	K	Drayton Margaret—†	9	housewife	24	"
	L	Maddox Charlotte—†	11	housekeeper	54	"
	M	Juitt Eva—†	11	housewife	39	"
	N	Burrell Edna—†	11	checker	38	44 Cabot
	O	Burrell Harold	11	U S A	21	here
	P	Williams Shellie—†	13	housekeeper	38	"
	R	Snowden Samuel	13	porter	61	"
	S	Burns Fannie—†	13	domestic	48	"
	T	Burns Thelma—†	13	clerk	25	
	U	Philips Jeffrey	15	laborer	40	
	V	Woods Henrietta—†	15	domestic	47	"
	W	Woods Irving	15	welder	46	"
	X	Whitehead Elizabeth—†	15	housewife	29	29 Sterling
	Y	Whitehead Lincoln	15	laborer	40	29 "
	Z	Armour Edward	17	"	50	449 Walnut av
919						
	A	Armour Margaret—†	17	housewife	37	449 "
	B	Brown Nannie B—†	17	housekeeper	72	here
	C	Brown Walter	17	painter	48	"
	D	Williams Carmen—†	17	waitress	37	"
	E	Williams Frank	17	porter	38	

Madison Street

Page.	Letter.	Full Name.	Residence, Jan. 1, 1943.	Occupation.	Supposed Age.	Reported Residence, Jan. 1, 1942. Street and Number.
	N	*Gould Catherine—†	2	housewife	40	2644 Wash'n
	O	Gould Raymond	2	painter	42	2644 "
	P	Roberts Alfred M	2	retired	75	here
	R	Roberts Elizabeth—†	2	at home	44	"
	S	*Romano Agnes—†	2	housewife	41	"
	T	Romano Letterio	2	plasterer	51	"
	U	Gagliardi Frank	2	laborer	50	
	V	*Gagliardi Mary—†	2	housewife	39	"

Page.	Letter.	Full Name.	Residence, Jan. 1, 1943.	Occupation.	Supposed Age.	Reported Residence, Jan. 1, 1942. Street and Number.

Madison Street—Continued

	W	Wright Anna—†	4	at home	75	here
	X	Dunn Andrew	4	boilermaker	59	19 Rutland sq
	Y	Dunn Gladys—†	4	counter girl	23	19 "
	Z	*Dunn Jen—†	4	housewife	49	19 "
920						
	A	*Turner David	4	carpenter	58	here
	B	*Turner Martha—†	4	housewife	59	"
	C	Smith Stella M—†	4	at home	66	"
	D	Wilson Byron	4	pressman	43	"
	E	Humphrey John G	6	millhand	70	"
	F	Humphrey Sarah—†	6	housewife	66	"
	G	Stoner Marie E—†	6	waitress	50	"
	K	*Guizzi Ada—†	6	at home	68	53 W Dedham
	L	Halpin Emma G—†	7	"	75	here
	M	Halpin William J	7	retired	73	"
	N	Marshall Lena—†	8	at home	70	"
	O	Cargo Benjamin	8	baker	60	"
	R	Buckman Mary H—†	8	at home	56	11 Yeoman
	S	Strother Charles P	9	operator	58	here
	T	Strother Gertrude—†	9	housewife	47	"
	U	Strother Leonard	9	fireman	21	"
	V	DeVenosa Clara—†	10	housewife	70	"
	W	DeVenosa Gustave	10	retired	77	
	X	Buckley Elizabeth G—†	11	at home	52	
	Y	Buckley William J	11	U S N	28	
	Z	Campbell Jane E—†	11	packer	30	
921						
	A	Reiser Gladdys—†	11	at home	24	
	B	Hurley Anna—†	12	"	71	"
	C	Smith Eva—†	12	W A A C	31	"
	D	Smith Samuel	12	chauffeur	31	"
	E	Smith Henry	13	chef	52	
	F	Lynch Alice M—†	14	housewife	50	"
	G	Lynch John	14	chauffeur	59	"
	H	Thompson Mary E—†	14	at home	70	
	K	Coleman Alfred	15	U S N	30	
	L	Coleman Lillian—†	15	housewife	60	"
	M	Geddis Edward	15	laborer	52	
	N	LeFevre Anna—†	15	at home	70	"
	O	*Ferguson Jessie—†	16	"	92	8 Nawn
	P	Wylie Mildred—†	16	"	70	18 Madison

Page.	Letter.	FULL NAME.	Residence, Jan. 1, 1943.	Occupation.	Supposed Age.	Reported Residence, Jan. 1, 1942. Street and Number.

Madison Street—Continued

	R	Boulay Arthur	16	carpenter	64	here
	S	Morris John E	16	plumber	58	"
	T	Morris Lillian—†	16	housewife	59	"
	U	Khan Fazil	17	builder	54	"
	V	Cook Mary E—†	18	maid	65	22 Madison
	W	Fay Ruth—†	18	housewife	22	21 Worcester sq
	X	Fay Thomas	18	mechanic	25	21 "
	Y	Coleman Alice—†	18	housewife	20	50 Mall
	Z	Coleman Edward	18	packer	20	50 "
922						
	A	Gaskins Emma J—†	19	at home	73	here
	B	Gaskins Louise—†	19	housewife	31	"
	C	Gaskins Peter	19	painter	31	"
	D	Merrill Lila—†	20	stitcher	48	32 Madison
	E	Nasuti Concetta—†	20	at home	43	here
	F	Nasuti Maria—†	20	clerk	20	"
	G	Taylor John	20	laborer	42	"
	H	*Taylor Rita—†	20	housewife	44	"
	K	Patterson Gertrude—†	21	clerk	27	2 Greenwich
	N	*Farrara Angelo	22	laborer	48	here
	O	*Farrara Lucy—†	22	housewife	46	"
	P	Bruno Elizabeth—†	22	factoryhand	20	"
	R	Gutro Bessie—†	24	domestic	58	"
	S	Donohue John	24	laborer	65	"
	T	Donohue Mary—†	24	housewife	67	"
	U	White Bertha F—†	26	at home	68	"
	V	Bernard Joseph	26	machinist	29	"
	W	Bernard Wilma—†	26	housewife	28	"
	X	Wilson Victoria—†	28	at home	37	
	Y	Allen Frank B	28	baker	49	
	Z	Sullivan George	28	clerk	22	
923						
	A	*Sullivan John	28	laborer	57	"
	B	*Sullivan Julia—†	28	housewife	53	"
	C	Ford George	30	salesman	49	"
	D	Paige Lena—†	30	at home	47	
	E	Crosby George	30	machinist	55	"
	F	Crosby Helen—†	30	housewife	43	"
	G	Reinhardt Frederick A	32	retired	76	100 Roxbury
	H	Reinhardt Rebecca—†	32	housewife	69	100 "
	K	Lanigan Ellen—†	32	"	28	here
	L	Lanigan James J	32	superintendent	35	"

Page.	Letter.	Full Name.	Residence, Jan. 1, 1943.	Occupation.	Supposed Age.	Reported Residence, Jan. 1, 1942. Street and Number.

Ruggles Street

	O	Alden Cora V—†	9	maid	57	672 Shawmut av
	P	Arnold George P	9	musician	42	672 "
	R	Tolman James	9	laborer	30	here
	S	Tolman Mary—†	9	housewife	32	"
	T	Moore Alzater—†	9	"	23	41 Cabot
	U	Moore Ernest	9	metalworker	27	41 "
	V	Jones Annie—†	9	laundryworker	37	here
	W	Jones Phyllis—†	9	packer	22	"
	X	Gayle Anna—†	9	housewife	27	225 W Canton
	Y	Gayle Reginald	9	waiter	28	225 "
	Z	Williams Asberrie	9	packer	39	Georgia
924						
	A	Williams Barry	9	presser	39	17 Hammond
	B	Williams Grace—†	9	"	34	Georgia
	C	Williams Lillian—†	9	laundryworker	37	17 Hammond
	U	Christmas Mary—†	11	housewife	20	Hull
	E	Christmas Walton	11	mechanic	23	74 Bower
	F	McMillan Almeda—†	11	housewife	33	here
	G	Fernandes Margaret—†	11	operator	26	Brookline
	H	Pires Margaret—†	11	stitcher	26	"
	K	Pires Mary—†	11	housewife	23	Ohio
	L	Pires Vasco	11	chipper	28	"
	M	Barros Manuel	11	millhand	35	here
	N	Pina Frank	11	operator	26	Ohio
	O	Murphy Bessie—†	11	laundryworker	37	here
	P	Halfpenny Beatrice—†	11	housewife	43	"
	R	May Bertha—†	13	"	24	"
	S	May James	13	chipper	38	
	T	Sandiford Frances—†	13	housewife	30	"
	U	Sandiford Preston	13	musician	35	"
	V	Mendes Albert	13	laborer	45	69 Ruggles
	W	Thomas Jennie—†	13	housewife	40	here
	X	Thomas Joseph	13	laborer	42	"
	Y	Patterson Arthur	13	packer	45	"
	Z	Patterson Lucy—†	13	clerk	38	
925						
	A	Wiggins Emerson	13	chipper	26	
	B	Wiggins Hazel—†	13	housewife	23	"
	C	Phelan Elizabeth—†	15	"	53	
	D	Phelan William	15	agent	54	"
	E	McGrath Thomas	15	retired	82	643 Hunt'n av
	F	Scullin Margaret—†	15	cook	47	643 "

Page.	Letter.	Full Name.	Residence, Jan. 1, 1943.	Occupation.	Supposed Age.	Reported Residence, Jan. 1, 1942. Street and Number.

Ruggles Street—Continued

Page.	Letter.	Full Name.	Residence, Jan. 1, 1943.	Occupation.	Supposed Age.	Reported Residence, Jan. 1, 1942. Street and Number.
	G	Baird Della G—†	15	housewife	58	here
	H	McGuire Marion—†	15	finisher	30	"
	K	Fountain Arsine	15	mechanic	38	"
	L	Fountain Mary—†	15	attendant	32	"
	M	*Whittingham Frank	15	bookbinder	60	906 Col av
	N	*Whittingham May—†	15	housewife	53	906 "
	O	Stewart Edith—†	15	"	23	here
	P	*Stewart Leroy	15	janitor	41	"
	S	McRae John	41	operator	25	76 Kendall
	T	McRae Martha—†	41	laundryworker	23	76 "
	U	Springs Ethel—†	41	hairdresser	41	here
	V	Springs James	41	seaman	43	"
	W	Lassiter Eugene	41	U S C G	41	"
	X	Lassiter Grace—†	41	housewife	37	"
	Y	Fields Mary—†	41	"	48	
	Z	Fields William C	41	mechanic	52	"
926						
	A	Fields William E	41	U S A	32	
	B	Harris Anna—†	41	housewife	44	"
	C	Harris Charles	41	laborer	43	
	D	Moore Irene—†	41	housewife	49	"
	E	Moore Spurgeon	41	porter	42	"
	F	Pierce Edna—†	41	housewife	28	30 Symphony rd
	G	Pierce Fred	41	porter	31	30 "
	H	Catherwood Cleveland	41	U S A	25	here
	K	Catherwood Ivy—†	41	dressmaker	24	"
	L	*Catherwood Louise—†	41	housewife	50	"
	M	Catherwood Wilbert	41	U S A	23	
	N	Drayton Minnie—†	53	stitcher	38	"
	O	Luacaw Clyde	53	laborer	40	31 Newbern
	P	Luacaw John	53	"	46	14 Oakland av
	R	Williams Walter	53	"	40	Lowell
	S	McDuffie Jonnie—†	53	housewife	43	here
	T	Turnage William	53	seaman	29	"

Shawmut Avenue

Page.	Letter.	Full Name.	Residence, Jan. 1, 1943.	Occupation.	Supposed Age.	Reported Residence, Jan. 1, 1942. Street and Number.
	V	Blake Amy—†	608A	housewife	40	here
	W	Blake Thomas	608A	retired	57	"
	X	Johnson James B	608A	mortician	36	"
	Y	Robinson Mary J—†	608A	housekeeper	53	"

Page.	Letter.	FULL NAME.	Residence, Jan. 1, 1943.	Occupation.	Supposed Age.	Reported Residence, Jan. 1, 1942. Street and Number.

Shawmut Avenue—Continued

	z	Allen Clementine—†	608A	housewife	34	here
927						
	A	Allen Ethan A	608A	printer	48	
	C	Costa Albert E	610A	welder	60	
	D	Costa Rachel—†	610A	housewife	60	"
	E	Costa Reynold M	610A	U S A	35	
	F	Green Augusta—†	610A	housekeeper	23	"
	G	Green Charles	610A	retired	60	"
	H	Green Charles B	610A	U S A	21	
	K	Green Gladys—†	610A	housewife	43	"
	L	Green Leslie H	610A	welder	26	9 Lattimore ct
	O	*French Augusta—†	612A	housekeeper	34	101 Camden
	P	Butler Bertha—†	612A	"	56	here
	R	Butler Bruce	612A	foundryman	31	"
	S	Butler Eleanor—†	612A	housewife	30	"
	T	Hart Robert	612A	rigger	42	"
	U	Daway Helen R—†	612A	housewife	30	49 Hammond
	V	Daway Michael	612A	laborer	35	49 "
	X	Briggs Louis	614A	"	48	here
	Y	Jones Louise—†	614A	housekeeper	42	"
	Z	Smith Pearl—†	614A	domestic	23	"
928						
	A	Winn Charles E	614A	retired	63	
	B	Armstrong Alberta—†	614A	stitcher	23	
	C	Fuller John A	614A	laborer	43	
	D	Fuller Nelson	614A	tailor	42	
	E	Jefferson Matilda—†	614A	"	39	
	F	Butler Arthur	614A	chauffeur	48	"
	G	Butler Mary—†	614A	bookkeeper	56	"
	H	Moseley Catherine—†	614A	housekeeper	37	"
	L	Beale Carlotta—†	616A	"	34	"
	M	Jenkins Ethel—†	616A	"	49	
	N	Harding Elizabeth—†	616A	housewife	45	"
	O	Harding Wesley	616A	machinist	48	"
	R	Wilson Joseph	618A	butler	42	
	S	Wilson Mary—†	618A	domestic	40	"
	T	Dixon Sarah—†	618A	housewife	66	"
	U	Dixon William	618A	druggist	71	
	V	Brown Annie—†	618A	housekeeper	63	"
	W	Sykes James	618A	meatcutter	45	"
	X	Walker Virginia—†	618A	presser	43	

Page.	Letter.	Full Name.	Residence, Jan. 1, 1943.	Occupation.	Supposed Age.	Reported Residence, Jan. 1, 1942. Street and Number.
929		**Shawmut Avenue**—Continued				
	A	Wilson Cyril	626	carpenter	43	here
	B	Byers Bertha—†	626	seamstress	64	"
	C	Lee Jessie—†	626	housewife	34	"
	D	Lee Robert H, jr	626	porter	38	
	E	Davis Mattie—†	626	housekeeper	36	"
	F	Mitchell Valarie—†	626	"	29	"
	K	Fox Frederick	630	laborer	29	
	L	Fox Gussie—†	630	housewife	25	"
	M	Shepard Clarence	630	painter	46	
	N	Walker Singer—†	630	housewife	45	"
	T	Engermann Gertrude—†	638	"	40	
	U	Engermann Isaiah	638	molder	44	
	V	Reddick Cornelius	638	electrician	60	"
	W	Reddick Kenneth	638	U S A	20	
	X	Reddick Ruthena—†	638	housewife	49	"
	Y	Matthews Ena C—†	638	"	67	
	Z	Matthews Walter H	638	clerk	67	
930						
	D	Jeffries Anna—†	646	housewife	47	"
	E	Jeffries Oliver	646	laborer	56	
	F	Hawkins Mary—†	646	housekeeper	72	"
	G	Warwick Eugene	646	chef	42	"
	H	Warwick Ida—†	646	housewife	42	"
	K	Cook Aaron	646	watchman	60	"
	L	Miller Adolph	646	laborer	29	"
	M	Wiley John	646	"	37	"
	N	Davis James	646	"	23	129 Lenox
	O	Davis Vera—†	646	housewife	22	129 "
	S	Reid Fay—†	660	domestic	42	662 Shawmut av
	T	Reid John	660	houseman	50	662 "
	V	Freeman Dora A—†	660	housekeeper	68	41 Windsor
	W	Thacker Thelma—†	660	housewife	21	156 Columbia rd
	X	Thacker William	660	mechanic	23	156 "
	Y	Matthews Beatrice—†	662	housewife	37	here
	Z	Matthews Leon	662	waiter	40	"
931						
	A	Robinson Mary—†	662	housekeeper	29	"
	B	Robinson William K	662	painter	27	"
	C	Nathan Mattie—†	662	instructor	44	"
	E	Richardson Annie M—†	664	housekeeper	67	11½ Greenwich

Page.	Letter.	Full Name.	Residence, Jan. 1, 1943.	Occupation.	Supposed Age.	Reported Residence, Jan. 1, 1942. Street and Number.
		Shawmut Avenue—Continued				
	F	Richardson Edward T	664	porter	69	11½ Greenwich
	G	Nelson Ella B—†	664	housekeeper	50	here
	H	Nelson Floyd	664	laborer	20	"
	K	Wade Mary—†	664	housewife	51	"
	L	Wade William H	664	laborer	59	
	M	Clark Anna—†	664	clerk	24	"
	N	Clark George H, jr	664	U S A	23	
	O	Harley Emma—†	664	housekeeper	42	"
	P	Campbell Harry	666	retired	47	"
	R	Campbell Rosanna—†	666	housewife	45	"
	S	Burns Joseph	666	laborer	40	"
	T	Brown John D	666	"	25	64 Cabot
	U	Brown Julius	666	"	47	here
	V	Bullock Lucy—†	666	housewife	35	"
	W	Bies Rose—†	666	cook	52	"
	X	Hodges Lacey	666	laborer	39	"
	Z	Fonseca Frank V	670	"	42	
932						
	A	Fonseca Lillian—†	670	housewife	36	"
	B	Hudson Adelaide M—†	670	domestic	51	Newton
	C	Cardwell Robert	670	clerk	28	here
	D	Carrington Carol—†	670	housekeeper	24	"
	E	Carrington Lee	670	laborer	33	"
	F	Nelson Mary—†	672	clerk	40	
	G	Haynes Helena—†	672	housekeeper	37	"
	H	Haynes Leslie	672	machinist	40	"
	K	Bibby Maud—†	672	domestic	50	"
	L	Butler Ernest E	672	boilermaker	27	"
	M	Francis Arline—†	672	waitress	30	
	N	Francis John	672	mover	32	
	O	Dickenson Bessie C—†	674	at home	55	
	P	Gaskins Emma A—†	674	"	86	
	R	Northern Margaret A—†	674	domestic	51	"
	S	Schenck Ruth—†	674	"	62	
	T	Goodrich Lillian—†	674	housewife	44	"
	U	Rochester Alice—†	676	hairdresser	59	"
	V	Williams Anna—†	676	domestic	49	"
	W	Dickson Esther—†	676	"	46	
	X	Dickson Lena—†	676	"	39	
	Y	Mimms Emma—†	676	at home	56	
	Z	Rice Beulah—†	676	domestic	61	"

Page.	Letter.	FULL NAME.	Residence, Jan. 1, 1943.	Occupation.	Supposed Age.	Reported Residence, Jan. 1, 1942. Street and Number.

933
Shawmut Avenue—Continued

	B	Ferrish John	686	waiter	63	here
	C	Henry Frances—†	686	housekeeper	46	"
	D	Lewis Florence—†	686	seamstress	42	"
	E	Richardson Eva—†	686	operator	37	"
	F	Williams Juanita—†	686	at home	60	
	G	Bryant Carrie—†	688	domestic	25	"
	K	Glover Roy	688	porter	45	
	H	Grant Thomas	688	laborer	45	
	L	Singletary Richard	688	"	33	
	M	Terry Matthew	688	"	47	
	N	Roberts Alexander L	690–692	physician	57	"
	O	Brown Edward W, jr	690–692	welder	25	18 Windsor
	P	Brown Mary E—†	690–692	housewife	20	18 "
	R	Carney Albert F	690–692	laborer	55	here
	S	Carney Julia L—†	690–692	housekeeper	47	"
	T	Terrell Joel	690–692	retired	70	"
	U	Wells Josephine—†	690–692	clerk	23	
	V	Wells Mabel G—†	690–692	housekeeper	48	"
	W	Wells Mildred—†	690–692	clerk	21	"
	X	Ferriea John	690–692	laborer	47	
	Y	Lopez Joseph	690–692	chauffeur	39	"
	Z	Lopez Ruth A—†	690–692	housekeeper	43	"
934						
	A	Morris Benjamin	690–692	retired	67	
	B	Lewis Edward	690–692	U S A	23	
	C	Lewis Everett L	690–692	cook	49	
	D	Lewis Gwendolyn—†	690–692	housekeeper	22	"
	E	Lewis Imogene—†	690–692	domestic	50	"
	F	Lewis Leon E	690–692	U S A	21	
	G	Carey Daisy—†	690–692	housekeeper	58	"
	H	Cheeks Lillian—†	690–692	laundress	36	"
	K	Harris Winston	690–692	cutter	45	
	L	Williams Edward B	690–692	laborer	47	
	M	Hawkins Doris—†	690–692	housekeeper	34	"
	N	Hawkins Hunter L	690–692	clerk	35	"
	O	Bowen Etta—†	694	housekeeper	49	"
	P	Bowen Fritz	694	laborer	22	"
	R	Bowen Leonard	694	"	66	
	S	Bowen Thelma—†	694	clerk	21	
	T	Brooks Elizabeth—†	696	domestic	55	"

Page.	Letter.	FULL NAME.	Residence, Jan. 1, 1943.	Occupation.	Supposed Age.	Reported Residence, Jan. 1, 1942. Street and Number.

Shawmut Avenue—Continued

	U	Martin James	696	cook	22	here
	V	Philips Robert	696	student	27	"
	W	Shepard Amy J—†	696	housewife	58	"
	X	Shepard Charles W	696	engineer	65	"
	Y	Duncan Philip	698	laborer	23	Walpole
	Z	Martin John	698	storekeeper	40	here
935						
	A	Roberts Edith—†	698	domestic	37	741 Shawmut av
	B	Silva Dominga—†	698	housekeeper	26	here
	C	Silva Manuel	698	storekeeper	43	"
	E	Oliver Elizabeth—†	699	housekeeper	47	12 Westminister
	G	Brooks Geneva—†	699	"	59	here
	H	Wright Erminie—†	699	housewife	40	"
	K	Wright William	699	longshoreman	36	"
	L	Numes Mabel—†	701	housewife	53	"
	M	*Numes Manuel	701	gardener	73	"
	N	Lee Georgiana—†	701	housewife	45	"
	O	Lee Stannard	701	laborer	47	"
	P	Jaynes Martha—†	701	housekeeper	71	121 Warwick
	R	Dison Thomas	701	laborer	60	here
	T	Smith David P	703	waiter	63	"
	U	Mitchell Laura—†	703	housewife	56	"
	V	Mitchell Rufus	703	retired	73	
	X	*Walter Clifford	703	janitor	42	"
	Y	Walter Norris	703	cable splicer	20	"
	Z	*Walter Thomasina—†	703	housewife	40	"
936						
	A	Mattox Mary—†	704	housekeeper	38	18 Hollander
	B	Williams Ernestine—†	704	domestic	41	here
	C	Miller Sally—†	704	at home	46	"
	E	James James	705	laborer	69	57 Camden
	F	Wolf Bertha—†	705	domestic	59	here
	G	Green Doris—†	705	housewife	32	14 Sterling
	H	Green Thomas	705	laborer	41	14 "
	O	*Trotman Frances—†	707	domestic	28	here
	M	Nelson Marjorie—†	707	housewife	25	101 W Springfield
	N	Randolph Luteria—†	707	housekeeper	26	38 Sussex
	R	Weeks Helen—†	708	"	48	here
	S	Weeks Thomas	708	laborer	22	"
	T	Jones Henry	708	"	25	"
	U	Jones Janey—†	708	housekeeper	69	"

Page.	Letter.	Full Name.	Residence, Jan. 1, 1943.	Occupation.	Supposed Age.	Reported Residence, Jan. 1, 1942. Street and Number.

Shawmut Avenue—Continued

Page.	Letter.	Full Name.	Residence, Jan. 1, 1943.	Occupation.	Supposed Age.	Reported Residence, Jan. 1, 1942. Street and Number.
	v	Stevens Mary—†	708	housekeeper	58	here
	w	Stevens Randolph	708	laborer	60	"
	y	Kelley Charles	710	porter	59	"
	z	Kelley Edith M—†	710	housekeeper	63	"
937						
	A	Coleman James A	710	retired	75	
	B	Coleman Nancy—†	710	housekeeper	59	"
	C	Simmons Clarence	710	painter	54	"
	D	Simmons Lillian—†	710	housewife	52	"
	G	Lewis Charles H	714	laborer	49	
	H	Lewis Susan E—†	714	housewife	46	"
	K	Harris William D	714	porter	39	"
	M	Silvia Agnes—†	716	housewife	27	22 Weston
	N	Silvia Anthony L	716	shipper	28	22 "
	O	Andrews Emily—†	716	housewife	25	New Bedford
	P	Andrews John	716	shipper	32	"
	R	Barry Oscar	716	laborer	23	here
	S	Barry Ruby—†	716	housekeeper	26	"
	T	Harris Lucy—†	716	presser	39	"
	U	Painter Narcissa—†	716	nurse	61	"
	W	Gordon Mary—†	718	hairdresser	47	"
	X	Gordon Robert	718	barber	63	
	Y	Pope Gladys—†	718	domestic	32	"
	Z	DeLong Edward R	718	retired	71	
938						
	A	DeLong Minnie A—†	718	housekeeper	73	"
	E	Phillips Harold	720	laborer	50	"
	F	Strother Francis R	720	"	29	
	G	Strother Louise—†	720	housewife	26	"
	H	Moody Cora B—†	720	housekeeper	67	"
	K	Moody Viola F—†	720	domestic	26	"
	L	McCall Edith—†	720	"	51	
	M	McCall Jean—†	720	clerk	23	
	S	Crockett Marie—†	722A	housekeeper	45	"
	T	Crockett Samuel	722A	porter	50	"
	R	Stevenson Adam	722A	retired	58	
	X	Braxton Joseph	724A	laborer	30	
	Y	Hurd Josephine—†	724A	housekeeper	50	"
	Z	Hurd Marion W—†	724A	baker	30	"
939						
	D	Cunningham Eustis	726½	laborer	63	

Page.	Letter.	Full Name.	Residence, Jan. 1, 1943.	Occupation.	Supposed Age.	Reported Residence, Jan. 1, 1942. Street and Number.

Shawmut Avenue—Continued

Page.	Letter.	Full Name.	Residence, Jan. 1, 1943.	Occupation.	Supposed Age.	Reported Residence, Jan. 1, 1942. Street and Number.
	C	Ford Alice—†	726½	domestic	56	here
	E	Hill Catherine—†	726½	"	75	"
	F	Lincoln Beulah—†	726½	maid	51	12 Northfield
	G	Brown Emily C—†	726½	housewife	25	156 Lenox
	H	Brown Stanley L	726½	machinist	26	here
	K	Thomas Homer	726½	porter	26	526 Col av
	L	Thomas Margaret P—†	726½	housewife	36	526 "
	P	Smith Henry	732	laborer	51	here
	R	Griger James	732	clerk	40	"
	S	Griger Laura—†	732	housewife	38	"
	U	Gallaway Mary E—†	732	housekeeper	47	"
	T	Callahone Ella—†	732	domestic	35	"
	V	Lee Charles	732A	laundryman	62	"
940						
	A	*White Charles A	742	chauffeur	43	1117 Harrison av
	B	*White Edith E—†	742	housewife	44	1117 "
	C	Lyons Sarah—†	742	housekeeper	45	here
	D	Nichols Avis E—†	742	housewife	42	"
	E	Nichols John A	742	chauffeur	45	"
	F	Thomas Arnold	742	laborer	40	
	G	Thomas Josephine—†	742	housewife	37	"
	H	Taggart Martha L—†	742	housekeeper	42	"
	K	Hoffman Alice—†	742	domestic	27	"
	L	Hoffman Clara B—†	742	housewife	31	"
	M	Hoffman James A	742	carcleaner	52	"
	O	Carrington Moses L	746	laborer	41	
	P	Williams Joyce C—†	746	domestic	40	"
	S	Morris Elizabeth—†	746	housewife	25	"
	T	Morris William	746	U S A	28	
	U	Henderson James E	746	chauffeur	52	"
	V	Henderson Mahalia—†	746	housewife	42	"
	W	Broder Cynthia—†	746	domestic	39	"
	X	Leite Florencio F	746	welder	42	
	Y	Lynn Thelma N—†	746	domestic	54	"
	Z	Carter James M, jr	746	painter	35	
941						
	A	Hinds Lincoln	746	student	28	
	B	Witherspoon Emma J—†	746	housewife	60	"
	C	Etridge Ida—†	746	"	23	41 Ruggles
	D	Etridge Louis	746	cook	27	41 "
	E	Marshall John	746	welder	41	here

Page.	Letter.	Full Name.	Residence, Jan. 1, 1943.	Occupation.	Supposed Age.	Reported Residence, Jan. 1, 1942. Street and Number.

Shawmut Avenue—Continued

	F	Lane Lydia—†	746	housewife	30	here
	G	Allen Charles F	746	U S N	31	981A Tremont
	H	Allen Eva L—†	746	maid	31	981A "
	K	Ward Rebecca—†	746	domestic	31	here
	L	McRay Catherine—†	746	housewife	23	"
	M	McRay George	746	laborer	29	"
	N	Smith Albert	746	"	44	Ohio
	O	Smith Grace R—†	746	housewife	36	"
	P	Leir Leroy A	746	welder	40	here
	R	Simmons Bessie R—†	750	housewife	59	"
	S	Simmons John J	750	laborer	60	"
	T	Ellis Mae—†	750	domestic	34	"
	U	Oliver Agnes—†	750	"	35	
	V	Miller Flossie J—†	750	matron	43	
	W	Tyler Edward D	750	laborer	28	"
	X	Tyler Vera L—†	750	housewife	23	"
	Y	Seales Charles	750	laborer	45	
	Z	Seales Inez—†	750	housewife	40	"
942						
	A	Clark Mack	750	laborer	38	
	B	Clark Vivian—†	750	housewife	28	"
	C	Kent Albert	750	laborer	60	
	D	Price Christopher C	750	watchman	64	"
	E	Price Clifford E—†	750	housewife	62	"
	F	Robinson George D	750	laborer	51	
	G	Howard Florence—†	750	at home	62	
	H	Priolean Thelma—†	750	entertainer	21	"
	K	Sorrell Marie E—†	750	housekeeper	51	"
	L	*Tarvares Jose L	750	retired	72	"
	M	Johnson Hester—†	750	housewife	45	"
	N	Johnson Robert	750	laborer	45	
	O	Burrells Elmer	750	chipper	49	
	P	Thompson Edward	750	chauffeur	45	"
	R	Thompson Janie—†	750	housewife	45	"
	S	Upshaw Gertrude—†	750	domestic	50	"
	T	Reid Laura L—†	762	housewife	48	"
	U	Reid Philip A	762	laborer	60	
	V	Clark Eleanor—†	762	domestic	49	"
	W	Clark Louise—†	762	at home	78	
	X	Berry Willis	762	chipper	61	
	Y	Berry Winifred—†	762	housewife	61	"

Page.	Letter.	FULL NAME.	Residence, Jan. 1, 1943.	Occupation.	Supposed Age.	Reported Residence, Jan. 1, 1942. Street and Number.
943						
		Shawmut Avenue—Continued				
	B	Harris Jesse	764A	laborer	30	here
	C	Washington Annie V—†	764A	housewife	49	"
	D	Washington William A	764A	machinist	50	"
	E	Simmonds Richard	764A	shoemaker	40	"
	F	Simmonds Rose—†	764A	housewife	40	"
	H	Haynes Daisy—†	766A	domestic	30	"
	K	Young Millicent—†	766A	housekeeper	45	"
	L	Young Olga—†	766A	maid	20	"
	M	Brown Albert E	766A	bookbinder	65	"
	N	Mayers Allister	766A	mechanic	53	"
	O	Mayers Edna M—†	766A	student	21	
	P	Miller Lena—†	766A	domestic	61	"
	R	Dudley Annie J—†	770	housewife	71	"
	S	Dudley James S	770	laborer	58	
	T	Shepherd Bessie—†	770	housewife	61	"
	U	Shepherd Earl	770	U S A	22	
	V	Shepherd John	770	laborer	24	
	W	Shepherd Samuel M	770	clerk	60	
	X	Shepherd Samuel M	770	U S A	26	
	Y	Brown Robert	770	waiter	56	
	Z	*Brown Sophie—†	770	housewife	52	"
944						
	A	*Snape Dita—†	770	domestic	25	"
	B	Mayers Floyd	772	laborer	27	Illinois
	C	Mayers Mildred—†	772	housewife	25	"
	D	Gittens Elizabeth L—†	772	"	27	here
	E	Gittens William A	772	laborer	30	"
	F	Rosa Evelyn H—†	772	maid	28	"
	G	Hutchins Jeremiah	772	porter	29	
	H	Hutchins Palmira—†	772	housewife	29	"
	L	Hutchins Arthur R	774	U S A	22	
	M	Hutchins Isabell—†	774	housewife	66	"
	N	Hutchins Jeremiah	774	retired	80	
	O	Betts James W	774	musician	47	"
	P	Betts Sadie M—†	774	housewife	60	"
	R	Tasco Elinor—†	774	operator	29	
	S	Turner Clifford B	774	musician	46	"
	T	Jones Marion	rear 780	painter	45	
	U	Jones Victory—†	" 780	housewife	32	"
	V	Reed Arthur B	782	chauffeur	50	"

Page.	Letter.	FULL NAME.	Residence, Jan. 1, 1943.	Occupation.	Supposed Age.	Reported Residence, Jan. 1, 1942. Street and Number.

Shawmut Avenue—Continued

	W	Reed Grace D—†	782	laundress	56	here
	X	Reed Lillian M—†	782	housewife	48	"
	Y	Johnson Mary—†	782	domestic	26	"
	Z	Jones Grace—†	782	housewife	30	"
945						
	A	Jones Harold	782	chauffeur	38	"
	B	*Douglin Adriana—†	784	housewife	53	"
	C	*Douglin Benjamin	784	janitor	53	"
	D	Alves James	rear 786	welder	30	10 Willard pl
	E	Dias Joseph	" 786	laborer	36	10 "
	F	Dias Olinda—†	" 786	housewife	31	10 "
	G	Kilduff Louis V	788	chauffeur	50	here
	H	Kilduff Mary E—†	788	housewife	50	"
	K	Thomas Francis T	788	machinist	25	"
	L	Kilduff Leila K—†	788	housewife	24	"
	M	Kilduff Vincent J	788	electrician	21	"
	O	Farnsworth Melvin	rear 792	U S N	33	
	P	Fitzgibbons John	" 792	janitor	67	
	R	Gould Annie—†	" 792	housewife	65	"
	S	Gould Charles	" 792	laborer	37	"
	T	Gould William	" 792	"	30	
	U	Stricker Mary—†	" 792	saleswoman	35	"
	W	Hazzard Laura E—†	794	clerk	35	
	X	Smith Florence J—†	794	housewife	55	"
	Y	Smith James N	794	retired	76	
	Z	Gonsalves Ruth—†	794	domestic	25	"
946						
	A	Mewett Minnie—†	794	housekeeper	71	"
	B	Dent Martha E—†	794	"	88	
	C	King Carrie—†	794	at home	79	
	D	Tucker Isadore E	794	retired	67	
	E	*Doherty James	rear 794	laborer	49	
	F	Doherty James T	" 794	"	23	
	G	*Doherty Katherine—†	" 794	housewife	57	"
	1G	Salisbury Adele—†	" 794	maid	58	
	H	Wickson Carrie—†	796	housekeeper	51	"
	K	Molinelli George P	796	chauffeur	44	"
	L	Molinelli Mary A—†	796	housekeeper	70	"
	M	Needle Bessie—†	796	housewife	42	"
	N	Needle Rubin	796	storekeeper	38	"

Page.	Letter.	FULL NAME.	Residence, Jan. 1, 1943.	Occupation.	Supposed Age.	Reported Residence, Jan. 1, 1942. Street and Number.

Sterling Street

Page.	Letter.	FULL NAME.	Residence, Jan. 1, 1943.	Occupation.	Supposed Age.	Reported Residence, Jan. 1, 1942. Street and Number.
	R	Jones Ella R—†	28	at home	67	here
	S	Winston Clarence L	28	musician	66	"
	T	Winston Mary—†	28	housewife	65	"
	U	Taylor Edmund S	28	laborer	52	
	V	Taylor Edna—†	28	housewife	50	"
	W	Cannon Alice—†	29	at home	56	
	X	Rosa Isadore	29	operator	24	"
	Y	Washington George	29	mechanic	47	Maine
	Z	Whitehead Laura—†	29	housewife	70	here
947						
	A	Whitehead Mabel—†	29	laundress	38	"
	B	Whitehead Viola—†	29	housekeeper	35	"
	C	Whitehead William E	29	laborer	53	"
	D	Pires Charlotte—†	30	housewife	24	"
	E	Pires Lawrence	30	laborer	28	
	F	White Elizabeth B—†	30	housewife	73	"
	G	White Lillian R—†	30	"	38	
	H	Johnson Irene J—†	30	domestic	48	"
	K	Johnson William H	30	laborer	48	Connecticut
	L	Matthew Charles H	30	clerk	52	here
	N	Kerzirian Anne M—†	31	"	29	"
	O	Kerzirian Edward M	31	laborer	25	"
	P	Kerzirian Nicholas W	31	"	28	
	R	*Kerzirian Rose—†	31	housekeeper	54	"
	S	Garrett Charles	32	retired	78	12 Cunard
	T	Chisholm Mary J—†	33	housewife	59	here
	U	Chisholm William H	33	baker	64	"
	V	Banks John	34	porter	28	"
	W	Banks Rosaline A—†	34	clerk	24	
	X	Smith William E	34	retired	64	
	Y	Thomas Ida—†	34	housekeeper	46	"
948						
	H	Depew Irene—†	39	hairdresser	41	"
	K	White Gertrude—†	39	laundress	42	"
	L	Kezirian Jacob K	39	mechanic	35	"
	M	*Kezirian Taquie—†	39	housekeeper	60	"
	P	Bishop George W	40	houseman	42	673 Shawmut av
	R	Bishop Grace A—†	40	housewife	39	673 "
	T	Keeling Blanche—†	41	housekeeper	42	here
	U	Keeling William B	41	baker	50	"

Page.	Letter.	Full Name.	Residence, Jan. 1, 1943.	Occupation.	Supposed Age.	Reported Residence, Jan. 1, 1942. Street and Number.

Sterling Street—Continued

	V	Dillon Mary—†	41	laundress	43	here
	W	Patterson John	41	laborer	28	"
	X	Smith Elizabeth—†	43	at home	50	"
	Y	Tyler Jane—†	43	housekeeper	65	"
	Z	Webster Daniel	43	laborer	55	"
949						
	B	Durant Mary—†	49	housekeeper	69	"
	C	Hoyt Martha—†	49	at home	61	"
	D	*Currie Frances E—†	49	domestic	56	"
	G	Bruce Ernest	58	porter	52	"
	K	Mason Betsy—†	60	housewife	53	N Carolina
	L	Mason Mary—†	60	domestic	28	here
	M	Monroe Ophelia—†	60	"	42	"
	N	Willis Judith—†	60	at home	83	"
	O	Felix Albert	62	laborer	67	
	P	*Bourne Bertie S	68	seaman	48	
	S	Washington Arthur	68	laborer	35	
	T	Sutton Arthur	70	U S A	31	
	U	Sutton Elsie—†	70	housewife	21	"
	V	Ramsey Jeanette—†	70	housekeeper	31	"
	W	Brooks Ernest	70	laborer	40	"
	X	Brown George	70	"	42	
	Y	Postlock James	70	porter	42	"
	Z	Brown Rosa—†	72	domestic	35	"
950						
	A	Smith Ada—†	72	housekeeper	52	"
	B	Smith Mabel—†	72	domestic	54	"
	C	Smith Vivian—†	72	"	48	
	D	Worthy Blanche M—†	72	"	55	
	E	Crute Kiezie—†	74	housewife	45	"
	F	Crute William	74	porter	52	
	K	Caldwell Rose—†	76	domestic	50	"
	L	Perry Elbert	76	manager	22	"
	M	Grace Dorothy A—†	76	housewife	22	"
	N	Grace Samuel	76	cook	25	
	O	Waitears Eliza—†	78	housekeeper	67	"
	P	Perry Katherine L—†	78	domestic	56	"
	R	McGruder Jasper	78	U S N	28	"
	S	Washington Laura—†	78	domestic	35	Texas
	T	Jenkins Rachel—†	80	at home	65	here
	U	Brown Flora—†	80	matron	45	"

Page.	Letter.	FULL NAME.	Residence, Jan. 1, 1943.	Occupation.	Supposed Age.	Reported Residence, Jan. 1, 1942. Street and Number.

Sterling Street—Continued

	W	Cummins Harriet—†	82	domestic	50	here
	X	Jackson Albert	82	U S A	26	"
	Y	Jackson Edna—†	82	housewife	26	"
	Z	Taylor John	82	baker	32	
951						
	A	Gray Jacqueline—†	82	housewife	21	"
	B	Gray Lillian—†	82	domestic	57	"
	C	Gray William	82	painter	30	
	D	Sanderson John	84	laborer	37	
	E	Cash Charles	84	porter	54	
	F	Cash Gertrude—†	84	housekeeper	27	"
	G	Berry Blanche—†	84	laundress	53	"
	H	Berry Leo	84	laborer	36	
	K	Berry Osbourne	84	porter	32	"
	L	Fraser Melvina—†	84	domestic	38	Brookline
	M	McClark Mary—†	84	"	42	here
	N	Wilson Joseph	84	garageman	22	"
	O	Robart Margaret—†	84	domestic	40	"
	P	McPherson Ethel—†	84	housewife	31	"
	R	Morris Bertha—†	84	waitress	35	
	S	Morris John	84	laborer	45	
	T	Walker Helen L—†	84	housewife	37	"
	U	Walker Quinnie	84	mechanic	38	"
	X	Armstrong Charles H	132	cook	28	
	Y	Armstrong Gloria—†	132	clerk	21	"
	Z	Armstrong Louise F—†	132	housekeeper	50	"
952						
	A	Chase Susanne—†	132	domestic	57	"
	B	Joseph Donald	132	porter	32	
	C	Joseph Ernest	132	U S A	33	
	D	*Joseph Frances—†	132	housekeeper	59	"
	E	Joseph Garibena—†	132	"	30	"
	F	Joseph George	132	U S A	25	"
	G	Joseph Victor	132	"	27	
	H	Miles John W	134	laborer	42	
	K	Pitts Josephine T—†	134	housewife	43	"
	L	Greenidge Charles	134	laborer	42	
	M	Greenidge James	134	clergyman	56	"
	N	Lewis Emma L—†	134	housewife	52	"
	O	Lewis Ferdinand H	134	U S A	35	
	P	Lewis George W	134	laborer	56	

Page.	Letter.	Full Name.	Residence, Jan. 1, 1943.	Occupation.	Supposed Age.	Reported Residence, Jan. 1, 1942. Street and Number.

Sterling Street—Continued

	R	*Lewis James M	134	chef	57	here
	S	Monroe Edith—†	134	seamstress	24	"
	T	Ramsey Charles B	134	mechanic	52	"
	U	*Ramsey Gladys E—†	134	housewife	46	"
	V	Doley Georgia—†	136	housekeeper	61	"
	W	Washington Lillian—†	136	"	59	"
	X	Middlebrooks Edna E—†	138	housewife	34	"
	Y	Middlebrooks Howard	138	laborer	38	

953 Tilden Place

953	A	Tyson Lucy A—†	1	housekeeper	72	here
	B	Gilliard Catherine M—†	1	"	45	6 Auburn
	C	Broadard Janet—†	1	"	28	Worcester
	D	Duchett Anne B—†	2		80	here
	E	Williams Isabel—†	2		68	"

Warwick Street

	G	Howard John	95	laborer	47	here
	H	Walker Alex	95	"	47	"
	K	Ross Alberta—†	95	operator	21	21 Edgeworth
	L	Walker Mildred—†	95	domestic	28	Brookline
	M	Young Doucious	95	laborer	21	Georgia
	N	Emerson Charles	95	cooper	61	here
	O	Emerson Inez—†	95	housewife	52	"
	P	Emerson Ruth—†	95	clerk	28	"
	R	Thompson Alice—†	95	housekeeper	38	12 Bush
	S	Thomas Daniel H	95	welder	53	here
	T	Thomas Ethel—†	95	housewife	50	"
	U	Jeannette Carrie—†	97	"	74	"
	V	Middleton Minnie—†	97	"	67	
	W	Starks Robert H	97	laborer	38	
	X	Logan Benjamin	97	rigger	47	
	Y	Logan Mary—†	97	housewife	30	"
	Z	Vinson Mildred—†	97	maid	37	
954						
	A	Gay Redmond	97	waiter	66	
	B	Perkins John B	97	laborer	62	"
	C	Boyd Ernestine—†	97	housekeeper	33	698 Shawmut av
	D	Hill Laura—†	97	attendant	21	698 "

Page.	Letter.	Full Name.	Residence, Jan. 1, 1943.	Occupation.	Supposed Age.	Reported Residence, Jan. 1, 1942. Street and Number.

Warwick Street—Continued

Page.	Letter.	Full Name.	Residence, Jan. 1, 1943.	Occupation.	Supposed Age.	Reported Residence, Jan. 1, 1942. Street and Number.
	E	McKain Eliza—†	97	laundress	60	here
	F	Kelly Alfred	99	cook	58	“
	G	Kelly Sarah—†	99	housewife	47	“
	H	Kelly William H	99	welder	21	
	K	Bee Celia—†	99	housekeeper	48	“
	L	Bee Edward	99	laborer	21	“
	M	Day Emma—†	99	domestic	48	“
	N	Martin Wilhelmina—†	99	waitress	27	
	O	Knight Rebecca—†	99	housewife	46	“
	P	Mayberry Amelia—†	99	laundress	54	“
	R	Pasket John J	99	machinist	58	“
	S	Williams Irene S—†	99	housewife	26	Florida
	T	Williams Ralph S	99	welder	29	“
	U	Latson Ida—†	rear 99	housewife	24	“
	V	Latson Robert	“ 99	laborer	30	“
	X	Jackson Mary—†	“ 99	domestic	42	here
	Y	Morse William S	“ 99	pipefitter	39	“
	Z	Dixon Armstead	“ 99	clerk	32	“
955						
	A	Dixon Iola—†	“ 99	dressmaker	29	“
	B	Adams Mary—†	“ 99	domestic	27	“
	C	Adams Percival	“ 99	U S A	26	
	D	Noiles Mildred—†	“ 99	mattressmaker	25	“
	E	Bowers Anna—†	“ 99	“	25	“
	F	Jackson Elizabeth—†	“ 99	maid	23	Salem
	G	Lord Helen—†	“ 99	clerk	33	38 Sussex
	H	Roundtree Delia—†	“ 99	housekeeper	23	38 “
	K	Johnson Arthur	“ 99	laborer	47	here
	L	Johnson Dora—†	105	housekeeper	57	“
	M	Johonson Jacob	105	repairman	27	“
	N	Johnson Marie—†	105	housewife	28	“
	O	Diggins Emma L—†	107	housekeeper	69	“
	P	Maxey Charles	107	waiter	69	“

956 Washington Street

Page.	Letter.	Full Name.	Residence, Jan. 1, 1943.	Occupation.	Supposed Age.	Reported Residence, Jan. 1, 1942. Street and Number.
	C	Currie Mary—†	1911	waitress	53	here
	D	Hanson John	1911	molder	57	“
	E	Higgins Thomas	1911	chauffeur	48	673 Mass av
	F	Scannell Walter	1911	waiter	39	here
	K	Stolle Francis	1911	retired	67	“

Page.	Letter.	Full Name.	Residence, Jan. 1, 1943.	Occupation.	Supposed Age.	Reported Residence, Jan. 1, 1942. Street and Number.

Washington Street—Continued

Page.	Letter.	Full Name.	Residence, Jan. 1, 1943.	Occupation.	Supposed Age.	Reported Residence, Jan. 1, 1942. Street and Number.
	G	Stolle William	1911	tilesetter	58	here
	H	Tation Richard	1911	houseman	59	"
	L	Burke John J	1913	laborer	63	Middleboro
	M	Finn William F	1913	retired	75	here
	N	Gibbons Thomas	1913	farmer	52	151 Appleton
	O	Glover Elijah C	1913	printer	62	here
	P	McCormack Stephen	1913	retired	70	4 Cedar
	R	Norton Mary—†	1913	domestic	56	here
	S	Webguish Allen	1913	laborer	69	"
	U	*Anderson Gustave	1917	cementworker	64	"
	W	Conray Joseph M	1917	agent	58	
	X	Frazier John	1917	laborer	62	"
	Y	Landsburg William	1917	chauffeur	39	1911 Wash'n
	Z	Montgomery John	1917	clerk	50	here
		957				
	A	*McDonald Joseph	1917	retired	82	1913 Wash'n
	B	O'Connor James	1917	"	67	here
	1B	Palmer Edward	1917	"	79	"
	C	*Sylvain Alphonsine—†	1917	housekeeper	61	"
	D	*Sylvain Gabrielle F—†	1917	"	30	"
	G	Johnson Grace M—†	1927	housewife	44	New Bedford
	R	King Peter	1947	waiter	35	18 Ball
	S	Shepard Julia M—†	1947	housewife	33	here
	T	Williams Lanice—†	1947	maid	39	"
	U	Williams Stephen A	1947	seaman	39	"
	V	Davis Frank	1947	painter	67	
	W	Davis Gertrude—†	1947	radios	20	
	X	Davis Helen—†	1947	housewife	55	"
	Y	Marshall Lloyd	1947	U S A	31	1967 Wash'n
	Z	Marshall Mary—†	1947	housewife	26	1967 "
		958				
	A	White Alfred	1947	welder	20	1967 "
	E	Newton Ella M—†	1957	at home	63	here
	F	Layne Frederick W	1957	waiter	41	"
	G	Layne Marie D—†	1957	housewife	47	"
	K	Mattier Constantine D	1957	laborer	57	
	L	Mattier Constantine D	1957	U S A	20	
	H	Mattier Eleanor—†	1957	housewife	47	"
	N	Tunnell David	1959	chauffeur	33	"
	O	Tunnell Elizabeth—†	1959	laundryworker	32	"
	P	Hurley Margaret—†	1959	dishwasher	34	"

Page.	Letter.	Full Name.	Residence, Jan. 1, 1943.	Occupation.	Supposed Age.	Reported Residence, Jan. 1, 1942. Street and Number.

Washington Street—Continued

	R	Murray Stephen	1959	laborer	31	N Hampshire
	S	Robinson Etta—†	1959	housewife	36	here
	U	*Davis Mary—†	1959	"	37	"
	Y	Coleman Lucy—†	1963	domestic	43	"
	Z	Sims Florence—†	1963	housewife	38	"
959						
	A	Sims John	1963	laborer	45	
	B	Johnson Catherine—†	1963	examiner	28	"
	C	Mynick Amelia—†	1963	housewife	34	"
	D	Weldon Maybelle—†	1963	nurse	41	
	E	White Rose—†	1963	housewife	45	"
	F	*White William	1963	porter	55	"
	H	Adams Clara L—†	1967	waitress	22	Chelsea
	K	Sharp William	1967	U S A	28	24 Reed
	L	Sweet Mary B—†	1967	waitress	23	24 "
	N	Thomas Elizabeth—†	1967	housewife	24	24 "
	M	Thomas Phillip A	1967	U S A	26	Winchester
	P	Ridgley Mamie V—†	1969	housewife	71	here
960						
	O	Griffith James H	2049	operator	55	23 Thorndike
	P	Yetsook Edith—†	2049	housewife	50	23 "
	R	*Yetsook George	2049	carpenter	48	23 "
	S	Buckland Frank	2049	shipper	56	here
	T	Buckland Marion—†	2049	housekeeper	26	"
	U	Buckland Mattie—†	2049	housewife	60	"
961						
	G	Fiandaca Isabelle—†	2079	"	40	
	H	Fiandaca Rosario	2079	laborer	48	
	K	*Knight Richard	2079	installer	39	
	L	*Knight Rose—†	2079	housewife	40	"
	M	Little Albert	2079	laborer	35	119 W Brookline
	N	Little Olive—†	2079	housewife	22	119 "
	P	Reardon George J	2083	electrician	47	2 Cliff pl
	R	Reardon Mary E—†	2083	housewife	42	2 "
	S	Lymneos Eileen—†	2083	clerk	22	4 Renfrew
	T	*O'Mara James	2083	laborer	62	4 "
	U	O'Mara Margaret—†	2083	housekeeper	73	4 "
	X	Suddard Albertine—†	2085	housewife	54	here
	Y	Suddard Clayton	2085	contractor	65	"
	Z	Suddard Gerald	2085	U S A	21	"
	[1]Z	Benfield James A	2085	U S N	21	1 Regent

Page.	Letter.	Full Name.	Residence, Jan. 1, 1943.	Occupation.	Supposed Age.	Reported Residence, Jan. 1, 1942. Street and Number.
962		**Washington Street**—Continued				
	A	Collier Alice E—†	2085	housekeeper	50	here
	B	Collier Walter H	2085	U S A	20	"
	D	Skinner Alice E—†	2093	housekeeper	65	"
	V	Cavanaugh Homer	2145	laborer	25	25 Burgess
	W	Denomme Joseph	2145	attendant	48	41 Roxbury
	Y	Donnelly William P	2145	repairman	42	6 Circuit
	X	Donovan Thomas J	2145	guard	52	Rhode Island
	Z	Essayan Boghos	2145	storekeeper	57	722 Shawmut av
963						
	A	Farrell John H	2145	oiler	38	820 Parker
	B	Hewitt Stephen B	2145	chauffeur	28	Hyannis
	C	Liddell John	2145	shipper	61	here
	D	Morse Russell J	2145	baker	35	"
	E	Murray Patrick A	2145	retired	67	"
	F	O'Brien Jeremiah D	2145	operator	26	28 Coffey
	G	Roach Mabel A—†	2145	housekeeper	56	here
	H	Roach Robert L	2145	U S N	47	"
	K	Sullivan Cornelius J	2145	chauffeur	50	New York
	N	Plummer George L	2161	counterman	56	18 Thornton
	O	Plummer Margaret K–†	2161	housekeeper	44	18 "
	P	Hanscom Harriet—†	2161	"	69	here
	R	Cunningham Katherine–†	2161	waitress	30	"
	S	Perkins Frances—†	2161	"	47	"
	T	Wood Della L—†	2161	cashier	49	
	W	Williams Henry	2161	janitor	48	"
	X	Joyce Mabel E—†	2161	clerk	48	219 Harvard av
	Y	Joyce Myles J	2161	"	22	219 "
	Z	Cano Albert	2161	checker	60	here
964						
	A	Cano Florence—†	2161	housewife	52	"
	B	Darcy Ella—†	2161	housekeeper	44	"
	C	Vale Rena—†	2161	waitress	40	"
	D	Johnson Desinda G—†	2161	housewife	74	"
	E	Johnson William H	2161	operator	72	
	F	Sprague Katherine E–†	2161	housewife	53	"
	G	Mooney Anna R—†	2161	"	41	
	H	Mooney Peter M	2161	mechanic	47	"
	M	Thompson Jennie—†	2161	waitress	47	
	O	Ebbitts Elizabeth—†	2161	housewife	60	"
	P	Ebbitts William H	2161	painter	62	

Page.	Letter.	Full Name.	Residence, Jan. 1, 1943.	Occupation.	Supposed Age.	Reported Residence, Jan. 1, 1942. Street and Number.

Washington Street—Continued

Page.	Letter.	Full Name.	Residence, Jan. 1, 1943.	Occupation.	Supposed Age.	Reported Residence, Jan. 1, 1942. Street and Number.
	R	Gardiner Marie—†	2161	stitcher	64	9 Regent sq
	S	Tully Alice—†	2161	finisher	43	9 "
	T	Campbell Annie M—†	2161	housewife	61	here
	U	Campbell John V	2161	stagehand	64	"
	V	Dyer Kenneth M	2161	chauffeur	36	231 W Newton
	W	Dyer Theresa M—†	2161	housewife	30	231 "
	X	MacDonald James W	2161	warehouseman	64	here
	Y	MacDonald Madeline-†	2161	housewife	60	"
	Z	Whitehouse May—†	2161	housekeeper	42	530 Mass av
965						
	A	Whitehouse William E	2161	chauffeur	38	530 "
	B	Capen Roy	2161	"	37	here
	C	Tolman Joseph J	2161	molder	24	39 Norwell
	D	Tolman Mabel A—†	2161	housewife	23	39 "
	E	Deininger Caroline—†	2161	stitcher	55	10 Goodrich rd
	F	Doherty Jeremiah	2161	toolmaker	50	here
	G	Doherty Theresa—†	2161	housekeeper	50	"
	H	O'Malley Bridie—†	2161	housewife	33	"
	K	O'Malley Thomas	2161	chauffeur	36	"
	L	Smith Helen—†	2161	operator	23	29 Worcester sq
	M	Perkins Elizabeth R—†	2161	at home	81	here
	N	Whalen Agatha S—†	2161	housewife	22	"
	O	Whalen John G	2161	operator	26	"
	P	Suby Helen C—†	2161	housewife	39	30 Magnolia
	R	Suby Helen C—†	2161	stenographer	21	30 "
	S	Colbert Bertha—†	2161	housewife	56	here
	T	Colbert Edward L	2161	U S A	23	"
	U	Colbert John E	2161	letter carrier	63	"
	V	Speth Julia L—†	2161	housekeeper	67	"
	W	Myerstein Mary E—†	2161	"	75	"
	X	Glover Mary—†	2161	stitcher	32	"
	Y	Hayes Katherine—†	2161	waitress	42	
	Z	Brown Mabel R—†	2161	stitcher	63	
966						
	A	Black Elaine—†	2161	"	38	Rhode Island
	B	Carlson Sadie B—†	2161	waitress	40	here
	C	Smith Howard A	2161	electrician	58	"
	D	Lewis Guerwood	2161	fisherman	35	"
	E	Lewis Margaret—†	2161	housewife	32	"
	F	Moyer Frances G—†	2161	housekeeper	54	"
	G	Moyer Warren C	2161	buffer	29	

Page.	Letter.	Full Name.	Residence, Jan. 1, 1943.	Occupation.	Supposed Age.	Reported Residence, Jan. 1, 1942. Street and Number.

Washington Street—Continued

	K	*Grant Mary—†	2161	housewife	29	here
	L	*Grant Pius	2161	lineman	38	"
	M	Connolly Evelyn—†	2161	housewife	31	Somerville
	N	Connolly John	2161	warehouseman	33	"

Westminster Street

	Z	Bethune Elizabeth—†	64	housekeeper	53	here
967						
	A	Bethune Owen	64	mechanic	41	"
	B	Minner Marion—†	64	domestic	42	"
	C	Minner Myrtle—†	64	"	43	"
	D	Hawkins Annie—†	64	presser	31	751 Shawmut av
	E	Jackson Juanita—†	64	clerk	23	751 "
	F	Sands Carrie—†	64	"	29	751 "
	G	Bruce Estelle—†	66	domestic	45	here
	H	Bruce William	66	cleaner	54	"
	K	Cobbs Annie—†	66	housewife	52	"
	L	Cobbs James	66	retired	67	"
	M	Wilson Mary—†	66	cook	45	"
	N	Furlman Myrtle—†	66	clerk	30	32 Holyoke
	P	Davis John	68	retired	67	here
	R	Haliday Florence—†	68	housewife	26	"
	S	Haliday James	68	grinder	26	"
	U	Foster Irene—†	70	seamstress	34	"
	T	Moseley Ellen—†	70	domestic	77	"
	W	Lee Milton	70	laborer	36	
	X	Lee Viola—†	70	housewife	36	"
	Y	Jordan Mamie—†	74	at home	76	68 Westminster
	Z	Tate Elizabeth—†	74	"	73	here
968						
	A	Watson Martha—†	74	domestic	42	"
	B	Henderson Annie—†	76	at home	80	233 Cabot
	C	Gainville Ida—†	76	housewife	67	here
	D	Montero John	76	U S A	20	"
	E	Burney George	76	bottler	34	60 Williams
	F	Burney Ida—†	76	housewife	27	here
	G	Cooper Jamie—†	76	housekeeper	26	Florida
	H	Glover Naomi—†	84	seamstress	22	12 Elbert
	K	Glover Sadie—†	84	housewife	47	12 "

Page.	Letter.	Full Name.	Residence, Jan. 1, 1943.	Occupation.	Supposed Age.	Reported Residence, Jan. 1, 1942. Street and Number.

Westminster Street—Continued

	L	Glover Thomas	84	metalworker	47	12 Elbert
	M	Bryant Griffith	84	carpenter	53	here
	N	Gilbert Lewis	84	fireman	44	"
	O	Irving Brady	84	laborer	24	"
	P	Irving Stella—†	84	housewife	24	"
	R	Hooker Minnie—†	86	"	66	22 Genesee
	S	Smith Henry	86	laborer	55	New York
	T	Smith Mabel—†	86	housewife	46	"
	X	Farrar Frank H	86	retired	72	here
	U	Farrar Garnett B	86	U S A	25	"
	V	Farrar Joseph H	86	"	27	"
	W	Farrar Mary—†	86	housewife	46	"
	Y	Davis Edwin	86	laborer	51	"
	Z	Northington Charles	88	longshoreman	51	716 Shawmut av
969						
	A	Robinson Julia—†	88	housekeeper	68	here
	B	Rodrigues Benvinda—†	88	housewife	29	69 Ruggles
	C	Rodrigues Iris	88	pinboy	42	69 "
	D	Hudgins Adelaide—†	88	domestic	53	here
	E	Russell Jane—†	88	"	24	"
	F	Shepherd Laura—†	90	"	27	20 Elbert
	G	Wagner Julia—†	90	"	30	56 Sterling
	H	Williams Minnie—†	90	housewife	60	56 "
	K	Taylor Carrie—†	90	domestic	50	21 Hammond
	M	Bennett Ruby—†	92	"	39	3 Cunard
	N	Rose Charles	92	contractor	45	63 Ruggles
	O	Rose Pauline—†	92	housewife	35	63 "
	P	Lee Hazel—†	92	"	28	here
	S	Allen Francis	94	laborer	45	"
	T	Allen Frank	94	"	27	"
	U	Allen Sarah—†	94	domestic	45	"
	V	Baker Geraldine—†	94	"	35	
	W*	Andrews Bertha—†	94	"	40	
	X	Andrews Manuel	94	longshoreman	57	"
	Y	Jones David	96	retired	55	111 Ruggles
	Z	Jones Laura—†	96	housewife	49	111 "
970						
	A	McFarlane Catherine—†	96	"	37	here
	B	Gomes Melvin	96	seaman	28	91 Camden
	C	Snow Adele—†	96	housewife	26	91 "
	D	Snow Williams	96	chauffeur	28	91 "

Page.	Letter.	Full Name.	Residence, Jan. 1, 1943.	Occupation.	Supposed Age.	Reported Residence, Jan. 1, 1942. Street and Number.

Weston Street

Page.	Letter.	Full Name.	Residence, Jan. 1, 1943.	Occupation.	Supposed Age.	Reported Residence, Jan. 1, 1942. Street and Number.
	E	Dore Daniel	9	cook	47	here
	F	Dore Elizabeth—†	9	housekeeper	46	"
	G	*Allen Etha—†	9	dressmaker	30	"
	H	*Allen Leila—†	9	housewife	32	"
	K	Hill Charles	9	laborer	55	
	L	Lloyd Sadie—†	9	dressmaker	60	"
	M	Williams Alice—†	11	domestic	67	"
	N	Foster Helen—†	11	housekeeper	62	"
	O	Williams Lewis	11	chauffeur	44	"
	P	Paul Mattie—†	11	domestic	43	"
	R	Paul William	11	U S A	44	
	S	Flowers Ellen—†	13	housewife	72	"
	T	Flowers Thomas	13	retired	75	
	U	Washington Helen—†	13	housewife	35	"
	V	Washington William	13	laborer	36	

Williams Street

Page.	Letter.	Full Name.	Residence, Jan. 1, 1943.	Occupation.	Supposed Age.	Reported Residence, Jan. 1, 1942. Street and Number.
	Z	Buzzell Amos	18	seaman	42	here
971						
	A	Buzzell Enid—†	18	at home	26	
	B	Dyer Alice—†	18	"	48	
	C	Dyer Joseph R	18	teamster	52	"
	D	Flower Roy	18	mechanic	36	"
	E	Grant Thomas	18	tailor	56	
	F	Wilkie Edward	18	laborer	53	
	G	Coles Jessie—†	20	at home	54	
	H	Coles Lawrence	20	laborer	25	
	K	Garica Margaret—†	20	domestic	29	"
	L	Garica Robert	20	laborer	28	
	M	Griffin Carinthia—†	20	waitress	27	"
	N	Griffin Elizabeth—†	20	at home	41	"
	O	Owens Dorothy—†	20	teacher	32	
	P	Owens James T	20	barber	57	"
	S	Dawson Edward	22	cook	39	32 Hammond
	T	Green William R	22	machinist	44	here
	U	Parks Ella—†	22	at home	26	228 W Canton
	V	Parks James	22	laborer	22	Missouri
	W	Tatum James	22	"	27	Louisiana
	X	Martin Bertha—†	24	at home	62	here
	Y	Martin Blanche—†	24	domestic	55	"

Page.	Letter.	Full Name.	Residence, Jan. 1, 1943.	Occupation.	Supposed Age.	Reported Residence, Jan. 1, 1942. Street and Number.

Williams Street—Continued

	Z	Martin George	24	clerk	37	here
972						
	A	Martin Solomon	24	porter	67	"
	C	James Nathan	26	retired	66	
	D	James Thirza—†	26	housewife	54	"
	E	Carter Abia—†	26	clerk	20	N Carolina
	F	Small James	26	mechanic	25	12 Marble
	G	Small Josephine—†	26	at home	24	12 "
	H	Miller Edward	26	baker	48	here
	K	Miller Roselyn—†	26	at home	39	"
	L	Miller Wilhelmina—†	26	stenographer	21	"
	M	Hill Carrie—†	28	housewife	36	"
	N	Hill Harold	28	mechanic	37	"
	O	Marshall Carrie—†	28	at home	70	
	P	Marshall John	28	laborer	29	
	R	Marshall Lillian—†	28	at home	31	
	S	Marshall Thomas H	28	retired	70	
	T	Bynoe Edna—†	30	at home	46	
	U	Bynoe Edna B—†	30	"	24	"
	V	Bynoe George	30	welder	21	
	W	Bynoe John	30	carpenter	47	"
	X	Bynoe Victor	30	engineer	29	
	Z	Corbin Clarence	34	physician	27	"
973						
	A	Corbin Darnley	34	social worker	28	"
	D	Lewis Alma—†	34	at home	22	
	B	Lewis Clairmonte	34	mechanic	45	"
	C	Lewis Edwardina—†	34	housewife	45	"
	E	Morrison Yvonne—†	34	waitress	35	
	F	Strother Virginia—†	34	clerk	26	
	G	Barber Frances—†	36	superintendent	50	"
	H	Stone Lillian R—†	36	director	55	
	N	Bowles Joseph B	57	plumber	69	
	O	Wallace Irene M—†	57	clerk	31	"
	P	Wallace James B	57	U S A	32	Somerville
	R	Wong Irene—†	57	at home	30	here
	S	Wong Mary M—†	57	housewife	57	"
	T	Coss Phyllis—†	59	clerk	22	29 Wellington
	U	Williams Clifford	59	U S A	28	29 "
	V	Calhoun Lillian—†	59	clerk	29	here
	W	Furtado Margaret—†	59	housewife	32	"

Page.	Letter.	Full Name.	Residence, Jan. 1, 1943.	Occupation.	Supposed Age.	Reported Residence, Jan. 1, 1942. Street and Number.

Williams Street—Continued

Page.	Letter.	Full Name.	Residence, Jan. 1, 1943.	Occupation.	Supposed Age.	Reported Residence, Jan. 1, 1942. Street and Number.
	X	Archibald Eldora M—†	59	at home	79	here
	Y	Shepherd Catherine—†	59	housewife	47	"
	Z	Shepherd Nathaniel	59	mechanic	44	"
974						
	A	Carter Bessie M—†	60	at home	55	
	B	Marshall Catherine—†	60	"	31	
	C	Thompson Calvin	60	laborer	21	
	D	Thompson Leslie E	60	cook	50	
	E	*Thompson May—†	60	at home	41	"
	F	Barboza George	60	mechanic	27	Ohio
	G	Barrows Frank	60	"	27	Falmouth
	H	Merenda Flora—†	60	at home	34	Ohio
	K	*Washburn Victoria—†	60	"	66	"
	L	Dean Alice M—†	61	"	42	801 Tremont
	M	Dean Ellen F—†	61	domestic	24	801 "
	N	Dean George W	61	U S A	20	801 "
	O	*Daniels Vera—†	61	waitress	30	here
	P	Smith Conway, jr	61	teamster	24	"
	R	Smith Evelyn—†	61	housewife	25	"
	S	Brooks Carrie—†	61	"	48	156 Lenox
	T	Brooks George	61	carpenter	53	156 "
	U	Jones Arthur W	61	U S A	25	156 "
	V	*Midgett Delcina—†	62	at home	32	46 Cabot
	W	Midgett Joseph	62	clerk	34	46 "
	X	Harrel Robert	62	U S M C	34	here
	Y	Harrel Theresa—†	62	at home	31	"
	Z	Levy Freda—†	62	clerk	24	1 Auburn
975						
	A	Green Josephine—†	62	at home	31	here
	B	Green William	62	laborer	31	"
	C	Bordly Florence—†	63	at home	31	"
	D	Bordly Francis	63	teamster	29	"
	E	Brisbane Henry	63	laborer	56	"
	F	Brisbane Sinnie—†	63	housewife	56	"
	G	Haltwanger Mattie B—†	63	domestic	43	"
	H	*Farrell John	63	porter	42	
	K	*Waithe Gwendolyn—†	63	housewife	36	"
	L	*Waithe Winston	63	laborer	39	
	M	Ross Josephine—†	64	at home	28	"
	N	Ross Thomas	64	porter	39	
	O	Carrick Ida—†	64	at home	56	

Page.	Letter.	Full Name.	Residence, Jan. 1, 1943.	Occupation.	Supposed Age.	Reported Residence, Jan. 1, 1942. Street and Number.

Williams Street—Continued

	P	Carrick William	64	U S A	34	here
	R	Davis Norvell	64	retired	61	"
	S	Reddick Aaron	64	grinder	27	"
	T	Reddick Charles	64	welder	23	
	U	Reddick Preston	64	U S A	39	
	V	Reddick Stephen	64	clerk	39	
	W	Reddick Viola—†	64	at home	64	
	X	*Knight Adella—†	66	"	58	
	Y	*Knight Charles	66	laborer	59	
	Z	Knight Lottie L—†	66	clerk	21	
976						
	A	Knight Patrick	66	electrician	20	"
	B	Burgo Joseph	66	cook	39	
	C	Burgo Mary—†	66	at home	30	
	D	Braxton Annie—†	66	"	74	
	E	Foskey Catherine—†	67	housewife	25	"
	F	Foskey George	67	porter	61	
	G	Hutchinson David	67	seaman	70	
	K	Hiutchnson David, jr	67	U S A	22	"
	H	Pena Eliza—†	67	saleswoman	28	"
	L	Gray Wellington	67	baker	40	19 Greenwich pk
	M	Pleasant May—†	67	waitress	34	12 Marble
	N	Jackman Audley	68	operator	39	here
	O	Jackman Linda—†	68	housewife	41	"
	R	Mewett Chester	68	porter	44	"
	P	Walker Caroline—†	68	at home	69	
	S	Davis Alonzo	68	molder	50	
	T	Davis Kathleen—†	68	at home	48	"
	U	Fowler Edgar	69	laborer	33	"
	V	Fowler Mary—†	69	housewife	32	"
	W	*Brown Clara—†	69	at home	46	
	X	Mosely Osford	69	blacksmith	42	"
	Y	*Henry Charles A	69	"	45	
	Z	Tucker Edward	70	oiler	53	
977						
	A	Tucker Mary—†	70	at home	49	
	B	Steven Marie—†	70	"	58	
	C	Steven Wilson	70	"	61	
	D	*Ferreira Antonio	70	porter	50	
	E	Ferreira Martha—†	70	at home	39	
	G	Sapp Bernice—†	71	housewife	25	"

Page.	Letter.	Full Name.	Residence, Jan. 1, 1943.	Occupation.	Supposed Age.	Reported Residence, Jan. 1, 1942. Street and Number.

Williams Street—Continued

	F	Sapp Renzybell	71	welder	30	here
	H	Walker Rose—†	71	domestic	28	"
	K	*Alleyne Joseph	71	laborer	50	"
	L	Marshall Lloyd	71	U S A	30	"
	M	Smith Alberta—†	71	domestic	34	15 Ball
	N	Smith Frank L	71	electrician	44	15 "
	O	Smith Grace—†	71	housewife	63	15 "
	P	Whitaker Amelia—†	72	at home	65	here
	R	Nellon Esther—†	72	"	66	"
	S	Nellon Nina—†	72	domestic	20	"
	T	Andrews Edith—†	72	"	50	
	U	Wiggins Emma—†	73	at home	73	
	V	Wiggins James	73	retired	83	
	W	Johnson Georgia—†	73	housewife	47	"
	Y	Johnson Neal	73	laborer	46	
	X	Morgan Mary—†	73	clerk	25	
	Z	Smith Catherine—†	73	at home	62	
978						
	A	Smith Winifred—†	73		42	
	B	Graham Scottie—†	74	"	36	
	C	*Mitchell Linford	74	porter	41	
	D	Simmonds Mabel—†	74	housewife	42	"
	E	Rogers Sarah—†	74	at home	59	
	F	Callender Ella—†	75	"	26	
	G	Callender Granville	75	mechanic	29	"
	H	Jacobs Ora—†	75	at home	61	
	K	Carlton Nathaniel	75	laborer	39	
	L	Carlton Virginia—†	75	housewife	35	"
	M	Murphy Lillian—†	75	operator	21	"
	N	Robinson Adelaide—†	76	at home	42	
	O	Robinson William	76	laborer	41	
	P	Otley Emma—†	76	at home	63	
	R	*Otley Joseph	76	laborer	67	"
	S	Johnson Hazel—†	76	at home	29	77 Sterling
	T	Smith Hattie—†	76	"	84	here
	U	Smith Marion—†	76	domestic	47	"
	V	Martin Eulasee	77	laborer	35	"
	W	*Martin Letitia—†	77	housewife	35	"
	X	Flippo Cora—†	77	clerk	62	
	Y	Pride Estella—†	77	housewife	67	"

Page.	Letter.	FULL NAME.	Residence, Jan. 1, 1943.	Occupation.	Supposed Age.	Reported Residence, Jan. 1, 1942. Street and Number.

Williams Street—Continued

	Z	Pride William G	77	laborer	62	here
979						
	A	Sledge Dorothy—†	78	housewife	36	"
	B	Sledge William	78	boilermaker	49	"
	C	Holmes Odell—†	78	at home	51	
	D	*Semedo Simplicio	78	laborer	54	
	E	*Belgrave Mary—†	78	at home	78	
	F	Douglas Beatrice—†	78	domestic	56	"
	G	*Ferry Michael	79	salesman	52	"
	H	*Ferry Pauline—†	79	housewife	48	"
	K	Murphy Bessie—†	79	at home	31	
	L	Murphy Dessie—†	79	"	61	
	M	Murphy John	79	cook	31	"
	N	Wade Eva M—†	79	maid	58	17 Walnut pk
	O	Sewell George	80	carpenter	59	here
	P	Sewell Sadie—†	80	at home	63	"
	R	Chapman Emma—†	80	domestic	57	"
	S	Hazard Bertha—†	80	at home	49	
	T	Hazard John	80	retired	74	"
	U	Washington Irene—†	81	at home	45	
	V	Washington Irene—†	81	leatherworker	21	"
	W	Washington Isaac	81	cook	59	
	X	Brown Elmer	81	longshoreman	39	"
	Y	Brown Lena—†	81	at home	55	
	Z	Andonian Joseph	81	laborer	35	
980						
	A	Andonian Kachadoor	81	factoryhand	67	"
	B	*Andonian Mary—†	81	at home	63	"
	C	Monroe Catherine—†	82	"	78	603 Shawmut av
	D	Foskey Clara—†	82	"	58	here
	E	Foskey Roger	82	mechanic	25	"
	F	Gomes Clarissa—†	82	clerk	20	"
	G	Gomes Gladys—†	82	"	37	
	H	Hall Herbert	82	laborer	22	
	K	Hall Herbert	82	"	59	
	L	Hall Leopold	82	U S A	23	
	M	*Hall Susan—†	82	at home	58	
	N	Brisbane Joseph	84	laborer	51	
	O	Brisbane Sarah—†	84	at home	59	
	P	Simmons Henry	84	retired	66	

Page.	Letter.	Full Name.	Residence, Jan. 1, 1943.	Occupation.	Supposed Age.	Reported Residence, Jan. 1, 1942. Street and Number.
		Williams Street—Continued				
	R	*Lall Elvira—†	84	at home	54	here
	S	Lall Holden	84	U S A	32	"
	T	*Lall James	84	laborer	54	"
	U	Lall Leonice—†	84	secretary	23	"
	V	Brady Charles	86	laborer	35	
	W	Brady Ethel—†	86	housewife	33	"
	X	Wilson Emma—†	86	at home	29	
	Y	Williams Odessa—†	86	"	25	
	Z	Williams Walter	86	laborer	30	
981		**Williams Street Terrace**				
	A	Hill Anna—†	2	domestic	29	here
	B	White Thelma—†	2	housewife	26	23 Westminister
	C	Brown John	2	laborer	50	here
	F	Wyatt George T	3	operator	39	"
	G	Wyatt Thomas	3	laborer	32	"
	H	*Chase Mary E—†	4	at home	45	16 Newbern
	K	Wesley Charles, jr	4	salesman	23	here
	L	Wesley Francis	4	U S A	21	"
	M	Wesley Sarah—†	4	housewife	42	"
	P	McDaniels Fendell—†	5	"	30	
	R	McDaniels Leon	5	laborer	48	
	T	Payne John	6	"	60	
	U	Walcott Hezekiah—†	6	tailor	66	
	V	Ferguson Lucy M—†	6	housewife	56	"
	W	*MacFarland Florence—†	7	housekeeper	69	"
	X	Young Sandy	7	mechanic	32	"
	Y	Granger Barbara—†	7	domestic	42	"
982						
	A	Wood Edith—†	8	housekeeper	68	"
	B	Gray James	8	laborer	32	89 Hammond ter
	C	Gray Lora—†	8	housewife	24	89 "
	D	Moody Helen—†	8	housekeeper	48	Malden
	E	Wood David	8	shipfitter	51	4 Fairweather
	F	Hayes Laura—†	9	presser	31	95 Warwick
	G	Wilkes Mary—†	9	"	52	95 "
	H	*Edwards Rebecca—†	9	housekeeper	57	here

Page.	Letter.	FULL NAME.	Residence, Jan. 1, 1943.	Occupation.	Supposed Age.	Reported Residence, Jan. 1, 1942. Street and Number.

Williams Street Terrace—Continued

	K	Benjamin Adelaide—†	9	dressmaker	33	here
	L	Benjamin Mary E—†	9	domestic	53	"

Winthrop Place

	M	Chandler Joseph	6	retired	68	here
	N	Walker Lucinda—†	6	housekeeper	62	"
	O	Walker William	6	mechanic	41	"
	P	*Wilson Richard A	6	janitor	65	

Woodbury Street

	T	*Poem John	2	retired	83	here
	U	Lewis Arthur	2	laborer	56	34 Wellington
	V	Hubbard George	2	janitor	55	here
	Z	White George	4	operator	43	"
983						
	A	White Irene—†	4	housewife	41	"
	B	*Berlin Morris	5	retired	70	
	C	Harris Spencer	5	laborer	50	
	E	Kryskow Joseph S	10	"	26	
	F	Kryskow Veronica—†	10	cook	47	
	G	Suckecki Wladek M	10	operator	23	
	K	*Pohorecky Catherine—†	12	housewife	67	"
	L	Sprague Vera—†	12	"	33	
	M	Philips Sarah—†	14	at home	74	
	N	Goodwin Augustine	14	janitor	49	"
	O	Lee Robert F	14	retired	67	27 Woodbury
	P	Johnson Martha—†	14	domestic	43	here
	X	Kernisky Stephen	18	U S N	22	"
	Y	*Perechodnuck Anthony	18	chef	55	"
	Z	Perechodnuck Elizabeth—†	18	housewife	57	"
984						
	A	Murphy Andrew	21	janitor	45	Saugus
	B	*Wales Alberta N—†	21	housewife	49	here
	D	Kimber Christina—†	27	clerk	25	"
	E	Kimber William	27	janitor	53	"

Page.	Letter.	FULL NAME.	Residence, Jan. 1, 1943.	Occupation.	Supposed Age.	Reported Residence, Jan. 1, 1942. Street and Number.

Woodbury Street—Continued

	G	Harris James	27	retired	59	here
	H	Tanaszuk Anthony	28	U S A	21	"
	K	Tanaszuk Delia—†	28	housewife	50	"
	L	Tanaszuk Demetra	28	laborer	53	
	M	Tanaszuk Rosanna—†	28	housewife	21	"
985						
	A	Crawford Ruth—†	34	domestic	35	"
	B	Crosby Elva—†	34	at home	67	
	C	Davis Ursula—†	34	housekeeper	48	"
	D	Morse Emma—†	34	housewife	59	77 Sterling
	E	Morse Richard	34	laborer	56	77 "
	F	Pyburn James	35	"	47	here
	G	Aikins Edna—†	35	housekeeper	34	"
	H	White Laura—†	35	housewife	67	"
	K	Cisco Christina—†	35	at home	63	"
	L	Jeffrey Tina—†	35	cook	59	79 Camden
	M	Anderson Helen—†	35	housekeeper	56	here
	N	Mitchell Lucy—†	35	"	71	666 Shawmut av
	R	Pate William	39	mechanic	70	here
	S	Lee Alfreda—†	39	housewife	29	"
	T	Lee James H	39	U S A	36	"

Worcester Place

	U	Allen Joseph	2	baker	43	here
	V	Bass James	2	laborer	40	"
	W	Bass Ruby—†	2	housewife	40	"
	X	Alsterberg Frank S	3	retired	91	
	Y	Smith Emma—†	4	housekeeper	60	"
	Z	Weathers Caleb	4	retired	58	
986						
	B	Henry Alonzo	5	barber	54	
	D	Johnson Hazel—†	5	laundress	47	"
	E	Johnson Mary—†	5	"	41	
	F	Braithwaite Una—†	6	housekeeper	35	"
	G	Carr Frank	6	ironworker	33	"
	H	Carr Julia—†	6	housewife	32	"
	K	Carr Nellie—†	6	domestic	32	"

Page.	Letter.	FULL NAME.	Residence, Jan. 1, 1943.	Occupation.	Supposed Age.	Reported Residence, Jan. 1, 1942. Street and Number.

Worcester Place—Continued

	M	Nestor Sanot	7	porter	41	here
	N	Johnson Mary—†	7	housekeeper	68	"
	O	Manerson Alfred	7	clerk	23	"
	P	Manerson Ruth—†	7	housewife	21	"
	R	Ricks Elsie—†	8	domestic	36	"
	S	Brice Robert E	8	retired	62	
	T	Jackson John	8	mechanic	40	"
	U	Robinson Charles	9	welder	29	55 Humboldt av
	V	Robinson Rosamond—†	9	housewife	25	55 "
	W	Prear Barbara—†	9	"	24	673 Shawmut av
	X	Proctor Ruth—†	9	domestic	35	610 "
	Y	Santos Elinor—†	10	at home	27	here
	Z	Santos John J	10	barber	67	"
987						
	A	Burt Chester	10	chauffeur	42	31 Newcomb
	B	Burt Iola—†	10	housekeeper	54	31 "

10

11

12

1

1

1

Ward 9—Precinct 10

CITY OF BOSTON

LIST OF RESIDENTS
20 YEARS OF AGE AND OVER

(NON-CITIZENS INDICATED BY ASTERISK)
(FEMALES INDICATED BY DAGGER)

AS OF

JANUARY 1, 1943

JOSEPH F. TIMILTY, *Chairman*
FREDERIC E. DOWLING, *Secretary*
WILLIAM A. MOTLEY, JR.
FRANCIS B. McKINNEY
EVERETT R. PROUT
Listing Board.

CITY OF BOSTON PRINTING DEPARTMENT

Page.	Letter.	Full Name.	Residence, Jan. 1, 1943.	Occupation.	Supposed Age.	Reported Residence, Jan. 1, 1942. Street and Number.

1000

Auburn Street

	A	Waters Harold	3	porter	28	here
	B	Waters Herman	3	laborer	50	"
	C	Waters Hubert	3	porter	29	"
	D	Waters Mabel—†	3	housewife	46	"
	E	Waters Mary—†	3	maid	25	
	F	Jessamy Clarissa—†	3	housewife	58	"
	G	*Jessamy William	3	porter	56	"
	H	*Adams Charles	3	laborer	51	Worcester
	K	Adams Julia—†	3	housewife	53	"
	L	Logan Jessie—†	5	maid	26	here
	M	Logan Susie—†	5	housewife	50	"
	N	Medley Edna—†	5	"	46	"
	O	Medley Kenneth	5	porter	21	"
	P	Ward Minerva—†	5	maid	65	987 Tremont
	R	Daughtry Ionia—†	5	housewife	49	here
	S	Daughtry Joan—†	5	student	23	"
	T	Daughtry Paul L	5	porter	24	New York
	U	Lewis Ionia—†	5	clerk	26	"
	W	Carr Harriet L—†	6	housekeeper	60	here
	X	Gray Emma—†	6	at home	88	"
	Y	Crickson Christopher	7	U S A	28	"
	Z	Crickson Estelle—†	7	clerk	27	
1001						
	A	DaLomba Barbara—†	7	"	22	
	B	DaLomba Joseph	7	chef	37	
	C	Harrison Charles	7	U S A	21	
	D	Harrison George T	7	welder	25	
	E	Harrison Olive—†	7	housewife	50	"
	F	*McIntyre Sidney	7	porter	27	
	G	Stewart James	7	machinist	50	"
	H	Singer Esther—†	rear 7	housewife	70	"
	K	Singer William	" 7	constable	31	"
	L	Cain Harriet—†	8	housekeeper	24	"
	M	Reed Alonzo N	8	laborer	64	"
	N	Reed Harriet—†	8	housewife	61	"
	O	Reed Leon S	8	laborer	22	"
	P	Johnson Henrietta—†	8½	maid	25	34 Hammond
	S	Sanders Gertrude—†	8½	housewife	45	here
	R	Sanders Oliver	8½	laborer	51	"
	T	Smith Gertrude—†	8½	attendant	24	"

Page.	Letter.	Full Name.	Residence, Jan. 1, 1943.	Occupation.	Supposed Age.	Reported Residence, Jan. 1, 1942. Street and Number.

Auburn Street—Continued

	U	Jordan Warren	8½	porter	21	126 Cabot
	V	Barnett Robert	8½	retired	75	here
	W	Jacobs Beatrice—†	8½	housekeeper	43	"
	X	Earley Richard R	10	clergyman	33	"
	Y	Davis Irene—†	11	housekeeper	34	1270 Col av
	Z	Goldman Eda—†	11	housewife	52	here
1002						
	A	Goldman Louis	11	clerk	23	"
	B	Goldman Morris	11	"	58	"
	C	Goldman Rose—†	11	"	30	"
	D	Dell Ella—†	11	housewife	42	"
	E	Dell Thomas	11	porter	54	"
	F	Cordice Constance—†	13	clerk	22	Winchester
	G	Cordice Florence—†	13	housewife	42	"
	H	Crookman Harley	13	laborer	30	N Hampshire
	K	Darby Dalton	13	welder	30	Texas
	L	Darby Georgia—†	13	housewife	30	"
	M	Durham Isaac	13	laborer	22	N Carolina
	N	Durham Vivian—†	13	housewife	30	"
	O	Jones Elmer	13	welder	33	Nebraska
	P	Smith Milton H	13	machinist	44	here
	R	Smith Ruth—†	13	housewife	40	"
	S	Johnson Daniel	14	porter	56	370 Blue Hill av
	T	Johnson Helen A—†	14	housewife	59	370 "
	U	*Hill Clementine—†	14	maid	66	72 Kendall
	V	Landrum Amy—†	14	"	48	here
	W	McGee Blanche—†	14	housekeeper	43	"
	X	Singletary John	15	retired	65	"
	Y	Singletary Rachel—†	15	housewife	62	"
	Z	Howard Rachel—†	15	stitcher	25	"
1003						
	A	King Ernest	15	U S A	25	"
	B	Singletary Catherine—†	15	presser	35	"
	C	Singletary Clifton	15	laborer	22	"
	D	Singletary John, jr	15	"	36	"
	E	Singletary Joseph	15	"	38	"
	F	Singletary Nathaniel	15	"	25	"
	G	Singletary Richard	15	"	33	"
	H	Oliva Ann—†	16	housewife	26	18 Reed
	K	Oliva John	16	toolmaker	28	here
	L	Gervasi Angelina—†	16	housewife	58	"

Page.	Letter.	Full Name.	Residence, Jan. 1, 1943.	Occupation.	Supposed Age.	Reported Residence, Jan. 1, 1942. Street and Number.

Auburn Street—Continued

	M	*Gervasi Joseph	16	laborer	64	here
	N	Oliva Andrew	16	U S A	25	"
	O	Oliva Angelo	16	designer	21	"
	P	*Oliva Frances—†	16	operator	55	
	R	Oliva Mary—†	16	stitcher	23	
	S	*Oliva Santo	16	laborer	58	
	T	Wilson Rose—†	18	housekeeper	48	"
	U	Morle Emily—†	18	housewife	65	"
	V	Morle Hubert N	18	porter	65	
	W	Morle Ruth L—†	18	maid	24	
	X	Smith Louisa—†	19	"	60	
	Y	Bennett Marion—†	19	clerk	23	
	Z	Bennett Maud—†	19	waitress	46	
1004						
	A	Raynor Alice A—†	20	dressmaker	28	"
	B	Raynor Arain—†	20	operator	22	"
	C	Raynor John H	20	laborer	57	
	D	Raynor Mabel—†	20	housewife	58	"
	E	Reid Clementine—†	20A	cook	51	
	F	Reid Joseph B	20A	"	53	
	K	Harris Charles	22	laborer	33	
	L	Harris Frances—†	22	housewife	36	"
	M	Smith Ethel R—†	22	"	43	
	N	Smith Ossian R	22	machinist	45	"
	O	Lall Bernice—†	22A	housewife	26	"
	P	Lall Deweth	22A	welder	26	
	R	Dabbs Fedora—†	24	stenographer	31	"
	S	Manning Mahalia—†	24	stitcher	50	"
	T	Smith Herbert K	24	chauffeur	44	"
	U	Smith Lillian—†	24	housewife	43	"
	V	Taylor Robert	24	welder	42	
	W	Taylor Virginia—†	24	clerk	21	

Bicknell Avenue

	X	Marquis Clara—†	1	at home	65	here
	Y	Campbell Florence M—†	1	housewife	20	"
	Z	Campbell Robert P	1	machinist	20	"
1005						
	A	Jaggy Ethel—†	1	housewife	30	"
	B	Jaggy Joseph E	1	chauffeur	33	"

Page.	Letter.	Full Name.	Residence, Jan. 1, 1943.	Occupation.	Supposed Age.	Reported Residence, Jan. 1, 1942. Street and Number.

Bicknell Avenue—Continued

	C	Shea Ann—†	3	clerk	50	here
	D	Steinberg Alfred	3	pedler	33	"
	E	Steinberg Lillian—†	3	housewife	33	"
	F	Linehan John	3	operator	23	
	G	Ross Mary—†	3	housekeeper	47	"
	K	Brockel Mary—†	5	at home	74	866 Albany
	L	Fraser Christine—†	5	"	63	here
	M	Belanger Cecile—†	6	housewife	49	"
	N	Belanger Louis	6	meatcutter	47	"
	O	Chausse Ernest	6	U S A	39	
	P	Coleman Ethel—†	6	housewife	40	"
	R	O'Brien George J	6	letter carrier	65	"
	S	Williams Chester R	6	laborer	39	Connecticut
	T	Williams Rose M—†	6	clerk	27	"
	U	*Vicar Bessie M—†	8	housewife	42	here
	V	Vicar John M	8	laborer	46	"
	W	Paxton Kathleen—†	8	housewife	20	50 Cliff
	X	Paxton Ralph E	8	mechanic	33	50 "
	Y	Geiger Gertrude—†	8	at home	46	here

Cabot Street

	Z	Cooper Harry M	226	leatherworker	53	79 Highland
1006						
	A	Kostick Alex	226	salesman	52	42 Corona
	B	Kostick Sarah—†	226	housewife	39	42 "
	C	MacPhee Christine—†	226	"	75	7 Anita ter
	D	MacPhee Michael	226	retired	86	7 "
	E	Cohan Margaret E—†	226	housewife	24	237 Cabot
	F	Cohan Maurice	226	U S A	21	237 "
	G	Dingle Edgar U	240	transitman	38	here
	H	Dingle Theresa V—†	240	housewife	59	"
	K	Motherville Catherine—†	240	"	66	"
	L	Motherville Hugh	240	retired	75	
	M	Hughes Bridget A—†	240	housewife	57	"
	N	Hughes Patrick J	240	fireman	54	"
	O	Hughes Raphael E	240	U S N	21	"
	P	Hughes Richard J	240	clerk	26	"
	R	Kelly Richard T	240	U S A	26	
	S	Kelly Ruth A—†	240	housewife	23	"
	U	Linsky Margaret G—†	242	"	36	

Page.	Letter.	Full Name.	Residence, Jan. 1, 1943.	Occupation.	Supposed Age.	Reported Residence, Jan. 1, 1942. Street and Number.

Cabot Street—Continued

	V	Linsky Philip A	242	operator	46	here
	X	Gallagher Francis P	250	investigator	51	"
	Y	Gallagher Mary A—†	250	housewife	48	"
	Z	Gallagher Robert W	250	U S N	20	"
1007						
	A	Bader George	262	laundryworker	36	"
	B	Lynch Mary E—†	262	housewife	63	"
	C	Lynch Walter E	262	salesman	36	"
	D	Sanborn Ida B—†	262	housewife	59	"
	E	Norris Charles F, jr	rear 262	guard	48	
	F	Norris Sadie C—†	" 262	housewife	68	"
	G	*Costello John J	" 262A	retired	59	
	H	Costello John J, jr	" 262A	U S A	26	"
	K	*Costello Margaret—†	" 262A	housewife	59	"
	M	Greenfield Ethel—†	266	clerk	21	
	N	*Greenfield Rose—†	266	housewife	48	"
	O	Greenfield Samuel	266	pipecoverer	48	"

Goldsmith Place

	P	Winiger Mabel—†	1	housekeeper	55	51 Vermont
	R	Navis John J	1	welder	32	8 Comins ter
	S	*Navis Margaret—†	1	housewife	34	8 "
	V	Bourne Mary—†	3	"	58	here
	W	Bourne Robert L	3	U S A	20	"
	X	Bourne Rose M—†	3	cashier	26	"
	Y	Mason John N	3	window cleaner	64	"
	Z	Ryan Frances E—†	3	stitcher	60	
1008						
	C	Keffer Diamond—†	5	at home	56	
	D	Langman Almeda—†	5	housewife	54	"
	E	Langman William C	5	packer	55	
	H	Benson Anna L—†	7	housewife	40	"
	K	Benson Anna M—†	7	"	76	
	L	Benson Jenny A—†	7	dressmaker	47	"
	M	Brennan Bernard	9	machinist	41	"
	N	Heath Beulah—†	9	shoeworker	66	"
	O	Muir Kenneth	9	bricklayer	46	Virginia
	P	Daggett Duke	9	U S A	39	here
	R	Daggett Helen—†	9	housewife	37	"

Page.	Letter.	FULL NAME.	Residence, Jan. 1, 1943.	Occupation.	Supposed Age.	Reported Residence, Jan. 1, 1942. Street and Number.

Haskins Street

Page.	Letter.	FULL NAME.	Residence, Jan. 1, 1943.	Occupation.	Supposed Age.	Reported Residence, Jan. 1, 1942. Street and Number.
	S	White Irene—†	20	housewife	49	here
	T	Pina Bella—†	22	"	69	"
	U	Pina Frank	22	laborer	58	"
	V	Arthur Edwin M	24	machinist	47	"
	W	Arthur Marietta P—†	24	housewife	39	"
	X	Gervais Treffle	24	retired	79	"
	Y	Haynes Cameron V	30	U S A	21	1086 Tremont
	Z	Haynes Douglas O	30	"	26	here
1009						
	A	Haynes Edna G—†	30	housewife	42	"
	B	Haynes Gustave	30	laborer	45	"
	C	Haynes Mildred E—†	30	housewife	21	1086 Tremont
	D	*Nehalsingh Claudia—†	34	"	40	44 Haskins
	E	*Nehalsingh Walter J	34	clerk	45	44 "
	G	Manifold Herman	36	U S N	27	here
	H	*Manifold Preston A	36	retired	64	"
	K	*Manifold Sarah E—†	36	housewife	54	"
	L	Williams Gwendolyn O—†	36	presser	22	730 Shawmut av
	M	Williams Ivan O	36	U S A	35	here
	N	Benders George F	38	mechanic	68	"
	O	Benders Susie D—†	38	housewife	67	"
	P	Benders William E	38	seaman	39	
	R	Wynn Marjorie—†	38	stitcher	32	
	T	Roache Bessie—†	46	housewife	57	"
	U	Roache Francis M	46	U S A	23	
	V	Roache James H	46	machinist	61	"
	W	Roache James H, jr	46	shipfitter	32	"
	X	Bavuso Carrio	54	retired	68	
	Y	*Bavuso Rosa—†	54	housewife	79	"

Hubert Street

Page.	Letter.	FULL NAME.	Residence, Jan. 1, 1943.	Occupation.	Supposed Age.	Reported Residence, Jan. 1, 1942. Street and Number.
	Z	Brown Garnell	2	laborer	27	here
1010						
	A	Brown Rebecca—†	2	domestic	56	"
	B	Tavares Alice—†	2	housewife	32	Falmouth
	C	Andrews Conway	2	U S A	22	here
	D	Andrews Ida—†	2	housewife	38	"
	E	*Andrews Manuel	2	laborer	48	"
	F	Andrews Raphael	2	U S A	21	"
	G	Burnett Marie—†	2	housewife	35	"

Page.	Letter.	FULL NAME.	Residence, Jan. 1, 1943.	Occupation.	Supposed Age.	Reported Residence, Jan. 1, 1942. Street and Number.

Hubert Street—Continued

	H	Burnett William	2	meatcutter	38	here
	K	Lewis Hattie—†	2	at home	27	"
	L	Snelling Queenie—†	2	"	30	"
	M	Haynes David	2	laborer	39	
	N	Haynes Evelyn—†	2	housewife	37	"
	O	*Martin Beatrice—†	2	"	50	
	P	Martin Wilfred	2	rigger	45	
	R	Selby William	2	clerk	55	
	S	Carter Otie—†	2	domestic	40	"
	T	Fauntleroy Mary—†	2	at home	90	
	U	Monteiro Corinne—†	2	housewife	20	"
	V	Monteiro Roger	2	U S A	20	"
	W	Tatch Herbert	4	repairman	31	1 Comet pl
	X	Tatch Rose—†	4	housewife	42	1 "
	Z	Dreyton Louise—†	4	"	22	here
1011						
	A	Dreyton Sidney	4	laborer	29	
	B	Cook Nellie—†	4	domestic	40	"
	C	Geary Gordon	4	laborer	30	
	D	Geary Laura—†	4	housewife	24	"
	E	Vanderbilt Martha—†	4	domestic	56	"
	F	*Harvey Constance—†	4	housewife	40	"
	G	Harvey Ida—†	4	stitcher	25	
	H	Luacow Irving	4	laborer	36	
	K	Luacow Marjorie—†	4	housewife	35	"
	L	Luacow Wilbur	4	welder	20	
	M	Powell Annie—†	4	at home	55	
	N	Scroggins Luther	4	U S A	23	
	O	Campbell Clifford	4	U S N	27	
	P	Campbell Laura—†	4	stitcher	26	
	R	Mitchell David	4	U S A	21	
	S	Mitchell Hattie—†	4	at home	57	"
	T	*Carney Estelle—†	6	domestic	41	Illinois
	U	Williams Jessie—†	6	"	32	Wellesley
	V	Hill Charles L	6	janitor	66	542 Shawmut av
	W	Hill John	6	clerk	27	542 "
	X	Hill Lessie—†	6	housewife	62	542 "
	Y	*Bramble Rose—†	6	"	60	here
	Z	*Davis Samuel	6	laborer	35	"
1012						
	A	Haynes Walker	6	meatcutter	43	"

Page.	Letter.	Full Name.	Residence, Jan. 1, 1943.	Occupation.	Supposed Age.	Reported Residence, Jan. 1, 1942. Street and Number.

Hubert Street—Continued

Page.	Letter.	Full Name.	Residence, Jan. 1, 1943.	Occupation.	Supposed Age.	Reported Residence, Jan. 1, 1942. Street and Number.
	B	Lewis Martha—†	6	domestic	31	here
	C	Lewis Robert	6	laborer	30	"
	D	Lewis Zenia—†	6	housewife	24	"
	E	Harrison Susie—†	6	at home	59	
	F	Bassett William A	6	retired	72	
	G	*Gomes Frank	6	laborer	46	
	H	*Gomes Luna—†	6	housewife	56	"
	K	Dennison Laura A—†	6	"	57	
	L	Dennison Phillip J	6	janitor	67	"
	M	Hampton Jennie B—†	6	at home	38	New York
	N	Evans John	8	laborer	45	here
	O	Evans Marion—†	8	housewife	35	"
	P	Kurn Dorothy—†	8	"	29	80 Sterling
	R	Kurn Quillo	8	chipper	46	80 "
	S	Porter Clara—†	8	operator	33	here
	T	Smith Gladys—†	8	"	21	"
	U	Smith Kathleen—†	8	housewife	50	"
	V	Smith Robert	8	riveter	50	
	W	Brown Joseph	8	laborer	38	
	X	Grice Anna—†	8	cutter	27	
	Y	Coles Dorothy—†	8	housewife	41	"
	Z	Johnson Herbert	8	longshoreman	42	"
1013						
	A	Griffin Carrie—†	8	housewife	60	"
	B	Howes Jane—†	8	clerk	31	"
	C	Jones Harriett—†	8	domestic	41	9 Hubert
	D	Jones Lewis	8	laborer	42	9 "
	E	Graves Albert	8	"	39	here
	F	*Graves Hilda—†	8	housewife	37	"
	G	Lee Hazel—†	10	"	28	"
	H	Hays Iola—†	10	"	28	
	K	Hays William	10	laborer	33	
	L	Jeffers Pearl—†	10	housewife	37	"
	M	Wornum Cornelius	10	laborer	37	17 Hubert
	N	Thomas Matthew L	10	U S A	21	here
	O	Thomas Vera—†	10	housewife	37	"
	T	*Lall Frances—†	14	"	25	"
	U	Lall Winston	14	machinist	31	"
	V	Hopkins George R	14	laborer	48	
	W	Hopkins Louella—†	14	housewife	53	"
	X	Thompson Gladys—†	14	waitress	26	

Page.	Letter.	Full Name.	Residence, Jan. 1, 1943.	Occupation.	Supposed Age.	Reported Residence, Jan. 1, 1942. Street and Number.

Hubert Street—Continued

	Y	Harris Mary—†	14	housewife	50	here
	Z	Harris Vernice—†	14	operator	27	"
1014						
	A	Burnett Beatrice—†	16	housewife	20	34 Kent
	B	Burnett Edgar	16	pipefitter	38	34 "
	C	Collins Eula—†	16	domestic	21	Florida
	D	Jenkins Abraham	16	carpenter	23	New Jersey
	E	*Salmore Noel G	16	cook	50	here
	F	*Toy Bertha—†	16	housewife	60	203 Camden
	G	Wright Francine—†	16	"	20	203 "
	H	Badgett Joseph	18	cook	51	here
	K	Badgett Mary—†	18	housewife	44	"
	L	Willis Mary—†	18	"	32	"
	M	Holmes Herbert	18	laborer	26	9 Oakburn av
	N	Holmes Marie—†	18	housewife	24	9 "
	O	Thompson Rose—†	18	"	40	here
	P	Simmons Frank	18	driller	43	Falmouth
	R	Simmons Marion—†	18	housewife	35	"
	S	Williams Essie—†	18	"	21	Alabama
	T	Williams Moses	18	laborer	22	"
	U	Johnson Nellie—†	18	housewife	43	here
	V	Ramos Frances—†	18	at home	35	"
	W	Roderick James	18	laborer	46	"

Kent Street

	X	Rolfe Charles O	6	U S A	44	here
	Y	Rolfe Charles O, jr	6	welder	22	4 Danforth pl
	Z	Rolfe Louise M—†	6	housewife	21	54 E Cottage
1015						
	A	Rolfe Miriam F—†	6	presser	20	here
	B	Bishop Alfred G	6	chauffeur	38	"
	C	Bishop Anna M—†	6	typist	36	"
	D	*Maslauskas Martha—†	6	housewife	41	"
	E	DeRoche James	6	operator	27	"
	F	McPeck Elizabeth—†	9	at home	80	
	G	Woods Edward	9	U S A	23	
	H	Shuris Bessie—†	9	housewife	59	"
	K	Shuris Constance—†	9	stitcher	25	
	L	Shuris George	9	U S A	31	
	M	Shuris John	9	"	20	

Page.	Letter.	Full Name.	Residence, Jan. 1, 1943.	Occupation.	Supposed Age.	Reported Residence, Jan. 1, 1942. Street and Number.

Kent Street—Continued

	N	Shuris Netta—†	9	operator	22	here
	O	Shuris William	9	cashier	60	"
	P	Slavinsky Jennie—†	9	houseworker	31	"
	R	Slavinsky John	9	retired	74	
	S	Slavinsky John O	9	guard	26	
	T	Slavinsky Minnie—†	9	housewife	69	"
	U	Libby Hazen R	11	clerk	45	
	V	Libby Olive G—†	11	housewife	63	"
	W	Hayes John	11	U S N	45	
	X	Higgins Catherine T—†	11	housewife	65	"
	Y	Higgins James E	11	mechanic	30	"
	Z	Higgins John E	11	clerk	35	
1016						
	A	Benoit Elizabeth—†	11	housewife	66	"
	B	Benoit Wilfred	11	laborer	37	
	D	Brown Ruth S—†	12	housewife	58	"
	E	Boudreau Eva—†	12	domestic	35	"
	F	Keating Delia—†	13	at home	66	
	G	Seeley Joseph	13	laborer	26	
	H	Bradley Kathleen P—†	13	clerk	40	
	K	West John R	13	stenographer	22	"
	L	*Gouthro Margaret M—†	13	housewife	34	"
	M	*Gouthro Simon	13	mechanic	35	"
	N	Milligan Joseph D	13	floorlayer	42	"
	O	Sexton Barbara—†	15	housewife	43	"
	P	Sexton John	15	laborer	41	
	R	Morgan Agnes N—†	15	housewife	49	"
	S	Morgan Everett J	15	U S A	22	"
	T	Morgan James H	15	coremaker	54	"
	U	DeMars Antonio H	15	diemaker	43	"
	V	Kalberg Celena R—†	15	housewife	64	"
	W	Kalberg Joseph A	15	laborer	54	
	X	Hanley Annie A—†	16	housewife	74	"
	Y	Cranston Cora A—†	16	"	78	
	Z	Lane Rita E—†	17	"	28	
1017						
	A	Lane Timothy	17	chauffeur	33	"
	B	Gauthro Anna—†	17	housewife	30	"
	C	Gauthro Edward W	17	laborer	30	"
	D	MacDougall Mae W—†	17	housewife	49	82 Roxbury
	E	Curran Ellen E—†	20	"	60	here

Page.	Letter.	FULL NAME.	Residence, Jan. 1, 1943.	Occupation.	Supposed Age.	Reported Residence, Jan. 1, 1942. Street and Number.

Kent Street—Continued

	F	Curran William J	20	U S A	31	here
	G	Maloney Katherine V—†	20	at home	75	"
	H	Sullivan Eugene	21	laborer	59	"
	K	*Sullivan Mary—†	21	housewife	58	"
	L	Greenan Hugh F	21	U S N	27	
	M	Greenan Joseph B	21	chauffeur	28	"
	N	Greenan Josephine C—†	21	housewife	51	"
	O	Greenan Paul F	21	U S N	22	
	P	Greenan William B	21	chauffeur	53	"
	R	Moroney Elsie—†	21	housewife	50	8 Kingsbury
	S	Moroney William	21	cook	62	8 "
	T	Fitzgerald Ernest	22	retired	71	here
	U	Fitzgerald Mary—†	22	teacher	53	"
	V	Kerr Helen—†	24	housewife	63	12 Kent
	W	*Pelechowicl Frances—†	24	"	57	51 Marcella
	X	*Pelechowicl John	24	carpenter	68	51 "
	Z	Burrell Amedee A	26	U S A	23	55 Newland
1018						
	A	Burrell Eliza J—†	26	dyer	45	55 "
	D	Peters Helen E—†	31	housewife	41	20 Springfield
	E	Peters Robert	31	painter	51	20 "
	F	Hurley John J	31	realtor	70	here
	G	Morse Lucy J—†	31	at home	97	"
	K	Hicks Andrew	32	chauffeur	32	"
	L	Hicks Gertrude M—†	32	domestic	32	"
	M	Reid Marion M—†	32	housewife	35	"
	N	Reid Thomas H	32	laborer	40	
	O	Burnett George	34	"	28	
	P	Jones James S	34	"	34	
	R	Walker Julia—†	34	housewife	35	"
	S	*Watson Dudley	37	carpenter	48	"
	T	*Watson Evelyn E—†	37	housewife	44	"
	U	Watson Sylvia M—†	37	stitcher	21	"
	V	Burnett Freda—†	37	housewife	21	37 Weston
	W	Key Katherine—†	37	factoryhand	43	here
	X	Key Tina—†	37	waitress	22	"
	Y	Simmons Robert	37	laborer	31	37 Weston
	Z	White Flora—†	37	housewife	34	here
1019						
	A	White Oliver N	37	operator	35	"
	B	Adams Julius	38	retired	79	

Page.	Letter.	Full Name.	Residence, Jan. 1, 1943.	Occupation.	Supposed Age.	Reported Residence, Jan. 1, 1942. Street and Number.

Kent Street—Continued

	c	*Dixon Mary E—†	38	housewife	67	here
	D	Gibson Josephine—†	38	"	75	181 Dudley
	E	Schaffer Frank M	40	retired	82	here
	F	Talios Pauline P—†	40	housewife	42	"
	G	Talios William E	40	waiter	51	"

Linden Park Street

	H	Barnes Anna M—†	7	seamstress	46	here
	K	Barnes Henry F	7	dishwasher	64	"
	L	Gilmore Josephine—†	7	at home	76	"
	M	Laval Richard	7	laborer	28	3 Roxbury
	N	Ramsdell Frank	7	retired	75	3 Glenwood
	O	Velesco Helen—†	7	housewife	43	Connecticut
	P	Velesco William	7	U S N	38	Iceland
	R	Austin Arthur W	9	cook	50	Worcester
	S	Austin Sarah—†	9	housewife	51	"
	T	*Holland John	9	houseman	60	here
	U	*Holland Louise—†	9	at home	63	"
	V	Lorenzo Gregorio	9	U S N	33	657 Tremont
	W	Lorenzo Vernie—†	9	operator	24	657 "
	X	St Clair Inez—†	9	at home	33	Malden
	Y	Azzariti Louis	11	repairman	55	here
	Z	Blaisdell Edith—†	11	operator	39	"
1020						
	A	Deshon Alfred M	11	retired	73	
	B	Deshon Laura—†	11	housewife	58	"
	C	Guiffre Liberal	11	chef	79	"
	D	Harvey Alfred	11	engineer	71	Reading
	E	Harvey Katherine—†	11	housewife	72	"
	F	Barry Margaret—†	13	at home	52	538 Mass av
	G	Chase Anna—†	13	housewife	37	168 Humboldt av
	H	Chase Clifton	13	guard	43	168 "
	K	Foley Walter	13	mechanic	35	here
	L	*Giambusso Gaetano	13	proprietor	55	"

Marble Street

	O	Jones Josie—†	1	housewife	49	here
	P	Marshall Lucy W—†	1	"	40	"
	R	Marshall Samuel W	1	cook	44	"

Page.	Letter.	Full Name.	Residence, Jan. 1, 1943.	Occupation.	Supposed Age.	Reported Residence, Jan. 1, 1942. Street and Number.

Marble Street—Continued

	s	Warrick Hattie—†	1	at home	65	here
	u	Cook Anna M—†	2	operator	32	"
	v	Ramos John	2	chef	38	"
	w	Ramos Viola—†	2	housewife	28	"
	x	Ranford Carrie—†	2	domestic	28	"
	y	Marshall Anna—†	2	operator	35	"
	z	Marshall Thomas E	2	cook	45	
1021						
	A	Williams Dolores—†	2	housewife	31	"
	B	Mason Eleanora—†	3	domestic	64	"
	C	Mason Fannie—†	3	"	44	
	D	McKane Alice W—†	3	at home	81	
	E	McKane Cornelius	3	U S A	45	
	F	McKane William F	3	laborer	40	
	H	Woodruff Maude E—†	11	teacher	39	"
	K	Frye Dorothy F—†	11	clerk	33	Brookline
	L	Frye Robert S	11	electrician	42	"
	M	Tucker Lucille—†	11	operator	40	here
	N	Brown Pinkie—†	11	presser	25	"
	O	Brown William	11	laborer	32	"
	P	Smith Vera—†	11	housewife	30	998 Tremont
	R	Smith Vincent	11	laborer	32	998 "
	S	Barrett Yulee—†	11	at home	32	here
	T	Brown Ruth—†	11	domestic	21	"
	U	Jackson John	11	laborer	34	"
	V	Howard Henry C	11	welder	34	
	W	Howard Louise—†	11	housewife	32	"
	X	Price Charles H	11	mechanic	63	"
	Y	Crawford Christine M—†	11	housewife	50	"
	Z	Crawford John C	11	chef	50	
1022						
	A	Mosely Ardell	11	welder	33	Newton
	B	Mosely Marian—†	11	housewife	32	"
	C	Oliver Daisy—†	11	"	30	here
	D	Oliver Harry F	11	waiter	36	"
	E	Moore John R	11	U S A	24	"
	F	Moore Ruth—†	11	housewife	24	19 Westminster
	G	Allen Joe C	11	laborer	27	N Carolina
	H	Allen Yva—†	11	messenger	21	here
	K	Singleton Mattie—†	11	housewife	25	"
	L	Singleton Walter	11	attendant	25	"

Page.	Letter.	Full Name.	Residence, Jan. 1, 1943.	Occupation.	Supposed Age.	Reported Residence, Jan. 1, 1942. Street and Number.

Marble Street—Continued

Page.	Letter.	Full Name.	Residence, Jan. 1, 1943.	Occupation.	Supposed Age.	Reported Residence, Jan. 1, 1942. Street and Number.
	M	Hall Carrie—†	11	housewife	31	42 Sarsfield
	O	Williams Robert J	11	oiler	39	23 Rutland sq
	N	Williams Willie M—†	11	housewife	29	23 "
	P	Dancy Joseph R	11	welder	26	here
	R	Dancy Susie—†	11	housewife	23	"
	S	Edwards Samuel	11	porter	48	"
	T	Spells Charles	11	laborer	40	70 Ruggles
	U	*Spells Daisy—†	11	stitcher	38	70 "
	V	Gomez Mary L—†	11	at home	58	Onset
	W	Jackson Beatrice—†	11	housewife	23	New York
	X	Jackson Phillip A	11	machinist	28	"
	Y	Dixon Willa—†	11	mechanic	24	here
	Z	Dunn Kenneth	11	laborer	20	8 Hubert
1023						
	A	Brabson Susie—†	11	maid	51	Hingham
	B	Jacklin Leon V	11	painter	40	70 W Rutland
	C	Jacklin Ruth E—†	11	stitcher	35	70 "
	D	Thomas Madeline—†	11	housewife	31	12 Sussex
	E	Thomas Walter	11	laborer	36	12 "
	F	Hinds Goldbert	12	musician	34	here
	G	Hinds Maud—†	12	housewife	35	"
	H	Ferguson Emily—†	12	maid	41	"
	K	Ramsey Alfreda—†	12	housewife	37	"
	L	Jordan Theresa—†	12	operator	31	59 Bromley
	M	Benford William C	12	porter	47	here
	N	Folks Calvin	12	U S A	21	181 Northampton
	O	Gary Roger	12	laborer	24	here
	P	Gary Rosalie—†	12	clerk	23	"
	R	Barlow Francis J	12	operator	46	"
	S	Barlow Violet O—†	12	housewife	30	"
	T	Simms John C	12	laborer	32	
	U	Simms Ruth—†	12	housewife	30	"
	V	Leake Howard J	12	laborer	37	
	W	Leake Josephine—†	12	housewife	32	"
	X	Stephens Cordelia—†	12	at home	34	"
	Y	Allen Eileen—†	12	housewife	32	Cambridge
	Z	Allen Kenneth	12	welder	26	"
1024						
	A	Strickland Millie—†	12	housekeeper	28	here
	B	Winbush Irene—†	12	housewife	53	8 Gertrose
	C	Winbush Nelson	12	guard	49	8 "

Page.	Letter.	Full Name.	Residence, Jan. 1, 1943.	Occupation.	Supposed Age.	Reported Residence, Jan. 1, 1942. Street and Number.

Marble Street—Continued

	D	*Dias Thomas	12	retired	69	here
	E	Gomez Andre	12	laborer	24	"
	F	*Gomez Fred	12	contractor	40	"
	G	Sylvia Joseph T	12	laborer	42	69 Ruggles
	H	Lofton William	12	porter	39	here
	K	Bovelle Deather—†	12	housewife	43	"
	L	Bovelle Henry	12	porter	46	"
	N	Gooding Charles A	12	waiter	34	34 Greenwich
	O	Massey Katherine—†	12	housewife	30	here
	P	Massey Wesley	12	cook	32	"
	R	Luster Florence—†	12	housewife	27	"
	S	Phillips Charles A	12	painter	27	
	T	Phillips Rose A—†	12	housewife	26	"
	U	Nurse Gladstone	12	clergyman	48	15 Rockland
	V	Drake Ruth—†	12	housewife	26	here
	W	Drake William	12	waiter	31	"
	X	Amis George	12	machinist	25	"
	Y	Amis Vera—†	12	housewife	23	"
	Z	Lee Gertrude—†	12	operator	38	
1025						
	A	Turner Henrietta—†	12	housewife	23	"
	B	Turner John	12	laborer	26	"
	C	Hylton Ursula—†	12	secretary	30	137 Harold
	D	Jewel Frances—†	12	housewife	26	here
	E	Jewel Robert	12	chauffeur	30	"
	F	Watson Brunette—†	12	housekeeper	40	"
	G	Tufts Commer	12	laborer	22	"
	H	Tufts Evelyn—†	12	housewife	22	"
	K	Mathews Oscar S	12	porter	41	Maine
	L	Romaine Rose—†	12	housewife	38	here

Oakburn Avenue

	M	Johnson Emma—†	4	housewife	46	here
	N	Johnson James H	4	boilermaker	51	"
	O	Corbett Annie—†	4	housewife	43	"
	P	Corbett Samuel	4	janitor	46	
	R	Jefferson Julian	4	laborer	34	
	S	Jefferson Rebenna—†	4	housewife	35	"
	T	Fernandes Frank	6	laborer	54	
	U	Fernandes Jennie—†	6	housewife	48	"

Page.	Letter.	Full Name.	Residence, Jan. 1, 1943.	Occupation.	Supposed Age.	Reported Residence, Jan. 1, 1942. Street and Number.

Oakburn Avenue—Continued

	v	*Smith Harold	6	operator	21	here
	w	*Smith Henrietta—†	6	housewife	49	"
	x	Smith Mildred—†	6	"	23	"
	Y	Lowell Corbett	6	laborer	42	
	Z	Lowell Louise—†	6	housewife	36	"
1026						
	A	Bonds Edith—†	7	"	27	8 Grinnell
	B	Bonds Frank	7	U S A	27	8 "
	C	Johnson Christine—†	7	housewife	36	here
	D	Johnson Roy	7	longshoreman	42	"
	E	Chavers Mary—†	7	housewife	62	"
	F	Graham Ruby—†	7	"	38	
	G	Ellis Georgiana—†	8	"	38	
	H	Pumphery Rachel—†	8	"	51	
	K	Stevens Laura—†	8	operator	21	"
	L	Cole Hagar—†	8	"	26	
	M	Lew Ethel—†	8	housewife	46	"
	N	Lew Harold	8	operator	44	"
	O	Brown James W	9	cook	64	35 Weston
	P	Johnson John	9	laborer	51	47 Westminster
	R	Talbot Louise—†	10	housewife	51	here
	S	Talbot Robert	10	laborer	22	"
	T	Talbot Stanley	10	"	59	"
	U	*Caines Phoebe—†	10	housewife	45	"
	V	*Richardson Carmelia—†	10	"	49	
	W	*Richardson George	10	carpenter	49	"
	X	Richardson Robert	10	laborer	22	"
	Y	Armstrong Georgianna—†	11	housewife	61	74 Westminster
	Z	Carter Eva—†	11	"	64	74 "
1027						
	A	Hawkins David	11	laborer	61	74 "
	B	Smith Florence—†	11	housewife	29	here
	C	Smith Harold	11	presser	35	"
	D	Smith Louise—†	11	housewife	51	"
	E	Calhoun Esterene—†	12	"	36	
	F	Latimer Willa—†	12	stitcher	38	
	G	Wilson Hester—†	12	housewife	60	"
	H	Robinson William	12	longshoreman	50	"
	K	Ogilvie George	12	chef	54	
	L	Ogilvie Geraldine—†	12	at home	22	
	M	Ogilvie Josephine—†	12	housewife	50	"

Page.	Letter.	Full Name.	Residence, Jan. 1, 1943.	Occupation.	Supposed Age.	Reported Residence, Jan. 1, 1942. Street and Number.

Oakburn Avenue—Continued

	O	Jones Clarence	13	laborer	47	here
	P	Jones Elizabeth—†	13	housewife	45	"
	R	Knight Muriel—†	14	"	20	21 Hammond
	S	Knight William	14	laborer	24	21 "
	T	Williams Oscar	14	clergyman	49	21 "
	U	Bradley Julia—†	14	operator	40	here
	V	White Joseph	14	retired	73	"
	W	Graves Maria—†	14	machinist	21	"
	X	*Graves Sevena—†	14	housewife	45	"
	Y	*Horton Cyril	15	porter	42	
	Z	*Horton Ethel—†	15	housewife	38	"
1028						
	A	*Peters Edna—†	15		39	
	B	*Santos Josephine—†	15	"	53	
	C	Santos Julia—†	15	operator	22	"
	D	*Santos Martin	15	laborer	63	
	E	Santos Vivian	15	U S A	24	
	F	Mendes Philip	16	laborer	48	
	G	Gray Emma—†	16	housewife	43	"
	H	Gray Gerald	16	messenger	46	"
	K	Gray Marcellus	16	U S A	21	
	L	Hayes Elizabeth—†	16	housewife	35	"
	M	Hayes Stanley	16	laborer	42	
	N	*Peters Isabella—†	17	housewife	40	"
	O	*Peters Manuel	17	barber	40	
	P	Robinson Joseph	17	retired	77	
	R	Young Mary—†	17	housewife	62	"
	S	Meikle Alfred E	17	welder	22	"
	T	Paschal Aida V—†	17	housewife	50	"
	U	Winbush Dorothy—†	18	"	27	
	V	Winbush Robert	18	fireman	40	
	W	Richards Irene—†	18	housewife	62	"
	X	Fergerson Lovet—†	18	"	45	
	Y	Holmes Abraham	18	kitchenman	51	"
	Z	Joiner Benjamin	19	laborer	58	"
1029						
	A	Joiner Louise—†	19	housewife	55	"
	B	*Murray Hilda—†	19	"	45	
	C	*Murray Lawrence	19	porter	46	"
	D	Smith Mary R—†	19	housewife	32	"
	E	Smith Raymond	19	chipper	34	

F Frances Charles	20	laborer	60	here
G Jackson Lula—†	20	housewife	62	"
H Warner Reginald	20	operator	42	"
K Warner Vivian—†	20	housewife	35	"
L Hayes Raymond	20	seaman	22	
M Semedo Addie—†	20	housewife	43	"
N*Semedo Domingo	20	operator	52	
O Brown Mary—†	21	housewife	70	"
P Bruce Harrison	21	laborer	54	
R Rodrigues Beatrice—†	21	housewife	34	"
S*Rodrigues John D	21	operator	46	
T*Campbell Grace—†	21	housewife	42	"
U*Campbell Jerome	21	laborer	45	
V Ruger Elizabeth—†	22	housewife	75	"
W*Shorupshy Helen—†	22	"	47	
X*Shorupshy Michael	22	laborer	54	
Y Shorupshy Michael, jr	22	salesman	26	
Z Shorupshy William	22	U S A	21	
1030				
A Johnson Columbus	23	janitor	27	
B Johnson Dorothy—†	23	operator	24	
C Peterson Eliza—†	23	housewife	74	"
D Gordon Dorothy—†	23	"	31	
E Gordon George	23	laborer	34	
F Williams Victoria—†	23	seamstress	40	"
H Nickes Andrew	25	cook	50	"
K*Singletary William	25	laborer	38	13 Oakburn av
L Evans Frances—†	27	housewife	24	here
M Evans Leroy	27	laborer	25	"
N Grabouski Adam	27	tailor	59	"
O Grabouski Edmund	27	U S M C	25	"
P Grabouski Veronica—†	27	housewife	63	"
R Cornish Mary L—†	27	"	34	
S Cornish Ralph	27	janitor	39	
U Walker Levinia—†	29	housewife	67	"
X*Lopez Bessie—†	31–33	"	50	
Y*Lopez James	31–33	operator	57	
Z Loveless Annie—†	31–33	housewife	35	"
1031				
A Crowley Ruth—†	35	"	37	
B Farrell Ruth—†	35	stenographer	28	"

Page.	Letter.	Full Name.	Residence, Jan. 1, 1943.	Occupation.	Supposed Age.	Reported Residence, Jan. 1, 1942. Street and Number.

Oakburn Avenue—Continued

Page.	Letter.	Full Name.	Residence, Jan. 1, 1943.	Occupation.	Supposed Age.	Reported Residence, Jan. 1, 1942. Street and Number.
	C	Sellon Burton	35	U S A	35	here
	D	Sellon Henry D	35	retired	97	"
	E	Wolff Mabel—†	35	housewife	52	"

Prentiss Place

Page.	Letter.	Full Name.	Residence, Jan. 1, 1943.	Occupation.	Supposed Age.	Reported Residence, Jan. 1, 1942. Street and Number.
	F	DeAngelo Angeline—†	2	housewife	60	here
	G	DeAngelo Dominic	2	retired	68	"
	H	Haberger Antoinette—†	2	housewife	25	"
	K	Haberger Joseph L	2	mechanic	25	"
	L	Ernshaw Celia—†	3	housewife	72	"
	M	Ernshaw John E	3	operator	38	"
	N	Hennessey John	4	retired	69	
	O	Hennessey Joseph	4	"	65	
	P	Hennessey Mary—†	4	housewife	70	"
	R	Hennessey Theresa—†	4	waitress	64	

Roxbury Court

Page.	Letter.	Full Name.	Residence, Jan. 1, 1943.	Occupation.	Supposed Age.	Reported Residence, Jan. 1, 1942. Street and Number.
	S	Hayes Helen—†	6	housewife	54	here
	U	Coyne Mary—†	6	at home	69	"
	V	Newlands Mary E—†	8	housewife	35	"
	W	Newlands William	8	painter	46	
	X	Doyle Edward	8	steamfitter	40	"
	Y	Leonard Ruth—†	8	saleswoman	25	636 E Fifth
	Z	Lozier Ethel—†	8	housewife	58	here
1032						
	A	Lozier George	8	U S A	24	
	B	*White Louis	8	laborer	50	"
	C	Gustafson Daniel	9	operator	21	"
	D	*Gustafson John	9	retired	64	
	E	Gustafson Nellie—†	9	housewife	57	"
	F	Golias Evanthia—†	9	"	45	
	G	Golias Milton S	9	retired	60	"
	L	Keilty Helen—†	11	housewife	56	"
	M	Keilty James J	11	U S M C	26	"
	N	Keilty John J	11	laborer	58	
	O	Keilty Mary—†	11	clerk	22	
	P	Keilty Thomas P	11	U S A	24	"
	R	Waldron John	11	houseman	50	Brewster
	S	Perry Joseph L	11A	chauffeur	44	here

Page.	Letter.	Full Name.	Residence, Jan. 1, 1943.	Occupation.	Supposed Age.	Reported Residence, Jan. 1, 1942. Street and Number.

Roxbury Court—Continued

Page.	Letter.	Full Name.	Residence, Jan. 1, 1943.	Occupation.	Supposed Age.	Reported Residence, Jan. 1, 1942. Street and Number.
	T	Perry Mildred F—†	11A	housewife	40	here
	U	Perry Robert J	11A	U S N	20	"
	V	Hartnett Annie—†	11A	housewife	62	"
	W	Hartnett John	11A	painter	61	
	X	Moore Catherine—†	12	housewife	34	"
	Y	Moore Peter	12	mechanic	38	"
	Z	Sheehan Clifford	12	janitor	23	
1033						
	A	*Femino Flavia—†	14	housewife	50	"
	B	Femino Letterio	14	barber	53	
	C	*Biondi Grace—†	14	saleswoman	32	"
	D	*Raymond Petrina—†	14	at home	64	
	F	Delaney Ada—†	15	housewife	34	"
	G	Delaney Kenneth	15	operator	32	
	H	Fiander John	15	retired	74	
	K	McNulty Alphonsus	16	clerk	42	
	L	McNulty Dellrese—†	16	housewife	37	"
	M	Corbo Guy	16	boxmaker	55	"
	N	Corbo Jane—†	16	housewife	51	"
	O	Bishop Mabel—†	17	at home	49	115 Worcester
	P	Duffley Bessie—†	17	"	57	14 Huckins
	R	Duffley Mary—†	17	"	67	14 "
	S	*Delaney Sophia—†	19		71	here
	T	Watson Elizabeth—†	19	"	60	"
	U	Day Francis	20	clerk	30	"
	V	*Day Mabel—†	20	housewife	29	"
	W	Wollman Anna—†	20	"	49	
	X	Wollman Edward	20	U S C G	24	"
	Y	Wollman Frieda W—†	20	nurse	21	"
	Z	Wollman Paul	20	painter	47	

1034 Roxbury Street

Page.	Letter.	Full Name.	Residence, Jan. 1, 1943.	Occupation.	Supposed Age.	Reported Residence, Jan. 1, 1942. Street and Number.
	O	*Flynn William G	81	painter	50	here
	P	MacLean Anna—†	81	at home	38	"
	R	*MacLean Elizabeth—†	81	"	76	"
	S	Dann Oscar	81	shipfitter	27	11 Malbon pl
	T	Dann Theresa—†	81	housewife	29	11 "
	U	Brewster Edward A	81	fireman	48	here
	V	Brewster George W	81	mechanic	72	"

Page.	Letter.	FULL NAME.	Residence, Jan. 1, 1943.	Occupation.	Supposed Age.	Reported Residence, Jan. 1, 1942. Street and Number.

Roxbury Street—Continued

	W	Brewster Sarah E—†	81	housewife	69	here
	X	Mitchell John B	81	machinist	53	"
	Y	Mitchell Margaret—†	81	stitcher	43	"
	Z	Mitchell William J	81	clerk	24	
1035						
	A	Leary Josephine—†	81	saleswoman	55	"
	B	Leary Nellie—†	81	domestic	48	"
	C	Baker Maurice J	81	manager	52	39 Harvard
	D	Baker Sophia—†	81	housewife	49	39 "
	E	Savosik Julia—†	81	"	22	23 Dana
	F	Savosik Walter	81	laborer	25	23 "
	G	McRae Albert	81	clerk	20	11 Dudley
	H	McRae Anna P—†	81	"	24	11 "
	K	McRae Anna V—†	81	housewife	47	11 "
	L	McRae Kathryn—†	81	saleswoman	27	11 "
	O	Miller Harold T	83A	machinist	44	here
	P	Miller Janet E—†	83A	housewife	39	"
	R	Miller Marilyn R—†	83A	bookkeeper	20	"
	S	Wall Bertha E—†	83A	housewife	53	"
	T	Wall Joseph F	83A	repairman	55	"
	U	Wagner Evelyn—†	85	waitress	33	"
	V	Kelley Ellen C—†	85	housewife	68	"
	W	Kelley James J	85	laborer	37	"
	X	Kelley Leo G	85	watchman	33	"
	Y	Kelley Richard	85	retired	79	
	Z	Kelley Thomas J	85	welder	40	
1036						
	A	Barry Margaret—†	85	housewife	58	"
	B	Garbey Nora—†	85	"	35	"
	E	Davidson Jeffrey R	87A	wireworker	20	139 Hillside
	F	Marson Marjorie L—†	87A	saleswoman	34	here
	G	Marson Walter S	87A	mechanic	34	"
	H	Cottrell Marjorie—†	87A	laundress	39	3 Willis ter
	L	Brewster Harold A	93	manager	45	here
	N	Richard Elizabeth M—†	99	operator	65	"
	O	Harding Caroline A—†	99	housewife	77	"
	P	Harding George M	99	retired	76	
	R	Buonopane Francis P	103	U S A	26	"
	S	Buonopane Joseph J	103	"	22	"
	T	Buonopane Lorenzo	103	watchman	67	"
	U	Buonopane Mary A—†	103	housewife	45	"

Page.	Letter.	Full Name.	Residence, Jan. 1, 1943.	Occupation.	Supposed Age.	Reported Residence, Jan. 1, 1942. Street and Number.
1037						

Ruggles Street

	D	*Lee George	24	operator	71	here
	E	Norton Harry J	24	ironworker	61	"
	F	Schappell Maude—†	24	teacher	65	"
	G	*Banzonie Michael	24	porter	67	
	H	Vayo Josephine—†	24	housekeeper	65	"
	K	Aylwood Grace—†	26	housewife	24	"
	L	Bowles Mildred—†	26	"	36	9 Goldsmith pl
	M	Foley James J	26	janitor	40	9 "
	N	Foley Joseph W	26	foreman	68	Belmont
	O	Straub Maude—†	26	housewife	56	here
	R	Bentley Arthur	30	welder	21	"
	S	Bentley Helen—†	30	housewife	45	"
	U	Abrams Roberta—†	58	packer	36	"
	V	Stewart Ella—†	58	housekeeper	55	33 Oakburn av
	W	King Leola—†	58	"	37	here
	X	Straks William	58	laborer	59	"
	Y	Jordan Marion—†	58	domestic	43	"
1038						
	B	Stephens Ida L—†	59	housewife	63	"
	C	Stephens William H	59	laborer	55	
	D	*Rock Erma—†	59	housewife	40	"
	E	*Rock Walter N	59	cook	45	
	G	Mosby Emma—†	60	housekeeper	63	"
	H	Robinson Lucy—†	60	housewife	42	"
	K	Robinson Snowden	60	porter	46	
	L	Fisher Bayard C	60	U S A	33	
	M	Hoyt Helen E—†	60	typist	30	
	N	White Aubrey	60	metalworker	35	"
	P	Snowden Alice A—†	61	housewife	45	"
	R	Snowden William J	61	janitor	53	"
	S	Fletcher Florence—†	61	maid	38	"
	T	Stewart Carrie—†	61	operator	23	"
	U	Stewart Frank R	61	U S A	21	
	V	Woods Florine—†	61	housewife	47	"
	W	Woods Louis	61	bottler	47	
	X	Santos Eva—†	61	housewife	41	"
	Y	*Santos Frank	61	laborer	47	
	Z	Holston Dina M—†	61	operator	49	"
1039						
	A	Howcutt Martin L	61	laborer	50	

Page.	Letter.	Full Name.	Residence, Jan. 1, 1943.	Occupation.	Supposed Age.	Reported Residence, Jan. 1, 1942. Street and Number.
		Ruggles Street—Continued				
	B	Smith Amelia—†	61	housewife	60	here
	C	West Mark P	62	laborer	31	533 Mass av
	D	*Taylor Julia—†	62	domestic	34	here
	E	*Taylor Robert	62	laborer	43	"
	F	Hammond Catherine—†	62	housewife	35	"
	K	Brannon Edward	63	retired	72	
	L	Francis Emma—†	63	domestic	74	"
	M	Johnson Edna—†	63	"	24	
	N	McGirt Cora—†	63	"	25	
	O	McGirt Ellen—†	63	housewife	70	"
	R	McMullan Alma—†	63	clerk	22	
	S	McQueen Susie—†	63	operator	26	"
	T	Sylvia Amos	63	laborer	38	
	U	Sylvia Thelma—†	63	housewife	38	"
	V	Bowden James A	63	janitor	69	10 Hammond
	W	Bowden John F	63	cook	68	Illinois
	X	Davis Anna—†	63	housewife	40	here
	Y	Davis Milton	63	U S A	22	"
	Z	Madrey Elizabeth—†	63	housewife	47	"
1040						
	A	Madrey Samuel	63	rigger	46	"
	B	Love Mattie—†	64	housewife	35	Alabama
	C	Love Robert	64	laborer	50	"
	D	McAllister Ida—†	64	housewife	39	here
	E	McAllister Pinkston	64	attendant	39	"
	F	Hinds Estella—†	64	housekeeper	56	"
	H	Gett George	65	laborer	73	"
	K	Jones Albert	65	"	47	"
	M	Wilson Gussie—†	65	housewife	34	15 Gertrose
	N	Wilson Milton	65	clergyman	34	15 "
	O	Wilson Rosetta—†	65	at home	55	15 "
	[1]O	*Robert Gerald	66	laborer	64	here
	P	Robert Geraldine—†	66	domestic	23	"
	R	Robert Mary—†	66	housewife	64	"
	S	Lomax Estella—†	66	"	42	"
	T	Lomax Henry	66	laborer	46	
	U	Gaines Andrew	66	retired	65	
	V	Gaines James	66	U S A	26	
	W	Gaines Luther	66	laborer	29	
	X	Gaines Mattie—†	66	housewife	59	"
	Y	Kent Mattie—†	66	domestic	20	"

Page.	Letter.	FULL NAME.	Residence, Jan. 1, 1943.	Occupation.	Supposed Age.	Reported Residence, Jan. 1, 1942. Street and Number.

Ruggles Street—Continued

	Z	Williams Langford G	66	laborer	31	here
1041						
	B	Johnson Anna—†	67	housekeeper	46	78 Ruggles
	C	Hollins Emma—†	67	housewife	50	Illinois
	D	White Benjamin F	67	laborer	24	"
	E	Hawkins Aline P—†	67	housekeeper	40	here
	F	Ray Irving	67	cook	43	129 Lenox
	H	Wright Samuel	68	"	55	here
	K	Wright Susan—†	68	housewife	65	"
	L	Franklin William J	68	musician	49	"
	M	Franklin William J	68	U S A	21	
	N	Senedo Dorothy—†	68	typist	25	
	O	Senedo Estelle—†	68	housewife	52	"
	P	Senedo Margaret—†	68	domestic	22	"
	S	Lopes Adeline—†	69	student	23	
	T	Lopes Joseph	69	retired	61	"
	U	Lopes Louise—†	69	housewife	54	"
	V	Whitfield Lucy—†	69	"	41	
	W	Whitfield William	69	laborer	64	
	X	Ross Harriet—†	69	housewife	40	"
	Y	Bowes Marion—†	69	"	68	
	Z	Bowes Virginia—†	69	at home	75	
1042						
	A	Sylvia Edith—†	69	operator	35	
	B	Williams Zilla—†	69	housekeeper	54	"
	D	Redmond Charles W	69	painter	56	"
	E	Redmond Viola—†	69	housewife	67	"
	F	Santos Henry	69	laborer	45	97 Warwick
	G	Santos Kandis—†	69	housewife	39	97 "
	K	Johnson Daisy—†	70	domestic	28	here
	L	Johnson Dorothy—†	70	packer	28	"
	M	Phillips David N	70	cook	58	"
	N	Phillips Dora—†	70	housewife	63	"
	O	*Wilson Joan—†	70	"	50	
	P	*Wilson Nathan	70	laborer	60	
	R	McGirt Joseph H	70	"	59	
	S	McGirt Nancy—†	70	housewife	69	"
	T	Scott Sally—†	70	operator	49	"
	U	Weston Lula—†	70	at home	85	
	W	*Jones Meta—†	72	housewife	39	"
	X	*Jones Thomas	72	laborer	50	

Page.	Letter.	Full Name.	Residence, Jan. 1, 1943.	Occupation.	Supposed Age.	Reported Residence, Jan. 1, 1942. Street and Number.

Ruggles Street—Continued

Page.	Letter.	Full Name.	Residence, Jan. 1, 1943.	Occupation.	Supposed Age.	Reported Residence, Jan. 1, 1942. Street and Number.
	Y	Brown Irene—†	72	housewife	58	here
	Z	Brown William A	72	seaman	68	"
1043						
	A	Jackson Thomas E	72	bootblack	22	"
	B	Jackson Violet—†	72	housewife	23	"
	C	White Walter	72	laborer	59	"
	E	Williams James A	73	"	51	66 Warwick
	F	Williams Rita—†	73	housewife	35	66 "
	G	McQueen Cyrus	73	shipper	28	here
	H	McQueen Willa—†	73	housewife	28	"
	L	Wells Priscilla—†	74	stitcher	41	"
	M	Wells Roy	74	musician	40	"
	N	Cobb Alvin	74	welder	35	
	O	Cobb Odessa—†	74	housewife	34	"
	P	Smith Eleanor—†	74	at home	22	N Carolina
	R	Adams Isadora—†	74	housewife	48	here
	S	Raynor Aubrey	74	retired	81	"
	T	Williams Ethel—†	75	housewife	25	"
	U	Williams Gettis	75	clergyman	60	"
	V	*Cruz John J	75	laborer	58	60 Ruggles
	W	Williams Alice E—†	75	housekeeper	60	60 "
	X	Carter Dell—†	75	domestic	58	8 Taber
	Y	Hutchinson Robert	75	retired	38	Maryland
	Z	Walcott Theodore	75	laborer	44	8 Taber
1044						
	A	Williams Ann—†	76	housewife	25	here
	B	Williams Kenneth	76	laborer	26	"
	C	Culbert Rose—†	76	domestic	25	"
	D	Floyd Joseph	76	laborer	40	"
	E	Lewis Mabel—†	76	housewife	25	"
	F	Drakeford Catherine—†	76	stitcher	22	
	G	Rhodes Elizabeth—†	76	at home	41	
	H	Dotten Carroll	77	chipper	33	
	K	Dotten Nora—†	77	housewife	29	"
	L	Miller Edna—†	77	stitcher	27	
	M	Miller Eric E	77	U S A	21	
	N	Miller Samuel	77	retired	68	"
	O	Ross Annie M—†	77	housewife	60	13 Auburn
	P	Ross Robert L	77	chef	64	13 "
	R	Gardner Beulah—†	78	stitcher	42	here
	S	Smith William W	78	ironworker	44	"

Page.	Letter.	Full Name.	Residence, Jan. 1, 1943.	Occupation.	Supposed Age.	Reported Residence, Jan. 1, 1942. Street and Number.

Ruggles Street—Continued

	T	Bowden Inez—†	78	housewife	41	here
	X	Lawson John	82	porter	50	"
	Y	Rogers Charles	82	"	49	"
	Z	Rogers Sarah—†	82	housewife	47	"
1045						
	A	Posler Helen—†	82	domestic	61	"
	B	Posler Mary—†	82	housewife	40	"
	C	Thompson Jane—†	82	domestic	23	18 Gertrose
	D	Bowden James H	82	chauffeur	21	7 "
	E	Bowden Mary M—†	82	housewife	23	7 "
	F	Faris Benjamin	82	laborer	48	here
	G	Faris Mildred—†	82	housewife	40	"
	H	Granville Mamie—†	82	operator	24	"
	M	Boyd Lucinda—†	82	housekeeper	66	"
	N	Dames Frederick B	82	packer	30	"
	W	*Speers Robert	101	baker	60	
	X	*Wagner Georgianna—†	101	housewife	75	"
	Y	Hayes John E	101	U S A	30	
	Z	Hayes Naomi—†	101	housewife	50	"
1046						
	A	Sullivan Ada—†	101	housekeeper	52	"
	B	Crispbee Edward	101	retired	50	69 Ruggles
	C	Hayes Issahates	101	laborer	49	here
	E	Hassett Dora—†	105	housekeeper	63	"
	G	McGee George	105	bricklayer	42	"
	F	McGee Gertrude—†	105	housewife	38	"
	K	Sumlin Elizabeth—†	109	housekeeper	38	"
	L	Wray Susan—†	109	"	37	"
	N	Sultis Malvin M	111	operator	20	781 Shawmut av
	O	Baddett Louise H—†	111	housewife	27	99 Warwick
	P	Baddett William R	111	packer	28	99 "
	U	Freeman Rose—†	117	housewife	65	28 Rose
	V	Foster Charlotte—†	117	housekeeper	71	here
	W	Herbert Amanda—†	117	"	55	"
	X	Wiggins Edward	119	laborer	79	"
	Y	Morris Ida—†	119	housekeeper	55	"

1047 Saint Francis de Sales Street

	C	Schools Leo	7	cook	36	here
	D	Schools Madeline—†	7	housewife	33	"

Page.	Letter.	FULL NAME.	Residence, Jan. 1, 1943.	Occupation.	Supposed Age.	Reported Residence, Jan. 1, 1942. Street and Number.

Saint Francis de Sales Street—Continued

	E	Alvarez Josephine—†	7	laundress	69	here
	F	Hall Agnes—†	7	domestic	72	"
	H	Bartlett Edna—†	11	housewife	33	16 Texas
	K	Bartlett John C	11	machinist	35	16 "
	L	Reid Mary—†	12	domestic	61	here
	N	Hope Mary—†	15	housewife	66	"
	O	Renault Albinia—†	15	"	47	"
	P	Renault Wallace	15	painter	45	
	R	Miskell William	15	mechanic	52	"
	S	Wanat Antonina—†	17	housewife	37	"
	T	*Small Anne—†	18	"	67	
	U	*Small Frank	18	retired	74	
	V	Estabrook Stella—†	18	domestic	68	"
	W	Blair Bertha—†	18	housewife	55	"
	X	Blair Vivian—†	18	waitress	21	
	Z	Hartigan Mary C—†	19	housewife	56	"
1048						
	A	Carlson Walter	19	guard	40	117 Cabot
	B	Heavey John	19	retired	67	here
	C	Keenan Earl	19	laborer	30	"
	D	Keenan Gertrude—†	19	housewife	65	"
	E	*Frazier Victoria—†	20	domestic	73	"
	F	Minnahan Mary—†	20	"	78	
	K	Crowley Margaret—†	32	"	46	
	O	McLellan Arthur	33	retired	74	
	P	*O'Connor Nora—†	33	domestic	72	"
	S	Jones Esther—†	34	housewife	37	Randolph
	U	Kenny George	35	clerk	65	here
	V	Ryan Anthony	35	cook	28	11 Dudley
	W	Ryan Catherine—†	35	housewife	51	11 "
	Y	Postizzi Julia—†	36	laundress	27	here
	Z	Marshall Edna—†	36	housewife	28	"
1049						
	B	Dineen Elizabeth—†	38	"	45	17 Roxbury ct
	C	Dineen John	38	laborer	53	17 "
	D	Walsh Margaret—†	38	domestic	70	here
	E	*Morgan Catherine—†	40	housewife	62	222 Cabot
	F	*Morgan John	40	laborer	50	222 "
	G	Kelly Celia A—†	40	nurse	35	here
	H	Kelly Nora—†	40	housewife	63	"
	K	Barry John	40	retired	65	195 Vernon

Page.	Letter.	Full Name.	Residence, Jan. 1, 1943.	Occupation.	Supposed Age.	Reported Residence, Jan. 1, 1942. Street and Number.

Saint Francis de Sales Street—Continued

Page.	Letter.	Full Name.	Residence, Jan. 1, 1943.	Occupation.	Supposed Age.	Reported Residence, Jan. 1, 1942. Street and Number.
	L	Barry Nora—†	40	housewife	65	195 Vernon
	M	Cameron Anne—†	44	"	53	here
	N	Cameron Thomas	44	machinist	56	"
	O	Fountain Claude A	44	U S N	39	"
	P	Fountain Martha C—†	44	housewife	63	"
	R	Fountain William	44	laborer	66	

Shawmut Avenue

Page.	Letter.	Full Name.	Residence, Jan. 1, 1943.	Occupation.	Supposed Age.	Reported Residence, Jan. 1, 1942. Street and Number.
	T	Graham Frederick E	741	clerk	42	Cambridge
	U	Grant George	741	blacksmith	56	here
	V	Grant Olivia E—†	741	housewife	46	"
	W	Lockman Beryl—†	741	"	32	"
	X	Lockman Lycurgas	741	painter	32	"
	Y	Alfred Josephine—†	741	domestic	30	New York
	Z	Madrey Abraham	741	rigger	35	here
1050						
	A	Madrey Jennie—†	741	housewife	30	"
	B	Phippin Frank H	741	porter	37	
	C	Phippin Hattie—†	741	housewife	64	"
	D	Stigler Earl	741	laborer	50	"
	F	Rose Thomas	741	janitor	50	129 Boylston
	K	Morgan Rita—†	745A	social worker	38	here
	M	Meade Christine—†	745A	housewife	42	"
	L	Meade John	745A	laborer	52	"
	N	Weaver Blossom—†	745A	housewife	22	"
	O	Weaver Curtis S	745A	laborer	26	
	P	Weaver Elsie L—†	745A	housewife	27	"
	R	Weaver Robert	745A	clerk	32	
	S	Munnally Hilda—†	747	housewife	45	"
	T	Munnally Lawrence	747	mechanic	45	"
	U	Henry John	747	laborer	40	"
	V	Henry Lucille—†	747	housewife	40	"
	W	Waterhouse Eugene	747	mechanic	45	"
	X	Waterhouse Julia—†	747	presser	42	
	Y	Lamb Obeline—†	747	housewife	43	"
	Z	Lamb Richard C	747	waiter	48	
1051						
	A	Randolph Ulysses	749	laborer	47	
	B	Banks Ethel—†	749	operator	37	
	C	Tenney Nellie—†	749	housekeeper	48	"

Page.	Letter.	Full Name.	Residence, Jan. 1, 1943.	Occupation.	Supposed Age.	Reported Residence, Jan. 1, 1942. Street and Number.

Shawmut Avenue—Continued

	D	Tenney Nettie—†	749	housewife	70	here
	E	Walker Rose—†	749	operator	33	"
	F	Wornum Foster	749	porter	55	"
	G	Wornum Julia—†	749	housewife	60	"
	H	Bailey Laura—†	749	"	55	
	K	Bailey William	749	mechanic	55	"
	L	Banks William	749	retired	72	
	M	Humbert William A	749	porter	62	"
	N	McCoy Beatrice—†	751	housewife	45	3 Wentworth pl
	O	McCoy Thomas	751	laundryman	53	3 "
	P	Morris Irene—†	751	housewife	57	here
	R	*Morris James E	751	watchman	56	"
	S	Douglas Frances—†	751	housewife	44	"
	T	Douglas Mortimer	751	longshoreman	40	610 Shawmut av
	U	Smith Clarone A—†	751	housewife	44	here
	V	Smith Joseph E	751	porter	45	"
	W	Smith Mildred B—†	751	operator	22	"
1052						
	B	Clark Evelyn L—†	763	housekeeper	75	"
	C	Field Evangeline J—†	763	"	74	
	D	Jordan Florence A—†	763	"	72	
	E	Jordan George E	763	salesman	65	"
	K	Murray John B	779	janitor	60	Brookline
	L	Murray Winifred—†	779	housewife	56	"
	M	Cross Nina—†	781	domestic	47	here
	N	Myers Mary E—†	781	housekeeper	69	"
	O	Sulthis Edith—†	781	housewife	45	"
	P	Bland Albert	781	laborer	47	
	R	Bland Ella W—†	781	domestic	53	"
	S	Myers Daisy E—†	783	housewife	28	20 Elbert
	T	Myers Ralph E	783	mechanic	43	20 "
	U	Davis Bessie—†	783	housewife	46	here
	V	Davis Maurice M	783	presser	48	"
	W	Harris Eunice—†	783	dressmaker	25	Greenfield
	X	Harris Walter	783	laborer	27	"
	Y	Seavey Ethel—†	783	dressmaker	44	here
	Z	Seavey Walter	783	laborer	61	"
1053						
	A	Anderson Albert	787	clergyman	62	"
	B	Atone Mary A—†	789	housewife	33	"
	C	Lewis Mollie L—†	789	"	51	"

Page.	Letter.	Full Name.	Residence, Jan. 1, 1943.	Occupation.	Supposed Age.	Reported Residence, Jan. 1, 1942. Street and Number.

Shawmut Avenue—Continued

	D	McClain Bessie—†	793	housewife	56	here
	E	McClain Henry J	793	laborer	48	"
	F	Carter Robert L	793	fireman	48	"
	G	Carter Viola—†	793	housewife	54	"
	H	Carter Gertrude—†	795	dressmaker	41	"
	K	Carter Marguerite B—†	795	housewife	67	"
	L	Griffin Hattie B—†	795	housekeeper	68	"

Vernon Court

	T	Fisher Anna E—†	2	housewife	32	here
	U	Fisher Joseph G	2	guard	36	"
	V	Pappas Mary—†	3	housewife	35	"
	W	Pappas Teddy	3	waiter	50	

Vernon Place

	X	Ball Delia—†	2	housekeeper	46	here
	Y	*Laird John	2	retired	74	"
1054						
	A	Lynch Henry P	2	roofer	25	
	B	Lynch Marion—†	2	housewife	25	"
	D	Pendergast John W	4	undertaker	53	"
	E	Powell Alice—†	4	housewife	27	"
	F	Powell Joseph	4	chauffeur	29	"
	G	Gallagher Arthur	4	"	37	
	H	Gallagher Dorothy—†	4	housewife	34	"
	K	Eames Charles F	6	rigger	29	"
	L	Eames Loretta—†	6	housewife	25	"
	M	Hayes Annie E—†	6	"	33	
	N	Hayes George W	6	optician	32	
	O	Dewire Madeline—†	6	housewife	27	"
	P	Dewire Robert J	6	carpenter	29	"

Vernon Street

	R	Campbell James	23	social worker	56	here
	S	Mennes Donald	23	"	64	"
	T	Twitchell Benjamin H	27	motorman	44	"
		Twitchell Gertrude—†	27	housewife	46	"
	V	Callahan Hilma M—†	29	"	54	

Page.	Letter.	Full Name.	Residence, Jan. 1, 1943.	Occupation.	Supposed Age.	Reported Residence, Jan. 1, 1942. Street and Number.

Vernon Street—Continued

	W	Callahan Patrick F	29	clerk	55	here
	X	Oran Francis X	29	“	31	“
	Y	Oran Marie T—†	29	housewife	28	“
	Z	Morton Ellsworth	31	porter	29	
1055						
	A	Morton Irene—†	31	housewife	26	“
	B	Caswell Rose—†	31	“	53	
	C	Caswell Silas A	31	pipecoverer	55	“
	E	Reavis George H	35	laborer	32	
	F	Reavis Katie J—†	35	housewife	65	“
	G	Reavis Levi H	35	retired	72	
	H	Dyott Alfred	39	machinist	38	“
	K	Dyott Mary—†	39	housewife	34	“
	L	McBarron Edward L	45	clerk	62	
	M	McBarron Sarah A—†	45	at home	81	
	N	DeLong Albert W	46	U S A	33	
	O	*DeLong Eli	46	painter	62	
	P	DeLong Florence—†	46	housewife	56	“
	R	Ewanosky Michael	46	finisher	46	
	S	Brennan Helen G—†	46	clerk	35	
	T	Kenny Daniel F	46	U S A	22	“
	U	Kenny John F	46	“	43	
	V	McCarthy Catherine E—†	46	matron	65	
	W	Campbell Charles	47	retired	67	
	X	Rogers Loretta—†	47	operator	53	“
	Y	Scholey Edward T	47	chauffeur	51	“
	Z	Scholey Florence—†	47	housewife	48	“
1056						
	B	*Campbell Lillian—†	48	“	36	
	D	LaPorte Lillian—†	48	at home	39	
	E	Moore Sadie—†	48	“	56	“
	F	Rockwood Albert E	48	painter	46	
	G	Rockwood John H	48	“	44	
	H	Ryan Thomas L	48	teamster	57	“
	K	Gill Annie—†	48A	domestic	56	“
	L	Gill Robert	48A	clerk	28	
	M	Powers Edward	49	custodian	56	“
	N	Powers Helen—†	49	housewife	62	“
	R	Boudreau Charles	50	metalworker	32	“
	S	Boudreau Katherine—†	50	housewife	28	“
	T	Chaperon Daniel J	50	carpenter	48	“

Page.	Letter.	FULL NAME.	Residence, Jan. 1, 1943.	Occupation.	Supposed Age.	Reported Residence, Jan. 1, 1942. Street and Number.

Vernon Street—Continued

	U	Chaperon Stella M—†	50	housewife	46	here
	V	Colleran Ellen—†	50	"	65	"
	W	Colleran Helen—†	50	inspector	38	"
	X	Colleran Margaret—†	50	at home	30	
	Y	Colleran Mildred—†	50	clerk	22	
	Z	Colleran Patrick	50	retired	71	
1057						
	A	Colleran Patrick E	50	electrician	36	"
	B	Connelly Annie—†	50	clerk	33	"
	D	Babcock Mary—†	51	housewife	55	19C Palmer
	E	Babcock Richard	51	U S A	20	19C "
	F	Behnke Charles W	51	machinist	55	here
	G	Behnke Irene G—†	51	housewife	52	"
	K	Roche John	52	U S A	36	Plymouth
	L	*Roche Mary—†	52	packer	37	Brookline
	M	Bolduc Blanche—†	52	housewife	50	here
	N	Bolduc Loretta—†	52	waitress	23	"
	O	Fisher James	52	seaman	27	223 Cabot
	P	Fisher Marie—†	52	clerk	28	223 "
	R	Pearson Avis—†	52	housewife	39	here
	S	Pearson Malcolm	52	mechanic	48	"
	T	Urch Mabel—†	52	nurse	63	"
	V	Wolfe Herman H	53	clerk	31	
	W	Wolfe Mary J—†	53	housewife	30	"
	X	Hardiman Grace—†	53	"	36	"
	Y	Bornstein Dora—†	55	storekeeper	35	"
	Z	Bornstein Harry	55	"	46	"
1058						
	A	Haynes Mary A—†	60	teacher	52	
	B	Knightly Helen G—†	60	"	53	
	C	McKenna Mary—†	60	"	38	"
	D	McTigue Sabina—†	60		69	
	E	Scavitto Pauline C—†	60	"	37	
	F	Schaeffner Katherine—†	60	"	61	"
	G	Price Richard	70	U S M C	21	3 Tupelo
	H	Wheeler Annie L—†	70	at home	57	3 "
	K	Wheeler Chester L	70	janitor	59	3 "
	L	Dunn Annie R—†	70	at home	70	here
	M	Dunn John T	70	laborer	39	"
	N	Dunn Patrick F	70	retired	75	"
	O	Lally Anna G—†	70	at home	35	"

Page.	Letter.	Full Name.	Residence, Jan. 1, 1943.	Occupation.	Supposed Age.	Reported Residence, Jan. 1, 1942. Street and Number.

Vernon Street—Continued

Page.	Letter.	Full Name.	Residence, Jan. 1, 1943.	Occupation.	Supposed Age.	Reported Residence, Jan. 1, 1942. Street and Number.
	P	Lally William E	70	U S A	37	96 Centre
	R	*Cheveary Edward	76	carpenter	49	19 Glenwood
	S	*Cheveary Laura—†	76	at home	37	19 "
	T	McDermott George J	76	roofer	47	15 Rockville pk
	U	McDermott Loretta R—†	76	housewife	44	15 "
	V	Callahan Elizabeth—†	76	at home	47	here
	W	Callahan John	76	cook	47	"
	X	Callahan Joseph	76	laborer	25	"
	Y	Caldwell Lillian—†	78	at home	33	"
	Z	Miller John	78	U S A	21	69 Cabot
1059						
	A	Miller John H	78	timekeeper	52	69 "
	B	Miller Margaret—†	78	housewife	54	69 "
	C	Crawford John F	78	mechanic	27	here
	D	Crawford Rita—†	78	housewife	26	"
	E	Guitard Alphonsine—†	78	stitcher	52	"
	F	Connor Anne T—†	80	clerk	21	
	G	Connor Elizabeth—†	80	housewife	50	"
	H	Connor William A	80	painter	57	
	K	Lacey Mary—†	80	at home	63	"
	L	Gerraughty Ethel—†	80	"	34	79 Highland
	M	Bornetzky Laura P—†	82	housewife	36	here
	N	Bornetzky Walter J	82	teacher	36	"
	O	McLaughlin Lillian—†	82A	housewife	26	"
	P	McLaughlin William	82A	salesman	30	"
	R	Stanlake Blanche—†	84	at home	33	"
	S	Stanlake John	84	clerk	54	"
	T	Slawsby Harriet—†	84	at home	39	60 Cliff
	U	Slawsby John	84	U S A	29	60 "
	V	Mulrey Rosa A—†	84	at home	57	here
	W	Pettigrew Mary—†	86	"	68	"
	X	Hanrahan Margaret—†	86	"	74	"
	Y	Welch Elinor D—†	86	W A V E	22	"
	Z	Van Orden Sarah J—†	86	saleswoman	60	Cambridge
1060						
	A	Abbott Horatio	87	carpenter	61	here
	B	Anderson Gustave	87	chauffeur	51	Brockton
	C	Anderson John	87	electrician	40	Wash'n D C
	D	*Anderson Robert L	87	mechanic	65	here
	E	Baker Henry	87	laborer	80	"
	F	Beard Vernon P	87	"	58	"

Page.	Letter.	FULL NAME.	Residence, Jan. 1, 1943.	Occupation.	Supposed Age.	Reported Residence, Jan. 1, 1942. Street and Number.

Vernon Street—Continued

Page.	Letter.	FULL NAME.	Residence, Jan. 1, 1943.	Occupation.	Supposed Age.	Reported Residence, Jan. 1, 1942. Street and Number.
	G	Brodie Harold J	87	laborer	51	Hudson
	H	*Buckley Thomas J	87	"	37	here
	K	Casey James T	87	"	61	"
	L	*Christie Joseph	87	cook	48	"
	M	Churchill Albert	87	clerk	46	New York
	N	Clark Joseph	87	chauffeur	57	here
	O	Cole Byron	87	"	52	"
	P	*Covert Harold G	87	laborer	52	"
	R	*Drummy John	87	"	49	
	S	Dupre Regis	87	"	74	
	T	*Ericson Eric	87	"	49	
	U	Farnsworth Harry L	87	chauffeur	50	"
	V	Farrell Christopher	87	laborer	64	"
	W	*Ferguson James	87	carpenter	75	"
	X	*Ferguson Peter C	87	cook	55	
	Y	*Flaherty Patrick	87	laborer	46	
	Z	Flanagan Thomas J	87	"	63	
1061						
	A	Flynn John	87	"	39	
	B	*Forsyth Andrew	87	boilermaker	58	"
	C	*Forsyth William	87	"	62	
	D	Gaffey John H	87	laborer	52	
	E	Galvin Thomas F	87	"	36	
	F	Geary Edward R	87	"	49	"
	G	Geibe Edward F	87		51	Missouri
	H	Grady Andrew F	87		50	here
	K	Grady John	87	"	66	"
	L	Graham Thomas J	87	chauffeur	37	"
	M	Groody William H	87	accountant	47	"
	N	Haggerty Patrick D	87	laborer	66	
	O	Hearon Henry M	87	storekeeper	60	"
	P	Helender Victor E	87	shoeworker	64	"
	R	Henry Elizabeth—†	87	housewife	26	Ohio
	S	Henry Everett	87	accountant	28	"
	T	Holland John	87	laborer	56	here
	U	Hurley Joseph P	87	clerk	50	"
	V	Kenney Thomas E	87	laborer	64	"
	W	Kuhn Joseph	87	upholsterer	62	"
	X	LaJoie Louis J	87	shoemaker	34	Framingham
	Y	*Leavitt John P	87	salesman	55	here
	Z	Leith Helmuth	87	seaman	47	"

Page.	Letter.	Full Name.	Residence, Jan. 1, 1943.	Occupation.	Supposed Age.	Reported Residence, Jan. 1, 1942. Street and Number.

1062
Vernon Street—Continued

Page.	Letter.	Full Name.	Residence, Jan. 1, 1943.	Occupation.	Supposed Age.	Reported Residence, Jan. 1, 1942. Street and Number.
1062	A	Linblad Stephen T	87	laborer	44	here
	B	Love Robert	87	"	60	"
	C	Lowe William H	87	porter	62	"
	D	Lynch Timothy J	87	laborer	62	
	E	Lyons John J	87	"	48	
	F	MacDonald William	87	painter	64	
	G	*MacGregor Hector	87	laborer	62	
	H	*Matlock Leo F	87	carpenter	42	"
	K	McLeod John	87	laborer	55	
	L	*McSweeney John M	87	"	60	
	M	Milliken William	87	clerk	59	
	N	Millman Harry	87	"	59	
	O	*Mitchell James J	87	laborer	51	"
	P	Moran Edward	87	"	75	
	R	Moran Michael	87	"	58	
	S	Morrill Frank E	87	"	49	"
	T	Morse Lester	87	cook	43	Springfield
	U	Mulvey Patrick F	87	laborer	60	here
	V	Mummey Dale H	87	accountant	52	"
	W	Murphy Edward M	87	laborer	32	"
	X	*Nicholson Martin J	87	"	50	"
	Y	Nicholson William	87	painter	62	Lawrence
	Z	Nute Herbert T	87	laborer	57	here
1063	A	O'Neil Charles S	87		70	Tewksbury
	B	*O'Neill Jeremiah	87	"	57	Malden
	C	*Pitchers Edward	87	seaman	56	here
	D	Powers William F	87	laborer	49	"
	E	Quigley Alexander	87	"	51	"
	F	Raymond George	87	"	72	
	G	Reed Fred W	87	"	58	
	H	Riley William	87	"	65	
	K	Ross David	87	painter	65	
	L	Rossitt Harry	87	laborer	77	
	M	Rowe Burton J	87	"	46	
	N	Sargeant Edward	87	"	62	
	O	Shaw Samuel C	87	engineer	63	"
	P	Smith Charles F	87	laborer	58	Pennsylvania
	R	Smith George	87	"	64	Rhode Island
	S	Snow Charles L	87	"	56	here

Page.	Letter.	Full Name.	Residence, Jan. 1, 1943.	Occupation.	Supposed Age.	Reported Residence, Jan. 1, 1942. Street and Number.

Vernon Street—Continued

	T	Stewart Charles J	87	tailor	58	here
	U	Sullivan John	87	laborer	57	"
	V	*Sutherland Howard	87	salesman	53	"
	W	Taylor William J	87	laborer	60	Newton
	X	Townsend Burton W	87	"	65	here
	Y	Tracey Frank B	87	cigarmaker	60	"
	Z	*Trites Arthur H	87	laborer	61	"
1064						
	A	Troy James W	87	carpenter	35	Quincy
	B	*Wall Thomas	87	laborer	51	here
	C	*Wasson James	87	"	53	"
	D	*Webster William H	87	"	71	"
	E	Welch John P	87	"	65	
	F	Wenning Walter K	87	painter	59	"
	G	White Edward F	87	salesman	53	Lincoln
	H	Daniels Lillian—†	88	maid	51	here
	K	*Henry Cornelia—†	88	at home	56	"
	L	*Johnson Ida—†	88	"	35	"
	M	Johnson Oscar	88	chipper	39	
	N	Johnson Stanley L	88	waiter	40	
	O	Johnson Viola—†	88	at home	33	"
	P	Pollard Lyle—†	88	cook	51	N Hampshire
	R	Stuart Gladys—†	88	maid	38	here
	S	Bergland Corinne—†	90	clerk	21	"
	T	Bergland Ruth—†	90	"	44	"
	U	Brown Corinne—†	90	"	33	
	V	Tyler Mildred—†	90	at home	40	
	W	Tyler William	90	U S A	20	
	X	Burton Elizabeth—†	92	maid	63	
	Y	Chaverie Catherine—†	92	waitress	60	
	Z	Gracey Sadie—†	92	maid	25	
1065						
	A	McGeever Catherine—†	92	at home	69	"
	B	Tate Aurelia S—†	94	"	40	79 Windsor
	C	Tate Phineas W	94	porter	40	79 "
	D	Savoy Clara M—†	94	at home	51	here
	E	Savoy Joseph J	94	janitor	52	"
	F	Clark Marvin W	94	welder	28	Brookline
	G	Clark Mary—†	94	housewife	26	"
	H	White Helen—†	94	at home	24	Georgia
	K	White William	94	laborer	47	"

Page.	Letter.	FULL NAME.	Residence, Jan. 1, 1943.	Occupation.	Supposed Age.	Reported Residence, Jan. 1, 1942. Street and Number.

Vernon Street—Continued

	L	Ray Sylvia G—†	94	clerk	28	540 Col av
	M	McCarthy Albert	96	"	37	here
	N	McCarthy Margaret—†	96	at home	36	"
	O	Sequin Albert	96	welder	46	"
	P	Sequin Louise—†	96	clerk	43	
	R	Brennan Louise—†	96	matron	57	
	S	Cass Louise—†	96	at home	29	
	T	*Doyle James C	rear 97	barber	46	
	U	*Jesso Mary—†	" 97	laundress	63	"
	V	Burke Catherine—†	98	at home	76	
	W	Burke Jeremiah	98	retired	76	
	X	McKernan John	98	welder	24	
	Y	McKernan Mary E—†	98	at home	49	
	Z	McKernan Thomas	98	U S N	22	
1066						
	A	McKernan Walter F	98	clerk	28	
	B	McKernan William J	98	fireman	51	
	C	McKernan William J, jr	98	U S A	26	
	D	Campbell Frederick	98	pipefitter	52	"
	E	O'Brien Catherine—†	98	clerk	29	
	F	Parsikian Charles	98	laborer	49	
	G	Parsikian Jean—†	98	at home	31	
	H	Hartford Glen	99	machinist	35	"
	K	Hartford John	99	cobbler	68	
	L	Hartford Margie—†	99	housewife	57	"
	M	Lawless Nellie—†	100	"	59	
	N	Lawless Patrick	100	laborer	59	
	O	Fitzgerald Mary J—†	100	housewife	50	"
	P	Fitzgerald Patrick J	100	laborer	48	
	R	Matthews Anna—†	100	clerk	23	
	S	McBride Catherine M—†	100	at home	55	"
	T	Harris Adelaide P—†	102	housewife	24	1186½ Tremont
	U	Harris Edward D	102	welder	23	1186½ "
	V	Giblin James	102	retired	76	here
	W	Giblin Sarah E—†	102	at home	40	"
	X	Morrison Sarah E—†	102	"	65	"
	Y	Fleming Agnes—†	102	"	28	
	Z	Fleming Thomas H	102	brakeman	30	"
1067						
	A	O'Neil John J	102	laborer	53	
	B	Burns Thomas J	116	clergyman	45	"

Page.	Letter.	FULL NAME.	Residence, Jan. 1, 1943.	Occupation.	Supposed Age.	Reported Residence, Jan. 1, 1942. Street and Number.

Vernon Street—Continued

	C	Lawlor Patrick H	116	clergyman	39	here
	D	O'Brien Mary C—†	116	maid	37	"
	E	Quill Patrick J	116	clergyman	60	"
	F	Brady Esther B—†	122	teacher	36	
	G	Decher Helen M—†	122	"	49	
	H	Degnan Sarah—†	122	"	42	
	K	Frawley Elizabeth R—†	122	"	46	"
	L	Hedderman Marie F—†	122	"	49	74 Union Park
	M	Maisey Margaret H—†	122	"	27	here
	N	McAllister Sally P—†	122	"	28	"
	O	*O'Donnell Catherine C—†	122	cook	35	"
	P	Yarnell Bernice A—†	122	teacher	30	"
	R	*Cupner Leah—†	124	at home	60	

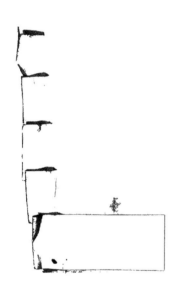

Ward 9—Precinct 11

CITY OF BOSTON

LIST OF RESIDENTS
20 YEARS OF AGE AND OVER

(NON-CITIZENS INDICATED BY ASTERISK)
(FEMALES INDICATED BY DAGGER)

AS OF

JANUARY 1, 1943

JOSEPH F. TIMILTY, *Chairman*
FREDERIC E. DOWLING, *Secretary*
WILLIAM A. MOTLEY, JR.
FRANCIS B. McKINNEY
EVERETT R. PROUT
Listing Board.

CITY OF BOSTON PRINTING DEPARTMENT

Page.	Letter.	Full Name.	Residence, Jan. 1, 1943.	Occupation.	Supposed Age.	Reported Residence, Jan. 1, 1942. Street and Number.
1100						

Cabot Street

1100	A	Smith Benjamin A	136	U S M C	21	here
	B	Smith Frances M—†	136	housewife	44	"
	C	Smith Harry W	136	U S A	20	"
	E	Darby James	142	butler	43	Waban
	F	Floyd Theresa—†	146	at home	80	here
	G	Forney Hattie—†	146	maid	59	"
	H	Jones Julius E	146	porter	63	"
	K	Jones Mae—†	146	housewife	42	"
	L	*Shea Mary—†	150	at home	72	
	M	Cramer Frank	150	laborer	55	"
	N	Cramer Helen—†	150	housewife	65	"
	O	Ford Edward	150	U S A	27	
	P	Ford George	150	"	28	
	S	*Chorkofsky Sophie—†	152	at home	55	"
	T	Walker Mary C—†	154	housewife	60	Rhode Island
	U	Jones Caroline A—†	154	presser	53	here
	V	Ruffin Fannie B—†	154	housewife	77	"
	W	Clifton Alice—†	154	matron	32	"
	X	Fortune Alvin U	154	welder	31	"
	Z	Balthrop Eleanor—†	157	housekeeper	36	189 Cabot
1101						
	A	Smith James	157	laborer	60	here
	B	Welsh John	159	"	48	"
	C	Welsh Mary—†	159	housewife	46	"
	D	Cunard Mary—†	159	clerk	21	"
	E	Perry Richard	159	U S A	24	
	K	Gibbs Addie M—†	161	housekeeper	65	"
	L	Hudson Ella—†	161	housewife	65	"
	M	Grayson Jennie—†	161	housekeeper	65	"
	N	Brooks Blanche—†	162	housewife	24	"
	O	Brooks Sebron	162	pipecutter	44	"
	P	Middleton Charles E	162	laborer	43	
	R	Middleton Charlotte E–†	162	housewife	42	"
	T	MacDonald Rose—†	163	domestic	43	19 Newbern
	U	Owens James R	163	seaman	42	here
	V	Owens Louise—†	163	housewife	62	"
	W	Martin James	163	machinist	50	"
	X	Martin Mary—†	163	housewife	46	"
	Y	Cisco Janie—†	164	at home	68	"
	Z	*Forbes Walter	164	janitor	45	60 Ball

Page.	Letter.	FULL NAME.	Residence, Jan. 1, 1943.	Occupation.	Supposed Age.	Reported Residence, Jan. 1, 1942. Street and Number.

1102
Cabot Street—Continued

A	Black Edna—†	164	social worker	43	here
B	Cox Lionel A	164	metalworker	25	"
C	Vaughan Julie E—†	164	housewife	25	"
D	Jones Carrie—†	164	housekeeper	51	"
E	Wilson Mary—†	166	housewife	53	"
F	Wilson Robert	166	laborer	54	
G*	Durkin Edward	168	"	64	
H*	Durkin Winifred—†	168	housewife	61	"
K	Cabral Annie R—†	168	"	54	
L	Cabral John	168	salesman	56	"
M	Coffey Elizabeth J—†	168	housewife	53	"
N	Coffey John G	168	porter	66	"
O	Doucette Joseph F	170	welder	42	137 Cabot
P	Doucette Marion A—†	170	housewife	35	137 "
R	Donohue Helen—†	170	"	43	here
S*	Mahar Joseph V	170	freighthandler	61	"
T*	Mahar Mary E—†	170	housewife	65	"
U	Blackman Robert T	174	choreman	70	"
V	Goodwin Jennette P—†	174	housewife	77	"
W	Benders Carl H	174	shipfitter	36	"
X	Benders Dorothy M—†	174	housewife	32	"
Y	Johnston Grace A—†	181	"	54	
Z	Johnston Osceola	181	laborer	51	
	1103				
A	Almeida Antone	182	mechanic	25	"
B	Almeida Rose—†	182	housewife	25	"
C*	Arauzo Frank	182	retired	59	
D	Stevens Cornelia L—†	182	housewife	66	"
E	Stevens Edward M	182	retired	42	
F	Jones Alice—†	182	stitcher	27	"
G	Jones Charles	182	engineer	26	New York
H	Jones Gladys—†	182	stitcher	24	here
K	Jones William	182	U S A	21	"
M	Curtis Agnes—†	184	at home	37	"
N	Brown Arthur J	184	operator	50	
O	Martin Rose E—†	184	cleaner	66	
P	Moses Ann—†	184	at home	68	
R	Moses Roy	184	musician	42	"
T	Maddon Alice—†	185	housewife	34	"
U	Maddon John J	185	chauffeur	44	"

Page.	Letter.	Full Name.	Residence, Jan. 1, 1943.	Occupation.	Supposed Age.	Reported Residence, Jan. 1, 1942. Street and Number.

Cabot Street—Continued

	v	McLean Harry	185	finisher	64	here
	w	Shapiro Elizabeth—†	185	housewife	39	“
	x	Shapiro Lewis	185	merchant	41	“
	y	Furey James	185	laborer	64	
	z	Furey Margaret—†	185	housewife	56	“
1104						
	A	Lavery Christina—†	187	“	31	“
	B	Lavery James	187	laborer	28	41 Mozart
	C	Shapiro Dora—†	187	at home	71	here
	D	Gordon Charles J	187	clerk	23	“
	E	Gordon Emanuel	187	“	48	“
	F	Gordon Sarah—†	187	housewife	45	“
	G*	Webber Anna—†	188	“	67	
	H	Cupples Margaret—†	188	wrapper	28	
	N	McEachern Donald A	192	packer	37	
	O*	McEachern Ethel M—†	192	housewife	36	“
	P	Flood Mary—†	192	“	39	
	R*	Madsen Emaline—†	192	at home	69	“
	S	Gordon Sarah—†	194	clerk	25	
	T	Gray Joseph	194	seaman	46	
	U	Gray Mary—†	194	housewife	48	“
	Y*	Roach Elizabeth M—†	214	“	40	
	Z	Roach John P	214	chauffeur	49	“
1105						
	A	Johnson Josephine—†	215	housekeeper	50	“
	B	McGowan Thomas	215	laborer	54	“
	C	Collier Anna—†	215	housewife	43	“
	D	Collier Frank	215	clerk	52	
	E	Collier John	215	U S N	22	
	F	Cosgrove Edward J	216	chauffeur	47	“
	G*	Cosgrove Helen F—†	216	housewife	44	“
	H	Cosgrove William J	216	U S A	24	
	K	Harris Olive—†	216	at home	67	
	M	Ball Clarence	217	laborer	55	
	O	Fallon John F	219	blueprinter	43	“
	P	Downey Annie M—†	219	housewife	56	“
	R	Downey Gertrude M—†	219	clerk	23	
	S	Downey Joseph F	219	“	58	
	V	Boogusch Edward	221	chauffeur	50	“
	W	Boogusch Elizabeth A—†	221	housewife	40	“
	X	Clark Henry, jr	221	chauffeur	24	“

Page.	Letter.	Full Name.	Residence, Jan. 1, 1943.	Occupation.	Supposed Age.	Reported Residence, Jan. 1, 1942. Street and Number.

Cabot Street—Continued

Page.	Letter.	Full Name.	Residence, Jan. 1, 1943.	Occupation.	Supposed Age.	Reported Residence, Jan. 1, 1942. Street and Number.
	Y	Clark Margaret J—†	221	housewife	24	here
	Z	Connor Louise—†	222	at home	80	“
1106						
	A	Hangis Loretta—†	222	housewife	53	“
	B	Hangis Louis	222	shoecutter	54	“
	C	Vincent Charles	222	rigger	37	2 Highland
	D	Vincent Ethel—†	222	housewife	34	39 Haskins
	E	Horsman Marion—†	223	at home	77	here
	F	Taylor Thomas E	223	printer	65	“
	G	Chase Frank H	223	chauffeur	27	142 George
	H	Chase Theresa—†	223	housewife	52	here
	K	Hines Bernard A	223	nurse	50	“
	N	Girten Charles S	235	upholsterer	43	“
	O	Girten Esther—†	235	mechanic	22	“
	P	Girten Lydia—†	235	housewife	42	“
	R	Kilduff Ellen V—†	235	“	57	
	S	Kilduff Helen M—†	235	clerk	39	
	T	Kilduff Joseph T	235	chauffeur	63	“
	U	Kilduff William L	235	fireman	37	
	V	Steward Dorothy—†	237	housekeeper	37	“
	W	Pothier Mary—†	237	“	45	“
	X	Glendenning Jennie—†	237	“	34	“
	Z	Dwyer Katherine L—†	243	housewife	36	1 Hayden ter
1107						
	A	Dwyer Thomas	243	cutter	39	1 “
	B	Albee Hattie—†	243	housewife	46	here
	C	Albee Percy	243	cigarmaker	47	66 Waltham
	D	Lego Florence C—†	243	housewife	40	Norwell
	N	Quigley Margaret—†	259	at home	73	here
	O	Cameron Carrie—†	259	housewife	61	“
	P	Cameron Daniel	259	carpenter	74	“
	R	Devine Sarah—†	259	at home	72	
	U	Rosner George	263	clerk	44	
	V	Carney George	263	fireman	44	
	W	Carney Mary—†	263	housewife	43	“
	X	Griffin Delia—†	263	clerk	46	
	Z	Mudge Charles R	265	laborer	40	
1108						
	A	Mudge William F	265	rodman	44	
	B	Mudge William F, jr	265	chauffeur	20	“
	C	DeGaust Alice—†	265	housewife	34	“

Page.	Letter.	Full Name.	Residence, Jan. 1, 1943.	Occupation.	Supposed Age.	Reported Residence, Jan. 1, 1942. Street and Number.
		Cabot Street—Continued				
	D	Brooks Anne A—†	271	housewife	63	here
	E	MacDonald Francis, jr	271	printer	20	"
	F	MacDonald Margaret—†	271	saleswoman	21	"
	G	MacDonald Mary—†	271	housewife	41	"
	H	MacDonald Theresa—†	271	clerk	24	
	L	Linehan Alice—†	273	housewife	30	"
	M	Linehan Michael J	273	U S N	29	
	N	Hurley Albert	273	mechanic	29	"
	O	Hurley Margaret—†	273	housewife	24	"
	P	Snow Herbert	273	telegrapher	52	"
	R	Snow Robert	273	clerk	22	
	S	Snow Ruth—†	273	housewife	44	"
	T	Winters Rose—†	283	"	62	
	U	Winters Theodore C	283	laborer	62	
	V	Fennell Julia—†	283	housewife	34	"
	W	Fennell Paul	283	laborer	35	
	X	Barry John	283	"	48	
	Y	Barrett Earl	285	painter	41	
	Z	Barrett Ethel—†	285	housewife	41	"
1109						
	A	Ganim Sigrid—†	285	"	48	
	B	Ganim Thomas	285	laborer	49	
	C	Kirstead Donald	285	U S A	42	
	D	Kirstead Ella—†	285	housewife	63	"
	E	Kirstead Samuel	285	baker	47	32 Linden Park
	F	Hooper Myrtle—†	287	housewife	32	36 Greenleaf
	G	Salmon Dorothy—†	287	"	31	here
	H	Glynn Anne—†	287	"	67	"
	K	Glynn Lillian—†	287	laundress	23	"
	L	Glynn Patrick J	287	laborer	37	
		Church Place				
	N	*Nolan Katherine—†	1	at home	76	136 Cabot
	O	Sears Elizabeth—†	1	"	67	21 Valentine
	P	Todaro Domenico	2	laborer	34	here
	R	Todaro Helen—†	2	housewife	29	"
	S	Claffey Jennie—†	2	"	31	"
	T	Claffey Joseph	2	cook	36	
	U	Novack Anna—†	3	housewife	29	"
	V	Novack George	3	diemaker	30	"

Page.	Letter.	Full Name.	Residence, Jan. 1, 1943.	Occupation.	Supposed Age.	Reported Residence, Jan. 1, 1942. Street and Number.

Church Place—Continued

	W	Pollastretti Carmine A	3	oiler	28	here
	X	Pollastretti Lorraine—†	3	housewife	22	"
	Y	Webber Della—†	4	"	59	"
	Z	Wontz Tekla—†	4	housekeeper	49	287 Cabot
1110						
	A	Martini Ellen—†	5	"	54	here
	B	Palmer Rilla—†	7	"	44	"
	C	Palmer William	7	U S N	22	"
	D	Roger Eleanor—†	7	clerk	21	
	M	Main Harold D	10	painter	48	
	N	Maine Mary—†	10	housewife	42	"
	O	Golden Annie—†	10	housekeeper	60	"
	P	*Osaskaw Ceoxida—†	10	"	60	"
	R	Cook James	12	laborer	55	
	S	Cook Mary—†	12	housewife	55	"
	T	Hynes John	12	laborer	42	52 Elmwood
	U	Hynes Mary—†	12	housewife	31	52 "

1111 Columbus Avenue

	A	Joyce Mary—†	967	at home	80	5 Pratt ct
	B	Kierstead Mary—†	967	laundress	62	here
	C	Kierstead Russell	967	laborer	45	"
	D	Ferriera Elizabeth—†	967	housewife	65	5 Paris pl
	F	Roseman Frances—†	969	"	57	here
	G	Roseman John E	969	clergyman	71	"
	H	Kelley Mary A—†	969	housewife	69	"
	K	Kelley Michael J	969	retired	67	
	M	Bussey George E	971	"	77	
	N	Bussey Lula M—†	971	housewife	65	"
	O	Linskey Mary—†	971	housekeeper	66	"
	P	Kinnehan Ellen—†	971	housewife	39	"
	R	Kinnehan George	971	U S A	21	
	S	Stemmler Amelia—†	973	housewife	45	"
	T	Stemmler Charles	973	laborer	48	
	U	Stemmler Charles, jr	973	U S A	22	
	V	Stemmler Mildred—†	973	clerk	20	
	W	Graham Arthur J	975	laborer	54	
	X	Graham Catherine K—†	975	housewife	46	"
	Y	Graham Dorothy—†	975	clerk	20	"
	Z	Graham Eleanor—†	975	"	24	

Page.	Letter.	Full Name.	Residence, Jan. 1, 1943.	Occupation.	Supposed Age.	Reported Residence, Jan. 1, 1942. Street and Number.

1112 Columbus Avenue—Continued

Page.	Letter.	Full Name.	Residence, Jan. 1, 1943.	Occupation.	Supposed Age.	Reported Residence, Jan. 1, 1942. Street and Number.
1112	A	Graham Ruth—†	975	clerk	22	here
	C	Callanan Joseph L	979	U S A	43	Vermont
	D	Callanan Katherine—†	979	housewife	29	here
	E	Cass Frank	979	laborer	58	"
	F	Donahue Catherine—†	979	housekeeper	65	"
	G	St Lawrence Agnes—†	981	housewife	34	"
	H	St Lawrence Edward	981	laborer	36	
	L	Nolan Joseph	984	chauffeur	42	"
	M	Nolan Marie—†	984	housewife	38	"
	N	Dinsmore Juanita—†	984	"	27	
	O	Dinsmore Theodore	984	laborer	30	
	V	Mills Evelyn—†	987	housekeeper	31	"
	X	Tobin Joseph P	988	laborer	47	"
	Y	Tobin Nellie—†	988	housewife	61	"
	Z	Reagan Daniel J	988	retired	76	
1113	A	*Reagan Hannah—†	988	housewife	84	"
	B	Reagan James A	988	chauffeur	46	"
	C	Fuller Clarence E	989	carpenter	70	"
	D	Royce John E	989	mechanic	34	23 Elmwood
	E	Royce Lulu—†	989	housewife	29	23 "
	F	Cleary Elaine—†	989	"	35	here
	G	Cleary Eugene F	989	chauffeur	36	"
	K	Wallace Jessie—†	991	housewife	60	"
	L	Wallace Joseph H	991	janitor	50	993 Tremont
	N	Cullen Henry J	991	foreman	47	371 Col av
	O	Cullen Mary C—†	991	housewife	38	371 "
	P	White Agnes E—†	992	"	31	here
	R	White Edward S	992	U S M C	33	"
	S	Volz Annie R—†	992	housewife	47	1275 Col av
	T	Volz James H	992	chauffeur	48	1275 "

1114 Dallas Place

Page.	Letter.	Full Name.	Residence, Jan. 1, 1943.	Occupation.	Supposed Age.	Reported Residence, Jan. 1, 1942. Street and Number.
1114	G	Wisnevsky Helen—†	1	stenographer	20	here
	H	Wisnevsky Ludmilla—†	1	at home	59	"
	K	Wisnevsky Richard	1	retired	68	"
	L	Portras Mathew	2	laborer	62	
	M	Costello Theresa—†	3	stenographer	45	"
	O	McDonald Margaret—†	6	at home	72	"

Page.	Letter.	Full Name.	Residence, Jan. 1, 1943.	Occupation.	Supposed Age.	Reported Residence, Jan. 1, 1942. Street and Number.

Dallas Place—Continued

Page.	Letter.	Full Name.	Residence, Jan. 1, 1943.	Occupation.	Supposed Age.	Reported Residence, Jan. 1, 1942. Street and Number.
	R	*Tausevich Earl	7	janitor	57	here
	S	Tausevich Elizabeth—†	7	at home	54	"
	T	Clark Dorothy—†	9	laundress	20	"
	U	Clark Henry C	9	clerk	51	
	V	Clark Mary—†	9	"	43	
	W	Clark Robert E	9	operator	22	"

Downing Street

Page.	Letter.	Full Name.	Residence, Jan. 1, 1943.	Occupation.	Supposed Age.	Reported Residence, Jan. 1, 1942. Street and Number.
	X	Palmieri Catherine—†	10	at home	41	Vermont
	Y	*Barry John	10	laborer	44	here
	Z	Barry Mary A—†	10	at home	44	"
1115						
	A	Kilroy John	20	laborer	37	
	B	Kilroy Sarah—†	20	domestic	55	"
	C	Watson Mary A—†	20	at home	77	
	D	Watson Patrick J	20	retired	79	
	E	Maxwell Julia M—†	20	at home	54	
	F	Maxwell William L	20	laborer	60	

Hampshire Street

Page.	Letter.	Full Name.	Residence, Jan. 1, 1943.	Occupation.	Supposed Age.	Reported Residence, Jan. 1, 1942. Street and Number.
	G	West Edward	5	U S A	26	here
	H	West Joseph E	5	sexton	51	"
	K	West Margaret—†	5	saleswoman	21	"
	L	West Olga A—†	5	housewife	47	"
	M	West Paul J	5	student	23	
	O	*Sullivan Hannah—†	8	at home	39	
	S	Lindberg Irene—†	10	"	22	
	T	Lindberg Ossian	10	laborer	25	
	V	Fagan Mary—†	12	at home	78	
	W	Henderson Alexander	18	chef	55	
	X	Henderson Ora—†	18	housewife	50	"
	Y	Gray Elnore—†	18	at home	77	"
	Z	Frazer Mary—†	18	waitress	25	Arlington
1116						
	A	McCabe Annie—†	20	housewife	60	22 Hampshire
	B	*McCabe Edward	20	retired	63	22 "
	C	Somerville Mamie—†	20	at home	50	here
	D	Brown Mattie S—†	20	domestic	29	"
	H	Kalinoski Mary—†	28	housewife	52	"
	K	Kalinoski Stanley	28	machinist	50	"

Page.	Letter.	Full Name.	Residence, Jan. 1, 1943.	Occupation.	Supposed Age.	Reported Residence, Jan. 1, 1942. Street and Number.

Haskins Street

	R	Griffin Margaret—†	9	housekeeper	36	here
	S	Falcetta Inez S—†	9	hairdresser	30	"
	T	Roach Ethelinda—†	9	housewife	53	"
	U	Roach Horace	9	U S A	22	
	V	Roach James	9	operator	55	"
	W	Walton Jerry	11	"	28	1 Trotter ct
	X	Walton Mary—†	11	housewife	33	1 "
	Y	Victor Christina—†	11	"	41	here
	Z	Victor Gustave	11	laborer	54	"
1117						
	A	Truell Joseph	11	U S A	28	
	B	Waterman Annie—†	11	housewife	49	"
	C	Waterman William	11	laborer	35	
	E	Irish Lillian—†	15	housewife	48	"
	F	Irish William	15	janitor	47	
	G	Queely Ann—†	15	housewife	44	"
	H	Queely Samuel W	15	laborer	45	
	K	Patterson Grace—†	17	housewife	26	"
	L	Patterson Wilfred	17	metalworker	28	"
	M	Hayes Theresa—†	17	housekeeper	37	"
	N	Jennings Christine—†	17	clerk	29	"
	O	Plett Minnie H—†	17	housewife	62	"
	P	Plett Wallace	17	clerk	20	
	R	Small Muriel—†	17	"	22	"
	S	Finch Ruth—†	19	housewife	29	29 E Lenox
	T	Finch William	19	molder	29	29 "
	U	Moore Mary L—†	19	laundress	26	29 "
	V	*Duguid Marie—†	19	housewife	41	144 Ruggles
	W	*Duguid Samuel	19	laborer	49	144 "
	X	Mapp George D	19	U S A	21	144 "
	Y	*Goodrich Allen F	19	porter	49	here
	Z	Goodrich Elmer	19	student	22	"
1118						
	A	*Goodrich Stella—†	19	housewife	44	"
	B	Platt Elliot	21	chauffeur	23	58 Sterling
	C	Platt Ethel—†	21	housewife	23	58 "
	D	Lewis Albert	21	clerk	33	here
	E	Lewis Minnie—†	21	housewife	27	"
	F	*Lewis Mary J—†	21	"	46	"
	G	Lewis Samuel A	21	laborer	48	
	H	Roberts Bertha—†	23	housewife	32	"

Page.	Letter.	Full Name.	Residence, Jan. 1, 1943.	Occupation.	Supposed Age.	Reported Residence, Jan. 1, 1942. Street and Number.

Haskins Street—Continued

	K	Roberts James	23	attendant	34	here
	L	Banks Lawrence H	23	attorney	45	"
	M	Stubbs Henry L	23	pipefitter	34	Virginia
	N	Stubbs Virginia—†	23	operator	31	"
	P	*Munro Charles G	35	laborer	57	here
	R	Munro Ora E—†	35	housewife	73	"
	S	Reynolds Anna J—†	35	housekeeper	69	"
	T	Fraser Helen M—†	35	housewife	27	"
	U	Fraser William A	35	chauffeur	39	"
	V	Brosnahan George A	35	machinist	58	"
	W	Doyle Anna E—†	35	at home	63	
	X	Doyle Catherine A—†	35	"	75	
	Y	Doyle Ellen M—†	35	housewife	71	"
	X	*Boroian Alma—†	35	housekeeper	29	1117 Tremont
1119						
	A	*Boroian Samuel	35	laborer	49	1117 "
	B	*Ford Catherine—†	35	housekeeper	45	20 Lansing
	D	Hanson Betty—†	37	"	24	13 Seneca
	E	Dudley Annie—†	37	"	53	here
	F	Malk John	37	machinist	71	"
	G	Holt William	37	chef	38	"
	H	Fraser George B	37	painter	49	35 Haskins
	K	Prinz Gustav	39	laborer	69	here
	M	Barbrick Nora—†	39	at home	70	"
	N	*Nalbandian Margaret—†	39	"	70	"
	P	Polykonis Adam	39	shoemaker	45	"
	R	Myrick Bishop	41	laborer	38	
	S	Myrick Celestina—†	41	teacher	28	
	T	Myrick Laura E—†	41	housewife	67	"
	U	Lomax Georgie—†	43	housekeeper	65	2 Williams ter
	V	Roberts Andrew	43	mattressmaker	25	S Carolina
	W	Roberts Pinky—†	43	housewife	30	"
	X	O'Brien Agnes V—†	45	"	61	here
	Y	O'Brien James E	45	laborer	60	"
	Z	Corner Annie—†	45	housewife	73	"
1120						
	A	Corner William N	45	janitor	61	"
	B	Diggs Alfred C	47	packer	23	
	C	Doles Clara L—†	47	clerk	26	
	D	O'Sullivan Annie—†	49	housewife	37	"
	E	O'Sullivan John P	49	boilermaker	37	"

Page.	Letter.	FULL NAME.	Residence, Jan. 1, 1943.	Occupation.	Supposed Age.	Reported Residence, Jan. 1, 1942. Street and Number.

Haskins Street—Continued

	F	Schwartz Hyman	51	salesman	31	here
	G	Schwartz Sarah—†	51	seamstress	24	"
	H	Flattish Margaret—†	53	housekeeper	65	29 Kent

Lamont Street

	K	Barnett Mabel—†	8	housewife	37	here
	L	Barnett Russell	8	laborer	40	"
	M	Doyle Henrietta—†	8	housewife	56	"
	N	Doyle Norma—†	8	W A A C	21	"
	O	Herd Kenneth W	8	undertaker	37	"
	P	Herd Louise—†	8	housewife	26	"
	R	Sullivan Charles	8	U S A	23	
	S	Sullivan Marion—†	8	domestic	49	"
	T	Sullivan Marion—†	8	clerk	21	
	U	Kreckler Catherine—†	9	"	21	
	V	Kreckler Francis	9	painter	51	
	W	Kreckler Francis, jr	9	U S A	21	
	X	Kreckler Martha—†	9	clerk	22	
	Y	Kenney Anne—†	9	housewife	60	"
	Z	Kenney Joseph	9	mechanic	32	"
1121						
	A	Tatroult Ella—†	9	housewife	41	"
	B	Tatroult Laurier	9	chef	37	
	D	Slavin James L	12	retired	67	"
	E	*Romano Frank	12	laborer	44	1352 Tremont
	F	*Romano Mary—†	12	housewife	40	1352 "
	G	Blanchard Sarah V—†	12	"	53	here
	H	Durham James E	12	U S N	28	"
	K	Durham Rita—†	12	housewife	22	"
	L	Melinsky Abraham	13	U S N	29	
	M	Melinsky Gidia	13	orderly	34	"
	N	Melinsky Jennie—†	13	housewife	56	"
	O	Flynn Annie—†	13	weaver	48	
	P	Ryan Lawrence	13	laborer	28	
	R	Hannon Alice—†	13	stenographer	35	"
	S	*Hannon Mary—†	13	housewife	74	"
	T	Hannon Walter	13	U S A	38	
	U	Vierkant Charles	14	janitor	37	
	V	Vierkant Julia—†	14	housewife	65	"
	W	Day Earl	14	machinist	39	"

Page.	Letter.	Full Name.	Residence, Jan. 1, 1943.	Occupation.	Supposed Age.	Reported Residence, Jan. 1, 1942. Street and Number.

Lamont Street—Continued

	X	Day Etta—†	14	housewife	32	here
	Y	Foley Lillian—†	14	"	40	8 Church pl
	Z	Foley Patrick	14	laborer	47	8 "
		1122				
	A	Clark Charles	16	mechanic	28	here
	B	Clark Rita—†	16	housewife	24	"
	C	Franklin Harold T	16	bartender	28	"
	D	Franklin Hilda—†	16	housewife	30	"
	E	*Garnett Theora—†	16	"	27	29 Lambert
	F	*Garnett William	16	lithographer	26	29 "
	G	Fallon Margaret E—†	19	at home	76	here
	K	Early Delia—†	19	housewife	70	"
	L	Earley John F	19	laborer	43	"
	M	Golden John F	19	U S A	24	
	N	Hagelstein Theresa—†	21	housewife	60	"
	O	Bieler Julia—†	21	"	42	
	P	Bieler Leo	21	machinist	45	"
	R	Minkle Anna G—†	21	housewife	43	"
	S	Minkle Harry	21	printer	45	
	T	Campbell Margaret—†	24	housekeeper	68	"
	V	Anagnostou Anna—†	28	stitcher	31	"
	W	Anagnostou Basilion	28	laborer	35	
	X	Kilroy Sarah—†	28	bookkeeper	33	"
	Y	Schubert Mary—†	28	housewife	28	"
	Z	Schubert William	28	meat smoker	32	"
		1123				
	A	Deveney Elizabeth—†	35	at home	86	
	B	Deveney Thomas	35	chauffeur	59	"
	C	Peterson John	35	painter	36	
	D	Healey Annie—†	35	domestic	50	"
	E	Healey Margaret—†	35	clerk	25	
	F	Kelley Esther—†	35	housewife	52	"
	G	Kelley Gilbert W	35	U S A	23	
	H	Kelley James W	35	retired	66	
	K	*Fancey Fred	35	chauffeur	44	"
	L	Fancey Gladys—†	35	housewife	43	"
	M	Cleary Ann—†	36	"	28	"
	N	Cleary Joseph	36	laborer	32	
	O	Ruzzano Alice—†	36	housewife	27	"
	P	Ruzzano Frank	36	machinist	31	"
	R	Doyle Daniel	36	laborer	34	

Page.	Letter.	Full Name.	Residence, Jan. 1, 1943.	Occupation.	Supposed Age.	Reported Residence, Jan. 1, 1942. Street and Number.
		Lamont Street—Continued				
	S	Doyle Margaret—†	36	housewife	29	here
	T	Noble Frank	37	clerk	45	"
	U	Noble Mary—†	37	housewife	42	"
	V	Beardsley Bessie—†	37	"	38	
	W	Beardsley George	37	sexton	42	
	X	Gary Edward	37	laborer	38	
	Y	Gary Mary—†	37	housewife	38	"
	Z	Cerone Andrea	38	shoemaker	55	"
1124						
	A	Cerone Marion—†	38	housewife	44	"
	B	Moschos George	38	cook	46	103 Vernon
	C	Moschos Velma—†	38	housewife	42	103 "
	D	*McCarthy Daniel	38	retired	68	242 Cabot
	E	McCarthy John	38	U S A	28	242 "
	F	McCarthy Margaret—†	38	baker	22	242 "
	G	Donnelly James C	39	laborer	48	here
	H	Donnelly John J	39	chauffeur	51	"
	K	Donnelly Mary—†	39	domestic	46	"
	L	Sullivan Elizabeth A—†	39	at home	22	
	M	Sullivan Helena—†	39	housewife	56	"
	N	Sullivan Richard J	39	shipper	33	"
	O	Burns Dorothy—†	39	stitcher	21	11 Malbon pl
	P	Burns Evelyn—†	39	housewife	40	11 "
	R	Slattery Edward	40	retired	72	746 Parker
	S	Slattery Mary—†	40	housewife	68	746 "
	T	Carchire Barnham	40	U S A	24	here
	U	Carchire Mary—†	40	stenographer	22	"
	V	Lennell Frank	40	laborer	38	"
	W	Lennell Mary A—†	40	housewife	68	"
	X	Lennell Nelson E	40	retired	73	"
	Y	McCarthy Delia—†	40	domestic	25	243 Cabot
	Z	McCarthy Thomas M	40	mechanic	26	243 "
1125		**Linden Avenue**				
	A	Heid Dorothy—†	2	at home	42	here
	B	*Beaulieu Margaret—†	2	"	39	"
	C	*Beaulieu Oliver A	2	shoemaker	46	"
	D	Cain Farrell	2	U S A	26	67 E Brookline
	E	Page Florence—†	2	at home	41	here
	F	Page John	2	laborer	44	"

Linden Avenue—Continued

Page.	Letter.	Full Name.	Residence, Jan. 1, 1943.	Occupation.	Supposed Age.	Reported Residence, Jan. 1, 1942. Street and Number.
	G	Blaney Henry J	4	U S A	24	here
	H	*Blaney John	4	retired	59	"
	K	Blaney Rita A—†	4	clerk	20	"
	L	Blaney Rosaline H—†	4	"	22	
	M	Blaney Rosetta—†	4	at home	55	"
	N	Dunn Annie—†	4	"	65	109 Vernon
	O	Dunn Donald F	4	U S A	30	109 "
	P	Dunn Francis O	4	machinist	52	109 "
	R	Furkart Bessie—†	4	housewife	35	255 Eustis
	S	Furkart Robert	4	mechanic	40	255 "

Linden Park Street

Page.	Letter.	Full Name.	Residence, Jan. 1, 1943.	Occupation.	Supposed Age.	Reported Residence, Jan. 1, 1942. Street and Number.
	U	Duffley Margaret E—†	23	housewife	47	here
	V	Ferreira Caroline V—†	23	housekeeper	45	"
	W	Carter Abbie T—†	23	housewife	50	"
	X	Carter John J	23	operator	46	"
	Y	Higgins James	25	pipefitter	56	"
	Z	Higgins Mary V—†	25	housewife	59	"
1126	A	Champ Helen A—†	25	"	45	
	B	O'Connell John J	25	finisher	47	
	C	*O'Connell Josephine—†	25	housewife	76	"
	D	Hall Mary—†	27	"	29	
	E	Hall Robert	27	U S A	30	
	F	Eckert Katherine—†	27	housewife	32	"
	G	Lynch Catherine K—†	27	"	66	
	H	Lynch Samuel E	27	gilder	62	
	K	Glynn Anna A—†	27	housewife	33	"
	L	Glynn Thomas H	27	laborer	39	
	M	Carter Agnes—†	29	attendant	26	"
	N	Carter George	29	laborer	48	
	O	Richards Grace—†	29	housewife	51	"
	P	Bolton Agnes M—†	29	housekeeper	49	18 Burnett
	R	Bolton Alice M—†	29	housewife	28	18 "
	S	Bolton Granville B	29	carpenter	25	18 "
	T	Duffey Alfred E	29	guard	30	78 Vernon
	U	Duffey Loretta P—†	29	housewife	27	78 "
	V	Glynn Daniel	31	operator	40	10 Linden Park
	W	Glynn Dennis P	31	clerk	37	10 "
	X	Glynn Sophie P—†	31	housewife	31	10 "

Page.	Letter.	FULL NAME.	Residence, Jan. 1, 1943.	Occupation.	Supposed Age.	Reported Residence, Jan. 1, 1942. Street and Number.

Linden Park Street—Continued

	Y	Rand Louis	31	draftsman	38	10 Linden Park
	Z	Ferguson William	31	clerk	43	10 "
1127						
	A	Ryan Mary—†	33	at home	65	here
	B	Leppert Vera E—†	37	housewife	30	521 Mass av
	C	Leppert Woodrow	37	candymaker	30	521 "
	D	McNulty Emma M—†	37	housewife	25	here
	E	McNulty William	37	clerk	27	"
	F	Wohlgemuth Frank B	37	operator	53	"
	G	Wohlgemuth Raymond T	37	roofer	20	"
	H	Tice Grant G	39	shipper	40	
	K	Tice Mae E—†	39	housewife	39	"
	L	Dolan John	39	ironworker	52	"
	M	Reilly Helen—†	39	housewife	22	"
	N	Reilly John	39	ironworker	20	"
	O	Reilly Mildred—†	39	housewife	42	"
	P	Reilly William	39	U S A	23	
	R	Leahy John	39	retired	76	
	S	Thomas Margaret—†	39	housewife	39	"
	T	Lapio Mary—†	41	"	43	38 Wait
	U	Lapio Rocco	41	mechanic	36	38 "
	V	Zapponi John	41	laborer	62	here
	W	Zapponi Marguerita—†	41	housewife	60	"
	Y	*Casale Charles	43	laborer	52	"
	Z	Kolbe Helena—†	43	housewife	44	"
1128						
	A	Kolbe Ursula—†	43	stenographer	22	"
	B	Kolbe Walter	43	operator	50	"
	C	Rembetsy Bessie—†	43	housewife	42	"
	D	Rembetsy George	43	U S A	24	
	E	Rembetsy Helen—†	43	clerk	21	
	F	Rembetsy Peter	43	operator	23	
	G	Mangan Helen J—†	43	maid	59	"
	H	Manning Margaret K—†	43	clerk	38	
	K	McNulty Mary A—†	43	housewife	65	"
	L	McNulty William J	43	laborer	66	
	M	Sullivan Julia F—†	45	housewife	35	"
	N	Sullivan Peter F	45	foreman	38	"
	O	Tutunjian Manuel	45	manager	49	"
	P	Tutunjian Rose—†	45	housewife	47	"

Page.	Letter.	FULL NAME.	Residence, Jan. 1, 1943.	Occupation.	Supposed Age.	Reported Residence, Jan. 1, 1942. Street and Number.

Linden Park Street—Continued

Page.	Letter.	FULL NAME.	Residence, Jan. 1, 1943.	Occupation.	Supposed Age.	Reported Residence, Jan. 1, 1942. Street and Number.
	R	Goode Lawrence	45	U S M C	23	here
	S	Goode Mary—†	45	housewife	45	"
	T	Goode William	45	clerk	25	"
	V	Rallis Speros	47	baker	57	
	W	Rallis Victoria—†	47	housewife	46	"
	X	Samaras Stavroula—†	47	"	40	"
	Y	Noonan Hazel—†	49	"	47	51 Linden Park
	Z	Noonan John	49	laborer	55	51 "
1129						
	A	Alvarez Joseph A	49	U S A	24	3 Gay
	B	Alvarez Mary—†	49	laundryworker	24	here
	C	Duffey John	49	watchman	65	"
	D	Duffey Mary—†	49	housewife	65	"
	E	Noun James	49	U S A	20	
	F	Noun Jennie—†	49	housewife	42	"
	G	Noun Pandy	49	laborer	47	
	K	Lannaville Mary E—†	51	housewife	53	"
	L	Lannaville Oliver N	51	roofer	64	
	M	Gormley Catherine M—†	51	at home	70	
	N	Gormley Francis H	51	clerk	33	
	O	Gormley James F	51	"	38	
	P	Gormley Thomas M	51	U S A	28	"
	R	Martonelli Angelina—†	53	housewife	33	275 Sumner
	S	Broom Jennie—†	53	"	32	556 Tremont
	T	Broom Leroy	53	U S C G	39	556 "
	U	Daw Viola—†	53	tel operator	55	Cambridge
	V	Smolinsky Marion—†	63	housewife	27	4 St Francis de Sales
	W	Smolinsky Stephen	63	baker	30	4 "
	X	Slavin Ann—†	63	housekeeper	37	here
	Z	Tracey Helen—†	65	clerk	26	"
1130						
	A	Tracey Nora—†	65	housewife	56	"
	B	Fleming Bernice—†	65	"	30	
	C	Fleming Robert A	65	operator	31	"
	E	Battalio Inez—†	67	"	29	"
	F	Kelley John J	67	"	47	
	G	Kelley Marion V—†	67	housewife	41	"
	H	Capuzzo Arthur	67	U S A	22	
	K	Capuzzo Celia—†	67	millhand	20	"
	L*	Capuzzo Mary—†	67	at home	54	

Page.	Letter.	FULL NAME.	Residence, Jan. 1, 1943.	Occupation.	Supposed Age.	Reported Residence, Jan. 1, 1942. Street and Number.

Linden Park Street—Continued

	M	Capuzzo Patrick	67	salesman	24	here
	N	Stephenson John	69	retired	72	"
	P	Carr Catherine—†	69	housekeeper	50	"

Motley Street

	R	Fowler George A	1	retired	70	here
	S	Rosapane Modestino	1	"	63	"
	U	*Driscoll Ellen—†	3	housewife	78	"
	V	*Driscoll James	3	laborer	65	
	X	Beatty Charles B	3	doorman	47	"
	Y	Beatty Emily F—†	3	at home	43	"
	Z	Wind Harry N	5	shipper	35	"
1131						
	A	Wind Wilhelmina—†	5	at home	35	
	B	Godin Blanche—†	5	"	42	
	C	Godin David	5	U S A	21	
	D	Godin Frank	5	janitor	47	
	E	Berkeley Johanna—†	5	at home	44	
	F	Murphy Daniel F	5	U S A	45	
	G	*Murphy Matthew F	5	retired	75	
	H	Walsh Josephine—†	5	at home	21	

Ruggles Street

	U	*Simmion Samuel	133	cobbler	64	here
1132						
	L	Miles Charlotte—†	144	at home	39	
	M	Miles Dorothy—†	144	messenger	20	"
	N	*Nauwinger Frank	144	painter	62	
	O	*Nauwinger Nora—†	144	housewife	43	"
1133						
	B	Hare Christina—†	214	clerk	65	
	C	Walsh Annie—†	214	at home	74	
	D	Walsh Ella J—†	214	waitress	42	"
	E	Walsh Luke J	214	retired	76	
	F	Brown Richard P	214	U S A	29	
	G	Brown Thelma M—†	214	saleswoman	23	"
	H	Garvey Annie F—†	214	at home	72	"
	K	Garvey George H	214	retired	74	
	L	Sennott Mary F—†	214	nurse	50	

Page.	Letter.	FULL NAME.	Residence, Jan. 1, 1943.	Occupation.	Supposed Age.	Reported Residence, Jan. 1, 1942. Street and Number.

Ruggles Street—Continued

	M	O'Neil Annie L—†	216	at home	43	here
	N	O'Neil Robert L	216	conductor	45	"
	O	McGreevey Annie E—†	216	at home	74	"
	P	McGreevey Michael T	216	retired	77	

Sumner Place

	V	Gordon Maxwell N	2	U S A	25	here
	W	Gordon Robert	2	storekeeper	47	"
	X	Gordon Sarah—†	2	housewife	45	"
	Y	Coyne Margaret E—†	2	housekeeper	41	"
	Z	Drury Anna F—†	2	secretary	37	"
1134						
	A	Drury Catherine—†	2	at home	80	
	B	Campbell Francis F	2	U S A	27	
	C	Campbell Grace C—†	2	housewife	50	"
	D	Campbell Helen P—†	2	clerk	22	
	E	Brewster Bridget T—†	3	housewife	45	"
	F	Brewster John F	3	laborer	46	
	G	Chenette Alice B—†	3	housewife	58	"
	H	Chenette Francis T	3	U S N	22	
	K	Chenette Genevieve—†	3	stenographer	30	"
	L	Chenette John F	3	U S N	24	"
	M	Chenette Louis L	3	electrician	57	"
	N	Chenette Louis L, jr	3	U S N	26	
	O	Merrithew Harry	4	letter carrier	53	"
	P	Parker Anna—†	4	housewife	57	"
	R	Parker Chester T	4	foundryman	55	"
	S	Parker Henry E	4	"	33	
	T	McCarthy Austin	4	laborer	35	
	U	McCarthy Sophia—†	4	laundryworker	33	"
	V	Lombardi Fortunato	4½	laborer	46	2 Ward
	W	Lombardi Jean—†	4½	housewife	37	2 "
	X	Warren Agnes T—†	4½	"	25	here
	Y	Warren Frank E	4½	operator	25	"
	Z	Tonaszuck Leocadia O—†	4½	housewife	26	"
1135						
	A	Tonaszuck Walter T	4½	shipper	26	
	B	Conroy Jean C—†	5	housewife	35	"
	C	Conroy William C	5	chauffeur	33	"
	D	Early Bernard T	5	plumber	40	"

Page.	Letter.	Full Name.	Residence, Jan. 1, 1943.	Occupation.	Supposed Age.	Reported Residence, Jan. 1, 1942. Street and Number.

Sumner Place—Continued

Page.	Letter.	Full Name.	Residence, Jan. 1, 1943.	Occupation.	Supposed Age.	Reported Residence, Jan. 1, 1942. Street and Number.
	E	Early Lillian R—†	5	housewife	38	here
	F	MacKenzie Mertice E—†	6	housekeeper	38	"
	G	Wallace A May—†	6	"	32	15 Centre
	H	Dority Elizabeth L—†	6A	manager	22	here
	K	Wedgewood Roswell G	6A	welder	46	"
	L	Wedgewood Sarah K—†	6A	housewife	49	"
	M	McCluskey Catherine F—†	6A	"	40	
	N	McCluskey Charles E	6A	fireman	44	"
	O	Kenney John T	7	U S A	34	12 Hawthorne
	P	Kenney Laura H—†	7	housewife	34	12 "
	R	MacLeod Catherine R—†	7	"	36	here
	S	Kirby Margaret M—†	8	"	39	1223 Tremont
	T	Kirby William M	8	rigger	44	1223 "
	U	Burnham Astrid D—†	8	housekeeper	46	here
	V	Burnham Phyllis V—†	8	wrapper	21	"
	W	Burnham Russell O	8	U S N	22	"
	X	Foley Dorothea M—†	8A	secretary	26	"
	Y	Foley John A	8A	mechanic	50	"
	Z	Foley Mary D—†	8A	housewife	48	"
1136						
	A	Schnetzer Benjamin	9	clerk	59	
	B	Schnetzer Benjamin G	9	U S N	21	
	C	Schnetzer Bertram M	9	pressman	30	"
	D	Schnetzer Margaret G—†	9	housewife	48	"
	E	Schnetzer Thomas A	9	U S A	23	
	F	Norton Elizabeth A—†	10	secretary	44	"

Terry Street

Page.	Letter.	Full Name.	Residence, Jan. 1, 1943.	Occupation.	Supposed Age.	Reported Residence, Jan. 1, 1942. Street and Number.
	G	Schoen Charles	2	laborer	43	66 Weston
	H	Schoen Edwina—†	2	housewife	32	66 "
	K	Allen John	2	chauffeur	57	47 St Botolph
	L	Connors Mary—†	2	housewife	38	1273 Tremont
	M	Connors William L	2	chauffeur	39	1273 "
	N	Vasco Frank	4	machinist	33	26 Pompeii
	O*	Vasco Rita—†	4	housewife	25	26 "
	P	Young Effie—†	4	"	27	694 Tremont
	R	Young Ralph	4	pipefitter	37	694 "
	S	Chabot Hermeline—†	4	housewife	35	59 Whittier
	T	Chabot Normand P	4	painter	44	59 "
	U	Magee Annie—†	6	housewife	53	here

Page.	Letter.	Full Name.	Residence, Jan. 1, 1943.	Occupation.	Supposed Age.	Reported Residence, Jan. 1, 1942. Street and Number.

Terry Street—Continued

Page.	Letter.	Full Name.	Residence, Jan. 1, 1943.	Occupation.	Supposed Age.	Reported Residence, Jan. 1, 1942. Street and Number.
	V	Magee Percival F		lineman	55	here
	W	Brady John J		painter	68	"
	X	Brady Katherine—†		housewife	61	"
	Y	Brady Mary F—†		at home	73	"
	Z	Flynn Joseph F	6	U S A	42	

1137 Tremont Street

Page.	Letter.	Full Name.	Residence, Jan. 1, 1943.	Occupation.	Supposed Age.	Reported Residence, Jan. 1, 1942. Street and Number.
	S	Gainer Charles D	1177A	carpenter	53	New Bedford
	T	Kelly Katherine—†	1177A	factoryhand	46	here
	U	Kelly William	1177A	guard	26	"
	V	Long Emma—†	1177A	at home	69	137 Vernon
	W	Reynolds Leroy	1177A	factoryhand	42	here
	X	Reynolds Violet—†	1177A	housewife	39	"
	Y	Benner Clifford	1177A	factoryhand	26	"
	Z	Benner Marie—†	1177A	housewife	21	"
1138						
	A	McDonald James	1177A	clerk	67	
	B	Pelleran Beatrice—†	1177A	factoryhand	65	"
	C	Cauthier Beatrice—†	1177A	housewife	21	987 Col av
	D	Cauthier Phillip	1177A	factoryhand	24	987 "
	E	Ferber Ellen—†	1177A	housewife	58	here
	F	Ferber Michael	1177A	clerk	56	"
	G	Kinahan Catherine—†	1177A	housewife	23	28 Gurney
	H	Kinahan James	1177A	laborer	23	24 Halleck
	K	Carlson Christine—†	1177A	at home	42	here
	L	Smith Blanche—†	1177A	"	38	"
	O	Ford Bessie—†	1180	housewife	34	"
	P	Ford Jay	1180	porter	36	
	R	Waller Betty—†	1180	housewife	31	"
	S	Waller Isaac	1180	cleanser	35	
	T	Perry Eleanor—†	1180	housekeeper	46	"
	U	White Gladys—†	1180	clerk	64	"
	V	White Hattie—†	1180	"	28	
	W	Williams Bernice—†	1180	housewife	44	"
	X	Williams Hamilton	1180	clerk	64	
	Y	Montgomery Ruth—†	1180	housekeeper	47	"
	Z	Antonia Eunice M—†	1180	housewife	50	"
1139						
	A	Antonia Leon	1180	clerk	29	
	C	Matthews George	1182	librarian	73	

Page.	Letter.	Full Name.	Residence, Jan. 1, 1943.	Occupation.	Supposed Age.	Reported Residence, Jan. 1, 1942. Street and Number.

Tremont Street—Continued

Page.	Letter.	Full Name.	Residence, Jan. 1, 1943.	Occupation.	Supposed Age.	Reported Residence, Jan. 1, 1942. Street and Number.
	D	Matthews Walter	1182	laborer	26	here
	E	Reavis Anna—†	1182	housewife	23	"
	F	Brown Penny—†	1182	housekeeper	37	8 Hubert
	G	Walker David	1182	laborer	71	8 "
	H	Thiebault Desire E	1182	janitor	63	here
	L	Saunders Clara L—†	1182	stitcher	61	37 Tremlett
	M	Jones Inez M—†	1182	housewife	41	here
	N	Jones John	1182	waiter	39	"
	O	Dillon Lemuel	1182	laborer	55	"
	P	Gregory Carrie—†	1182	housekeeper	48	"
	S	Katsis Aspice—†	1183	housewife	54	"
	T	Katsis Theodus	1183	laborer	65	"
	U	Martinowski John	1183	retired	63	
	V	*Martinowski Pauline—†	1183	housewife	59	"
	W	*Auciello Anna—†	1183	"	48	
	X	*Auciello Phillip	1183	retired	77	
	Y	Auciello Phillip, jr	1183	U S A	25	"
	Z	Auciello Ralph	1183	chauffeur	48	"
1140						
	A	*Auciello Sarah—†	1183	at home	76	
	B	Foley Annamae—†	1183	saleswoman	33	"
	C	LoCore Josephine—†	1183	stenographer	26	"
	D	Lorusso John	1183	laborer	51	"
	E	Lorusso Phyllis—†	1183	operator	22	"
	L	Randall Burton E	1186½	watchman	63	"
	M	Zagame Erna—†	1186½	housewife	43	"
	N	Zagame Samuel	1186½	mechanic	50	"
	O	Dorman Burton	1186½	"	35	Cambridge
	P	Dorman Dolly—†	1186½	housewife	27	"
	T	Panogopoulos Kostantinos	1187	laborer	57	here
	U	Goodridge Odella—†	1187	housewife	30	"
	W	Murray Ella—†	1187	at home	58	29 Benton
	X	Murray Stephen	1187	clerk	22	29 "
1141						
	E	*Tisi Louise—†	1195	at home	55	here
	F	Tisi Pasquale	1195	laborer	60	"
	G	Tisi Rocco	1195	U S A	22	"
	H	Jones Charles	1195	laborer	42	
	K	Jones Laura—†	1195	at home	60	
	L	Yeghigian Bagdasar	1195	laborer	55	
	M	*Yeghigian Elizabeth—†	1195	housewife	48	"

Page.	Letter.	Full Name.	Residence, Jan. 1, 1943.	Occupation.	Supposed Age.	Reported Residence, Jan. 1, 1942. Street and Number.

Tremont Street—Continued

Page.	Letter.	Full Name.	Residence, Jan. 1, 1943.	Occupation.	Supposed Age.	Reported Residence, Jan. 1, 1942. Street and Number.
	N	*Nicholson Minnie—†	1195	at home	75	here
	O	Garabedian Charles	1195	U S A	30	“
	P	Garabedian Peter	1195	U S N	25	“
	R	Garabedian Yegsa—†	1195	at home	48	
	S	Plummer Lloyd	1195	U S A	32	
	T	Plummer Mary—†	1195	clerk	28	
	U	Carlino Angelo	1195	laborer	36	“
	V	Carlino Anna—†	1195	housewife	28	“
	X	Murray John J	1196	laborer	43	
	Y	Murray Margaret—†	1196	housewife	33	“
	Z	Poret Anna—†	1196	“	50	
1142						
	A	Poret Robert	1196	printer	51	
	B	Doherty James J	1196	tinsmith	63	“
	C	Doherty Mary—†	1196	housewife	74	“
	D	Doherty Phillip J	1196	retired	70	“
	E	Howie Grace—†	1196	housewife	71	76 Bennington
	F	Howie William W	1196	retired	73	76 “
	G	Silva Helen—†	1196	housewife	31	here
	U	*Ciano Anna—†	1199	“	42	“
	V	Ciano Charles	1199	storekeeper	51	“
	W	*Fostolo Nicola—†	1199	factoryhand	43	“
	X	Whalen Michelina—†	1199	housewife	29	“
	Y	Whalen Walter	1199	laborer	34	
	Z	Kakatolis Antonio	1199	“	61	“
1143						
	A	*Kakatolis Bessie—†	1199	housewife	55	“
	B	*Anderson Carl E	1199	oiler	57	
	C	Pratt Lillian M—†	1199	housewife	50	“
	D	*Coniaris George	1199	laborer	62	
	E	Coniaris Pauline—†	1199	stitcher	22	
	F	*Coniaris Stella—†	1199	housewife	46	“
	K	*Kaperelle Michael	1201	pedler	66	
	O	Green Arrie—†	1204B	housewife	47	“
	P	Green James	1204B	laborer	46	“
	R	Wilson Eleanor—†	1204B	student	23	42 Cunard
	S	Wilson John W	1204B	“	20	42 “
	T	Wilson Reginald	1204B	laborer	49	42 “
	U	*Wilson Violet—†	1204B	housewife	48	42 “
	V	Perry Euphemia A—†	1204B	“	50	here
	W	Perry Samuel P	1204B	clergyman	51	“

Page.	Letter.	FULL NAME.	Residence, Jan. 1, 1943.	Occupation.	Supposed Age.	Reported Residence, Jan. 1, 1942. Street and Number.

Tremont Street—Continued

	X	Perry Samuel P, jr	1204B	student	21	here
	Y	Mason Leola—†	1204B	housewife	58	"
	Z	Mason Leonard F	1204B	guard	58	"
1144						
	A	Coleman Walter	1204B	watchman	51	"
	B	Vaughn Dennis	1204B	foreman	56	
	C	Vaughn Muriel—†	1204B	clerk	21	
	D	Vaughn Raymond	1204B	U S A	23	
	E	Vaughn Sabania—†	1204B	housewife	50	"
	F	Reed Adele—†	1204B	"	38	
	G	Reed Richard	1204B	watchman	40	"
	V	Brown Emma—†	1223	housewife	54	"
	W	Heaney Mildred—†	1223	at home	49	
	X	Lambert Sadie—†	1223	"	55	
	Y	Hughes John Q, jr	1223	painter	43	
	Z	Hughes Mary E—†	1223	housewife	42	"
1145						
	A	Hall Elizabeth—†	1225	merchant	53	"
	B	Arancio Salvatore	1225	laborer	35	Brookline
	C	Meade Nellie—†	1225	clerk	63	here
	F	Dimock Edward	1237	laborer	50	10 Lamont
	G	Dimock Julia—†	1237	housewife	50	10 "
	K	Roache Joseph P	1241	laborer	38	1100 Col av
	L	Roache Mabel—†	1241	housewife	25	1100 "
	M	Johnson Lily—†	1241	"	20	57 Woodford
	N	Johnson Raymond	1241	chauffeur	24	57 "

Vernon Street

	V	MacDonald John	103	pipefitter	32	221 Cabot
	W	MacDonald Katherine-†	103	housewife	28	221 "
	X	Brown Theresa—†	105	"	22	N Hampshire
	Y	Iknaian George	105	laborer	54	here
	Z	*Iknaian Mary—†	105	housewife	36	"
1146						
	B	*Verderber Louis	107	chauffeur	47	"
	C	*Verderber Mary—†	107	housewife	41	"
	D	Innaco Josephine—†	107	stitcher	45	
	E	*Schlappi Bertha—†	107	housewife	69	"
	F	Schlappi John	107	cabinetmaker	46	"
	H	Cooperstein Benjamin	109	engineer	27	

Page.	Letter.	Full Name.	Residence, Jan. 1, 1943.	Occupation.	Supposed Age.	Reported Residence, Jan. 1, 1942. Street and Number.

Vernon Street—Continued

	K	*Cooperstein Esther—†	109	housewife	63	here
	L	Cooperstein Harry	109	retired	63	"
	M	Tracy Harold	109	fireman	45	"
	N	Tracy Lillian—†	109	housewife	37	"
	O	Evelyn Donald	111	checker	62	
	P	Holbert Arless	111	machinist	39	"
	R	Holbert Winifred—†	111	housewife	33	"
	S	Thomas Fred	111	U S A	26	
	T	Thomas Helen—†	111	housewife	65	"
	U	Thomas Marjorie—†	111	"	28	31 Lambert
	V	MacGregor Alice G–† rear	113	"	65	here
	W	Chase Emily A—† "	113	"	70	"
	X	Chase George S "	113	retired	76	"
	Y	O'Hara Francis	115	U S A	22	"
	Z	O'Hara Mary E—†	115	housewife	55	"
1147						
	A	O'Hara William J	115	janitor	56	
	B	Allen Jenny—†	119	at home	68	
	C	Baker Dorothy—†	119	housewife	47	"
	D	Baker George	119	painter	58	
	E	Avant Clarence I	119	hostler	59	
	F	Avant Cora B—†	119	housewife	50	"
	G	Pullins Catherine—†	119	"	44	
	H	Pullins Edward	119	laborer	43	"
	K	Jordan Margaret—†	121	housewife	67	"
	L	*Douglas Nora—†	121	at home	29	Pennsylvania
	M	*Douglas Roy	121	laborer	30	"
	N	Holmes Burns	121	porter	39	here
	O	Flannery Colby S	125	laborer	37	65 Rutland
	P	Flannery Marion—†	125	housewife	37	65 "
	R	Atkins Francis A	125	laborer	47	here
	S	Atkins Frank	125	retired	81	"
	T	Atkins Mary E—†	125	housewife	40	"
	U	Henderson Francis	127	metalworker	27	Malden
	V	Henderson Josephine—†	127	housewife	25	"
	W	Becotte Delia—†	127	at home	37	14 Oscar
	X	Becotte Emil	127	laborer	44	14 "
	Y	Fallon Elizabeth—†	127	at home	78	here
	Z	Fallon William J	127	laborer	35	"
1148						
	B	*Weiner Eli	129	plumber	40	

Page.	Letter.	FULL NAME.	Residence, Jan. 1, 1943.	Occupation.	Supposed Age.	Reported Residence, Jan. 1, 1942. Street and Number.

Vernon Street—Continued

Page.	Letter.	FULL NAME.	Residence, Jan. 1, 1943.	Occupation.	Supposed Age.	Reported Residence, Jan. 1, 1942. Street and Number.
	c	*Weiner Elizabeth—†	129	housewife	36	here
	D	Johnson Minnie B—†	129	"	44	"
	E	Jurek Anna—†	130	"	29	"
	F	Jurek Louis L	130	painter	30	
	G	Quinlan Bernard F	130	laborer	31	
	H	Quinlan Eleanor—†	130	housewife	27	"
	K	Savage Marguerite—†	130	"	48	
	L	Savage Paul A	130	steamfitter	50	"
	M	Skelly Delia K—†	131	housewife	23	10 Roxbury ct
	N	*Skelly William J	131	laborer	40	10 "
	P	Chiuchiolo Assunta—†	136	at home	73	here
	R	DiManno Angelo	136	carpenter	47	"
	S	DiManno Henrietta—†	136	housewife	35	"
	T	*DiManno John	136	musician	38	"
	V	Kenney Catherine A—†	137	housewife	67	"
	W	Kenney John P	137	retired	65	
	X	Hebert Susan—†	137	maid	48	
1149						
	A	*Myers James	138	salesman	46	"
	B	Spencer Bertha M—†	138	stitcher	47	"
	E	Rogers Bessie—†	140	housewife	39	108 Hunneman
	F	Rogers Frederick	140	painter	50	108 "
	H	Lydon Doris—†	140	housewife	47	here
	K	*Lydon Michael	140	roofer	47	"
	M	Cobb Charles H	142	retired	68	"
	N	Cobb Cora A—†	142	housewife	69	"
	O	Haggerty Charles W	142	U S N	24	
	P	Haggerty Charlotte M—†	142	housewife	50	"
	R	Haggerty Pearl M—†	142	stenographer	26	"
	S	Haggerty William J	142	shipper	68	"
	T	Flynn John J	142	"	51	
	U	Flynn John J	142	U S N	21	
	V	Flynn Thomas H	142	clerk	20	
	Z	*Hing Chin	193	laundryman	61	"
1150						
	A	Wong Hung	193		50	
	B	*Ginsing Wong	193	"	38	
	C	*Kucknan Wong	193	engineer	68	"
	D	Gilligan Mary—†	195	at home	86	Weymouth
	E	Gilligan Nellie—†	195	"	76	"

Page.	Letter.	FULL NAME.	Residence, Jan. 1, 1943.	Occupation.	Supposed Age.	Reported Residence, Jan. 1, 1942. Street and Number.

Vernon Street—Continued

	F	Daley George J	195	dishwasher	57	10 Hampshire
	G	Daley Mary—†	195	housewife	65	10 "
	H	Caswell Warren F	195	welder	50	here
	K	Hutchinson Francis H	197	laborer	22	"
	L*	Hutchinson Margaret—†	197	housewife	59	"
	M	Hall Doris E—†	197	"	31	53 Newland
	N	Hall William E	197	chef	39	53 "
	O*	Vigneaux Sophie—†	197	at home	70	here
	P	Parker Sarah—†	199	housewife	58	"
	R	Dockham Patrick F	199	U S A	24	"
	S	Dragon Anna E—†	199	operator	46	"
	T	Ford Walter J	199	"	37	10 Hampshire

Warwick Street

	V	Jackson Jean—†	115	maid	33	Cambridge
	W	Johnson Martha—†	115	housewife	39	here
	X	Johnson Mary—†	115	domestic	61	"
	Z	Pearman Louise—†	117	housewife	53	115 Warwick
1151						
	A	Pearman Reginald	117	teacher	24	115 "
	B	Durbin Jesse O	117	porter	61	here
	C	Johnson Lizzie D—†	117	domestic	63	"
	D	Hunter Joseph	119	laborer	42	"
	E	Hunter Lucy—†	119	domestic	40	"
	F	Lilley Frederica—†	119	"	40	"
	G	Scott Edison	119	clergyman	30	Illinois
	H	Scott Latona—†	119	housewife	35	"
	K	Stallworth Andrew	119	cook	31	here
	L	White Mary—†	121	domestic	50	"
	M	Williams Lodia—†	121	housewife	26	"
	N	Williams Morgan	121	operator	30	"
	O	Robinson Emma—†	121	housewife	47	"
	P	Best Ida M—†	121	domestic	53	55 Westminster
	R	Peay Bella—†	123	housewife	58	here
	S	Peay Hilbert	123	U S N	54	"
	U	Fernandes Eva—†	123	housewife	65	"
	V	Fernandes Peter	123	retired	87	
	W	Anderson Mary J—†	125	housewife	58	"

Page.	Letter.	Full Name.	Residence, Jan. 1, 1943.	Occupation.	Supposed Age.	Reported Residence, Jan. 1, 1942. Street and Number.

Warwick Street—Continued

	X	Anderson Robert M	125	retired	64	here
	Y	Anderson Robert M, jr	125	student	21	"
	Z	Williams Pauline—†	125	domestic	50	"
1152						
	A	Cooper Charles	127	retired	68	
	B	Peay Moses	127	laborer	55	"
	C	Richman James	127	"	53	37 Flagg
	D	*Samuel Charles	127	waiter	70	here
	E	*Samuel Martha—†	127	housewife	58	"
	F	Young John	127	retired	73	37 Flagg
	G	Merchant Sadie Y—†	129	clerk	40	here
	H	Brooks William H	129	laborer	60	"
	K	Davis Gus	129	cook	55	"
	L	Palmer Mary—†	129	operator	25	Ohio
	M	Smith Earl	129	clerk	32	here
	N	Smith Emily—†	129	housewife	24	"
	O	Allen Rita J—†	131	waitress	21	"
	P	Cooke Ernest D	131	attorney	59	"
	R	Evans Abraham	131	retired	79	"
	S	Wiles Rita—†	131	housewife	36	23 Munroe
	T	Cooper Dorothy B—†	133	clerk	34	New York
	U	Cooper Frederica—†	133	housewife	66	here
	V	*Gaskin Gertrude—†	133	domestic	67	"
	W	Jenkins Clara B—†	133	maid	42	"
	X	Jenkins Sebron A	133	shipper	41	"
	Y	Ballard Emerson	135	operator	31	20 Ball
	Z	Ballard Frances—†	135	housewife	31	20 "
1153						
	A	*Broome Gordon	135	fireman	41	here
	B	Clarke Alfred E	135	U S A	28	"
	C	*Clarke Edith—†	135	housewife	46	"
	D	Harrison Doris—†	135	laundress	23	"
	E	*King Allen	135	shipper	39	Cambridge

Weston Street

	F	Blagdon Irene—†	10	housewife	43	here
	G	Blagdon William A	10	machinist	58	"
	H	Cahill Jennie—†	10	at home	61	Maine
	K	Wheat Louisa—†	10	housekeeper	43	here
	L	Oakes Elizabeth—†	10	housewife	58	1063 Harrison av

Page.	Letter.	Full Name.	Residence, Jan. 1, 1943.	Occupation.	Supposed Age.	Reported Residence, Jan. 1, 1942. Street and Number.

Whittier Street

Page.	Letter.	Full Name.	Residence, Jan. 1, 1943.	Occupation.	Supposed Age.	Reported Residence, Jan. 1, 1942. Street and Number.
	N	Sorenson Arlene—†	3	clerk	20	here
	O	Sorenson John	3	fisherman	45	“
	P	Sorenson Margaret—†	3	housewife	39	“
	G	Gardner James	5	laborer	25	
	S	Gardner Mary—†	5	housewife	26	“
	T	McCormick James	5	laborer	40	
	U	*McCormick Margaret—†	5	housewife	35	“
	W	Haley Charles	15	U S A	35	
	X	Haley Mary—†	15	clerk	62	
	Y	Cox Thomas	15	retired	72	
	Z	Haley James	15	U S A	30	
1154						
	A	Haley Nellie—†	15	housewife	58	“
	B	Anderson Alice—†	17	“	34	
	D	Amato Paul	19	janitor	44	
	E	*Amato Rose—†	19	housewife	37	“
	F	*Amato Salvatore	19	retired	72	
	L	*Fitzgerald Ellen—†	56	housewife	43	“
	M	Fitzgerald Patrick	56	laborer	52	
	N	Hays John	56	U S M C	21	“
	O	*Moogan Bridget—†	56	housekeeper	58	“
	P	Marshman Margaret—†	56	at home	86	“
	R	*Marshman Robert	56	janitor	56	“
	S	*Connolly Alice—†	56	housewife	54	39 Delle av
	T	*Connolly Martin	56	laborer	61	39 “
	U	Magee Delphina—†	56	housewife	36	here
	V	Magee Ernest C	56	welder	38	“
	W	Newell Louise—†	56	housewife	73	“
	X	MacIntyre Henry	56	sailmaker	53	“
	Y	MacIntyre Jennie—†	56	housewife	55	“
	Z	Harrington John	56	mechanic	36	“
1155						
	A	Harrington Mary—†	56	housewife	66	“
	B	Harrington William	56	U S A	40	
	C	Zollinger Edwin A	59	rigger	42	
		Zollinger Mathilde—†	59	housewife	69	“
	E	Daly Charles	59	waiter	36	3 Motley
	F	Daly Daniel F	59	retired	57	3 “
	G	Daly Elizabeth—†	59	housewife	40	3 “
	H	Farinella Phyllis—†	59	“	26	1197 Tremont
	K	Farinella Vincenzo B	59	machinist	25	1197 “

Ward 9—Precinct 12

CITY OF BOSTON

LIST OF RESIDENTS
20 YEARS OF AGE AND OVER

(NON-CITIZENS INDICATED BY ASTERISK)
(FEMALES INDICATED BY DAGGER)

AS OF

JANUARY 1, 1943

JOSEPH F. TIMILTY, *Chairman*
FREDERIC E. DOWLING, *Secretary*
WILLIAM A. MOTLEY, JR.
FRANCIS B. McKINNEY
EVERETT R. PROUT
Listing Board.

CITY OF BOSTON PRINTING DEPARTMENT

Page.	Letter.	Full Name.	Residence, Jan. 1, 1943.	Occupation.	Supposed Age.	Reported Residence, Jan. 1, 1942. Street and Number.

Allard Court

Page.	Letter.	Full Name.	Residence, Jan. 1, 1943.	Occupation.	Supposed Age.	Reported Residence, Jan. 1, 1942. Street and Number.
1200	A	Priesing Elsie—†	1	housewife	50	154 Warren
	B	Priesing Gustaf W	1	architect	68	here
	C	Ingham Eva—†	1	housewife	52	"
	D	Heinemann Anna—†	1	cook	41	Brockton
	E	Lanois Edward J	1	chauffeur	50	Groton
	K	Tracey Elizabeth—†	4	housewife	28	here
	L	Tracey Herman J	4	laborer	37	"
	M	Strater Burns	4	"	40	"
	N	Strater Catherine—†	4	housewife	39	"
	O	McEachern Ellen—†	4	"	45	
	P	McEachern Joseph	4	laborer	47	

Columbus Avenue

Page.	Letter.	Full Name.	Residence, Jan. 1, 1943.	Occupation.	Supposed Age.	Reported Residence, Jan. 1, 1942. Street and Number.
	S	Ganley Mary—†	1038	housewife	75	71 Bromley
	T	Kilduff Sarah—†	1038	at home	80	here
	U	Levangi Julia—†	1038	housewife	69	"
	V	White Anna—†	1038	"	40	"
	W	Powell Mary E—†	1038	nurse	67	
	X	Straus Dora—†	1038	housewife	69	"
	Y	Straus Theodore C	1038	draftsman	32	"
	Z	Gibbons Olivia—†	1040	housewife	43	"
1201	A	Guarneri Joseph	1040	laborer	31	
	B	Guarneri Lillian—†	1040	housewife	30	"
	E	*Burns Catherine—†	1046	"	55	"
	G	Nye Alfred F	1048	oiler	32	195 Vernon
	H	Nye Dorothy C—†	1048	housewife	28	195 "
	K	Schutt Russell J	1048	painter	36	1118 Dor av
	L	DeLalo Frank	1048	laborer	40	here
	M	DeLalo Irene—†	1048	housewife	30	"
	N	Ricci John J	1048	baker	28	"
	O	Ricci Rose—†	1048	housewife	26	"
	P	Calais Rita—†	1048	"	67	
	R	Papas Charles	1048	laborer	40	"
	S	Papas Eva—†	1048	housewife	32	"
	T	*Munro Elsie—†	1048	"	47	9 Dempster
	U	Munro John	1048	leatherworker	26	9 "

Page.	Letter.	Full Name.	Residence, Jan. 1, 1943.	Occupation.	Supposed Age.	Reported Residence, Jan. 1, 1942. Street and Number.

Columbus Avenue—Continued

Page.	Letter.	Full Name.	Residence, Jan. 1, 1943.	Occupation.	Supposed Age.	Reported Residence, Jan. 1, 1942. Street and Number.
	Y	Hinds Catherine—†	1051	housewife	46	here
	Z	Hinds Edward	1051	laborer	44	"
1202						
	A	Williams Jeremiah	1051	chauffeur	39	"
	B	Williams Mary—†	1051	housewife	37	"
	C	Bruce Elmer	1051	laborer	34	Everett
	D	Bruce Grace—†	1051	housewife	35	"
	K	Ahern John	1055	steamfitter	51	here
	L	*McEachern James	1055	carpenter	73	"
	N	*O'Brien Anna—†	1057	housekeeper	44	"
	O	Czwinski Frederick	1057	laborer	45	
	P	Czwinski Mary—†	1057	housewife	40	"
	U	Doherty Lillian—†	1077	"	36	"
	V	Doherty Mary—†	1077	clerk	26	
	W	Doherty Richard	1077	U S N	21	"
	X	*Booras Helen—†	1077	housewife	42	3 Johnston pk
	Y	Booras Nicholas	1077	grocer	43	3 "
1203						
	P	Newton Ellen—†	1100	housewife	54	here
	R	Newton William J	1100	U S A	21	"
	U	Connolly Joseph	1101	clerk	54	"
	V	Connolly Margaret—†	1101	"	47	
1204						
	B	D'Amore Fred	1107A	U S A	29	
	C	D'Amore Henrietta—†	1107A	clerk	30	
	D	D'Amore Mary—†	1107A	"	24	
	E	D'Amore Pasquale	1107A	shoeworker	56	"
	F	D'Amore Rose—†	1107A	stitcher	28	
	G	*D'Amore Theresa—†	1107A	housewife	52	"
	H	Connolly Josephine—†	1107A	"	45	
	K	Connolly Mary E—†	1107A	clerk	23	
	L	Connolly Patrick	1107A	painter	58	
1205						
	L	Greene Edgar	1140	retired	84	Brookline
	M	Stack Isabelle—†	1140	housewife	41	"
	N	Stack Joseph J	1140	janitor	41	"
1206						
	L	Nyhan Francis W	1174	director	31	here
	M	Nyhan Nora J—†	1174	matron	60	"
	N	Kyriacos Christos	1174	baker	47	"

Page.	Letter.	Full Name.	Residence, Jan. 1, 1943.	Occupation.	Supposed Age.	Reported Residence, Jan. 1, 1942. Street and Number.

Columbus Avenue—Continued

	o	*Kyriacos Mary—†	1174	housewife	33	here
	s	Raditsis Argyro—†	1184	beautician	29	"
	T	Raditsis James A	1184	barber	32	"
	U	Jenkins Margaret—†	1184	beautician	43	"
	V	Jenkins William	1184	U S A	30	

1207

Conant Place

	F	Gildea Nora—†	3	housekeeper	66	here

Crawshaw Place

	H	McDonnell Richard	1	retired	76	Long Island
	K	Stier John A	1	metalworker	51	here
	L	Cosgrove Sarah A—†	1	housekeeper	69	"

Crossin Place

	O	Doyle Edward A	4	rubberworker	39	here
	P	Romanos Sina—†	4	housewife	56	7 Tupelo
	R	Sorenson Robert	4	retired	66	2½ Putnam pl
	S	Dimock Alma K—†	5	housekeeper	62	here
	T	Ingsterup Anna M—†	5	"	65	2½ Putnam pl
	U	Nutter Nellie—†	5	housewife	59	here
	V	Logan John	6	laborer	51	"
	W	Pratt Mary—†	6	housewife	57	"
	X	Nelson John	6	watchman	63	"
	Y	Chase Confucious	7	engineer	75	
	Z	Boothman Annie—†	7	housewife	70	"
1208						
	A	Leahy Ellen—†	7	"	61	
	B	Leahy John J	7	retired	74	

Dunlow Street

	C	*Keskula Elizabeth—†	8	housewife	50	here
	D	*Keskula John	8	carpenter	57	"
	G	Goode William	10	porter	60	"
	H	Donnell Ellna V—†	36	housewife	23	"
	K	Marston George M	36	engineer	51	
	M	Glennon Edward	38	laborer	42	

Dunlow Street—Continued

Page.	Letter.	Full Name.	Residence, Jan. 1, 1943.	Occupation.	Supposed Age.	Reported Residence, Jan. 1, 1942. Street and Number.
	N	Glennon Nellie—†	38	housewife	41	here
	O	Davis Edward J	40	mechanic	42	"
	P	Davis Julia A—†	40	housewife	34	"

Elmwood Court

Page.	Letter.	Full Name.	Residence, Jan. 1, 1943.	Occupation.	Supposed Age.	Reported Residence, Jan. 1, 1942. Street and Number.
	S	Glynn Grace—†	1	housewife	66	here
	T	Glynn Henry	1	retired	73	"
	U	Ross Margaret T—†	1	housewife	35	"
	V	Moriarty John E	1	U S C G	40	"
	W	Moriarty Mary L—†	1	housewife	30	"
	X	Crowley Catherine—†	5	housekeeper	58	"
	Y	Obert Frank C	5	policeman	55	"
	Z	McGrath Edward J	7	optician	21	
1209						
	A	McGrath James L	7	shipper	23	
	B	McGrath John J	7	U S A	26	
	C	McGrath Margaret C—†	7	housewife	50	"
	D	McGrath William F	7	shipfitter	24	"
	E	McGrath William J	7	bookbinder	50	"
	F	Favor Clarence A	9	packer	53	
	G	Favor Mary N—†	9	housewife	38	"

Elmwood Place

Page.	Letter.	Full Name.	Residence, Jan. 1, 1943.	Occupation.	Supposed Age.	Reported Residence, Jan. 1, 1942. Street and Number.
	H	Rodd Annie A—†	1	housewife	65	here
	K	Rodd Edward L	1	carpenter	68	"
	L	Rodd Warren	1	assembler	24	"
	M	Keaveny Daniel F	1	seaman	41	
	N	Keaveny Mary A—†	1	housewife	72	"
	O	Murphy James J	2	porter	28	
	P	Murphy Margaret—†	2	domestic	26	"
	R	Murphy Mary C—†	2	housewife	67	"
	S	Murphy Michael	2	U S A	20	"
	T	Ferrullo Anna E—†	3	housewife	37	113 Cedar
	U	Ferrullo Phillip	3	laborer	38	113 "
	V	Aristide Constance—†	3	housewife	28	here
	W	Aristide Misto	3	salesman	38	"
	X	Deering Helen—†	3	housewife	40	"
	Y	Deering William	3	checker	50	
	Z	Hurley Andrew	4	dishwasher	55	"

1210
Elmwood Place—Continued

Page.	Letter.	Full Name.	Residence, Jan. 1, 1943.	Occupation.	Supposed Age.	Reported Residence, Jan. 1, 1942. Street and Number.
1210	A	Murphy Joseph A	4	chauffeur	38	here
	B	Murphy Lucille M—†	4	housewife	39	"
	C	Boisvert Jeanette—†	5	"	45	Dracut
	D	Boisvert Rita—†	5	operator	20	"
	E	Boisvert Victor	5	laborer	50	"
	F	Ellis Annie—†	5	housewife	42	11A Elmwood pl
	G	Ellis Irving	5	laborer	38	11A "
	H	Costello Arthur F	5	U S A	27	here
	K	Costello Robert	5	"	24	"
	L	Tobin Marie F—†	5	housewife	35	"
	M	Tobin Thomas P	5	metalworker	40	"
	N	Furkart Catherine—†	7	housewife	21	78 Vernon
	O	Furkart Russell	7	chauffeur	26	78 "
	P	Petro Constantine	7	butcher	28	here
	R	Petro Pandora—†	7	housewife	21	"
	S	Petro Peno—†	7	"	44	"
	T	Maloney Joseph D	9	chauffeur	51	38 Norfolk
	U	Maloney Marion J—†	9	housewife	51	38 "
	V	Crosby Evelyn—†	9	"	35	here
	W	Crosby Harold E	9	U S C G	38	"
	X	Harrison Ernest	11	supervisor	34	83 C
	Y	Harrison Ruth—†	11	housewife	33	83 "
	Z	Daly James J	11A	U S A	34	1190 Col av
1211	A	Daly Lois—†	11A	housewife	29	1190 "
	B	Haggerty Helen—†	11A	"	51	1190 "
	C	Haggerty John J	11A	laborer	51	1190 "

Elmwood Street

Page.	Letter.	Full Name.	Residence, Jan. 1, 1943.	Occupation.	Supposed Age.	Reported Residence, Jan. 1, 1942. Street and Number.
	D	Briggs Cecelia—†	1	housewife	52	here
	E	Briggs Frederick	1	clerk	53	"
	F	Briggs Frederick J	1	U S N	21	"
	G	Saunders Hannah K—†	1	at home	73	
	H	Shydecker Elfreda—†	2	bookkeeper	25	"
	K	Shydecker Martha—†	2	housewife	63	"
	L	Shydecker Otto	2	florist	66	"
	M	Hartford Alice L—†	7	housewife	42	"
	N	Hartford Raymond J	7	lawyer	46	
	O	Hartford William	7	retired	75	

Elmwood Street—Continued

Page.	Letter.	Full Name.	Residence, Jan. 1, 1943.	Occupation.	Supposed Age.	Reported Residence, Jan. 1, 1942. Street and Number.
	P	Goehring John C	10	retired	74	here
	R	Goehring Katherine—†	10	housewife	80	"
	S	Barry David J	10	retired	65	"
	T	Barry David J, jr	10	laborer	24	
	U	Barry Mary F—†	10	housewife	64	"
	V	Goehring John A	10	laborer	48	
	W	Goehring Minna—†	10	housewife	48	"
	X	Schlotzhauer Marie A—†	10	at home	32	
	Y	Boucher Alice—†	11	housewife	32	"
	Z	Boucher George	11	laborer	39	
1212						
	A	Economo Milton	11	machinist	24	"
	B	Economo Muriel—†	11	dressmaker	24	"
	C	Campbell Alice—†	11	housewife	28	12 Lamont
	D	Campbell James	11	laborer	32	12 "
	F	Kent Charles	15	machinist	30	here
	G	Kent Florence—†	15	housewife	30	"
	H	Kent Fred	15	salesman	64	"
	K	*Jacovides Garifolia—†	15	housewife	40	"
	L	Bendery Joseph S	15	retired	63	
	M	Bendery Theresa—†	15	housewife	62	"
	N	Evenish Andrew	15	laborer	33	
	O	*Lannon Mary—†	18	housewife	66	"
	P	Lannon William	18	chauffeur	58	"
	R	Pilling Ethel—†	18	operator	42	"
	S	*Pilling Harry	18	barber	58	
	T	Bowen Guy	19	laborer	62	
	U	Bowen Helen—†	19	housewife	39	"
	V	Bowen Robert F	19	U S N	20	
	W	Longo Domenic	21	fisherman	38	"
	X	Longo Sarah A—†	21	housewife	34	"
	Y	Kelley Mary—†	22	"	45	"
	Z	Murphy Mathew	22	U S C G	26	11 Frawley
1213						
	A	Murphy Rose E—†	22	stenographer	24	11 "
	B	Quigley Francis D	22	retired	60	here
	C	Quigley Mary E—†	22	housewife	55	"
	D	Mulcahy Katherine—†	22	stitcher	46	"
	E	Mulcahy Mary E—†	22	at home	50	"
	F	Niland Helen—†	23	housewife	31	34 Vine
	G	Niland Patrick T	23	houseman	37	34 "

Page.	Letter.	FULL NAME.	Residence, Jan. 1, 1943.	Occupation.	Supposed Age.	Reported Residence, Jan. 1, 1942. Street and Number.

Elmwood Street—Continued

	H	McIsaac Angus	23	laundryman	32	here
	K	McIsaac Ethel—†	23	housewife	32	"
	L	Bavley Rebecca—†	26	"	39	"
	M	Bavley Reuben	26	laborer	42	
	N	Donohue Helen—†	26	seamstress	24	"
	O	Donohue John J	26	clerk	28	
	P	Donohue Mary—†	26	housewife	57	"
	R	Donohue Patrick	26	chauffeur	58	"
	S	Durfee Margaret—†	26	factoryhand	26	"
	T	Cadogan Catherine—†	26	housewife	48	"
	U	Cadogan John J	26	laborer	48	
	V	Tobin Francis	26	U S M C	21	"
	W	Donnelly James E	30	guard	56	
	X	Russell Catherine—†	30	housewife	42	"
	Y	Russell Mary D—†	30	clerk	23	
	Z	Carroll Anna—†	32	at home	80	
1214						
	A	Page Alice—†	32	nurse	28	
	B	Page Ellen L—†	32	housewife	67	"
	C	Page Helen—†	32	clerk	31	
	D	Page Michael A	32	retired	69	
	E	Tremblay Arthur J	34	operator	53	
	G	Healey Mary—†	36	housewife	66	"
	H	Healey Thomas W	36	retired	68	3 Newark
	K	Nicotera Frank	36	clerk	21	9 Leniston
	L	Coutlis Irene—†	38	housewife	46	here
	M	*Hogan Raymond	38	mechanic	33	"
	N	*Leopold Sarah—†	38	domestic	35	"
	O	*Leopold Wallace	38	chef	37	
	P	King William	38	"	56	
	T	Cusimano Leonard	43	roofer	27	
	U	Cusimano Marie—†	43	housewife	24	"
	X	Andonian Agavni—†	45	"	49	
	Y	Baker Albert	45	chef	64	
	Z	Baker Sadie—†	45	housewife	70	"
1215						
	B	Fraser Archibald	48	carpenter	63	"
	C	Kimball Harriet—†	48	housekeeper	76	"
	D	McDonald Helen—†	48	"	65	"
	E	Swift Henry W	48	clerk	62	
	F	Swift John F	48	retired	67	

Page.	Letter.	Full Name.	Residence, Jan. 1, 1943.	Occupation.	Supposed Age.	Reported Residence, Jan. 1, 1942. Street and Number.
		Elmwood Street—Continued				
	G	Cutting Alfred F	49	retired	59	16 Dana pl
	H	Cutting Beatrice—†	49	housewife	53	16 "
	K	Fay James S	49	electrician	45	here
	L	Fay Mary—†	49	housewife	34	"
	M	*Burgess Hattie—†	50	"	50	37 Orchard
	N	Burgess Joseph E	50	laborer	37	37 "
	O	Dearborn Ella L—†	50	housewife	60	here
	P	Dearborn Herbert W	50	plumber	64	"
	S	Nason Annie S—†	52	housewife	49	"
	T	Nason Joseph P	52	upholsterer	62	"
	U	King Bridget—†	52	housewife	70	"
	V	King Peter J	52	chauffeur	39	197 Vernon
	W	Busby Elizabeth—†	52	housewife	71	73 Smith
	X	Busby John	52	retired	68	73 "
	Y	Hayes Edna C—†	54	housewife	39	here
	Z	Penney Philip R	54	shipper	20	"
1216						
	A	*McConnellogue Bridget–†	54	housekeeper	67	6 Myrtle pl
	B	*McConnellogue Catherine—†	54	"	66	6 "
	C	McPherson John	54	carpenter	56	119 Savin Hill av
	D	McPherson Mary—†	54	laundress	54	119 "
	E	Carey Elton E—†	56	housewife	64	9 Elmwood pl
	F	Carey Paul T	56	U S A	27	here
	G	Carey William J	56	"	22	"
	H	Sheldon Mary J—†	56	housekeeper	80	63 Marcella
	K	Burgess Charles	56	laborer	22	5 Peyear pl
		Gurney Street				
	M	Connor Martin	2	laborer	57	here
	N	Lydon Mary—†	2	housekeeper	76	"
	O	Totten Mary—†	2	nurse	44	15A Alleghany
	P	Lowe Bessie—†	2	housekeeper	64	here
	R	Battaglia Delia—†	2	"	68	"
	S	Flynn Margaret—†	2	"	44	"
	T	Hooley John	2	clerk	31	
	V	Hebron Annie—†	12	housekeeper	61	"
	W	Hebron Ralph	12	laborer	65	"
	X	Swartz Abraham	12	clerk	21	
	Y	Swartz Ethel—†	12	"	26	
	Z	Swartz Fannie—†	12	housewife	55	"

Page.	Letter.	Full Name.	Residence, Jan. 1, 1943.	Occupation.	Supposed Age.	Reported Residence, Jan. 1, 1942. Street and Number.
1217						

Gurney Street—Continued

	A	Swartz Samuel	12	clerk	61	here
	B	Burton Francis H	12	mechanic	35	"
	C	Burton Teresa—†	12	housewife	30	"
	D	Lenane Johanna—†	14	nurse	45	
	E	Resnick Aaron	14	clerk	35	
	F	Resnick Sadie—†	14	housewife	33	"
	G	Leonard Delia A—†	14	domestic	50	1429 Tremont
	H	Leonard Martin J	14	clerk	60	1429 "
	K	Curdo Agnes C—†	20	housewife	49	here
	L	Curdo Walter	20	chauffeur	52	"
	M	Hammond Amy—†	20	housewife	35	"
	N	Hammond Robert	20	chauffeur	34	"
	O	Keane John	20	U S A	22	
	P	McQuillan Anne—†	20	housewife	55	"
	R	McQuillan Catherine—†	20	clerk	25	
	S	Quinlan John	22	laborer	50	
	T	Murphy Joseph	22	B F D	35	
	U	Murphy Marion C—†	22	housewife	39	"
	V	O'Hare Anna—†	22	housekeeper	37	"
	W	Tynan Alice M—†	28	clerk	21	"
	X	Tynan Benjamin J	28	shipper	46	
	Y	Tynan Mary—†	28	housewife	47	"
	Z	Kane James	28	laborer	44	
1218						
	D	Keough George F	28	chauffeur	39	"
	A	Kinnehan Catherine—†	28	at home	24	
	B	Long Helen F—†	28	housewife	41	"
	C	Long John J	28	U S A	21	
	E	Long William	28	policeman	42	"
	F	Lynskey Anna—†	28	housewife	31	72 Hillside
	G	Lynskey John	28	chauffeur	35	70 Bartlett
	H	Gill Alfred K	30	U S A	38	here
	K	Gill Margaret T—†	30	housekeeper	74	"
	L	Davis Frank J	30	clerk	57	"
	M	Davis Matilda E—†	30	housewife	50	"
	N	Davis Paul J	30	clerk	21	
	O	Davis Robert A	30	U S A	24	
	P	Davis William H	30	"	22	
	R	Homsey Evelyn—†	30	housewife	45	"
	S	Homsey Frank	30	clerk	45	

Page.	Letter.	Full Name.	Residence, Jan. 1, 1943.	Occupation.	Supposed Age.	Reported Residence, Jan. 1, 1942. Street and Number.

Gurney Street—Continued

Page.	Letter.	Full Name.	Residence, Jan. 1, 1943.	Occupation.	Supposed Age.	Reported Residence, Jan. 1, 1942. Street and Number.
	T	Barry Catherine—†	36	housewife	55	here
	U	Barry James	36	retired	59	"
	V	McCarthy Julia—†	36	housekeeper	43	64 Terrace
	W	McFarland Mae—†	36	"	41	64 "
	X	Windows Harry	36	clerk	57	64 "
	Y	Blanchard Catherine—†	36	housewife	49	here
	Z	Bourdouris George	54	clerk	49	1267 Tremont
1219						
	A	Bourdouris Mary—†	54	housewife	40	1267 "
	B	McShane Anna—†	56	"	53	here
	C	McShane Edward	56	laborer	23	"
	D	McShane Evelyn—†	56	clerk	26	"
	E	McShane Florence—†	56	"	30	
	F	McShane Michael	56	butcher	62	
	G	McShane Paul	56	U S A	28	

Halleck Street

Page.	Letter.	Full Name.	Residence, Jan. 1, 1943.	Occupation.	Supposed Age.	Reported Residence, Jan. 1, 1942. Street and Number.
	P	Selfridge Robert J	130	metalworker	56	here
	S	McClendon Bernard R	132	chauffeur	44	8 Ward
	T	McClendon Rose—†	132	housewife	44	8 "
	U	Webb Dorella—†	132	"	52	27 Burbank
	W	Darcy Josephine—†	134	"	29	here
	X	Darcy Oscar	134	chauffeur	37	"
	Y	Beattie Catherine L—†	134	housewife	52	"
	Z	Westcott John	134	chauffeur	28	7 Templeton way

1220 Hampshire Street

Page.	Letter.	Full Name.	Residence, Jan. 1, 1943.	Occupation.	Supposed Age.	Reported Residence, Jan. 1, 1942. Street and Number.
	A	Hatfield Joseph H	91	laborer	64	here
	C	Bratton Mary—†	91	housewife	60	"
	D	Hilson Meleda—†	93	"	68	"
	E	McDonald Florence—†	93	factoryhand	25	"
	F	McDonald Margaret—†	93	housewife	69	"
	G	Dalton Charles	97	oiler	38	
	H	Dalton Mary B—†	97	housewife	39	"
	L	Snyder Francis	101	chauffeur	25	"
	M	Snyder John T	101	U S A	23	
	N	Snyder Mary E—†	101	housewife	63	"
	O	Lynch Richard W	101	U S M C	20	"
	P	Thorpe Anna E—†	101	housewife	40	"

Page.	Letter.	Full Name.	Residence, Jan. 1, 1943.	Occupation.	Supposed Age.	Reported Residence, Jan. 1, 1942. Street and Number.

Hampshire Street—Continued

	R	Thorpe Catherine—†	101	housewife	68	here
	S	Thorpe Rita M—†	101	factoryhand	29	"
	T	Conaty Thomas	103	metalworker	51	"
	U	MacIntosh Alexander	107	sexton	60	
	V	MacIntosh Edith M—†	107	nurse	24	
	W	MacIntosh Lucy C—†	107	housewife	49	"

Johns Court

	X	Horton Edith—†	2	housewife	46	7 Malbon pl
	Y	Horton John	2	chauffeur	44	7 "
1221						
	B	Mulholland Gertrude—†	8	housewife	34	here
	C	Mulholland Harry W	8	painter	49	"

King Street

	D	Hokinson Lynn	15	laborer	52	Connecticut
	E	Hokinson Mabel—†	15	housewife	48	"
	G	Bristol Edmond	15	mechanic	27	25 Station
	H	Bristol Gertrude—†	15	housekeeper	60	25 "
	M	Masotta Giovanni	18	laborer	51	here
	N	Masotta Josephine—†	18	housewife	51	"
	O	Masotta Liborio	18	U S A	26	"
	R	Haynes May—†	18	stitcher	39	37 Linden Park
	T	Kennedy Esther—†	20	housewife	32	here
	U	Kennedy Joseph	20	laborer	36	"
	V	Ross Elizabeth—†	20	housewife	54	"
	W	Ross Norman	20	clerk	53	"
	X	McCormack Archibald	20	salesman	34	4 Allard ct
	Y	McCormack Lillian—†	20	housewife	29	4 "
	Z	Christiansen Helma—†	24	domestic	51	here
1222						
	A	Soderberg Ivan	24	mechanic	45	"
	B	Hagen John F	24	machinist	45	4 Cable
	C	Hagen John F, jr	24	U S A	21	4 "
	D	Williams Elena E—†	28	housekeeper	43	17 Kearsarge av
	E	Nelson August	28	laborer	69	here
	F	Nelson Pauline—†	28	housewife	64	"
	G	Schefler Ella G—†	28	"	49	"
	H	Schefler John J	28	clerk	21	

Page.	Letter.	FULL NAME.	Residence, Jan. 1, 1943.	Occupation.	Supposed Age.	Reported Residence, Jan. 1, 1942. Street and Number.

King Street—Continued

	K	Schefler Walter L	28	upholsterer	27	here
	L	Tobin Elizabeth—†	31	housewife	32	"
	M	Tobin Harold	31	foreman	37	"
	N	Dineen Dorothy—†	31	housewife	29	"
	O	Dineen William	31	chauffeur	32	"
	P	Jones Mildred—†	33	housewife	25	"
	R	Jones Walter J	33	chauffeur	31	"
	S	Morrow Mary A—†	33	housekeeper	58	"
	T	Morrow Robert F	33	clerk	23	"
	U	Morrow Robert R	33	fireman	59	

King Terrace

	V	Barbour Charles	1	laborer	54	88 W Springfield
	W	Barbour Julia—†	1	housewife	62	88 "
	X	Connor Henry	1	laborer	31	here
	Y	Connor Louise—†	1	housewife	30	"
	Z	Christian Roberta—†	1	"	26	1818 Wash'n
		1223				
	A	Wells Anna—†	3	"	31	Norwood
	B	Wells Clarence	3	laborer	31	"
	C	Murray John	3	"	55	here
	D	Gleason Arthur	3	"	37	"
	E	Lewis John E	5	"	40	"
	F	Lewis Julia E—†	5	housewife	35	"
	G	Morrissey John M	5	laborer	40	
	H	Morrissey Madeline M—†	5	housewife	35	"
	K	McDonough Catherine—†	5	"	37	"
	L	McDonough Joseph P	5	laborer	37	
	M	McGrath John J	5	U S A	20	

Linden Park Street

	N	Eaton Effie—†	125	housewife	66	here
	O	Eaton Perry W	125	policeman	71	"

Luteman Place

	R	Hulbert Josephine A—†	3	housewife	52	here
	S	Alerding Edward J	5	optician	36	"
	T	Alerding Helen E—†	5	housewife	33	"

Page.	Letter.	FULL NAME.	Residence, Jan. 1, 1943.	Occupation.	Supposed Age.	Reported Residence, Jan. 1, 1942. Street and Number.

Luteman Place—Continued

	V	Lamond Catherine M—†	7	operator	51	here
	U	*Lamond Mary—†	7	housekeeper	89	"
	W	Lamond Robert	7	mechanic	57	"

Mindoro Street

	Y	O'Neil James	18	chauffeur	34	here
	Z	O'Neil Ruth—†	18	housewife	32	"
1224						
	A	Miller Bridget A—†	18	"	58	
	B	Miller Charles J	18	laborer	56	
	C	Miller Charles J, jr	18	"	28	
	D	Nesbitt Catherine L—†	21	housewife	54	"
	E	Nesbitt George J	21	U S A	22	"
	F	Nesbitt William J	21	mechanic	48	"
	G	Huber George G	21	laborer	47	"
	H	Muller Adolph	21	retired	79	"
	K	Doherty Hannah J—†	22	housewife	60	157 Roxbury
	L	Doherty John E	22	U S A	20	here
	M	Doherty Mary J—†	22	packer	36	157 Roxbury
	N	Doherty Thomas F	22	shipper	62	157 "
	O	Blum Ethel M—†	22	housewife	50	here
	P	Blum George E	22	U S A	25	"
	R	Blum Percy A	22	carpenter	52	"
	T	*Sullivan Michael	42	retired	72	"
	U	*Sullivan Winifred—†	42	housewife	66	"

Parker Street

	W	Scannell Mary—†	586	housewife	42	here
	X	Scannell Timothy J	586	coppersmith	52	"
	Y	Lenhardt Charles	588	chauffeur	68	"
	Z	Lenhardt Mary—†	588	housewife	68	"
1225						
	B	Kelley Catherine—†	596	at home	83	
	C	Kelley James H	596	laborer	39	
	D	Kelley Robert E	596	"	54	"
	E	Cadwell Catherine C—†	596	housewife	30	"
	F	Cadwell Henry L	596	U S A	40	
	G	Cadwell Joseph F	596	retired	72	"
	H	Cadwell Mary—†	596	winder	35	"

Page.	Letter.	Full Name.	Residence, Jan. 1, 1943.	Occupation.	Supposed Age.	Reported Residence, Jan. 1, 1942. Street and Number.

Parker Street—Continued

	K	Cleary John	596	U S A	39	here
	L	Edwards Elizabeth—†	596	housekeeper	53	"
	M	Manning Agnes—†	596	operator	26	"
	N	Manning Nora—†	596	housewife	61	"
	O	Hayes Annie—†	598	"	32	
	P	Hayes John	598	retired	67	
	R	Hayes Thomas	598	laborer	36	
	S	Hayes William	598	salesman	26	"
	T	Doyle Catherine—†	598	secretary	32	"
	U	O'Rourke Charles J	598	yardman	51	"
	V	O'Rourke Margaret—†	598	winder	42	
	W	O'Rourke Mary—†	598	housewife	46	"
	Y	Thomas Katherine—†	604	"	39	
	Z	Thomas Nicholas	604	chef	47	
1226						
	C	Fitzgerald Edward A	608	painter	66	
	D	Looney Cornelius J	608	dishwasher	65	"
	E	Looney John J	608	retired	67	
	F	Looney Mary C—†	608	housekeeper	50	"
	H	Apostol Gilo—†	612	housewife	67	"
	K	Apostol Naum	612	pedler	66	
	L	John Esther—†	614	clerk	20	
	M	John Mary—†	614	housewife	25	"
	N	*John Sophia—†	614	"	50	
	O	John Vasil	614	pedler	31	
	V	*Adams Anastasia—†	654	housewife	76	"
	W	*Adams Catherine—†	654	"	40	
	X	Adams John	654	baker	50	"
	Y	*Adams Theodore	654	retired	76	
1227						
	A	Reidy John J	668	laborer	23	
	B	Reidy Nora A—†	668	housewife	49	"
	C	Reidy Stephen T	668	laborer	58	
	D	Athas Stavros	668	retired	55	
	E	Athas Steryiani—†	668	housewife	49	"
	F	Clinton John J	668	laborer	55	
	G	Clinton Margaret J—†	668	housewife	79	"
	H	Healy Delia—†	670	"	52	36 Gurney
	K	Healy Robert B	670	chemist	43	36 "
	L	*Cobb Alma—†	670	housewife	36	here
	M	*Cobb John	670	laborer	37	"

Page.	Letter.	Full Name.	Residence, Jan. 1, 1943.	Occupation.	Supposed Age.	Reported Residence, Jan. 1, 1942. Street and Number.

Parker Street—Continued

Page.	Letter.	Full Name.	Residence, Jan. 1, 1943.	Occupation.	Supposed Age.	Reported Residence, Jan. 1, 1942. Street and Number.
	N	*McDougall Christine—†	670	housewife	39	here
	O	*McDougall Michael	670	laborer	41	“
	P	Donahue Jeremiah	670	machinist	48	“
	R	Donahue John	670	operator	40	“
	S	Donahue Mary—†	670	packer	46	
	Y	*Sacco Jennie—†	684	housewife	56	“
	Z	Sacco John	684	barber	59	
1228						
	A	Sacco John J	684	U S A	24	
	B	Kelley Mary—†	686	housewife	74	“
	C	Kelley Mary—†	686	“	39	
	D	Kelley Michael	686	retired	73	
	E	Kelley Michael E	686	clerk	46	
	F	Shine Edward T	688	U S A	23	
	G	Shine Robert J	688	chauffeur	20	“
	H	Travers Annie J—†	688	housewife	51	“
	K	Travers Patrick H	688	breweryman	56	“
	L	Winn Owen J	688	laborer	46	
	N	McDonald John W	692	clerk	64	
	O	McDonald Sadie E—†	692	housewife	65	“

Prentiss Street

Page.	Letter.	Full Name.	Residence, Jan. 1, 1943.	Occupation.	Supposed Age.	Reported Residence, Jan. 1, 1942. Street and Number.
	S	*King Laura—†	6	seamstress	41	here
	T	*Richardson Emily—†	6	housewife	58	“
	V	Harrison Leopold	6	waiter	40	“
	U	Harrison Lola—†	6	housewife	33	“
	W	Laird Mabel—†	6	“	27	
	X	Laird Robert	6	cook	29	
	Y	Graves John H	6	porter	41	
	Z	Vest Flora M—†	6	housewife	38	“
1229						
	A	Francis Alda—†	6	“	43	
	B	Brown Marjorie—†	6	maid	45	
	C	Hammond Dennis	6	porter	47	
	D	Youngblood Evelyn—†	6	seamstress	29	“
	E	Hector Pearl—†	6	maid	24	
	F	Best Julian	6	porter	47	
	G	Best Marie—†	6	housewife	41	“
	H	*Howes William	6	porter	34	
	K	*Howes Winifred—†	6	housewife	28	“

Page.	Letter.	Full Name.	Residence, Jan. 1, 1943.	Occupation.	Supposed Age.	Reported Residence, Jan. 1, 1942. Street and Number.

Prentiss Street—Continued

Page.	Letter.	Full Name.	Residence, Jan. 1, 1943.	Occupation.	Supposed Age.	Reported Residence, Jan. 1, 1942. Street and Number.
	L	Moore Charles E	6	janitor	39	here
	M	*Moore Stella—†	6	housewife	34	"
	N	Daniels Howell C	6	watchman	49	"
	S	Roberts Emma A—†	31	housewife	49	"
	T	Roberts Ruth A—†	31	clerk	25	
	U	Leonard James	31	janitor	27	
	V	Leonard Mary C—†	31	clerk	26	"
	W	Wotton George H	33	seaman	39	485 Shawmut av
	X	*Wotton Mary A—†	33	housewife	25	485 "
	Y	*O'Flaherty Mary—†	33	"	38	here
	Z	O'Flaherty Raymond	33	waiter	38	"
1230						
	C	Dobkin Samuel	37	metalworker	53	"
	E	Feeley Daniel	37	painter	40	
	F	Feeley Delia—†	37	housewife	38	"
	G	Kinahan George T	37	marbleworker	66	"
	H	Kinahan Margaret M—†	37	housewife	77	"
	L	MacDonald Alex J	39	musician	67	"
	M	McConologue Nora—†	39	laundress	55	"
	N	McDermott Joseph	39	laborer	56	
	S	Lindenman Elizabeth S–†	45	operator	24	"
	T	Lindenman Josephine V–†	45	matron	62	
	U	Schroth Anthony J	45	painter	64	
	V	Schroth George A	45	"	54	
	W	Wanders Ann E—†	47	housewife	85	"
	X	Wanders Florence T—†	47	"	64	"
	Y	Cogan Martha G—†	47	"	63	
1231						
	A	Adelman Elizabeth—†	49	"	84	
	B	Adelman Frank	49	laborer	53	
	C	Adelman Mary F—†	49	housewife	52	"
	D	Adelman Peter	49	laborer	52	"
	K	*Abolin Mary—†	65	housewife	78	8 Romar ter
	L	Kadeg Elizabeth—†	65	"	63	here
	M	Kahps Emma—†	65	"	63	"
	N	Kemp Gloria—†	65	"	25	183 Centre
	O	Kemp Richard	65	U S N	23	183 "
	P	Nee Delia—†	66	housewife	49	here
	R	Nee Luke	66	laborer	50	"
	S	Freiberg Mary—†	66	at home	80	"
	T	Doherty Elizabeth—†	66	housewife	70	"
	U	Doherty Hugh	66	clerk	54	

Page.	Letter.	Full Name.	Residence, Jan. 1, 1943.	Occupation.	Supposed Age.	Reported Residence, Jan. 1, 1942. Street and Number.

Roxbury Street

	W	Allen Charlotte—†	221	housekeeper	53	here
	X	Allen Elizabeth—†	221	housewife	21	63 Terrace
	Y	Allen Vernon	221	U S A	24	63 "
	Z	Saunders Harry	221	operator	64	2161 Wash'n
1232						
	A	Saunders Jessie—†	221	housewife	43	2161 "
	B	Pierone Edward	223	storekeeper	48	here
	C	Pierone Margaret—†	223	housewife	39	"
	D	*Wilbur Rachel—†	223	"	49	"
	E	Robinson Helen—†	223	"	32	
	F	Robinson Roy	223	custodian	44	"
	G	McGonagle Catherine—†	227	housewife	50	"
	H	McGonagle Catherine—†	227	manager	21	"
	K	McGonagle Francis J	227	laborer	24	
	L	McGonagle John F	227	chauffeur	52	"
	M	McGonagle John J	227	U S A	22	
	N	Gallagher Catherine—†	227	housewife	58	"
	O	Gallagher Christina—†	227	operator	23	"
	P	Gallagher Thomas	227	shoeworker	68	"
	R	Stillings Theresa—†	227	housekeeper	26	"
	S	Padula Carmela—†	227	housewife	46	"
	T	Padula Carmine	227	shoeworker	46	"
	U	Padula Phyllis—†	227	bookkeeper	21	"
	V	Bulger Bridie—†	227	housekeeper	39	"
	W	Bulger Charles	227	baker	62	"
	X	Campbell Marie—†	227	housewife	37	275 Roxbury
	Y	Campbell William A	227	painter	39	275 "
	Z	*Driscoll Mary—†	227	housewife	38	here
1233						
	A	Driscoll William	227	electrician	58	"
	B	McLaughlin Angus	243	U S A	25	
	C	*McLaughlin James	243	laborer	67	
	D	*McLaughlin Mary—†	243	laundryworker	22	"
	E	*McLaughlin Minnie—†	243	housewife	57	"
	F	Murphy Mary—†	243	inspector	23	25 Paul Gore
	G	Brooks Bridget J—†	243	housewife	39	here
	H	Brooks Thomas M	243	pipefitter	43	"
	K	Brooks Thomas M, jr	243	U S M C	20	"
	L	Kellard Anna—†	245	housewife	37	"
	M	Kellard Walter	245	laborer	39	"
	N	Fay Anna—†	245	housewife	28	87 Albion

Page.	Letter.	Full Name.	Residence, Jan. 1, 1943.	Occupation.	Supposed Age.	Reported Residence, Jan. 1, 1942. Street and Number.

Roxbury Street—Continued

Page.	Letter.	Full Name.	Residence, Jan. 1, 1943.	Occupation.	Supposed Age.	Reported Residence, Jan. 1, 1942. Street and Number.
	O	Fay Joseph	245	shipworker	31	87 Albion
	P	Christopher Ellen—†	245½	housekeeper	31	175 Boylston
	R	McClintock Georgia—†	247	housewife	24	15 Castle
	S	McClintock John	247	chauffeur	28	15 "
	T	Biedermann Eleanor—†	247	housewife	30	7 Gay
	U	Biedermann John	247	electrician	32	7 "
	V	Clifford Josephine—†	249	housewife	32	here
	W	Clifford Timothy	249	laborer	36	"
	X	Fleming Anne—†	249	saleswoman	46	"
	Y	Fleming James G	249	mechanic	44	"
	Z	Fleming Jane—†	249	housewife	74	"
1234						
	A	Rodd Albert E	251	carpenter	35	"
	B	Rodd Margaret—†	251	housewife	32	"
	C	McLaughlin Catherine-†	251	"	60	
	D	McLaughlin Dennis	251	laborer	62	
	E	McLaughlin Dennis, jr	251	factoryhand	33	"
	F	McLaughlin John J	251	shoeworker	30	"
	G	McLaughlin Mary—†	251	clerk	37	
	H	Grottendeck Mary—†	251	housekeeper	33	"
	K	Mulkern Bridget—†	251	"	62	"
	L	Mulkern Coleman J	251	U S A	30	
	M	Mulkern James	251	"	27	
	N	Mulkern Thomas	251	"	26	
	R	Quinn Alice P—†	259	housekeeper	35	"
	S	Quinn Steven E	259	shipper	32	"
	V	Crittenden Edna—†	265	housewife	43	245 Roxbury
	W	*Crittenden Frank	265	U S A	22	245 "
	X	*Crittenden James	265	"	20	245 "
	Y	Shevlin John	265	retired	49	245 "
	Z	Armstrong Anna—†	267	housewife	39	986 Harris'n av
1235						
	A	Armstrong Emile	267	garageman	37	986 "
	B	McMillan Bessie—†	269	housewife	69	here
	C	King Laura—†	271	housekeeper	41	"
	E	O'Leary Helen—†	275	housewife	32	39 Delle av
	F	Scanlan Jeremiah	275	retired	65	39 "
	G	Rose Margaret L—†	275	"	63	40 "
	H	Rose Marguerite F—†	275	clerk	31	40 "
	K	Covell Helen—†	275	housewife	28	117 F
	L	Covell Ralph	275	laborer	32	117 "

Page.	Letter.	Full Name.	Residence, Jan. 1, 1943.	Occupation.	Supposed Age.	Reported Residence, Jan. 1, 1942. Street and Number.
		Roxbury Street—Continued				
	M	Goldsmith Douglass L	277	U S A	24	here
	N	*Goss Joseph	277	painter	51	"
	O	Goss May—†	277	housewife	60	"
	P	*Russ Mary—†	277	housekeeper	40	22 Anita ter
	R	Mahoney Margaret—†	277	"	72	here
	S	Wagner Frederick	279	oiler	41	"
	T	Wagner Mary—†	279	housewife	39	"
	U	Pomerleau Helen—†	279	bus girl	21	2536 Wash'n
	V	Pomerleau Leondine—†	279	housewife	43	2536 "
	W	Pomerleau Lorenzo	279	barber	42	2536 "
	Y	Magrath Clara—†	285	housewife	39	here
	Z	Magrath Samuel	285	chauffeur	40	"
1236						
	C	Buckman Helen—†	311	housekeeper	46	"
		Station Street				
	T	Clinton John	15	laborer	59	here
	Z	Langers Conrad C	25	barber	53	"
1237						
	A	McLellan Lucy E—†	25	housewife	41	"
	D	Keaney Charles J	25	laborer	43	
	E	Keaney Mary E—†	25	housewife	46	"
	H	*Calapai Leo	25	barber	66	
	K	Calapai Mary—†	25	housekeeper	66	"
	L	Newton John J	27	retired	68	"
	M	Rainville Frederick	27	laborer	53	987 Col av
	N	Rainville Nora—†	27	housekeeper	38	987 "
	O	Freeson Henry	27	retired	81	here
	R	Trudel Anne—†	29	housekeeper	66	"
	S	Brehm Arthur A	29	laborer	71	"
	T	Brehm Joseph H	29	attendant	31	"
	U	Brehm Rose O—†	29	housewife	66	"
	V	Cleary Mary A—†	29	housekeeper	74	1275 Col av
1238						
	A	Weinberg Otto	70	iceman	66	612 Parker
	B	Clark Mary E—†	70	at home	66	141 Ruggles
	C	Dujsik Theofil	70	laborer	57	here
	D	Dujsik Vendelin	70	"	24	"
	F	Panos Catherine—†	72	housewife	30	75 Burbank

Page.	Letter.	Full Name.	Residence, Jan. 1, 1943.	Occupation.	Supposed Age.	Reported Residence, Jan. 1, 1942. Street and Number.
		Station Street—Continued				
	G	*Panos William H	72	chef	36	75 Burbank
	H	*Theodorkis John	72	retired	38	here
	K	*Theodorkis Stella—†	72	housewife	32	"
		Texas Street				
	T	*Marko Nicholas	16	cook	56	here
	V	Yeomans George C	16	laborer	35	"
	W	Yeomans Julia L—†	16	housewife	30	"
1239		**Tremont Street**				
	B	Ferrari Frank	1214	laborer	66	here
	C	Ferrari Genevieve—†	1214	waitress	42	"
	D	Gatley Bernard	1214	laborer	54	"
	E	Lamoretti Clotilde—†	1214	storekeeper	60	"
	O	Heinrich Helen—†	1238	polisher	43	
	P	Heinrich Joseph	1238	U S N	22	
	R	Malloy Edward	1238	porter	69	
	S	Malloy Hattie M—†	1238	housewife	64	"
	U	Krotman Bessie—†	1240	"	52	
	V	Krotman Frank	1240	merchant	62	"
	W	Lazaris Anthony P	1240	laborer	58	
	X	*Lazaris Lena—†	1240	housewife	46	"
	Y	Lazaris Mary—†	1240	stitcher	22	
1240						
	B	Gervasi Anthony	rear 1242	storekeeper	54	"
	C	Gervasi Centina—†	" 1242	dressmaker	25	"
	D	Gervasi Dominic	" 1242	U S A	28	
	E	Gervasi Joseph	" 1242	"	22	
	F	Gervasi Josephine—†	" 1242	housekeeper	32	"
	G	*Gervasi Lucy—†	" 1242	housewife	53	"
	N	Driscoll Margaret—†	1248½	"	38	"
	O	Driscoll Peter	1248½	mover	38	
	R	Wilkie Joseph	1248½	laborer	45	"
	S	Wilkie Mary—†	1248½	housewife	36	"
	T	Dora Agnes—†	1250	"	26	251 Cabot
	U	Dora Cecil	1250	operator	36	251 "
	W	Masse Bridget—†	1250	housewife	58	here
	X	Masse Chester	1250	machinist	55	"
	Y	McHugh Winifred—†	1250	nurse	38	"

Page.	Letter.	Full Name.	Residence, Jan. 1, 1943.	Occupation.	Supposed Age.	Reported Residence, Jan. 1, 1942. Street and Number.

Tremont Street—Continued

Page.	Letter.	Full Name.	Residence, Jan. 1, 1943.	Occupation.	Supposed Age.	Reported Residence, Jan. 1, 1942. Street and Number.
	Z	Metalo James	1250A	cobbler	68	1273 Tremont
1241						
	A	Killion Annie—†	1252	housekeeper	64	here
	B	DePrizio Joseph	1252	laborer	45	“
	D	Roberts Eugene	1252	“	39	2558 Wash'n
	E	Roberts Florence—†	1252	housewife	32	2558 “
	F	Roberts Albert	1252	laborer	35	56 E Newton
	G	Roberts Mary—†	1252	housewife	37	56 “
	L	*Orchanian Peter	1263	carpetmaker	65	Palmer
	M	Hall James	1263	U S A	21	47 Vernon
	N	Hall Vera—†	1263	housewife	45	47 “
	O	Moore Otis	1263	U S N	22	Texas
	R	Taylor Albert	1265	U S A	34	here
	S	*Taylor Elizabeth—†	1265	housewife	56	“
	T	*Primas John	1265	chef	50	“
	U	*Primas Sarah—†	1265	housewife	39	“
	W	Fitzgerald Francis P	1267	chauffeur	53	197 Hampden
	X	Jones George E	1267	factoryhand	20	Randolph
	Y	Jones Violet—†	1267	housewife	43	197 Hampden
	Z	Vassile Alexander	1267	baker	24	here
1242						
	A	Vassile Anna—†	1267	wrapper	21	
	B	*Vassile Virginia—†	1267	housewife	59	“
	C	*Skambas Charles	1267	helper	50	
	D	Skambas Christopher	1267	U S A	20	
	E	Skambas Elaine—†	1267	housewife	43	“
	F	Gordon Annie—†	1267	housekeeper	61	“
	G	Gordon Esther—†	1267	winder	59	“
	H	Gordon Miriam—†	1267	housewife	65	“
	K	Gordon Raphael	1267	cutter	71	
	L	Gordon Sarah—†	1267	clerk	63	
	P	Callahan Eugene A	1273	trackman	44	“
	R	Callahan Eugene F	1273	mover	21	
	S	Callahan John J	1273	seaman	20	
	T	Callahan Mary E—†	1273	housewife	42	“
	U	Edwards Peter	1273	laborer	23	7 Gay
	V	Elliott Margaret E—†	1273	housekeeper	34	12 Roxbury ct
	W	Hayes Daniel C	1273	U S A	27	7 Gay
	X	Hayes Daniel F	1273	shipper	63	7 “
	Y	Hayes Hilda—†	1273	housewife	63	7 “
	Z	Hayes Mary T—†	1273	cutter	31	7 “

Page.	Letter.	FULL NAME.	Residence, Jan. 1, 1943.	Occupation.	Supposed Age.	Reported Residence, Jan. 1, 1942. Street and Number.
1243		**Tremont Street**—Continued				
	A	Apostle Celia—†	1273	clerk	52	here
	B	Apostle Dennis	1273	dishwasher	64	"
	C	Wong Faith—†	1273	housewife	35	"
	D	Wong Samuel	1273	chauffeur	42	"
	M	*Athanasopoulos Julia–†	1280A	housewife	42	"
	N	Athanasopoulos Peter	1280A	shoeworker	45	"
	O	Byrne Mary—†	1280A	housewife	32	106 Linden Park
	P	Byrne Thomas L	1280A	salesman	38	106 "
	R	*Quinn John T	1280A	shipper	36	2872 Wash'n
	S	*Quinn Katherine—†	1280A	housewife	38	2872 "
	T	Arnold Helen—†	1282	factoryhand	21	1137 Tremont
	U	Arnold Louis	1282	finisher	24	here
	V	Mitsiaris George J	1282	chauffeur	50	"
	W	Mitsiaris Xanthi—†	1282	housewife	49	"
	X	Arnold Bessie—†	1282	"	47	
	Y	Arnold Catherine—†	1282	waitress	21	
1244						
	G	Burke Michael J	rear 1293	laborer	37	
	E	O'Brien Helen—†	" 1293	housewife	42	"
	F	O'Brien John J	" 1293	fireman	49	"
	H	Heinrich Peter	" 1293	laborer	49	139 Vernon
	K	Sawyer Stephen A	" 1293	retired	82	139 "
	M	McFadden William L	" 1297	electrician	30	43 Smith
	N	Plunkett Sadie—†	" 1297	housewife	50	here
	O	Plunkett William	" 1297	chauffeur	45	"
	P	Conroy Mary—†	" 1297	housekeeper	52	r 1293 Tremont
	R	Clark Emily—†	" 1297	at home	50	here
	W	Tully Elizabeth—†	1301	operator	26	"
	X	Tully Frank	1301	machinist	22	"
	Y	Tully Joseph	1301	U S A	21	"
	Z	Tully Mary—†	1301	operator	25	"
1245						
	A	Tully Philip	1301	manager	24	"
	B	*Tully Susan—†	1301	housewife	57	"
	C	Tully Thomas	1301	clerk	23	
	N	Catarius Cornelius	1309	oiler	41	
	O	Catarius Edith A—†	1309	housewife	42	"
	P	Mealey Helen—†	1309	"	20	
	R	Mealey Thomas	1309	U S A	22	
	S	McDonald Margaret—†	1309	housekeeper	76	"

Page.	Letter.	FULL NAME.	Residence, Jan. 1, 1943.	Occupation.	Supposed Age.	Reported Residence, Jan. 1, 1942. Street and Number.

Tremont Street—Continued

	T	Dawson Mary—†	1309	housekeeper	62	here
	U	Kelley Peter	1309	floorman	66	"
	V	Myers Delia—†	1309	housewife	61	"
	W	Myers William	1309	laborer	61	
	Y	Dexter Benjamin T	1309	operator	59	
	Z	Dexter Frances L—†	1309	housewife	50	"
1246						
	A	Shaughnessey Mary—†	1309	"	45	
	B	Shaughnessey Michael	1309	laborer	56	"
	D	Freeman Lula J—†	1309	housewife	48	617 Shawmut av
	W	Trask Charles	1324	retired	70	here
	Z	Buckley Michael	1326	laborer	51	"
1247						
	A	Sullivan Frank	1326	chauffeur	24	"
	B	Trask Charles	1326	laborer	63	
	C	Trask Effie—†	1326	housewife	69	"
	D	Dwyer David	1326	student	22	
	E	Dwyer Maurice	1326	laborer	53	
	S	Daniels John J	1346½	boilermaker	36	"
	T	Daniels Lillian—†	1346½	housewife	36	"
1248						
	A	Yee Harry	1413	laundryman	36	"
	K	Marotto Eligio	1429	machinist	25	31 Mall
	L	Marotto Rose—†	1429	housewife	21	31 "
	M	Marotto Carmella—†	1429	tailor	27	24 Winthrop
	N	Marotto Gaetano	1429	laborer	67	24 "
	O	Marotto Marguerite—†	1429	tailor	24	24 "
	P	Marotto Mary—†	1429	housewife	56	24 "
	W	Mulligan George	1441	rigger	25	here
	X	Mulligan Mary—†	1441	cleaner	42	"
	Y	Mulligan William	1441	U S A	23	"
	Z	Megna Albert	1441	"	23	
1249						
	A	Megna Dominica—†	1441	housewife	59	"
	B	Megna John	1441	blacksmith	59	"
	C	Megna Josephine—†	1441	clerk	22	
	D	Megna Marie—†	1441	operator	20	"
	H	Angelopulos Angelo	1443B	counterman	47	Medford
	K	*Angelopulos Poli—†	1443B	housewife	45	"
	L	Lyons John J	1445	counterman	64	1682 Tremont
	M	Lyons Louise—†	1445	housewife	59	1682 "

Page.	Letter.	Full Name.	Residence, Jan. 1, 1943.	Occupation.	Supposed Age.	Reported Residence, Jan. 1, 1942. Street and Number.

Tremont Street—Continued

	N	Cullen Edward M	1445	retired	67	here
	O	Cullen Jennie—†	1445	housewife	56	"

Vernon Street

	R	McManus Edward F	186	retired	77	48 Elmwood
	S	McCall Alice D—†	186	stenographer	35	here
	T	McCall Elizabeth A—†	186	housewife	62	"
	U	McCall Lewis	186	chauffeur	54	"
	V	Flanagan Joseph F	190	laborer	60	
	W	Flanagan Mary T—†	190	housewife	48	"
	X	Ryley Anna M—†	190	maid	45	1077 Col av
	Y	Ryley Dorothy—†	190	housewife	78	1077 "
1250						
	A	Rogers James R	192	retired	70	here
	E	*Latheras James	rear 196	cook	49	1125A Tremont
	F	Latheras Margaret–†	" 196	housewife	49	1125A "
	G	Gannon Michael	" 196	chauffeur	38	here
	H	Gannon Ruth—†	" 196	housewife	35	"
	K	*Bazinas Condillia–†	" 196	"	41	"
	L	Bazinas Theodore	" 196	laborer	52	"
	M	McDonnell Helen—†	198	housewife	29	251 Cabot
	N	McDonnell Patrick J	198	laborer	33	251 "
	O	Quinn Charles	198	"	34	here
	P	Quinn Helen—†	198	housewife	29	"
	S	Powlowski Charles	200	chauffeur	41	"
	T	Powlowski Esther—†	200	housewife	38	"

Ward Street

	Z	Carey John	2	laborer	50	here
	X	Doucette Henry	2	"	42	"
1251						
	A	*Colpron Phidime	6	"	45	"
	D	Donnelly Lydia B—†	8	housewife	70	6 Ward
	E	Donnelly William G	8	retired	71	6 "
	G	Audet John	16	barber	50	here
	H	Audet Mary—†	16	housewife	51	"
	K	Kelly Mary A—†	16	at home	74	"
	L	*McCarthy Helen—†	16	"	60	
	M	Chapman Ellen G—†	20	"	27	

Page.	Letter.	Full Name.	Residence, Jan. 1, 1943.	Occupation.	Supposed Age.	Reported Residence, Jan. 1, 1942. Street and Number.

Ward Street—Continued

Page.	Letter.	Full Name.	Residence, Jan. 1, 1943.	Occupation.	Supposed Age.	Reported Residence, Jan. 1, 1942. Street and Number.
	N	Locke Charles M	20	chauffeur	30	here
	O	Nolan James W	20	clerk	50	"
	P	Nolan Margaret E—†	20	housekeeper	71	"
	R	Allgaier Anna J—†	24	housewife	70	"
	S	Allgaier Charles	24	shipper	68	
	T	Barton Herbert P	24	foreman	43	
	U	Barton Marie J—†	24	housewife	42	"
	V	Perz Dora—†	24	at home	76	"
	W	Brown Agnes C—†	38	housewife	35	6 O'Callaghan way
	X	Brown Florence M—†	38	housekeeper	55	here
	Y	Brown Thomas J	38	chauffeur	36	6 O'Callaghan way
	Z	Smith Esther—†	38	housewife	29	here
1252						
	A	Smith Eugene W	38	shipper	40	"
	B	Ochs Florence—†	42	housewife	42	"
	C	Ochs William A	42	welder	46	32 St Francis de Sales
	E	Dolan Alton W	44	metalworker	39	here
	F	Dolan Helen—†	44	housewife	39	"
	G	Sullivan Alice O—†	44	nurse	32	"
	H	Sullivan Catherine—†	44	housewife	33	"

13

14

15

Ward 9—Precinct 13

CITY OF BOSTON

LIST OF RESIDENTS
20 YEARS OF AGE AND OVER

(NON-CITIZENS INDICATED BY ASTERISK)
(FEMALES INDICATED BY DAGGER)

AS OF

JANUARY 1, 1943

JOSEPH F. TIMILTY, *Chairman*
FREDERIC E. DOWLING, *Secretary*
WILLIAM A. MOTLEY, JR.
FRANCIS B. McKINNEY
EVERETT R. PROUT
Listing Board.

CITY OF BOSTON PRINTING DEPARTMENT

Page.	Letter.	FULL NAME.	Residence, Jan. 1, 1943.	Occupation.	Supposed Age.	Reported Residence, Jan. 1, 1942. Street and Number.

1300
Alvah Kittredge Park

	A	Murphy William D	2	salesman	54	here
	B	Allen Earl	3	"	54	N Hampshire
	C	Allen Frances—†	3	housewife	52	"
	D	Boynton Abbie W—†	3	housekeeper	58	here
	E	Callahan Helen—†	3	"	50	268 Dudley
	F	Callahan Thomas	3	laborer	50	268 "
	G	*Duggan Anna—†	3	housekeeper	59	here
	H	Dunn Robert E	3	laborer	70	"
	K	Glynn Mary—†	3	housekeeper	71	268 Dudley
	L	Maxwell Anna—†	3	housewife	28	here
	M	Maxwell Richard	3	watchman	31	"
	N	Minkkinen Bertha—†	3	factoryhand	22	Gardner
	O	Sparks Beatrice M—†	3	housewife	46	here
	P	Sparks Richard	3	upholsterer	58	"
	R	Winterbottom Lillian—†	3	saleswoman	26	N Hampshire
	S	Wood Clara—†	3	factoryhand	30	here
	W	Vickers Charles D	5	U S A	23	"
	X	Vickers Lillian—†	5	housewife	45	"
	Y	Vickers William D	5	porter	62	
	Z	Smith Thelma—†	5	saleswoman	37	"
1301						
	A	Randall Doris—†	5	housewife	27	"
	B	Randall John W	5	laborer	27	
	C	Tolin Anne—†	6	waitress	25	
	D	Finneran John	6	laborer	48	"
	E	Pitts Alice—†	6	housewife	51	27 Norfolk
	F	Pitts Joseph	6	chauffeur	48	27 "
	G	Carey Joseph	6	laborer	38	14 Cortes
	H	Carey Mary—†	6	housewife	35	here
	K	Martin Raymond	7	carpenter	46	19 Highland av
	L	Martin Vera—†	7	housewife	38	19 "
	N	Hardy Joseph	7	welder	27	13 Linden Park
	O	Hardy Marie—†	7	housewife	25	13 "
	P	Marsden Edna—†	7	"	20	81 Highland
	R	Marsden Joseph	7	chauffeur	22	81 "
	T	Hines Sarah E—†	8	housekeeper	69	here
	U	Williams Regina M—†	8	at home	81	"
	V	Finney Theresa A—†	8	"	70	"

Page.	Letter.	Full Name.	Residence, Jan. 1, 1943.	Occupation.	Supposed Age.	Reported Residence, Jan. 1, 1942. Street and Number.

Bartlett Street

Page.	Letter.	Full Name.	Residence, Jan. 1, 1943.	Occupation.	Supposed Age.	Reported Residence, Jan. 1, 1942. Street and Number.
	W	Kilduff Alice C—†	56	clerk	26	here
	X	Kilduff Frances B—†	56	housewife	64	"
	Y	Kilduff James F	56	U S A	22	"
	Z	McFarland Susan M—†	56	card cutter	60	"
1302						
	A	McLellan Ann—†	56	clerk	25	
	B	Roberts Arthur J	56	rigger	60	
	C	Townson George	56	foreman	32	
	D	Townson Mary E—†	56	housewife	31	"
	E	Leavitt Geraldine—†	58	housekeeper	71	"
	F	Lopez James	58	laborer	36	
	G	Murphy Charles F	58	rubberworker	39	"
	H	Murphy Helen M—†	58	housewife	42	"
	K	*Postlewaite Mary—†	58	housekeeper	55	"
	L	Rowley Frank M	58	laborer	83	54 Roxbury
	M	Twomey Thomas	58	"	52	here
	N	Donnelly Sarah A—†	60	housewife	63	"
	O	Donnelly Walter J	60	woodworker	68	"
	P	Gillis Marie—†	60	housekeeper	68	"
	R	Berger Leo	64	roofer	43	"
	S	Graham Francis	64	caretaker	45	"
	T	Graham Lillian—†	64	cook	40	
	U	Grover Mirdza —†	64	housewife	30	"
	V	Kerr Janet—†	64	milliner	60	
	W	Maurin Edward	64	carpenter	52	"
	X	Maurin Mirdza—†	64	housewife	54	"
	Y	Poore Guy L	64	chef	34	
	Z	Poore Lillian—†	64	housewife	35	"
1303						
	A	Daly Dorothy—†	68	clerk	22	25 Lambert av
	B	Daly Edward	68	U S A	28	25 "
	C	Lyle Charlotta L—†	68	housewife	50	here
	D	Lyle Everett D	68	porter	55	"
	E	Nickerson Mary—†	68	housewife	40	25 Lambert av
	F	Nickerson Warren	68	clerk	38	25 "
	G	Tempori Herbert	68	laborer	20	28 Moreland
	H	Ahern Helen—†	70	stitcher	57	here
	K	Blum James G	70	janitor	54	"
	L	Blum Lillian—†	70	housewife	54	"

Page.	Letter.	Full Name.	Residence, Jan. 1, 1943.	Occupation.	Supposed Age.	Reported Residence, Jan. 1, 1942. Street and Number.

Bartlett Street—Continued

	M	Duggan Jeremiah	70	laborer	60	here
	N	Greely Julia—†	70	housekeeper	65	60 Cliff
	O	Kelly Anna O—†	70	secretary	50	here
	P	Kelly Mary T—†	70	housekeeper	52	"
	R	Reynolds Martin J	70	U S A	35	"
	S	Reynolds Mary—†	70	housewife	33	"
	T	Calapa Nicholas	70	barber	44	
	U	Calapa Palma—†	70	dressmaker	40	"
	V	Higgins Catherine—†	70	housewife	54	"
	W	Timmons Arthur T	70	chauffeur	50	"
	X	Hamilton George	70	clerk	35	
	Y	Hamilton Mary—†	70	housewife	28	"
	Z	Ryan Thomas J	70	operator	66	
1304						
	A	Garrison Florence N—†	70	clerk	47	
	B	Garrison Jessie I—†	70	nurse	56	
	C	MacDonald John H	70	fireman	68	
	D	MacDonald Mary C—†	70	housewife	61	"
	E	Weldon Ethel L—†	70	operator	34	"
	F	Vaughn Geneva—†	70	housekeeper	67	"
	G	Lewin Dean B	70	painter	57	"
	H	Lewin Gertrude A—†	70	housewife	61	"
	K	Piscitelli Andrew	70	U S A	28	
	L	Piscitelli Anna—†	70	housewife	42	"
	M	Farley Germaine—†	70	"	26	
	N	Farley Leo	70	billposter	38	"
	O	Reisinger John C	70	mechanic	49	"
	P	Reisinger Marguerite—†	70	housekeeper	22	"

Blanchard Street

	R	Eaton Doris—†	4	stenographer	21	here
	S	Eaton Mary E—†	4	housewife	48	"
	T	Richardson Alvon	5	machinist	35	276 Dudley
	U	Richardson Ruth—†	5	clerk	27	276 "
	V	Doyle Joseph	5	shipper	48	4 Linwood
	W	Doyle Lillian—†	5	seamstress	47	4 "
	X	Lipper Lewis	5	clerk	46	here
	Y	Lipper Lillian—†	5	housewife	38	"
	Z	Governor William F	5	operator	43	6 Linwood

Page.	Letter.	Full Name.	Residence, Jan. 1, 1943.	Occupation.	Supposed Age.	Reported Residence, Jan. 1, 1942. Street and Number.
1305						
		Blanchard Street—Continued				
	A	Lazuri Norman	6	clerk	31	here
	B	Lazuri Rachael—†	6	housewife	29	"
	C	Conrad Ada M—†	8	waitress	58	94 W Newton
	D	Mosiz Anne—†	8	housekeeper	56	here
	E	Tansey Bernard H	10	U S A	33	"
	F	Tansey John F	10	clerk	42	"
	G	Tansey Katherine J—†	10	housewife	39	"
	H	Tansey Patrick J	10	salesman	39	"
	K	Forester Joseph	16	pipefitter	28	"
	L	Forester Katherine—†	16	housewife	26	"
	M	Forester Anna—†	18	housekeeper	48	181 Winthrop
	N	Forester Otis	18	electrician	24	181 "
	O	Forester Ruth—†	18	housewife	20	Maine
		Centre Street				
	R	Fountain Arsine	2	mechanic	40	4 Louise pk
	U	Baasner Henry	4	seaman	50	86 Lawn
	V	Crowe Anna H—†	4	housekeeper	52	86 "
	W	Oliver George F	4	guard	48	86 "
1306						
	A	Reilly Charles	4½	retired	66	here
	B	Reilly Francis A	4½	U S A	33	"
	C	Reilly Mary—†	4½	operator	29	"
	D	Reilly Sarah—†	4½	housewife	66	"
	E	Reilly Warren T	4½	U S A	38	
	F	Donovan Agnes E—†	4½	housewife	57	"
	G	Donovan Agnes K—†	4½	secretary	32	"
	H	Donovan John J	4½	clerk	70	"
	L	Libbey Albert J	6	realtor	53	Hingham
	M	Doucette Arthur J	7	welder	39	247 Roxbury
	N	Doucette Gladys M—†	7	housewife	47	247 "
	O	Graffam Joseph F	7	retired	79	247 "
	P	Misciewicz Bertha—†	7	clerk	37	here
	R	Misciewicz Felix J	7	pipefitter	48	"
	S	*Stowinska Julia—†	7	housewife	63	"
	T	Fillon Charles	7	machinist	23	"
	U	*Triftriantafillou Anna—†	7	housewife	45	"
	V	Triftriantafillou William	7	cook	53	"
	W	Alger Mabel J—†	8	at home	69	Wrentham

Page.	Letter.	Full Name.	Residence, Jan. 1, 1943.	Occupation.	Supposed Age.	Reported Residence, Jan. 1, 1942. Street and Number.

Centre Street—Continued

	X	Allard Lillian—†	8	at home	68	20 Homes av
	Y	Bell Catherine S—†	8	housekeeper	65	here
	Z	Bell Edna—†	8	clerk	27	"
1307						
	A	Ezzo Anthony	8	mechanic	34	171 Centre
	B	Francis George	8	retired	78	142 Cedar
	C	Lynch Jeremiah	8	"	71	here
	D	Madden Hannah—†	8	at home	67	"
	E	Maguire James	8	retired	77	"
	F	Moritz Pius	8	grocer	66	"
	G	Ryan George	8	retired	65	"
	H	*Landers Annie—†	9	housewife	60	4 Linwood sq
	K	*Landers Joseph	9	mechanic	60	4 "
	L	Landers Margaret—†	9	clerk	22	4 "
	M	Mousechian Arshaloos—†	9	housewife	44	137 Ruggles
	N	Mousechian Nahabed	9	finisher	58	137 "
	O	*MacDonald Charlotte—†	9	at home	88	here
	P	Parker Anna C—†	9	stenographer	45	"
	R	Parker William B	9	U S A	21	"
	S	Guinessy James P	13	U S N	32	
	T	Guinessy Mary R—†	13	housewife	28	"
	U	Hurley Eugene J	13	U S A	25	
	V	Hurley John E	13	"	26	
	W	Hurley Margaret—†	13	housewife	55	"
	X	Hurley Margaret L—†	13	clerk	21	
	Y	Hurley Michael	13	plumber	65	
	Z	McElwaine Arthur L	13	manager	32	"
1308						
	A	Jones Elizabeth—†	14	housekeeper	77	"
	B	Arlington Annie—†	15	housewife	64	"
	C	Arlington George	15	clerk	30	
	E	Arlington Walter	15	shipper	28	
	D	Arlington William H	15	engineer	64	"
	F	Willis Albina—†	15	packer	26	8 Putnam pl
	G	Hansen Catherine—†	16	housewife	48	here
	H	Hansen Otto	16	blacksmith	50	"
	K	Pickett Anna—†	16	domestic	24	"
	L	Pickett George T	16	U S A	22	
	M	Pickett Grace—†	16	clerk	34	
	N	Pickett John G	16	U S A	28	
	O	Pickett Margaret—†	16	housewife	63	"

Page.	Letter.	Full Name.	Residence, Jan. 1, 1943.	Occupation.	Supposed Age.	Reported Residence, Jan. 1, 1942. Street and Number.

Centre Street—Continued

Page.	Letter.	Full Name.	Residence, Jan. 1, 1943.	Occupation.	Supposed Age.	Reported Residence, Jan. 1, 1942. Street and Number.
	P	Pickett Willard B	16	clerk	30	here
	R	Pickett Willard G	16	mason	62	"
	S	Murphy Dorothy—†	16	domestic	35	Medford
	T	Walsh Arthur	16	U S A	24	here
	U	Walsh David	16	clerk	28	"
	V	Walsh Janet—†	16	housewife	61	"
	W	Walsh Jeremiah	16	laborer	62	
	X	Murphy Annie—†	rear 16	housewife	71	"
	Y	Greene Frank	17	receiver	37	
	Z	Greene Lulu—†	17	housewife	31	"
1309						
	A	Sullivan Nora M—†	17	housekeeper	75	"
	B	Brindley Mary E—†	18	housewife	56	"
	C	Hebald Lafayette	18	clerk	35	
	D	Sullivan Charles D	18	U S N	22	
	E	Sullivan Ellen V—†	18	secretary	25	"
	F	Sullivan Mary A—†	18	cutter	53	
	G	Scrufutis Charles H	18	grocer	65	
	H	Scrufutis Demetria—†	18	housewife	60	"
	K	Scrufutis Ethel C—†	18	student	20	
	L	Scrufutis Helen C—†	18	chemist	24	
	M	Scrufutis James H	18	grocer	60	
	N	Scrufutis William C	18	U S N	27	
	O	Giodano Anthony	19	woodcarver	44	"
	P	Giodano Lena—†	19	housewife	41	"
	R	Visconti Ursula—†	19	winder	22	
	T	Brunick Margaret—†	19½	at home	20	
	U	Brunick Mary J—†	19½	operator	23	"
	V	Brunick Mary J—†	19½	housewife	50	"
	W	Canning Elizabeth—†	19½	"	60	
	X	Canning James	19½	machinist	35	"
	Y	Vaccaro George	rear 20	realtor	57	
	Z	Vaccaro George W	" 20	U S A	21	
1310						
	A	Vaccaro Olga—†	" 20	housewife	57	"
	B	King Helen—†	21	topographer	32	"
	C	King Nellie—†	21	housewife	60	"
	D	Collins Francis E	21	paver	36	
	E	Collins Mary E—†	21	housewife	37	"
	F	Conway Margaret—†	21	"	70	
	G	Conway Patrick	21	retired	79	

Page.	Letter.	Full Name.	Residence, Jan. 1, 1943.	Occupation.	Supposed Age.	Reported Residence, Jan. 1, 1942. Street and Number.

Centre Street—Continued

Page.	Letter.	Full Name.	Residence, Jan. 1, 1943.	Occupation.	Supposed Age.	Reported Residence, Jan. 1, 1942. Street and Number.
	K	*Scott Anna—†	23	at home	67	here
	L	Cremins Katherine—†	23	governess	27	"
	M	Cremins Katherine E—†	23	housewife	53	"
	N	Knowlton Margaret—†	23	"	40	
	O	Dietel Edwin	26	painter	38	
	P	Dietel Hannah—†	26	housewife	40	"
	R	Dietel Sophie M—†	26	"	68	"
	T	Marshall Elizabeth—†	29	"	39	Florida
	U	Marshall Stanley N	29	supervisor	37	"
	V	Shaffner Nita—†	29	housewife	50	here
	W	Dunn Anne M—†	29	"	48	"
	X	Dunn Peter	29	laborer	50	"
	Y	*Miskel Delia—†	31	dressmaker	48	"
	Z	Miskel Leo	31	houseman	21	"
1311						
	A	Miskel Stanley	31	janitor	54	
	B	Braunfield Arlene—†	31	housekeeper	63	"
	C	Hannon Fred	31	forger	57	33 Highland
	D	Jezerman Gottfried W	31	bartender	35	110 Broadway
	E	Lindsay Genevieve—†	31	at home	70	here
	F	Atherton James	45	retired	87	"
	G	Davis Hattie C—†	45	nurse	74	"
	H	Gaham Annie—†	45	cook	63	"
	K	Rush James	45	houseman	51	Chelsea
	L	Taylor Frederick L	45	physician	72	here
	M	Taylor Gwen Q—†	45	housewife	59	"
	N	White Joseph	48	U S A	38	"
	O	White Rebecca—†	48	housewife	60	"
	P	White Ada J—†	48	"	65	
	R	White Alfred N	48	U S A	25	
	S	White Ernest W	48	bellhop	28	
	T	White George F	48	retired	73	
	U	Guinessy Bridget—†	64	housewife	60	"
	V	Guinessy Christopher	64	U S N	24	
	W	Guinessy George	64	chauffeur	30	"
	X	Guinessy Vincent	64	U S A	28	
	Z	Higgins Bernard	66	"	27	
1312						
	A	Higgins Helen—†	66	housewife	62	"
	B	Higgins James	66	clerk	24	
	C	Higgins Kathleen—†	66	"	29	

Page.	Letter.	Full Name.	Residence, Jan. 1, 1943.	Occupation.	Supposed Age.	Reported Residence, Jan. 1, 1942. Street and Number.

Centre Street—Continued

	D	Higgins Patrick J	66	pipefitter	58	here
	E	Solazzo Anthony	66	laborer	59	"
	F	*Solazzo Peter	66	"	63	"
	G	*Solazzo Rose—†	66	factoryhand	30	"
	H	*Solazzo Seraphina—†	66	housewife	51	"
	L	Watson Blanche—†	68	"	50	
	M	Watson Evelyn—†	68	typist	21	
	N	Watson Fred	68	custodian	54	"
	O	Watson George	68	U S N	22	
	P	Campbell Helen J—†	68	stitcher	69	"
	R	Patterson Agnes—†	68	housewife	58	"
	S	Patterson John K	68	carpenter	58	"

Eliot Terrace

	U	Lindman Charles W	1	boilermaker	52	883 Hunt'n av
	V	Wainwright Josephine—†	1	housekeeper	48	883 "
	W	*Boyd Benjamin	1	watchman	62	here
	X	Boyd Mary—†	1	housewife	54	"

1313 Highland Avenue

	A	Arnett Ruby—†	10	waitress	35	here
	B	Anderson Albert B	10	oiler	31	68 Horadan way
	C	Anderson Levilla M—†	10	housewife	34	68 "
	D	O'Donnell Gertrude A—†	10	"	41	here
	E	O'Donnell James J	10	machinist	40	"
	F	Connolly Alice—†	11	operator	33	"
	G	Connolly Loretta—†	11	"	37	
	H	Connolly Margaret—†	11	tel operator	40	"
	K	Connolly Mary—†	11	"	39	
	L	Kucharski Catherine—†	11	housewife	35	"
	M	Kucharski Joseph	11	mechanic	37	"
	N	Lowry Anita M—†	12	housekeeper	63	"
	O	Moody Charles F	12	chef	52	"
	P	Gould Cora—†	12	housekeeper	64	"
	R	Murphy James	12	steamfitter	49	49 Linden Park
	S	Murphy Mary—†	12	clerk	25	49 "
	U	Detry Mary A—†	13	housewife	44	Connecticut
	V	Detry Walter O	13	salesman	44	1621 Wash'n
	W	Lyon Arthur W	13	U S N	23	71 Symphony rd

Page.	Letter.	FULL NAME.	Residence, Jan. 1, 1943.	Occupation.	Supposed Age.	Reported Residence, Jan. 1, 1942. Street and Number.

Highland Avenue—Continued

	X	Lyon Margaret—†	13	housewife	20	71 Symphony rd
	Z	Yates Ralph	14	U S A	29	here
1314						
	A	Yates Thelma—†	14	secretary	20	"
	B	Yurawitz Lucy—†	14	housewife	53	"
	C	Cavanaugh Elizabeth—†	14	"	65	
	D	Cavanaugh Henry M	14	clerk	38	"
	E	Sherriff Eileen—†	14	housewife	23	1 Hillview av
	F	Gagnon Iva—†	15	"	42	here
	G	Holmes Daniel J	15	builder	63	"
	H	Holmes Laura M—†	15	housewife	52	"
	K	Townsend Hartley	15	clerk	57	"
	L	Gagnon Francis	15	chauffeur	34	"
	M	Dever Frances—†	15	housewife	22	32 Prospect
	N	Dever William	15	trimmer	23	32 "
	O	Diamond Mary—†	15	housewife	28	here
	P	Zirul Anna—†	17	"	63	"
	R	Zirul Christopher	17	carpenter	63	"
	S	Anderson August	17	molder	60	
	T	Anderson Charles A	17	"	29	
	U	*Anderson Christina—†	17	housewife	56	"
	V	Selin Emma—†	17	clerk	21	
	W	Selin Greta—†	17	housewife	57	"
	X	Arildsen Dorothea—†	17	"	45	"
	Y	*Arildsen Marius A	17	shipfitter	40	"
1315						
	A	Davis Laura—†	19	housewife	65	"
	B	Isberg Eric	19	machinist	36	"
	C	Isberg Hilda—†	19	housewife	40	"
	D	McCue James	19	clerk	49	
	E	Merritt Joseph	19	machinist	39	"
	F	Merritt Winifred—†	19	housewife	39	"
	K	Brennan Michael	21	retired	75	
	L	Cremins Irene M—†	21	bookkeeper	41	"
	M	Cremins Julia—†	21	housewife	79	"
	N	O'Connor Julia L—†	21	clerk	46	"
	O	*Spracklin Florence M—†	22	housewife	42	"
	P	Spracklin Florence R—†	22	typist	20	
	R	Spracklin Wallace A	22	janitor	42	
	S	Foster Douglas	22	U S A	21	
	T	*Foster Elizabeth—†	22	housewife	44	"

Page.	Letter.	FULL NAME.	Residence, Jan. 1, 1943.	Occupation.	Supposed Age.	Reported Residence, Jan. 1, 1942. Street and Number.

Highland Avenue—Continued

	U	Foster Jennie—†	22	clerk	20	here
	V	Foster John	22	laborer	49	"
	W	Foster Oscar	22	U S A	22	"
	Y	Christopherson Michael	24	receiver	60	
	Z	*Christopherson Ragnhild-†	24	housewife	59	"
1316						
	A	Carroll Helen D—†	25	housekeeper	51	"
	B	Carroll Johanna T—†	25	"	56	
	C	Carr Marguerite A—†	26	"	67	"
	D	Farrell Eva—†	26	fitter	46	Lynn
	E	Forester Ellen E—†	26	housewife	62	here
	F	King Sarah A—†	26	at home	70	Brookline
	G	Kelley Mary—†	27	operator	34	127 Roxbury
	H	Phillips John	27	chauffeur	44	here
	K	Reall Jennie—†	27	housewife	35	6 Centre
	L	Reall John	27	clerk	45	6 "
	M	Vincent Mary C—†	27	housewife	77	here
	N	Vincent Richard S	27	mechanic	45	"
	O	West Clara—†	27	housewife	63	"
	P	West Henry	27	machinist	53	"
	S	*Needham Mary K—†	32	housewife	33	"
	T	Needham Michael P	32	chauffeur	47	"
	U	*Quinn Arlene—†	32	waitress	22	Maine
	V	*Quinn Florence—†	32	folder	28	Medford
	W	Dakin George W	32	retired	70	here
	X	Dakin Hattie M—†	32	housewife	65	"
	Y	Cook Alice S—†	32	housekeeper	68	26 Highland av
	Z	Mandosa Frank	32	laborer	33	here
1317						
	A	Mandosa Helen—†	32	housewife	33	"
	B	*Arundell Julia—†	34	"	43	42 Guild
	C	Goldstein Myer	34	realtor	54	here
	D	Knightly Harry C	34	storekeeper	56	249 Wash'n
	E	Knightly Lillian F—†	34	housewife	58	249 "
	F	Porter Mary M—†	38	"	48	here
	G	Riemer Barbara—†	38	"	24	"
	H	Thyng Mabel—†	38	saleswoman	53	"
	K	Merton Hadie—†	40	at home	50	
	L	Merton Minnie—†	40	housekeeper	42	"
	M	*Costa Mary—†	40	housewife	40	"
	N	*Costa Phyllis—†	40	teacher	49	

Page.	Letter.	Full Name.	Residence, Jan. 1, 1943.	Occupation.	Supposed Age.	Reported Residence, Jan. 1, 1942. Street and Number.

Highland Avenue—Continued

Page.	Letter.	Full Name.	Residence, Jan. 1, 1943.	Occupation.	Supposed Age.	Reported Residence, Jan. 1, 1942. Street and Number.
	O	Everett Amelia M—†	42	housewife	63	here
	P	Everett Edward	42	clergyman	63	“
	R	O'Connor Ellen F—†	42	teacher	62	“
	S	Oliver Austin	42	engineer	58	
	T	Oliver Jennie—†	42	housewife	50	“

Highland Place

Page.	Letter.	Full Name.	Residence, Jan. 1, 1943.	Occupation.	Supposed Age.	Reported Residence, Jan. 1, 1942. Street and Number.
	U	Cochis Arthur	1	mechanic	30	here
	V	Cochis Sally—†	1	housewife	24	“
	W	Perkins Annie E—†	1	at home	77	“
	X	Smith George E	1	clerk	56	
	Y	Smith Katherine T—†	1	housewife	55	“
	Z	Connors Helen M—†	2	“	26	
1318						
	A	Connors William R	2	electrician	29	“
	B	Hill George H	2	clerk	53	21 Bucknam
	C	Hill Mary K—†	2	housewife	53	21 “
	H	Dollman Hugo R	3	shipper	71	here
	K	Dollman Margaret A †	3	housewife	50	“
	L	McDonald Daniel W	3	custodian	54	“
	N	Egan Alice—†	4	housewife	62	“
	O	Egan John P	4	chef	64	“
	P	Laiveneck Emily—†	4	operator	56	Gardner
	R	Mittelholzer Marie—†	4	at home	77	58 Bickford
	S	Weed Catherine—†	4	waitress	36	here
	T	Gillis Viola—†	5	musician	45	“
	U	Smith Fred O	5	retired	82	“
	W	Hanna Alfred J	5	machinist	48	“
	X	Hanna Helen C—†	5	waitress	22	
	Y	Hanna Susie M—†	5	housewife	48	“
	Z	Joy Annie C—†	6	at home	70	
1319						
	A	Joy Harriet E—†	6	waitress	37	
	B	Otto Anna T—†	6	operator	40	..
	C	Stanley John A	6	retired	68	
	D	Ward Edmund F	6	chauffeur	65	“
	E	Ward Edmund F	6	executive	36	“
	F	Ward John B	6	U S A	34	

Page.	Letter.	Full Name.	Residence, Jan. 1, 1943.	Occupation.	Supposed Age.	Reported Residence, Jan. 1, 1942. Street and Number.

Highland Place—Continued

	G	Ward Lewis F	6	shipfitter	26	here
	H	Ward Marie G—†	6	housewife	65	"
	K	Linquist Harold	6	clerk	22	"
	L	Linquist Hilda—†	6	housewife	54	"
	M	*Iuvarra Nicolina—†	6	at home	60	"
	N	Iuvarra Salvatore	6	retired	63	

Highland Street

	O	Canfield Esther L—†	1	housewife	54	here
	P	Canfield Pierce R	1	plumber	57	"
	R	Fisher William L	1A	mortician	45	"
	S	Walker Arnold E	1A	student	28	"
	T	Clifford John	2	plumber	28	5 Eustis
	U	Dineen John	2	janitor	43	14 Lambert
	V	Feeley Ralph	2	porter	25	71 Bartlett
	W	Grybas Adolph	2	U S A	26	here
	X	*Kressler Emma—†	2	at home	73	"
	Y	Kressler Johanna—†	2	housekeeper	45	"
	Z	Lavassa William	2	laborer	36	Marlboro
1320						
	A	Levine Samuel	2	ironworker	30	here
	B	Lewis Samuel	2	iceman	79	"
	C	Dallas Herbert A	3	supervisor	61	"
	D	Dallas Margaret T—†	3	housewife	59	"
	E	Dallas Marie I—†	3	clerk	54	"
	F	Melady Frank A	3	"	62	
	G	Salter Herbert J	3	"	63	"
	H	Ryan Francis R	4	janitor	42	32 Woodcliff
	K	Ryan Isabelle C—†	4	housewife	44	32 "
	L	Faenza Elizabeth—†	5	bookkeeper	20	here
	M	Faenza Frank	5	draftsman	59	"
	N	*Faenza Giovina—†	5	housewife	48	"
	O	Joyce Albert F	7	laborer	31	20 Dorr
	P	Kelleher Edward F	7	foreman	43	20 "
	R	Kelleher Margaret F—†	7	housewife	35	20 "
	S	McManus George	7	steward	33	20 "
	T	Nayers John E	7	printer	34	20 "
	U	Scannell Richard A	7	engineer	53	284 Talbot av

Page.	Letter.	Full Name.	Residence, Jan. 1, 1943.	Occupation.	Supposed Age.	Reported Residence, Jan. 1, 1942. Street and Number.

Highland Street—Continued

	W	Reddish Herbert B	8	U S N	22	752 Parker
	X	Reddish Hilda—†	8	housewife	24	752 "
	Z	Bagley Joseph D	9	U S A	32	here
1321						
	A	Carroll John	9	lather	35	
	B	Proctor Russell	9	roofer	39	"
	C	Sullivan Daniel	9	retired	63	
	D	Sullivan Daniel F	9	salesman	31	"
	E	Sullivan Joseph T	9	teacher	33	"
	F	Sullivan Mary M—†	9	housewife	31	40 Savin
	G	Sullivan Mary N—†	9	clerk	35	here
	H	Sliwa John W	10	lawyer	45	"
	K	Sliwa Stella R—†	10	housewife	39	"
	L	Dennis Annie—†	10	"	70	
	M	Dennis George F	10	retired	77	
	N	Walker Alfred	10	U S A	34	
	O	Walker Annie—†	10	housekeeper	59	"
	P	Walker David	10	U S A	23	"
	R	Walker Joseph	10	laborer	25	
	S	Glynn James D	10	U S M C	20	"
	T	Glynn John F	10	foreman	45	36 Linden pk
	U	Glynn John F, jr	10	U S A	24	here
	X	Cusimano Maurice	12	"	25	"
	V	DiLegami Peter	12	shoemaker	49	"
	W	*DiLegami Theresa—†	12	housewife	47	"
	Y	Alaimo John	12	operator	32	"
	Z	Alaimo Suzanne—†	12	housewife	29	"
1322						
	A	Campbell Lawrence H	12	transitman	35	65 Fort av
	B	Campbell Mary C—†	12	housewife	32	65 "
	C	Glynn Elizabeth M—†	14	"	47	here
	D	Glynn John H	14	salesman	51	"
	E	Neilsen Albert F	14	carpenter	51	"
	F	Neilsen Dorothy—†	14	waitress	21	
	G	Neilsen Myra—†	14	housewife	50	"
	H	Rice Mary E—†	14	at home	77	"
	L	Erickson Albert F	16	laborer	56	144 Dudley
	M	Erickson Sophie—†	16	housewife	45	144 "
	N	Trepanies Dennis W	16	shipworker	23	144 "
	O	Tompkins Esther—†	16	housewife	38	here
	P	Tompkins Frank	16	bottler	48	"

Page.	Letter.	Full Name.	Residence, Jan. 1, 1943.	Occupation.	Supposed Age.	Reported Residence, Jan. 1, 1942. Street and Number.

Highland Street—Continued

	R	Jackson Eleanor—†	16	housewife	28	Everett
	S	Lamson Walter C	18	counterman	60	here
	T	Glynn Anna M—†	18	housewife	49	"
	U	Glynn John H	18	chauffeur	48	"
	V	Sullivan Mary—†	18	housewife	40	"
	W	Sullivan Michael	18	laborer	40	
	X	Connelly James H	18	rubberworker	76	"
	Y	Small Agnes T—†	18	at home	68	
	Z	*Campagnone Angelo	19	contractor	55	"
1323						
	A	*Campagnone Mary—†	19	housewife	52	"
	C	Donahue Bridget—†	19	"	77	"
	D	Bishop Martha—†	20	at home	71	
	E	Crump Willie—†	20	domestic	35	"
	F	Harris Edward	20	porter	47	
	G	Robinson Ada—†	20	housewife	41	"
	H	Robinson Charles A	20	mechanic	42	"
	K	Simpson Reuben	20	porter	50	14 Linwood pk
	L	Plunkett Anna F—†	21	housewife	36	here
	M	Plunkett Thomas F	21	baker	38	"
	N	Hogan Edward F	21A	U S N	30	86 Vernon
	O	Hogan Matilda M—†	21A	housewife	25	86 "
	P	Smolinsky Anna—†	21A	"	56	here
	R	Smolinsky Frank	21A	gardener	56	"
	S	Smolinsky Frank J	21A	U S A	33	"
	T	Smolinsky Matthew F	21A	"	21	
	U	Smolinsky Rose V—†	21A	secretary	35	"
	V	Barry Philip	22	shipper	40	"
	W	Barry Rose—†	22	housewife	38	"
	X	Piscatelli John	22	U S A	45	
	Y	Piscatelli Marie—†	22	housewife	75	"
	Z	Piscatelli Nunzio	22	U S A	32	
1324						
	A	Cunneen John M	23	"	42	
	B	Liddy Nora M—†	23	housewife	69	"
	C	Burke Theresa W—†	23A	"	43	
	D	Burke William J	23A	chauffeur	42	"
	E	Dunn Edward J	23A	U S A	25	
	F	Dunn James E	23A	serviceman	41	"
	G	Dunn James J	23A	U S A	30	
	H	Brown John	25	clerk	51	

Page.	Letter.	Full Name.	Residence, Jan. 1, 1943.	Occupation.	Supposed Age.	Reported Residence, Jan. 1, 1942. Street and Number.

Highland Street—Continued

	K	Demeritt Mark C	25	lithographer	41	here
	L	Hickey Edward	25	retired	72	"
	M	Lents Louise—†	25	stitcher	45	"
		McCauley Beatrice—†	25	waitress	40	
		Miller Catherine—†	25	clerk	53	
	N O	Swininer Catherine—†	25	at home	67	
	R	Taft Dora D—†	25	housekeeper	75	"
	S	Ball Joseph D	28	machinist	43	"
	T	Hagerty William	28	laborer	53	
	U	*O'Neill Cornelius	28	retired	89	
	V	O'Neill Margaret M—†	28	housewife	45	"
	W	O'Neill Patrick J	28	checker	50	"
	X	O'Neill Richard P	28	clerk	21	
	Y	*Giardini Charles J	30	radios	34	
	Z	Giardini Sue J—†	30	housewife	29	"
1325						
	A	Rindone Anthony	30	U S A	22	"
	B	Connors Anna P—†	30	examiner	26	5 Elmwood pl
	C	Connors Nina—†	30	housewife	55	5 "
	D	Connors Nina M—†	30	clerk	24	5 "
	E	Connors Ruth E—†	30	"	20	5 "
	F	Croumey Anna M—†	33	"	25	here
	G	Croumey Carl A	33	machinist	52	"
	H	*Croumey Katherine—†	33	at home	76	"
	K	Croumey Mary—†	33	housewife	47	"
	L	Powelkopf Louise—†	33	laundress	52	"
	M	Chute Alfred E	33	metalworker	31	62 Neponset av
	N	Chute Edith E—†	33	housewife	26	62 "
	O	*Griffin Margaret E—†	33	"	54	here
	P	Griffin Patrick	33	steamfitter	57	"
	R	Wadon Helen K—†	33	housewife	31	"
	S	Wadon John	33	patternmaker	33	"
	T	Brown Rebecca—†	34	waitress	40	181 Northampton
	U	Edison Annie—†	34	housewife	68	181 "
	V	Katchings James	34	porter	59	106 W Springfield
	W	Lewis Robert P	34	longshoreman	37	181 Northampton
	X	Beattie Arthur W	36	ironworker	58	here
	Y	Beattie Eleanor—†	36	housewife	43	"
	Z	Beattie James	36	U S A	22	"

Page.	Letter.	FULL NAME.	Residence, Jan. 1, 1943.	Occupation.	Supposed Age.	Reported Residence, Jan. 1, 1942. Street and Number.

1326

Highland Street—Continued

	A	Beattie Pearl—†	36	factoryhand	20	here
	B	Beattie Philip	36	U S A	23	"
	C	Dann Albert	42	laborer	20	"
	D	Dann August	42	watchman	61	"
	E	*Dann Martha—†	42	housewife	55	"
	F	Dann Paul	42	U S A	23	"
	G	Rodonis Joseph	42	laborer	45	38 Vinton
	H	*Rodonis Rose—†	42	housewife	43	38 "
	K	Diaferio Jean—†	42	"	22	here
	L	Diaferio Michael	42	salesman	25	"
	M	Ross Catherine C—†	44	clerk	33	"
	N	Ross Harvey D	44	U S A	31	
	O	*Ross Helen—†	44	housewife	62	"
	P	*Ross Hugh G	44	U S A	39	
	R	*Ross Irad J	44	foreman	68	

Highland Terrace

	S	Ahearn May—†	1	housewife	21	here
	T	Ahearn Timothy	1	laborer	22	"
	U	Gowing Hattie—†	1	at home	67	"
	V	Peasler Helen L—†	1	laundress	45	"
	W	Pratt Ida M—†	1	housewife	23	6 Jarvis pl
	X	Pratt Leonard	1	tester	24	6 "
	Y	Weeks George F	1	machinist	28	here
	Z	Weeks Hattie M—†	1	at home	25	"
1327						
	A	*Levy Jean—†	1	housewife	38	"
	B	*Levy Morris	1	carpenter	49	"
	C	Howard Dorothy—†	1	domestic	37	"
	D	Howard George B	1	laundryman	33	"
	E	Howard Mary—†	1	stitcher	32	
	F	Brinkert Catherine—†	2	at home	42	
	G	Brinkert Herbert R	2	chauffeur	45	"
	H	*Haroutunian Catherine—†	3	at home	39	
	M	Haroutunian Michael	3	shoeworker	29	"
	K	Caffarelli Anna—†	3	saleswoman	31	"
	L	Caffarelli Joseph	3	merchant	40	"

Page.	Letter.	Full Name.	Residence, Jan. 1, 1943.	Occupation.	Supposed Age.	Reported Residence, Jan. 1, 1942. Street and Number.

John Eliot Square

	N	Armstrong Marjorie—†	14	teacher	35	here
	O	Brown Carleton W	14	student	24	N Hampshire
	P	Bydeley Elsie—†	14	"	30	Montana
	R	Clark Eve—†	14	clerk	26	here
	S	Forsythe Thomas	14	student	24	Rhode Island
	T	Greenwood Sibyl L—†	14	social worker	26	Winchendon
	U	Hager Russell P	14	student	26	Rhode Island
	V	Hawley Jean—†	14	teacher	25	N Hampshire
	W	Helseth Jane—†	14	secretary	26	here
	X	Hobley Esther M—†	14	upholsterer	40	"
	Y	*Holmes Anna—†	14	housekeeper	65	"
	Z	Lynch Sophia G—†	14	"	65	"
1328						
	A	Mannel Elizabeth—†	14	student	25	Connecticut
	B	March Viola R—†	14	teacher	50	here
	C	McLaughlin Esther—†	14	housewife	45	"
	D	McLaughlin Francis X	14	clerk	48	"
	E	Menclum Estelle M—†	14	social worker	65	"
	F	Olsen Marion—†	14	student	24	Connecticut
	G	Pierce Willette C—†	14	clerk	30	here
	H	Robie Natalie A—†	14	teacher	25	"
	K	Robie Theodore	14	physician	25	"
	L	Ryan Mary P—†	14	student	24	Connecticut
	M	Sawitsky Anne—†	14	clerk	30	Cambridge
	N	Soule Frederick J	14	social worker	59	here
	O	Soule Grace M—†	14	housewife	57	"
	P	Soule Richard H	14	U S A	22	"
	R	Soule Robert M	14	"	27	"
	S	*Subac Hans C	14	student	24	5 Adelaide
	T	Tye Raymond A	14	"	21	Haverhill
	U	Weir Barbara L—†	14	clerk	24	Minnesota
	V	Wyman Martha A—†	14	"	55	here
	X	Mulkeen Catherine V—†	26	beautician	50	"
1329						
	M	Brennan John A	50	repairman	45	"
	N	Brennan Marie J—†	50	housewife	45	"
	O	Brennan Thomas T	50	U S A	21	
	R	Lee Goon	50C	laundryman	65	"

Page.	Letter.	Full Name.	Residence, Jan. 1, 1943.	Occupation.	Supposed Age.	Reported Residence, Jan. 1, 1942. Street and Number.

Lambert Avenue

Page.	Letter.	Full Name.	Residence, Jan. 1, 1943.	Occupation.	Supposed Age.	Reported Residence, Jan. 1, 1942. Street and Number.
	Y	Richards Caroline C—†	5	teacher	68	here
	V	Battalia Elizabeth—†	5	saleswoman	44	2754 Wash'n
	W	Battalia Marino	5	U S A	26	2754 "
	X	Battalia Rosena—†	5	housekeeper	46	2754 "
	Z	Spinella Josephine—†	5	at home	42	2754 "
1330						
	A	Hennessey Austin	17	U S A	34	here
	1A	Horgan Dorothy—†	17	nurse	22	"
	B	Horgan John	17	U S A	28	"
	C	Kennedy Janet—†	17	nurse	40	
	D	Kennedy Mary—†	17	at home	67	"
	F	Kiernan Anna—†	17	housewife	39	"
	G	Kiernan Frank	17	shipfitter	38	"
	H	Stapleton Ethel—†	17	at home	62	
	K	Stapleton Joseph	17	retired	60	
	L	Carlson Oscar	19	machinist	58	"
	M	Dysart Fred	19	blacksmith	63	"
	N	Kessler Mabel—†	19	seamstress	48	"
	O	Lancy Emma—†	19	housekeeper	64	"
	P	McSweeney Mary—†	19	domestic	57	"
	R	Shuman Henry	19	chauffeur	46	"
	S	Doyle Catherine P—†	21	winder	21	
	T	Doyle Francis E	21	guard	56	
	U	Doyle Mary C—†	21	at home	23	
	V	Doyle Mary T—†	21	housekeeper	55	"
	W	Cunniff Eleanor M—†	21	clerk	20	"
	X	Cunniff Elizabeth N—†	21	housewife	49	"
	Y	Cunniff Mary P—†	21	clerk	22	
	Z	Cunniff Patrick	21	fireman	56	
1331						
	A	Scott Catherine—†	21	housewife	45	"
	C	Scott George T	21	fireman	45	
	B	Scott Katherine M—†	21	stenographer	23	"
	D	Scott William	21	chauffeur	51	"
	E	Drew Cecile—†	23	housewife	27	"
	F	Drew Lawrence	23	painter	33	
	G	Gillis Alexander F	23	supervisor	24	"
	H	Gillis John W	23	U S A	22	

Page.	Letter.	Full Name.	Residence, Jan. 1, 1943.	Occupation.	Supposed Age.	Reported Residence, Jan. 1, 1942. Street and Number.

Lambert Avenue—Continued

	K	Gillis Joseph	23	U S N	23	here
	L	Gillis Lawrence	23	"	20	"
	M	Gillis Marie—†	23	housewife	50	"
	N	Gillis Mary—†	23	secretary	25	"
	O	Gillis Michael B	23	carpenter	60	"
	P	Foley Joseph	23	painter	39	
	R	Foley Lola—†	23	housewife	36	"
	S	Hoyle Elizabeth—†	25	"	43	
	T	Hoyle John C	25	mechanic	41	"
	W	Power John H	27	electrician	59	"
	X	Power Margaret L—†	27	housewife	59	"
	Y	Dakin George P	27	U S A	21	"
	Z	Dakin Harold P	27	storekeeper	44	"
1332						
	A	Dakin Margaret G—†	27	housewife	44	"
	B	Cameron Cora L—†	27	"	65	
	C	Cameron William H	27	retired	66	
	D	Mehan Faye A—†	27	waitress	43	
	E	Stearns Howard J	27	manager	52	"
	F	Turner Inez C—†	27	treasurer	47	"

Lambert Street

	G	McClutchy John H	4	U S A	23	here
	H	McClutchy Margaret C—†	4	housewife	41	"
	K	McClutchy Mary A—†	4	operator	20	"
	L	McClutchy Thomas F	4	inspector	47	"
	M	Potter Margaret—†	4	housewife	20	"
	N	Potter William H	4	U S A	20	"
	O	Costello Loretta—†	8	housewife	57	"
	P	Wheatley Robert	8	U S A	21	"
	R	Newton Dorothy—†	8	housewife	40	629 Tremont
	S	Newton Guy	8	electrician	45	629 "
	T	Conlon Charles F	8	U S N	23	here
	U	Conlon Delia—†	8	housewife	57	"
	V	Conlon Paul E	8	U S A	22	"
	W	Lally Michael	8	machinist	51	New York
	X	*Robbins Elizabeth—†	10	housewife	31	9 Oakland
	Y	Robbins Frederick H	10	porter	37	9 "

Lambert Street—Continued

Page.	Letter.	Full Name.	Residence, Jan. 1, 1943.	Occupation.	Supposed Age.	Reported Residence, Jan. 1, 1942. Street and Number.
1333	A	Boltin Anna—†	10	housewife	61	here
	B	Boltin Bernard G	10	toolmaker	34	"
	C	Boltin John	10	retired	64	"
	D	Robbins Ida M—†	12	housewife	67	27 Linwood
	E	Letteney Edith—†	12	"	65	11 Meshaka
	F	Wood Chester R	12	U S A	42	here
	G	Wood Mary E—†	12	housewife	43	"
	H	LaShoto Antonia—†	13	"	48	"
	K	LaShoto Michael	13	buffer	48	
	L	LaShoto Stanley	13	pipefitter	24	"
	M	McClellan Elizabeth—†	13	housewife	54	12 Cedar pk
	N	McClellan James V	13	metalworker	21	12 "
	O	McClellan Marilyn—†	13	stitcher	20	12 "
	P	Hekinian Kirkor	14	welder	28	59 Whittier
	R	Jamgochian Mihran	14	cleaner	59	59 "
	S	Jamgochian Rose—†	14	housewife	42	59 "
	T	MacLeod Christina—†	15	"	55	here
	U	MacLeod Malcolm	15	baker	55	"
	V	Drury Elizabeth—†	16	housewife	37	"
	W	Drury Vincent	16	U S A	35	
	X	Rainer Blanche—†	16	wireworker	41	"
	Y	Neugebauer Carl	17	counterman	49	"
	Z	Neugebauer Ida K—†	17	housewife	52	"
1334	A	Roherty Ida—†	17	beautician	26	"
	B	Roussopolos Apostolos C	17	U S A	34	15 Codman pk
	C	Roussopolos Jennie—†	17	housewife	32	15 "
	D	Trottier Bernard	20	operator	37	here
	E	Trottier Helen—†	20	housewife	31	"
	F	Farrell Mary—†	21	beautician	23	33 Alaska
	G	O'Keefe John	21	clerk	27	33 "
	H	O'Keefe Margaret—†	21	housewife	26	33 "
	K	Foy Rita—†	22	"	29	Danvers
	L	Foy Roland	22	foreman	34	"
	M	Richards Beatrice—†	23	housewife	32	here
	N	Bornstein Abram	24	storekeeper	43	"
	O	Bronstein Sara—†	24	housewife	45	"
	P	Carney Jane E—†	24	"	33	16 Lamont
	R	Carney Robert F	24	cleaner	36	16 "

Page.	Letter.	FULL NAME.	Residence, Jan. 1, 1943.	Occupation.	Supposed Age.	Reported Residence, Jan. 1, 1942. Street and Number.

Lambert Street—Continued

	S	Godsoe Rita J—†	24	housewife	20	Brookline
	T	Godsoe Robert E	24	laborer	26	"
	V	Ryan Mary A—†	26	housewife	68	here
	W	Pottle Raymond	26	U S A	23	64 Circuit
	X	Rotondi Lois—†	26	housewife	27	24 Greenville
	Y	Swenson Arthur	26	laborer	66	39 Mt Pleasant av
	Z	Burnhan Harry	26	"	53	here
1335						
	A	Pineau Harry	26	clerk	42	
	B	Pineau Mary—†	26	housewife	27	"
	C	Giblin Mary R—†	27	"	71	5 Brookfield
	D	Giblin Peter P	27	retired	71	5 "
	E	Lohmann Esther—†	27	housewife	48	here
	F	Lohmann Frank	27	chef	48	"
	G	Cobb Gertrude—†	28	housewife	27	"
	H	Cobb Sumner	28	laborer	28	"
	K	Fay Frank J	28	welder	39	30 Lambert
	L	Fay Joan—†	28	housewife	38	30 "
	M	Curtis Christina—†	28	"	53	here
	N	Curtis James B	28	laborer	63	"
	O	Curtis Milton J	28	U S A	23	"
	P	Grant Harry C	30	clerk	53	127 Eustis
	R	Grant Margaret J—†	30	housewife	33	127 "
	S	O'Keefe Gertrude—†	30	"	35	here
	T	O'Keefe Timothy F	30	chauffeur	37	"
	U	Verranault Carmela—†	30	housewife	37	3 Gay
	V	Verranault Henry E	30	laborer	34	3 "
	W	Clark Joan—†	31	housewife	25	37 Howard av
	X	Clark Thomas	31	fireman	33	37 "
	Y	Krebs Carl A	31	artist	41	here
	Z	Krebs Madeline—†	31	housewife	39	"
1336						
	A	Tierney Michael J	31	retired	75	
	B	Ericson Oscar R	31	U S A	34	
	C	Secord Jessie—†	31	housewife	67	"
	D	Secord Margaret E—†	31	operator	43	"
	E	Handren James T	31	candymaker	45	"
	F	Handren John F	31	laborer	52	"

Page.	Letter.	Full Name.	Residence, Jan. 1, 1943.	Occupation.	Supposed Age.	Reported Residence, Jan. 1, 1942. Street and Number.

Lambert Street—Continued

	G	Handren John J	31	U S A	20	here
	H	Harrington Edward J	31	"	21	"
	K	Harrington John P	31	"	22	"
	L	Magoon Margaret—†	31	housewife	67	"
	M	Soper Frank	31	manager	47	"
	N	Soper Margaret—†	31	housewife	40	"
	O	Johnson Oscar	31	boilermaker	31	"
	P	Riesner Jacob	31	engineer	60	
	R	Smith Harold	31	metalworker	26	"
	S	*Wadon Lucy—†	31	housewife	56	"
	T	Wadon William	31	ironworker	50	"
	U	*Minsky Anne—†	31	housewife	30	"
	V	*Minsky Saul	31	laborer	35	
	W	Feller Esther—†	31	housewife	27	"
	X	Feller John G	31	clerk	39	
	1X	DelTufo Helen—†	31	housewife	30	"
	Y	Godsoe Herbert D	31	salesman	64	"
	Z	Godsoe Kenneth H	31	shipper	21	
1337						
	A	Godsoe Mary C—†	31	housewife	52	"
	C	Lefevre Dorothy—†	34	"	32	
	D	Lefevre Kenneth A	34	mover	38	
	E	Tebeau Harold R	34	fireman	27	
	F	Tebeau Nellie—†	34	housewife	25	"
	G	McInnis Helen—†	36	"	40	"
	H	McInnis John	36	engineer	65	"
	K	Gillis Florence—†	38	housewife	43	"
	L	Gillis John J	38	operator	45	"
	M	*Roper Kathleen E—†	40	housewife	28	"
	N	Roper Martin J	40	storekeeper	40	"
	O	McCarren Barbara M—†	40	housewife	59	"
	P	McCarren Barbara M—†	40	clerk	21	
	R	McCarren Edward C	40	U S A	31	
	S	McCarren Edward J	40	retired	67	"
	T	McCarren John F	40	U S A	26	"
	U	McCarren Joseph D	40	clerk	28	
	V	Foshey Charles A	40	machinist	38	"
	W	Foshey Helen E—†	40	housewife	66	"

Page.	Letter.	Full Name.	Residence, Jan. 1, 1943.	Occupation.	Supposed Age.	Reported Residence, Jan. 1, 1942. Street and Number.

Lambert Street—Continued

Page.	Letter.	Full Name.	Residence, Jan. 1, 1943.	Occupation.	Supposed Age.	Reported Residence, Jan. 1, 1942. Street and Number.
	X	Potter Mary—†	42	teller	45	here
	Y	Potter Ruth—†	42	housewife	22	"
	Z	Kapp Arthur	42	baker	55	"
1338						
	A	Kapp Gertrude R—†	42	housewife	35	"
	B	Logan Joseph	42	salesman	44	"
	C	Logan Laura M—†	42	housewife	47	"

Linwood Square

Page.	Letter.	Full Name.	Residence, Jan. 1, 1943.	Occupation.	Supposed Age.	Reported Residence, Jan. 1, 1942. Street and Number.
	D	Perry John	2	chauffeur	30	here
	E	Perry Theresa—†	2	housewife	28	"
	F	McGran Ellen M—†	2	housekeeper	50	1922 Col av
	G	Moynihan Amelia—†	2	at home	78	1922 "
	K	Grasso Antoinette—†	4	housewife	20	1 Eliot ter
	L	Grasso Leonard J	4	coremaker	23	1 "
	M	Mastrobattista Elenora—†	4	housewife	35	here
	N	Mastrobattista Ostilio	4	cook	39	"
	O	Fornaro Angelina F—†	5	wrapper	31	"
	P	Fornaro Catherine—†	5	presser	27	
	R	Fornaro Guy J	5	U S N	22	
	S	Fornaro John C	5	chauffeur	20	"
	T	Fornaro Nicola	5	retired	63	
	U	Fornaro Rosa—†	5	housewife	56	"
	V	Russo John	5	barber	52	"
	W	Connors Annie—†	5	at home	70	5 Chilcott pl
	X	Connors Michael	5	machinist	68	5 "
	Y	Connors Thomas W	5	"	58	5 "
	Z	Seeds Catherine L—†	5	housekeeper	65	5 "
1339						
	A	Lugrin Berne	6	finisher	33	13 Highland av
	B	Lugrin Charles B	6	retired	61	13 "
	C	Lugrin Florence—†	6	housewife	67	13 "
	D	Witol Selma L—†	6	housekeeper	42	Revere
	E	Lord Agnes—†	6	"	40	here
	F	Carter Bertha H—†	7	housewife	54	"
	G	Carter Walter W	7	painter	46	"
	H	Hall Mary E—†	7	at home	67	"
	K	Weir Charles M	7	chauffeur	41	97 St Alphonsus
	L	Weir Mary—†	7	housewife	42	97 "
	N	Townsend James	8	laborer	23	76 Fort av

Page.	Letter.	Full Name.	Residence, Jan. 1, 1943.	Occupation.	Supposed Age.	Reported Residence, Jan. 1, 1942. Street and Number.

Linwood Square—Continued

	o	Townsend Margaret—†	8	housewife	21	76 Fort av
	p	Power Alice G—†	8	housekeeper	30	14 Day
	r	Shelton Howard J	9	shipper	44	here
	s	Shelton Joseph P	9	janitor	72	"
	t	Shelton Ruth—†	9	housewife	35	"
	u	Stewart Archie E	9	clerk	29	
	v	Stewart Letitia E—†	9	housewife	27	"
	x	Carrigan John F	10	lather	43	
	y	Carrigan Loretta A—†	10	housewife	38	"
	z*	Groden Catherine—†	10	"	53	319 E
1340						
	a	Groden Edward J	10	metalworker	24	319 "
	b	Groden Patrick C	10	laborer	63	319 "
	c	Groden Thomas I	10	U S A	26	319 "
	d	Groden Winifred C—†	10	nurse	22	319 "
	f	Tobias Abraham	12	packer	60	here
	g	Wisentaner Anna—†	13	housewife	62	"
	h	Wisentaner Frank R	13	operator	39	"
	k	Wisentaner Hope V—†	13	clerk	24	
	l	Wisentaner John B	13	machinist	70	"
	m	Wisentaner Leo A	13	U S N	26	
	n	Wisentaner Ruth A—†	13	secretary	29	"
	p	Crosby Lillian—†	16	housekeeper	37	"
	r	Keene Edith F—†	16	housewife	36	"
	s	Keene Francis L	16	chauffeur	29	"
	t	Tebeau Francis D	16	sign painter	32	"
	u	Tebeau Helen A—†	16	housewife	28	"
	v	Tebeau Walter L	16	painter	37	"
	w	Murphy George A	20	conductor	28	"
	x	Murphy Jennie T—†	20	clerk	22	
	y	Murphy Katherine T—†	20	housewife	62	"
	z	Murphy Michael J	20	upholsterer	62	"
1341						
	a	Murphy Olga—†	20	housekeeper	29	"
	b	Finneran Andrew J	22	pipefitter	20	"
	c	Finneran Catherine M—†	22	housewife	45	"
	d	Finneran Patrick B	22	watchman	50	"
	e	O'Connor Helen E—†	22	bookbinder	47	"
	f	Clonan Arthur M	24	cleaner	26	
	g	Clonan Coleman J	24	retired	70	
	h	Clonan Coleman J, jr	24	clerk	31	"

Page.	Letter.	Full Name.	Residence, Jan. 1, 1943.	Occupation.	Supposed Age.	Reported Residence, Jan. 1, 1942. Street and Number.

Linwood Square—Continued

	K	Clonan Edward F	24	packer	28	here
	L	Clonan Helen C—†	24	housekeeper	36	"
	M	Donnelly Eleanor M—†	26	clerk	22	"
	N	Donnelly Mary A—†	26	housewife	48	"
	O	Donnelly Michael F	26	porter	52	
	P	Donnelly Michael	26	U S N	20	
	R	Donnelly Thomas H	26	U S A	26	

Linwood Street

	S	Shaughnessy Rosella—†	1	housekeeper	34	here
	T	Smith Albert C	1	U S A	24	14 Alpine
	U	Smith Margie—†	1	housewife	37	here
	V	Graham Elizabeth T—†	1	housekeeper	43	133 Warren
	W	Willey Karl T	1	U S N	25	Somerville
	X	Willey Martha E—†	1	housewife	20	133 Warren
	Y	Bragg Blanche—†	19	"	32	Revere
	Z	Bragg John	19	chauffeur	33	"
1342						
	A	Laefer Fannie—†	19	housekeeper	68	here
	C	Burjoice Marion—†	21	housewife	50	"
	D	Burjoice Morris	21	inspector	50	"
	E	Gildea Florence—†	21	saleswoman	51	"
	F	Haarer Marion—†	21	clerk	42	
	G	Gilliland Carl	21	foreman	43	
	H	Gilliland Dorothy—†	21	housewife	39	"
	K	Davies Ann—†	23	"	69	
	L	Davies William H	23	carpenter	65	"
	M	Hutchinson Ruth M—†	23	clerk	34	
	N	Kirkpatrick Charles T	23	cooper	64	
	O	Kirkpatrick Janet—†	23	housewife	61	"
	P	Martin Mary—†	23	housekeeper	54	"
	R	Martin William G	23	U S A	34	
	S	Shruhan Frank P	25	machinist	39	"
	T	Shruhan Margaret E—†	25	housewife	37	"
	U	McCoy Alma R—†	27	"	27	155 Thornton
	V	McCoy Predore A	27	mechanic	39	155 "
	W	Williams Katherine—†	27	housewife	57	68 Codman pk
	X	King Dorothy—†	27	packer	23	here

Linwood Street—Continued

Page.	Letter.	Full Name.	Residence, Jan. 1, 1943.	Occupation.	Supposed Age.	Reported Residence, Jan. 1, 1942. Street and Number.
	Y	King Florence—†	27	housekeeper	44	here
	Z	King Owen	27	laborer	47	"
1343						
	A	Molloy Sarah—†	27	stitcher	52	
	C	O'Brien Edward V	39	clerk	27	
	D	O'Brien Elsie—†	39	housekeeper	27	"
	E	Rosenbloom Katherine—†	39	housewife	32	"
	F	Rosenbloom Samuel I	39	pipefitter	36	"
	K	Coughlin Frank A	41	plumber	42	
	L	Coughlin Mary C—†	41	housewife	41	"
	N	Greer Anna A—†	41	housekeeper	30	"
	O	Greer John J	41	shoemaker	42	"
	P	Greer Joseph G	41	carcleaner	38	"
	R	*Maguire Mary—†	41	housekeeper	59	"
	T	Kelley Catherine C—†	43	laundress	55	"
	U	Kelley Henry M	43	retired	67	
	V	Gallagher Eugene F	43	chauffeur	36	"
	W	Gallagher Mary A—†	43	housekeeper	65	"
	X	Donnelly Winifred C—†	43	"	46	"
1344						
	B	Cotter Bernard T	45	laborer	27	16 Highland
	A	Cotter Carmella M—†	45	housewife	21	16 "
	D	Lucey Jessie M—†	45	"	46	2 Fenwick
	E	Lucey Michael	45	engineer	59	2 "
	F	Felides Athena—†	51	housewife	48	here
	G	*Felides Harry	51	cook	62	"
	H	Felides Lena—†	51	clerk	21	"
	K	Felides Mary—†	51	"	23	
	L	Felides William	51	chauffeur	23	"
	M	Georgenes George	51	restaurateur	46	"
	N	*Georgenes Victoria N—†	51	housewife	40	"
	O	Perkins Jennie L—†	53	at home	81	75 Centre
	P	Perkins Susie B—†	53	bookkeeper	59	75 "
	R	Richards Louise K—†	53	housekeeper	62	75 "

Millmont Street

Page.	Letter.	Full Name.	Residence, Jan. 1, 1943.	Occupation.	Supposed Age.	Reported Residence, Jan. 1, 1942. Street and Number.
	S	Walsh Ella T—†	4	shoeworker	58	here
	T	Walsh James J	4	laborer	55	"

Page.	Letter.	FULL NAME.	Residence, Jan. 1, 1943.	Occupation.	Supposed Age.	Reported Residence, Jan. 1, 1942. Street and Number.

Millmont Street—Continued

	U	Walsh Margaret M—†	4	housekeeper	48	here
	W	Cannon Rita B—†	6	"	26	"
	X	Stefany Anna—†	6	housewife	57	"
	Y	Stefany Anthony R	6	U S N	22	
	Z	Stefany John A	6	floorlayer	59	"
1345						
	A	Pratt George	6	U S A	29	
	B	Pratt Margaret—†	6	housewife	26	"
	C	White Julia—†	6	manufacturer	25	"
	D	White Margaret—†	6	housekeeper	59	"
	E	Bradley Mary H—†	8	housewife	38	"
	F	Bradley Milton H	8	guard	37	
	G	Shepard James W	8	painter	49	
	H	Shepard Mary—†	8	housekeeper	50	"
	L	Mohr Carl	10	chauffeur	44	592 Park
	M	Mohr Edna—†	10	housewife	34	592 "
	N	Curtis John H	10	bricklayer	62	here
	O	Whaley Audrey U—†	12	housewife	23	"
	P	Whaley Rusell E	12	welder	26	"
	R	Wyche Chester A	12	chef	62	
	S	Chisholm Louise B—†	12	operator	50	"
	T	Vaughn Betty—†	12	housewife	36	"
	U	Vaughn Thomas	12	chef	39	
	Y	Callaway Beatrice—†	16	housekeeper	40	"
	Z	Peace Alice R—†	16	domestic	47	11 Dartmouth pl
1346						
	A	Kenny Margaret—†	24	at home	64	here
	B	Page Catherine L—†	24	housewife	25	"
	C	Page William V	24	pipefitter	26	"
	D	Hanna Dorothy—†	24	housewife	36	"
	E	Hanna Francis	24	welder	39	
	F	Camp Catherine—†	26	clerk	40	
	G	Davis Lena—†	26	nurse	59	
	H	Regele Albert L	26	machinist	49	"
	K	Regele Catherine—†	26	housekeeper	47	"
	L	Regele Catherine—†	26	secretary	23	"
	M	Kantzian George	30	clerk	38	"
	N	Kantzian Lillian—†	30	housewife	32	"
	O	Paretchan Esther—†	30	"	52	
	P	Paretchan Harold R	30	U S A	21	

Page.	Letter.	Full Name.	Residence, Jan. 1, 1943.	Occupation.	Supposed Age.	Reported Residence, Jan. 1, 1942. Street and Number.

Millmont Street—Continued

Page.	Letter.	Full Name.	Residence, Jan. 1, 1943.	Occupation.	Supposed Age.	Reported Residence, Jan. 1, 1942. Street and Number.
	R	Ames Mary E—†	30	librarian	68	here
	S	Reed Anna M—†	30	housekeeper	79	Indiana

Morley Street

Page.	Letter.	Full Name.	Residence, Jan. 1, 1943.	Occupation.	Supposed Age.	Reported Residence, Jan. 1, 1942. Street and Number.
	U	Robinson Beatrice E—†	11	housekeeper	52	here
	V	Robinson Dorothea C—†	11	clerk	21	"
	W	Robinson Grace E—†	11	housewife	57	"
	X	Robinson William A	11	janitor	60	
	Y	Deassacos Demetrios	12	retired	69	
	Z	Deassacos Despina—†	12	housewife	69	"
1347						
	A	Deassacos Charles	12	chef	38	
	B	Deassacos Nicholas	12	clerk	41	
	C	Deassacos Theodore	12	U S A	30	"
	D	Habeeb Mary—†	12	clerk	25	2 Highland pl
	E	Lenardis George	12	"	29	here
	F	Lenardis Georgia—†	12	housewife	29	"
	G	Lenardis Peter	12	clerk	50	"
	H	Dunne Ernest	14	fisherman	46	"
	K	Vargas Damaso	14	janitor	46	
	L	Vargas Frances—†	14	housewife	42	"
	O	Friedholm Carl	15	clerk	25	
	P	Friedholm Lillian—†	15	housewife	22	"
	R	Barnes Bert	16	mechanic	54	"
	S	Barnes Fay—†	16	operator	53	
	T	Frazer Winifred—†	16	clerk	59	
	U	Robinson Flora M—†	16	at home	80	
	V	Reynolds Mary—†	17	housekeeper	57	"
	W	Dorgan Elizabeth—†	18	housewife	59	"
	X	Dorgan John J	18	retired	69	
	Y	Dorgan John J	18	clerk	38	
	Z	Dorgan Joseph	18	"	31	
1348						
	A	McAdam Harold	19	laborer	47	
	B	McAdam Nellie—†	19	housewife	47	"
	C	Thoma Anna—†	19	"	52	
	D	Thoma Elsie—†	19	clerk	28	
	E	Thoma John	19	mechanic	58	"
	F	Thoma John	19	U S A	22	

Page.	Letter.	Full Name.	Residence, Jan. 1, 1943.	Occupation.	Supposed Age.	Reported Residence, Jan. 1, 1942. Street and Number.

Morley Street—Continued

	G	Crapo Nina—†	20	housekeeper	61	here
	H	Jefson Celina—†	20	"	32	224 Dudley
	K	Venti Catherine—†	20	housewife	32	here
	L	Venti George W	20	mechanic	34	"
	M	White Angelina—†	20	housekeeper	65	224 Dudley
	N	Kingsley Anna C—†	21	housewife	60	here
	O	Kingsley Charles L	21	contractor	67	"
	P	Evans Mary E—†	22	housewife	32	"
	R	Evans William	22	clerk	34	
	S	Galicher Lucille—†	22	housekeeper	47	"

Norfolk Street

	T	Conlogue Francis	5	U S A	25	here
	U	Conlogue James	5	rigger	59	"
	V	Conlogue Mary—†	5	housewife	51	"
	W	McGrath John	5	U S A	29	287 Highland
	X	McGrath Mary—†	5	housewife	26	287 "
	Y	Wallace Coleman	5	pipefitter	39	here
	Z	Wallace Marion—†	5	housewife	35	"
1349						
	A	VanAuken Anthony	7	laborer	32	"
	B	VanAuken Doris—†	7	housewife	28	Maine
	C	Brownell Christina—†	7	housekeeper	53	here
	D	Cronin Irene—†	7	housewife	40	"
	E	Bailey Anna—†	9	"	42	"
	F	Bailey Anna B—†	9	clerk	23	
	G	Bailey Peter A	9	shipper	21	"
	H	Gardner Jean—†	9	clerk	21	
	K	*Gardner Nellie—†	9	housewife	53	"
	L	Qualter Blanche—†	9	"	23	
	M	Qualter John	9	rigger	25	
	N	Higgins Ethel G—†	9	housewife	32	"
	O	Higgins Joseph T	9	salesman	34	"
	P	King Mary—†	10	housewife	45	"
	R	Semenuck Mary F—†	11	housekeeper	21	"
	S	Twombly Amanda—†	11	housewife	38	"
	T	Twombly Robert	11	cook	41	"
	U	Allen Anna—†	11	leather sorter	43	15 Concord sq
	V	Lowney Rachel—†	12	housewife	48	here
	W	Lowney Stanley J	12	U S A	26	"

Page.	Letter.	FULL NAME.	Residence, Jan. 1, 1943.	Occupation.	Supposed Age.	Reported Residence, Jan. 1, 1942. Street and Number.

Norfolk Street—Continued

Page.	Letter.	FULL NAME.	Residence, Jan. 1, 1943.	Occupation.	Supposed Age.	Reported Residence, Jan. 1, 1942. Street and Number.
	X	Lowney Stanley W	12	toolmaker	52	here
	Z	Rose Inez—†	14	housewife	43	"
1350						
	A	Rose Inez—†	14	stitcher	21	
	B	Daley Bridget—†	15	housewife	61	"
	C	Daley Daniel J	15	laborer	58	
	D	Daley Daniel J	15	U S A	21	
	E	Stefanilo Alma—†	15	housekeeper	55	"
	F	Stefanilo Almonen—†	15	waitress	59	"
	G	Stefanilo Catherine—†	15	"	20	
	H	Cayse Edna—†	15	housewife	30	"
	K	Cayse James L	15	U S C G	32	"
	L	McDougall Charles	17	steelworker	29	46½ Cedar
	M	McDougall Eleanor—†	17	housewife	24	46½ "
	N	Curley Ethel—†	17	"	29	4 Cliff pl
	O	Paquette Celina—†	17	"	63	here
	P	Holman Luther	19	barber	46	"
	R	Laverty Minnie—†	21	housewife	33	"
	S	Laverty William	21	wool sorter	34	"
	T	Leon Anna—†	23	housewife	54	"
	U	Leon George	23	laborer	53	
	V	Leon Mary—†	23	clerk	21	"
	W	Ford Eleanor—†	23	housewife	29	23 Draper
	X	Ford John	23	laborer	30	23 "
	Y	Potter Jeremiah	23	foreman	54	191 W Fourth
	Z	Potter Mary—†	23	housewife	54	here
1351						
	A	Potter Raymond	23	laborer	25	"
	B	Lanouette Evelyn—†	25	housewife	26	Dedham
	C	Lanouette William	25	chauffeur	25	25 Circuit
	D	Nolan Mary E—†	25	houseworker	74	here
	E	Nolan William F	25	baker	44	"
	F	Walsh Charles	25	chauffeur	30	32 Warrenton
	G	Cobb Minnie—†	27	housekeeper	61	25 West
	H	Ferguson William D	27	U S A	24	47 Fort av
	L	Stone Gertrude—†	30	housewife	31	N Hampshire
	M	Stone Robert	30	clerk	31	"
	N	*Plourd Metharde—†	30	housewife	40	Maine
	O	*Plourd Pia	30	machinist	39	"
	P	Towey Mary—†	31	housewife	48	here
	R	Towey Michael	31	laborer	45	"

Page.	Letter.	Full Name.	Residence, Jan. 1, 1943.	Occupation.	Supposed Age.	Reported Residence, Jan. 1, 1942. Street and Number.

Norfolk Street—Continued

	S	Ryan Joseph	31	laborer	39	here
	T	Ryan Mary—†	31	housewife	37	"
	U	Carmody Edward F	31	laborer	50	"
	V	Carmody Theresa—†	31	housewife	50	"
	W	Gallagher Mary—†	31	"	67	"
	Z	Pollock George	40	clerk	26	2786 Wash'n
1352						
	A	Pollock Ruby—†	40	housewife	32	2786 "
	B	Brown Ethel M—†	40	"	41	here
	C	Stone Mary A—†	45	"	41	"
	D	Hanna Christine—†	49	"	42	"
	E	Hanna Henry	49	machinist	50	"
	F	McGee Alice T—†	49	housekeeper	45	"
	G	McGee William C	49	chauffeur	43	"
	H	Shaw Florence C—†	51	housewife	48	"
	K	Shaw William	51	clerk	51	
	L	*Paskow Joseph	53	laborer	49	
	M	Shirkoff Alice—†	53	housekeeper	45	"
	N	Shirkoff Nicholas	53	painter	48	"
	O	Borowski Anthony	53	laborer	32	
	P	Borowski Edward	53	carpenter	22	"
	R	Borowski Frank	53	laborer	61	"
	S	Borowski Nellie—†	53	housewife	65	"

Roxbury Street

	T	*Fay Della—†	224	domestic	43	here
	U	Fraser Christopher D	224	stableman	65	"
	V	Fraser Christopher S	224	fireman	30	"
	W	Morse Charles M	224	brakeman	32	"
	X	Morse Mabel—†	224	housewife	32	"
	Z	Burns John	224	janitor	56	
	Y	Burns Mary—†	224	housewife	55	"
1353						
	B	Lynch Celia—†	234	"	34	
	C	Lynch Joseph	234	laborer	47	
	D	Lynch Margaret—†	234	domestic	65	"
	E	Cantone Salvatore	234	laborer	38	
	F	Cantone Susan—†	234	housewife	30	"
	G	Habeeb Anna—†	234	stitcher	51	"
	H	Souther Helen—†	234	housekeeper	38	40 Circuit

Page.	Letter.	Full Name.	Residence, Jan. 1, 1943.	Occupation.	Supposed Age.	Reported Residence, Jan. 1, 1942. Street and Number.

Roxbury Street—Continued

Page.	Letter.	Full Name.	Residence, Jan. 1, 1943.	Occupation.	Supposed Age.	Reported Residence, Jan. 1, 1942. Street and Number.
	K	Koehler Martha—†	244	housekeeper	65	here
	M	Davidson Harriet—†	244	housewife	70	"
	N	Spaulding Alice—†	244	"	64	"
	O	Ford John	246	laborer	67	
	P	Ford Mary—†	246	housewife	61	"
	R	Cross Mary—†	246	housekeeper	73	"
	S	Cross Mary E—†	246	usher	41	"

Willoughby Place

Page.	Letter.	Full Name.	Residence, Jan. 1, 1943.	Occupation.	Supposed Age.	Reported Residence, Jan. 1, 1942. Street and Number.
	V	McInnes Daniel	1	guard	59	here
	X	Shine William	1	laborer	49	Milton
	W	Poles Edward	1	clerk	43	Wrentham
	Z	Morris Dorothy—†	2	housewife	38	here
1354						
	A	Morris James	2	printer	47	
	B	Egan Anna—†	2	housekeeper	62	"
	C	McDonald Evelyn—†	2	housewife	59	"
	D	McDonald Frank	2	mechanic	61	"
	E	Regan Louise—†	2	at home	71	
	F	Crosby Margaret—†	3	clerk	49	
	G	Wertz Arthur L	3	mechanic	57	"
	H	Wertz Kathleen D—†	3	housewife	49	"
	K	Connelly Charles	4	chauffeur	57	"
	L	Connelly Mary—†	4	housewife	44	"
	M	Chapman Irene—†	5	housekeeper	39	"
	N	Chapman Melvin	5	clerk	51	"
	O	Knight Henry W	6	engineer	34	21 Bromley
	P	Knight Josephine E—†	6	housewife	33	21 "

14

1

Ward 9—Precinct 14

CITY OF BOSTON

LIST OF RESIDENTS
20 YEARS OF AGE AND OVER

(NON-CITIZENS INDICATED BY ASTERISK)
(FEMALES INDICATED BY DAGGER)

AS OF

JANUARY 1, 1943

JOSEPH F. TIMILTY, *Chairman*
FREDERIC E. DOWLING, *Secretary*
WILLIAM A. MOTLEY, JR.
FRANCIS B. McKINNEY
EVERETT R. PROUT

Listing Board.

CITY OF BOSTON PRINTING DEPARTMENT

Page.	Letter.	Full Name.	Residence, Jan. 1, 1943.	Occupation.	Supposed Age.	Reported Residence, Jan. 1, 1942. Street and Number.

1400

Bartlett Street

Page.	Letter.	Full Name.	Residence, Jan. 1, 1943.	Occupation.	Supposed Age.	Reported Residence, Jan. 1, 1942. Street and Number.
1400	E	Lamb Mary E—†	7	at home	26	here
	F	Marcotte Ethel—†	7	"	39	1 Fountain sq
	G	Gatt Edward J	7	chauffeur	43	here
	H	Gatt Ethel M—†	7	housewife	41	"
	K	Stewart Floyd	9	foreman	33	"
	L*	Stewart Marion M—†	9	housewife	30	"
	M	Gilboy Catherine—†	9	"	34	
	N	Gilboy John H	9	U S C G	39	"
	O	McAuliffe Ada M—†	9	housewife	51	"
	P	McAuliffe James F	9	musician	23	"
	R	McAuliffe Marjorie I—†	9	clerk	20	
	S	Mann John T	11	laborer	48	
	T	Mann Katherine M—†	11	housewife	39	"
	U	Tallent Kenneth	11	machinist	30	"
	V	Tallent Rose—†	11	housewife	29	"
	W	Volz James L	11	laborer	25	"
	X	Volz Lydia G—†	11	housewife	22	"
	Y	Booth John D	13	rigger	44	
	Z	Booth Lillian M—†	13	housewife	48	"
1401	A	Hurley Ellen—†	13	at home	35	
	B	Little Margaret—†	13	"	68	
	C	Raymond Alfred W	13	laborer	41	"
	D	Raymond Harold W	13	mechanic	39	"
	E	Raymond Kathleen J—†	13	housewife	29	"
	F	Eastwine Helene W—†	15	"	39	
	G	Lohnes Gertrude—†	15	"	39	
	H	Lohnes Harry	15	machinist	43	"
	K	Bennett Merton P	15	checker	28	
	L	Bennett Millicent T—†	15	housewife	27	"
	M	Blair Doris—†	17	"	32	
	N	Hall Ambrose C	17	shipper	30	
	O*	Hall Ambrose T	17	cook	72	"
	P	Hall Charles A	17	laborer	25	
	R	Olsen Alice B—†	17	waitress	24	
	S	Kelliher Beatrice F—†	17	housewife	52	"
	T	Kelliher Ernest G	17	engineer	26	
	U	Kelliher Francis E	17	roofer	54	
	V	Homan Harry	19	watchman	53	"
	W	Campagnone John J	19	electrician	27	27 Norfolk

Page.	Letter.	Full Name.	Residence, Jan. 1, 1943.	Occupation.	Supposed Age.	Reported Residence, Jan. 1, 1942. Street and Number.

Bartlett Street—Continued

	X	Sharkowitz Sophie—†	19	laundress	22	27 Norfolk
	Y	McDonald John J	21	chauffeur	47	here
	Z	McDonald Lillian—†	21	housewife	46	"
1402						
	A	Cameron Agnes A—†	21	"	47	"
	B	Cameron Edwin F	21	ironworker	29	Woburn
	C	Cameron Robert A	21	"	51	here
	E	Roy Azildor	23	painter	42	"
	F	Roy Irene—†	23	housewife	32	"
	G	*Luks Anna—†	25	"	62	
	H	Luks Leo	25	retired	67	
	K	Chiampa Helen P—†	25	housewife	32	"
	L	Chiampa Salvatore	25	contractor	38	"
	M	Kronmiller Karl	37	pipefitter	37	"
	N	Kronmiller Nora E—†	37	housewife	33	"
	O	Melanson Mary G—†	37	operator	36	"
	P	Phillips Margaret M—†	37	"	54	
	R	Maginnis Mary C—†	37	housewife	30	"
	S	Lombard Clyde R	39	boxmaker	48	"
	T	Lombard Myrtle E—†	39	housewife	35	"
	U	Granskis Helen J—†	39	waitress	35	
	V	McBurnie Clifford F	39	shipfitter	42	"
	W	McBurnie Valerie C—†	39	housewife	39	"
	X	Hall Agnes—†	41	at home	40	17 Bartlett
	Y	Connolly Lena—†	41	housewife	49	here
	Z	Connolly William H	41	gardener	50	"
1403						
	A	Harrington Dean H	41	painter	39	33 Blue Hill av
	B	Harrington Lillian—†	41	housewife	56	33 "
	D	Reardon Mae T—†	55	"	48	here
	E	Reardon Marie T—†	55	saleswoman	21	"
	F	Reardon William F	55	bartender	53	"
	G	Richardson George W	55	U S N	23	
	H	Richardson Kathleen M—†	55	housewife	23	"
	K	Gilson Agnes—†	55	stitcher	45	
	L	Gilson Margaret—†	55	"	56	
	M	Godfrey Marie—†	55	"	50	
	N	Mullaney Harold	57	carpenter	53	"
	O	Mullaney Mary E—†	57	housewife	50	"
	P	Rosenfeld Clara—†	59	at home	69	
	R	Rosenfeld Rosa—†	59	"	57	

Page.	Letter.	FULL NAME.	Residence, Jan. 1, 1943.	Occupation.	Supposed Age.	Reported Residence, Jan. 1, 1942. Street and Number.

Bartlett Street—Continued

Page.	Letter.	FULL NAME.	Residence, Jan. 1, 1943.	Occupation.	Supposed Age.	Reported Residence, Jan. 1, 1942.
	S	Couillard Viola—†	67	stitcher	36	here
	T	Kinsman Louise—†	67	clerk	39	574 Newbury
	U	O'Keefe Daniel	67	laborer	55	29 Hancock
	V	Scott Catherine—†	67	at home	75	here
	W	Spinney Eva—†	67	housekeeper	46	"
	X	Zwickes Jessie—†	67	stitcher	27	"
	Y	Cahill Delia A—†	69	housewife	59	"
	Z	Cahill Mary C—†	69	tel operator	29	"
1404						
	A	Clark Henry	69	retired	65	
	B	Morgan James	69	"	69	
	C	Summers Beulah G—†	69	domestic	51	"
	D	Walsh John J	69	bartender	47	"
	E	Yrauel William	69	baker	60	56 Heath
	F	Carlson Charles	71	painter	42	here
	G	Connors Frank	71	laborer	42	56 Whittier
	H	Gilio Catherine—†	71	housewife	22	4 Moreland
	K	Gilio Leonard	71	operator	24	4 "
	L	Goldsmith Charles	71	factoryhand	30	38 Dudley
	M	Hart Harold	71	porter	46	here
	N	Horan Ellen—†	71	stitcher	57	"
	O	McGuiness Howard	71	laborer	40	15½ Wendover
	P	McGuiness Mary—†	71	housewife	35	121 Highland
	R	Walsh Annie E—†	71	"	47	here

Bartlett Terrace

Page.	Letter.	FULL NAME.	Residence, Jan. 1, 1943.	Occupation.	Supposed Age.	Reported Residence, Jan. 1, 1942.
	S	Reid James	1	chef	27	Maynard
	U	*Russo Angelo M	1	barber	52	49 Vernon
	V	Russo Irene A—†	1	housekeeper	46	49 "
	W	Russell Althea—†	3	housewife	60	20 Fairbury
	X	Russell George H	3	upholsterer	69	20 "
	Y	*Potter Kathleen—†	3	housewife	27	81 Westland av
	Z	Potter Ralph	3	chauffeur	28	81 "
1405						
	A	*Sullivan Barbara—†	3	housewife	42	here
	B	Sullivan Edward	3	U S A	22	"
	C	Sullivan William G	3	U S N	20	"
	F	Santamaria Eugenio	4	laborer	63	
	H	Thompson Vera—†	5	housekeeper	40	"
	K	Kemp Bessie—†	5	housewife	34	"

Page.	Letter.	FULL NAME.	Residence, Jan. 1, 1943.	Occupation.	Supposed Age.	Reported Residence, Jan. 1, 1942. Street and Number.

Bartlett Terrace—Continued

Page.	Letter.	FULL NAME.	Residence, Jan. 1, 1943.	Occupation.	Supposed Age.	Reported Residence, Jan. 1, 1942. Street and Number.
	L	Kemp Harry C	5	laborer	34	here
	N	Horne Edward	6	"	42	"
	O	Horne Ruth—†	6	housewife	42	"
	P	Hendricks Gracia—†	6	"	24	Medford
	R	Hendricks Philip	6	chauffeur	33	"
	T	Rafferty Agnes—†	7	factoryhand	40	here
	U	Gillespie Irene—†	7	housekeeper	34	"
	V	Shine Daniel	8	retired	77	"
	W	Shine Timothy	8	laborer	45	
	X	Farezoco Nicholas	8	riveter	43	
	Y	Pederson Helen B—†	8	housewife	30	"
	Z	Pederson Warren	8	laborer	35	
1406						
	C	Sevene Albina—†	8	housekeeper	49	10 Bartlett ter
	A	*Sevene Alice—†	8	housewife	32	Somerville
	D	Sevene David	8	laborer	41	10 Bartlett ter
	B	Sevene Jeremiah	8	chauffeur	33	Somerville
	F	*Brown Louise—†	10	housewife	34	here
	G	McAulay Catherine—†	10	housekeeper	23	"
	H	*McAulay Edith—†	10	housewife	48	"
	K	*McAulay John	10	machinist	50	"
	M	*Robinson John	12	laborer	49	927 Albany
	N	Robinson Marie—†	12	housewife	45	927 "
	O	Sabin Catherine K—†	12	"	43	here
	P	Sabin Edgar	12	pipefitter	49	"

Dudley Place

Page.	Letter.	FULL NAME.	Residence, Jan. 1, 1943.	Occupation.	Supposed Age.	Reported Residence, Jan. 1, 1942. Street and Number.
	R	Williams Laura P—†	3	housewife	27	here
	S	Williams Phillip B	3	expressman	51	"
	T	Somes Mabel R—†	3	factoryhand	36	"
	U	Somes Margaret F—†	3	housewife	80	"
	V	Marshall Celia B—†	4	"	66	
	W	*Marshall Daniel F	4	operator	36	
	X	Marshall Joseph G	4	U S A	22	
	Y	Marshall Leo P	4	clerk	29	
	Z	Marshall Mary B—†	4	cashier	27	
1407						
	A	Marshall Ruth E—†	4	hostess	25	
	B	*Marshall Thomas	4	retired	68	"
	C	Marshall William	4	U S A	32	

Page.	Letter.	Full Name.	Residence, Jan. 1, 1943.	Occupation.	Supposed Age.	Reported Residence, Jan. 1, 1942. Street and Number.

Dudley Street

Page.	Letter.	Full Name.	Residence, Jan. 1, 1943.	Occupation.	Supposed Age.	Reported Residence, Jan. 1, 1942. Street and Number.
	E	Wetmore Grace—†	1	at home	71	here
	F	Brennan Katherine I—†	1	saleswoman	52	53 Dudley
	G	Brennan Rose V—†	1	"	62	53 "
	H	Vaughn Ellen G—†	1	domestic	64	here
	M	*MacDonald Sophie—†	1	at home	73	"
	P	Manning Alice M—†	1	stitcher	59	"
	R	Erner Alice M—†	1	at home	65	
	T	Kingsley Etta M—†	1	"	65	
	U	Kingsley Mary E—†	1	housekeeper	67	"
	V	Connor Mary—†	1	domestic	82	"
	W	MaCready Mary E—†	1	nurse	69	
	Z	Flynn Mary—†	1	matron	60	
1408						
	A	Hill Theresa C—†	1	saleswoman	57	"
	D	McDermott Margaret A—†	1	at home	73	"
	E	Murnane Anna B—†	1	saleswoman	56	Quincy
	L	Baclay Isabelle—†	3	housekeeper	36	here
	M	Cronin Leo	3	janitor	40	"
	N	Daley Daniel	3	dishwasher	55	48 Elmwood
	O	Dorsey Joseph	3	chauffeur	48	271 Roxbury
	P	Harden Leo	3	laborer	53	here
	R	Manley Mark	3	bricklayer	48	"
	S	McGowan John	3	dishwasher	24	215 Cabot
	T	Potter Albert	3	carpenter	58	40 Kenilworth
	U	Rooney John	3	laborer	56	here
	V	Trainor Robert	3	painter	53	"
	W	Walsh Albert	3	toolmaker	32	"
	X	Walsh Helen—†	3	housewife	27	"
	Y	Bowman William	5	roofer	54	
	Z	Crowley Margaret—†	5	operator	54	"
1409						
	A	Fitzgerald John	5	rigger	39	"
	B	Lavin Wilbur	5	bricklayer	40	58 Oak rd
	C	MacLeod Bernard	5	shipfitter	34	here
	D	MacLeod Irene—†	5	housewife	27	"
	E	McCarthy Francis	5	laborer	37	"
	F	*McManus James	5	"	65	
	G	Reynolds Nora—†	5	operator	37	"
	H	Reynolds Roland	5	upholsterer	27	"
	K	Ryan Owen	5	laborer	50	21 Cabot
	L	Tucker Edward	5	"	37	991 Col av

Page.	Letter.	FULL NAME.	Residence, Jan. 1, 1943.	Occupation.	Supposed Age.	Reported Residence, Jan. 1, 1942. Street and Number.

Dudley Street—Continued

	N	Carrigan James J	9	orderly	48	here
	O	Geddry Grace M—†	9	matron	44	"
	P	Geddry Grace M—†	9	nurse	21	"
	R	Geddry Walter A	9	U S A	45	
	S	O'Toole Mary—†	9	matron	40	
	T	Crowley Ethel F—†	9	housewife	52	"
	U	Crowley William J	9	clerk	65	
	W	Brown Clarence	11	machinist	40	"
	X	Brown Frances—†	11	housewife	38	"
	Y	Crandall Frederick J	11	laundryworker	23	"
	Z	Crandall Helena T—†	11	housewife	63	"
1410						
	A	Crandall Joseph	11	manager	65	"
	B	Doyle Cornelius, jr	11	U S A	37	130 Warren av
	C	Doyle Helen C—†	11	clerk	31	here
	E	McIntyre Julia—†	13	storekeeper	54	"
	F	Sullivan Daniel	13	chauffeur	27	"
	G	Sullivan John	13	pressman	26	"
	H	Sullivan Margaret—†	13	housewife	54	"
	K	Sullivan Mary—†	13	clerk	23	
	L	Sullivan Michael H	13	machinist	55	"
	M	Sullivan Thomas	13	laborer	21	"
	N	Brown George A	13	repairman	64	"
	O	Brown Myrtle—†	13	housewife	61	"
	U	MacCormack Mark J	21	machinist	52	"
	V	MacCormack Mary—†	21	housewife	48	"
	W	Bayer Arthur J	27	cutter	72	
	X	Bayer Helen M—†	27	housekeeper	55	"
	Y	Camenick Francis	38	painter	49	2401 Wash'n
	Z	Corliss Catherine—†	38	housekeeper	70	here
1411						
	A	Douglas Samuel	38	laborer	38	57 W Dedham
	B	Langan Thomas	38	chauffeur	60	here
	C	Mahn Rose J—†	38	housekeeper	55	"
	D	Manson Henry	38	retired	55	"
	E	Meskill Edward	38	laborer	59	
	F	Sullivan Eugene	38	"	43	
	G	Young Robert	38	machinist	47	"
	K	DeYoung Irene A—†	40	housewife	49	"
	L	McCabe James A	40	chauffeur	32	"
	M	*Menezes Delphine—†	40	domestic	60	"

Page.	Letter.	Full Name.	Residence, Jan. 1, 1943.	Occupation.	Supposed Age.	Reported Residence, Jan. 1, 1942. Street and Number.

Dudley Street—Continued

	R	Carmichael George W	46	clerk	25	here
	S	Carmichael Martha C—†	46	retailer	50	"
	T	Cushman Sylvia F—†	46	housekeeper	83	"
	U	Evelyn Mary—†	46	at home	73	"
	V	Hovanesian Vahan	46	tailor	36	279 Dudley
	W	McAlister Mary R—†	46	clerk	53	here
	X	Spencer Harry W	46	steamfitter	61	"
	Y	Spencer Maude A—†	46	housewife	67	"
1412						
	A	Bakshoian Apar	48	laborer	47	"
	B	Bakshoian Kiarig—†	48	housewife	43	"
	C	Boucher Alberta—†	48	"	39	
	D	Boucher Paul	48	machinist	49	"
	E	Calderara Charles A	50	chauffeur	52	"
	F	Costello James	50	retired	65	25 Putnam
	G	Costello John F	50	machinist	34	here
	H	Diehl Charles E	50	retired	50	"
	K	Falvey Patrick J	50	house officer	55	Pennsylvania
	L	Flinn George H	50	laborer	40	462 Shawmut av
	M	*Hoy Mary—†	50	at home	43	here
	N	Hughes James E	50	chauffeur	36	2401 Wash'n
	O	McKay William	50	retired	79	here
	P	*Petria Michael	50	"	67	"
	R	Watson Mary—†	50	at home	60	50 Moreland
	T	Ananiades Ananias	rear 52	laborer	50	here
	U	Ananiades Despinia—†	" 52	clerk	23	"
	V	*Ananiades Mary—†	" 52	housewife	56	"
	W	Ananiades Nicholas	" 52	U S A	24	"
	X	Crawford George F, jr	53	machinist	22	33 Highland
	Y	Crawford Stella—†	53	housewife	22	33 "
	Z	Igo Edward	53	chauffeur	24	40A Newbern
1413						
	A	Igo Frances—†	53	housewife	22	40A "
	B	Brinkert Alfred	54	metalworker	37	here
	C	Brinkert Julia—†	54	housewife	30	"
	D	Helein Catherine—†	54	"	53	"
	E	Ludvigsen John	54	laborer	40	"
	F	Connolly Mary—†	55	clerk	69	Wakefield
	G	Donovan Andrew	55	retired	47	here
	H	Hughes Evelyn—†	55	housekeeper	51	"
	K	Mahon John	55	painter	40	"

Dudley Street—Continued

Page.	Letter.	Full Name.	Residence, Jan. 1, 1943.	Occupation.	Supposed Age.	Reported Residence, Jan. 1, 1942. Street and Number.
	L	McInnis William	55	clerk	38	here
	M	Mulligan Helen—†	55	"	41	"
	N	Mulligan James	55	painter	45	"
	O	Newmire Joseph	55	laborer	57	
	P	Ryan Minnie—†	55	housekeeper	59	"
	R	Sullivan John V	55	clerk	49	"
	S	McLaughlin Edwin W	56	painter	41	
	T	McLaughlin Wenonah F–†	56	housewife	45	"
	U	Anderson George	57	laborer	35	679 Mass av
	V	Crockett Elmer E	57	retired	75	72 W Newton
	W	Durant Christine—†	57	housekeeper	52	here
	X	Gass Frederick E, jr	57	laborer	41	"
	Y	Manthorne Roland	57	"	40	"
	Z	O'Brien Richard	57	"	62	
1414						
	A	Olsen Christian	57	clerk	62	
	B	Pantermoler Ernest W	57	"	49	
	C	Pantermoler Laura—†	57	housekeeper	53	"
	D	Rogers Charles	57	retired	75	Maine
	E	Ryan Patrick	57	"	61	513 Dudley
	F	Sahlehuber George	57	"	71	227 Roxbury
	G	Benda Arthur	58	motorman	43	here
	H	Benda Helen—†	58	housewife	38	"
	K	Burton George	59	clerk	73	"
	L	Coleman John	59	"	55	"
	M	Erisman Jeremiah	59	mechanic	35	Medway
	N	Fallon Joseph A	59	clerk	47	here
	O	Fitzgerald Edward J	59	laborer	24	N Hampshire
	P	Higgins Frank	59	"	35	here
	R	Higgins John	59	clerk	48	"
	S	Lundberg Emma—†	59	"	66	"
	T	Maguire William	59	mechanic	47	"
	U	Sharkey Catherine—†	59	housekeeper	56	"
	V	Lehtola George F	rear 60	chauffeur	44	"
	W	Lehtola Julia E—†	" 60	housewife	33	"
	X	Donovan Daniel M	61	retired	71	
	Y	Donovan John D	61	electrician	37	"
	Z	Jones John	64	retired	74	
1415						
	A	Kilroy Anna C—†	64	housewife	40	"
	B	Kilroy John M	64	U S A	35	

Page.	Letter.	Full Name.	Residence, Jan. 1, 1943.	Occupation.	Supposed Age.	Reported Residence, Jan. 1, 1942. Street and Number.

Dudley Street—Continued

Page.	Letter.	Full Name.	Residence, Jan. 1, 1943.	Occupation.	Supposed Age.	Reported Residence, Jan. 1, 1942. Street and Number.
	C	O'Rourke Peter	64	U S N	28	here
	D	Roach Patrick	64	laborer	63	"
	E	Yvaskian William	64	chef	50	38 Dudley
	F	Barthel Albert D	65	chauffeur	44	here
	G	Barthel Veronica—†	65	housewife	43	"
	H	Finnergan Peter	rear 66	clerk	45	"
	K	Kennedy Nora—†	" 66	housewife	46	"
	L	Kennedy Thomas E	" 66	U S A	32	
	M	O'Donnell John J	" 66	"	38	"
	N	O'Donnell Mary A—†	" 66	housewife	37	"
	O	Maree Bartholomew	67	guard	47	
	P	Maree Catherine—†	67	housewife	42	"
	R	Crawford Bertha—†	rear 68	"	65	52 Rockland
	S	McCorrison Clarence A	" 68	operator	20	52 "
	T	McCorrison Gladys—†	" 68	checker	46	52 "
	U	McCorrison Sears B	" 68	U S A	23	52 "
	V	Rubin Bessie—†	69	housekeeper	61	here
	W	Rubin Harry	69	clerk	66	"
	Z	Ayer James	79	machinist	36	"
1416						
	A	Ayer John	79	laborer	65	"
	B	Ayer Mary—†	79	housekeeper	55	"
	C	Doherty Catherine—†	79	clerk	32	"
	D	Watson Margaret—†	79	housewife	61	"
	E	Watson William W	79	clerk	66	
	H	Weymouth Elizabeth L—†	85	at home	76	
	K	Weymouth Malcolm L	85	clerk	36	
	L	Weymouth Regina O—†	85	bookkeeper	38	"
	M	Horsman William	87	retired	75	"
	P	Sullivan Joseph K	93	clerk	67	230 Dudley
	R	Sullivan Joseph T	93	U S N	38	230 "
	S	Sullivan Martha E—†	93	housewife	67	230 "
	T	Sullivan Thomas E	93	U S N	36	230 "
	U	Faysal Anna—†	95	housewife	38	here
	V	Faysal Samuel	95	machinist	46	"
	X	Law Albert C	95	cook	54	"
	Y	Law Albert H	95	U S A	32	
	Z	Law James P	95	operator	33	"
1417						
	A	Law Laura—†	95	housewife	54	"
	B	Law Robert H	95	U S A	32	

Dudley Street—Continued

Page.	Letter.	Full Name.	Residence, Jan. 1, 1943.	Occupation.	Supposed Age.	Reported Residence, Jan. 1, 1942. Street and Number.
	V	Bard Alice—†	144	housekeeper	55	here
	W	Good James	144	foreman	53	"
	X	Bourassa Georgiana—†	144	laundress	46	"
	Y	Cronin Helen—†	144	waitress	24	
	Z	Cronin Mary—†	144	housekeeper	53	"
1418						
	A	Howes Ann—†	144	dressmaker	21	"
	B	Campbell Frederick	144	clerk	28	
	C	Campbell Mary—†	144	housewife	26	"
	D	Duffy Alice—†	144	"	54	
	E	Duffy Charles	144	laborer	54	
	F	Cooley Letha—†	144	housekeeper	54	"
	G	Gill Annie—†	144	operator	55	"
	H	Mank Margaret—†	144	housekeeper	68	"
	K	*O'Neil Ann—†	144	housewife	46	"
	L	*O'Neil Frederick	144	chef	46	
	M	Hardy John	144	operator	44	"
	N	Moran Walter	144	chauffeur	34	"
	O	Pothier Albert	144	fireman	49	
	P	Walsh John	144	operator	50	"
	R	Wheaton Ernest	144	"	52	

Dunlow Place

Page.	Letter.	Full Name.	Residence, Jan. 1, 1943.	Occupation.	Supposed Age.	Reported Residence, Jan. 1, 1942. Street and Number.
	U	Lawler Mary—†	41	housewife	74	here
	V	Lawler Thomas	41	machinist	46	"

Elmwood Street

Page.	Letter.	Full Name.	Residence, Jan. 1, 1943.	Occupation.	Supposed Age.	Reported Residence, Jan. 1, 1942. Street and Number.
	W	Luby Mary—†	87	housewife	38	here
	X	Luby William	87	clerk	38	"
	Y	O'Donnell Stella—†	87	operator	33	"
	Z	Travers Dorothy—†	87	laundress	44	"
1419						
	A	Travers Florence—†	87	operator	21	"
	B	Bannow Bernard	93	"	32	
	C	Bannow Victoria—†	93	housewife	31	"
	D	Couturier Adjutor	93	electrician	42	96 Albion
	E	Couturier Barbara—†	93	housewife	38	96 "

Page.	Letter.	Full Name.	Residence, Jan. 1, 1943.	Occupation.	Supposed Age.	Reported Residence, Jan. 1, 1942. Street and Number.

Gay Street

	F	McHatton Helen—†	1	housewife	53	here
	G	McHatton James H	1	packer	53	"
	H	Greenlaw Alice M—†	1	housewife	54	7 Ball
	K	Cullinan Catherine—†	3	housekeeper	71	53 Dale
	L	*Morrison Frances B—†	3	housewife	36	3A Gay
	M	*Morrison Sidney S	3	salesman	36	3A "
	O	Tibbetts Ellen—†	3A	housewife	59	8 Alvah Kittredge pk
	P	Tibbetts James	3A	laborer	59	8 "
	R	*Johnson Edward B	7	cook	37	14 Terrace
	S	Johnson Elizabeth T—†	7	housewife	36	14 "
	T	Alvarez Edward F	7	machinist	51	3 Gay
	U	Alvarez Edward F	7	laborer	25	3 "
	V	Alvarez Mary D—†	7	clerk	21	3 "
	W	Alvarez Rebecca M—†	7	housewife	42	3 "
	X	Ruzzano Anthony	7	operator	63	here
	Y	Ruzzano Josephine—†	7	housekeeper	25	"

Hayden Terrace

1420	M	Pollack Evelyn—†	1	housewife	50	98 E Newton
	N	Wilkins Pearl—†	1	factoryhand	21	98 "
	O	DeChane Francis J	1	"	20	here
	P	DeChane Gertrude—†	1	housekeeper	38	"
	R	Cayton Nancy—†	1	"	27	133 Moreland
	Z	Pemberton Margaret—†	4	housewife	33	35 Fort av
1421	A	Pemberton Ralph	4	clerk	36	35 "
	B	McLaughlin Beatrice—†	4	housewife	30	2464 Wash'n
	C	McLaughlin William C	4	rigger	37	2464 "

John Eliot Square

	G	Paulery Eva L—†	3	at home	61	1 Dudley
	H	Pooler Clifford J	3	janitor	61	here
	K	Sullivan Alice—†	3	housewife	37	69 Bartlett
	L	Sullivan Edward	3	machinist	40	69 "

Kenilworth Street

	N	Toohey Harold B	1	clerk	52	here
	O	Toohey Minnie V—†	1	housewife	30	"

Page.	Letter.	Full Name.	Residence, Jan. 1, 1943.	Occupation.	Supposed Age.	Reported Residence, Jan. 1, 1942. Street and Number.

Kenilworth Street—Continued

Page.	Letter.	Full Name.	Residence, Jan. 1, 1943.	Occupation.	Supposed Age.	Reported Residence, Jan. 1, 1942. Street and Number.
	P	O'Connell John	1	operator	42	here
	R	O'Connell Rose—†	1	housewife	40	"
	S	Cook Fred A	1	machinist	53	Malden
	T	Cook Margaret A—†	1	housewife	49	"
	U	Pease Adele—†	1	"	72	here
	V	Pease Dorothy—†	1	waitress	40	"
	W	Griswold Margaret—†	1	"	53	59 Dudley
1422						
	A	Connors Patrick	7	yardman	34	here
	B	Kelly John J	7	trackman	37	"
	C	Kelly Mary E—†	7	housewife	42	"
	D	Dixon Charles F	13	sign writer	36	"
	E	Dixon Ruby M—†	13	clerk	36	
	F	Hughes Robert J	13	"	34	
	G	Hughes Ruth—†	13	housewife	34	"
	H	Butler Dorothy—†	15	"	28	"
	K	Butler Nathan	15	mechanic	32	"
	L	Hastings Ada E—†	15	housewife	28	"
	M	Hastings Samuel H	15	waiter	62	
	N	Jacobs Bertha—†	15	domestic	66	"
	O	Jacobs Hilda—†	15	clerk	50	"
	P	Morris Viola—†	15	assembler	25	Mashpee
	R	Campbell Mary A—†	17	housewife	78	here
	S	Campbell William D	17	superintendent	78	"
	T	Marshall Carl L	17	U S A	28	Ohio
	U	Marshall Mary E—†	17	housewife	26	"
	V*	Earle Martha—†	19	laundress	54	here
	W	King Drew	19	physician	56	"
	X	King Drew, jr	19	U S A	22	"
	Y	King Evelyn W—†	19	housewife	46	"
	Z	Taylor Edna—†	19	cleaner	52	"
1423						
	A	Taylor Emma—†	19	teacher	22	
	B	Taylor Florence—†	19	secretary	20	"
	C	Cox Emile—†	21	domestic	58	21 Kenilworth
	D	Haines William	21	tester	21	Nebraska
	E	Jordan Lilla E—†	21	at home	71	50 Windsor
	F	Lewis Alfred C	21	chauffeur	49	35 Vine
	G	Lewis Lottie—†	21	housewife	47	35 "
	H	Richardson Mary—†	21	at home	62	here
	K	Scott Harold	21	foreman	47	"

Page.	Letter.	Full Name.	Residence, Jan. 1, 1943.	Occupation.	Supposed Age.	Reported Residence, Jan. 1, 1942. Street and Number.

Kenilworth Street—Continued

Page.	Letter.	Full Name.	Residence, Jan. 1, 1943.	Occupation.	Supposed Age.	Reported Residence, Jan. 1, 1942. Street and Number.
	L	Hughes Fannie—†	22	housewife	63	here
	M	Hughes Joseph B	22	porter	70	"
	N	Hughes Robert J	22	retired	69	"
	P	Gammon Elwood G	24	sexton	64	
	R	Gammon Margaret—†	24	housewife	62	"
	V	*Foster Bartlett	38	at home	89	
	W	Foster Grace—†	38	housewife	47	"
	X	Foster Herbert	38	painter	46	"
	Y	Jonason Christine—†	38	housewife	33	92 Waltham
	Z	*Jonason Samuel R	38	meatcutter	41	92 "
1424						
	B	Fish Esther—†	40	matron	49	here
	C	Rooney Marjorie—†	40	cashier	23	1 Willoughby pl
	D	Rooney Philip	40	serviceman	27	1 "
	E	Berardinelli Antonio	40	boilermaker	31	here
	F	Loewen Doris—†	40	housewife	21	Dedham
	G	Wiley Grace—†	40	at home	50	here
	H	Qualters Margaret E—†	40	housewife	46	"
	K	Qualters Thomas M	40	foreman	52	"
	L	*McDonald Bernard	42	chauffeur	26	237 Dudley
	M	McDonald Edith—†	42	housewife	26	237 "
	N	Dolan Catherine A—†	42	at home	78	here
	O	McLaughlin Annie G—†	42	clerk	49	"
	P	Curtis Frederick J	42	manager	45	"
	R	Curtis Isabelle—†	42	telegrapher	47	"
	S	Cosgrove Elizabeth R—†	44	librarian	36	
	T	Rush Charles	44	rigger	42	
	U	Rush Evelyn—†	44	housewife	32	"
	V	Cosgrove Helen C—†	44	operator	37	"
	W	Cosgrove Joseph T	44	porter	67	
	X	Cosgrove Sarah J—†	44	housewife	66	"
	Y	Calnan James G	44	laborer	37	
	Z	Calnan James M	44	superintendent	67	"
1425						
	A	Calnan Mary W—†	44	housewife	63	"
	B	Anderson Christine—†	50	at home	73	
	C	Blass George	50	U S A	36	
	D	Buck Robert	50	"	42	"
	E	Carlson Minnie—†	50	at home	72	Watertown
	F	Piper Frances M—†	50	housekeeper	52	Attleboro
	G	Thompson Mildred A—†	50	clerk	53	here

Page.	Letter.	FULL NAME.	Residence, Jan. 1, 1943.	Occupation.	Supposed Age.	Reported Residence, Jan. 1, 1942. Street and Number.

Kenilworth Street—Continued

	H	Tyler Delilah—†	50	hostess	76	here
	K	Voye Hannah—†	50	at home	82	"
	L	White Edna—†	50	matron	52	"
	M	*Wolfe Mabel—†	50	nurse	60	

Lambert Avenue

	N	LaCourse Julia—†	4	stitcher	47	54 Elmwood
	O	Lyons Mildred E—†	4	housewife	46	54 "
	P	Whalen Theresa—†	4	housekeeper	70	54 "
	R	McMann Emma F—†	4	"	70	here
	S	Wagner Annie E—†	4	"	75	"
	T	Wagner Florence M—†	4	operator	40	"
	U	Wagner Joseph F	4	receptionist	41	"

Linden Park Street

	Z	Tressel Alfred	8	machinist	23	here
1426						
	A	*Tressel Catherine—†	8	housewife	56	"
	B	Tressel Frank	8	U S N	24	
	C	Tressel Leon	8	shipper	24	
	D	Khoshabjian Lucy—†	8	housewife	38	"
	E	Khoshabjian Mugerdich	8	laborer	48	
	H	McKenna Catherine—†	10	housewife	47	"
	K	McKenna Madeline—†	10	clerk	22	"
	L	Muldoon Helen—†	12	"	30	
	M	Muldoon Thomas A	12	agent	42	
	N	Devine Catherine—†	18	housekeeper	65	"
	O	Devine Margaret—†	18	at home	66	"
	R	Flannery John J	24	retired	78	
	S	Mountain James E	24	foreman	53	
	T	Conroy Mary E—†	24	housekeeper	51	"
	U	Murphy Chester	26	chauffeur	36	61 Terrace
	V	Murphy Helen—†	26	housewife	37	61 "
	X	Larkin James W	30	clerk	46	here
	Y	Larkin Katherine—†	30	housewife	45	"
1427						
	B	Fuller Ann—†	36	housekeeper	52	927 Albany
	C	Plant James A	36	watchman	64	927 "
	D	Gabree Hannah—†	36	housewife	33	2729 Wash'n

Page.	Letter.	Full Name.	Residence, Jan. 1, 1943.	Occupation.	Supposed Age.	Reported Residence, Jan. 1, 1942. Street and Number.

Linden Park Street—Continued

Page.	Letter.	Full Name.	Residence, Jan. 1, 1943.	Occupation.	Supposed Age.	Reported Residence, Jan. 1, 1942. Street and Number.
	E	Gabree Joseph	36	rigger	34	2729 Wash'n
	F	Flannery Michael	36	retired	75	here
	G	Gittens Mary—†	36	matron	40	"
	H	Harding Marie—†	42	stitcher	40	38 Cabot
	K	Pierce Everett E	42A	storekeeper	59	here
	L	Pierce Mary—†	42A	housewife	60	"
	N	Pellegrino Charles	44	fireman	40	"
	O	Pellegrino Margaret—†	44	housewife	30	"
	P	Kelley Martin J	44A	chauffeur	52	"
	R	O'Toole Anna T—†	44A	housewife	51	"
	S	O'Toole James	44A	inspector	50	"
	T	Gaffney Alice—†	44A	housewife	29	"
	U	Gaffney John	44A	shipper	30	
	V	Hardy William	46	chauffeur	45	"
	W	Bunker Esther L—†	46A	clerk	23	
	X	Pelichowicz John J	46A	U S A	28	
	Y	Warren Charles F	46A	engineer	57	
	Z	Warren Susan L—†	46A	housewife	56	"
1428						
	A	Brany John	46A	retired	64	
	B	Brany Rae—†	46A	housewife	64	"
	C	Downey Elizabeth L—†	48	"	29	
	D	Downey John J	48	U S N	34	
	E	Sweeney Stella—†	48A	housewife	45	"
	F	Sweeney Walter	48A	chauffeur	45	"
	G	Gray Joseph A	48A	U S N	27	
	H	Gray Manuel A	48A	rigger	47	
	K	Gray Mary J—†	48A	housewife	47	"
	L	Foster Margaret H—†	50	"	53	
	M	Foster William E	50	optometrist	27	"
	N	Klempa Anthony	50A	U S M C	21	"
	O	*Klempa Eva—†	50A	housewife	50	"
	P	*Klempa Frank	50A	laborer	62	
	R	Klempa Theresa—†	50A	laundryworker	25	"
	S	Thibodeau Gladys—†	50A	housewife	42	"
	T	Thibodeau Henry	50A	chauffeur	42	"
	Z	McCullough Edward T	94	laborer	52	
1429						
	A	McCullough Margaret E–†	94	housewife	49	"
	C	Kelly Julia—†	98	housekeeper	55	"
	E	Laughlin Helen—†	102	clerk	42	"
	F	Laughlin John	102	"	45	

Page.	Letter.	FULL NAME.	Residence, Jan. 1, 1943.	Occupation.	Supposed Age.	Reported Residence, Jan. 1, 1942. Street and Number.

Malbon Place

	K	Nestor Delia—†	1	housewife	70	131 Centre
	L	Nestor Patrick J	1	painter	60	131 "
	M	Allen Rose—†	1	housewife	78	here
	N	Blumenfield Mary—†	1	"	57	"
	O	Blumenfield Max	1	printer	56	"
	P	Blumenfield Paul	1	U S A	27	
	S	Anderson Helen—†	2	housewife	29	"
	T	Senott Dorothy—†	2	"	34	
	U	Senott John	2	U S N	37	
	W	Croft Charles	3	chauffeur	30	"
	X	Croft Margaret—†	3	housewife	30	"
	Y	Horner Elizabeth—†	3	"	25	
	Z	Horner John E	3	laborer	29	
1430						
	B	Moulton Mary—†	4	saleswoman	30	"
	C	Greer Edna—†	4	housewife	27	"
	D	Greer Edward	4	chauffeur	30	"
	E	Willamson Mary—†	5	laundress	38	"
	G	Jurow Minnie—†	5	factoryhand	55	6 Prentiss pl
	H	Jurow Walter	5	laborer	32	6 "
	K	McGonagle John	6	"	33	here
	L	McGonagle Mary—†	6	housewife	30	"
	M	Goode Ellen T—†	6	clerk	62	11 Juniper
	N	Goode James	6	laborer	30	108 Canton
	O	Goode William	6	"	42	11 Juniper
	P	Archibald Almena—†	6	housewife	47	here
	R	Henry Ada M—†	7	"	43	8 Hampshire
	S	Perkins Katherine—†	7	cutter	22	8 "
	T	Fournier Dorothy—†	7	factoryhand	25	here
	U	Fournier Elizabeth—†	7	housewife	54	"
	V	Horner Flora—†	7	"	50	"
	W	Horner Hayden	7	janitor	54	
	X	Horner Mary L—†	7	clerk	27	
	Y	Horner Raymond N	7	U S A	33	
	Z	Rockwood Charlotte—†	8	housewife	21	"
1431						
	A	Rockwood Walter	8	laborer	25	
	B	Leonard Margaret—†	8	housewife	35	"
	C	Leonard William	8	bellboy	36	
	D	Curley Gertrude—†	8	housewife	31	"
	E	Curley John	8	bartender	32	"
	F	Frieburger Rose—†	9	at home	60	

Page.	Letter.	FULL NAME.	Residence, Jan. 1, 1943.	Occupation.	Supposed Age.	Reported Residence, Jan. 1, 1942. Street and Number.

Malbon Place—Continued

	G	D'Entremont Harriett—†	9	at home	69	here
	H	Lyons John	9	orderly	57	"
	K	Hollett Alice—†	10	laundress	55	"
	L	*Ballin Wilbur	10	janitor	38	
	M	O'Gallagher Andrew	10	laborer	64	
	N	O'Gallagher Mary—†	10	housewife	62	"
	O	Earley Mary—†	11	at home	54	Quincy
	P	Murphy Mary—†	11	waitress	46	82 Roxbury
	R	Doyle Audrey—†	11	clerk	27	here
	S	Doyle Kenneth	11	laborer	29	"
	T	Moran Ora—†	12	housewife	65	"
	U	Musanti Louis	12	longshoreman	55	16 Blue Hill av
	V	Ball Mary—†	12	clerk	42	1 Malbon pl
	W	Ball Peter	12	laborer	29	1 "

Percy Place

	Y	Homer Frank A	1	oiler	42	here

Perkins Place

1432	B	McKenna John	3	repairman	57	here
	C	McKenna Katherine C—†	3	housewife	52	"
	D	McKenna Lorraine F—†	3	clerk	23	"

Putnam Place

	F	Flynn Bridget—†	1	at home	69	here
	G	Flynn Patrick J	1	repairman	67	"
	H	Sweet Florence A—†	2	housewife	42	"
	K	Sweet James M	2	seaman	47	"
	L	Currie Addie—†	2	housewife	38	6 Dolan's ct
	M	Currie Eugene A	2	U S M C	20	6 "
	N	Currie George	2	laborer	48	6 "
	O	Cox Catherine—†	2	operator	58	here
	P	German George	2	plumber	56	"
	R	Kenny Mary G—†	2	stitcher	65	"
	S	O'Toole Mary—†	2	at home	73	
	T	Neugebauer Anna—†	2	"	65	
	U	Neugebauer Bertha—†	2	"	79	"
	V	Lewis Annie—†	2½	"	82	3 Warren pl

Putnam Place—Continued

Page.	Letter.	Full Name.	Residence, Jan. 1, 1943.	Occupation.	Supposed Age.	Reported Residence, Jan. 1, 1942. Street and Number.
	W	Lewis David	2½	painter	47	3 Warren pl
	X	Lewis James A	2½	retired	82	3 “
	Y	Jewett Caretha M—†	2½	clerk	21	here
	Z	Jewett Elizabeth A—†	2½	cook	43	“
1433						
	A	Jewett Harold L	2½	U S N	43	
	B	Trueman Carleton	rear 2½	chauffeur	28	“
	C	Trueman Doris—†	“ 2½	at home	26	
	D	Meegan Mary A—†	3	“	68	
	E	Stanley Minnie C—†	3	nurse	57	“
	F	Harrington Edward	3	machinist	36	“
	G	McLelland Harold	3	inspector	27	18 Dana
	H	McLelland Olivia—†	3	at home	53	here
	K	Parker Helen B—†	3	housewife	28	154 E Cottage
	L	Parker Richard W	3	toolmaker	27	154 “
	M	Ludington Alice L—†	4	at home	25	3 Glenwood
	N	Ludington Annie L—†	4	“	56	here
	O	Ludington Charlotte E—†	4	typist	20	“
	P	Ludington Homer J	4	letter carrier	58	“
	R	Ludington Margaret E—†	4	draftswoman	32	“
	S	Ludington Richard O	4	U S M C	21	“
	T	Ludington Robert E	4	U S A	25	
	U	Lucas Theresa—†	5	at home	49	
	V	Massiglia Sadie—†	5	waitress	48	
	W	Lekbelos Alex G	5	janitor	57	
	X	*Polydor George	5	cook	43	
	Y	Vougouthimos George	5	“	50	
	Z	Murray Bridget—†	8	at home	55	
1434						
	A	Murray John J	8	shipfitter	60	“
	B	Murray Margaret—†	8	clerk	22	
	C	Murray Rose A—†	8	“	24	

Putnam Street

Page.	Letter.	Full Name.	Residence, Jan. 1, 1943.	Occupation.	Supposed Age.	Reported Residence, Jan. 1, 1942. Street and Number.
	D	Corthell Melville R	13	shipper	65	here
	E	Dunn Frances—†	13	housekeeper	76	“
	F	Ward Arthur F	15	foreman	46	“
	G	Ward Edward F	15	U S A	23	
	H	Ward Madeline E—†	15	housewife	45	“
	K	*Beegan Margaret J—†	25	maid	53	

Putnam Street—Continued

Page.	Letter.	Full Name.	Residence, Jan. 1, 1943.	Occupation.	Supposed Age.	Reported Residence, Jan. 1, 1942. Street and Number.
	L	Clasby Alice F—†	25	housewife	43	24 Robinwood av
	M	Conley John G	25	retired	75	here
	N	Derrick Robert B	25	coppersmith	44	Connecticut
	O	DiGiacomo Arthur	25	shoeworker	55	Somerville
	P	*Grady Anna M—†	25	manager	49	here
	R	Manley Leona V—†	25	stitcher	44	"
	S	*McNeil Mary C—†	25	domestic	36	"
	T	Reardon Mary T—†	25	at home	65	"
	U	Smeniglio Elaine L—†	25	waitress	25	Cambridge
	V	Steffani Richard D—†	25	carpenter	46	here
	W	*Sullivan Bella—†	25	stitcher	70	89 Cedar

Roxbury Street

Page.	Letter.	Full Name.	Residence, Jan. 1, 1943.	Occupation.	Supposed Age.	Reported Residence, Jan. 1, 1942. Street and Number.
1435						
	K	Eastman Warren	41	laborer	50	64 Dudley
	L	Fisher Forrest E	41	machinist	67	here
	M	Flynn Patrick	41	laborer	70	"
	N	Greenwood John J	41	"	37	"
	O	Hanley James P	41	clerk	42	181 Dudley
	P	Rockwell Howard	41	dishwasher	40	259 Highland
	R	*Walsh Elizabeth M—†	41	domestic	66	53 Dudley
	U	Arnold George W	47	mechanic	47	2 Kittredge ter
	V	Ashworth Anna—†	47	at home	79	47 Roxbury
	W	Cleary Edward J	47	steamfitter	51	47 "
	X	Cove Thomas J	47	fisherman	46	14 Highland
	Y	Duggan Gerard J	47	plumber	35	Cambridge
	Z	Dunn Stephen	47	fisherman	35	14 Highland
1436						
	A	Grant Frederick	47	machinist	36	47 Roxbury
	B	*Hallowell Mary B—†	47	housekeeper	57	here
	C	Hudon Joseph T	47	machinist	64	"
	D	Scott Charles L	47	floorman	44	165 W Canton
	E	Foley Mark F	49	paver	74	here
	F	Kelley Katherine—†	49	domestic	35	23 Highland
	G	Raymond Rose—†	49	"	59	25 Alexander
	H	Rose Charles V	49	carpenter	52	14 Norfolk
	K	Schmitt Agnes—†	49	housewife	68	here
	L	Schmitt Otto A	49	textileworker	47	"
	M	Scott Ralph E	49	clerk	46	"
	N	*Sousa Frank	49	cook	35	"
	O	Vincent Manuel	49	"	55	25 Dean

Page.	Letter.	Full Name.	Residence, Jan. 1, 1943.	Occupation.	Supposed Age.	Reported Residence, Jan. 1, 1942. Street and Number.
		Roxbury Street—Continued				
	R	Harris John P	54	embalmer	50	here
	S	Norton John	54	watchman	55	"
	X	Rae Marion—†	rear 82	entertainer	41	"
	Y	Rae Mary E—†	" 82	housekeeper	71	"
	Z	Whalen Edna—†	" 82	housewife	32	1 Hayden ter
1437						
	A	Whalen Martin	" 82	shipfitter	34	1 "
	B	Glennon Esther I—†	" 82	housewife	38	here
	C	Glennon Timothy	" 82	chauffeur	52	"
	D	Bond Philomena—†	98	at home	72	"
	E	Wickman Charles	98	engineer	67	
	F	Carmos Angeline—†	98	at home	29	
	G	Carmos John	98	chef	34	
	H	Carmos Rose—†	98	housewife	29	"
	L	Bowes George T	100	machinist	46	"
	M	Bowes Hazel—†	100	housewife	40	"
	N	Tanck Arthur W	100	welder	39	
	O	Tanck Ethel—†	100	housewife	30	"
	R	Norton Edward M	104	retired	69	
	S	Norton Elizabeth A—†	104	at home	72	
	T	Norton John F	104	machinist	39	"
	U	Re Cesare G	106	"	55	
	V	Re Francis C	106	U S C G	24	"
	W	Re Janet—†	106	clerk	23	
	X	Re John E	106	U S A	20	"
	Y	Re Joseph A	106	operator	22	
	Z	Re Nancy—†	106	housewife	52	"
1438						
	B	Driscoll Ruth—†	120	"	46	
	C	Driscoll William G	120	roofer	46	
	D	Fitzgerald Anna—†	120	at home	76	"
	E	Fitzgerald David	120	mechanic	52	"
	F	Malloy John J	122	U S A	22	
	G	Malloy Peter P	122	"	27	
	H	Malloy William	122	finsher	57	
	K	McManus James	127	laborer	46	
	L	McManus Mary—†	127	housewife	44	"
	M	McCarthy Mary F—†	127	saleswoman	62	37 Edgewood
	N	Watson Evelyn A—†	127	"	65	37 "
	O	Foley Mary E—†	127	housewife	62	7 Horan way
	P	Foley Robert J	127	operator	64	7 "
	R	Bell Elizabeth—†	129	housekeeper	47	here

Page.	Letter.	Full Name.	Residence, Jan. 1, 1943.	Occupation.	Supposed Age.	Reported Residence, Jan. 1, 1942. Street and Number.

Roxbury Street—Continued

	S	Sheedy Catherine—†	129	housekeeper	67	here
	T	Roche Anna R—†	129	housewife	47	"
	U	Roche John J	129	laborer	55	"
	V	Roche John W	129	U S A	22	
	X	Marsh Dorothy—†	130	operator	26	
	Y	Marsh George C	130	carpenter	62	"
	Z	Marsh Mary—†	130	housekeeper	60	"
1439						
	A	McKenna Mary—†	130	at home	50	
	C	Reader Arthur P	131	laborer	59	
	D	Reader Catherine M—†	131	seamstress	56	"
	E	Churchward James A	131	salesman	54	"
	F	Churchward Mary—†	131	housewife	54	"
	G	Nickerson Carl H	133	chipper	34	
	H	Nickerson Florence R—†	133	housewife	26	"
	K	Frieburger Julia C—†	133	"	41	
	L	Frieburger William F	133	chauffeur	41	"
	M	McMurray Helen M—†	133	housewife	21	"
	N	Lucas Helen F—†	133	"	67	
	O	Lucas Thomas S	133	packer	73	
	P	Pitts Marie A—†	135	housekeeper	45	"
	R	Pitts Noel R	135	U S A	22	"
	S	Keay Winford J	135	student	25	
	T	Keay Winford L	135	clerk	74	
	U	Fitzpatrick James E	135	"	65	
	V	Lyons Edward A	135	machinist	35	"
	X	Purvis Chiquita C—†	139	clerk	45	
	Y	Purvis Thomas E	139	baker	45	
	Z	Lee Genevieve M—†	139	housekeeper	59	"
1440						
	A	Wells Anna L—†	139	"	59	
	B	Hoskins Albert J	139	clerk	70	
	C	Hoskins Alice E—†	139	"	60	
	E	Jardine Margaret A—†	149	waitress	57	"
	F	Ling Bertha M—†	149	domestic	49	252 Newbury
	D	McGrale Amy O—†	149	cook	67	Newton
	G	Peabody Gertrude M—†	149	superintendent	47	here
	H	Reynolds Helen E—†	149	nurse	48	"
	K	White Pearl F—†	149	"	36	40 Lochstead av
	M	Gilbert Lee—†	157	seamstress	40	here
	N	Crockett Elmer H	157	welder	29	42 Terrace

Page.	Letter.	Full Name.	Residence, Jan. 1, 1943.	Occupation.	Supposed Age.	Reported Residence, Jan. 1, 1942. Street and Number.

Roxbury Street—Continued

	O	Crockett Mary E—†	157	housewife	25	42 Terrace
	P	MacKenzie Alexander M	157	foreman	47	here
	R	York Grace—†	157	domestic	50	"
	S	Flanagan Clara—†	157	housekeeper	67	"
	T	Flanagan Dorothy—†	157	domestic	25	"
	U	McGrath Jennie—†	157	housekeeper	67	"
	V	McMeniman Jennie—†	157	cashier	50	"
	W	Toohey Joan E—†	157	nurse	38	
	Y	Colton Carrie A—†	165	housekeeper	78	"
	Z	Colton Clara E—†	165	"	75	"
1441						
	A	Warren Louise—†	167	laundress	55	"
	B	*Babin Amanda—†	167	waitress	40	"
	C	*Babin Joseph E	167	finisher	40	
	D	Bradley Tekla—†	167	housekeeper	52	"
	E	Carson Harold	167	machinist	24	"
	F	Gore Elizabeth A—†	169	housekeeper	78	"
	G	*Dalley Fred	169	chauffeur	38	"
	H	Dalley Grace E—†	169	housewife	32	"
	K	Clark Frank J	169	machinist	67	"
	L	Clark Lillian P—†	169	waitress	45	
	M	Selig Ada M—†	171	housewife	68	"
	N	Selig Charles R	171	U S A	38	
	O	*Selig Herbert A	171	carpenter	70	"
	P	Hamill Emily A—†	171	housekeeper	66	68 Bartlett
	R	*Fetler Bette—†	171	housewife	62	here
	S	Romans Victor	171	storekeeper	67	"
	T	Giancola Arthur A	173	shoeworker	43	"
	U	Giancola Emma E—†	173	cook	43	"
	V	Aylward Sadie M—†	173	housewife	25	43 Shirley
	W	Aylward Thomas F	173	machinist	22	43 "
	X	Hurdy Helen M—†	173	domestic	55	here
	Y	Nickerson Frances M—†	173	clerk	22	"

1442 Shawmut Avenue

	D	Carpenter Albert J	806	architect	59	here
	E	Carpenter Benjamin	806	U S A	33	"
	F	Carpenter Elizabeth M—†	806	at home	85	"
	G	Carpenter Irma L—†	806	bookkeeper	36	"
	H	Charles Julia A—†	806	at home	60	"

Page.	Letter.	Full Name.	Residence, Jan. 1, 1943.	Occupation.	Supposed Age.	Reported Residence, Jan. 1, 1942. Street and Number.

Vernon Street

	L	Bennett Gertrude L—†	18	housewife	38	here
	M	Bennett LeRoy F, sr	18	engineer	45	"

1443 Warren Street

	A	Hardy Ernest	53	welder	37	here
	B	Hardy Lorraine—†	53	housewife	23	"
	C	Brisbois Joseph	53	butcher	36	"
	D	Young Joseph	53	chauffeur	42	132 Warren
	E	Brown Donald	53	welder	26	here
	F	Morris Michael	53	coppersmith	31	"
	G	Morris Phillip	53	operator	35	"
	H	LeMann Rose—†	53	housekeeper	26	"
	K	O'Leary Gerald	53	machinist	28	"
	L	O'Leary Mary—†	53	housewife	30	"
	M	Coughlin Agnes—†	53	housekeeper	50	"
	N	Coughlin Paul	53	U S A	22	
	O	Healey Agnes—†	53	housekeeper	44	"
	P	Healey Marie—†	53	bookkeeper	40	"
	R	Galbraith Christine—†	53	teacher	68	"

1445 Washington Street

	C	Hodsdon Charles J	2401	operator	52	here
	D	Mulrey Bernard G	2401	checker	52	53 Dudley
	E	Murphy Josephine M–†	2401	waitress	54	here
	F	Burnett Philip	2401	metalworker	66	"
	G	Cox Peter	2401	foreman	46	17 Highgate
	H	Downing John	2401	motorman	45	Everett
	K	Seymour Emma N—†	2401	stitcher	61	here
	L	Wilson Elizabeth—†	2401	"	62	48 Winslow
	M	Snow Marion E—†	2401	laundress	39	4 Dana pl
	N	*Snow Wallace P	2401	exterminator	39	4 "
	O	Clancy Francis S	2401	plumber	47	here
	P	Lowe Alfred A	2401	painter	54	"
	R	McIsaac Mary E—†	2401	realtor	43	"
	S	Sarro Carmine	2401	linoleum layer	39	7 Dennis
	T	Sherburne Margaret M–†	2401	waitress	24	here
	U	Buckley Timothy	2401	plumber	50	62 Cliff
	V	Cook Eva J—†	2401	housewife	58	here
	W	Cook William G	2401	foreman	63	"

Page.	Letter.	Full Name.	Residence, Jan. 1, 1943.	Occupation.	Supposed Age.	Reported Residence, Jan. 1, 1942. Street and Number.

Washington Street—Continued

	x	*Hayden Charles E	2401	superintendent	74	75 W Brookline
	Y	Hayden Susan A—†	2401	housewife	64	75 "
	Z	Holland John J	2401	retired	73	75 "
1446						
	A	McLaughlin Dorothy E–†	2401	secretary	22	15 Allston
	B	McMillan Alexander	2401	retired	80	100 Warren
	C	McMillan Eleanor M–†	2401	housewife	72	100 "
	D	Buzzell Annabelle—†	2401	housekeeper	42	here
	E	Buzzell Charles S	2401	laborer	24	"
	F	Coffey Charles C	2401	fireman	65	"
	G	Lelacheur James	2401	retired	79	
	H	*Payzant Alice N—†	2401	at home	77	
	K	Rhodes William L	2401	laborer	57	
	L	Wilson Helen B—†	2401	housewife	46	"
	M	Kemmett Alice F—†	2401	"	57	1464 Tremont
	N	Kemmett Catherine—†	2401	stitcher	20	1464 "
	O	Kemmett Helen E—†	2401	waitress	27	1464 "
	P	Kemmett Mary L—†	2401	operator	22	1464 "
1447						
	B	*Black Frances—†	2457	housewife	37	354 Harris'n av
	C	*Black Samuel	2457	painter	37	here
	N	Lyons Cornelius	2459	merchant	85	"
	O	White Eleanor—†	2459A	maid	44	"
	P	White Palmer	2459A	cleaner	45	"
	R	Gifford Ella—†	2459B	at home	52	7 Kearsarge av
	S	Gifford Orianna—†	2459B	"	89	7 "
	X	Toner Francis J	2459B	shipper	44	4 Hayden ter
	Y	Toner Francis J	2459B	U S A	20	here
	Z	Toner Margaret G—†	2459B	housewife	39	4 Hayden ter
1448						
	B	Gill Flora—†	2493	"	53	26 Kent
	C	Harrold Joseph	2493	porter	32	here
	D	Harrold Loretta—†	2493	housewife	23	"
	E	Conti Guy	2493	laborer	49	"
	F	VerKampen Charles W	2495	painter	36	2493 Wash'n
	G	VerKampen Mary C—†	2495	at home	66	2493 "
	H	Scharbius Bessie—†	2495	housekeeper	63	42½ Warren

Willis Terrace

	O	Sheedy Josephine—†	1	housewife	76	1 Glenwood
	P	Hanley Michael	2	laborer	47	here

Page.	Letter.	FULL NAME.	Residence, Jan. 1, 1943.	Occupation.	Supposed Age.	Reported Residence, Jan. 1, 1942. Street and Number.

Willis Terrace—Continued

	R	McGowan Mary—†	2	housewife	49	here
	S	Bodge Grace—†	2	"	61	"
	T	Bodge Vernon J	2	janitor	48	"
	U	*Kalis Alma—†	2	housewife	52	"
	V	Kalis Jacob	2	laborer	58	
	W	Benson Mary—†	2	at home	82	"
	X	Ford Helen Q—†	2	housewife	36	130 Roxbury
	Y	Ford Peter P	2	printer	38	130 "
	Z	Pye James	3	factoryhand	39	Weymouth
1449						
	A	Pye Mary A—†	3	housewife	32	"
	B	Burblies Emma—†	3	"	48	here
	C	Burblies Fritz	3	cook	42	"
	D	Duffy Caroline—†	3	housewife	47	28 Lambert
	E	Duffy George	3	janitor	48	28 "
	F	*Sheedy Julia—†	4	housewife	41	here
	G	Hardy Charles W	4	laborer	25	"
	H	Hardy Dorothy—†	4	clerk	24	"
	K	Hardy Helen B—†	4	housewife	58	"
	L	Downing Corinne E—†	4	"	27	2484 Wash'n
	M	Downing William J	4	chauffeur	30	2484 "

Ward 9—Precinct 15

CITY OF BOSTON

LIST OF RESIDENTS
20 YEARS OF AGE AND OVER

(NON-CITIZENS INDICATED BY ASTERISK)
(FEMALES INDICATED BY DAGGER)

AS OF

JANUARY 1, 1943

JOSEPH F. TIMILTY, *Chairman*
FREDERIC E. DOWLING, *Secretary*
WILLIAM A. MOTLEY, JR.
FRANCIS B. McKINNEY
EVERETT R. PROUT
Listing Board.

CITY OF BOSTON PRINTING DEPARTMENT

Page.	Letter.	Full Name.	Residence, Jan. 1, 1943.	Occupation.	Supposed Age.	Reported Residence, Jan. 1, 1942. Street and Number.
1500		**Cathedral Street**				
	B	Kenney Bridget—†	4	housewife	75	here
	C	Burke James J	4	shipper	41	"
	D	Burke Mary J—†	4	housewife	42	"
	E	*Donovan Anna M—†	4	"	36	16 Fenwick
	F	Donovan Leonard E	4	U S A	39	16 "
	G	Whitney Louise—†	6	operator	41	here
	H	Whitney Louise N—†	6	"	23	"
	K	Lawler Andrew	6	retired	76	"
	L	Lawler Margaret—†	6	housewife	44	"
	M	O'Brien Charles J	6	machinist	20	"
	N	*O'Brien John C	6	retired	59	
	O	Minton Bernard F	8	U S N	21	
	P	Minton Bridget M—†	8	housewife	51	"
	R	Minton Mary J—†	8	saleswoman	24	"
	S	Minton Michael	8	retired	84	
	T	Minton Patrick J	8	porter	58	
	U	Corbett Christine A—†	8	housewife	62	"
	V	Corbett Daniel P	8	molder	26	
	W	Corbett Mary B—†	8	baker	28	
	X	Gallagher Elizabeth M—†	8	housewife	37	"
	Y	Gallagher Patrick J	8	butcher	41	
		Cedar Square				
	Z	Sardello Angelo E	1	plumber	38	here
1501						
	A	Sardello Fannie—†	1	housewife	33	"
	B	Sarno Almerindo	1	constable	60	"
	C	Sarno Theresa—†	1	housewife	50	"
		Cedar Street				
	D	McPhee Elizabeth—†	1	housekeeper	59	here
	E	Menton Nyrike—†	1	"	65	"
	F	Menton William H	1	retired	64	"
	L	Corliss Cecelia M—†	3	housewife	57	"
	M	Corliss James H	3	retired	88	
	N	Corliss Joseph E	3	laborer	60	
	O	Corliss Joseph H	3	U S A	26	
	P	Harding Francis B	4	painter	62	

Page.	Letter.	Full Name.	Residence, Jan. 1, 1943.	Occupation.	Supposed Age.	Reported Residence, Jan. 1, 1942. Street and Number.

Cedar Street—Continued

	R	Harding Mary H—†	4	housewife	42	here
	S	Finn Nora—†	5	clerk	33	"
	V	Finn Helen—†	12	student	21	"
	W	Finn John J	12	U S A	47	
	X	Finn Margaret—†	12	housewife	46	"
	Y	Finn Mary A—†	12	teacher	21	
	Z	Finn William J	12	U S A	24	
1502						
	A	Lomax Ira—†	16	housewife	39	"
	B	Lomax Leon	16	electrician	40	"
	C	McGourthy Joanna—†	18	housewife	52	"
	D	McGourthy Katherine—†	18	housekeeper	50	"
	E	McGourthy Patrick J	18	retired	74	"
	F	Haslan Harry G	18	salesman	37	"
	G	Sullivan Josephine A—†	20	teacher	32	
	H	Sullivan Julia T—†	20	stenographer	35	"
	K	Sullivan Mary R—†	20	teacher	38	"
	L	Husbands Beltide—†	22	housewife	46	"
	M	Husbands Wilbur	22	porter	47	
	N	McReynold Aurelia—†	22	waitress	32	"
	O	Pugh Julia—†	22	housewife	55	"
	P	Sampson Dominick	24	laborer	42	
	R	Sampson Dorothy—†	24	housewife	38	"
	S	Dannenhoffer Marion—†	24	"	44	"
	T	Dannenhoffer Rosanna—†	24	"	77	
	U	Holland John	24	laborer	40	
	V	Holland Rose—†	24	housewife	41	"
	Y	Brown Joseph E	26	chauffeur	33	"
	Z	Brown Marie J—†	26	housewife	26	"
1503						
	B	Farrar Mabel M—†	29	clerk	67	
	C	Porter Edward W	29	machinist	59	"
	D	Welman Charles	29	plumber	52	
	E	Cameron Helen—†	29	housewife	57	"
	F	Cooper Jessie—†	29	clerk	37	
	G	Williams Joseph	29	painter	60	
	H	Williams Mary—†	29	housewife	60	"
	K	Carmichael Albert	29	machinist	35	"
	L	Carmichael Mabel—†	29	housewife	29	"
	M	Romano Rosario	35	cobbler	65	
	N	Votta Carmella—†	35	housewife	27	"

Page.	Letter.	FULL NAME.	Residence, Jan. 1, 1943.	Occupation.	Supposed Age.	Reported Residence, Jan. 1, 1942. Street and Number.

Cedar Street—Continued

	O	Votta John	35	cobbler	32	here
	P	Johnston Anna—†	37	housewife	34	"
	R	Johnston Norman H	37	painter	34	"
	S	Anton Charles	49	instructor	31	"
	T	Anton Valia—†	49	housewife	27	"
	U	Ganota Charles	49	clerk	30	
	V	Ganota Helen—†	49	housewife	26	"
	W	Lewin Dorothea—†	49	bookkeeper	32	"
	X	Morgan Edward	49	mechanic	50	"
	Y	Nickerson Catherine M—†	49	housewife	33	"
	Z	Nickerson Harold	49	cook	36	
1504						
	A	Lewin Ernest H	49	clerk	64	
	B	Lewin Maude A—†	49	housewife	53	"
	D	Wolohowicz Frank	49	painter	48	
	E	Wolohowicz Lena—†	49	housewife	48	"
	F	Wolohowicz Stanley	49	U S A	24	

Circuit Street

	K	McGillvary John	50	machinist	38	6 Galena
	L	*McGillvary Mary—†	50	housewife	29	6 "
	M	Downey Agnes V—†	50	operator	57	here
	O	Theall Catherine—†	64	housewife	42	50 Rockland
	P	Berberian Julia—†	64	clerk	21	here
	R	*Berberian Mary—†	64	housewife	48	"
	S	Berberian Misak	64	storekeeper	51	"
	W	Autuori Americo	68	musician	22	"
	X	Autuori Angelina—†	68	housewife	47	"
	Y	Autuori Annette—†	68	saleswoman	23	"
	Z	Autuori Frank	68	laborer	46	
1505						
	A	Autuori Yolanda—†	68	stenographer	21	"
	B	Nevara Doris—†	68	housewife	35	"
	C	Nevara Rudolph	68	painter	34	
	E	Cross Eleanor—†	70	housewife	22	"
	F	Perry May—†	70	"	46	
	G	Smallcomb Lillian—†	70	"	44	
	H	Rogers Morris	70	laborer	48	
	K	Rogers Rita—†	70	housewife	45	"
	O	Fromara Elias	74	baker	55	

Page.	Letter.	Full Name.	Residence, Jan. 1, 1943.	Occupation.	Supposed Age.	Reported Residence, Jan. 1, 1942. Street and Number.

Circuit Street—Continued

Page.	Letter.	Full Name.	Residence, Jan. 1, 1943.	Occupation.	Supposed Age.	Reported Residence, Jan. 1, 1942. Street and Number.
	P	Fromara Julia—†	74	housewife	40	here
	R	Abraham Fandi	74	laborer	31	"
	S	Abraham Mary—†	74	housewife	26	"
	T	Kovachi Christopher	74	laborer	48	
	U	Kovachi Nellie—†	74	factoryhand	45	"
	V	Dyer Nellie C—†	76	housewife	69	"
	W	Dyer Warren C	76	retired	71	
	X	Tenney Charles W	76	carpenter	70	"
	Y	Tenney Velma M—†	76	housewife	50	"
	Z	Ryan Florence C—†	76	"	50	
1506						
	A	Ryan William	76	cook	50	4 Circuit
	B	O'Shea John	78	laborer	36	here
	C	O'Shea Sheila—†	78	housewife	33	"
	D	Sulkey Helen—†	80	"	38	"
	E	Sulkey Herbert	80	welder	40	"
	F	Ashe Margaret—†	82	clerk	45	
	G	*Cresto Alexandra—†	82	housewife	64	"
	H	Cresto Elizabeth—†	82	clerk	22	
	K	Bath Annie J—†	82	laundress	68	"

Dale Street

Page.	Letter.	Full Name.	Residence, Jan. 1, 1943.	Occupation.	Supposed Age.	Reported Residence, Jan. 1, 1942. Street and Number.
	N	Sherman Margaret—†	111	housewife	32	here
	O	Sherman Paul	111	machinist	40	"
	P	Hayes Rita M—†	111	operator	24	2894 Wash'n
	R	*Hickey Alexander J	111	laborer	57	2894 "
	S	*Hickey Ida G—†	111	housewife	52	2894 "
	T	Hickey John	111	U S A	23	2894 "
	U	Hickey Lawrence	111	chauffeur	49	2894 "
	V	Brennan Anna—†	111	attendant	22	here
	W	Brennan Helen—†	111	factoryhand	25	"
	X	Brennan John	111	U S N	20	"
	Y	Brennan Lawrence L	111	laborer	50	"
	Z	Brennan Leo	111	cleaner	21	"
1507						
	A	Brennan Mary—†	111	housewife	50	"
	B	Stapleton John W	113	clerk	44	
	C	Stapleton Priscilla—†	113	housewife	42	"
	D	Stapleton Ruth—†	113	clerk	20	
	E	MacEachern Ann—†	113	housewife	35	"

Page.	Letter.	FULL NAME.	Residence, Jan. 1, 1943.	Occupation.	Supposed Age.	Reported Residence, Jan. 1, 1942. Street and Number.

Dale Street—Continued

	F	MacEachern Joseph	113	chauffeur	34	here
	G	Maher Catherine—†	113	housewife	43	284 N Harvard
	H	*McIntyre Peter	115	carpenter	40	4 Southwood
	K	*McIntyre Theresa—†	115	housewife	34	4 "
	L	Wiley Ernest	115	hotelworker	38	here
	M	Chapple Helen—†	115	waitress	32	"
	N	MacQuarrie Laura—†	115	housewife	20	"
	O	MacQuarrie Raymond	115	ironworker	35	"
	P	*Robertson Helena—†	115	attendant	53	"
	R	Maloney Lorin	115	salesman	38	"
	S	Maloney Rose C—†	115	housewife	36	"
	T	Trainor Catherine—†	115	at home	65	"
	U	Egleston Margaret L—†	115	clerk	35	156 Thornton
	V	Woods Ellen E—†	115	at home	58	156 "
	W	Woods George A	115	mechanic	22	156 "
	X	Woods Ruth E—†	115	W A V E	20	156 "
	Y	Carmichael Emma—†	115	at home	68	here
	Z	Carmichael Walter	115	instruments	27	"
1508						
	A	Krouson Elaine—†	115	housewife	24	"
	B	Krouson Walter	115	photographer	24	"
	D	Hoey Mary—†	115	housewife	47	"
	C	Hoey Michael	115	clerk	53	
	E	Curry Charles D	115	inspector	35	"
	F	Curry Delia—†	115	at home	74	
	G	Curry George D	115	retired	74	
	H	Day Mary A—†	115	housewife	45	"
	K	McMillen John A	115	salesman	52	"
	L	Bergstrom Rose—†	117	laundress	48	"
	M	Chancholo Edward	117	machinist	32	"
	N	Chancholo Mary—†	117	housewife	23	"
	O	Chuplis Amelia—†	117	nurse	28	
	P	McLeod Dorothy—†	117	housewife	41	"
	R	Moore James	117	machinist	21	"
	S	Phelan Augusta—†	117	laundress	35	"
	T	Walsh Blanche—†	117	housewife	60	"
	U	Walsh James	117	retired	58	
	V	Wardwell Horace E	117	U S A	41	
	W	Wilkins Mary—†	117	housewife	64	"
	X	Gormley Patrick	119	U S A	38	20 Sheridan
	Y	McDonnell James E	119	checker	39	20 "

Page.	Letter.	Full Name.	Residence, Jan. 1, 1943.	Occupation.	Supposed Age.	Reported Residence, Jan. 1, 1942. Street and Number.

Dale Street—Continued

	Z	McDonnell Mary—†	119	housewife	56	20 Sheridan
1509						
	A	Moors Edward	119	machinist	46	here
	B	Moors Lettie—†	119	housewife	44	"
	C	McDonald Charles	119	chauffeur	45	"
	D	McDonald Dorothy—†	119	operator	22	"
	E	McDonald Evelyn—†	119	"	20	"
	F	McDonald Lawrence	119	molder	33	New York
	G	O'Neil John	119	laborer	57	here
	H	O'Neil Mary A—†	119	housewife	65	"
	K	O'Neil William J	119	clerk	23	"
	L	Manthorne Margaret—†	121	housewife	88	"
	M	Manthorne Mina—†	121	at home	75	
	N	Manthorne Theopolous	121	guard	68	
	P	Coogan Josephine—†	121	at home	63	
	R	Coogan Mary—†	121	"	65	
	S	Coogan Robert E	121	clerk	30	"
	T	Campbell James F	131	machinist	40	2 Hayden ter
	U	Campbell Mary—†	131	housewife	30	2 "
	V	Russell Anna—†	131	"	44	here
	W	Russell John	131	counterman	42	"
	X	Vena Amelia—†	133	housewife	56	"
	Y	Vena Ernesto	133	storekeeper	57	"
	Z	Vena John	133	clerk	27	"
1510						
	A	Camillo Florence—†	133	housewife	22	1 Walnut ct
	B	Camillo Vincent J	133	U S A	26	217 Eustis

Dorr Street

	D	Brownstein Samuel	6	bartender	41	here
	E	Brownstein Verna—†	6	housewife	30	"
	F	Block Mary—†	6	"	43	"
	G	Jones Frances—†	6	waitress	31	
	H	Broderick Anna—†	6	housewife	59	"
	K	Nee Francis	6	operator	28	"
	L	Nee Gladys—†	6	housewife	25	"
	N	Blank Albert	8	druggist	42	
	O	Blank Frances—†	8	housewife	42	"
	P	Kane John	8	carpenter	35	"
	R	Glynn Anna—†	10	housewife	27	"

Page.	Letter.	Full Name.	Residence, Jan. 1, 1943.	Occupation.	Supposed Age.	Reported Residence, Jan. 1, 1942. Street and Number.
		Dorr Street—Continued				
	S	Glynn James	10	shipwright	28	here
	T	Dermody Harry J	10	foreman	42	"
	U	Dermody Lucia—†	10	housewife	42	"
	V	Finkler Jacob	10	tailor	52	
	W	McDonnell Catherine L—†	10	housewife	68	"
	X	McDonnell Isabelle R—†	10	inspector	47	"
	Y	Anderson August, jr	12	U S A	32	
	Z	Anderson Rita M—†	12	housewife	27	"
1511						
	A	Roche Edna M—†	12	typist	21	
	B	Roche Joseph	12	metalworker	46	"
	C	Roche Mary—†	12	housewife	44	"
	D	Roche Mary H—†	12	typist	22	
	E	Dobson Harry	12	florist	48	
	F	Kenney Esther—†	12	clerk	22	
	G	Kenney Joseph	12	plumber	57	
	H	Kenney Mary—†	12	housewife	48	"
	K	Kenney Mary—†	12	clerk	29	
	L	Muriaty Eugene	14	retired	71	
	M	Muriaty Eugene J	14	U S N	26	
	N	Muriaty Josephine M—†	14	housekeeper	29	"
	O	Behnke Della F—†	14	housewife	45	"
	P	Behnke Frederick	14	clerk	45	
	R	Behnke Hilda—†	14	"	38	
	S	Wells Edgar S	14	leatherworker	62	"
	T	Wells Frederick J	14	chauffeur	29	"
	U	Wells Gertrude A—†	14	housewife	62	"
	V	Wells Herbert L	14	shoeworker	33	"
	X	Capillo Jennie—†	18	housewife	60	"
	Y	Capillo Louis	18	barber	60	
	Z	Capillo Margaret—†	18	at home	34	
1512						
	A	Cornelli Domenick	18	salesman	40	"
	B	Cornelli Frances—†	18	housewife	36	"
	C	McKeon Herbert C	18	foreman	44	"
	D	McKeon Stella A—†	18	housewife	36	"
	E	Caulfield Rita—†	20	"	23	
	F	Caulfield Thomas	20	machinist	26	"
	G	Brown Anna V—†	20	clerk	29	
	H	Brown Carl E	20	painter	59	
	K	Brown Florence—†	20	housewife	52	"

Dorr Street—Continued

Page.	Letter.	Full Name.	Residence, Jan. 1, 1943.	Occupation.	Supposed Age.	Reported Residence, Jan. 1, 1942. Street and Number.
	L	Gaffrey Grace—†	20	housewife	27	here
	M	Caulfield Mary—†	20	"	50	"
	N	Sullivan Ellen—†	22	"	76	"
	O	Sullivan Mary C—†	22	"	47	
	P	Sullivan Michael J	22	janitor	48	
	R	Glennon Patrick J	22	engineer	52	
	S	Nelson Eldon	22	operator	42	"
	T	Nelson Martha—†	22	housewife	48	"
	V	McGettrick Andrew F	24	clerk	35	
	W	McGettrick Anna—†	24	housewife	72	"
	X	McGettrick Charles E	24	clerk	40	
	Y	McGettrick Helen M—†	24	teacher	27	
	Z	Smith Kenneth J	26	clerk	45	
1513						
	A	Smith Susanna—†	26	housewife	72	"
	B	Dempster Linden G	26	machinist	34	"
	C	Gately Martin J	26	packer	52	
	D	Gately Mary J—†	26	housewife	54	"
	E	Clark Catherine—†	26	"	58	
	F	Clark Raymond H	26	grocer	58	
	G	Vogel Catherine V—†	26	at home	49	
	H	Harrington Lucy—†	28	"	34	
	K	Seifert Hazel—†	28	housewife	41	"
	L	Carey Mary G—†	28	clerk	42	
	M	Carey Nellie V—†	28	housewife	62	"
	N	Roche John	28	laborer	65	
	O	Donnelly Anna F—†	28	housewife	76	"
	P	Donnelly Walter E	28	salesman	43	"
	R	Ayers Barbara E—†	32	hairdresser	45	"
	S	McCarthy Elizabeth M–†	32	housewife	73	"
	T	McCarthy Joseph M	32	U S A	31	

Fenwick Street

Page.	Letter.	Full Name.	Residence, Jan. 1, 1943.	Occupation.	Supposed Age.	Reported Residence, Jan. 1, 1942. Street and Number.
	V	Clune Annie F—†	2	at home	86	here
	W	Murray Mary J—†	2	housewife	45	"
	Y	Crawford Elizabeth—†	4	"	54	"
	Z	Crawford William	4	retired	69	
1514						
	A	Gardner Ethel—†	6	housewife	45	"
	B	Gardner John H	6	laborer	44	

Page.	Letter.	Full Name.	Residence, Jan. 1, 1943.	Occupation.	Supposed Age.	Reported Residence, Jan. 1, 1942. Street and Number.

Fenwick Street—Continued

Page.	Letter.	Full Name.	Residence, Jan. 1, 1943.	Occupation.	Supposed Age.	Reported Residence, Jan. 1, 1942. Street and Number.
	c	*Bolger Elizabeth—†	6	housewife	50	here
	D	Bolger James T	6	carpenter	49	"
	E	Holmberg Alfred	8	machinist	47	Quincy
	F	Holmberg Lois—†	8	housewife	43	"
	G	Arnold Caroline—†	8	"	28	here
	H	Arnold James	8	metalworker	32	"
	K	Feeley Elizabeth T—†	10	housewife	69	"
	L	Feeley Henry F	10	retired	71	
	M	Kucherer Mary—†	10	housewife	70	"
	N	Fleming Richard W	10	clerk	23	
	O	Fleming William R	10	machinist	52	"
	P	Murphy Mary—† 1st r	10	at home	76	
	s	*Cameron Hannah–† 2d "	10	"	67	"
	T	Cadlick Catherine–† 2d "	10	housewife	42	2644 Wash'n
	U	Cadlick Joseph 2d "	10	machinist	43	2644 "
	V	Tobin John	14	painter	35	5 Codman pk
	w	*Tobin Mary—†	14	housewife	31	5 "
	X	Langdon Elizabeth—†	14	"	42	here
	Y	McDermott John	14	butcher	32	9 Codman pk
	Z	McDermott Mary—†	14	housewife	27	9 "
1515						
	B	Cronin Margaret—†	16	maid	45	here
	c	*McDonald Margaret—†	16	housewife	38	"
	D	McKenna Catherine—†	16	"	40	"
	E	McKenna Michael	16	gardener	43	"
	F	Ryan David	18	retired	65	
	G	Dolan Catherine—†	18	housewife	57	"
	H	Dolan Edward J	18	porter	60	
	K	Dolan Mary—†	18	clerk	21	
	L	Cauden Helen M—†	18	housewife	63	"
	M	Cauden John	18	retired	62	
	N	Hayes Catherine M—†	18	clerk	23	
	o	*Brown Catherine—†	20	housewife	55	"
	P	Brown Frank	20	U S A	23	
	R	Brown Henry	20	"	26	
	S	Bresnahan John	20	retired	86	
	T	Gaughan Anna—†	20	housewife	48	"
	U	Gaughan James	20	laborer	51	
	V	Delaney Sarah—†	20	housewife	46	"
	W	Lander Frank E	20	clerk	54	439 Shawmut av
	X	Thompson Joseph A	22	laborer	28	here

Page.	Letter.	Full Name.	Residence, Jan. 1, 1943.	Occupation.	Supposed Age.	Reported Residence, Jan. 1, 1942. Street and Number.

Fenwick Street—Continued

	Y	Thompson Mary V—†	22	matron	50	here
	Z	Riordan Cornelius	22	porter	40	"
1516						
	A	Riordan Mary—†	22	housewife	39	"
	B	Corkery Hannah M—†	22	"	63	
	C	Corkery Jeremiah	22	retired	59	
	D	Corkery Jeremiah, jr	22	U S A	25	
	E	Corkery John F	22	"	23	
	F	Clift Herbert	24	retired	66	
	G	Clift Margaret—†	24	housewife	62	"
	H	Fitzpatrick Helen—†	24	waitress	49	57 Codman pk
	K	*Ryan Hannah—†	24	housewife	56	here
	L	*Ryan Mary T—†	24	at home	60	"

Guild Street

	M	Perry John	32	superintendent	44	here
	N	Perry Helen M—†	32	housewife	39	"
	O	Hennessey Anna—†	34	"	60	"
	P	Hennessey Ruth—†	34	inspector	30	"
	R	Hennessey Thomas	34	laborer	65	
	S	Langdon Frances V—†	36	housewife	36	"
	T	Langdon James F	36	U S A	20	
	U	Langdon Thomas J	36	chauffeur	44	"
	V	Clark Doris I—†	38	factoryhand	36	"
	W	*Meaney Helen—†	40	housewife	42	"
	X	Meaney James	40	U S A	23	
	Y	*Meaney Mary T—†	40	waitress	22	
	Z	Hajenian Armena—†	40	housewife	52	"
1517						
	A	Hajenian Stephen	40	storekeeper	61	"
	B	Bergen Henry	40	inspector	51	"
	C	Bergen Mary—†	40	housewife	48	14 Linwood
	D	Smith Alice—†	42	"	49	22 Lambert
	E	Egersheim Albert E	42	mechanic	34	100 Regent
	F	Egersheim Emma M—†	42	housewife	54	100 "
	G	Egersheim William V	42	guard	58	100 "
	K	Collins Elaine—†	44	housewife	29	here
	L	Collins Wilfred	44	electrician	30	"
	M	Edwards Rebecca—†	44	housewife	35	"

Page.	Letter.	FULL NAME.	Residence, Jan. 1, 1943.	Occupation.	Supposed Age.	Reported Residence, Jan. 1, 1942. Street and Number.

Guild Street—Continued

	N	Edwards Martin	44	laborer	42	here
	O	*Herbert Egbert	44	engineer	56	"
	P	*Herbert Ivy—†	44	housewife	44	"
	R	*Lamond Alice—†	46	"	72	
	S	Balabanis Doris—†	46	"	35	
	T	Balabanis Ernest	46	cook	45	"
	U	Wolff Anna J—†	46	housewife	43	102 Fellows
	V	Wolff Everett W	46	mechanic	39	102 "
	W	Wolff Mary L—†	46	clerk	21	102 "
	Y	Makara Eugene	48	cutter	31	4 Bartlett ter
	Z	Makara Mary—†	48	housewife	31	4 "
1518						
	A	Healey Margaret—†	48	"	65	here
	B	Healey Patrick	48	retired	74	"
	D	Eisner Josephine—†	50	housewife	41	"
	E	*Eisner Ray	50	carpenter	46	"
	F	White Catherine F—†	50	housewife	33	"
	G	White George H	50	shipbuilder	44	"
	H	Egan Gladys M—†	52	housewife	33	2461 Wash'n
	K	Egan James E	52	chauffeur	35	2461 "
	L	Horton Helen—†	52	factoryhand	31	here
	M	Sturgis Margaret—†	52	housewife	54	"
	N	Bussey Anita—†	52	"	20	"
	O	Bussey Harold F	52	U S A	26	237 Warren
	P	Rodde Herbert	52	"	23	here
	R	Rodde Marie—†	52	maid	53	"

Highland Street

	T	Frongello Frances—†	52	factoryhand	21	here
	U	Frongello Joseph	52	U S N	25	"
	V	*Frongello Mary—†	52	housewife	47	"
	W	*Calarese Ann—†	52	"	48	
	X	Calarese Eugene	52	barber	49	
	Y	Calarese Frank	52	U S A	25	"
	Z	Calarese John	52	mechanic	22	"
1519						
	A	Calarese Vincent	52	U S A	21	"
	C	Tollo Mabel—†	54	housewife	26	"
	D	*Tollo Placido	54	barber	33	
	E	Carey Charles	54	U S A	24	

Page.	Letter.	Full Name.	Residence, Jan. 1, 1943.	Occupation.	Supposed Age.	Reported Residence, Jan. 1, 1942. Street and Number.
		Highland Street—Continued				
	F	Carey Elizabeth A—†	54	housewife	65	here
	G	Carey James	54	U S A	22	"
	H	Carey Marie—†	54	factoryhand	23	"
	K	Carey Walter L	54	plumber	65	
	L	McLaughlin Irene—†	54	factoryhand	31	"
	M	Clark Frances—†	56	housewife	31	"
	N	Doyle Mary E—†	56	"	30	
	O	Doyle Thomas F	56	bartender	35	"
	P	Burns Sadie—†	56	housewife	54	29 Linden Park
	R	Carson Alice—†	56	"	36	29 "
	S	Carson Lester	56	freighthandler	37	29 "
	T	Girban Harold	56	janitor	46	29 "
	U	Lawler John	56	laborer	27	29 "
	V	Gaeta Agnes—†	58	housewife	22	Quincy
	W	Gaeta Frank	58	mover	27	"
	X	Valanzola Albert	58	janitor	52	100 E Newton
	Y	Valanzola Angelena—†	58	housewife	42	100 "
	Z	Valanzola Salvatore	58	U S A	22	100 "
1520						
	A	Foti Carmella—†	58	housewife	38	here
	B	Sweezey Doris—†	60	chauffeur	26	18 Ray
	C	Tarr Edward	60	"	39	18 "
	D	Tarr Jessie L—†	60	housewife	45	18 "
	E	Grady Geraldine—†	60	"	35	here
	F	Grady William	60	accountant	39	"
	G	Perella Albert	60	U S A	26	"
	H	Perella Alphonso	60	cook	60	
	K	Perella Felicia—†	60	factoryhand	23	"
	L	Perella Linda—†	60	clerk	20	
	M	*Perella Theodora—†	60	housewife	60	"
	N	Shedd Fred	62	mechanic	30	"
	O	Shedd John	62	chauffeur	62	"
	P	Shedd Joseph	62	U S A	25	
	R	Shedd Richard	62	U S N	23	
	S	Shedd Robert	62	U S A	28	"
	T	Tabbi Joseph	62	mechanic	26	1279 Col av
	U	*Tabbi Josephine—†	62	housewife	47	1279 "
	V	Tabbi Leo	62	U S A	21	1279 "
	W	Tabbi Salvatore	62	laborer	53	1279 "
	X	Tabbi Salvatore, jr	62	U S A	27	1279 "
	Y	Tabbi Tina—†	62	factoryhand	25	1279 "

Page.	Letter.	Full Name.	Residence, Jan. 1, 1943.	Occupation.	Supposed Age.	Reported Residence, Jan. 1, 1942. Street and Number.

Highland Street—Continued

Page.	Letter.	Full Name.	Residence, Jan. 1, 1943.	Occupation.	Supposed Age.	Reported Residence, Jan. 1, 1942. Street and Number.
	Z	Norton Anne R—†	62	housewife	51	here
1521						
	A	Norton John	62	cleaner	54	
	B	Norton John	62	operator	24	“
	C	Norton Lillian—†	62	clerk	20	“
	D	Norton Mary—†	62	“	22	
	E	Ashe Charlotte—†	64	housewife	25	“
	F	Ashe John J	64	switchman	36	“
	G	Casteldo Mary—†	64	housewife	24	“
	H	Casteldo Michael	64	mechanic	27	“
	K	Dawber Helen—†	64	housewife	25	73 Cedar
	L	Dawber John	64	chauffeur	36	73 “
	M	Kenney Florence—†	66	housewife	24	here
	N	Kenney Joseph	66	assembler	27	“
	O	Hill David	66	machinist	48	“
	P	Hill Helen—†	66	housewife	38	“
	R	Cass Catherine—†	66	“	32	15 Dorr
	S	Cass John	66	chauffeur	35	15 “
	T	Milliken Pauline B—†	68	housewife	50	here
	U	Milliken Walter R	68	collector	29	“
	V	Milliken Walter S	68	storekeeper	57	“
	W	Hawes Florence—†	68	housewife	59	153 Cedar
	X	Snell Charles N	68	engineer	57	153 “
	Y	Snell Frances—†	68	housewife	40	153 “

1522 Hulbert Street

Page.	Letter.	Full Name.	Residence, Jan. 1, 1943.	Occupation.	Supposed Age.	Reported Residence, Jan. 1, 1942. Street and Number.
1522						
	A	Perry Evelyn—†	2	housewife	28	22 Ottawa
	B	Perry Robert	2	chef	32	22 “
	C	West Anna—†	2	housewife	30	here
	D	West Walter J	2	painter	42	“
	F	McElroy Francis	12	janitor	33	“
	G	McElroy James E	12	U S A	29	“
	H	McElroy John W	12	clerk	26	
	K	McElroy Mary A—†	12	housewife	60	“
	L	McElroy Mary A—†	12	clerk	34	
	M	McKeever Elizabeth—†	12	housewife	58	“
	N	Boyle Martha—†	12	clerk	59	
	P	Neville Elizabeth—†	14	operator	37	“
	R	Coffey Dennis	14	clerk	52	

Page.	Letter.	Full Name.	Residence, Jan. 1, 1943.	Occupation.	Supposed Age.	Reported Residence, Jan. 1, 1942. Street and Number.

Hulbert Street—Continued

Page.	Letter.	Full Name.	Residence, Jan. 1, 1943.	Occupation.	Supposed Age.	Reported Residence, Jan. 1, 1942. Street and Number.
	S	Coffey John	14	student	22	here
	T	Needham Catherine—†	14	housewife	40	"
	U	Needham George	14	laborer	40	"
	V	Needham John J	14	U S A	20	
	X	Katsianes Christo	16	bookkeeper	42	"
	Y	Katsianes Louise—†	16	housewife	32	"
	Z	Cheney Claire—†	16	"	32	133 Dale
1523						
	A	Doyle Elizabeth—†	16	at home	68	here
	B	Doyle Marie—†	16	clerk	35	"
	C	Sebastian Clifton	17	shoeworker	50	"
	D	Sebastian Clifton, jr	17	U S M C	20	"
	E	Sebastian Grace—†	17	housewife	42	"
	F*	Rogers Delia—†	17	"	65	
	G	Rogers Thomas	17	retired	74	
	H	Brennan Marion A—†	19	clerk	50	
	K*	Brophy Catherine J—†	19	at home	68	
	L	Dunn Henry	19	retired	72	
	M	Fitzmorris Irene R—†	19	clerk	21	
	N	Fitzmorris Mary T—†	19	"	26	
	O	Fitzmorris Winifred A—†	19	housewife	64	"
	P	Newton John F	21	janitor	41	
	R	Newton Margaret M—†	21	housewife	40	"
	S	Daly Helen G—†	23	saleswoman	31	"
	T	Daly Joseph M	23	chauffeur	37	"
	U	Collins Mary—†	23	housewife	65	"
	V	Boretti Charles J	23	mason	46	
	W	Boretti Mary—†	23	housewife	39	"
	X*	Bilodeau Alfreda—†	25	"	35	
	Y	Bilodeau Louis	25	packer	37	"
	Z	McDermott Bartholomew	25	fireman	50	
1524						
	A	McKenna Evelyn F—†	25	housewife	27	"
	B	McKenna John J	25	fireman	29	
	C	Guinan Rose H—†	27	housewife	64	"
	D	Mooney Mary—†	27	at home	66	
	E	Easton Edward H	27	pressman	47	"
	F	Easton Eileen—†	27	housewife	29	"
	G	MacDonnell John	27	plasterer	63	"
	H	MacDonnell John J	27	clerk	27	
	K	MacDonnell Mary A—†	27	housewife	66	"

Page.	Letter.	Full Name.	Residence, Jan. 1, 1943.	Occupation.	Supposed Age.	Reported Residence, Jan. 1, 1942. Street and Number.
		Juniper Street				
	L	Campbell Donald W	1	machinist	23	here
	M	Campbell Dorothy E—†	1	housewife	22	"
	N	Callahan Evelyn—†	1	"	26	"
	O	Heindl Martha—†	1	factoryhand	65	"
	P	Arey Chandler C	5	gaugemaker	41	"
	R	Arey Mabel—†	5	saleswoman	38	"
	S	Cavanaugh Gertrude B—†	5	housewife	43	"
	T	Cavanaugh John J	5	U S A	22	
	U	Cavanaugh William F	5	engineer	20	"
	W	Goodman Charles J	7	"	37	
	X	Goodman Mary S—†	7	housewife	33	"
	Y	Hyland Katherine C—†	7	"	71	
	Z	Hyland William G	7	mechanic	38	"
1525						
	A	Hunt Douglas A	7	clerk	38	"
	B	Kane Josephine—†	9	housewife	63	"
	C	McMurray Fredric	9	clerk	63	
	D	*Beattie Letta—†	9	housewife	70	"
	E	Gillespie William	9	laborer	46	"
	G	Dykes Agnes—†	11	housewife	24	24 King
	H	Dykes David	11	clerk	30	24 "
	K	Bresnahan Jeremiah	11	laborer	42	2767 Wash'n
	L	Bresnahan Mildred—†	11	housewife	34	2767 "
	M	Hardy George	11	machinist	25	here
		Hardy Helen—†	11	housewife	23	"
		Kenney Eugene L	1	U S A	29	"
		Kenney John J	1	retired	67	
		Kenney Katherine T—†	1	housewife	60	"
		Kenney Phyllis G—†	15	machinist	20	"
	N	Vaughan Alfred	15	chemist	55	Everett
	U	Vaughan Katherine—†	15	housewife	49	"
	V	Jaravinos Angelus	21	seaman	25	here
	W	Jaravinos Anna—†	21	stitcher	22	"
	X	Jaravinos Charles	21	U S N	27	"
	Y	Jaravinos Mary—†	21	machinist	22	"
	Z	Jaravinos Peter	21	retired	65	
1526						
	A	*Zafferes Bessie—†	21	stitcher	35	
	B	Zafferes Thomas	21	bartender	48	"
	C	Sarno Adeline—†	22	clerk	23	
	D	Sarno Angelina—†	22	housewife	56	"

Page.	Letter.	Full Name.	Residence, Jan. 1, 1943.	Occupation.	Supposed Age.	Reported Residence, Jan. 1, 1942. Street and Number.
		Juniper Street—Continued				
	E	Sarno Beatrice—†	22	clerk	24	here
	F	Sarno Edward V	22	U S A	31	"
	G	Sarno Frank	22	retired	66	"
	H	Sarno Richard F	22	U S A	32	
	K	Sarno William J	22	machinist	26	"
	L	Crane Catherine—†	23	at home	77	
	M	Kearney Nellie—†	23	cleaner	59	
	N	Jianos Aristotle	23	chef	53	
	O	Jianos Frances—†	23	nurse	26	
	P	Jianos Martha—†	23	investigator	24	"
	R	Jianos Mary—†	23	housewife	53	"
	S	Tankiewicz Helen—†	25	inspector	22	"
	T	*Tankiewicz Pauline—†	25	housewife	52	"
	U	*Tankiewicz Peter	25	cook	56	"
	V	Davis Charles	25	molder	48	8 Galena
	W	Davis Jessie—†	25	housewife	45	8 "
	X	Peterson Anna C—†	25	"	44	25 Lamartine
	Y	Peterson William J	25	welder	44	25 "
	Z	Baker Elizabeth F—†	26	housewife	71	here
1527						
	A	Haley Arthur F	26	U S C G	37	"
	B	Haley Pierce S	26	appraiser	73	"
	C	Haley William E	26	"	35	
	H	Higgins Patrick	30	retired	74	
	F	Rooney Anna B—†	30	housewife	42	"
	G	Rooney Anthony G	30	machinist	42	"
	K	Gumpright Frances—†	30	housewife	75	"
	L	Gumpright Herbert L	30	teacher	33	
	M	Gumpright Walter L	30	piano tuner	50	"
	N	Murray Catherine—†	34	housewife	52	"
	O	Murray Margaret—†	34	clerk	25	
	P	Murray Mary D—†	34	paper worker	27	"
	R	McLaughlin Charles	34	milkman	51	"
	S	McLaughlin Robert J	34	U S A	25	
	T	McLaughlin Rose—†	34	housewife	51	"
	U	Lena Josephine—†	38	housekeeper	20	"
	V	Lena Patrick	38	fireman	59	"
	W	Polin Andrew	38	floorlayer	46	"
	X	Polin Frances—†	38	housewife	46	"
	Y	Campbell Archibald	42	retired	69	
	Z	Campbell Rita—†	42	housekeeper	26	"

Page.	Letter.	Full Name.	Residence, Jan. 1, 1943.	Occupation.	Supposed Age.	Reported Residence, Jan. 1, 1942. Street and Number.

1528

Juniper Street—Continued

	A	Blitzer Conrad	42	engineer	73	here
	B	Blitzer Lina E—†	42	housewife	71	"
	C	Henderson May—†	47	"	34	"
	D	Henderson Roy	47	electrician	39	"
	E	Jones Mary E—†	47	housekeeper	56	"
	F	Menter George	47	foreman	42	"
	G	Menter Marie—†	47	stenographer	40	"
	H	Mitchell Henry S	47	electrician	40	"
	K	Mitchell Violet—†	47	housewife	36	"
	L	Richardson Annie—†	47	at home	68	
	M	Woodson Bernice—†	47	operator	21	"
	N	Scully Eleanor F—†	48	housewife	42	"
	O	Arbuckle Catherine B—†	48	clerk	60	
	P	*Andrews Emanuel	49	tailor	47	
	R	*Andrews Gertrude—†	49	finisher	45	

Juniper Terrace

	S	Bouchard Charles	1	inspector	50	here
	T	Bouchard Dorothy—†	1	housewife	42	"
	U	Bouchard Marion—†	1	clerk	21	"
	V	Mulhern Joseph F	2	mechanic	46	"
	W	Mulhern Mary—†	2	housewife	40	"
	X	Mulhern Warren T	2	U S A	22	
	Y	Chace Chester	4	painter	43	
	Z	Chace Prudence—†	4	housewife	42	"

1529 Lambert Avenue

	B	Breslow Ellen F—†	45	at home	76	25 Millmont
	C	Flanagan Richard M	45	retired	72	here
	D	Killeen Mary E—†	45	at home	86	732 Parker
	E	McQuaid James D	45	retired	73	here
	F	Reese Mary A—†	45	matron	73	"
	G	Seifert Sarah—†	45	at home	67	101 M
	H	Sorenson Christian C	45	retired	72	here
	K	Willard Mary L—†	45	at home	76	42 W Newton
	L	Young Edwin B	45	retired	83	here
	M	Bowie Jeanette S—†	46	housewife	33	"
	N	Bowie Leon E	46	clerk	45	"

Page.	Letter.	Full Name.	Residence, Jan. 1, 1943.	Occupation.	Supposed Age.	Reported Residence, Jan. 1, 1942. Street and Number.

Lambert Avenue—Continued

	O	Rehn Barbara C—†	46	housewife	23	Dedham
	P	Rehn Elvin G	46	U S N	33	"
	R	Gallagher James F	46	U S A	50	here
	S	Gallagher Lillian F—†	46	operator	48	"
	T	Hipson Jessie M—†	46	at home	84	"
	U	Damatin Alice A—†	48	operator	27	"
	V	Damatin Lawrence S	48	machinist	28	"
	W	Damatin Vasil S	48	bellboy	25	"
	X	Goslin James E	48	painter	58	1 Bartlett ter
	Y	Goslin Lena M—†	48	housewife	58	1 "
	Z	Goslin Mary M—†	48	operator	23	1 "
1530						
	A	Goslin Norman E	48	U S A	21	1 "
	B	Goslin Thomas J	48	"	24	1 "
	C	Ekberg Astrid M—†	48	housewife	38	here
	D	Ekberg Erik B	48	welder	37	"
	E	Fee Josephine—†	50	operator	40	55 Waverly
	F	Silvey Alice—†	50	housewife	65	here
	G	Silvey John J	50	attendant	35	"
	H	Silvey Leo F	50	chauffeur	42	"
	K	Carrigg Anna F—†	50	housewife	40	"
	L	Carrigg Edward J	50	electrician	40	"
	M	*Sullivan Mary J—†	52	housewife	43	"
	N	Sullivan Patrick	52	laborer	43	
	O	Spillane Ellen—†	52	housewife	42	"
	P	Spillane James H	52	laborer	46	
	R	McNally Bertha A—†	52	bookkeeper	26	"
	S	McNally Hugh J	52	shipper	58	"
	T	Paris George J	52	operator	25	1022 Bennington
	U	Paris Marguerite E—†	52	housewife	24	here
	V	Austin Myrtle L—†	60	"	38	Vermont
	W	Austin William W	60	laborer	34	80 Clifford
	X	Thorpe Edward A	60	rigger	32	here
	Y	*Thorpe Pasqualena—†	60	housewife	31	"
	Z	Mooney Daniel P	60	operator	60	"
1531						
	A	Mooney Sarah V—†	60	W A A C	21	"
	B	O'Connor James E	60	cook	34	Virginia
	C	O'Connor Mary E—†	60	housewife	22	here
	D	Combie Andrew A	62	operator	30	Somerville
	E	Tucker Ira O	62	guard	51	Stoughton

Page.	Letter.	FULL NAME.	Residence, Jan. 1, 1943.	Occupation.	Supposed Age.	Reported Residence, Jan. 1, 1942. Street and Number.

Lambert Avenue—Continued

Page.	Letter.	FULL NAME.	Residence, Jan. 1, 1943.	Occupation.	Supposed Age.	Reported Residence, Jan. 1, 1942. Street and Number.
	F	Tucker Viola I—†	62	housewife	58	Stoughton
	G	Bushey Helen J—†	62	waitress	25	here
	H	Bushey Oliver P	62	U S M C	23	"
	K	*Flynn John J	62	houseman	52	"
	L	Reynolds Frank	62	chef	28	
	M	Reynolds Margaret—†	62	housewife	27	"
	N	Aldridge Byron A	64	U S A	24	
	O	Gleason Mary B—†	64	housewife	34	"
	P	Murray Arthur P	64	painter	72	
	R	Abramowicz Anna S—†	64	housewife	62	"
	S	Abramowicz John	64	laborer	57	
	T	Cohen Hedwig—†	64	waitress	32	"
	U	Cohen Louis	64	U S A	32	12 Stanwood
	V	Feinberg Mildred E—†	64	housewife	24	here
	W	Feinberg Samuel	64	U S A	24	"
	X	MacMasters Charles G	64	woodworker	57	"
	Y	*MacMasters Rose M—†	64	housewife	47	"
	Z	Madden John J	80	contractor	45	"
1532						
	A	Madden Ruth H—†	80	housewife	42	"
	B	Abbott Nellie—†	88	at home	68	
	C	*Derranski Benjamin	88	retired	50	"
	D	*Ellison Rose—†	88	housewife	23	Dedham
	E	Murphy Helen—†	88	operator	52	here
	F	Pozerska Edna—†	88	housewife	46	"
	G	Pozerska Stanley	88	laborer	24	"

Logan Street

Page.	Letter.	FULL NAME.	Residence, Jan. 1, 1943.	Occupation.	Supposed Age.	Reported Residence, Jan. 1, 1942. Street and Number.
	H	Collins Jeremiah E	4	laborer	45	here
	K	Collins Winifred E—†	4	housewife	47	"
	L	Holly William R	4	U S C G	23	"
	M	O'Neil Edna C—†	4	housewife	39	39 Fort av
	N	O'Neil Franklin D	4	custodian	44	39 "
	O	Kenny Catherine G—†	4	secretary	51	here
	P	Kenny George J	4	cashier	59	"
	R	Kenny John F	4	shipper	63	"
	S	Kenny Mary A—†	4	housekeeper	64	"
	T	Nestor Eleanor J—†	6	cashier	45	"

Page.	Letter.	FULL NAME.	Residence, Jan. 1, 1943.	Occupation.	Supposed Age.	Reported Residence, Jan. 1, 1942. Street and Number.

Logan Street—Continued

	U	Nestor Gerald J	6	U S A	22	here
	V	Nestor James J	6	mechanic	47	"
	W	Paull Eleanor J—†	6	housewife	20	"
	X	Paull George F	6	U S N	25	515 Saratoga
	Y	McDonald Michael R	6	U S A	22	here
	Z	McDonald Russell A	6	shipwright	51	"
1533						
	A	McDonald Walburga—†	6	housewife	45	"
	B	Winter Catherine—†	6	"	43	
	C	Winter Frederick W	6	machinist	43	"
	D	Winter Jean A—†	6	clerk	21	
	E	*Hodne Aslaugh—†	9	housekeeper	26	"
	F	Hodne Nils	9	shipfitter	36	"
	G	Steele Helen H—†	11	housekeeper	42	56 Bartlett
	H	Steele Philip E	11	lineman	45	56 "
	K	Koton Alice—†	12	housewife	47	here
	L	Koton Hugh	12	policeman	41	"
	M	Hurley Ethel M—†	14	housewife	39	"
	N	Hurley John C	14	agent	41	
	O	Mahoney Albert F	15	U S A	26	
	P	Mahoney Ellen E—†	15	housekeeper	65	"
	R	Mahoney Helen R—†	15	clerk	33	"
	S	Mahoney Marcella T—†	15	"	28	
	T	Ferrara Raymond	16	cobbler	32	
	U	Ferrara Vera—†	16	housewife	28	"
	V	Barry Ann—†	17	"	42	
	W	Barry Daniel A	17	molder	47	"
	X	Coakley Edward	18	laborer	45	
	Y	*Coakley Mary C—†	18	housewife	40	"
	Z	Sampson Elizabeth—†	18	inspector	34	"
1534						
	A	*Sampson Lloyd J	18	laborer	30	
	B	Flaherty Everett	20	B F D	35	
	C	Flaherty Margaret—†	20	housekeeper	32	"
	D	Roumacher Clara P—†	21	housewife	33	"
	E	Roumacher Francis J	21	letter carrier	41	"
	F	Lyons Elizabeth M—†	22	housewife	52	"
	G	Lyons William J	22	chauffeur	50	"
	H	O'Brien Beatrice—†	23	housewife	41	11 Logan
	K	O'Brien Harold	23	policeman	46	11 "

Page.	Letter.	Full Name.	Residence, Jan. 1, 1943.	Occupation.	Supposed Age.	Reported Residence, Jan. 1, 1942. Street and Number.

Millmont Street

	L	Moore Grace—†	5	housewife	26	here
	M	Moore Harry	5	painter	37	"
	N	Gaeta Anna—†	5	housewife	31	66 Highland
	O	Gaeta Anthony J	5	laborer	33	66 "
	P	Maloof Debby—†	5	housewife	55	4 "
	R	Maloof Victoria—†	5	saleswoman	23	4 "
	S	Scarmogino Agnes—†	5	housewife	25	236 Saratoga
	T	Scarmogino Joseph	5	shoeworker	28	236 "
	U	Maxwell Myra M—†	9	housewife	32	here
	V	Maxwell Raymond G	9	welder	32	"
	W	*Adami Edgardo	9	tailor	35	"
	X	Adami Helen—†	9	housewife	27	"
	Y	Frazier Claire—†	9	laundress	23	"
	Z	Maxwell Lorenz	9	U S A	24	
1535						
	A	Dunn Anna—†	15	housewife	72	"
	B	Dunn Elizabeth—†	15	"	42	
	C	Dunn James	15	retired	75	
	D	Dunn Joseph	15	U S A	38	
	E	Dunn William	15	policeman	45	"
	F	*Lawless Christopher J	15	laborer	41	"
	G	McAuliffe Anna L—†	15	housewife	42	"
	H	McAuliffe William H	15	laborer	44	"
	K	Donlon Catherine—†	23	housewife	72	11 Elmwood
	L	Jones Catherine—†	23	"	30	11 "
	M	Vivada Francis A	23	laborer	21	Plymouth
	N	Waldmeyer Charles D	23	"	50	29 Vernon
	O	Breault Chester	25	retired	32	10 Edgewood
	P	*Fitzgerald Elizabeth—†	25	housewife	57	here
	R	Fitzgerald Joseph W	25	constable	32	"
	S	Fitzgerald Virginia—†	25	housewife	20	N Hampshire
	T	Vega Dante G	29	barber	43	here
	U	Vega Josephine—†	29	housewife	42	"
	V	Dale Charles J	29	electrician	28	"
	W	Dale Ethel L—†	29	housewife	23	"
	X	*Keany Ellen—†	29	"	26	53 Forest Hills
	Y	*Keany Patrick	29	U S A	36	7 Westville rd
	Z	Rivera Rachel—†	31	housewife	59	here
1536						
	A	*Xavier Alice—†	31	"	58	
	B	Stewart Reginald	31	operator	38	

Millmont Street—Continued

Page.	Letter.	Full Name.	Residence, Jan. 1, 1943.	Occupation.	Supposed Age.	Reported Residence, Jan. 1, 1942. Street and Number.
	C	Stewart Ruth A—†	31	housewife	34	here
	D	Allen Thomas	31	welder	30	"
	E	Allen Winifred—†	31	housewife	29	"
	F	Bennett Arthur A	39	machinist	48	"
	G	Bennett Catherine J—†	39	housewife	45	"
	H	Halleran John J	39	salesman	48	"
	K	Waldmyer Arthur	39	U S A	24	
	L	Waldmyer Catherine—†	39	housewife	21	"
	M	Polishook Benjamin	39	U S A	26	
	N	*Polishook Celia—†	39	housewife	58	"
	O	Polishook Grace—†	39	"	24	11 Hildreth
	P	Polishook Louis	39	lawyer	25	here
	R	Polishook Samuel	39	U S A	21	"
	S	Curley Gertrude—†	39	housewife	43	"
	T	Curley Hubert	39	installer	44	

Oakland Street

Page.	Letter.	Full Name.	Residence, Jan. 1, 1943.	Occupation.	Supposed Age.	Reported Residence, Jan. 1, 1942. Street and Number.
	W	Aries Peter	5	cook	56	here
	X	*Aries Teresa—†	5	housewife	53	"
	Y	Massaglia Madaline—†	5	"	30	"
	Z	Massaglia Marguerita—†	5	seamstress	63	"
1537	A	Massaglia Rudolph	5	welder	31	
	B	Crugnola Angelo	7	U S A	21	
	C	*Crugnola Orlandina—†	7	housewife	50	"
	D	Crugnola Vito	7	shoecutter	52	"
	E	*Lippie Palmiro	7	laborer	66	
	F	Forster Helen M—†	9	housewife	36	"
	G	Forster John S	9	laundryman	40	"
	H	Cronin Rita—†	11	stitcher	20	48 Hampden
	K	Reynolds Agnes—†	11	housewife	69	48 "
	L	Timmins Harry D, jr	11	machinist	25	105 Regent
	M	Timmins Katherine L—†	11	housewife	22	105 "
	N	O'Hare Joseph	13	welder	32	4 Hogan ct
	O	Timmins Anna R—†	13	clerk	26	here
	P	Timmins Cecelia J—†	13	housewife	62	"
	R	Timmins Harry	13	carpenter	59	"
	S	Manfredi Phyllis—†	15	clerk	24	
	T	Manfredi Russell	15	machinist	28	"
	U	Marotta Bridget—†	15	housewife	23	"

Oakland Street—Continued

Page.	Letter.	Full Name.	Residence, Jan. 1, 1943.	Occupation.	Supposed Age.	Reported Residence, Jan. 1, 1942. Street and Number.
	V	Marotta Louis	15	baker	26	here
	W	Parisse Mary—†	15	housewife	57	"
	X	Parisse Rose—†	15	saleswoman	20	"
	Y	Kelley Sarah I—†	17	housewife	45	4 Sunderland
	Z	Kelley William E	17	pipefitter	42	4 "
1538						
	A	Sprague Josephine M—†	17	housewife	38	17 Roxbury ct
	B	Willett Charles A	17	toolmaker	21	here
	C	Willett Charles B	17	machinist	64	"
	D	Willett Marguerite—†	17	housewife	61	"
	E	Duato Henry D	19	metalworker	42	83 Ferrin
	F	Krusvich Bessie—†	19	housewife	58	Brockton
	G	Priolo Anna—†	19	"	30	here
	H	Grossi Anna—†	19	operator	26	"
	K	*Grossi Loretta—†	19	housewife	51	"
	L	Grossi Pasquale	19	carpenter	49	"
	M	*Crangelo Frederick	19	chef	55	
	N	*Smith Freda—†	19	housewife	35	"
	O	Smith Henry H	19	rigger	32	

Osgood Court

Page.	Letter.	Full Name.	Residence, Jan. 1, 1943.	Occupation.	Supposed Age.	Reported Residence, Jan. 1, 1942. Street and Number.
	P	McPhail James W	2	cutter	64	here

Ray Street

Page.	Letter.	Full Name.	Residence, Jan. 1, 1943.	Occupation.	Supposed Age.	Reported Residence, Jan. 1, 1942. Street and Number.
	R	Kelley Arthur J	8	mechanic	33	here
	S	Kelley Evelyn—†	8	housewife	30	"
	T	Buckley George A	8	U S A	24	"
	U	Buckley John R	8	sorter	43	
	V	Buckley Josephine T—†	8	housewife	42	"
	W	Shugrue Ann—†	8	"	38	
	X	Shugrue Daniel	8	plasterer	42	"
	Y	Sullivan Annie—†	9	housewife	67	12 Ray
	Z	Sullivan Joseph M	9	U S A	28	12 "
1539						
	A	Sullivan Michael	9	retired	66	12 "
	B	Sullivan John	9	clerk	37	2 Fenwick
	C	Sullivan Margaret—†	9	at home	63	2 "
	D	Sullivan Nora—†	9	laundress	58	2 "
	E	Regan Charles	9	U S M C	30	here

Page.	Letter.	Full Name.	Residence, Jan. 1, 1943.	Occupation.	Supposed Age.	Reported Residence, Jan. 1, 1942. Street and Number.

Ray Street—Continued

	F	Regan Francis J	9	clerk	26	here
	G	Regan Martin	9	rigger	55	"
	H	Regan Mary—†	9	housewife	52	"
	K	Donovan Frank	10	laborer	38	
	L	Donovan Sarah—†	10	at home	83	
	M	Daley Elizabeth—†	10	housewife	65	"
	N	Daley James P	10	watchman	65	"
	O	Cass Frank	10	orderly	40	
	P	Cass Rose—†	10	housewife	55	"
	R	Monaghan Madeline—†	12	"	30	8 Valentine
	S	Monaghan Maurice	12	chauffeur	36	8 "
	T	Bell Nora E—†	12	housewife	35	here
	U	Sands Edward A	12	watchman	53	"
	V	Sands Effie M—†	12	"	42	"
	W	*Foley Bridie—†	14	housewife	30	"
	X	Foley Jeremiah	14	packer	35	
	Y	O'Hanley Grace—†	14	housewife	28	"
	Z	O'Hanley Raymond	14	electrician	30	"
1540						
	A	Fucile Silvestro	14	clerk	32	
	B	Fucile Thelma—†	14	housewife	29	"
	C	Habeeb Catherine—†	16	"	29	
	D	Habeeb Joseph	16	chauffeur	32	"
	E	McPhee Katherine—†	16	housewife	32	57 Codman pk
	F	*McPhee Michael	16	chauffeur	39	57 "
	G	McQuarrie Joan—†	16	nurse	37	57 "
	H	Daley Joseph	16	metalworker	32	here
	K	Daley Margaret—†	16	housewife	28	"
	L	Bussey Daniel	18	shipper	24	65 Fort av
	M	Bussey Lorraine—†	18	housewife	21	65 "
	N	Ross George F	18	fireman	42	here
	O	Ross Ruth—†	18	factoryhand	23	"
	P	Dailey Celia—†	18	clerk	23	"
	R	Dailey Mary—†	18	saleswoman	21	"
	S	Dailey Michael	18	retired	72	
	T	Cunningham Ann—†	20	housewife	22	"
	U	Cunningham William	20	operator	25	"
	V	Kline Margaret A—†	20	housewife	50	4 Rock
	W	Kline Thomas J	20	clerk	49	4 "
	X	Brown Eugenie—†	20	housewife	39	890 Harris'n av
	Y	Brown Lucien	20	operator	44	890 "

Page.	Letter.	Full Name.	Residence, Jan. 1, 1943.	Occupation.	Supposed Age.	Reported Residence, Jan. 1, 1942. Street and Number.

Ray Street—Continued

Page.	Letter.	Full Name.	Residence, Jan. 1, 1943.	Occupation.	Supposed Age.	Reported Residence, Jan. 1, 1942. Street and Number.
	z	Boisvert Euclive	22	laborer	50	here
1541						
	A	Boisvert Mary—†	22	housewife	42	"
	B	Burns Annie G—†	22	"	59	
	C	Burns Isabelle P—†	22	clerk	29	
	D	Burns Joseph F	22	retired	80	
	E	Boisvert Exilda—†	22	housewife	49	"
	F	Boisvert Odilon	22	chauffeur	58	"
	G	Cavelius Ann—†	24	housewife	64	"
	H	Cavelius Marie—†	24	secretary	29	"
	K	Cavelius Peter	24	machinist	66	"
	L	Cooper George	24	U S A	25	"
	M	Cooper Rosalie—†	24	housewife	24	"
	N	McCarthy Charles G	26	laundryman	23	"
	O	McCarthy Dennis	26	retired	76	
	P	McCarthy Katherine—†	26	at home	64	
	R	McCarthy Margaret M—†	26	clerk	25	
	S	McCarthy Rita C—†	26	operator	21	"
	T	*Meyers Annie—†	28	at home	80	
	U	*Meyers Henry	28	retired	84	
	V	Donlan Annie—†	28	housewife	74	"
	W	Donlan Peter	28	retired	76	
	X	Gallagher Delia—†	28	at home	70	
	Y	Doyle Margaret—†	30	"	73	
1542						
	A	Hogan Ellen—†	30	housewife	57	"
	B	Hogan William	30	laborer	60	
	C	O'Connell Daniel	30	clerk	55	
	D	Harney John J	35	steamfitter	66	"
	E	Harney Mary E—†	35	housewife	61	"
	F	Harrow Annie—†	35	at home	68	
	G	*Stewart Samuel W	35	painter	64	
	H	Lapsley Michael	35	retired	70	
	K	Lapsley Sarah—†	35	housewife	68	"

Regent Street

Page.	Letter.	Full Name.	Residence, Jan. 1, 1943.	Occupation.	Supposed Age.	Reported Residence, Jan. 1, 1942. Street and Number.
	N	Daley Joseph D	85	clergyman	33	here
	O	Dunn Joseph	85	"	47	"
	P	Kelley Mary—†	85	cook	62	"
	R	*McCarthy Anna—†	85	maid	34	

Page.	Letter.	Full Name.	Residence, Jan. 1, 1943.	Occupation.	Supposed Age.	Reported Residence, Jan. 1, 1942. Street and Number.

Regent Street—Continued

	s	Minigan Frederick	85	clergyman	31	here
	T	Ring Charles J	85	"	69	"
	U	Bradley Margaret T—†	91	teacher	21	"
	V	Brown Julia J—†	91	housekeeper	54	"
	W	Corrigan Catherine A—†	91	teacher	34	"
	X	Crowley Mary E—†	91	"	41	
	Y	Dolan Helen—†	91	"	61	
	Z	Donohoe Mary—†	91		34	
1543						
	A	Finnegan Mary A—†	91	"	38	
	B	Glynn Margaret M—†	91	"	54	
	C	Hartigan Marie F—†	91	"	46	
	D	Keefe Margaret—†	91	"	52	
	E	Kelly Anna—†	91		43	
	F	Lally Teresa M—†	91		50	
	G	MacDougall Jessie A—†	91	"	34	
	H	MacLelland Mary M—†	91	"	27	
	K	McCloskey Frances X—†	91	"	23	
	L	McCusker Mary M—†	91	"	38	
	M	McHale Mary A—†	91	"	46	
	N	Sullivan Therese M—†	91	"	24	"
	O	Whooley Alice J—†	91	"	57	"
	P	Whitney Lettie—†	95	housewife	43	Springfield
	R	Whitney Thomas	95	laborer	50	"
	S	Fallon Catherine—†	95	housewife	57	here
	T	Fallon Malachi J	95	U S N	23	"
	U	Fallon Mary C—†	95	clerk	22	"
	V	Fallon Patrick J	95	mechanic	54	"
	W	Fahey James	95	guard	55	
	X	*Fahey Mary A—†	95	housewife	46	"
	Y	Otto Frederick	97	mechanic	37	"
	Z	Otto Josephine—†	97	housewife	34	"
1544						
	B	Gould Elsie—†	97	"	48	
	C	Mardirosian Armnag	99	laborer	58	
	D	Mardirosian Dorothy—†	99	housewife	33	"
	E	Campbell Margaret—†	99	"	21	34 Lindsey
	F	MacDonald Margaret—†	99	"	48	34 "
	G	MacDonald Roderick	99	steamfitter	52	34 "
	H	MacDonald William	99	laborer	23	34 "
	K	Dzengelewski Witold	99	baker	62	33 Copeland

Page.	Letter.	Full Name.	Residence, Jan. 1, 1943.	Occupation.	Supposed Age.	Reported Residence, Jan. 1, 1942. Street and Number.

Regent Street—Continued

	L	Gladki Regina—†	99	housewife	26	144 Winthrop
	M	Gladki Vincent	99	steamfitter	36	144 "
	N	Dekas Anna B—†	103	housewife	45	here
	O	Dekas James	103	gardener	47	"
	P	Alcorn Ernest R	105	chauffeur	38	Medford
	R	Alcorn Frances A—†	105	housewife	36	"
	S	McMullen Allen J	105	laborer	71	Canada
	T	McMullen Marion—†	105	clerk	32	here
	U	McMullen Thomas S	105	cook	34	"
	V	Foley Bartholomew	113	shipfitter	36	"
	W	Foley Helen M—†	113	housewife	30	"
	X	Salmon John	113	storekeeper	47	"
	Y	Salmon Nora—†	113	housewife	38	"
	Z	Rogers Jesse	113	musician	31	"
1545						
	A	Rogers Mary—†	113	housewife	28	"
	B	MacDonald Anna—†	115	"	25	
	C	MacDonald Roderick J	115	welder	26	
	D	Feeley George	115	U S A	40	
	E	Feeley John J	115	welder	37	
	F	Feeley Mary—†	115	housewife	32	"
	G	Bergman Albert W	115	painter	63	"
	H	Bergman Catherine E—†	115	housewife	62	"
	K	Miller Evangeline E—†	117	"	25	"
	L	Miller John T	117	electrician	31	2654 Wash'n
	N	Noiseaux Alice—†	117	waitress	31	here
	O	Noiseaux John B	117	cook	47	"
	P	*Chiklas Goldie—†	119	housewife	30	15 Highland av
	R	Chiklas Louis	119	chauffeur	30	15 "
	S	Lake Arthur R	119	retired	73	here
	T	Lake Ruby—†	119	housewife	66	"
	U	Deady Blanche—†	119	clerk	24	"
	V	Deady Charles A	119	laborer	50	
	W	McGonagle Helen—†	119	clerk	22	
	X	McGonagle James J	119	U S A	24	"

Rockledge Street

	Y	McCormick Thomas H	2	laborer	38	here
	Z	Turner Edward S	2	retired	76	"

Page.	Letter.	Full Name.	Residence, Jan. 1, 1943.	Occupation.	Supposed Age.	Reported Residence, Jan. 1, 1942. Street and Number.
		1546				
		Rockledge Street—Continued				
	A	Turner Maude—†	2	housewife	62	here
	B	Thompson Allan P	2	pipefitter	30	Harwich
	C	Thompson Anna—†	2	housewife	28	"
	D	Strudas Edward	4	baker	32	here
	E	Strudas Mary—†	4	housewife	23	"
	F	Strudas Adam	4	baker	63	"
	G	Strudas Josephine—†	4	housewife	58	"
	H	Strudas Vincent	4	U S A	24	"
	K	Birt Pearl E—†	4	housewife	46	14 Linwood
	L	Birt Rubin L	4	operator	45	14 "
	M	Morrissey Lena A—†	4A	housewife	45	here
	N	Morrissey Leo	4A	maint'n'ceman	44	"
	O	Desmond Alice F—†	4A	housewife	64	"
	P	Desmond Joseph F	4A	mechanic	65	"
	R	Gorman Donald G	4A	U S A	23	
	S	Gorman Edward M	4A	stenographer	25	"
	T	Gorman Margaret A—†	4A	housewife	58	"
	U	Gorman Mary E—†	4A	clerk	28	
	V	Gorman Virginia—†	4A	operator	26	
	W	Brady Catherine M—†	8	housewife	66	"
	X	Brady Margaret—†	8	stenographer	27	"
	Y	Brady Patrick J	8	retired	67	"
	Z	Narseff Michael	8	welder	35	
		1547				
	A	*Narseff Nezzera—†	8	housewife	62	"
	B	Manning John F	8	policeman	44	"
	C	Manning Wilhelmina—†	8	housewife	43	"
	D	Quigley Mary A—†	10	seamstress	59	"
	E	Dantona Joseph	12	laborer	51	
	F	Dantona Joseph	12	welder	24	
	G	Dantona Josephina—†	12	housewife	50	"
	H	Dantona Tina—†	12	seamstress	26	"
	K	Moran John	14	U S A	24	
	L	Moran Mary—†	14	housewife	55	"
	M	Moran Thomas	14	fireman	59	
	N	Moran Thomas	14	laborer	30	
	O	Moran Walter	14	U S A	21	"
	P	Abizaid George	16	laundryman	41	"
	R	Abizaid Josephine—†	16	housewife	29	"
	S	Cronin Florence—†	19	"	43	

Page.	Letter.	Full Name.	Residence, Jan. 1, 1943.	Occupation.	Supposed Age.	Reported Residence, Jan. 1, 1942. Street and Number.

Rockledge Street—Continued

	T	Cronin John	19	machinist	44	here
	U	Minkel Flora—†	19	housewife	69	"
	V	Barry Joan—†	21	"	53	"
	W	Barry Mary L—†	21	seamstress	47	"
	X	Kean John J	21	electrician	46	"
	Y	Nestef Josephine—†	23	housewife	27	"
	Z	Nestef Solomon	23	laborer	30	
1548						
	A	Coffey Beatrice—†	25	housewife	53	"
	B	Coffey Jeremiah	25	clerk	60	

Thornton Street

	D	*Unni Fabio M	1	barber	40	here
	C	Unni Santa—†	1	housewife	32	"
	E	McDonald Ann—†	2	"	32	"
	F	McDonald George	2	operator	34	"
	G	Barry Irene—†	3	housewife	37	"
	H	Barry Robert F	3	B F D	45	
	K	Normile Catherine—†	4	typist	33	
	L	Normile Margaret—†	4	inspector	21	"
	M	Normile Mary—†	4	housewife	60	"
	N	Stilphen Carl E	4	riveter	23	
	O	Stilphen Ruby M—†	4	housewife	43	"
	P	Darcy Ann—†	5	"	28	
	R	Darcy John M	5	laborer	28	
	S	Fleming Francis J	6	U S A	31	
	T	Fleming Gertrude E—†	6	stenographer	35	"
	U	Fleming Helen L—†	6	clerk	27	"
	V	Fleming Jane E—†	6	teacher	33	"
	W	Fleming John P	6	retired	63	
	X	Fleming Margaret M—†	6	clerk	22	
	Y	Fleming Mary E—†	6	housewife	62	"
1549						
	A	Rock Frank J	7	retired	68	
	B	*Caulfield Mary—†	8	nurse	67	
	C	Fleming Gertrude M—†	8	clerk	67	
	D	*Bickerstaffe Anna E—†	9	housewife	73	"
	E	Bickerstaffe Cyril	9	clerk	33	
	F	Mitchell Lillian—†	11	housewife	31	"

Page.	Letter.	Full Name.	Residence, Jan. 1, 1943.	Occupation.	Supposed Age.	Reported Residence, Jan. 1, 1942. Street and Number.

Thornton Street—Continued

	G	Mitchell Michael J	11	bartender	38	here
	H	Rosit Olga—†	12	housekeeper	56	"
	K	Heumiller Annette—†	12	housewife	47	"
	L	Pare Alice M—†	12	secretary	47	"
	M	Ministeri Gaetano	19	laborer	44	
	N	Ministeri Jennie—†	19	housewife	39	"
	O	Higgins Francis X	21	U S A	34	
	P	Jenkins Mary E—†	21	housewife	33	"
	R	Jenkins Robert W	21	laborer	38	
	S	McManus Mary M—†	21	housekeeper	74	"
	T	Dalton Mildred—†	23	tel operator	37	"
	U	Hickey Harry F	23	chauffeur	41	"
	V	Hickey Mary M—†	23	housewife	64	"
	W	Fitzgibbon David P	25	policeman	42	"
	X	Fitzgibbon Mary F—†	25	nurse	42	"
	Y	Tardanico Henry	27	chauffeur	24	24 Pompeii
	Z	Tardanico Irene—†	27	clerk	21	2656 Wash'n
1550						
	A	Gramer Bertha H—†	28	housewife	48	here
	B	Gramer Paul J	28	manufacturer	49	"
	C	Gramer Albert L	28	clerk	40	"
	D	Gramer Anna M—†	28	housekeeper	70	"
	E	Gramer Joseph H	28	electrician	37	"
	F	*Tardanico Mary—†	29	housewife	46	24 Pompeii
	G	*Tardanico Salvatore	29	chauffeur	56	24 "
	H	Condry Florence—†	31	housewife	24	46 Lambert av
	K	Condry Thomas	31	operator	27	46 "
	L	Theodore Kleopatra—†	32	housewife	36	here
	M	Theodore Paskal	32	salesman	40	"
	N	Bower Anna—†	32	housekeeper	65	"
	O	Redmond Helen B—†	33	housewife	23	17 O'Meara ct
	P	Redmond William J	33	operator	27	17 "
	R	Reader Evelyn—†	35	housewife	24	here
	S	Reader William	35	inspector	28	"
	T	O'Dea Madeline—†	36	clerk	20	"
	U	O'Dea Marie—†	36	housewife	48	"
	V	O'Dea Thomas J	36	guard	48	"
	W	Compos Florence—†	36	forewoman	50	"
	X	Pendexter Albert	36	U S A	23	
	Y	Pendexter Mildred—†	36	nurse	23	
	Z	Plageman Clara—†	36	clerk	52	

Page.	Letter.	FULL NAME.	Residence, Jan. 1, 1943.	Occupation.	Supposed Age.	Reported Residence, Jan. 1, 1942. Street and Number.
		1551				
		Thornton Street—Continued				
	A	Plageman Joseph	36	foreman	42	here
	B	Plageman Teresa—†	36	clerk	54	"
	C	Pace Frederick	37	foreman	46	"
	D	Pace Gertrude—†	37	housewife	46	"
	E	Pace Veronica—†	37	clerk	22	"
	F	Kendrick Edgar	38	foreman	58	
	G	Kendrick Emma—†	38	clerk	46	
	H	Kendrick Marion—†	38	"	21	
	K	Zipper Amelia—†	38	seamstress	60	"
	L	Lathuras Charles J	38	clerk	22	
	M	Lathuras John A	38	"	63	
	N	Lathuras Kimon J	38	"	20	
	O	Lathuras Mary—†	38	housewife	52	"
	P	Papajohn Katherine—†	39	"	35	
	R	Papajohn Peter	39	cook	44	
	S	Ginty Elizabeth C—†	41	clerk	25	
	T	Ginty Margaret—†	41	tel operator	35	"
	U*	Ginty Mary—†	41	housekeeper	59	"
	V	Ginty Mary T—†	41	clerk	28	"
	W	Stewart Rose—†	41	housewife	32	157 Deforest
	X	Todd John P	45	painter	48	41 Bartlett
	Y	Todd John W	45	U S A	21	41 "
	Z	Todd Josephine—†	45	housewife	40	41 "
		1552				
	A	Todd William J	45	U S A	20	41 "
	B	Grube Alexander	45	"	29	here
	C	Grube Frances—†	45	stitcher	25	"
	D*	Grube Mildred—†	45	"	52	"
	E	Gebauer Alma—†	45	housewife	46	"
	F	Gebauer Fritz	45	shipfitter	46	"
	G	Dunlop Annie J—†	51	housewife	56	"
	H	Dunlop Cecelia A—†	51	teacher	35	
	K	Dunlop Henry B	51	meter reader	36	"
	L	Dunlop Michael J	51	retired	74	
	M	Dunlop William F	51	U S A	40	
	N	Banks Clara V—†	76	housewife	63	"
	O	Banks John W	76	waiter	63	"
	P	Bruce Charles H	76	retired	58	30 Greenwich pk
	R	Bruce Lucy M—†	76	housewife	56	30 "
	S	Davidson Harriett—†	80	nurse	40	here

Page.	Letter.	Full Name.	Residence, Jan. 1, 1943.	Occupation.	Supposed Age.	Reported Residence, Jan. 1, 1942. Street and Number.

Thornton Street—Continued

	T	Davidson John P	80	chauffeur	40	here
	V	Baker George F	82	U S N	21	"
	W	Baker Violet T—†	82	housekeeper	46	"
	X*	Hipson Irvin F	84	chauffeur	40	"
	Y	Hipson Mabel L—†	84	housewife	36	"
	Z	Bunker Arthur G	86	U S A	20	
1553						
	A	Bunker Hazel G—†	86	housewife	48	"
	B	Bunker Raymond S	86	welder	46	
	C	Bunker Harold D	86	custodian	43	"
	D	Bunker Violet E—†	86	housewife	43	"

Washington Street

	E	Sadowski Anthony	2595	laborer	64	570 Dor av
	G	McMillan Hugh	2612	retired	71	here
	H	McMillan Marie—†	2612	housekeeper	57	"
	M	O'Connor Frederick D	2614	painter	32	"
	N	O'Connor Margaret—†	2614	housewife	60	"
	O	O'Connor Margaret A–†	2614	clerk	35	
	P	O'Connor Mary—†	2614	housewife	37	"
	S	Gilboy Cecelia—†	2618	"	67	
	T	Gilboy Edward F	2618	retired	74	
	U	Gilboy Mary A—†	2618	housewife	39	"
	V	Rich Marian M—†	2618	"	25	
	W	Rich Michael F	2618	electrician	27	"
	Z	Bartino Delphine—†	2622	housewife	72	"
1554						
	A	Connick Mary—†	2622	saleswoman	21	2560 Wash'n
	B	Robinson Mildred—†	2622	housewife	58	2560 "
	C	Donnelly Arthur	2624	machinist	35	here
	D	Donnelly Geraldine—†	2624	housewife	35	"
	F	Bostwick Maude P—†	2626	"	67	"
	G	Mackintosh Elizabeth–†	2626	housekeeper	66	"
	H	McDonald John J	2626	chauffeur	56	"
	L	Hoberman Beatrice—†	2628	housewife	52	"
	M	Hoberman Maurice L	2628	attorney	55	
	O	Kelley Mary E—†	2630	housewife	63	"
	P	Kelley Mary E—†	2630	clerk	25	
	R	Corby Catherine—†	2632	housewife	60	"
	S	Moore Frank L	2632	salesman	48	New York

Page.	Letter.	Full Name.	Residence, Jan. 1, 1943.	Occupation.	Supposed Age.	Reported Residence, Jan. 1, 1942. Street and Number.

Washington Street—Continued

	T	McGran Edward F	2641	machinist	52	here
	U	McGran Lillian V—†	2641	housewife	48	"
	V	Lynch James J	2644	guard	29	24 Kent
	W	Lynch Mary J—†	2644	housewife	29	24 "
	Y	Hobson John F	2644	porter	42	212 Highland
	Z	Hobson Viola—†	2644	housewife	49	212 "
1555						
	G	Kelly Ann—†	2648	"	29	here
	H	Kelly Francis	2648	welder	30	"
	K	McLaughlin Delia—†	2648	housewife	55	"
	L	McLaughlin Michael	2648	plumber	22	"
	R	Smalley Ada—†	2654	housewife	52	"
	S	Smalley Samuel C	2654	U S A	28	
	T	Ericson Agnes—†	2654	housewife	61	"
	U	Ericson Fritz	2654	machinist	68	"
	V	Smith Ethel M—†	2654	operator	34	"
	X	DosPassos Edythe—†	2656	housewife	55	"
	Y	DosPassos Pedro	2656	seaman	51	
	Z	Hernandez Cruz	2656	U S A	23	
1556						
	A	Mercer William R	2656	retired	71	
	B	Arnold Helen—†	2656	housekeeper	50	"
	C	*Saunders Jessie—†	rear 2656	"	70	"
	N	Brooks Edna—†	2671	housewife	48	144 Dudley
	O	Brooks Harry	2671	plumber	49	144 "
	T	Heath Linnie V—†	2677	housewife	81	here
	U	Parsell Lillian G—†	2677	"	83	"
	Y	Matheson Chester P	2680	U S C G	21	"
	Z	Matheson Lillian—†	2680	housewife	58	"
1557						
	A	Matheson Peter	2680	chef	58	
	C	Chin Wong	2682	laundryman	28	"
	E	Thayer Eugene	2683	physician	76	"
	F	Thayer Idella—†	2683	housewife	75	"
	G	Harding Lucy B—†	2684	"	58	
	H	Murray Bridget—†	2684	"	69	"
	K	Schroeder Robert	2684	cigarmaker	58	"
	L	Archibald Hattie S—†	2684	housewife	65	"
	M	Katzlberger Alice—†	2684	"	47	2778 Wash'n
	N	Katzlberger Joseph	2684	waiter	56	2778 "

Lightning Source UK Ltd.
Milton Keynes UK
UKHW021246301118
333254UK00010B/776/P

9 780365 256410